CENTENARY EDITION

THE
LETTERS OF
SIR WALTER SCOTT
1787—1807

PUBLISHED BY

Constable and Company Ltd.
LONDON

·

Oxford University Press
BOMBAY CALCUTTA MADRAS

·

*The Macmillan Company
of Canada, Limited*
TORONTO

THE
LETTERS OF
SIR WALTER SCOTT
1787—1807

EDITED BY

H. J. C. GRIERSON
LL.D., LITT.D., F.B.A.

REGIUS PROFESSOR OF ENGLISH LITERATURE
AT THE UNIVERSITY OF EDINBURGH

ASSISTED BY

DAVIDSON COOK
W. M. PARKER
and others

LONDON
CONSTABLE & CO LTD
1932

B

15671

PRINTED IN GREAT BRITAIN BY ROBERT MACLEHOSE AND CO. LTD.
THE UNIVERSITY PRESS, GLASGOW

EDITOR'S PREFACE

THE origin of the present attempt to bring together in a final form as many of Sir Walter Scott's Letters as is practicable was the gift made to the National Library of Scotland by Sir Alfred J. Law, M.P., of Honresfeld, Littleborough. Mr. Davidson Cook had access to this large collection of letters—letters to Morritt, to Lockhart, to Sir Walter Scott's family and others—before it was thus gifted to the Scottish nation ; and his reprint of some of the letters and comments upon others showed that Lockhart's treatment of these letters, for his purpose as biographer, had been a very free one ; that, to use his own word, he had " manipulated " the letters in a variety of ways. The transcriptions are seldom minutely accurate ; Scott's mis-spellings and Scotticisms are freely corrected ; omissions are sometimes indicated by stars, but quite as often the letter runs on without any such indication of important omissions. Moreover, letters are occasionally " contaminated," *i.e.* what appears as one consists really of two letters written at different dates.

It was this fact, brought to light by Mr. Cook's preliminary survey of the Honresfeld collection, that suggested to Messrs. Constable and Co. the bold idea of making an edition as complete as can ever be done of all the discoverable letters of any importance, and of issuing at least the first part of it on the date of the Centenary of Scott's death. When they requested me to act as Editor, assisted by Mr. Cook, who had already copied most of the Law collection, and by Miss Marguerite Wood (whose place was subsequently taken by Mr. W. M. Parker), I doubt if either editor or publisher quite realised the extent of the work or the complications likely to arise from the irregular arrival of desirable letters. Nor could our task be lightened by printing (in the manner adopted in Birkbeck Hill's edition of the Letters of Dr. Johnson) only letters hitherto unpublished, and referring the reader for others to Lockhart's *Life* and to Douglas's *Familiar Letters*, because in both these books the letters had been to some extent " manipulated " as described. Further, many letters are scattered through other files, memoirs, collections, periodicals, and even newspapers. Our design became, therefore, to bring together all available letters of any importance, printing them from the originals when available, from copies, or from already printed texts.

The first step was naturally to obtain the approval of the project from Major-General Sir Walter Maxwell Scott, Bart., D.S.O., the present head of the family and the owner of all Scott's literary copyrights. With the valuable co-operation of Mr. James Curle this approval was secured, and with a special and exclusive authority for printing in this edition those of Scott's letters which had not previously been published. Thus assured of the support and interest of the Scott family we could proceed.

To the Law Collection were added, as soon as our purpose became generally known, letters or copies of letters from a variety of sources, as our complete list will show. In the first place, Sir Alfred Law himself permitted us to transcribe a number of very important letters not included in his gift to the National Library. Mr. John H. Stevenson, K.C., generously gave us free access to the important Cadell correspondence, now in the possession of the National Library, but at that time in his personal possession. The Librarian of the Royal Library at Windsor and the late Archbishop of Canterbury, Lord Davidson, both volunteered letters under their care or in their possession, and were kind enough specially to prepare copies for our use. The Marquess of Northampton sent copies of Scott's letters to Miss Clephane, later Lady Compton. The Duke of Buccleuch put at our disposal the large collection of letters written to three successive

holders of the title as well as to Lord Montague, brother
to Duke Charles and guardian to the fifth Duke. Lord
Polwarth, chief representative of the Scotts of Mertoun
(the head of Sir Walter's branch of the family), did the
same with his letters. Mr. James Curle, Melrose, allowed
us to copy Scott's letters to his friend and Sheriff-Substitute, Charles Erskine. Mr. Isaac Bayley lent for tran-
scription an interesting volume of letters to members of
Scott's own family. To Professor H. E. Butler of London
University we are indebted for numerous and important
additions and corrections copied from the original letters
to Maria Edgeworth, now in the possession of his mother,
Mrs. Harriet J. Butler of Oxford. Messrs. Maggs, Francis
Edwards and Tregaskis, all well-known London booksellers, kindly permitted us to transcribe several letters in
their possession. Miscellaneous letters, copies of letters
or photostats, arrived from many sources, both British
and American, including a letter to Fenimore Cooper
which enabled us to trace the certificates of baptism
of Lady Scott and her brother, and a number of interesting photostats from the collection of Mr. Owen D.
Young. The letters to Lady Abercorn, from which Mr.
Douglas had printed a considerable number, were traced
to the Pierpont Morgan Library in New York, and,
having been examined by special permission by my
daughter, were found to be about twice as many as those
Mr. Douglas had included in his delightful volumes. The
letters to Mrs. Hughes were, when we began work, in the
possession of Mr. Heffer, Cambridge. With his permission we were able to collate the originals with these
letters as printed in the volume edited by Mr. Horace
G. Hutchinson in *Letters and Recollections of Sir Walter
Scott by Mrs. Hughes*. These letters were later purchased
by Mr. Gabriel Wells, New York, who confirmed the
permission granted. A comparison of these originals with
the letters in the volume referred to, and also with the
copies made by Mrs. Hughes for Lockhart, revealed some

interesting variations, for Mrs. Hughes had also a little
" manipulated " Scott's letters, in a manner flattering to
herself. To Mr. Hornel we are indebted for being able
to print from original autographs many of the letters to
Charles Kirkpatrick Sharpe. To the directors of Coutts
Bank ; to Col. John Murray, and to Major Morritt of
Rokeby Park, we also owe thanks for generously supplying important series of letters.

Two additions to this ever-increasing matter require a
word or two of description. The first consists of three
large volumes found at Abbotsford (now purchased by
the National Library of Scotland), containing copies of
letters obviously made for Lockhart when he was composing the *Life*. Many of these are in the handwriting
of Sophia Lockhart, others in that of Mrs. Hughes, but
there are various hands. These copies have aided us in
different ways, supplying letters of which we have been
unable to trace the originals, completing letters from the
originals of which portions have now been cut away or
become illegible, and enabling us to check later copies
with these earlier copies. Letters to Daniel Terry are
printed by us entirely from these copies or from printed
sources. None, I think, of the originals have come to hand.

The other important addition consists of letters to
Constable, to Cadell, and to James and John Ballantyne.
When Constable and Cadell parted company in 1826 the
bulk of the letters remained with Constable and were
used by his son (with careful selection) in his defence of
his father, *Archibald Constable and his Literary Correspondents*
(1873). But a number seem to have stayed with
Cadell, and Thomas Constable complains of want of
access to these. Cadell also remained Scott's publisher,
and there was therefore an active later correspondence
between them. Copies of the Cadell correspondence were,
as has been stated, supplied to us early by the kindness
of Mr. John H. Stevenson, K.C., who permitted them to
be copied by Miss Marguerite Wood. The letters have

since been purchased by the National Library of Scotland
and collated with the copies. The Constable correspondence with Scott, Cadell, Peter Constable and others was in
part presented to the Library some years ago through Mr.
Kilpatrick of the firm of T. & A. Constable, printers, and
was completed by gifts from Mrs. Forsyth, the grand-
daughter of Archibald Constable. Further, Archibald
Constable had printed a number of Scott's letters and
some others in a volume not intended for publication,
which, with several autograph letters, is in the possession
of Lord Rosebery at Barnbougle Castle. Most of the MS.
letters had been copied by Miss Wood with the permission
of the late Earl ; and after his death the present Earl of
Rosebery was good enough to allow us to use the printed
volume at the National Library. We had hardly begun
to copy these when the originals of almost all the letters
in the printed volume were found by Mr. Kilpatrick of
T. & A. Constable, and lent for our use.

The Ballantyne letters were available from a variety of
sources—from Lockhart's *Life* ; from the Ballantyne-
Humbug letter to Sir Adam Ferguson, and from the reply
to that letter issued by James Ballantyne's trustees ; from
a large collection gifted to the Library of the Writers to
the Signet by the representatives of Miss Douglas ; from
Mr. James Glen, Writer, Glasgow, to whose valuable
assistance throughout reference will be made. But almost
at the last moment was discovered, in the office of Messrs.
Mackenzie & Kermack, W.S., a volume of letters inscribed
in John Ballantyne's hand, " OPEN NOT, READ NOT." This
volume had been used by Lockhart in his Ballantyne-
Humbug letter to Sir Adam Ferguson, and these letters
are all in Scott's handwriting. In the parcel containing
the volume were also several copies of letters, one of Sir
Walter's, others of James and John to Scott. We have thus
been able to bring together a larger number of letters
dealing with Scott's business affairs than have been
accessible to any previous writer on the subject ; and the

letters which passed between Constable and Cadell have
enabled us to see what was going on, on the other side of
the curtain (so to speak), and to annotate Scott's letters.

Our letters are thus, it will be seen, drawn from a great
variety of sources—original autographs, copies of letters,
printed letters, and we have had to deal with each in a
different way. I had intended when an autograph letter
was actually before me to print it exactly as it stood, with
spelling, punctuation, contractions, etc., unaltered. Whatever may be said about reproducing or not reproducing
an older punctuation, there is very much to be said for
letting a reader see a letter exactly as the first reader saw
it—Morritt, Lady Abercorn or whoever it might be.
The careful brushing of the hair and adjusting of the
tie which Lockhart and Douglas effected by correction and punctuation (over-punctuation to my mind, for
Lockhart was as careful of punctuation as he was careless
of strict accuracy), give to Scott's letters an appearance
of deliberation quite other than that of impetuous haste
which the originals communicate.

I have had, however, to make some concessions to the
help of the reader and in the cause of economy. I have in
general supplied full-stops where Scott begins the next
sentence with a capital letter. My typists and printers
made the usual interval, and the interval without the stop
was merely irritating. Further, when a letter (for
example, the long letter to the Duke of Buccleuch on the
battle of Waterloo) had been set up from a printed version
before the original came into my hand, I have not always
thought it fair to the publishers to correct these details
throughout. In such cases a double source is quoted—
thus [*Law and Lockhart*] or [*Law and Familiar Letters*] etc.—
in order to indicate that the letter has been carefully
collated with the original but that the punctuation is that
of the printed source. If I have made any further alterations I have indicated them in a note. For accuracy in
these details I am much indebted to the care of Mr. Parker.

In printing from copies of letters I have made the minimum of change. That some corrections could be made was generally shown when an autograph came to hand. In letters taken from printed sources I have followed the punctuation, etc., of the book from which I have taken the letter. For letters sent me from a distance I have had, of course, to rely on the accuracy of my correspondents, when they did not send the original or a photostat.

Our thanks are due to the numerous persons who have given such generous aid by the loan of letters or by sending copies. I trust I have omitted none in the list. If by chance I have, I apologise, and I will try to make the omission good in a later volume. We are indebted to Messrs. Douglas for permission to print from their *Familiar Letters* such letters there printed as we have not been able to procure from other sources. My own thanks are specially due to my assistants. Mr. Cook copied the Law Collection and made himself primarily responsible for letters scattered through printed volumes. Mr. Parker has worked beside me, and I am indebted to him, not only for meticulously accurate copies of letters (including details of erasion, alteration, etc., that I have not always felt able to reproduce) and for correction of proofs, but also for valuable assistance with the notes. We have compared notes throughout, and I must be held responsible for errors, but very many of the notes are Mr. Parker's. In the annotation we have been very deeply indebted to Mr. Hugh Walpole, who lent us such volumes from his great collection of letter-books as we needed from time to time. By the help of these we have been able to explain what Scott is referring to, and also to date letters which he has left undated.

Towards the expense of copying and research, the burden of which has fallen on the Publishers, the University of Edinburgh has generously made a contribution from the Murray Fund.

In the matter of dating the letters we have done our best, but must ask for some leniency of criticism. Scott's only dates are often " Tuesday," " Friday," " 11th June," etc. ; and, if he gives a more precise date, it is not infrequently a wrong one. He has no scruples about giving a thirty-first day to June or September, or dating a March letter in September and a September letter in March.

Finally, I wish to acknowledge my quite special personal debt to Mr. James Glen. He has not only supplied many exceptionally interesting and valuable letters, but has given me constant assistance. He has made the details of the life of Scott a favourite study for years and has been good enough to give me the benefit of his accurate knowledge in the dating of letters, and in the explanation of allusions in letters to the Ballantynes and others. He has read the proofs throughout and saved me from many blunders ; and, finally, he has written for me a statement regarding Scott's financial troubles. We are indebted for consistent help throughout our work to Dr. Dickson, Dr. Meikle, Mr. Dobbie and the staff of the National Library of Scotland.

Editors have generally corrected Scott's spelling and supplied punctuation. Certain proper names he spells consistently in a way of his own—" Laswade," Lord Mellville, Adam Fergusson (the family used only one " s "), Francis Freling. My copyists have not *always* preserved these details.

The Introduction to this volume has passed through many changes of plan, and must be regarded as in the main provisional. I hope later to bring together the facts of Scott's life in a manner sufficient to correct and supplement Lockhart's great work, which, as a sympathetic picture by one who knew and loved the man, is never likely to be superseded.

H. J. C. GRIERSON.

THE UNIVERSITY,
    EDINBURGH, 18*th August* 1932.

CONTENTS

PUBLISHERS' NOTE

THE publishers of THE CENTENARY EDITION OF THE LETTERS OF SIR WALTER SCOTT desire to make grateful acknowledgment to Messrs. Robert MacLehose & Co. of Glasgow for their unfailing help in producing the work.

Particularly do they wish to express to Mr. James MacLehose, LL.D., the head of the firm, their great appreciation of his individual care and enthusiasm. Quite apart from the efficient craftsmanship and consideration shown by him as master-printer, he has taken so large a personal share in the arduous and protracted work of preparing for press the volumes of the CENTENARY EDITION, that his name must, from the outset and permanently, be associated with it.

LIST OF CORRESPONDENTS TO WHOM LETTERS IN THIS VOLUME ARE ADDRESSED

---

b

LENDERS OF LETTERS PRINTED IN THIS VOLUME FROM ORIGINAL MANUSCRIPT

*The words in Italics are the shortened title of lender,
as printed below each letter*

Abbotsford-Original
> From original letter now at Abbotsford

Abbotsford Copies
> From the collection of transcripts of Sir Walter Scott's letters made about 1834 by Mrs. Lockhart, Mrs. Hughes and others, and deposited at Abbotsford. In 1932 this collection was acquired by the National Library of Scotland

Bayley
> Isaac F. Bayley, Esq., Halls, Dunbar

Bell, C. F.
> C. F. Bell, Esq., Ashmolean Museum, Oxford

Blackwood-Copy
> From a MS. copy of the original letter lent by George Blackwood, Esq., Edinburgh

British Museum
> Manuscript Department, British Museum

Buccleuch
> His Grace the Duke of Buccleuch, Bowhill, Selkirk

Campbell-Colquhoun
> A. Campbell-Colquhoun, Esq., Garscadden, Drumchapel

Carre, Ralph Riddell
Major Ralph G. Riddell Carre, Cavers Carre, Lilliesleaf

Cave
C. J. P. Cave, Esq., Stoner Hill, Petersfield

Craig-Brown
Brigadier-General E. Craig-Brown, 9 Ainslie Place, Edinburgh

Curle
James Curle, Esq., LL.D., Priorwood, Melrose

Edin. Corp. Mus.
Edinburgh Corporation Museum

Edin. Univ. Lib.
Edinburgh University Library

Forster MS. Collection
Victoria and Albert Museum, South Kensington

Glen
James Glen, Esq., 14 Lynedoch Crescent, Glasgow

Hornel
E. A. Hornel, Esq., Broughton House, Kirkcudbright

Kerr, Mrs. Eveline
Mrs. Eveline Kerr, Belfast

Law
MSS. presented by Sir Alfred J. Law to the National Library of Scotland, Edinburgh

Law, Sir Alfred J.
Sir Alfred J. Law, Honresfeld, Littleborough

Lockhart, Miss Mary
Miss Mary Lockhart, Ashestiel, Selkirk

Maggs Bros.
Messrs. Maggs Brothers, 34 Conduit St., London, W.

Morgan, Pierpont
The Pierpont Morgan Library, New York

Nat. Lib. Scot.
The National Library of Scotland, Edinburgh

Owen, Mrs. Meilir
Mrs. Meilir Owen, Denbigh, Wales

Paterson, Miss, Banchory
Miss Hilda M. Leslie Paterson, Banchory

Rosebery
The Rt. Hon. the Earl of Rosebery, Dalmeny

Sands
The Hon. Lord Sands, 4 Heriot Row, Edinburgh

Scott, John T.
John T. Scott, Esq., 29 Newmarket Street, Ayr

Shirley
G. W. Shirley, Esq., Ewart Public Library, Dumfries

Stevenson
J. H. Stevenson, Esq., K.C., 9 Oxford Terrace, Edinburgh

Watson Collection
Deposited in the National Library of Scotland by the Trustees of the National Galleries of Scotland

Westwood
A. H. Westwood, Esq., Assay Office, Birmingham

Williams, Mrs.
Mrs. Marjorie Williams, St. Andrews

Wilson, Mrs.
Mrs. Wilson, 11 Drummond Place, Edinburgh

Young, Owen D.
    Owen D. Young, Esq., New York

PRINTED SOURCES OF LETTERS INCLUDED IN THIS VOLUME

Chambers's Journal

Diary illustrative of the Times of George IV
    Diary illustrative of the Times of George the Fourth. [By Lady Charlotte Bury (*nee* Campbell)]. 4 vols. London, 1838-39

Exhibition, 1871, Catalogue
    The Scott Exhibition Catalogue [1871]. Edinburgh, 1872

Familiar Letters
    Familiar Letters of Sir Walter Scott. Edited by David Douglas. 2 vols. Edinburgh, 1894

Fraser Memoir
    Memoir and Correspondence of General James Stuart Fraser. By Hastings Fraser. London, 1885

Hadden's George Thomson
    George Thomson, the Friend of Burns. His Life and Correspondence. By J. Cuthbert Hadden. London, 1898

Hawick Arch. Soc.
    Transactions of the Archaeological Society, Hawick

Historical MSS. Commission Reports

Lockhart
    Memoirs of the Life of Sir Walter Scott, Bart. [By J. G. Lockhart.] 7 vols. Edinburgh, 1837-38 ; and second edition. 10 vols. Edinburgh, 1839.

Notes and Queries

Pinkerton Correspondence
> The Literary Correspondence of John Pinkerton, Esq. Now first printed from the originals in the possession of Dawson Turner. 2 vols. London, 1830

Reply to the Ballantyne-Humbug
> Reply to Mr. Lockhart's Pamphlet, entitled *The Ballantyne-Humbug Handled*, by the authors of the *Refutation*. London, 1839

Scots Magazine

Scott, Letters of Sir Walter, 1832
> Letters of Sir Walter Scott, addressed to the Rev. R. Polwhele and others. London, 1832

Skene's Memories
> The Skene Papers. Memories of Sir Walter Scott. By James Skene. Edited by Basil Thomson. London, 1909

Smith's Kelso Grammar School
> History of Kelso Grammar School. By James Smith. Kelso, 1909

Surtees Memoir
> Memoir of Robert Surtees. By G. Taylor, with additions by J. Raine. (Publications of the Surtees Society.) Newcastle, 1852

Taylor's Memoir
> A Memoir of the Life and Writings of the late William Taylor of Norwich and Original Letters from Sir Walter Scott. Edited by J. W. Robberds. 2 vols. London, 1843

Thompson's A Scottish Man of Feeling
> A Scottish Man of Feeling. By H. W. Thompson. Oxford, 1931

INTRODUCTION

SIR WALTER SCOTT IN HIS LETTERS

When Lockhart in 1836 was approaching the end of his *Life of Scott*, Cadell, the publisher of that work and of the collected edition of Scott's work, seems to have suggested, as a supplement to the *Life*, a collection or selection of the letters. To this Lockhart replied on 20th June : " It is impossible that anything could be handsomer than what you propose touching Letters ; but indeed till I have done the *Life* I shall be unable to say anything distinctly about that matter. The great thing is to make the *Life* what it should be, and I don't wish you to be making bargains for a pudding out of which it should remain at another's discretion to pluck the plums. I must at once say that this matter must lie over until I shall have done the *Life* and *then* leisurely revised the unused correspondence. Indeed, I think we ought on many accounts to think of a much later appendix of Letters than your six months after the Biography in which so many of the best must be introduced. There is a world of repetition even in those to the same persons ; and, by the by, the perhaps dismalest thing for me (if I were to think of myself at all in the matter) is that very likely, when all his letters are thrown open to an unscrupulous after age, my manipulation may be thrown overboard entirely. . . . In the latter volumes I shall have more of my own and your recollections to draw on and (having already sufficiently exhibited his epistolary vein) may draw more moderately on that source of at least doubtful information as to the real feelings of one who *in his later days* must have felt that whatever he wrote would one day perhaps be printed. It is therefor probable that after using all of the Letters that I deemed needful for the first affair there may be a *very* rich appendix, we shall see." [1]

[1] Unpublished letter in possession of Mr. J. H. Stevenson, K.C.

No such appendix as Lockhart contemplated, with some trepidation, was published until 1894—nearly sixty years after—when Mr. David Douglas, at the request of the Hon. Mrs. Maxwell-Scott, edited the two volumes of *Familiar Letters*. Douglas's edition was carefully selected and also, like Lockhart's, " manipulated " by omissions, which are not always indicated, and occasionally by " contamination," or making one letter of what were really two. Douglas worked in the spirit of Lockhart, and his two volumes are a charming elaboration of the picture presented by the biography. And yet the effect produced on some minds, both by the *Life* and by *Familiar Letters*, shows that Lockhart was not altogether mistaken in contemplating with some misgiving the effect of a complete and unedited issue of the letters.

When the *Life* appeared Lord Cockburn, politically an opponent of Scott but none the less an ardent admirer of the man, wrote in 1838 : " Whether the publication of this portrait will do any good to his memory is a different matter. It has greatly dispelled the fascination connected with his name in the minds of those who only knew him through his work and his fame. They thought him purely a literary man. They have now been taught how much he was a tradesman even in the exercise of his genius ; and to what extent his taste for those feudal times, which formed the charm of some of his finest works, was united with the practical obeisance of a vassal to his superiors ; and how very narrow and shallow were his public views ; and how much less he valued fame and literature than those results of them which enabled him to exercise an intellectual and splendid hospitality." So far the *advocatus diaboli* ; but the man who had known Scott personally could not stop there : " On the other hand how much, how very much there is to admire and to love ! What extraordinary combination of genius with industry ; of the poetical powers without any of the defects of the poetical temperament. If the acquisition of money

entered too much into his literary thoughts, who ever made
so liberal a use of it, or one that so much extended the
renown of his country ? . . . Where shall we find a
steadier friend ? A better man in all the domestic
relations ? What author has ever passed through so
splendid a career, so utterly unspoiled ? To what rival
was he ever ungenerous ? How noble the spirit with
which he bore up against the wreck of his fortune ! How
honourable the feeling of justice, and the ambition of
ultimate independence, with which he struggled for his
creditors ! . . . Dear Scott ! When he was among us
we thought we worshipped him, at least as much as his
modesty would permit. And now that he has gone we
feel as if we had not enjoyed or cherished him half
enough. . . . I still hear his voice and see his form. I see
him in the court, and on the street, in company and by
the Tweed. The plain dress, the guttural burred voice,
the lame walk, the thoughtful heavy face with its mantling
smile, the honest hearty manner, the joyous laugh, the
sing-song feeling recitation, the graphic story—they are
all before me a hundred times a day." I have been
tempted to continue the quotation beyond what bears
immediately upon the effect of Lockhart's *Life*, because
it suggests so well the complex feeling which that *Life*,
with its fuller revelation of Scott's business dealings with
the Ballantynes and Constables, awakened in those who
had known him personally. Macaulay, a Whig like
Cockburn but with more of " the malevolence of his
party," and who had never thus known Scott, describes the impression produced on his mind by that
Life in sharper terms when declining Macvey Napier's
invitation to review Lockhart for the *Edinburgh* : " I have
not, from the little I do know of him, formed so high an
opinion of his character as most people seem to entertain.
. . . He seems to me to have been most carefully, and
successfully, on his guard against the sins which most
easily beset literary men. On that side he multiplied his

precautions, and set double watch. Hardly any writer of note has been so free from the petty jealousies and morbid irritabilities of our caste. But I do not think that he kept himself equally pure from faults of a very different kind, from the faults of a man of the world. In politics, a bitter and unscrupulous partisan ; profuse and ostentatious in expense ; agitated with the hopes and fears of a gambler ; perpetually sacrificing the perfection of his composition, and the durability of his fame, to his eagerness for money ; writing with the slovenly haste of Dryden, in order to satisfy wants which were not, like those of Dryden, caused by circumstances beyond his control, but which were produced by his extravagant waste or rapacious speculation ; this is the way that he appears to me. I am sorry for it, for I sincerely admire the greater part of his works ; but I cannot think he was a very high minded man." So Macaulay, not altogether unjustly, but with that touch of exaggeration which he could never escape once his pen was in his hand ; and without the qualifications which Cockburn makes, and which any fair consideration must make to every one of these charges. Scott's political partisanship was not a whit more bitter than that of many others on both sides, and Scott's conservatism had its root in the romantic cast of his sentiments and imagination. If his expense was " profuse and ostentatious," his liberality was equally profuse and far from ostentatious. His correspondence will reveal many faults in Scott's temper and errors in the conduct of his affairs ; but there is one thing that never fails from first to last, and that is his generosity to others—to his brothers and their children, to poor authors such as Maturin and Gillies, or a poor painter like Haydon, to anybody who had claims upon him or made appeal to him. I have " lost the best and most steady friend that I ever had in the world " were Hogg's words to Lockhart in 1832. The chief pleasure Scott derived from his wealth was this ability to help others, if he did also delight to

surround himself with all that appealed to his imagination
—land and trees and furniture and antiquities and
bric-à-brac, tenants and work people whom he could
befriend, animals to love and be loved by.

Nor is " a gambler's hopes and fears " quite a just
description of Scott's feelings as author and as co-partner
in James Ballantyne & Co. We shall learn from the
letters a good deal more than has been yet ascertained or
ascertainable concerning the storms through which Scott
passed in 1813 and the immediately following years, and
again when the final disaster overtook him. I have
concealed nothing that has come into my hands concerning Scott's financial dealings. Nor is it any part of my
plan to exculpate Scott at the expense of Constable or of
the Ballantynes, though they certainly made their contribution to that disaster. The impression made on my
mind by these letters is not that of a gambler fevered with
a thirst for gold, but of one to whom came, as in a dream,
fairy-gold, wealth which enabled him to gratify his
manifold desires and charities, but which, as is the way
with such gifts, disappeared as suddenly as it came. If he
had been intent on money for its own sake, he could easily
have made more and kept it longer. In all Scott did there
was the same blend of practical and imaginative interest.
He took up printing—bringing Ballantyne to Edinburgh—
as much because he loved books and wished to help
Ballantyne as from the hope to obtain a larger share of the
profits accruing from his work ; and when from printing
he went on to publishing, his personal taste induced him
to load the press with books which interested himself but
were not of the kind to interest the reading public. It is
easy for us looking back to blame Scott for these speculations and to perceive their unwisdom. We do not understand his position as it appeared to himself at the outset,
when he realised that it was to literature he must trust
rather than to the law to gain the wealth he desired. He
could not foresee the success of the poems, much less of the

novels. The *Border Minstrelsy* and *Tristrem* proved, indeed, that he had, as George Ellis saw, the power of making interesting reading even of an introduction and notes. But the *Lay of the Last Minstrel* was the first triumphant success. This was followed by Constable's offer of one thousand guineas for *Marmion*, before the poem was even completed ; and undoubtedly Scott's imagination was dangerously excited, but he knew quite well that no one could count on poetry as a permanent source of income.[1] A literary career, as Scott contemplated it at the outset, was to be for him, as it had been for Goldsmith and Johnson, one of heavy pieces of task-work for the publishers—editions of Dryden, Beaumont and Fletcher, a collection of the British poets, a life of Thomson and endless other works which suggested themselves to his fertile mind. The poems were to be—just as Johnson's and Goldsmith's had been—pleasant escapes from task-work, relieving the author and charming his readers. But they proved in addition to be what we call " best sellers," and Constable was there on the outlook for just such a possibility. In Scott he found what he was looking for ; and in the end, we shall see, Constable and Scott gambled upon one another. To Scott, Constable seemed an almost bottomless mine of wealth,[2] a publisher who knew his own business too well to pay the prices he did if he were not sure about himself. To Constable, Scott seemed to be an author whose services were to be secured and retained at almost any price.[3] But Scott was not a young author to be exploited. He was out for business

---

[1] The correspondence of Cadell and Constable shows that in 1813 they were afraid that the comparative failure of *Rokeby* and the greater failure of *Don Roderick* indicated the decline of Scott's popularity. See notes to the letters of that year.

[2] " No man thought the house worth less than £150,000. Constable told me when he was making his will that he was worth £80,000, etc."—*Journal*, i. 99.

[3] " All our books and schemes and plans are not worth a farthing compared with keeping up the Edinburgh Review, the Encyclopædia Britannica and the Author of Waverley, etc."—Cadell to Constable, 1823.

too and had the Ballantynes at hand to work through. Accordingly when he quarrelled with Constable, or rather with Constable's bibulous partner Hunter, who had already insulted and mortally offended Longman, Scott conceived the unfortunate thought of trying to double the part and play author and publisher in one.

This was the tragic error of Scott's life. He launched into the difficult and dangerous work of a publisher with insufficient capital and with partners who, like himself, knew really nothing about publishing. It was " Youth at the prow and Pleasure at the helm," and Scott's ardent, impatient, sanguine spirit to supply the driving power. It would have been better if Lockhart, unable, as he confessed later he was, to get to the bottom of Scott's financial affairs, had dealt more shortly with the subject and not attempted to apportion blame, for the result has been to provoke a reaction in favour of the Ballantynes and Constable which would represent them as Scott's victims rather than—as the Ballantynes certainly were—his protégés, who owed such success as they had in life to his unwavering friendship.[1] Scott cannot escape the blame that in the eyes of sober men will attach to his sanguine rashness and careless generosity ; and if John Ballantyne was tricky, was a little on the score of old Gobbo, " did somewhat smack, somewhat grow to " (III. 296), and James's " honesty " was perhaps synonymous with " simplicity," and both were as extravagant in their ways as Scott himself, used the funds and the credit of the firm to meet their personal needs, just as Scott did, nevertheless a man is responsible for his choice of friends. Scott had the weakness which is sometimes found in

---

[1] " Do pray leave out," Maria Edgeworth writes to Lockhart in 1838, " all the Accounts in Scott's life—only make one clear general statement and let there be an end of all that—Posterity will care nothing about Ballantyne and Constable or any one of them but Scott himself—And let me hear nothing more of Ballantyne *Humbug*—What a vulgar word quite unworthy of you."—MS. letters to Lockhart, now in the National Library of Scotland.

strong, commanding natures. He liked to have those
about him who would do exactly as he directed, who
were at his beck and command. For Scott's plunge into
printing and publishing was not inspired by a sordid
love of money. He was a dreamer, but his dreams had
always been of an active kind—not only of " the disposal
of ideal wealth," but " of wielding imaginary power." A
great captain like the Duke of Wellington would have been,
but for his lameness, the height of his ambition ; and
in Constable he saw something of a great captain—the
Napoleon of booksellers, a man who planned and achieved
greatly. When in 1809 he broke with him, it was to set
up John Ballantyne & Co. (*i.e.* himself) as a rival to
Constable, and the motive was not alone the desire for
ampler means but the temptation of a wider, more exciting
field for the exercise of his boundless energy. Lockhart
has described the activities and emotions of the years
1808-9, when he was writing *Marmion*, editing Dryden,
finishing Strutt's *Queenhoo Hall*, editing the memoirs of
Captain George Carleton, of Sir Robert Carey, and more
than one similar work, while at the same time busy
starting the *Quarterly Review* and contributing liberally to
the first numbers—and all the while also getting under
way himself as a publisher. " Aye, it was enough to tear
me to pieces, but there was a wonderful exhilaration about
it all ; my blood was kept at fever-pitch—I felt as if I
could have grappled with anything and everything ;
then there was hardly any one of my schemes that did not
afford me the means of serving some poor devil of a
brother author. There were always huge piles of
materials to be arranged, sifted and indexed—volumes of
extracts to be transcribed—journeys to be made hither
and thither for ascertaining little facts and dates—in
short, I could commonly keep half a dozen of the ragged
regiment of Parnassus in tolerable ease." That does not
seem to me to be the language of Macaulay's " fevered
gambler," but of a strong man finding an outlet for his

fully-developed powers [1] ; and the purchase of land, the planting and building, the electioneering, and the hospitality were all the outcome of the same boundless energy which, without ample means, would have been " cribb'd, cabin'd and confined." What Professor Herbert Read, basing himself on Fromentin's biography, has said of Rubens is largely applicable to Scott : " He never hesitated in his triumphal progress. However much we may regret his lack of self-criticism, it is to that he owed his surety. He was quite simply a man of action, and he painted as other men fenced or fought or made business. Quite frankly, art was his business. Once established he had his fixed price . . . nor did he confine his activities to painting. In this too he is a sharp contradiction of all romantic theories of genius. As is well known he was a considerable diplomatist . . . and always as triumphant in this rôle as he is painted. He lived a private life of luxury, or rather of largesse ; he needed ample space, comforts, possessions. And yet, again to the discomfort of romantic notions, he was strictly regular in his habits, faithful to his two successive wives, simple and straightforward with his friends, a kind father to his large family."

Three questions have been raised by the entrance of Scott into business, first as partner in James Ballantyne & Co., printers, in 1805, and then in John Ballantyne & Co., publishers, in 1809. These concern, first, the secrecy which he preserved, secondly, his relations with the Ballantynes, and thirdly, with Archibald Constable and

[1] Compare what he says in a novel written when he was just escaping from "awful uncertainty" :—" In the fluctuations of mercantile speculation there is something captivating to the adventurer even independent of the hope of gain. . . . This mixture of necessary attention and inevitable hazard—the frequent and awful uncertainty whether prudence shall overcome fortune or fortune baffle the schemes of prudence—affords full occupation for the powers as well as for the feelings of the mind, and trade has all the fascination of gambling without its moral guilt."— *Rob Roy*, c. I. The description of Frank's father " impetuous in his schemes as well as skilful and daring " acquires a fresh piquancy for the reader of Scott's letters from 1813 to 1817.

Robert Cadell. Mr. Buchan in his recent *Life* dismisses Scott's secrecy about his business connections as on a par with the silence which most of us preserve regarding our investments ; which seems to me hardly an exact parallel. If we hold brewery or oil shares we do not, as a rule, take active steps to promote the sale of beer and petrol among our friends. Did Scott then by this secrecy deceive the booksellers and procure orders for James Ballantyne & Co. on the strength of what were taken to be disinterested recommendations of works to be published ? It seems to me impossible to establish this. I know of no publisher who, after the crash, complained of having been deceived in this way. If Scott cared to make it a condition of his being the author or editor of a work that it should be printed by James Ballantyne & Co. it was free to the publisher to refuse. Are publishers alone to have the right to bargain ? They did reject more than one of his proposals. The scheme for an edition of the *British Poets*, to be edited by Scott and Campbell, came to nothing—or to *Chalmers' Poets* ; [1] and the proposal for an edition of the *English Chroniclers* met with a similar fate. Miller indeed paid a handsome price for " Dryden," but he made a good thing out of it. It was Constable's own choice to offer " one thousand guineas " for the unfinished *Marmion*, and if Constable undertook other memoirs and collections he did so either because he thought them reasonable speculations (and no man was a better judge) or because he was willing to risk some loss for the sake of retaining Scott's services. It was on his invitation that " Swift " was undertaken. Some doubt of Scott's capacity to complete the work in time, amid all his other tasks, seems to have led to the quarrel with the hot-headed Hunter.

[1] Campbell had looked forward to collaborating with Scott in this and reports with bitter disappointment in October 1805 : " They have taken Alex. Chalmers into keeping for £300 to perform the task." *Chalmers' Poets* is a useful compilation but of textual editing there is a minus quantity. It is a piece of what can justly be called " hack-work."

Constable refused to make the quarrel on his side a personal one ; and if he did grumble when the work was delayed till 1814 it is clearly because he was beginning in that year to fear—and Cadell was largely responsible —that Scott's popularity was on the wane. " Don Roderick helped to damn him—and the failure of Rokeby completed it "—so Constable writes in May of that year. *Waverley* dispelled his doubts. No ; the publisher who suffered most from Scott's recommendation of works to be undertaken was John Ballantyne & Co. (*i.e.* Scott himself), who undertook the publication of Jamieson's *History of the Culdees,* the poems of Anna Seward, Tixall Poetry, Weber's edition of Beaumont and Fletcher, the *Edinburgh Annual Register* and other works of the kind. A hitherto unpublished letter shows that Scott was eager in 1810 to issue an edition of Shakespeare with as accurate a text as Weber and James Ballantyne can make it ! The project illustrates well the amateurish character of Scott's activities as publisher.

If there is, as I think, something not entirely honourable in Scott's concealment—an error (as Professor Saintsbury has defined Aristotle's " tragic error ") " capable of infinite excuse but no positive justification "—it is in his treatment of his friends, the degree to which he kept them in the dark about his affairs. Hartstonge, Morritt, Charles Erskine—he borrowed from them all in the years of his first difficulties, 1813 ; and though he repaid them all there was a moment when it appeared that in order to do so he would have to pledge his entire income (see Vol. III. p. 320). Is it strictly honourable to pledge the credit of a friend without making clear to him the extent of the risk he is running—indeed without indicating that he is running any risk at all ? Even apart from that question, is it fair to accept a friend's confidences while concealing a fundamental fact in one's own life ? As Lockhart says : " I doubt not what gave him the bitterest pain, in the hour of his calamities, was the feeling of compunction with which he found himself obliged to stand before those with whom he had through life cultivated brotherly friendship convicted of having kept his heart closed to them on what they could not but suppose to have been the chief subjects of his thoughts and anxiety in times when they withheld nothing from him. These were perhaps the 'written troubles' that had been cut deepest into his brain. I believe it the more because it was never acknowledged."

The relation between Scott and the Ballantynes seems to me to have remained the same from the beginning to the end ; and can be stated in their own words.[1] In a memorandum, prepared for Lockhart, James Ballantyne writes : " My brother John though an active and pushing was not a cautious publisher, and the large sums received (*i.e.* for *The Lady of the Lake*) never formed an addition to stock. In fact they were all expended by the partners, who being young and sanguine men not unwillingly adopted my brother's hasty results." Scott's statement is much the same, with one important addition. Writing to James in November 1816, over the matter of a bill granted by James to his brother Alexander in the name of the firm but unknown to the other partner, he says : " You and your brother keeping the accompts we both drew according to our rated stocks with such indiscretion as it proved that the concern was run £4000 in debt, which £4000, containing *your* draughts as well as *my own*, I *alone* was under the necessity of replacing." They were all extravagant,[2] but Scott alone, then and in

---

[1] I refer a reader who wishes a closer analysis of the details, so far as now discoverable, to Mr. Glen's letter following this Introduction. I hope to deal with this and Scott's life generally in a subsequent volume.

[2] In a letter of 13th May 1814, that is, when the troubles and perils of the critical year 1813 were hardly yet over, Cadell describes to Constable an evening at the house of James Ballantyne : " Since you left this I was at a party he gave where there was an excellent display of Vocal and Instrumental music, the whole was finished by a most splendid Supper where there was the appearance of the first affluence and genteelity. Forty sat down to the Gala. What do you think of this ! ! for a ——

the end, had to pay the piper. Both John and James, it seems to me, despite constitutional defects—of trickiness in John, indolence and incompetence as an accountant in James—served Scott zealously and loyally. But they both benefited beyond their share in the profits of the business, and of some at any rate of the novels, and Scott had to pay for their overdrafts as well as his own. Nor can I find that he did them harm in any way. John, after a gay life, died believing himself able to leave legacies, which, like other of John's "states," was an illusion, for he left his wife (as she says herself), through his extravagance, in abject poverty, and Scott had to come to her help. James, who re-entered partnership with Scott in 1822 (a strange thing for him to do if he thought that Scott had ill-used him), owed his partner then £3000 besides other debts, all of which he had by 1826 cleared off save some £40. How this was done out of his *legitimate* share of the business or the novels is not clear from the accounts now in the Library of the Writers to the Signet. But whatever the trustees of the Ballantynes may have felt about Lockhart they have to admit, while busy placing the whole blame on Scott, that he never said an unkind word about either of them. He might be a little contemptuous of James's later liberal views and pious qualms, but he always lays it down to Cadell after the failure that they are in the same boat and that James must get all the printing they can give him.

The fatal amateurishness and recklessness with which the publishing business was conducted brought about the crisis of 1813-14, the history of which is pretty fully written in the letters here printed, and led to the appeal to Constable. Thereafter Constable becomes the chief sharer in the speculations and successes which began with the publication of *Waverley*. Longmans got *Guy Mannering* —and managed it badly, Scott thought, as compared

Printer!" They modelled themselves upon their patron, ultimately at his expense.

with Constable. Blackwood and Murray secured the first *Tales of my Landlord*, but with the second series of the *Tales* Constable took over what remained of the unsaleable stock of John Ballantyne & Co. and became the publisher of practically all the succeeding novels and other works [1] ; but always on the condition of granting bills on publication, or even in advance of publication, which could be discounted then and there—" discount— damn the very name—I shall hate it while I live," Scott writes to John Ballantyne in 1813—but, alas ! he forgot. The arrangements for a new *Travels on the Continent*, suggested by the success of *Paul's Letters to his Kinsfolk* in 1815, to be written if Scott went abroad again, is charac- teristic of the methods adopted. The journey itself was merely a project. Yet John hurries back to Edinburgh from Abbotsford to " raise my thousand pounds," *i.e.* his anticipated share, and counts on Constable accepting bills at once for " the two thousand pounds arising payable for your shares." Accordingly Constable under- takes to publish the work at half-profits and the canny Cadell, who in 1813-14 had spoken of Scott to Constable in the bitterest terms,[2] is convinced that a good bargain has been made, that the offer of half-profits from such an author is a very liberal one.

That, I think, indicates clearly the nature of the relations between Scott and Constable. Constable, with all his sagacity, was a dreamer too, a bold speculator who loved large schemes and lived extravagantly. It is a strange comment on the " canny Scot " to compare

----

[1] *The Monastery*, 1820, was given to Longman in order " to give Con- stable's credit a little repose " (see letter to John Ballantyne of 2nd August 1819), and Longman shared *The Abbot* with Constable.

[2] " I am not at all surprised at your spleen about Swift, he just appears to have cast it from him like as much dross that he longed to be quit of— it is needless for me to say anything here, you know pretty well my opinion of the gentleman."—Cadell to Constable, 6th May 1814. The whole correspondence of Scott and the Ballantynes and Constable and Cadell reads as commentary on what Aristotle has to say about friendships based on the quest of profit.—*Nic. Eth.* viii. c. 3.

Constable with the cautious and timid Murray, or Scott with the more successful and equally eager to grow rich Dickens. Constable too had operated on a narrow margin of capital and had experienced strokes of ill-fortune. His partnership with the bibulous and irritable Hunter involved him in a quarrel with Longman which led to the unfortunate attempt to establish a branch in London. The same partner's quarrel with Scott ostensibly set up John Ballantyne & Co., lost Constable a share of the *Lady of the Lake*, and quickened his suspicions of possible rivals ever afterwards to such a degree that he took risks on Scott which were beyond his means. Hunter's withdrawal from the partnership meant a loss of £17,000 worth of capital, and the later partnership with Cadell and Cathcart was interrupted by the almost immediate death of Cathcart, involving again a diminution of capital. " This has been a labouring concern for twelve years," Cadell writes to Constable in 1823 ; and again : " It is the want of capital that is the bane of all our operations." . . . " I cannot send Mrs. Constable's sum without stating to you explicitly that it is wholly impossible for the concern to afford so much to its partners. . . . I cannot discharge a more proper duty than that of warning you once more against what will in time assuredly sink this concern, that is its expense and the drains of the partners." " You said the other day that for two years you had done nothing to embark money—but you have *spent it*—in these two short years you have got nearly £9000 or £10,000 from the Company—is that not embarking—you say you will not longer live a life of misery —your family has drawn at the rate of £1400 from this embarrassed concern since June 1822."—Cadell to Constable, 23rd July 1823.

Scott and Constable, as I have said, gambled on one another. Scott was confident that Constable was a sagacious, crafty, well-to-do business man, able to take care of himself in any bargain he made, and who, though

he might at times, like all business men, have need of
" accommodation " from those to whom he would grant
the same in turn, was yet " rooted as well as branched
like the oak." It is usual to suggest that Scott's anger
with Constable after the failure was occasioned by his
having been induced by him to raise a loan over the
Abbotsford estate at the last moment.[1] But a careful
reading of Scott's words in the *Journal* shows that his
feeling went deeper than this. What Scott felt was that
he had lived in a dream for which Constable was largely
responsible : " Constable's business seems unintelligible.
No man thought the house worth less than £150,000.
Constable told me when he was making his will that he
was worth £80,000. Great profits on almost all the
adventures. No bad speculations—yet neither stock nor
debt to show. Constable might have eaten up his share ;
but Cadell was very frugal " ; and again : " Constable's
death might have been a most important thing to me if it
had happened some years ago, and I should then have
lamented it much. He has lived to do me some injury,
yet, excepting the last £5000, I think most unintentionally.
. . . I have no great reason to regret him ; yet I do. If
he deceived me, he also deceived himself." [2]

That is Scott's position. What was Constable's ? It is
clear now from the correspondence between Constable
and Cadell that Constable regarded Scott as an asset to
preserve which almost any risk must be taken, and,
whatever Cadell might have thought himself in 1813, he
came to be even more strongly of the same opinion. The
consequence was that Constable accepted bills, both
" value " bills for work done or undertaken, and " accommodation " bills, loans, to an extent that went far beyond

---

[1] As a fact the loan of £5000, to which Scott refers in the *Journal* as Constable's only intentional deceit, was not this loan over Abbotsford, but the sum
of £5000 borrowed from John Renwick of the Register House, at the instance
of Cadell, and used in an effort to save Hurst, Robinson & Co. The loan
over Abbotsford was also made at Cadell's instance. See Mr. Glen's Letter.

[2] *Journal*, i. 99, and ii. 11.

his means if, as at the end, there should come any pressure to realise.

If 1813 was the critical year in the relation between Scott and the Ballantynes, 1823, ten years later, is equally critical and decisive of the relation between Scott and Constable & Co., *i.e.* Archibald Constable and Robert Cadell. With the help of the now accessible correspondence, not only of Scott with Constable but of Constable and Cadell with each other, we can understand the position better than it has ever been possible to do, and see what led up to the disaster of three years later. In a letter written to Maria Edgeworth in December 1832 by Sir James Gibson-Craig,[1] who had been Constable's lawyer and consulted by him (he tells her) at every step, it is stated that in 1823 Constable, becoming alarmed by the amount of the bills granted " for Sir Walter's accommodation," went to Abbotsford carrying the whole of *his* bills and entreated Sir Walter to retire all the bills Constable & Co. held. This, Gibson-Craig says, owing to his own and Lady Scott's extravagance, Sir Walter could not do, whereupon Constable proceeded to put the counter-bills into circulation (not, apparently, having done so before), with the well-known result that ultimately Scott became liable for both sets of bills. In some notes [2] prepared for Lockhart when he was writing the *Life*, Cadell refers to the incident in a rather perfunctory way : " Constable & Co. made a strong remonstrance in the autumn of this year on the amount of the current accommodation bills." He then gives Scott's letter of 23rd August [3] and continues : " No change appears however to have taken place. A new novel was contracted for which was never destined to be

---

[1] See *Archibald Constable and his Literary Correspondents*, iii. 456. Sir James was a Whig and a friend of Lord Lauderdale, an old enemy of Scott. Gibson-Craig was anxious to challenge Scott over the articles in *The Beacon*, and was only dissuaded when it appeared that Scott had no personal share or knowledge of the libels.

[2] Unpublished ; now in the National Library of Scotland.

[3] *Archibald Constable*, etc., iii. 284-5, and in this edition later.

written, and Sir Walter deceived himself by thinking that such a course obliterated the accommodation bills ; at the same time that he thought a new bargain for works in advance wiped off such bills he asked for £1200 in addition—I allude to this the more particularly as Sir Walter often deceived himself in this way, even within a few months of his death." The episode is further and more fully dealt with in *Archibald Constable and his Literary Correspondents*, iii. c. xiii. There we learn that the visit to Abbotsford seems to have been postponed by the illness of Mrs. Constable,[1] but the letters which passed between Constable and Scott, on this occasion, both personal as from Constable and official in the name of A. C. & Co., are printed in full. I propose to reprint most of them in a later volume of this work. There is nothing in their tone to bear out Sir James's language of " entreating " nor Cadell's "strong remonstrance." They are most courteous and guarded letters, and that for very good reasons. What neither Cadell in his report to Lockhart nor Thomas Constable in his defence of his father tells is, that it was entirely against Cadell's wish that Constable took up the matter with Scott, and that at his instance the question raised was confined to that of " accommodation bills," *i.e.* loans, no mention being made of the bills " for value received," that is the bills which Constable & Co. had granted for work done, or in progress, or in prospect, by Scott, including the sum offered for the copyrights which they had purchased. The reason of Cadell's unwillingness to raise the question and to make Scott aware of the full extent of their obligations to him in one way and another is clearly brought out in his letters to his partner. " What can be the reason," he had written to Constable in July, " of your never failing remarks about Ballantyne's bills is a mystery to me but the utter ignorance of the absolute

[1] " A day having been fixed for a meeting at Abbotsford, my father found it necessary to postpone it in consequence of the illness of Mrs. Constable." —THOMAS CONSTABLE : *Constable, etc.*, iii. 280.

wants of your concern being as great if not greater than
those of J. B. & Co. [1]—I say *ours* are greater than theirs
—their bills to us I know are sooner cashed than ours to
them—do you suppose I have no alarms—I have many
but it is not for Ballantyne it *is for A. C. & Co.* I know
that Ballantynes have almost no other bills than ours and
Sir Walter's . . . but I also know that Sir Walter Scott has
a large estate—that it is *unencumbered*—that Jas. B. & Co.
have a good business—that they have nearly as much of
the Author of Waverley's works as we have and bills with
none else (at least if I am to believe Jas. B.) to any amount
worth a thought—more than that they have no sinks but
the interest of this sum and Sir Walter's present buildings
at Abbotsford—above all—the sum between them and
us appears much more than it is in reality. . . . As long
as A. C. & Co. are solvent there is no fear of Jas. B. &
Co.—there are three life-policies of Sir Walter's life if
anything happens the amount £20,000. Knowing
therefore what I do know I have no alarm in this quarter
for the quarter itself—my grief is that A. C. & Co. have
more from J. B. & Co. than J. B. & Co. from them.
. . . I am satisfied of their usefulness to A. C. & Co.—
without them and the bills and books A. C. & Co.
would not, in all likelihood, have existed. I am therefore
most grateful to them. I shall try to keep well with them
and at present do so, far from making any attempt to beat
down their bills I shall do my utmost to keep them on
smoothly, as I tell you honestly *we need them* and *must have
them*—the greatest fear I have in this quarter is Jas. Ballantyne's death." Despite Cadell's warning, Constable, who
had apparently (as he says to Scott) only just become fully
aware of the magnitude of the dealings between his firm
and J. B. & Co., insisted and wrote to Cadell asking for
a " state " to put before Scott as he wished " to lay a full

---

[1] " The miscreants of St. John Street," he had called them in 1815, but
that was when the negotiations with Murray and Blackwood were proceeding, for *Tales of my Landlord.*

view of all the pros and cons and engagements of every description before Sir Walter." Cadell replied on the 18th of August : " I shall do as you wish and write a scroll of what I would lay before Sir Walter—but I fear you and I will differ widely—in the first place—I would most strongly advise that it be delayed till we *are prepared*—that no statement be made of the actually existing sums—I would never allude to the value engagements—and I would propose no other plan but that of gradual reduction —so far from making up the statement as at 1 August I would delay it till 1 October—it will then be large enough —and quite large enough to make a case upon and a strong one—I say all this most deliberately—I regret if I am opposed to you in opinion in this—I always regret if I have to differ from you, but the importance of the quarter is so great that I would strongly and strenuously counsel cautious measures . . . as to anything like con- tracting for four new works and thus raising the funds I can assure you it appears to me . . . not one of your most judicious views." Constable then wrote to Scott and in his reply Scott makes what seems to me a very candid inquiry and a fair statement of his understanding of the relation between himself and the firm. " The first question I should candidly have asked you is whether the cause of your present correspondence arose merely out of the extent of those pecuniary transactions which I am as desirous as you to abridge, or whether the de- ficiency of the sale of *Quentin Durward* has diminished your general confidence in this sort of literature, and inclined you to restrict on all points our hitherto very extensive concerns ? Do not suppose me selfish enough to be vexed or angry if the latter should be the case ; and pray be candid and speak it out at once. I cannot expect, and do not wish, you to bestow the capital your skill and industry have acquired upon that which does not promise you profit ; nor do I think that because our former intercourse has been lucrative I have acquired or would wish to exercise any right to put my hand into your pocket any deeper than you desire." If Constable could have been equally candid he would have told Scott that he *was*, as his letters to Cadell show, in some anxiety about the rapid succession of novels, and he would have said that he could undertake no further engagements until those in hand were completed, and until the bills issued in advance, and especially those given by way of " accommodation," were retired. But with Cadell's warning in mind Constable replies : " I can at once assure you that I entertain no fears of any kind on the subject of the literary plans and undertakings in which my house is fortunately engaged with you, and it will unquestionably afford myself and my partner the greatest satisfaction to do all things and everything within our command which you can desire in continuing and extending the number of them. It was no dread of failure in these matters . . . which induced our present correspondence ; the motives were entirely confined to the extent of the money transactions . . . and I may also add the anxiety I have long had to see your high name free from the botheration of mercantile affairs." Accordingly the suggestions for reduction were confined to the accommodation bills. Nothing was said of the bills granted by Constable for work done or undertaken, which amounted to the gross sum of £35,000, in addition to the £27,000 of accommodation bills which Cadell found so useful. Scott made some effort to reduce the latter and at Constable's suggestion met them in part by fresh undertakings. " If by persevering reduction," says Constable (following Cadell's advice as to " gradual " reduction), " this sum could be brought down to £8000 or £10000 everything would move comfortably or easily ; but it must be apparent to your own excellent understanding that the sums in October and November and December are very large. The work now in progress would assist very considerably and we would suggest that, if in your power, it should appear early in November ; if its successor were to appear in February or March a farther sum will come in, and we might say that in December or January a new contract might come into play and with these operations the whole thing exhibit a more moderate appearance."

In view of all these facts taken together it is hard not to admit that Scott had a right to feel after the disaster that he had been deceived by Constable " if he also deceived himself," nor is it easy to acquit Cadell of being the more responsible partner in the deceit. Considering what Scott did after the crash it is difficult to believe that, had it been made clear to him in 1823 that their engagements were endangering both himself and Constable, he would not have made an effort to save the situation. If at a still earlier period Constable had not been induced to outbid other possible publishers Scott would doubtless have tried elsewhere. It is not likely that he would have found the timid Murray or the hard-headed Blackwood or Longman so complacent. In any case he would have divided his risks. I am not seeking to acquit Scott. His sanguine temper made him only too willing to be deceived. The hard terms he drove in his later works with Constable contributed to the disaster. He had early made up his mind that publishers were bargainers who must be met on their own ground. The lot of the literary man [1] at the

---

[1] " Constable is a deep draw-well—I was really duped by him but I have found him out—It is not two months since he absolutely made me believe he had not been meant by nature for a bookseller—but the cold grease has at last appeared—he is a piece of the most fallacious fat meat that ever was packed into a human skin—but God knows he is not the worst of the bunch."—Campbell to Scott, April 1815. Yet Cadell reports to Lockhart in 1834 : Scott was " throughout liberal to his publisher—he might have asked higher prices—if he had done so he would have got them—but when a price was once fixed for a book he took the same money for those that follow'd without making any change : in *Waverley* for example the First edition was published on the principle of the Booksellers taking the risk of paper & printing & dividing the gain with the author— this arrangement went on with all the after editions altho it is clear from the extraordinary popularity of the Author he might have exacted higher terms." Cadell to Lockhart, Abbotsford Copies, Vol. II. But Cadell's statements to Lockhart are not always to be reconciled with what he wrote to Constable at the time.

mercy of the publishers seemed to him, as he tells Bailey, one of the most wretched conceivable ; and he knew how Campbell and others fared. But it is equally impossible to prove that he treated the Ballantynes either unfairly or unkindly, or to acquit Constable and Cadell of having misled him as to their soundness and ability to offer such terms as they did. He paid the penalty. In the end the only person who profited by Scott's dreams and labours was Robert Cadell. He was an astute fellow. He wriggled out of his bankruptcy for a payment, if I understand his own letters, of some one and fivepence in the pound ; he started then as a publishing bookseller and retained Scott as his greatest asset, and one that he used to the utmost. If he tells Lockhart that to the end of his life Scott deceived himself about money matters he does not tell how much he was responsible by his encouragement to accept loans, or that it was he who urged Scott to keep the profits of *Tales of a Grandfather* for himself, a peccadillo which the trustees overlooked.

It has been necessary to describe at the outset how Scott's financial and business affairs appear seen in broad outline, because they bulk so largely in a fuller edition of the letters. The issue cannot be shirked. Scott is not, of course, the only author or artist who has been keenly interested in the business aspect of his work, has been a bargainer with publishers or patrons. Dickens hastened his death by profitable tours as a reader of his own works ; and Turner, as Scott will be found complaining, was not going to illustrate the *magnum opus*—the collected edition of the works—for an inadequate remuneraton. Balzac, like Scott, had a long fight with debt, but if he desired to be an honourable debtor he also liked the feeling that money was coming in. We all do. It is not Scott's acquisitiveness that is the disturbing factor, but his reckless expenditure on the purchase of land and in a large-handed hospitality. It was not really " ostentatious," as Macaulay with his so different temperament describes it, but rather imaginative—an aspect of that dream-life which, with all his air of the business man and man of the world, he lived throughout. Other men, Goethe for instance, have felt the double attraction of the poet—the creative artist in himself, on the one hand ; and of the man of the world, the power that seems to belong to the man of affairs, on the other. Tasso in the drama of that name and Antonio represent two sides of Goethe's own character, and the clash between them ; a clash which in the play he fails to reconcile. But if he failed to work out the conflict to a dramatic solution in the *Tasso*, Goethe's clear, analytic mind could hold the two tendencies apart, keep them from crossing one another in his life as Scott could not, with the result that the dreamer entered too much into the conduct of his affairs while the practical man kept a check—in general a wholesome one—upon the flights of the imagination, but sometimes with an inhibitory influence on quite justifiable sympathies, in the romances. We shall fail to do justice to Scott as man and creator if we fail to realise this blend of the dreamer and the practical man of the world.

For it was as a sensitive dreamer that Scott saw himself when he looked back on his delicate childhood, happy in the country with his grandparents and a devoted aunt, suffering at home from bullying brothers and servants impatient of his lameness,[1] although

> a fond mother's care and joy
> Was centered in her sickly boy,

and the memory of his own experience made him recur more than once to the dangers of a too early indulgence in the charms of feeling and imagination :

> Woe to the youth whom Fancy gains,
> Winning from Reason's hand the reins,

---

[1] " There is still the stile at which I can recollect a cross child's maid upbraiding me with my infirmity, as she lifted me coarsely and carelessly over the flinty steps which my brothers traversed with shout and bound. I remember the suppressed bitterness of the moment and, conscious of my own inferiority, the feeling of envy with which I regarded the easy move-

> Pity and woe ! for such a mind
> Is soft, contemplative, and kind ;
> And woe to those who train such youth,
> And spare to press the rights of truth,
> The mind to strengthen and anneal,
> While on the stithy glows the steel !

It is a little difficult to think of Wilfred in *Rokeby* as a self-portrait of Walter Scott rather than of a Shelley or a Lamartine ; but one will not understand his character or fate if one forgets how much of deliberate self-training had gone to make the strong, active, stoical man of the world and man of affairs when the delicacies of early youth were outgrown. It is those who know, or have known, what it is to be a little afraid of their own sensibility who will, like the young Swinburne, climb a dangerous cliff or undertake a feat of swimming to establish their own self-respect. And if Scott outgrew the timidity of delicacy and an acute sensibility he never outgrew the dreamer. Alike in his conduct of business and in his creative literary work the dreamer and the practical man were blended with one another in a way both fortunate and unfortunate for himself. " Since I was five years old I cannot remember the time when I had not some ideal part to play for my own amusement. . . . . My life, though not without its fits of waking and strong exertion, has been a sort of dream spent in

> Chewing the cud of sweet and bitter fancy.

I have worn a wishing cap, the power of which has often been to divert present griefs by a touch of the wand of imagination, and gild over the future prospect by prospects more fair than can ever be realised. . . . The love of solitude was with me a passion of early youth ; when in my teens I used to fly from company to indulge in visions and airy castles of my own, the disposal of ideal wealth and the exercise of imaginary power. This

ments and elastic steps of my more happily formed brethren."—*My Aunt Margaret's Mirror.*

feeling prevailed even till I was eighteen, when love and ambition threw me more into society, from which, however, I have at times withdrawn myself and have always been even glad to do so. I have risen from a feast satiated ; and unless it be one or two persons of very strong intellect, or whose spirits and good humour amuse me, I wish to see neither the high, the low, nor the middling class of society. This is a feeling without the least tinge of misanthropy, which I always consider as a kind of blasphemy of a shocking description."

This side of Scott's character he studied to suppress as contact with his robustious brothers—for Tom alone he seems to have had an affection which no misconduct could destroy—the brutalities of the High School Yards, and finally, the companionship of young Edinburgh advocates, a tough race intellectually, taught him what the world of men was really like, and what it thought of the dreamer. It was quite deliberately that he set himself to be a "roaring boy," and later a man of the world, so that when he took up authorship as his business it was, as he tells us, with the resolution "to keep as far as was in my power abreast of society, continuing to maintain my place in general company, without yielding to the very natural temptation of narrowing myself to what is called literary society . . . Like Gil Blas I resolved to stick by the society of my *Commis* . . . and to maintain my general interest in what was going on around me, reserving the man of letters for the desk and the library." Unless one realises this double strain in Scott's nature it will be difficult to understand or be just to—on the one hand the sensitive, imaginative dreamer building castles in the air for his own delight, and on the other the strong and active man who had learned from experience at home and contact with Edinburgh society that the only success which counted for anything in the world was that which gave one power and station, the means to gratify one's tastes, to indulge one's family, and to help and befriend depen-

dants and those who appealed to his acute sense of pity.
We might think more highly of Scott had he chosen with
Wordsworth a life of " plain living and high thinking " ;
but he might have paid for that by becoming the sublime
egoist that Wordsworth was in his later days, contemplating always his own effigy and with little sympathy for
younger men and poets. It might have been better if he
had cultivated the frugality and simplicity of Carlyle,
who in his way and measure was also generous to poorer
men, but for that too he might have paid by becoming
morose and irritable and wearing out the nerves of a
brilliant wife. As it was Scott's life was for many years
a happy one and brought happiness to others, to almost
everyone that came within his orbit. I can think of no
other man of letters to compare with him in this respect
unless it be to some extent Macaulay. The penalty of
Scott's errors—his impetuous extravagance in the purchase
of land and exercise of hospitality—was paid for by himself
and his family alone.

Moreover, to do justice to Scott, to understand, which
is now more important than to condemn, his weaknesses
as well as his virtues, it is necessary to be a little more
candid than Lockhart could be about his more immediate
inheritance, not the Auld Wats and Beardies on whom
it delighted his imagination to dwell as his ancestors,
but his own family in George Square. It has been said
that genius is not infrequently an emergence in a family
that shows a morbid, decadent tendency. It certainly
seems to be true of Walter Scott. Like Major Bridgenorth
in *Peveril of the Peak* Scott's parents had lost six children
before the eldest of Walter's brothers was born. The air
of College Wynd has been blamed, and doubtless justly
so far, but there must have been more than the locality to
blame. Robert, the eldest of those who survived, passed
from the navy in 1783 into the service of the East India
Company, for which service " his habits were ill-adapted,"
and he died—so says Scott—and the habits were doubtless

those to which Daniel fell a victim in the equally trying climate of Jamaica. John the soldier retired from the army with broken health and died at the early age of forty-seven, and Scott lets slip the betraying remark : " The poor major had been rather a free liver." It was the same weakness, Scott tells Charles after his uncle's death, that explains the checkered, and for Walter so costly, career of his favourite brother Tom. The only sister of the poet, Anne, was highly neurotic and died, partly as the result of an accident, in her thirtieth year. Walter was himself attacked in his second year by infantile paralysis, which left him permanently lame, and though the régime which he describes in *Peveril*—" a more sparing use of medicine, a bolder admission of fresh air, and a firm yet cautious attention to encourage rather than to supersede the exertions of nature "—saved his life, he continued to betray symptoms of delicacy till he had passed the age of fifteen. Thereafter he became not only healthy but robust, a man of powerful build and great endurance ; but he had inherited from his mother a tendency to gall-stones, which the hard work and financial anxiety of the years 1813 and after brought out in 1817, and more acutely in 1819. " With its disappearance," says Skene, " although restored to comparative health, disappeared also much of his former vigour of body, activity or power of sustaining fatigue, while in personal appearance he seemed in that short space to have advanced twenty years on the downward course of his life ; his hair became bleached and scanty ; the fire of his eye was much subdued, and his step more uncertain had lost the vigorous swinging gait with which he used formerly to proceed. . . . It was only after this period that I ever perceived that degree of abstraction and absence of mind which he sometimes exhibited when his thoughts had been deeply occupied."

Such was Scott's family inheritance, and if he had some of the faults that seem to have run in the blood, a certain careless handedness about money, let it be counted to him for virtue that he was not alone the genius but the pillar of his family. " You have become great, Walter," said his old uncle. " But you were always good," which did not mean that he was a model of all the " restrictive virtues " as Emerson calls them in speaking of Milton. What the word " good " indicates when it comes from the heart is a quality of the heart—kindness ; but Scott's was not capricious kindness like that of Byron, but steady and consistent kindness arising from an unfailing recognition of the rights or even the claims of others. I know no man of letters of the first rank to whom the word " dutiful " can be applied so justly as to Scott. It is an old-fashioned word, not much in favour to-day when the first of virtues is self-assertion ; when *sacro egoismo* is the great proof of character and genius. But Scott seemed able to combine it with a steady expansion of his own powers and tastes. He was dutiful to his parents—even to labouring in the office ; dutiful to his brothers, for if Daniel's cowardice repelled at the end his pride, and his estimate of courage as the ultimate virtue, he had got him his place in Jamaica, and after his death he made Daniel's natural child one of his many cares. No worry and loss of money ever alienated his affection for the easy-going Tom who had stood by him when a lame child. " I return you," writes Tom's wife from the Isle of Man, " the most heart-felt thanks for your brotherly conduct and affectionate expressions towards us." It is the same with everyone. Scott can be, when wounded or slighted, angry and even unjust but, unless the quarrel is obstinately maintained on the other side, he is easily placated. At the end he fights for James Ballantyne's claims as strongly as for his own, and lays aside his own labours to write an article on Molière and help the now impecunious Gillies, as he had in earlier days, when he could not help him to publish, sent Maturin an inclosure of fifty pounds. " But for you," writes

Laidlaw's brother to Scott, "my brother would have been reduced to depend for the necessaries of life upon his grudging creditors;" and, in acknowledging the gift of "a perspective glass," he writes : "It is another proof of the delight you take in making others happy." But no incident illustrates this fundamental trait in Scott's character better than that from the *Journal* which Mr. Buchan has cited : "A poor young woman came here this morning, well dressed, and well behaved, with a strong northern accent. She talked incoherently a long story of a brother and a lover both dead. I would have kept her here till I wrote to her friends, particularly to Mr Sutherland (an Aberdeen bookseller), to inform them where she is, but my daughter and her maidens were frightened, as indeed there might be room for it, and so I sent her in one of Davidson's chaises to the Castle at Jedburgh, and wrote to Mr Shortreed to see she is humanely treated. I have written also to her brother." But it is not the incident by itself that is remarkable. It is only one of many that might be cited of such consistent and persistent kindness. He could not leave a case that came in his way, or be content with a careless gift and a good wish. He had to see it through.

Indeed this aspect of Scott's character meets us at the threshold, when we turn from the troublesome matter of business and bills to other aspects of the letters, in the episode on which Lockhart has touched but which subsequent biographers have passed over generally, as the details remained somewhat obscure,—I mean Scott's friendship for and loyalty to young Charles Kerr, as we now know was the name of the friend whom Lockhart left unnamed. Scott's side of this early correspondence is still undiscovered but the letters of Kerr are in the National Library of Scotland, except a few which are in the University of Edinburgh Library. They bear out to the full all that Lockhart says of Scott's loyalty and helpfulness. "I shall keep your letters as the proof of an honest heart" are Kerr's first words. "God bless you for your past friendship, receive my warmest thanks—would to God I had more to offer." There can be no doubt, as Lockhart saw, that it was from this episode recalled in later life that *Redgauntlet* originated. The suggestion that William Clerk was the model of Darsie Latimer is not borne out by the character of Clerk as Scott describes him in the *Journal*— a typical Edinburgh advocate with a strong dose of *pruritus disputandi*, not the impulsive person that Charles Kerr shows himself from first to last and which is reproduced in Darsie combined with perhaps a greater amiability than one divines in Kerr. " Have nothing to do with Charles Kerr " says Scott's father, writing after the young man's return to Scotland—in the first of the letters of the older Scott to his son which I have come upon.

In 1792, writing to William Clerk, Scott says : " I have no chance of seeing ma chere adorable till winter if then " ; and in 1794 Kerr, speaking of some verses, says : " There are some delicate touches in them which to a man like you in love must prove acceptable." These are our earliest extant references to Scott's one great love affair. But there had been an earlier one, as letters here printed for the first time reveal—letters copied into a projected *Life* by some one unknown, now in the Forster MSS. in the South Kensington Museum. Of the originals, nothing is known, and I may be criticised for accepting these copies as genuine, or not at least reserving them for an appendix. They, to my mind, speak for themselves. Who the " Jessie " was is unknown, but she was the immediate source of the biographer's story ; she had married a medical student and settled in London. Who but Scott would have entertained a tradesman's daughter, for so the biographer describes the young woman, with old ballads, just as Jonathan Oldbuck might have done, and with his own youthful poems. The affair began, the story runs, at Kelso, probably in the early years of his law studies, but when the maiden was summoned to

Edinburgh to attend upon a sick relative Scott sought her out and frequently, to escape observation, was concealed for long periods in the china cupboard, where he passed the time in composing very mediocre verses :

Heed not what the world may say
Should they spy our goings-on ;
Put off till the evil day
What till then must be unknown.
They may blame ye—who would doubt it ?
Dinna fash your thumb about it.

Ever since Auld Adam's time
This good fashion hath prevailed,
To be happy in our prime
Ere each proper sense hath failed.
If they preach gainst this or flout it,
Dinna fash your thumb about it.

Gradually, as his social acquaintance widened, the young man's feelings cooled and he drew off, the damsel regarding his conduct " with a resentment that never subsided." It is an experience through which many young men have passed, and has left no mark on the novels (which reflect, if they also transfigure, so many of Scott's early experiences), unless indeed it be Edward Waverley's awakening regard for Miss Cicely Stubbs.

It was not so with his love for Miss Williamina Belsches, for a calf-love for a Jessie or a Rosaline is obliterated without leaving a trace on the sands of memory when the true Juliet appears, whereas no later love can ever breed entire forgetfulness of one sincere passion, especially if that has been a disappointed passion. The letters tell us no more than Lockhart does of Williamina Belsches, who remains almost as shadowy a figure as Jessie. But they do clear up some of the confusion in Lockhart's narrative of events.

From Clerk's letter to Sophia Lockhart, which is now in the National Library, it is evident that some of his friends did think Walter had been a little hardly used when the lady and her parents prudently preferred the banker to the young man with no apparent prospect of success either at the Bar or in any other direction. We can follow in his letter to Erskine of 24th March 1796 the agitations of the last year as he makes his way north to Aberdeen, casting longing looks towards Fettercairn, the home of Miss Belsches. A visit on his way back to Edinburgh in April-May reanimates his hopes while he excavates in Fenella's Castle ; and between hopes and fears he seems to have spent the summer and autumn, for the former are not yet quenched when on 26th September he writes to Erskine to communicate his joyful sympathy with his friend over the coming marriage of Ann Erskine to Campbell of Clathick. By the 12th of October his fate was sealed. The first verses of any worth he wrote, *The Violet*,[1] express his sense of injury, and long afterwards when his friend James Ballantyne met with the same treatment at the hands of a Glasgow fair one he recalls how he broke his wine-glass in anger on the occasion.

If, as one friend thought, Scott's sanguine and impatient temperament misled him as to Miss Belsches' sentiments, the same impetuous disposition led him a year later into a hasty marriage with a young woman

[1]   The violet in her green-wood bower
  Where birchen boughs with hazel mingle,
  May boast itself the fairest flower
   In glen or copse or forest dingle ;

  Though fair her gems of azure hue
   Beneath the dew-drop's weight reclining,
  I've seen an eye of lovelier blue,
   More sweet through wat'ry lustre shining.

  The summer sun that dew shall dry
   Ere yet the day be past its morrow ;
  Nor longer in my false love's eye
   Remained the tear of parting sorrow.

As Dame Una Pope-Hennessey says, "wat'ry lustre" is not a happy phrase, but the poem marks an advance on anything to Jessie. For the letter to Ballantyne see p. 296 where it is printed, but at too early a date.

of whose history he knew nothing. Reporting his parents' desire for some definite information he writes to the young lady : " They have not my apology for indifference upon the subject which is that my regard for Miss Carpenter herself was so great as to make me utterly careless upon all such matters " ; and long afterwards he tells Lockhart that into her family history " I never inquired ; there was, I believe, domestic distress and disagreement between Madame Charpentier and her husband—at least I conjectured so much." It is a strange statement, but the first confirms the later one. It was of a piece with Scott's impetuosity to ask no questions before the marriage ; and like his chivalrous delicacy to press for no confidences afterwards.

Of M. Charpentier we know really nothing, for Lockhart's account is rather a fairy-tale, except that he kept a riding-school at Lyons, a school apparently of the kind that the young Arthur Wellesley was sent to later, where young men learned not only to ride but the ways and manners of the French aristocracy. His wife, Margaret Charlotte Volère, bore to him three children—Margaret (later called Charlotte, who became Scott's wife) in December 1770 ; John David (known later as Charles Carpenter) in June 1772 ; and a third, Noël, in 1775, of whom we know nothing. About 1776 Madame Charpentier apparently left her home, and a report published by Robert Chambers in 1833 connected this departure with the name of Lord Downshire, then Lord Fairford, and not unnaturally conjecture has at times made him the parent of the two children of whom he certainly became the guardian in this country. The evidence does not bear this out. When the children came to England is not clear. They were brought over, Scott tells us, by Miss Jane Nicolson, whose own origin is difficult to ascertain.[1] Her sister Sarah was housekeeper

---

[1] According to Lockhart and herself she was " a daughter of Dr Nicolson, Dean of Exeter and grand-daughter of Bishop Nicolson of Carlisle "

to François Dumergue, also an émigré, who had settled in London and became dentist to the Prince Regent ; and the Dumergues, that is the father, his daughter Antoinette Adelaide and their housekeeper, were the closest friends of the two Charpentier children. The Dumergues were apparently respected people—intimate friends of Matthew Boulton, Watt's partner in Birmingham, in whose correspondence the names of the Dumergues and of Miss Charpentier frequently occur. With Dumergue's daughter the two Charpentiers were baptised into the Church of England at St. George's, Hanover Square, in 1787, giving then the correct dates of their births in France. Much later, after the death of Sir Walter, a sum of money which had been settled on Madame Charpentier, under circumstances which cannot now be traced, was recovered for Mrs. Charles Carpenter as her executrix, on the ground that her husband Charles

(1655-1727). But no Dr. Nicolson (or Nicholson as Lockhart spells the name) was ever Dean of Exeter or held any other ecclesiastical office there. Bishop Nicolson had three sons of whom Thomas lived only a few days ; Joseph, Chancellor of Lincoln, had two daughters ; and John, Rector of Donoughmore, had no children. Were then the two daughters Sarah and Jane ? No ; because Joseph died in 1728 and Sarah the elder sister of Jane was born in 1750. Her nephew S. N. Barber reports her death to M. R. Boulton (son of Matthew, Watt's partner) in 1838, " her only complaint may be said to have been her advanced age, 88." Moreover, there was an older sister Catherine (b. 1749) who married Stephen Barber. Concerning Jane the only fact discovered, beyond her connection with the Charpentier children, was that she was the person whom Mrs. Piozzi selected as companion for her children when she made up her mind to marry a second time. " Miss Thrale was of age now and I left Miss Nicholson, the Bishop's grand-daughter, whom they appeared to like exceedingly, with them, but she soon quitted her post on observing that they gave people to understand she was a cast mistress of Piozzi."—Hayward's *Piozzi*, i. 275. In another part of that confused work (of which there were two editions in the same year) Hayward says : " The lady Miss Nicolson, whom their mother had so carefully selected as their companion, soon left them, or, according to another version, was summarily dismissed by Miss Thrale (afterwards Viscountess Keith) who fortunately was endowed with high principles, firmness and energy." Jane and Mrs. Piozzi remained on friendly terms, for she is one of the persons most frequently mentioned, Hayward says, in her diary, which was " too private to be submitted to strangers." We gather from Mrs. Piozzi that her husband had old acquaintances in Lyons. It is just possible that it was through the Piozzis that she was introduced to the Charpentiers.

and Lady Scott, the only legitimate heirs of Madame Charpentier, had died without taking out letters of administration.

If this is so then Madame Charpentier may be allowed to drop out of the story. Why " draw her frailties from their dread abode ? " Whatever she may have done, and we do not know anything for certain, in no way affects her daughter or Scott. From a few letters which have come to light it seems that she lived for some years in Westminster, with occasional visits to Paris to see her mother. There she died in 1788, and Lord Downshire seems to have paid the few debts she left behind there and taken a steady and practical interest in the children. In March 1789 he secured for the son an appointment in the East India Company's service. Miss Jane Nicolson continued to act as Charlotte Carpenter's companion, and it was in her company that Walter Scott met her at Gilsland and on Christmas-Eve of the year 1797 was married to her. In the marriage-trust she is simply described as " Miss Charlotte Carpenter of Carlisle," that being the town in which she had lived during the weeks preceding the marriage.

Of Scott's own feelings for the lady who refused him and for her whom he married I must accept what he tells us himself. The first remained in his memory what she had been to his youthful imagination, the more easily that there followed no disillusioning experience. In his wife he found a woman with many tastes and humours that he shared—a natural gaiety and a love for society. She made an effort to enter into his literary tastes—at least so far as to make copies of his poems for friends. Leyden and others who knew her in the early days of her marriage remembered her with pleasure. " It is impossible not to beg to be remembered to dear Mrs. Scott and the fact is that the Laswade cottage, the blazing ingle &c. still recur as the happiest scenes of my youth." After her death Scott speaks of her as " the faithful and true companion of my fortunes," whose loss has left a blank that he is conscious of at every turn—in society, where he misses her courtesy to her guests ; in his study, where she came always to see if the fire burned and to ask a hundred kind questions ; at Mrs. Brown's lodgings, where the dirt is felt the more because of her almost oriental scrupulosity about cleanliness. How far she knew of his affairs we cannot tell, as he burned her correspondence. At the end she somewhat failed him. " Poor Charlotte was too much softened by prosperity to look adverse circumstances in the face." He wonders at her insensibility on leaving Castle Street. To others she hardly seemed the wife for Scott. Cockburn says, after reading the first volumes of Lockhart : " The two most extraordinary revelations to the people of Edinburgh are, that John Irving had once a particle of literary taste, and that there was a time when Lady Scott was pretty and agreeable." Whatever may have been her short-comings Scott was too little the typical man of letters to tell the whole world about it, in Byron's manner : " In the meanwhile I think my noble friend is something like my old peacock who chooses to bivouac apart from his lady and sit below my bedroom window to keep me awake with his screeching lamentation."

With his marriage ended Scott's *éducation sentimentale*. It has been suggested that the letters to Lady Abercorn betray a note of flirtation. I have printed here about twice as many as have hitherto appeared and have read the lady's numerous letters in the Walpole Collection, and to me it seems that what ardour there was is on her side. She is ever pressing him to meet them on their tours. She describes him as her dearest friend. It is evident from a late letter, written after *his* death (*i.e.* the marquess's), that she is a little hurt that the authorship of the *Tales of my Landlord* has never been confided to her by the author. Scott finds in her a lady patron who can help him in difficulties, a sympathetic friend to whom he can talk of many things, but I can see no more. He never opens his heart to her in quite such candid tones as to Lady Louisa Stuart. It seems to me a little absurd to suggest that his admission to her circle in 1806 turned Scott's head and made him discontented with Mrs. Scott. The marchioness, to tell the truth, is always much interested in Mrs. Scott and the children. Moreover, Scott had formed aristocratic friendships before 1806— the Buccleuchs, Lady Douglas, the Duke of Hamilton and his family ; and the letters of 1802 show that he had made as complete a conquest of Lady Anne Hamilton and Lady Susan as he did later of Lady Abercorn. Scott's attitude towards aristocratic society remained always the same. He respected their station, and was glad to be admitted to their society, but he never affected or aimed at becoming their social equal and treating them as such. There is no " dear Duke " or " dear Montague " as in the style of the tuft-hunter to-day. It is always " my dear Lord Duke " and " your Grace " and " my dear Lady Marchioness " as often as " my Dear Lady Abercorn " or " my dear friend," and that though they write to him with a blend of entire equality and sincere respect and affection. When in 1826 the egregious Sir John Sinclair proposed that he should seek a second wife in the Dowager Duchess of Roxburghe, he replied that if he contemplated a second marriage " I should endeavour to choose a person of my own condition."

No ; in the years following his marriage Scott's work— his career—has become his first thought, leaving him time and inclination for family life, for abundant friendships and social intercourse, but none for further romances of the heart. The years from his marriage in 1797 to the publication of the *Lay of the Last Minstrel* in 1805 seem to me among the happiest, the most care-free, of his life. He is finding himself in the editing and imitating of old ballads, the editing of *Sir Tristrem*, and the correspondence which this brings him with brother antiquaries, of whom

George Ellis becomes the chief friend. He measures him-self against the great "Monk" Lewis and soon begins to feel his superiority—if not in accuracy of rhymes, in capturing the spirit and manner of the old ballads. Nor are ballads the only form in which he is experimenting. Lewis finds for him a publisher of his version of Goethe's *Goetz von Berlichingen*, one of the several German plays he has translated ; and the drama is one of his ambitions. Heber gets Kemble to read and consider *The House of Aspen*, and expresses his own admiration for the play and his surprise at Kemble's rejection. Meanwhile he is still practising to some extent at the Bar and carrying on an active correspondence with Charles Erskine, his Sheriff-Substitute at Selkirk; for though I print only a few of these letters it must be remembered that there was a pretty steady flow of them, just as later, after 1805, the letters on business, of which also I can print only a fraction, form a strong under-current, at times a raging torrent, carried on without intermission, but of which there is only the faintest glimpse in the ever broadening, sparkling stream of his friendly and social correspondence. Gillies's picture of Scott with Erskine at Lasswade Cottage in these early years gives us a vivid glimpse of the man now in the prime of his strength and radiant with hopefulness :
" At this early period Scott was in appearance much more like the portrait by Saxon (with the favourite large dog Camp) engraved for the first edition of the *Lady of the Lake* than to any subsequent picture. He retained, in features and form, an impress of that elasticity and youthful vivacity which he used to complain wore off after he was forty ; and by his own account was exchanged for the plodding heaviness of an operose student. He had now indeed somewhat of a boyish gaiety of look, and in person was tall, slim and athletic."

> A face more fair you well might find,
> For Redmond knew the sun and wind,
> Nor boasted, from their tinge when free,

I   e

The charm of regularity ;
But every feature had the power
To aid the expression of the hour.

These lines, Erskine said, " give an excellent portrait of the author himself." The ill-health of 1819 and the troubles which helped to bring on that attack were to put an early end to Scott's youthfulness, as Skene tells us, but that gaiety of temper never quite forsook him— Mr. Scott or Sir Walter " has been here in great glee " is a phrase that recurs more than once in Cadell's often worried correspondence with Constable.

The Minstrelsy of the Scottish Border was the capital work of these first years, the germ of all that he was to do in the recovery of the past by the clue of that human nature which never changes in essentials. But the success of that work was limited enough to persuade Scott that " the practice of ballad writing was at present out of fashion " ; and by a series of accidents, with which most readers are familiar, a ballad on a goblin page became *The Lay of the Last Minstrel*, which appeared in January 1805. The instantaneous success of that poem determined the alliance with James Ballantyne, and that led to the further venture of John Ballantyne & Co., publishers, of which I have said enough.

From this moment literature becomes the chief business of his life, though he has many other official duties to carry through, and this fact raises another question, suggested by Macaulay's reference to Dryden. Mr. Buchan and other biographers speak of the editing of Dryden, Swift and such works mentioned above as " hack-work." Well, if that is so then one must be bold and admit that all Scott's poems and novels were hack-work, for, like Shakespeare's plays, they were written to make money. But it depends a little how one defines hack-work ; the *Oxford Dictionary* calls it " work done by a hack or hired drudge—esp. literary work which a person is hired by a publisher to do." That suggests

to my mind a biography or other piece of work undertaken at the request of a publisher by a person who has
given no particular attention to the subject before the
invitation was received, the brief delivered. That was
not so with Scott's Dryden or Swift—and he would like
to have edited Beaumont and Fletcher. He loved
literature and he loved history and antiquities. Dryden
was the third of English poets and Swift the greatest of
satirists and prose-writers. He poured into his lives
and introductions and notes the knowledge he had been
gathering for years, and communicated to them the gusto
with which he undertook anything in the nature of a
literary task. That he was a scientific editor I will not
aver—and it seems to be the fate of Dryden's plays to
incite the wrath of every editor against his predecessor—
but he had the gift of making even notes interesting.

Nor is very much gained by saying that Scott sacrificed
perfection in his art to love of money—or it is equally true
of Shakespeare. One is only substituting censure for an
effort to understand. Of perfection such as Macaulay
contemplates Scott was, as he confesses in the introduction to *The Monastery*, incapable. He had been telling
himself stories all his life, and when he found at last the
suitable form into which to pour them he had simply
to follow his daemon. He begins a novel such as *Rob Roy*
with the prospect of bills to be met by a certain date, and
with the printing press clattering at his heels ; but the
anxieties of which the letters are full seem to vanish as his
imagination gets to work, and one scene leads to another :
the son of a rich London merchant sent to Bordeaux to
learn the business and form the acquaintance of the chief
foreign correspondents ; his dislike for the business and
taste for poetry ; the breach with his father ; the journey
to the north and meeting with the timid Morris and the
cool Campbell ; the first encounter with his cousins and
Diana Vernon ; Andrew Fairservice and the start for
Scotland—the story flows on in an irresistible tide, one

scene rising after another in a way that suggests nothing
so much as Bergson's phrase, *Évolution créatrice*. It is not
true that he made no corrections at the suggestion of
James Ballantyne or Erskine—but, alas ! the letters to
Erskine were burned by a too conscientious lady. Even
between one edition and another there are improvements
of diction and phrase ; but the art of construction he
neither knew nor studied.

Meantime the stream of Scott's social life as reflected in
the letters broadens out. His visit to London in 1803 makes
him personally acquainted with George Ellis, with whom
he has already exchanged friendly letters on romances and
Sir Tristrem and problems connected therewith. He meets
Rogers, Rose and others, including Miss Anna Seward,
who is most largely represented in the correspondence
which follows. Wordsworth and his sister call upon him
in 1803 and Southey in 1805 and Wordsworth becomes
an occasional, Southey a more constant, correspondent,
for the good reason that for the more miscellaneous writer,
living by his pen, Scott can do a good turn from time to
time. He engaged him to write the historical part of
the unfortunate *Edinburgh Annual Register*, which involves
Southey in some of the anxieties of the year 1813 ; but
he also in that unfortunate year gets for him the laureate-
ship which had been offered to Scott himself. The
second visit to London in 1806 was made when Scott
had written a poem which was all the fashion, and he
was introduced to the Princess of Wales, whose side
he was a little inclined to take as against " our fat friend,"
but he changed his mind later. It was now he won the
enthusiastic friendship of the Marchioness of Abercorn,
the third wife of the Marquess " of Carabas " (as Scott
generally calls him in his letters—an addition which Lockhart suppresses.) She was Irish ; a daughter of the second
Earl of Arran in that country—and Scott seems always
to have felt a special sympathy with the Irish and to have
found some of his most devoted admirers among that

people. In her he found a good friend in two of the affairs which troubled the years after 1805 besides the business one. In 1809 his brother's mismanagement of the Scottish property of the marquess and flight from his creditors threw upon Scott a heavy burden of attorney work as well as involved him in losses. In 1811 he has to exert all his influence to secure the retiral of his predecessor on the clerks' bench and so secure the income, and in the same year he has to help his brother to return to active life as a paymaster in the army. The marchioness is his good friend in both the affairs that concerned himself—gaining for him the efficient aid of Arbuthnot of the Treasury, the " Gosh " of Greville's diary. It is not till 1808 that he makes the acquaintance, through Lady Louisa Stuart, of John Morritt, to whom he writes more constantly and more openly than to any one, except it be Lady Louisa Stuart. In 1806 he had met Joanna Baillie, and in 1808 she visited him in Scotland, and her letters to him fill a large part of the Walpole Collection. Miss Edgeworth comes in later but is the more interesting personality, for one cannot say that all Scott's correspondents are worth the trouble he took with them. He was too courteous to bores and self-seeking petitioners ; so courteous that it is not always easy for him to be entirely sincere, though he never fails in a case that appeals to his sense of pity.

It is as an accompaniment to Lockhart's *Life*—and occasionally a corrective—that the letters should be read, an addition to the impression which that work conveys of his amazing knowledge, interest and overflowing energy. " I have not," Miss Edgeworth writes to Lockhart, " Sir Walter Scott's Briareus power of doing hundreds of things at once with hundreds of arms of whatever length and power required for every imaginable purpose." In that capacity for accomplishing a hundred tasks at once Scott is a Napoleon of letters—criticism excellent of its kind, editing with all the requirements of

literary, historical and antiquarian knowledge, biography, history—and withal this flood of correspondence,
of which much has disappeared. It may be, as Lockhart
says, that Scott "must have felt that whatever he wrote
would one day perhaps be printed," but no letters written
by a literary man of distinction bear less evident marks
of any such thought. Neither the form nor the contents
suggest consciousness of a critical reader. They are
poured forth by a man who has no time to think of style or
punctuation—no time to cross t's or dot i's or supply even
full stops. They are at the opposite pole from the letters of
Pope or Byron or Stevenson, all palpable poseurs in
different ways. "We shall only see minds soon in prepared
undress (like Byron's)," writes Maria Edgeworth to
Lockhart—for Byron too is a stylist, if as anxious as Scott
to avoid the tone of the " literary person."

The impression given by the whole is broad and full
rather than deep, though there is no shallowness. Scott
does not easily write about his own feelings ; and he is
precluded from expatiating on his two main interests—
business and the novels—by the secrecy in which he had
chosen to invest them. His deeper feelings are reserved
for the *Journal*, and by the time that was begun the
stoicism which he had early learned to cultivate had
become a second nature. " In fact letters," he says of
those of Burns, " . . . very rarely contain the real opinions
of the writer. If an author sits down to the task of
formally composing a work for the use of the public he
has previously made up his mind both on the opinions
he is to express and on the mode of supporting them. But
the same man usually writes a letter only because the
letter must be written, is probably never more at a loss
than when looking for a subject, and treats it when
found rather so as to gratify his correspondent than
communicate his own feelings." In other than business
letters Scott obviously writes to entertain his correspondent,
but does so with a gusto that bespeaks his own enjoyment

of the theme and the communication.   Nor were the
deeper, more complex passions known to Scott.   Neither
in his letters nor in his novels do we catch any glimpse
of such storms as shook the heart of Shakespeare after
the first *joie de vivre* had abated ;   or the inner mystical
fervour of an Emily Brontë.   Scott could not have known
these and been quite what he was.   But he escaped also the
nervous irritation which for Carlyle clothed life in gloom
and could use the language of a deeper passion than the
occasion warranted.   To Carlyle, as he looked back in
the early morning, after a sea voyage, over the sparkling
waters of the Solway Firth to the blue hills of Cumberland in the distance, it seemed that " Tartarus itself and
the pale kingdoms of Dis could not have been more
preternatural to me—more stern, gloomy, sad, grand yet
terrible, yet steeped in woe."   It was not so that Scott
felt in the morning when he rose to his task so early :

> At morn the black-cock trims his jetty wing,
>   'Tis morning prompts the linnet's blithest lay,
> All Nature's children feel the matin spring
>   Of life reviving with reviving day.

" I wonder if others find so strongly as I do the truth
of the Latin proverb, *Aurora musis amica*.   If I forget a
thing over night I am sure to recollect it as my eyes open
in the morning.   The same if I want an idea or am
encumbered by some difficulty ; the moment of awaking
always supplies the deficiency, or gives me courage to
endure the alternative."   And even after the disaster
and when ill-health is increasing he is able to say, speaking
of the happy years he passed at Ashestiel : " But did
I ever pass unhappy years anywhere?   None that I
remember save those at the High School, which I
thoroughly detested on account of the confinement.   I
disliked serving in my father's office from the same
hatred of restraint.   In other respects I have had unhappy
days—unhappy weeks—even on one or two occasions
unhappy months ; but Fortune's finger has never been

able to play a dirge on me for a quarter of a year together." There is a virtue in being happy and communicating happiness ; and gloom is as often a nervous affection—the reflection of a bad digestion and excessive smoking—as of a deeper insight into life. Scott had no more illusions about the worth of life than Carlyle. Underneath his worldly and stoical temper lay an acute sensibility with which he had done battle from his youth. His sentiment—his romantic and passionate love of his country, of Scotland and Britain, and of the social order that was disappearing—astonished those who occasionally got glimpses of their depth and intensity, and his affections for those he lived with were as strong. " Walter and Jane appear cordial and happy in each other ; the greatest blessing Heaven can bestow on them or me who witness it. If we had Lockhart and Sophia there would be a meeting of the beings dearest to me in life." No man so constituted, and with Scott's clear insight into human nature and the conditions of life, can be happy in a merely shallow way. His favourite poetry was Johnson's—the *London* and *Vanity of Human Wishes*—and his views of this life and its necessary relation to the next were very much Johnson's. " What is this life ? A dream within a dream—as we grow older each step is an awakening. The youth wakes as he thinks from childhood—the full-grown man despises the pursuits of youth as visionary—the old man looks on manhood as a feverish dream."

The stream of Scott's active life broadened to its fullest in the years from 1815, when *Waverley* was published, to 1819, the years which the first five volumes of this edition will represent. " The publication of *Ivanhoe*," Lockhart says, " marks the most brilliant epoch in Scott's history as the literary favourite of his contemporaries. With the novel which he next put forth the immediate sale of these works began to decline gradually," though unfortunately for himself

Scott's sanguine temper refused to realise the fact and those who were gambling with him on that popularity were afraid of the effect of telling him the truth. These were the years of all the great " Scotch Novels," as they were generally called. Into them Scott was able to pour not only the sentiment and description which had delighted readers in the picturesque and sparkling but somewhat facile poems, but all his deeper knowledge of human nature—his humour and pathos ; and in these he was reviving the history of which he had the deepest and most intimate understanding, the history of Scotland in the seventeenth and eighteenth centuries and of the early nineteenth. For what Scott did best was not quite what won him his chief popularity in his own day and diffused his influence upon the Continent. Newman claimed Scott as a forerunner of the Oxford Movement, but it is not true that Scott had the power to reproduce the atmosphere of the Middle Ages, the illusion of the mediaeval, had any deep understanding of the Catholicism and the eroticism which colour mediaeval romance. In communicating to a reader what Flaubert calls the " frisson historique " he has been surpassed by some of his successors—Victor Hugo, Balzac, Flaubert, William Morris. Scott's achievement was not to transport you back into a strange past, making you share the feelings of men whose moral and spiritual life was remote from ours. It was rather the opposite, to dispel that feeling of strangeness and make you realise that the past was once a present and felt much as life does to us to-day. His closest affinity is not with modern mediaevalists, but with his great precedessors, Smollett and Fielding ; yes, and with Defoe, and that great, realistic, humorous handling of romance, the immortal forerunner of all modern fiction, *Don Quixote*. He brought the past out of the shadowy and strange lights in which we see it into the clear light of the present, of human nature which is always the same, even as Cervantes had in his way,

which could never be repeated, brought the hero and
exploits of chivalry out into the sunlight of the Spain of
his own day. How differently Hugo or Balzac would
have treated the story of *Waverley*. They would, I
believe, have for the purpose of the story identified
themselves with the Jacobite sentiment of the characters ;
at least made the centre of the interest a lover and a
passionate loyalist. Flora MacIvor and Edward Waverley
would have been the hero and heroine of a romance such
as that of Balzac's *Les Chouans*, to which might have been
given the second title of that novel, " Un jour sans lende-
main." That is not Scott's way at all. Flora MacIvor
is indeed the one passionate Jacobite in the story, but
that is a realistic touch, for our own history tells us—
witness Charlotte Corday and recent events in Ireland
and India—that it is women who most easily become the
romantic fanatics of a cause. Flora's brother is a Jacobite,
but for ambitious reasons. There is very little Jacobite
sentiment in the novel. What Scott gives is a picture,
realistic so far as it goes, and humorous, of how things
went in the past on the assumption that the men of the
past were like those of to-day, that then as now in any
great political movement you would find all sorts of men
engaged, and for the most diverse reasons, that the true
idealists would be few, the self-seeking numerous, and
perhaps even more numerous those who like Edward go
with the tide. What he did was, with a more interesting
story of the kind his age had been taught to expect, what
Defoe had done in the *Memoirs of a Cavalier* and the
History of the Plague. How differently again would
Balzac or Hugo have been affected by the original story
on which *Guy Mannering* was based. How much they
would have made of the tale of astrology and evil in-
fluences. Scott was not at ease in such a glamorous
atmosphere. He brings the whole thing out into the
clear light of a story of a district and a period when
gypsies and desperate smugglers were an actual ex-

perience, and weaves into it his pictures of folly and crime and loyalty and humour.

What he began with *Waverley* Scott continued on a higher level in the novels which followed with such breathless rapidity as the demands of business required— *Old Mortality*, *Rob Roy*, *The Heart of Midlothian*, *The Bride of Lammermoor*, *The Legend of Montrose*, and later *Redgauntlet*. On these rest his claim to an enduring fame ; give him his place, such as it is, and I still think it is a secure one, beside Shakespeare and Cervantes, for here he is on ground he knows thoroughly and dealing with times not so remote as to call for that impression of illusion which attaches to all attempts to reproduce a remote past. And the strength of these novels lies in the picture of the common people. I once, after spending two days admiring the beautiful interior of the Cathedral of Amiens, was standing in front of the cathedral looking at the figures and scenes from common life which decorate the front of that building, looking at them while the life of the town flowed past in the street, when suddenly the thought came to my mind how little change there was after all in the life of the people, those whose business it is from day to day to earn their living, who take life as it comes, welcoming the interludes of meals and pastimes, with little memory of the past and little forethought of more than the immediate future. The cathedral was there with its aisles and lofty arches and windows

> diamonded with panes of quaint device
> Innumerable of splendid stains and dyes
> As are the tiger-moth's deep-damasked wings ;
> And in the midst 'mongst thousand heraldries,
> And twilight saints, and dim emblazonings
> A thousand scutcheons blushed with blood of Kings
> and Queens.

But that belongs to a past we can never really revive— whereas the pictures on the outside represent a life that, despite trivial changes (motors for wagons and changes of

attire) is as vivid as the life of the streets beside them. And
so it is with Scott's greatest work. The soul of that work is
the Scottish people as they were and as in essentials they
are—the loyal Highlander Evan MacCombich, the Border
farmer Dandie Dinmont, the fisher people and the old
beggar Edie Ochiltree in *The Antiquary*, Mause and
Cuddie Headrigg in *Old Mortality* ; and on the outer
fringes of social life, smugglers and gypsies and poachers ;
and just a little above all these in the social scale, the
Glasgow merchant and baillie in *Rob Roy*, lawyers in
Guy Mannering and *The Heart of Midlothian*, doctors and
ministers and ministers' wives—all that go to make the
great body which we call the people, the people that work
to live. All these the old Tory Scott has, despite his
feudal sympathies and social ambitions, drawn with a
truth and gusto which his somewhat straw-stuffed kings
and captains—Cromwell and Mary and Richard and
Louis—seem to me never quite to exhibit. The greatest
of all the novels to us is the first part of *The Heart of Midlothian*, and the heroine is a simple, plain, not even quite
young Scottish maiden. In her life Scott, despite his
dislike for " high-flyers," whether in doctrine or in
evangelical sentiment and repressive morals, touches the
very core of Scottish character as Protestantism has given
it fibre and form, the unyielding attachment to principle
which André Gide has portrayed in some of his early
sketches of French Protestant character.

It cannot be said that the stream of Scott's correspondence grows narrower after 1819, as to some extent that
of his literary work does, but the letters do come to
include more of a conventionally social character. One
pays a heavy penalty for being the most popular literary
man of the age, as a glance through the Walpole Collection
of the letters to Scott show. Every bore thinks himself
entitled to write and to call : " I am annoyed beyond
measure with the idle intrusion of voluntary correspondents ; each man who has pen and ink and sheet of

foolscap to spare flies a letter at me. I believe the postage costs me £100 besides innumerable franks ; and all the letters regard the writer's own hopes or projects, or are filled with unasked advice or extravagant requests," and perhaps the most wearisome letters of all are those in which Scott relates to the Duke of Buccleuch or Lord Montague the local doings in politics, electioneering, and jobbery. But there are interesting additions to the deeper current as his children go from home, and when Lockhart is transferred to London to edit the *Quarterly Review*. The tide of Scott's prosperity reached its high-water mark in 1825 with the marriage of his son to a wealthy heiress and his triumphal visit to Ireland. He returned eager, as he tells Constable, to resume work and believing that with the completion of Abbotsford the worst of his expenses were at an end ; and then the storm broke. Lockhart's story of the alarming report he brought to Abbotsford and of Scott's drive to Polton to visit Constable in the night and return next morning when he breakfasted at Chiefswood, seems to be a tale in the manner of *Peter's Letters to his Kinsfolk*. Lockhart says that the incident occurred after his return from a visit to London, but Lockhart did not go to London on the business connected with the editorship of the *Quarterly* till October, when Constable was already in London. Lockhart is the bearer of a letter from Scott to Constable concerning a book wanted for the life of Napoleon, and Constable remained in London till the 3rd of November. By that time Scott was in Edinburgh, and it was in Edinburgh that he heard from Lockhart, who was then at Chiefswood, with apparently the first rumour of real trouble. Lockhart's letter was written on the 17th and Scott's reply of the 18th shows that this is the first suggestion of the kind : " Your kind and attentive letter gave me a shock for though I thought myself pretty safe knowing the situation of the house in question two years ago when their business was examined by an accountant to

settle matters between the partners—although I knew
that since that time the dogged and calculating prudence
of Cadell had been a check on the adventurous spirit of
his partner and had suffered nothing to be undertaken
without a sure view of the funds—although besides all
this I knew that a bond of £2500 to myself had been paid
to my agent John Gibson on the term day Messrs. Constable declining to hold the money though offered in case
they judged it an accomodation—although besides all
this I knew that Cadell had laid down a plan of re-
trenching discounts which made him wish to put off
payment of some cash due to me from November till
January and that nevertheless he had offered since I
came to town to shell out the ready if my occasions
required it—an offer voluntarily made—although I say
I knew all these things yet I could not read your note
without painful anxiety as doubtless I must have been put
to great inconvenience probably to loss by any such
event." Surely, if there had been a previous alarm, Scott
would have made some allusion to it now, but in no
letters of Scott or Constable or Cadell is there a hint of
any such event. Scott goes on in the letter cited to tell
how Cadell had dispelled his fears. The *Journal* relates
the stages by which he came to the complete discovery,
on 16th January 1826, of his bankruptcy.

The letters of 1825 are poignant reading. The note
conveyed by the young bridegroom to Constable on the
1st of February of that year has in it the hint of that
" hubris " which the Greeks thought awoke the envy and
anger of the gods : " By Walter Scott Esq. bridegroom
apparent—of the Kings Hussars by grace of God and the
Horseguards Lieutenant—younger of Abbotsford and
expectant of Lochore and a Baronet in posse to boot of all
that." If tragedy is the story of those who had risen high
upon the wheel of fortune and were then thrown down
Scott's story is a tragedy ; and that last and bitterest
ingredient, the consciousness of having been the agent

of one's proper woe, was not absent. Then it is, Bacon says, that "all strikes deadly inward and suffocateth." "I had a lesson," writes Scott when the first rumour reached him in November, "in 1814 which should have done good upon me, but success and abundance erased it from my mind." But Scott's disaster was in a deeper sense also his salvation. He made it the occasion for the noblest action of his life. It did not change his nature or make him exempt from the faults which had contributed to his disaster—a large carelessness about money, a sanguine readiness to believe the best. Nor did he become pious and penitent and sit down in sackcloth and ashes accepting bankruptcy as Carlyle thought he should have done. Like the Dutch poet of the seventeenth century, Vondel, when his son had involved himself in ruin, Scott surrendered his fortune and devoted his labours to satisfying his creditors. The laborious toil of his last years is painful to contemplate, and the readiness with which his publisher urged him on and friends still requisitioned his services. He meditated the Roman and stoical end, but that would have been to desert from the battle. The sanguine temper and failing brain gave him illusory hopes and beliefs. But when he died the principal of the debt was cleared with the help of the price paid for the outstanding copyrights by Cadell ; and by 1847 Lockhart had cleared the estate. The fairy-gold was flown. Many benefited by Scott's dreams and labours but not Scott or his children. Even the legacy of the Indian brother-in-law which in 1819 seemed to Scott to justify some more outlay on Abbotsford, some more help for Tom's children, never materialised till Scott and all his children were in their grave. The *Journal* remains as the finest and final record of a soul as manly as he was tender ; no saint, perhaps no hero—one can understand Carlyle's attitude, soured as his statement of it may be—but a man, a man with all his faults as lovable as he was great.

SIR WALTER SCOTT'S FINANCIAL
TRANSACTIONS

DEAR PROFESSOR GRIERSON,—I have pleasure in complying with your request that I should write you with reference to Sir Walter Scott's financial affairs. You do not, of course, ask for a statement showing in detail how the large indebtedness for which Sir Walter was held liable at the failure in January 1826 was from time to time incurred. It was not possible, even in 1826, for any such statement to be made up, as the books of the firm of James Ballantyne & Co., of which Scott was a partner, were not then in existence prior to May 1822, or at all events were not, even then, available. After May 1822 the books as kept by James Ballantyne were kept in such a manner as, according to Mr. John Gibson, W.S., who examined them in 1826, precluded any exact accounting between the partners being attempted. On 12th August 1833 he wrote to Mr. Bayley, W.S., who acted for Sir Walter's representatives : " I found it utterly impossible from the Books to discover how the accounts of the partners really stood. There was no account between them entered in the Books and neither they nor any other person could have told how much each had drawn from the concern."

There are, however, a number of books and documents still extant which throw a good deal of light on the financial transactions referred to, and with the help of these it is possible to get at least an insight into the complicated transactions in which Sir Walter was engaged, and to conjecture therefrom as to how the indebtedness for which he was held liable was incurred. There is, of course, no doubt as to the amount of the sums for which he was held liable, or with regard to the amount of the debts properly due by others outside his own firm which he was called upon to pay.

The printing business carried on by James Ballantyne had been removed from Kelso to Edinburgh in 1802, and in May 1805 Scott became a partner therein, with right to the profits to the extent of one-third. Those who are interested in the accounts of the partners, and in their drawings from the business during these early years, will find some information in Lockhart's pamphlet called *The Ballantyne-Humbug Handled* (1839) and in the pamphlet printed by the Ballantyne trustees in reply thereto.

In 1809 the firm of John Ballantyne & Co., booksellers and publishers, was started—Scott, James Ballantyne, and his younger brother John Ballantyne being the partners—Scott's share in the profits being one-half and each of the Ballantynes one-fourth. As is well known this business was unsuccessful, and it was arranged in 1813 to have it wound up. This seems to have been effected in 1817. The printing business of James Ballantyne & Co. was, however, carried on. It was understood to be a thriving business, but I am inclined to think that both Scott and James Ballantyne imagined that it was much more profitable than it really was. Owing to the losses sustained in the bookselling business, and to overdrafts made on the printing business, it was arranged in 1816 that the business should thereafter be carried on for Scott's behoof alone until such time as he was recouped for his losses. He accordingly became the sole partner in the business, James Ballantyne being merely manager at a salary of £400 per annum—raised for one year to £500. This continued down to 1821, when it was arranged that Ballantyne should be re-assumed as a partner as from May 1822. The missive letter by Scott embodying the terms of the new co-partnership, and which is dated 15th June 1821, is printed in the pamphlets referred to. In it Scott states that having drawn the full profits of the business since 1816 he considered that as at May 1822 he would thereby be indemnified for his " risk and advances " and was willing that Ballantyne should share equally in the profits after that date. He mentions that in the year 1816 Ballantyne was personally owing him a sum of £3000 and provides for its being liquidated by Ballantyne assigning to him his share of profits in five novels then contracted for. It is evident that no exact accounting was entered into, and it is provided that in the event of death between June 1821 and May 1822 there was to be no accounting other than the arrangement contained in the missive letter, " as it is not our purpose to go back on these complicated transactions."

The business of James Ballantyne & Co. was accordingly carried on for behoof of Scott and James Ballantyne until 17th January 1826, when it stopped payment. In the latter

1   *f*

part of the year 1825 there was throughout the country a severe financial crisis, causing the failure of several banks and of many firms. Among the latter Hurst, Robinson & Co., publishers, London, stopped payment on 14th January 1826. Their failure was due to the banks having restricted their discount facilities and also to their having engaged in speculations outside their legitimate business. At the same time they persisted then and for weeks afterwards that they were perfectly solvent, their assets being largely sunk in their stock-in-trade not readily realisable. They had for several years acted as the agents in London for Archibald Constable & Co., publishers, Edinburgh, and had carried on with them an exchange system of bills and counter-bills. Their stoppage brought down Constable & Co., and they in turn occasioned the failure of James Ballantyne & Co., who had been engaged in bill transactions with them.

Archibald Constable & Co. (whom I will refer to as " A. C. & Co.") were made bankrupt, and their affairs were wound up under the Bankruptcy Act by a process of sequestration. James Ballantyne & Co. (whom I will refer to as " J. B. & Co.") were not made technically bankrupt, but the creditors agreed to their affairs being wound up under a trust deed granted by the firm, and by Sir Walter Scott and James Ballantyne as partners and as individuals, under which they conveyed all their assets to trustees for the creditors, and by that deed Sir Walter undertook to employ his time and talents in the production of literary works, the sums arising from which to be applied to the payment of the debts owing by him.

A detailed list of the debts is given in the Sederunt Book of the trustees for the creditors, which has been deposited in the National Library of Scotland, Edinburgh. The amount of the debts, when the ranking was finally adjusted (apart from the mortgage of £10,000 secured over the estate of Abbotsford), came to £116,838 11s. 3d.

This sum can be considered as being made up as follows :

1. Sir Walter Scott's private debts - - £20,066 19 9
2. Debts (apart from bills) due by J. B. & Co. or for which both partners were liable (including £45 17s. 8d. for which J. B. alone was liable) - - 12,615 6 7
3. Bonds for which Sir Walter was liable, but which were the proper debts of A. C. & Co. - - - - - 9,129 9 0
4. Bills discounted and in the hands of third parties, £75,405 7s. 7d., but which, owing to small adjustments requiring to be made, ranked for - 75,026 15 11

Making up the total of - - £116,838 11 3

It is with regard to the amount of the bills, namely £75,405 7s. 7d., that the main difficulty arises in accounting for Sir Walter's large indebtedness.

These discounted bills may be analysed as follows :

1. Bills granted by A. C. & Co. to J. B. & Co. (or Sir W. S.).
   For value - - - £2,000 0 0
   For J. B. & Co's accommodation - - 27,088 2 6
   _____ £29,088 2 6
2. Bills granted by J. B. & Co. to A. C. & Co.
   For value - - - £1,005 18 4
   For A. C. & Co's accommodation - - 28,618 4 5
   _____ 29,624 2 9
3. Sir Walter's acceptances to J. B. & Co. without value - - - - - 15,365 13 2
4. Bills granted by Hurst, Robinson & Co. to J. B. & Co.
   For value - - - £563 15 10
   For J. B. & Co.'s accommodation - - 663 13 4
   _____ 1,227 9 2
5. A bill granted by J. B. & Co. to James Hogg (the Ettrick Shepherd) without value - - - - - - 100 0 0

£75,405 7 7

With reference to the above statement, I am including promissory notes under the term of bills. In some cases the name of the firm of J. B. & Co. did not appear on these documents but only Sir Walter's name, but I am treating them as bills due by J. B. & Co. as they formed part of the accommodation granted to the firm.

I may further explain that the course of dealing between A. C. & Co. and J. B. & Co. was that each firm paid their own acceptances—that is to say, although J. B. & Co. discounted A. C. & Co. acceptances granted without value, and received the money, it did not fall on them but on A. C. & Co. to provide funds to retire the bills when they fell due, the matter being kept right by J. B. & Co. retiring the acceptances without value which they granted to A. C. & Co. and which were discounted by that firm, the total amount of the acceptances running at any one time being kept nearly equal and any balance adjusted from time to time. I need scarcely say that each firm on the failure became liable for both sets of bills—in the case of one set of the bills as acceptors, and in the case of the other as endorsers. For example, although J. B. & Co. in discounting A. C. & Co.'s bill for say £1000 received only that sum (less discount), they became liable in the event of bankruptcy to a claim for £2000 in respect that they were also liable for the £1000 which A. C. & Co. received on discounting the counter-bill, and in the same way A. C. & Co. for each £1000 they received became liable on the bankruptcy taking place for £2000. There was thus a ranking on both estates by the banks who discounted the bills on which the names of both parties appeared. This double ranking, of course, did not apply in connection with the bills granted by Sir Walter Scott to J. B. & Co., as the banks who discounted these bills could only rank on the one estate, the estates of the firm and of Sir Walter being treated as one.

In addition to the above-mentioned bills, J. B. & Co. held bills granted by A. C. & Co. without value amounting to £4773 0s. 3d. which they had not discounted at the time of the failure and which accordingly did not rank. They also held bills granted by A. C. & Co. for value amounting to £7417 12s. 8d., but these bills were not discounted but lodged with bankers to secure overdrafts, and the bankers ranked on their overdrafts and not on the bills. I may further explain that I have included among the bills for £27,088 2s. 6d. above mentioned, granted by A. C. & Co. for J. B. & Co's accommodation, bills amounting to £4100, of which £2100 were granted as an advance on the *Life of Napoleon* which Sir Walter had undertaken to write and £2000 as an advance on a work he intended to write on *Continental Travels*, but as the former was not published till after the failure and A. C. & Co. were held to have no right to it, and as the latter was never written, I have treated these bills as among those granted without value.

What, then, it may be asked, was the amount of the debts which Sir Walter, or after his death his representatives, had to pay, which were properly debts due by others ? I have said that the two firms treated their own acceptances, even when granted without value, as being their own proper debts falling to be paid by them respectively. But in view that the totals ranking do not quite correspond it is, I think, right that the accommodation bills granted by J. B. & Co. for A. C. & Co.'s accommodation should be treated as being the proper debts of the latter firm ; these came to   - £28,618 4 5
Also the bills granted by A. C. & Co. for value   2,000 0 0
A. C. & Co. were also the proper debtors in
    the bonds above mentioned amounting to   9,129 9 0

Making as the debts properly due by A. C. &
    Co. which ranked on Sir Walter's estate £39,747 13 5
In addition the bill for value accepted by
    Hurst, Robinson & Co. was properly due
    by that firm -   -   -   -   -   -   563 15 10
And the bill without value by J. B. & Co. to
    James Hogg was properly due by the latter   100 0 0

The total debts accordingly properly due
    by others ranking on Sir Walter's estate
    were thus -   -   -   -   -   - £40,411 9 3

While it is, of course, the case that the bills granted by A. C. & Co. for the accommodation of J. B. & Co., amounting to £27,088 2s. 6d., being the proper debts of J. B. & Co., ranked not merely on their estate but also on that of A. C. & Co., who paid a dividend of 2s. 9d per £ thereon, yet Sir Walter or his representatives received no benefit therefrom, as the banks holding the bills, after receiving 20s. per £ from Sir Walter's estate, applied the dividends from A. C. & Co.' estate to account of interest on their debts.

Although it is also the case that the creditors of Sir Walter are considered to have ultimately received 20s. per £, yet the dividends paid only amounted to 18s. per £—the creditors having made a present to Sir Walter, in view of his exertions on their behalf, of his library, antiques and furniture, which were estimated to be equivalent to an additional 2s. per £. As the dividends actually paid were thus 18s. per £ the amount paid by Sir Walter and his representatives on the debts due by others, amounting as stated to £40,411 9s. 3d., was approximately £36,370.

While the above explanation accounts for some £40,411 of the debts due by bonds and bills, it will be noticed that after deducting from the debts due by bill, amounting to £75,405 7s. 7d., the bills for which others were properly liable, namely bills for £30,618 4s. 5d. so far as A. C. & Co. were concerned, £563 15s. 10d. properly payable by Hurst, Robinson & Co., and £100 properly payable by James Hogg —these amounting to £31,282 0s. 3d.—there still remains the large sum due on bill of £44,123 7s. 4d., as being the proper debt of J. B. & Co. or of Sir Walter Scott. As to how this debt was occasioned different answers have been given.

Lockhart considers that to the extent of over £30,000 it was due to old debts occasioned by the mismanagement of James Ballantyne, and to debts due by the bookselling and publishing business of John Ballantyne & Co., which had been wound up, and that the debt had been largely increased since 1822 by extravagant drawings out of the business by James Ballantyne. The Ballantyne trustees, on the other hand, attribute the debt to Sir Walter's land purchases, his building operations and expensive mode of living, and they allege that in the three years from January 1823 he drew from the business some £15,200 more than he paid in or was entitled to be credited with, and in one of their pamphlets they gave details of how this sum was arrived at.

I may say at once that I do not think that Lockhart is correct in attributing the debt of over £30,000 to old debts incurred by the printing and publishing firms in their legitimate businesses, and to the same having accumulated by renewals. In the missive letter referred to Scott says, as I have mentioned, that having received the full profits of the business of J. B. & Co. since 1816 he considers himself as being *fully indemnified* " for his risk and advances."

As regards the allegation made by Ballantyne's trustees

that Scott drew out of the business some £15,200 more than
he was entitled to, I am quite satisfied that this is erroneous.
The capital in the business was trifling and sunk in buildings
and plant and the whole profits of the business did not exceed,
on a very full average, £2000 per annum, so that if any sum
was drawn in excess of the share of the profits to which any
partner was entitled, it must have come out of an increase of
the accommodation bills, which were all debited to Sir Walter.
The detailed account which the Ballantyne trustees have
printed in their pamphlet (Appendix, pp. 74-87), showing
how they make out that Scott drew the large sum referred to
out of the business, while no doubt made up in all good faith,
will not stand examination.

It is evident the trustees have not understood several of
the entries in Ballantyne's cash book, as they have debited
Scott with sundry sums which should not have been put to
his debit, and, on the other hand, they have omitted to credit
him with substantial sums to which he was entitled. Among
these were his half share of the profits of the business ; bills
receivable to which he had right, amounting as at January
1823 to at least £7000 ; the author's copy money in respect
of the reserved one-third share of certain novels, and his
one-sixth of the profits on these. So far as I can make out the
sums to which Scott was entitled, but which have been omitted
from the account between January 1823 and the date of the
failure, come to over £20,000. I am corroborated in my view
by the ledger kept by James Ballantyne (now in the Signet
Library, Edinburgh) for the year 1823. It opens in January
1823 with a debit balance against Scott of £561 10s. 8d., being
the same figure as the Trustees' Account starts with, but in
place of a debit balance of £490 13s. at the end of that year,
as brought out in the Trustees' Account as at that date, there
is a credit balance in his favour of £8268 0s. 1d. in addition
to his share of profit, stated in the ledger to amount to
£1591 10s. 1d.—this profit being, however, I think, much
overestimated, as proper allowances for interest on capital
sunk in the business, depreciation, trade discounts, long
credit, etc. have not been given effect to. Taking, however,
the figure brought out by Ballantyne in his ledger, Scott had
a credit balance at the end of 1823 of £9859 10s. 2d. Nor is
this all, for it is evident that Scott has been erroneously debited
with certain sums—among others with the sum of £1250 on
23rd October 1823, being a sum which Ballantyne claims to

pay him, as mentioned in the ledger, "towards payment of cash as struck at the formation of new co-partnery J. B. to Sir W. Scott." The £1250 is merely placed to Scott's debit without any corresponding entry being placed to his credit. If this sum alone, apart from other sums wrongly debited to him, be added to the £9859 10s. 3d., it makes the sum at Scott's credit according to the ledger (as thus corrected) to be at 31st December 1823 £11,109 10s. 3d. in place of a debit balance of £490 13s. as brought out in the Trustees' Account, or a difference in the first year of their account of £11,600. The ledger, I may say, is not written up after 1823 with the exception of a few entries in January following, and the cash books of the firm are now amissing, so that the amount at the time of the failure which fell to be credited to Sir Walter in excess of his drawings cannot now be ascertained, but must, I think, have amounted to a very substantial sum.

As regards Ballantyne's position, his trustees claim that his share of profits for three and a half years from May 1822 to the date of the failure came to £5500, and that he had right to one-sixth of the profit on six novels, which, at £600 each, came to £3600, making in all £9100, and they say that he drew out £5356 3s. 9d., so that they allege he had a credit balance at the time of the failure of £3743 16s. 8d. There is no doubt, however, that this is a mistake. Ballantyne's share of the profits on two of the six novels referred to was assigned to Sir Walter in terms of the missive letter above mentioned. Further, the one half of the profits of the business for the first half year came to only about £325, and this sum was carried to Capital Account, and for the remaining three years I think a full estimate of half the profits would be £3000, this being much more than the profits were ascertained to be by an accountant when the business was carried on after the failure by the trustees for the creditors. The amount, accordingly, which he was entitled to draw on during the three and a half years at a full estimate would amount to say £5400. At May 1822 he was largely in debt. At the time of the failure his personal indebtedness had been practically extinguished, there being only some trifling accounts to shopkeepers, amounting in all to £45 17s. 8d. He seems, accordingly, to have paid off all his debts out of the business. In addition to doing so, according to Lockhart, he had lent his brother-in-law George Hogarth £1563, and in January 1826, although owning and occupying a house in Edinburgh, he was engaged in building another house, on which he had paid £400. His personal household and family expenditure, judging by the particulars given by Lockhart in his pamphlet (*The Ballantyne-Humbug Handled*, p. 87), was extravagant. Further, he was liable for one-half of the expense occasioned by borrowing to supply the capital requisite for carrying on the business. The conclusion to which I have come is that he was largely indebted to the firm, and thereby occasioned a considerable increase of the accommodation bills, with their expense. The ledger which he kept (but which it is impossible to check) shows that at the end of 1823 his debit balance was £9793 16s. 4d. (apart from his share of that year's profits), and there can be little doubt that this would be largely increased in the two following years.

As regards the printing office when the partnership was reconstituted in May 1822, the whole capital of the business was sunk in buildings and printing materials. It was arranged that each partner should put in £1000 in cash, but this was not done. At the end of the first half year—December 1822 —the half year's profits were carried to the Stock or Capital Account, but these only came to £655 3s. 10d. On the other hand the firm installed a steam printing press, paid off bonds and increased the printing materials. At the failure the value of the buildings and printing materials was estimated at £6855 11s. 10d., and no doubt cost more. In addition the nature of the business was to pay weekly wages ; these for 1823 came to about £4500. The accounts for printing were only rendered after the books were completed, and then long credit was given, in some cases from a year to eighteen months. The business accordingly required a very substantial capital, and this had in the circumstances to be raised by bills and partly by a bank overdraft, both of which methods were expensive.

I may sum up what I have to say regarding the cause of the great amount of bills—that I think this was largely owing to Sir Walter's land purchases, and his building and planting operations prior to 1823, but also, to a very considerable extent, owing to the business being carried on without sufficient capital and to James Ballantyne's excessive drawings.

There is no doubt that Sir Walter must take the chief blame for running the accommodation bills, both an expensive and hazardous system of borrowing. Nor does he disclaim his responsibility. Writing in his *Journal* on 18th October 1825 he says : "I have been rash in anticipating funds to buy land " ; and there are a number of similar entries. The accommodation bills, of course, began in a small way ; but in 1819 A. C. & Co. were under acceptance for some £7000. On 4th November in that year Constable wrote to his partner Cadell : "He (Scott) wants funds for the present month, besides carrying forward every bill accommodation—but unless with a view to our own decided and certain interest, I will not move." He communicated his resolve to Scott, and on 9th November Scott wrote to John Ballantyne : "Constable has declined accepting £1050 as we proposed and prefers going regularly to work accepting for work done and paying off bills when due . . . Constable will be vexed to lose M——y [*Monastery*] part 2 [*The Abbot*] the management that is—but he must e'en content himself and as he is so chary of his bills I shall be well pleased to have fewer of them. I am not very sorry ; he has lightened my conscience on this point and preserve his letter for him for *bonne bouche* in case he grumbles."

The result was that A. C. & Co. had either to grant bills or to risk the loss of their most valuable connection. In April 1823 Constable complained to his partner Cadell as to the extent of the bills then running, but Cadell, who, Lockhart says, was "an acute business man," replied that he was more afraid of A. C. & Co. than of J. B. & Co., and informed his partner that they could not do without J. B. & Co's counter-bills. In the beginning of August 1823 the bills to J. B. & Co. for which A. C. & Co. were liable had increased to £27,347 7s. 2d., and the counter-bills granted by J. B. & Co. to £27,375 4s. 2d., practically all of which had been put into circulation. Constable became somewhat alarmed, and he wrote to Scott suggesting that the bills should be reduced, and as to the best means of doing so. The correspondence is given in *Archibald Constable*, etc. (vol. iii. pp. 274-288). Scott then embarked on a scheme of retrenchment, and so far as appears did retrench. He paid into the business practically all his literary profits, such as the author's copy money for the novels contracted for after that date and his profits on these novels, and I confess I find it difficult to account for the bills not having been very substantially reduced at the time of the failure. As to any blame attaching to Constable's firm for carrying on accommodation bills to the extent to which they did, I think they were practically compelled by circumstances to do so. They could not very well disclose to J. B. & Co. any anxieties they might have as to their financial position; and so far as Constable himself was concerned, he does not seem to have fully realised the dangerous position his firm was placed in until very shortly before the disaster took place. As Scott very fairly puts it: " If he deceived others, he also deceived himself."

The charges made by Lockhart in his *Life of Scott* against Constable in connection with his actions at the time of the failure, I may say, are quite unwarranted. As these have been accepted as being correct by several authors when dealing with the life of Sir Walter, it is perhaps right that I should refer to them. Lockhart alleges that the counter-bills granted by J. B. & Co. were merely lodged with A. C. & Co. to protect them in case of the primary bills being dishonoured (overlooking that the primary bills fell to be retired by A. C. & Co. and not by J. B. & Co.), and he proceeds to state that the counter-bills " were allowed to lie unenquired about in Constable's desk until they had swelled to a truly monstrous ' sheaf of stamps.' Constable's hour of distress darkened about him, and he rushed with these to the money changers. They were nearly all flung into circulation in the course of this maddening period of panic. And by this one circumstance it came to pass that supposing Ballantyne & Co. to have, at the day of reckoning, obligations against them, in consequence of bill transactions with Constable to the extent of £25,000, they were legally responsible for £50,000."

What the original arrangement regarding the bills may have been I do not know. From a letter written by Sir James Gibson Craig, who acted as A. C. & Co.'s lawyer, it looks as if originally the counter-bills were not discounted. But whether this is so or not, for many years prior to the failure the counter-bills were regularly discounted by A. C. & Co., and this was known both to Scott and James Ballantyne. The counter-bills were made payable at Currie, Raikes & Co.'s banking house in London, and in Ballantyne's ledger—in the years 1822 and 1823—there are four or five entries each month of J. B. & Co. remitting money to London to retire the bills, the exchange costing a considerable sum of money, which, of course, would have been saved had the bills been undiscounted in A. C. & Co.'s premises in Princes Street, where Ballantyne could have paid them. On the bills being retired Ballantyne would see through whose hands they had passed. There is in the National Library of Scotland a statement made up by A. C. & Co.'s cashier in August 1823 showing how the counter-bills had been disposed of, and that they were not lying in Constable's desk. These amounted at that time, as I have said, to £27,375 4s. 2d., and had been sent as follows :

To Hurst, Robinson & Co. - - -	£11,401 10	0
Dixon, Langdale & Brooks, bankers, London (including two bills for £1542 lodged on deposit) - - -	5,328 13	2
D. Smith & Co., bankers, Edinburgh.		
Discounted - £1,663 6 0		
On deposit - 4,262 14 0		
	5,926 0	0
J. Carstairs, banker, London - -	3,219 11	0
Longman & Dickinson, stationers, London - - - - - -	1,499 10	0
	£27,375 4	2

On 25th September 1823 Constable wrote to Scott with reference to the bills maturing in October (*Archibald Constable*, etc., vol. iii. p. 287), sending a detailed list of these bills, headed, so far as those payable by A. C. & Co., " *A. C. & Co. have to pay*," and with reference to the counter-bills headed " *J. B. & Co. have to pay*." Sir Walter could not have supposed that the bills which his firm *had to pay* were lying in Constable's desk, and that Ballantyne had not to pay them, but merely to send round and receive them after they had matured.

The matter does not admit of any doubt. I find Scott writing to John Ballantyne (the letter undated, but probably about 1818) : " I fancy Constable's people find our counter-bills convenient which makes them preserve the present five of the renewals." I find Cadell writing to J. O. Robinson of Hurst, Robinson & Co. on 25th June 1822 : " I enclose

Ballantyne due	18/21 Octr.	£640
Do.	16/19 Novr.	640
Do.	21/24 ,,	640
		£1920

" They may be more useful to you than in our bill case ; if we have need we shall draw on you @ 3 & 4 months for their value fitting the matter.   Sending one by one makes them of no use to you."   Again on 23rd July 1823 Cadell, who was not so anxious as Constable was to have the bills reduced, wrote to his partner Constable with reference to Ballantyne's counter-bills : " At present so far from making any attempt to beat down their bills, I shall do my utmost to keep them on smoothly as I tell you honestly *we need them* and *must* have them."   In the same letter he says : " Their bills to us I know are sooner cashed than ours to them."

The account given by Lockhart in the *Life of Scott* of Constable's proceedings when in London at the time of the failure is very inaccurate, and indeed largely imaginary, as can be seen from the correspondence still extant.   There was no proposal, as he alleges, made by Constable that Scott should borrow £20,000 in Edinburgh and remit it to him in London. Constable's proposal, which, however, did not mature and, in any case, came too late, was that while his firm assigned their copyrights Scott should join by granting his personal obligation for £20,000 in an endeavour which was being made to obtain a loan in London on the footing that £40,000 or £45,000 was to be available for the purposes of A. C. & Co. and J. B. & Co. The particulars are given in *Archibald Constable*, etc. (vol. iii. p. 418).   If some such arrangement could have been effected in time and the money applied by each of the two firms in taking up £20,000 of the bills for which they were respectively primarily responsible, then, even if bankruptcy had ultimately taken place, Sir Walter's estate would have been saved from a ranking of £40,000 of bills, and benefited to the extent of £20,000.

In Sir Walter's *Journal* under date 23rd July 1827, on hearing of Constable's death, he records : " He has lived to do me some injury, yet excepting the last £5000 I think most unintentionally."   Scott's feeling regarding the £5000 was, of course, very natural, but I do not think he is quite fair to Constable in thinking that he intentionally injured him.   It is easy to be wise after the event, but on 23rd November 1825, when it was resolved to give the loan, it was strongly advocated by Cadell. Cadell, as is well known, became Scott's publisher after the failure and he would not, any more than Constable, have willingly done an intentional injury to Scott.   The circumstances were that Hurst, Robinson & Co. persisted that they were abundantly solvent but were in want of cash to an extent, unless they got relief, which would bring about their stoppage and the failure of A. C. & Co. and of J. B. & Co. A. C. & Co. had borrowed and sent them £5000, and the proposal was that Scott, along with them, should borrow an additional £5000. They were not asking Scott to do what they were not willing to do themselves, and the consequences of Hurst, Robinson & Co. stopping payment would be as serious for Scott—or more so—than for themselves. It was in these circumstances that Constable, Cadell, Ballantyne and Scott had a meeting and resolved to borrow on joint-security. Sir Walter in his *Journal*, under date 23rd November 1825, says : " I must be guided by them, and hope for the best. Certainly to part company would be to incur an awful risk." It is difficult in these circumstances to think that Constable intentionally did Scott an injury, or that the four parties who attended the meeting were not acting in accordance with what they thought was wise and prudent in view of the information which they then had.

As regards Scott's borrowing £10,000 on the security of Abbotsford, this has sometimes been charged against Constable as an injury he personally did to Scott. In Cadell's letter to Constable of 13th December 1825 (*Archibald Constable*, etc., vol. iii. p. 393) the history of the transaction is given. Cadell says that having called at Ballantyne's, " I have there done what I considered a duty. I found Jas. B.'s matters covered to Saturday only, and at once got him to agree to represent along with me the instant necessity of Sir W. borrowing £10,000 on Abbotsford. I wrote a letter on the spot which Jas. B. enclosed . . . I have at all events done my duty to Sir W., he cannot blame me after this."

Cadell, in acting as he did, was no doubt performing—as he thought—a kindness to Sir Walter, but it was he, and not Constable, who wrote advising Scott to borrow the money. I may say that Sir Walter did not succeed in borrowing £10,000 additional money. He had only reserved power under his son's marriage contract to borrow £10,000, taking into account any mortgages already affecting the estate. There was a mortgage for £3000 affecting the Kaeside portion of the estate, which had to be paid off out of the £10,000, so that only £7000 was received. This sum Scott paid into J. B. & Co., and £4000 of it was applied towards their own proper indebtedness and £3000 was advanced by Ballantyne to Cadell on 13th and 14th January 1826, when Constable was on his way to London.

My desire to correct the mis-statements referred to, which injuriously reflect on Constable's reputation and character, must be my apology for the length of this letter.

I am, Yours very truly,

JAMES GLEN.

14 LYNEDOCH CRESCENT,
    GLASGOW, *8th August*, 1932.

LETTERS

1787-1799

TO JESSIE ——, KELSO [1]

DEAR JESSIE,—I hope you will pardon my thus addressing you, after so short an acquaintance, but in truth I cannot commence writing to you in any other way. I do regard you as my dear Jessie, and if you will only allow me that favour be assured you shall have no cause to regret having done so. I cannot sufficiently express the impression your lovely features have made on my heart, but I am certain it is one that can never be effaced. Your gentleness, your goodness, your kindness have filled me with the sweetest feelings I have ever known. Might I believe I am not indifferent to you I should enjoy a comfort nothing else could give. I have scribbled the enclosed lines,[2] which, though I am well aware they are quite unworthy of their subject I hope will not be un-

---

[1] For the history of this early love episode see the Introduction. It rests on the authority of a chapter in an unpublished Life of Scott preserved in MS. in the Forster Collection at the Victoria and Albert Museum. The author is unknown. In general the biography is made up from Lockhart and Chambers and Hogg with padding in the nature of literary chapters on poetry and the novel. Its one feature is the history of this episode with some early poems, all apparently derived from the lady whoever she may have been.

[2] The enclosure was a song of four verses (unpublished) entitled "To Jessie" and initialled "W. S." The first stanza reads:

> Lassie can you love me weel?
> Ask your heart, and answer true.
> Doth that gentle bosom feel
> Love for one who loveth you?

I A

favourably recieved. They at least have one recommendation—the sentiments they contain are as sincere
as any that ever influenced a human bosom. If you
are not offended with my boldness I hope to see you
to-morrow morning. Sweet dreams attend you ! Allow
me to write myself Your obedient admirer

To Miss J.——, Kelso.   WALTER SCOTT

[*Forster MS. Collection*]

To JESSIE ——, KELSO

DEAREST JESSIE,—To my exceeding regret I am obliged
to start for Edinburgh to-morrow. With how extreme
a reluctance I tear myself away from your delicious
presence it would be in vain attempting to tell. As you
will not allow me to write from there for fear of a discovery
I know not how I shall get over the time that must elapse
before I can again possess the dear sweet happiness of
your society, but be fully convinced that the first opportunity that presents itself I will speed on the wings of
love to Kelso, relying on your kindness for a full recompense for the miserable hours I must pass before that
enjoyment can be obtained. I do not think our mutual
affection is suspected in any quarter, and as you have
honored me with your generous confidence there cannot
be the slightest probability of my allowing a syllable on
the subject to escape me. I have no doubt an end would
quickly be put to our meetings were they known by your
friends or by mine, but if I can help it they shall never
know it.

I do not see why young people should not be allowed
to be as happy as old ones, and dislike nothing so much
as seeing the latter hunt after the former like so many
staunch terriers if they are but suspected of following

their own honest inclinations. I have observed sufficient to be aware that your home cannot be a very agreeable one, and I can more easily sympathise with you on that point than on any other having had no little experience of a similar wretchedness, but as we cannot make its inmates more inclined towards the ordinary pleasures of life we may at least help ourselves to them when they should chance to come within our reach.

My stay here has been so exceedingly pleasant that I am afraid my dull doings at home will scarcely be tolerated. They cannot however prevent me thinking of you, which depend on it I shall do every hour as some means of helping me to get satisfactorily through the day. If I could satisfy myself that I should reign half as absolute in your thoughts as you will in mine, it would be a great consolation. But I hope the best ! You have honored me with the flattering avowal I most wished for, and relying on the duration of your love, which I prize above all the riches and honours of the world, I now for a time—Heaven grant it be brief—bid you adieu. Ever your devoted and attached　　WALTER

To Miss J——, Kelso.

[Forster MS. Collection]

To JESSIE ——, KELSO

Tuesday, midnight

DEAREST JESSIE,—I am glad that you have told me you like poetry, and you may be well assured I am not less so at your liking my poor efforts in that way. However since this is the case I can afford you as much as you can find time to read, for, for a long time past I have been spoiling a vast quantity of good paper with my attempts at the poetical. I have addressed the moon—that most be-rhimed of planets—so often I am ashamed to look her in the face. I have made odes to nightingales so numerous they might suffice for all that ever were hatched, and as for elegies, ballads, and sonnets and other small ware, truly I can assert their name is legion, for they are many. But besides these I have dared to attempt something of a more imposing character—an epic poem of hundreds upon hundreds of lines—a chronicle in verse of the wondrous doings of some famous Knights whose names, even, I doubt much you have ever heard. Indeed the extent of my industry in this way is something marvellous to those who know not that from the earliest period of my existence, ballads and other romantic poems I have read or heard as a favourite, and sometimes as an exclusive gratification.

I remember in my childhood when staying at Bath for my health with a kind aunt of mine, there was an Irish servant in the house where we lodged, and she once sung me two ballads which made a great impression on me at the time. One filled me with horror. It was about a mason who because he had not been paid for work he had done for a certain nobleman, when that lord was absent, conveyed himself into the castle with the assistance of a treacherous nurse and murdered the lady and her children with circumstances of great barbarity. The other was a tale of attempted murder signally foiled, the subject of which if I remember right is stated to have been a Scottish Knight, but it is to be hoped he was born elsewhere.[1]   I have enclosed an attempt at a ballad

---

[1] The second ballad referred to is given in full in the MS.   It is an unpublished version of *The Outlandish Knight* entitled by Scott "The False Knight and the King's Daughter."   The opening stanza runs :

> In Ireland once dwelt many Kings
> Who ruled in bower and hall,
> But though they very potent were
> One was more great than all.

The first-mentioned ballad is a version of *Lammikin*, described in an extract from a letter which I subjoin.   It is an interesting evidence of Scott's tenacious memory, for he is drawing on his recollection of the recitation of a maidservant when he was five years old :

The other Irish ballad you ask for although I am perfectly acquainted

[as] similar to the last as my memory will allow, but I am afraid it possesses nothing of the merit of the original. Still it may serve to amuse you, and after that it may be destroyed as soon as you please. I have burnt whatever notes I have recieved from you though very unwillingly,

with its most moving incidents I forget most of the very poor verse in which it is written   It however to the best of my recollection begins

> Laukin was as fine a mason
> As ever laid a stone
> He built a castle for Lord Blakeney
> But of payment got none

A result I imagine that happens to many builders   The ballad proceeds

> Said my Lord to my Lady
> And he going from home
> Have a care of that Laukin
> Until I come home

To which the lady answers

> What fear is there of him
> Or any of his kin
> I'll bar up my doors
> And my windows pin in

The Lord then sets off on his travels, but he has not long departed before the dreaded mason making his appearance

> Laukin came to the gate
> Knocked loud and did ring
> How ready was the false nurse
> To rise and let him in

The villain having obtained admittance to the castle by the assistance of his confederate whom he had bribed for the purpose proceeds to look after his victims and the following dialogue takes place between him and the false nurse

> " O where is your Lord
> Or is he within ? "
> " He's gone to fair England,
> To wait on the King."
>
> " O where is your Lady
> And is she within ? "
> " She's up in her chamber
> And her window's pinned in."
>
> " How shall we get her down ? "
> " Oh," says cruel Laukin,
> " We'll pierce the pretty baby
> With a silver bodkin."

This horrid suggestion is immediately put in practice and the cries of the

and I did so from the fear they might be discovered by
some curious person and the course of our true love made

child being so murdered quickly attract the attention of the alarmed
mother who cries out to the attendant

> " O nurse ! O nurse !
> How fast you do sleep,
> Don't you hear my pretty baby
> Crying out its last weep ? "

to which the old hag replies

> " I've fed him with the breast milk
> I've fed him with the pap
> I pray you fair lady
> To dandle him on your lap "
> " How can I come down "
> The lady she said
> " Without e'er a candle
> To light me from my bed."

The want of a candle the nurse suggests can be supplied in a manner
which may stagger the most credulous mind, for she says

> " You've two silk gowns
> As bright as the sun
> Put one of them on you
> While you are coming down."

The mistress unfortunately leaves her apartment but whether in any
belief that her " shining silks " will illuminate her path is more than
doubtful

> The Lady was coming down
> And felt no alarms
> How ready was Laukin
> To take her in his arms

She sees her fate and tries to escape from it

> " O Laukin, O Laukin !
> Spare my life, I pray
> And I'll give you as many jewels
> As you can carry away."

But the remorseless murderer was not to be led from his purpose and
replying

> " If you'll give me as many jewels
> As there are stones in the street
> I must with this dagger
> Pierce your white neck indeed "

and speedily accomplishes his brutal purpose : but Lord Blakeney returns
in time to prevent the escape of his relentless enemy from the scene of
slaughter and the mason and his accomplice are quickly fitted with halters
by the frantic nobleman and left hanging high up at the castle wall as a
monument of justice avenged."

A fragment of a ballad on the subject, *Lammikin. To the Tune of Gil
Morrice*, is printed in David Herd's *Ancient and Modern Scottish Songs*. It
differs markedly from Scott's version.

to run less smooth even than it does at present. I hope
you have or will follow my example, and then we need
entertain no fear. I hear my uncle coming to take me
with him to pay a visit to my aunt at the Garden [1] so
hastily conclude.   W. S.

Miss J——

[*Forster MS. Collection*]

To JESSIE ——, KELSO

ROSEBANK *Sunday morning one o'clock*

DEAR JESSIE,—Your praise of my poetic efforts em-
boldens me to make other attempts. Of Scottish songs
you are sufficiently familiar—you would not deserve to
be considered a Scottish lassie were you ignorant of them
—but of ancient English ballads it is very possible you
may not have heard once. Of ballads and romances I
think I have held a longer acquaintance than have I with
any other kind of learning, and lately I have managed
to get hold of more than one collection of old songs native
of the other side of the Border. The English have not so
many good old ballads as we have, yet they possess several
of a very interesting character, and among their early
love songs some are remarkable for a simplicity and
sweetness which have rarely been excelled. In the
examples here given I have modernised some of the words
so as to make them more easily understood by you—to
me however they lose much of their grace by being
deprived of their antique garment. Here is a commencement of a plaintive ditty and I doubt hugely
any of our living poets could so movingly express them-

---

[1] Writing to William Clerk on 6th August, 1790, Scott says : " Direct
to me at Miss Scott's, Garden, Kelso.   My letters lie there for me, as it saves
their being sent down to Rosebank."

selves. I need not add how truly it describes my own condition when I was prevented from obtaining that delicate surgery which makes any wound endurable.

> When the nightingale sings the woods waxen green
> Leaf and grass and blossom spring in April I ween,
> And love is to my heart gone with one spear so keen
> Night and day my blood it drinks my heart doth me teen.

That is to say he lies heart sore and heart sad as true lover must needs be till his mistress heal his heart and make him happy. Here is another fragment from another written in similar mood.

> For her love in sleep I slake (slack)
> For her love all night I wake
> For her love mourning I make
> More than any man.
> Blow northern wind
> Send thou me my Sweeting
> Blow northern wind
> Send thou me my Sweeting
> Blow, blow, blow.

But I have enclosed an entire ballad or rather a new version of one—having taken considerable liberties with some portions of it—which pleased me exceedingly. The original is supposed to have been written about the reign of the English King Henry 6th probably by some rival of him who wrote " Chevy Chace " and " The Battle of Otterburn " of which I have already I think sufficiently made you acquainted. The Minstrels of old were well rewarded. I trust your poor " Rymour " will taste of your sweet bounty without stint as a fitting reward for his labours in your service.

YOUR TRUE WALTER

For Miss J.

[*Forster MS. Collection*]

To WILLIAM CLERK [1]   [1788-1790 ?)

DEAR BARONET,—I am sorry to find that our friend
Colonel Grogg has behaved with a very undue degree
of vehemence in a dispute with you last night, occasioned
by what I am convinced was a gross misconception of
your expressions. As the Colonel, though a military
man, is not too haughty to acknowledge an error, he has
commissioned me to make his apology as a mutual friend,
which I am convinced you will accept from yours ever,

GIVEN AT CASTLE DUNS, *Monday*   DUNS SCOTUS
[*Lockhart*]

To MRS. SCOTT, GEORGES SQUARE, EDINBURGH

(With a parcel)
ROSEBANK, 5 *Sept.*, 1788

DEAR MOTHER,—I was favour with your letter, and
send you Annes Stockings along with this. I would have
sent them last week, but had some expectations of a private
opportunity. I have been very happy for this fortnight,
we have some plan or other for every day. Last week
My uncle, my Cousin Walter,[2] and I, rode to Smailholm,
and from thence walked to Sandiknow Craigs, where
we spent the whole day, and made a very hearty dinner

---

[1] "A smaller society, formed with less ambitious views, originated in a
ride to Pennycuik, the seat of the head of Mr. Clerk's family. . . . This
was called by way of excellence, *The Club.* . . . The members used to
meet on Friday evenings in a room in Carrubers Close, from which some
of them usually adjourned to sup at an oyster tavern in the same
neighbourhood. . . . At one of the merry suppers Walter Scott had said
something, of which, on recollecting himself next morning, he was sensible
that his friend Clerk might have reason to complain. He sent him
accordingly a note apologetical which has by some accident been preserved.
In it Scott contrives to make use of *both* his own club designations and
addresses his friend by another . . . which Clerk had received in consequence
of comparing himself to . . . Sir John Brute in the play."—LOCKHART. The
play in question is Vanbrugh's *The Provoked Wife*. William Clerk was the
second son of John Clerk of Eldin, author of the *Naval Tactics*, etc.
"Colonel Grogg" was Scott's nickname.

[2] Fourth son of Walter Scott of Raeburn, died 1802.

by the side of the Orderlaw well, on some Cold Beef and bread and cheese, we had also a small case Bottle of Rum to make Grogg in which we drank to the Sandiknow Bairns, and all their connexion.

This jaunt gave me much pleasure, and had I time, I would give you a more full account of it. The fishing has been hitherto but indifferent, and I fear I shall not be able to accomplish my promise with regard to the Wild ducks. I was out on friday, and only saw three. I may probably however send you a hare, as my Uncle has got a present of two Greyhounds from Sir H. MacDougall,[1] and as he has a License, only waits till the corn is of the ground to commence coursing.

Be it known to you, however, I am not altogether employ'd in amusements, for I have got two or three Clients, besides my Uncle, and am busy drawing tacks and Contracts,—not however of marriage. I am in a fair way of making money, if I stay here long.

Here I have written a pretty long letter, and nothing in it, but you know writing to ones friends is the next thing to seeing them. My Love to my father and the buoys, I am Dear Mother your dutifull and affectionate son,

WALTER SCOTT

[Law]

To WILLIAM CLERK

ROSEBANK, 6th August 1790

DEAR WILLIAM,—Here am I, the weather, according to your phrase, most bitchiferous ; the Tweed, within

---

[1] Sir Henry Hay Makdougal of Makerston : the fourth baronet succeeded his father Sir George Hay-Makdougal in 1777 and died in 1825. Scott's memory of Sir George " dragging his watch along the carpet to induce me to follow it " goes back to his fifth year or earlier. The wife of Walter Scott of Raeburn, the Quaker, and the mother of Beardie, was Isobel daughter of William Makdougal of Makerston, so that Sir Walter was a far distant cousin of the family. " There was always great friendship between us and the Makerston family. It singularly happened that at the burial of the late Sir Henry my cousin William Scott younger of Raeburn and I myself were the nearest blood relations present, though our connexion was of so old a date, and ranked as pall-bearers accordingly." (SCOTT, Journal, 1826.)

twenty yards of the window at which I am writing, swelled from bank to brae, and roaring like thunder. It is paying you but a poor compliment to tell you I waited for such a day to perform my promise of writing, but you must consider that it is the point here to reserve such within-doors employment as we think most agreeable for bad weather, which in the country always wants something to help it away. In fair weather we are far from wanting amusement, which at present is my business ; on the contrary, every fair day has some plan of pleasure annexed to it, in so much that I can hardly believe I have been here above two days, so swiftly does the time pass away. You will ask how it is employed ? Why, negatively, I read *no* civil law. Heineccius and his fellow worthies have ample time to gather a venerable coat of dust, which they merit by their dulness. As to my positive amusements,—besides riding, fishing, and the other usual sports of the country, I often spend an hour or two in the evening in shooting herons, which are numerous on this part of the river. To do this I have no farther to go than the bottom of our garden, which literally hangs over the river. When you fire at a bird, she always crosses the river, and when again shot at with ball, usually returns to your side, and will cross in this way several times before she takes wing. This furnishes fine sport ; nor are they easily shot, as you never can get very near them. The intervals between their appearing is spent very agreeably in eating gooseberries.

Yesterday was St. James's Fair, a day of great business. There was a great show of black cattle—I mean of ministers ; the narrowness of their stipends here obliges many of them to enlarge their incomes by taking farms and grazing cattle. This, in my opinion, diminishes their respectability, nor can the farmer be supposed to entertain any great reverence for the ghostly advice of a *pastor* (they literally deserve the epithet) who perhaps the day before overreached him in a bargain. I would not have you to suppose there are no exceptions to this character, but it would serve most of them. I had been fishing with my uncle, Captain Scott, on the Teviot, and returned through the ground where the Fair is kept. The servant was waiting there with our horses, as we were to ride the water. Lucky it was that it was so ; for just about that time the magistrates of Jedburgh, who preside there, began their solemn procession through the Fair. For the greater dignity upon this occasion, they had a pair of boots [1] among three men—*i.e.*, as they ride three in a rank, the *outer* legs of those personages who formed the outside, as it may be called, of the procession, were each clothed in a boot. This, and several other incongruous appearances, were thrown in the teeth of those cavaliers by the Kelso populace, and, by the assistance of whisky, parties were soon inflamed to a very tight battle, one of that kind which, for distinction sake, is called royal. It was not without great difficulty that we extricated ourselves from the confusion ; and had we been on foot, we might have been trampled down by these fierce Jedburghians, who charged like so many troopers. We were spectators of the combat from an eminence, but peace was soon after restored, which made the older warriors regret the effeminacy of the age, as, regularly, it ought to have lasted till night. Two lives were lost, I mean of horses ; indeed, had you seen them, you would rather have wondered that they were able to bear their masters to the scene of action, than that they could not carry them off.

I am ashamed to read over this sheet of nonsense, so excuse inaccuracies. Remember me to the lads of the

---

[1] Lockhart cites from a letter to himself from Andrew Shortreed : " The joke of the *one pair* of boots to *three pair* of legs. was so unpalatable to the honest burghers of Jedburgh, that they have suffered the ancient privilege of ' riding to the Fair,' as it was called . . . to fall into disuse. Huoy, the runaway forger, a native of Kelso, availed himself of the calumny in a clever squib on the subject :—

> The outside man had each a boot,
> The three had but a pair."

Literary, those of *the club* in particular. I wrote Irving.
Remember my most respectful compliments to Mr. and
Mrs. Clerk and family, particularly James ; when you
write, let me know how he did when you heard of him.
Imitate me in writing a long letter, but not in being long
in writing it. Direct to me at Miss Scott's, Garden,
Kelso. My letters lie there for me, as it saves their being
sent down to Rosebank. The carrier puts up at the
Grassmarket, and goes away on Wednesday forenoon.
Yours,

WALTER SCOTT

[*Lockhart*]

To WILLIAM CLERK

KIPPILAW, *Sept.* 3, 1790

DEAR CLERK,—I am now writing from the country
habitation of our friend Ramsay,[1] where I have been
spending a week as pleasantly as ever I spent one in my
life. Imagine a commodious old house, pleasantly
situated amongst a knot of venerable elms, in a fine
sporting, open country, and only two miles from an
excellent water for trouts, inhabited by two of the best
old ladies (Ramsay's aunts), and three as pleasant young
ones (his sisters) as any person could wish to converse
with—and you will have some idea of Kippilaw. James and
I wander about,—fish, or look for hares, the whole day,
and at night laugh, chat, and play round games at cards.
Such is the fatherland in which I have been living for some
days past, and which I leave to-night or to-morrow. This
day is very bad ; notwithstanding which, James has sallied
out to make some calls, as he soon leaves the country. I
have a great mind to trouble him with the care of this.

And now for your letter, the receipt of which I have

---

[1] Kippilaw, situated about five or six miles behind Abbotsford, on the
high ground between the Tweed and the Water of Ayle, is the seat of an
ancient laird of the clan Kerr, but was at this time tenanted by the family
of Scott's brother-apprentice, James Ramsay, who afterwards realized a
fortune in the civil service of Ceylon.—LOCKHART.

not, I think, yet acknowledged, though I am much obliged to you for it. I dare say you would relish your jaunt to Pennycuick very much, especially considering the solitary desert of Edinburgh, from which it relieved you. By the by, know, O thou devourer of grapes, who contemnest the vulgar gooseberry, that thou art not singular in thy devouring—*nec tam aversus equos sol jungit ab urbe* (*Kelsonianá scilicet*)—my uncle being the lawful possessor of a vinery measuring no less than twenty-four feet by twelve, the contents of which come often in my way ; and, according to the proverb, that enough is as good as a feast, are equally acceptable as if they came out of the most extensive vineyard in France. I cannot, however, equal your boast of breakfasting, dining, and supping on them. As for the civilians [1]—peace be with them, and may the dust lie light upon their heads : they deserve this prayer in return for those sweet slumbers which their benign influence infuses into their readers. I fear I shall too soon be forced to disturb them, for some of our family being now at Kelso, I am under the agonies lest I be obliged to escort them into town. The only pleasure I shall reap by this is that of asking you how you do, and, perhaps, the solid advantage of completing our studies before the College sits down. Employ, therefore, your mornings in slumber while you can, for soon it will be chased from your eyes. I plume myself on my sagacity with regard to C. J. Fox.[2] I always foretold you would tire of him—a vile brute. I have not yet forgot the narrow escape of my fingers. I rejoice at James's[3] intimacy with Miss Menzies. She promised to turn out a fine girl, has a fine fortune, and could James get her, he

---

[1] *i.e.* books on Civil Law, as the works of Johan Gottlieb Heineccius, mentioned in an earlier letter, and others.

[2] A tame fox kept by Clerk. The initials are, of course, those of the statesman, not beloved of Scott. See later.

[3] James Clerk, R.N., the younger brother of William. Miss Menzies is possibly an aunt or other relation of Lockhart's friend who saw Scott's hand writing *Waverley* or a later novel.

might sing, " I'll go no more to sea, to sea."   Give my
love to him when you write.—" God preserve us, what a
scrawl ! " says one of the ladies just now, in admiration at
the expedition with which I scribble.   Well—I was never
able in my life to do anything with what is called gravity
and deliberation.

I dined two days ago *tête à tête* with Lord Buchan.[1]
Heard a history of all his ancestors whom he has hung
round his chimney-piece.   From counting of pedigrees,
good Lord deliver us !   He is thinking of erecting a
monument to Thomson.   He frequented Dryburgh much
in my grandfather's time.   It will be a handsome thing.

---

[1] David Erskine, eleventh earl, 1742-1829.   " Lord Buchan is dead, a
person whose immense vanity, bordering upon insanity, obscured, or rather
eclipsed, very considerable talents.   His imagination was so fertile, that he
seemed really to believe the extraordinary fictions which he delighted in
telling.   His economy, most laudable in the early part of his life, when it
enabled him, from a small income, to pay his father's debts, became a
miserable habit, and led him to do mean things.   He had a desire to be a
great man and a Maecenas—*à bon marché*.   The two celebrated lawyers,
his brothers, were not more gifted by nature than I think he was, but the
restraints of a profession kept the eccentricity of the family in order.   Henry
Erskine was the best-natured man I ever knew, thoroughly a gentleman,
and with but one fault—He could not say *no*, and thus sometimes misled
those who trusted him.   Tom Erskine was positively mad. . . .   Both
Henry and Tom were saving men, yet both died very poor.   The latter at
one time possessed £200,000 ; the other had a considerable fortune.   The
Earl alone has died wealthy.   It is saving, not getting, that is the mother of
riches.   They all had wit.   The Earl's was crack-brained, and sometimes
caustic ; Henry's was of the very kindest, best-humoured, and gayest sort
that ever cheered society ; that of Lord Erskine was moody and muddish.
But I never saw him in his best days."—SCOTT, *Diary*, April 20, 1829.
    Among Mr. Hugh Walpole's MSS. is the following letter from Lord
Buchan to Scott's uncle :

" Captain Scott, Rosebank, near Kelso.

    DEAR SIR—John Smith the mason has now finished and erected the
    Tablet mural sarcophagus in the aisle of the Conventual Church here
    to mark my concession to you and to your Brothers to bury there, the
    inscription is as follows :

    Hunc locum sepulturae D. Seneschallus Buchaniae Comes Gualtero
        Thomae at Roberto Scott Haliburtoni nepotibus concessit.

    Smith is here who will give you in the charge of cutting and erecting
    the Stone.   Will you come and dine with me on Monday ?   I am my
    dear Sir Yrs sincerely   BUCHAN

    DRYBURGH ABBEY 28 *May* 91."

As to your scamp of a boy, I saw nothing of him ; but the face is enough to condemn there. I have seen a man flogg'd for stealing spirits on the sole information of his nose. Remember me respectfully to all your family.— Believe me yours affectionately,

WALTER SCOTT

[*Lockhart*]

To CAPTAIN ROBERT SCOTT

EDINBURGH, *Sept.* 30, 1790

DEAR UNCLE,—We arrived here without any accident about five o'clock on Monday evening. The good weather made our journey pleasant. I have been attending to your commissions here, and find that the last volume of Dodsley's Annual Register [1] published is that for 1787, which I was about to send you ; but the bookseller I frequent had not one in boards, though he expects to procure one for me. There is a new work of the same title and size, on the same plan, which, being published every year regularly, has almost cut out Dodsley's, so that this last is expected to stop altogether. You will let me know if you would wish to have the new work, which is a good one, will join very well with those volumes of Dodsley's which you already have, and is published up to the present year. Byron's Narrative [2] is not yet published, but you shall have it whenever it comes out.

---

[1] " The *Annual Register* was commenced by R. Dodsley and published by his house until 1790, when the copyright and stock were sold. The stock was purchased by Rivington, Baldwin and others, and each party published a distinct continuation of the Register."—*Edinburgh University Library Catalogue.* The new one referred to is probably Rivington's.

[2] *The Narrative of Admiral the Hon. John Byron, containing an account of the great distresses suffered by himself and his companions on the coast of Patagonia* &c. 1768. This is Foul-Weather Jack or Hardy Byron to whom the poet often refers :

> A strange doom is thy father's son's, and past
> Recalling, as it lies beyond redress ;
> Reversed for him our grandsire's fate of yore,—
> He had no rest at sea, nor I on shore.

Scott must refer to some reissue of the work, of which there were several.

Agreeable to your permission, I send you the scroll copy of an essay on the origin of the feudal system,[1] written for the Literary Society last year. As you are kind enough to interest yourself in my style and manner of writing, I thought you might like better to see it in its original state, than one on the polishing of which more time had been bestowed. You will see that the intention and attempt of the essay is principally to controvert two propositions laid down by the writers on the subject :—1st, That the system was invented by the Lombards ; and, 2dly, that its foundation depended on the King's being acknowledged the sole lord of all the lands in the country, which he afterwards distributed to be held by military tenures. I have endeavoured to assign it a more general origin, and to prove that it proceeds upon principles common to all nations when placed in a certain situation. I am afraid the matter will but poorly reward the trouble you will find in reading some parts. I hope, however, you will make out enough to enable you to favour me with your sentiments upon its faults. There is none whose advice I prize so high, for there is none in whose judgment I can so much confide, or who has shown me so much kindness.

I also send, as amusement for an idle half hour, a copy of the regulations of our Society, some of which will, I think, be favoured with your approbation.

My mother and sister join in compliments to aunt and you, and also in thanks for the attentions and hospitality

---

[1] " While attending Mr. Dugald Stewart's class, in the winter of 1790-91, Scott produced, in compliance with the usual custom of ethical students, several essays besides that . . . I believe, entitled " On the Manners and Customs of the Northern Nations.' But this essay it was that first attracted, in any particular manner, his Professor's attention. Mr. Robert Ainslie, well known as the friend and fellow-traveller of Burns [died 1838], happened to attend Stewart the same session, and remembers his saying, *ex cathedrâ*, ' The author of this paper shows much knowledge of his subject, and a great taste for such researches.' Scott became, before the close of the session, a frequent visitor in Mr. Stewart's family."—LOCKHART.

Scott seems to have read the same essay to his friends of the Speculative Society in November 1791.

which they experienced at Rosebank. And I am ever
your affectionate nephew,

WALTER SCOTT

P.S.—If you continue to want a mastiff, I think I can
procure you one of a good breed, and send him by the
carrier.

[*Lockhart*]

To WILLIAM CLERK

NORTHUMBERLAND, 26th Aug., 1791

DEAR CLERK,—Behold a letter from the mountains ; for
I am very snugly settled here, in a farmer's house, about
six miles from Wooler, in the very centre of the Cheviot
hills, in one of the wildest and most romantic situations
which your imagination, fertile upon the subject of
cottages, ever suggested. And what the deuce are you
about there ? methinks I hear you say. Why, sir, of all
things in the world—drinking goat's whey—not that I
stand in the least need of it, but my uncle having a slight
cold, and being a little tired of home, asked me last
Sunday evening if I would like to go with him to Wooler,
and I answering in the affirmative, next morning's sun
beheld us on our journey, through a pass in the Cheviots,
upon the back of two special nags, and man Thomas
behind with a portmanteau, and two fishing-rods fastened
across his back, much in the style of St. Andrew's Cross.
Upon reaching Wooler we found the accommodations so
bad that we were forced to use some interest to get
lodgings here, where we are most delightfully appointed
indeed. To add to my satisfaction, we are amidst places
renowned by the feats of former days ; each hill is crowned
with a tower, or camp, or cairn, and in no situation
can you be near more fields of battle : Flodden, Otterburn, Chevy Chase, Ford Castle, Chillingham Castle,
Copland Castle, and many another scene of blood, are

within the compass of a forenoon's ride. Out of the
brooks with which these hills are intersected, we pull
trouts of half a yard in length, as fast as we did the perches
from the pond at Pennycuick, and we are in the very
country of muirfowl.

Often as I have wished for your company, I never did
it more earnestly than when I rode over Flodden Edge.
I know your taste for these things, and could have undertaken to demonstrate, that never was an affair more
completely bungled than that day's work was. Suppose
one army posted upon the face of a hill, and secured by
high grounds projecting on each flank, with the river Till
in front, a deep and still river, winding through a very
extensive valley called Milfield Plain, and the only
passage over it by a narrow bridge, which the Scots
artillery, from the hill, could in a moment have demo-
lished. Add, that the English must have hazarded a
battle while their troops, which were tumultuously levied,
remained together ; and that the Scots, behind whom the
country was open to Scotland, had nothing to do but to
wait for the attack as they were posted. Yet did two-
thirds of the army, actuated by the *perfervidum ingenium
Scotorum*, rush down and give an opportunity to Stanley
to occupy the ground they had quitted, by coming over
the shoulder of the hill, while the other third, under Lord
Home, kept their ground, and having seen their king
and about 10,000 of their countrymen cut to pieces,
retired into Scotland without loss. For the reason of the
bridge not being destroyed while the English passed, I
refer you to Pitscottie,[1] who narrates at large, and to whom
I give credit for a most accurate and clear description,
agreeing perfectly with the ground.

My uncle drinks the whey here, as I do ever since I

---

[1] See *The historie and Cronicles of Scotland from the slauchter of King James I
to the ane thousand fyve hundreith thrie score fyftein yeir. Written and collected
by R. L. of Pitscottie, being a continuation of the translation of the Chronicles
written by Hector Boece and tr. by John Bellenden* . . . ed. by Æ. J. Mackay.
Scottish Text Society, 1899-1911. An Edinburgh edition appeared in 1728.

understood it was brought to his bedside every morning at six, by a very pretty dairy-maid. So much for my residence : all the day we shoot, fish, walk and ride ; dine and sup upon fish struggling from the stream, and the most delicious heath-fed mutton, barn-door fowls, poys,[1] milk-cheese, &c., all in perfection ; and so much simplicity resides among these hills, that a pen, which could write at least, was not to be found about the house, though belonging to a considerable farmer, till I shot the crow with whose quill I write this epistle. I wrote to Irving before leaving Kelso. Poor fellow ! I am sure his sister's death must have hurt him much ; though he makes no noise about feelings, yet still streams always run deepest. I sent a message by him to Edie,[2] poor devil, adding my mite of consolation to him in his affliction. I pity poor [3] * * * * * *, who is more deserving of compassion, being his first offence. Write soon, and as long as the last ;—you will have Perthshire news, I suppose, soon. Jamie's adventure diverted me much. I read it to my uncle, who being long in the India service, was affronted. Remember me to James when you write, and to all your family and friends in general. I send this to Kelso—you may address as usual ; my letters will be forwarded—adieu—*au revoir*.

WALTER SCOTT

[*Lockhart*]

To WILLIAM CLERK

ROSEBANK, 10th Sept., 1792

DEAR WILLIAM,—Taking the advantage of a very indifferent day, which is likely to float away a good deal

---

[1] *i.e.*, pies.

[2] Sir Adam Fergusson, of whom later we shall hear much. He was the son of Professor Adam Fergusson, at whose house Scott met Burns.

[3] I do not know to whom Scott refers. Charles Kerr of Abbotrule's trouble with his parents and departure from home was earlier, 1789 to 1791-1792, when he returned to claim his estates.

of corn, and of my father's leaving this place, who will
take charge of this scroll, I sit down to answer your
favour. I find you have been, like myself, taking
advantage of the good weather to look around you a
little, and congratulate you upon the pleasure you must
have received from your jaunt with Mr. Russell.[1] I
apprehend, though you are silent on the subject, that
your conversation was enlivened by many curious dis-
quisitions of the nature of *undulating exhalations*. I should
have bowed before the venerable grove of oaks at
Hamilton with as much respect as if I had been a Druid
about to gather the sacred mistletoe. I should hardly
have suspected your host Sir William[2] of having been the
occasion of the scandal brought upon the library and Mr.
Gibb[3] by the introduction of the Cabinet des Fées, of
which I have a volume or two here. I am happy to
think there is an admirer of *snug things* in the administration of the library. Poor Linton's[4] misfortune, though
I cannot say it surprises, yet heartily grieves me. I have
no doubt he will have many advisers and animadverters
upon the naughtiness of his ways, whose admonitions
will be forgot upon the next opportunity.

I am lounging about the country here, to speak
sincerely, as idle as the day is long. Two old companions
of mine, brothers of Mr. Walker of Wooden, having come
to this country, we have renewed a great intimacy. As
they live directly upon the opposite bank of the river,
we have signals agreed upon by which we concert a plan

---

[1] A surgeon, afterwards Professor of Clinical Surgery at Edinburgh
University.

[2] Sir William Miller (Lord Glenlee).

[3] The Librarian of the Advocates', now the National, Library of Scotland,
into which Sir William Miller, later Lord Glenlee, had introduced the
Cabinet des Fées.

[4] *i.e.* the Adam Fergusson mentioned above, so nicknamed because on
a boating expedition he had been hailed by a passing fisherman, who
mistook him for a friend, with the words : " Linton, you lang bitch, is that
you ? "

of operations for the day. They are both officers, and
very intelligent young fellows, and what is of some
consequence, have a brace of fine greyhounds. Yesterday
forenoon we killed seven hares, so you may see how
plenty the game is with us. I have turned a keen duck
shooter, though my success is not very great ; and when
wading through the mosses upon this errand, accoutred
with the long gun, a jacket, musquito trowsers, and a
rough cap, I might well pass for one of my redoubted
moss-trooper progenitors, Walter Fire-the-Braes, or rather
Willie wi' the Bolt-foot.

For about-doors' amusement, I have constructed a seat
in a large tree, which spreads its branches horizontally
over the Tweed. This is a favourite situation of mine for
reading, especially in a day like this, when the west wind
rocks the branches on which I am perched, and the river
rolls its waves below me of a turbid blood colour. I have,
moreover, cut an embrasure, through which I can fire
upon the gulls, herons, and cormorants, as they fly
screaming past my nest. To crown the whole, I have
carved an inscription upon it in the ancient Roman taste.
I believe I shall hardly return into town, barring accidents, sooner than the middle of next month, perhaps
not till November. Next week, weather permitting, is
destined for a Northumberland expedition, in which I
shall visit some parts of that country which I have not yet
seen, particularly about Hexham. Some days ago I had
nearly met with a worse accident than the tramp I took
at Moorfoot [1] ; for having bewildered myself among the
Cheviot hills, it was nearly nightfall before I got to the
village of Hownam, and the passes with which I was
acquainted. You do not speak of being in Perthshire
this season, though I suppose you intend it. I suppose
we, that is, *nous autres*, are at present completely dispersed.

Compliments to all who are in town, and best respects

---

[1] Where Scott had been nearly lost on a fishing expedition, as Irving tells
Lockhart in a letter of 8th April 1837.

to your own family, both in Prince's Street and at Eldin.—
Believe me ever most sincerely yours,

WALTER SCOTT

[*Lockhart*]

To WILLIAM CLERK

ROSEBANK, 30th Sept., 1792

DEAR WILLIAM,—I suppose this will find you flourishing
like a green bay-tree on the mountains of Perthshire, and
in full enjoyment of all the pleasures of the country. All
that I envy you is the *noctes cœnœque deum,* which I take it
for granted you three merry men will be spending
together, while I am poring over Bartholine [1] in the long
evenings, solitary enough ; for, as for the lobsters,[2] as you
call them, I am separated from them by the Tweed, which
precludes evening meetings, unless in fine weather and
full moons. I have had an expedition through Hexham
and the higher parts of Northumberland, which would
have delighted the very cockles of your heart, not so much
on account of the beautiful romantic appearance of the
country, though that would have charmed you also, as
because you would have seen more Roman inscriptions
built into gate-posts, barns, &c., than perhaps are to be
found in any other part of Britain. These have been all
dug up from the neighbouring Roman wall, which is still
in many places very entire, and gives a stupendous idea
of the perseverance of its founders, who carried such an
erection from sea to sea, over rocks, mountains, rivers,
and morasses. There are several lakes among the
mountains above Hexham, well worth going many miles

---

[1] Thomas Bartholinus, the younger, who wrote *Antiquitatum Danicarum de
causis contemptae a Danis adhuc gentilibus mortis libri tres,* 4to.   Hafniae, 1689.
The work was later recommended to Scott by John Ramsay of Ochtertyre,
on his reading Scott's translations, as " one of the noblest treasures of
antiquities any nation can boast of."—*Walpole Collection.*

[2] *i.e.* the young soldiers referred to above.   The use of the name for British
soldiers goes as far back as 1643.

to see, though their fame is eclipsed by their neighbourhood to those of Cumberland. They are surrounded by
old towers and castles, in situations the most savagely
romantic ; what would I have given to have been able to
take effect-pieces from some of them ! Upon the Tyne,
about Hexham, the country has a different aspect, presenting much of the beautiful, though less of the sublime.
I was particularly charmed with the situation of Beau-
front, a house belonging to a mad sort of genius, whom,
I am sure, I have told you some stories about. He used
to call himself the Noble Errington, but of late has
assumed the title of Duke of Hexham. Hard by the
town is the field of battle where the forces of Queen
Margaret were defeated by those of the House of York—
a blow which the Red Rose never recovered during the
civil wars. The spot where the Duke of Somerset and
the northern nobility of the Lancastrian faction were
executed after the battle, is still called Dukesfield. The
inhabitants of this country speak an odd dialect of the
Saxon, approaching nearly that of Chaucer, and have
retained some customs peculiar to themselves. They are
the descendants of the ancient Danes, chased into the
fastnesses of Northumberland by the severity of William
the Conqueror. Their ignorance is surprising to a
Scotchman. It is common for the traders in cattle,
which business is carried on to a great extent, to carry
all letters received in course of trade to the parish church,
where the clerk reads them aloud after service, and
answers them according to circumstances.

We intended to visit the lakes in Cumberland, but our
jaunt was cut short by the bad weather. I went to the
circuit at Jedburgh,[1] to make my bow to Lord J. Clerk,

---

[1] Scott's father had written to him on the 15th August : " lord J. Clerk
is in town . . . he called here yesterday and inquired very particularly for
you. I told him where you was, and he expects to see you at Jedburgh
upon the 21st. He is to be at Mellerstane on the 20th and will be there
all night. His Lordship said in a very pleasant manner that something
might cast up at Jedburgh to give you an opportunity of appearing, and

and might have had employment, but durst not venture. Nine of the Dunse rioters were condemned to banishment, but the ferment continues violent in the Merse. Kelso races afforded little sport—Wishaw [1] lost a horse which cost him £500, and foundered irrecoverably on the course. At another time I shall quote George Buchanan's adage of " a fool and his money," but at present labour under a similar misfortune ; my Galloway having yesterday thought proper (N.B., without a rider) to leap over a gate, and being lamed for the present. This is not his first *faux-pas*, for he jumped into a water with me on his back when in Northumberland, to the imminent danger of my life. He is, therefore, to be sold (when recovered), and another purchased. This accident has occasioned you the trouble of reading so long an epistle, the day being Sunday, and my uncle, the captain, busily engaged with your father's naval tactics, is too seriously employed to be an agreeable companion. Apropos (des bottes)— I am sincerely sorry to hear that James is still unemployed, but have no doubt a time will come round when his talents will have an opportunity of being displayed to his advantage. I have no prospect of seeing my *chère adorable* till winter, if then. As for you, I pity you not, seeing as how you have so good a succedaneum in M. G. ; and, on the contrary, hope, not only that Edmonstone may *roast* you, but that Cupid may again (as erst) *fry* you on the gridiron of jealousy for your infidelity. Compliments to our right trusty and well-beloved Linton, and Jean

that he would insist upon it and that in future he meant to give you a share of the criminal business in the Court all which is very kind. I told his Ldp. that I had disswaded you from appearing at Jedburgh but he said I was wrong in doing so I therefore leave the matter to you and him." Scott had gone as his father wished, but had shrunk from the business offered to him through the influence of Lord Braxfield. He had just been called and had not yet begun practice at the Parliament House.

[1] William Hamilton of Wishaw, afterwards Lord Belhaven, having established his claim to the title dormant since the death of the second baron, John Hamilton, whose speech against the Union was known as Belhaven's Vision.

Jacques.[1] If you write, which, by the way, I hardly have
the conscience to expect, direct to my father's care, who
will forward your letter. I have quite given up duck-
shooting for the season, the birds being too old, and the
mosses too deep and cold. I have no reason to boast of
my experience or success in the sport, and for my own
part, should fire at any distance under eighty or even
ninety paces, though above forty-five I would reckon
it a *coup désespéré* ; and as the bird is beyond measure shy,
you may be sure I was not very bloody. Believe me,
deferring, *as usual*, our dispute till another opportunity,
always sincerely yours,

                                        WALTER SCOTT

P.S.—I believe, if my pony does not soon recover, that
misfortune, with the bad weather, may send me soon to
town.

[*Lockhart*]

TO PATRICK MURRAY OF SIMPRIM, MEIGLE [2]

ROSEBANK, NEAR KELSO, *Sept.* 13, 1793

DEAR MURRAY,—I would have let fly an epistle at you
long ere this, had I not known I should have some

---

[1] John James Edmonstone of Newton. " The persons with whom I
chiefly lived at this period of my youth were William Clerk . . . James
Edmonstone of Newton ; George Abercromby ; Adam Fergusson . . .
John Irving . . . the Honourable Thomas Douglas, now Earl of Selkirk ;
David Boyle [later Lord Justice Clerk]—and two or three others, who
sometimes plunged deeply into politics and metaphysics, and not unfre-
quently ' daffed the world aside, and bid it pass.' "—*Autobiography*.

[2] The natural son of the fifth Lord Elibank, who in 1776 entailed on him
the estate of Simprim in Berwickshire. The estate was later disentailed
and sold in 1836. Murray acquired then Coupar Grange and other lands
in Perthshire. Robertson had been his tutor and in 1801 became minister
of Meigle in Perthshire—" a man of great worth, and an excellent scholar.
In his younger days he was fond of the theatre, and encouraged and
directed *Simprim, Grogg, Linton and Co.* in their histrionic diversions."—
LOCKHART. Murray will be found later an officer in the Perthshire Cavalry
or Dragoons. In 1808 Robertson was appointed Professor of Hebrew at
St. Andrews.

difficulty in hitting so active a traveller, who may in that respect be likened unto a bird of passage. Were you to follow the simile throughout, I might soon expect to see you winging your way to the southern climes, instead of remaining to wait the approach of winter in the colder regions of the north. Seriously, I have been in weekly hopes of hearing of your arrival in the Merse, and have been qualifying myself by constant excursions to be your Border *Cicerone*.

As the facetious Linton will no doubt make one of your party, I have got by heart for his amusement a reasonable number of Border ballads, most of them a little longer than Chevy Chase, which I intend to throw in at intervals, just by way of securing my share in the conversation. As for *you*, as I know your picturesque turn, I can be in this country at no loss how to cater for your entertainment, especially if you would think of moving before the fall of the leaf. I believe, with respect to the real *To Kalon*, few villages can surpass that near which I am now writing ; and as to your rivers, it is part of my creed that the Tweed and Teviot yield to none in the world, nor do I fear that even in your eyes, which have been feasted on classic ground, they will greatly sink in comparison with the Tiber or Po. Then for antiquities, it is true we have got no temples or heathenish fanes to show ; but if substantial old castles and ruined abbeys will serve in their stead, they are to be found in abundance. So much for Linton and you. As for Mr. Robertson, I don't know quite so well how to bribe him. We had indeed lately a party of strollers here, who might in some degree have entertained him,—*i.e.* in case he felt no compassion for the horrid and tragical murders which they nightly committed—but now, *Alas, Sir ! the players be gone.*

I am at present very uncertain as to my own motions, but I still hope to be northwards again before the commencement of the session, which (d—n it) is beginning to draw nigher than I could wish. I would esteem myself greatly favoured by a few lines informing me of your motions when they are settled ; since visiting you, should I go north, or attending you if you come this way, are my two grand plans of amusement

What think you of our politics now ? Had I been within reach of you, or any of the chosen, I suspect the taking of Valenciennes [1] would have been sustained as a reason for examining the contents of t'other bottle, which has too often suffered for slighter pretences. I have little doubt, however, that by the time we meet in glory (terrestrial glory, I mean) Dunkirk will be an equally good apology. Adieu, my good friend ;—remember me kindly to Mr. Robertson, to Linton, and to the Baronet. I understand both these last intend seeing you soon. I am very sincerely yours,

WALTER SCOTT

[*Lockhart*]

TO ROBERT SHORTREED [2]

To Robert Shortreed, Esq., Writer, Jedburgh

MY DEAR SIR,—I trouble you with the enclosed £1—1— for carrying on our joint operations at Hermitage Castle which I suppose our freind Dr. Elliot [3] will think of

---

[1] The city and fort fell to the Duke of Coburg on the 26th of July, but the further victories and the fall of Dunkirk which Scott anticipates were not to be. The allies were too busy dividing the skin of the bear ; " while France was preparing to arise with renewed vigour from her ashes, the Allies were courting their own doom."—*Cambridge Modern History*, vol. viii, 430.

[2] Robert Shortreed, later Sheriff of Roxburghshire, to whom Scott was introduced by his friend Charles Kerr of Abbotrule, was his companion in the seven years successive raids in quest of Border ballads. Unfortunately most of the early letters to Shortreed were accidentally destroyed. See a letter of Andrew Shortreed to Lockhart of 10th April 1837, etc. This letter from the Abbotsford copies refers to excavations at Hermitage Castle, from which Scott got a ring that had belonged to one of " The dark Knights of Liddesdale."—LOCKHART.

[3] Of Cleughhead. He was one of Scott's most devoted supporters in the quest of ballads and antiquities. From him Scott got the large horn that hung at Abbotsford. He was a doctor of medicine, not of divinity.

commencing about this time. I shall expect to hear from you if they prove successfull. Let the Cowt of Keelder [1] by no means be forgotten. I think it probable his grave may produce something. It will be proper to go as deep as the Till or we may lose our labour.

I expect to hear from the Dr. on the subject of our old Ballads, particularly Jemmy Tellferr which is a great favourite of mine. Tell the Dr. that I am tiring excessively for summer that I may visit Liddesdale again, and that I am saving the fees, to buy a *fringed Grey* that I may be independent of Mr. Lecks [2] charger, as I hope you will be of the Abbot's Palfrey—Apropos—I heard from him [3] the other day. He seems likely to get into a dispute with his brother—it would be happy for both parties if they would consent to arbitration. Best compliments to Mr. Rutherford & all Liddal water freinds when you see them, & do drop me a line when you can spare [time] from the weightier matters of the law to let me know you have received this. I am Dr Sir Ever yours sincerely,

WALTER SCOTT

EDINBURGH, 18 *Dec.*, 1793

[Abbotsford Copies]

[1] In his introduction to the ballad by John Leyden, called the *Cout of Keeldar*, Scott writes : " It is necessary to add, that the most redoubted adversary of Lord Soulis was the Chief of Keeldar, a Northumbrian district adjacent to Cumberland, who perished in a sudden encounter on the banks of the Hermitage. Being arrayed in armour of proof, he sustained no hurt in the combat ; but stumbling in retreating across the river, the hostile party held him down below water with their lances till he died ; and the eddy, in which he perished, is still called the Cout of Keeldar's Pool. His grave, of gigantic size, is pointed out on the banks of the Hermitage, at the western corner of a wall, surrounding the burial-ground of a ruined chapel." " If the country-people really designated him as *Cout* . . . they probably mean *Chief* . . .—

Muse I do,
A shepherd thus should blaize
The Coot of beauty. . . . WARNER'S *Albion*."

MS. letter of John Finlay to Sir W. S. 27th March 1803.

[2] A horsecouper in Jedburgh of whom many anecdotes were told.

[3] Charles Kerr ; his brother was afterwards General Thomas Kerr.

To PATRICK MURRAY

Wednesday 16*th* 7 *o'clock afternoon* [*April* 1794]

DEAR SIR,—Dr. Robertson being just about to inclose a letter to your honour I take the liberty to add a postscript. You will be glad to hear the *affair* of Saturday past over without any worse consequence to the Loyalists than that 5, including your friend & humble servant Coll. Grogg have been bound over to the peace, and obliged to give Bail for their good behaviour, which you may believe was easily found— The said Coll. had no less than three broken heads laid to his charge by as many of the Democrats.[1] Amidst my own military (I mean mock military) atchievements, let me not fail to congratulate you, & the Country, on the real character you have agreed to accept— Remember in case of real action I shall beg the honour of admission to your troop as a Volunteer. Believe me ever yours sincerely

WALTER SCOTT

[*Abbotsford Copies*]

To MISS CHRISTIAN RUTHERFORD [2] AT PITCULLEN, PERTH

EDINBURGH, 8*th June*, 1794

MA CHÈRE AMIE,—Nothing doubting that your curiosity will be upon the Tenters to hear the wonderfull events of the long-expected *fourth of June*, I take the pen to inform you that not one worth mentioning has taken place. Were I inclined to prolixity, I might, indeed, narrate at length

---

[1] See Lockhart's account of the row at the theatre with Irish medical students (*Life*, chap. vii). Kerr of Abbotrule refers to it in letters to Scott of 15th and 29th April 1794.

[2] Scott's aunt, the half-sister of his mother. In Lockhart this letter is wrongly dated 5th of June 1796. The original, in the possession of the Watson Collection, is dated as above. In Lockhart, too, the flag is to be hoisted on the Tron steeple. The town steeple would be St. Giles' steeple.

how near a Thousand gentlemen (myself among the number) offered their services to the Magistrates to act as *Constables* for the preservation of the peace—*how* their services were accepted—what fine speeches were made upon the occasion—*how* they were furnishd with pretty painted brown *battons*—*how* they were assembled in the Aisle of the New Church, and treated with Claret and sweetmeats—*how* Sir John Whiteford was chaced by the Mob, and *how* Tom, Sandy Wood, and I, rescued him, and dispersed his tormentors *à beaux coups de Battons*—*how* the Justice-Clerk's windows were broke by a few boys, and how a large body of constables and a press-gang of near two hundred men arrived, and were much disappointed at finding the coast entirely clear ; with many other matters of equal importance, but of which you must be contented to remain in ignorance till you return to your castle.

Seriously, everything, with the exception of the very trifling circumstances above mentiond, was perfectly quiet—much more so than during any King's birthday I can recollect : that very stillness, however, shews that something is brewing among our freinds the democrats, which they will take their own time of bringing forward. By the wise precautions of the Magts, or rather of the Provost, and the spirited conduct of the gentlemen, I hope their designs will be frustrated. Our association meets to-night, when we are to be divided into districts according to the place of our abode, places of Rendevous and captains named, so that, upon the hoisting of a flag on the town steeple, and ringing out all the large Bells, we can be on duty in less than five minutes. I am sorry to say that the complexion of the town seems to justify all precautions of this kind. I hope we shall all demean ourselves as *quiet* and *peaceable* Magistrates and intend, for the purpose of learning the duties of my new office, to con diligently the instructions delivered to the watch by our brother *Dogberry* of facetious Memory.

So much for information. By way of inquiry, pray let me know—that is, when you find a very idle hour—how you accomplishd the perillous passage of her majestie's ferry [1] without the assistance and escort of your preux-chevalier, and whether you will receive them on your return—how Miss R. and you are spending your time, whether stationary or otherwise—Above all, whether you have been at Indermay,[2] and all the &cs &cs which the question involves. Having made out a pretty long scratch, which, as Win Jenkins says, will take you some time to dessisfer,[3] I shall only inform you farther that I shall tire excessively till you return to your shop. I beg to be remembered to Miss Keir, and in particular to La belle Jeanne.[4] Best love to Miss Rutherford ; and believe me ever my dear Miss Chritty sincerely and affectionately your

W. S.

[*Watson Collection*]

TO CHARLES KERR

To Charles Kerr Esq Abbotrule by Jedburgh
   Care of Mr Shortreed Writer there

DEAR KERR,—I am extremely sorry to hear, which I only did the other day by chance, that your expedition to Keswick has been postponed on account of Mrs. Kerrs health—it gives me great concern to think it continues in so fluctuating a state. I do not know whether from the date of my intelligence this will find you still confined

[1] *i.e.* Queensferry.

[2] This should be " Inver-may," the home of Colonel John Hepburn Belsches, the half-brother of Miss Belsches' grandmother. Miss Chritty was evidently in the secret of this love-affair.

[3] So Scott here spells " decipher." He had probably in mind the following passage from one of Winifred Jenkins' letters in *Humphrey Clinker* : " Dear Mary Jones ! An please God when I return, I'll bring you a new cap, with a turkey-shell coom, and a pyehouse sermon, that was preached in the Tabernacle ; and I pray of all love, you will mind your vriting and your spilling ; for, craving your pardon, Molly, it made me swet to disseyffer your last scrabble, which was delivered by the hind at Bath."

[4] Joan Keir, afterwards Mrs. Aytoun.

to Abbotrule from this distressing cause. I shall direct
there at all events as I have no doubt my letter will find
you out. I have delayed writing for some time till I
should send you some account of your Commissions—
I have purchased for you Beatties Dissertations, Savages
Works, Derham on Physical Theology, and Masons
English Garden—which I shall either send or keep by
me as you please to direct in course of post— In addition
to the Roman Copper I have picked up two or three
silver coins at what I esteem a reasonable rate—I am in
treaty for a half Unicorn of James 3d and believe I can
get it for 18s. or 20s. It is a small gold coin rated by
Antiquarians as worth £2—2—. I intend it for you if you
so incline—I wish you could conveniently send me in
your next a note of the coins I have already sent you,
prices &c as my own is fallen aside and I should be sorry
to purchase duplicates for you. I have got you a *Canute*
among the silver coins.

No news here—except the disagreeable reports from
the Continent— The gentlemen here display a very
spirited intention of forming themselves into volunteer
corps—the only sure and effectual mode of self-protection,
as some of the late raised Regiments have displayed a
dangerous spirit of mutiny particularly Fullartons Legion.

You once sent me a very pretty little poem— Should
you meet with anything of the same kind that pleases
you, pray have the goodness to let me participate.
Apropos when you see Shortreed, if this finds you in his
neighbourhood, remind him to refresh Dr. Elliots
memory with regard to my Old Songs—I think you may
find some valuable curiosities of this kind in Cumberland
and need not add how much I shall be obliged to you, if
you can collect them. Believe me, with best Compliments to Mrs Kerr, ever sincerely yours

WALTER SCOTT

EDINBURGH 30 *June* 1794

[*Abbotsford Copies*]

I   C

To MISS C. RUTHERFORD, ASHESTIEL, BY SELKIRK

My dear Miss Chritty will perceive from the date of this Epistle that I have accomplishd my purpose of coming to town to be present at the trial of the Edinr. Traitors. I arrived here on Monday evening from Kelso & was present at Watts [1] trial on Wednesday which displayd to the public the most atrocious & deliberate plan of villany which has occurrd perhaps in the annals of G. Britain. I referr you for particulars to the papers & shall only add that the equivocations & perjury of the witnesses (most of them being accomplices in what they calld the *Great plan*) set the abilities of Mr. Anstruther, the kings council in the most striking point of view—The patience & temper with which he tried them on every side & screwd out of them the evidence they were so anxious to conceal, shewd much knowledge of human nature, & the art with which he arranged the information he receivd made the trial upon the whole the most interesting I ever was present at. Downies trial is just now going forwards over my head but as the evidence is quite the same formerly brought against Watt is not so interesting—You will easily believe that on Wednesday my curiosity was too much excited to retire at an early hour & indeed I sat in the court from 7 in the morning till two the next morning but as I had provided myself with some cold meat & a Bottle of Wine I contrived to support the fatigue pretty well. It strikes me upon the whole that the plan of these miscreants might from its very desperate & improbable nature have had no small

[1] Watt and Downie were tried for " organizing of a plot for a general rising in Edinburgh, to seize the Castle, the Bank, the persons of the Judges, and proclaim a Provisional Republican Government : all which was supposed to have been arranged in concert with the Hardies, Thelwalls, Holcrofts, and so forth, who were a few days later brought to trial in London for an alleged conspiracy to summon delegates to a National Convention, with a view to subvert the Government, and levy war upon the King." "The English prisoners were acquitted, but Downie and Watt were not so fortunate."— Lockhart.

chance of succeeding at least as far as concernd cutting off the soldiers & obtaining possession of the Banks besides shedding the Blood of the most distinguished Inhabitants —there I think the evil must have stoppd unless they had further support than has yet appeard. *Stook* was the prime mover of the whole & the person who supplied the money—& our theatrical disturbances are found to have formd one link of the scheme— So I have no doubt Messrs. Stooks Burk &c would have found out a new way of paying old debts—The *peuple* are perfectly quiescent upon this grand occasion & seem to interest themselves very little in the fate of their *soi disant freinds*. The Edr. Volunteers make a respectable & formidable appearance already—they are exercised four hours almost every day with all the rigour of military discipline—The Grenadier Company will consist entirely of men above six feet—So much for public news—as to home intelligence—know that my mother & Anne had projected a *jaunt* to Inverleithen—fate however had destined otherwise—The intended day of departure was usherd in by a most compleat deluge—to which & the consequent disappointment our proposed travellers did not submitt with that Christian meekness which might have beseemd—In short both within & without doors it was a *devil* of a day—The second was like unto it—The third day came a frost a killing frost [1] & in the shape of a letter from this fountain of health informd us no lodgings were to be had there, so whatever be its virtues or the grandeur attending a journey to its streams, we might as well have proposed to visit the River Jordan or the walls of Jericho—Not so our heroe John, he has been arrived here for some time (much the same as when he went away) & has formd the desperate resolution of riding out with me to Kelso to morrow morning. I have staid a day longer waiting

---

[1] *Henry VIII.* 3. 2. 355. This is the reading of the letter in Miss Lockhart's possession. Lockhart for some reason makes the words run " A post, a killing post," taking this apparently as an adaptation of the original. The only change that Scott has made is " came."

for the arrival of a pair of new boots & Buckskin &c's in
which the soldier is to be equipt. I ventured to hint the
convenience of a roll of diaculum plaister & a Box of the
most approved horseman's salve in which recommendation our Dr.[1] warmly joind. His impatience for the
journey has been somewhat coold by some inclination
yesterday displayd by his charger (a poney belonging to
Anne) to lay his warlike rider in the dust, a purpose he
had nearly effected—he next mounted Queen Mab who
treated him with little more complaisance & in carters
phrase, would neither *hap* nor *wynd* till she got rid of
him—Seriously however if Jack has not returnd coverd
with laurels, a crop which the *Rock* no longer produces,
he has brought back all his own goodnature & a manner
considerably improved, so that he is at times very
agreeable company—best love to Miss R.—Jean Anne
(I hope they are improved at the Battledore) & the Boys
—not forgetting my friend Acky tho least not last in my
remembrance. Best Comps. to the coll : I shall remember with pleasure Ashestiel hospitality & not without
a desire to put [it] to the proof next year. Adieu ma
chere Amie—when you write direct to Rosebank & I shall
be a good boy & write you another sheet of nonsense
soon—All friends here well—Ever yours affectionately

WALTER SCOTT

ADVOCATE'S LIBRARY 5 *Sept.* 1794

[*Miss Mary Lockhart*]

To MISS C. RUTHERFORD

[*October or November* 1794]

MY DEAR MISS CHRITTY may well be surprised at my
negligence in not acknowledging an epistle with which I
was favour'd some weeks ago, & the truth is that I have
little apology for my behaviour & must be content to

[1] Dr. Rutherford, Mrs. Scott's brother.

throw myself upon her clemency for an excuse. However as far as it can be admitted as a palliation be it known to you that since that time I have been in a constant state of restlessness during which I have hunted and pranced thro a good part of Perthshire & only returnd to town in the beginning of this week. I spent a few days very pleasantly at Mr. Stirling of Keir's, a family with which perhaps you may be acquainted, & where I accidentally met two freinds of yours who spent a night there—Mr. & Mrs. Belsches of Invermay.[1] When they understood who I was they enquired particularly after Miss Rutherford & you—I received a very polite Invitation to Invermay which want of time prevented my accepting of—they seem very pleasant folks—

Previous to my Ramble I stayd a single day in Town to witness the exit of the ci-devant Jacobin Mr. Watt. It was a very solemn scene, but the pusillanimity of the unfortunate victim was astonishing considering the boldness of his nefarious plans. It is matter of general regret that his Associate Downie should have received a reprieve which I understand is now prolonged for a second month—I suppose to wait the issue of the London Trials.

Our volunteers are now compleatly embodied & notwithstanding the heaviness of their dress have a martial & striking appearance—their accuracy in firing & manoevering excites the surprise of military Gentlemen who are the best judges of their merit in that way. Tom is very proud of the Grenadier company to which he belongs which has indisputably carried off the palm upon all publick occasions—

And now give me leave to ask you whether the approaching *Winter* does not remind you of your snug parlour in

---

[1] The Belsches of Invermay were the junior branch of the family of which the senior branch were the Belsches of Tofts, whose residence was at Fettercairn, Kincardineshire. It was to the Kincardineshire branch that Scott's lady belonged, but her grandmother was of Invermay.

Georges Street—Do you not feel a little uncomfortable
when you see

―― how bleak & bare
He wanders oer the heights of *Yair*

Amidst all this regard for your accomodation Dont
suppose I am devoid of a little self Interest when I press
your speedy return to Auld Reekie for I am really tiring
excessively to see the said parlour again inhabited :
Besides that I want the assistance of your eloquence to
convince my honourd father that nature did not mean
me either for a vagabond or *travelling Merchant* when she
honourd me with the wandering propensity lately so
conspicuously displayd.—I saw Dr. yesterday who is
well. I did not chuse to intrude upon the little lady this
being Sermon week. for the same reason we are looking
very religious & very sour at home. However it is with
some folks selon les regles that in proportion as they are
pure themselves they are entitled to render uncomfortable
those whom they consider as less perfect. Best love to
Miss R— cousins & friends in general & believe me ever
most sincerely yours   WALTER SCOTT

[*Miss Mary Lockhart*]

[*Postmarked May* 9] (*In another hand* 1795 Walter Scott)

To CHARLES KERR [1]

DEAR CHARLES,—I wrote you last week—a derangement
of the carriers days of arrival and departure owing to our
holy week again prevents you receiving the catalogue.
I hope however the Books from Manners came safe. I
have been introduced lately to a man whose acquaintance

[1] The laird of Abbotrule on the death of his father had returned from his
exile and claimed his inheritance. There are numerous letters from him
to Scott, and some from Scott's father to Walter about the trouble he has
caused by his various changes of plan. He entered the army, and later
letters from Dublin deal with his duels and adventures. His later letters
deal much with the collecting of coins and he refers to Scott's "reliable
and very compendious treatise on the Scots coinage".

has given me a great deal of pleasure and whose character I think will entertain you. He is a Dr. Jamieson [1] from Forfar, a man of Letters an author and a poet, an admirer of antiquities and a remarkably fortunate collector of coins of which he has a scarce and valuable selection. And withal this medallist and antiquarian is an *Antiburgher Seceding Clergyman* and does all these things not to mention the trifling expense attending the maintenance of a wife and only twelve children upon a princely salary of £60 a year, as well paid as such stipends generally are. I must not omit to add that he is a liberal well behaved man, which considering his situation really surprises me as much as his rigid economy. He has been of late obliged to part with several of his coins in order to purchase Books to enable him to carry on a work upon the Scottish language on which he is at present engaged. I have half concluded a bargain with him about a parcell at present in my possession and which I think are à bon marché. They are a few Scotch and some of the most beautifull and scarce Roman and Grecian Denarii which he had picked up in London. Now as I have compleatly given up the Roman line and as you have some which you might wish to increase I shall be happy if you chuse to join me in the concern. I give some Books and coins which I think more than worth the Scottish coins which are all that I care for and the Doctor asks £3—3 for Book [2]; this brings the Denarii to about 4/6 a piece which is very cheap as they are all worth that and five or six particularly a coin of Julius Caesar with the Elephant,

[1] The author of the *Etymological Dictionary of the Scottish Language*, 1808. After studying in Glasgow he became minister of an Anti-Burgher Church first at Forfar and then in Edinburgh. Princeton University made him a D.D. for his reply to Priestley's *History of Early Opinions*. Scott's friendship for the worthy man induced him to let the Ballantynes publish the same author's *An historical account of the ancient Culdees of Iona, &c.* (1811), which was not a paying investment, and he interested himself later in Jamieson's edition of the *Bruce* and *Wallace*, 1820.

[2] Word difficult to decipher. The sentence suggests something such as " for the lot."

and one of the plated coins reckoned so curious, and the Greek Pan, sell usually at from 10/6 to a guinea according to preservation. If therefore you chuse to be the purchaser you will take the trouble of remitting the cash in course of post as the long vacation has run me a little Bare. If not I shall take the risque upon myself as I have an opportunity of sending to London such coins as I do not chuse to keep. This subject like most others relating to the study has I perceive consumed my paper. So I have only to beg my best compliments to Mrs. Kerr and assure you that I remain yours sincerely

W. S.

[*Mrs. Eveline Kerr*]

To WILLIAM CLERK [1]

23d of August, 1795

IT gave me the highest satisfaction to find, by the receipt of your letter of the 14th current, that you have formed precisely the same opinion with me, both with regard to the interpretation of —— ——'s letter as highly flattering and favourable, and to the mode of conduct I ought to pursue—for, after all, what she has pointed out is the most prudent line of conduct for us both, at least till better days, which, I think myself now entitled to suppose, she, as well as I myself, will look forward to with pleasure. If you were surprised at reading the important billet, you may guess how agreeably I was so at receiving it ; for I had, to anticipate disappointment, struggled to suppress every rising gleam of hope ; and it would be very difficult to describe the mixed feelings her

---

[1] This letter is given by Lockhart as " to a friend." William Clerk's covering letter to Mrs. Lockhart shows that it was to him. See Introduction. The person referred to is Miss Belsches. Of the other friends referred to Lockhart says " *Crab* was the nickname of a friend [John Irving] who had accompanied [Adam] Fergusson [Linton] this summer on an Irish tour. Dr. Black, celebrated for his discoveries in chemistry, was Adam Fergusson's uncle ; and had, it seems, given the young travellers a strong admonition touching the dangers of Irish hospitality."

letter occasioned, which, *entre nous*, terminated in a very hearty fit of crying. I read over her epistle about ten times a-day, and always with new admiration of her generosity and candour—and as often take shame to myself for the mean suspicions which, after knowing her so long, I could listen to, while endeavouring to guess how she would conduct herself. To tell you the truth, I cannot but confess that my *amour propre*, which one would expect should have been exalted, has suffered not a little upon this occasion, through a sense of my own *unworthiness*, pretty similar to that which afflicted Linton upon sitting down at Keir's table. I ought perhaps to tell you, what indeed you will perceive from her letter, that I was always attentive, while consulting with you upon the subject of my declaration, rather to under than over-rate the extent of our intimacy. By the way, I must not omit mentioning the respect in which I hold your knowledge of the fair sex, and your capacity of advising in these matters, since it certainly is to your encouragement that I owe the present situation of my affairs. I wish to God, that, since you have acted as so useful an auxiliary during my attack, which has succeeded in bringing the enemy to terms, you would next sit down before some fortress yourself, and were it as impregnable as the rock of Gibraltar, I should, notwithstanding, have the highest expectations of your final success. Not a line from poor Jack—What can he be doing? Moping, I suppose, about some watering-place, and deluging his guts with specifics of every kind—or lowering and snorting in one corner of a post-chaise, with Kennedy, as upright and cold as a poker, stuck into the other. As for Linton, and Crab, I anticipate with pleasure their marvellous adventures, in the course of which Dr. Black's *self-denying ordinance* will run a shrewd chance of being neglected. They will be a source of fun for the winter evening conversations. Methinks I see the pair upon the mountains of Tipperary—John with a beard of three inches, united and blended with his shaggy black locks, an ell-wand-looking cane with a gilt head in his hand, and a bundle in a handkerchief over his shoulder, exciting the cupidity of every Irish raparee who passes him, by his resemblance to a Jew pedlar who has sent forward his pack—Linton, tired of trailing his long legs, exalted in state upon an Irish garron, without stirrups, and a halter on its head, tempting every one to ask—

"Who is that upon the pony,
So long, so lean, so raw, so bony?"

—calculating, as he moves along, the expenses of the salt horse—and grinning a ghastly smile, when the hollow voice of his fellow-traveller observes—" God ! Adam, if ye gang on at this rate, the eight shillings and sevenpence halfpenny will never carry us forward to my uncle's at Lisburn." Enough of a thorough Irish expedition.

We have a great marriage towards here—Scott of Harden, and a daughter of Count Bruhl, the famous chess-player, a lady of sixteen quarters, half-sister to the Wyndhams. I wish they may come down soon, as we shall have fine racketing, of which I will, probably, get my share. I think of being in town sometime next month, but whether for good and all, or only for a visit, I am not certain. O for November ! Our meeting will be a little embarrassing one. How will she look, &c. &c. &c., are the important subjects of my present conjectures— how different from what they were three weeks ago ! I give you leave to laugh when I tell you seriously, I had begun to " dwindle, peak, and pine," upon the subject— but now, after the charge I have received, it were a shame to resemble Pharaoh's lean kine. If good living and plenty of exercise can avert that calamity, I am in little danger of disobedience, and so, to conclude classically,

Dicite Io pæan, et Io bis dicite pæan ! [1]

Jubeo te bene valere,

GUALTERUS SCOTT

[Lockhart]

[1] Ovid, Ars Amatoria, II. 1

To GEORGE CHALMERS [1]

To George Chalmers Esq.
Office for Trade, Whitehall, London

[*17th February*, 1796]

SIR,—I should sooner have done myself the pleasure of replying to your polite favour if I had not been prevented by the interference of particular business—I am much concernd to find that the trifles you wish to see are scatterd among different miscellaneous collections some of which contain articles of a private nature—I send to the care of Mr. Anderson two MS. Books—the first consists chiefly of poems publishd and unpublishd collected at an early period of Life but containing I believe several Border songs—some of which have since appeard in a provincial publication but in a less perfect state. The few notes accompanying them are thrown together without any method & must in many instances be very imperfect—I cannot allow a consideration of their *undress* which can affect my own literary character & powers of composition only, to interfere with the gratification of your Request, but they are for your own eye only—I send another collection consisting chiefly of songs & Ballads in the Scottish dialect of indifferent merit & except the first unfortunately not historical.

These Ballads with a few others which I have pickd up from tradition & which lie scatterd thro' other MS of

---

[1] " Among other literary persons at a distance, I may mention George Chalmers, the celebrated antiquary, with whom he had been in correspondence from the beginning of this year, supplying him with Border ballads for the illustration of his researches into Scotch history. This gentleman had been made acquainted with Scott's large collections . . . by a common friend, Dr. Somerville, minister of Jedburgh, author of the *History of Queen Anne* ; and the numerous MS. copies communicated to him in consequence were recalled in the course of 1799, when the plan of the ' Minstrelsy ' began to take shape."—LOCKHART. George Chalmers (1742-1825) is best known now by his *Caledonia*, issued at intervals between 1807 and 1824. The Anderson referred to is, as Chalmers' letter of 10th February shows, " Wm. Anderson, Writer in the Advocates' Close." The ballads were recalled by June 1796, as a letter of Chalmers shows.

a more private nature I have sometimes thought of forming into a small collection, adding to them such of acknowledged merit as have already seen the light but I am discouraged by the multitude of similar publications —if therefore you can deduce from them any conclusions which can in the least illustrate your valuable labours, it will be only requiting in a very small degree the pleasure & instruction I have so often reapd from the perusal of your former publications—

If you wish any further information or communication I shall be happy to contribute whatever lies in my power— I have to regret that I have not committed to writing a number of little traditionary anecdotes which I have carelessly trusted to the fallible registry [or " register," *the paper is torn and repaired here*] of my memory— You will be able to judge from the jottings sent of what nature my researches have been & whether they can be of any service to you—in which case I shall get copies made of some articles of a similar nature for your perusal.

Permit me to conclude by congratulating my native country upon the hands into which the elucidation of her history has fallen & by assuring you of the sincere regard & respect with which I am Sir Your most Obedient Servant

WALTER SCOTT

[*Mrs. Williams*]

To WILLIAM ERSKINE

To William Erskine Esq Advocate London [1] Edinburgh.

WHEN I reflect how long I have been neglecting my promise to thee, when I consider, to let thee into a secret, that its present fullfillment is merely owing to the first

[1] The last word has been written in another hand, the London having been struck out. The letter had gone to London and been readdressed to Edinburgh. This is the letter, first printed by Lord Sands, and misdated September for April. See the Introduction.

rainy day which we have have had for these four weeks,
my very midriff would quiver with remorse were it not
for the quieting consideration that thou art now so
deeply engaged in the pleasures of thy beloved City that
it must dwell little in thy desires to learn the wanderings
of such a forlorn pilgrim as myself—My motions however
being at least as important to myself as those of P. P.[1]
the Parish Clerk I shall [take] the liberty of supposing
them equally so to thee (a strong supposition in most
cases, unless among Mountain[2] Boys) & thus I begin
my journal—Monday was three weeks I left the ancient
city of Edinr.—my equipage two ponies & Boy—or
if you will two palfreys & a foot page.—Beside me
pranced the Doughty Baron of Newton, John James
Edmonstoune, on a most splendid Bucephalus—Next
day view the same party drawn up with the addition
of Lieut. Drummond of the Perthsh: cavalry & the Laird
of Symprim upon the field of Bannockburn—hear the
Laird descant upon the position of the armies, Bruce
Douglas & Randolph familiar in his mouth as household
words, wheeling and caracolling as he became warmd
with his subject—Next see us at John Ramsay's—then
at Cambusmoir—& lastly, but how shall pen describe
the scenery or spell the names, view (bis) E— & me at the
Troshachs, a chain of most beautifull & romantic lakes
running North west from Callander into the highlands
Monday was a fortnight I set out on my solitary journey
up Loch Lubinich & round by Loch Earnhead to Crief
great part of which journey I performd on foot—I was
perfectly enchanted with your favourite (damn the

[1] *Memoirs of P. P. Clerk of this Parish.* Pope's skit upon Bishop Gilbert
Burnet's *History of My Own Times.*

[2] " The place [In the Outer House of the Court of Session] where these
idlers [young unemployed advocates] mostly congregated was called . . .
by a name which sufficiently marks the date, it was *The Mountain* . . . here
hour after hour passed away, week after week, month after month, and year
after year, in the interchange of light-hearted merriment among the circle
of young men, more than one of whom in after times, attained the highest
honours of the profession."—LOCKHART.

name I shall never hit it) Arbruchle,[1] which is compleatly *selon mon gout*—At Comrie I saw a very extensive camp & a fine waterfall above the house—At Perth I saw what gave me more pleasure than all the camps & cascades in my tour, for I saw Miss Erskine [2] tho only for half an hour—She has compleatly recoverd [from] her indisposition & is looking charmingly—Like a Cloud upon a whirlwind did I pass thro the fat Carse of Gowrie, thro Dundee, thro Arbroath, thro Montrose—At Benholm I was most cordially received by Geo: Robertson Scott who is a develish good fellow, aye and a moderate thinking rational man too, tho' the spleen of party has dubbd him a Democrat—For a thousand reasons I referrd any stay in that neighbourhood till my return Southwards so I tore myself from that quarter of the country & sad & slowly trotted on to Aberdeen with many an anxious thought upon the shadows clouds and darkness that involve my future prospects of happiness— I must not omit to tell you that Benholm consists of an elegant modern house built close to an ancient & venerable Tower the habitation of the old proprietors, which is preservd in compleat repair as it looks down a steep woody Glen to the sea commands a delightfull prospect— you will guess I was often to be found upon the Battlements straining my eyes towards the Distant Grampians— In Aberdeen I have been most hospitably received by several freinds of my father—I returnd yesterday from Freefield the seat of Mr. Leith [3] 30 miles to the Northwest

[1] Arbruikle, Arbuchle are successively struck out.

[2] Miss Erskine was at Perth when, in the course of this summer, she became engaged to Archibald Campbell of Clathick, after 1804 Campbell-Colquhoun, later Lord Advocate.

[3] Mr. G. M. Fraser, of the Public Library, Aberdeen, writes me : " Freefield is a property—once a Barony—with mansion house, in the parish of Rayne, about four miles north-east of Insch, and about 30 miles from Aberdeen. The property has been in the hands of the Leiths of Freefield (and Glenkindie), for centuries. The Leith of Freefield that Scott visited in 1796, must have been Alexander Leith of Freefield (and Glenkindie), who died 1828—succeeded by his son the well-known General Sir Alexander

who maintains very much the ancient hospitable character of an old Scottish Gentleman—he is married to a relation of mine—Of Traditions &c &c I have collected enough to set your Sister & you asleep after supper (unless when startled by the rumbling of an Earse name) for 20 nights successively—I say nothing of my future motions further than that I leave this tomorrow & shall be in Edinr. in about 8 days when I suppose I may almost expect to find you so that I shall have an answer in person to this long scrawl which I send merely to acquit me of my promise —I shall see your Sister on my return if she is still at Perth —I am you may believe anxious enough on one score & another & may well adopt the burden of an old song— 'If it were na my heart's light, I wad die "—Of the other Montagnards [1] I can say little—Clerk, Thomson, &c &c all in the country Cran—in town busy with Fountainhall & Mack with Goose upon Kant—In the mean time Monroe, as I hear, is annoying Miss Jane Dalrymple— from what I can see that damnd Anatomist has a mind to bring upon his head a rock from the mountain—I hope you will not omitt to pick up a few German books—& remember Agnes Bernauerinn   Well here's a long letter —quantity for quality—hay ! Billy ! hay !—Take of thyself in that Devil's drawing room into which thou hast gotten—As poor Tom says, Keep thy fingers from plackets & thy pen from Lenders Books & defy the foul fiend—But I know thee & the naughtiness of thy heart—

Leith, K.C.B. The present owner of Freefield is Alexander Leigh Henry Leith, Lord Burgh, who succeeded in 1926."

[1] See note, p. 45. Those in question are William Clerk of Penicuik ; Thos. Thomson, later Deputy Clerk Register ; George Cranston (later Lord Corehouse), who is busy with the decisions of Lord Fountainhall ; John Macfarlane of Kirkton, the only Kantist of the German class to which Scott had belonged . . . Jean Dalrymple is the daughter of Lord Hailes, and the Monroe who is paying her attentions is G. Alexander, the *third* Professor of Anatomy in Edinburgh University of that name. All this information Scott has derived from a letter sent to him at Montrose by Miss Cranston and forwarded to Aberdeen. It is now in the Walpole Collection, and bears the postmark, 18th April. Agnes Bernauerin is a tragedy by Graf Törring.

& how thou art proud in flesh & high in mind—As for
the trotting over four Inch Bridges that seems to be my
share of poor Toms exploits—till I break my neck over
one of them, believe me ever

　　　　　　　　　　　　　　Affectionately yours
　　　　　　　　　　　　　　　　WALTER SCOTT

ABERDEEN 24 *Septr.* [*April*] 1796
　　　　　　[*Written on Back*]
William Erskine Esq. Advocate Edinburgh. N.B.

　　　[*Written on other side*]
　　" tore by the seal of the cover."
[*Sands*]

　　　　　　　　　　　　　　[6*th May*, 1796]
TO THE REV. MR. WALKER, DUNNOTTAR MANSE [1]

MY DEAR SIR,—I take my first moment of disengage-
ment to let you know the result of my enquiries at Lady
Fenella's Castle, which is in my opinion at least decidedly
in favour of Tytlers opinion.　I was detaind at Fettercairn house by the hospitality of Sir John and Lady Jane
two or three days longer than I expected, from which you
will easily guess Miss Belsches was recoverd and able to

---

[1] This letter is to the minister of Dunnottar whom Scott had visited on his
way back from Aberdeen in April-May.　He had gone thence to Fettercairn,
the home of Miss Belsches, and there made excavations while the minister was
at his instigation doing the same at Dunnottar.　" Glencairn Castle, noted
as the residence of Fenella, wife and murderer of Kenneth II, in 994, was
originally an ancient fort erected at a very early period.　Like some other
strongholds of the same character . . . it consisted of a central building with
vitrified walls and an outer surrounding rampart or erection of dry stone."—
CAMERON, *History of Fettercairn*, in which work the letter is printed with
some errors.　It is here taken from the original in the possession of Miss
H. M. Leslie Paterson, Birkwood, Banchory, Kincardineshire.　Walker did
not report on his work at Dunnottar till 5th November 1796, and then only
to the effect that the proprietor had desired that the well should not be
further explored.　He has not been more successful in the quest for ballads.
" McHardy the highland schoolmaster has never yet got his collection but
promises fairly and my servant maid has not yet completed her search for
the Baron of Brackley, but has got notice where he is concealed."　A much

see company—Thus I had plenty of time on my hands
—which I employd in causing two labourers begin at
the ring or vallum immediately without the main rampart
and cut down till they came decisively to the original
soil—This outer embankment I found to consist of a
mound of stones of no very considerable size, none of
which as far as I could perceive had suffered from fire,
tho' I have upon this as well as several other occasions
to regret my want of chemical and mineralogical knowledge sufficient to enable me to decide with certainty—
We then continued opening our trench still digging
down to the soil, till we came to the very foundation of
the main and innermost Bulwark—You may guess my
satisfaction when on laying this bare I found the most
unequivocal marks of human industry—It consists of
oblong flat stones from 4 to 6 feet long, piled above each
other to the height of about 4 feet and breadth of 3 with
symmetry more exact than could have been expected—
This foundation formd a kind of casing within which
were piled apparently by the hand large bullet stones
which I presume were prevented from spreading
inwards by a similar pile of large flat stones corresponding
to that on the out side and thus a firm foundation had

later undated letter refers to this episode of the digging and may be
printed here :

"MY DEAR SIR GEORGE,—I received two or three days since your
interesting vindication of your opinion respecting the vitrified forts against
Dr Macculloch. I have not seen as yet the Doctors letters so that I am not
very competent to judge nor perhaps should I be so were I to investigate
the matter as deeply as I could having no science to aid me.

But I think our friend & associate cuts too short in disposing so very
absolutely both of Lord Woodhouselees opinion and of yours for I think
your pamphlet shows a strong probability that some of these structures
at least had been used as beacon stations. I cannot however think that all
of these were so because the only one which I ever examined particularly
with *spade & shovel* was in a low situation on the verge of a moss near
Fettercairn a place totally unfit for a signal light. Tradition terms this the
Castle of Fenella where Kenneth was murderd by that Lady & adds that
his castle was burnd in revenge of the Kings death by the royal followers.
If this could be trusted it would go far to shew that in one instance at least
Woodhouselees explanation had been just and that the vitrified appearance
arises from accidental combustion.

I　　　　　　　　D

been obtaind for the mound to be raised above which
as far as it now remains consists of Bullets etc diminishing gradually in size to the very top—Upon all this mass
the effect of fire was very visible and at the bottom I
found quantities of charcoal, but these effects were much
less remarkable below and appeard more and more
strong upon the higher stones till you came to the top
where the mass was completely vitrified—Thus the whole
was probably constructed as follows First two walls of
large flat stones were erected paralell to each other at a
distance corresponding to the height of rampart of
which this was to be the base—that rampart I take to
have been composed of branches of trees and stones the
latter gradually diminishing in size from that of the large
round bullets which occupied the interval between the
two casing walls of the foundation to a size which could
be more conveniently raised to the height of the top of
the mound—Supposing such a fabric to be surrounded
by 3 or 4 external ramparts of loose stones it wd compose
such a fortification as I take the fort of Balbegno to have
been when entire—Again supposing it to have been
stormd and set on fire, it is obvious that the lower part
being composed of huge stones would suffer little from
the heat, that the middle would suffer more, and that
the stones composing the uppermost part of the mass,
would if their substance admitted it be actually vitrified
both from their size and situation, the fire always operating
upwards—for the same reason what charcoal found its
way to the bottom of the mass would not be totally
consumed—and thus I account for the appearances I
have detaild above. My works are already almost
filld up with rubbish and some of the foundation stones
carried off, but I am convinced you will find upon
examination that the appearances are uniform—I am
dying to hear about the Well at Dunottar, &c., &c.,
&c. I am likewise anxious about my old Ballads and
I hope you will add to the many favours I have

already to acknowledge that of writing me very soon. My address is Georges Square, Edinr—Compliments to Messrs. Logie and Wood—I hope they do not faint in the good work—if so, I refer them to you for strength and consolation—I have visited a beautiful ruin called Eagle [1] Castle and was delighted—I have seen Cater Thun, and was astonishd—I hope this will find your whole famillé from Nelly to Macgriegar Inclusive in good health—Meantime We do most strictly charge you and command to keep an account of the Well expenditure and transmitt it to us for a settlement of accots and so we bid you heartily farewell.

Given from our Inn at Kinross the sixth day of May, jaivii and ninety-six years.

WALTER SCOTT

[Miss Paterson, Banchory]

TO WILLIAM ERSKINE [2]

To William Erskine,
47 Princes Street, Edinburgh

ROSEBANK, April [September] 9th, 1796

YOUR very interesting epistle reached me but to-day, as in the ordinary routine we send for our letters only three times a week; could I have anticipated the nature of the news it contained, I would not only have ransacked the post-house, but I verily believe I would have robbd the mail rather than its delivery should have been postponed one instant. Let me however take some credit

---

[1] i.e. "Edzell; thirteenth century Edale, popularly Aigle or Eagle." GROOM, Ordinary Gazetteer of Scotland. The dating at the end of the letter is strictly jmvii (1700), but Scott has reproduced the fashion it often takes the appearance of in old MSS.

[2] For the interest and importance of this letter, printed here for the first time except in a privately printed brochure, see the Introduction. Who the " unhallowed ourang-outang " was that dared to lift his eyes to Mary Anne Erskine I cannot say. " Dot-and-carry-one " is doubtless William Forbes or his father. " F——n " is " Fettercairn," the home of the Belsches.

for my observation, when I inform you that the important arrangement with which you acquaint me did not strike me with all the *surprise* you may perhaps have expected —in requital the *pleasure* which it gives me is inexpressible and it adds to it not a little that tho No. 47 must lose its amiable mistress she will still remain one of ourselves and if I know her aright will be as much the delight of her freinds as Mrs. C— as she has been as Miss E—. What intercourse I have had with Clathick tho not great has invariably been such as to entitle him to a very high place in my esteem, and I think I have told you how much I was obliged to him for the very freindly concern he took for my brother in the business of Morthland— But had I no personal knowledge of Mr. Campbell whatever, the excellence of his taste of itself would be sufficient to raise him high in my opinion and to induce me to believe he possesses a mind formed to make *our* beloved freind and sister happy—The man who can discern the value of a diamond independent of costly or fashionable *setting*, will surely be capable of prizing its inestimable worth when he has made it his own—Tell your sister that my best and *warmest* wishes for her welfare and happiness ever will, ever must attend her, and that there are not upon this earth two of her sex besides in whose happiness I feel myself equally interested and I rejoice to see in the alliance she is about to form everything which is likely to promote it— I could say very, *very* much upon this subject but I know she will understand me as well from these few words as if I had written volumes.[1] For you, my good freind, I certainly do feel a great deal, as I well know the blank in your domestic felicity which this felonious Sheriff is about to occasion, but I also well know the consolation you will find in the *reflected Happiness* of one so deservedly dear to you—You will now also have an opportunity of looking seriously around you for

[1] " Upon the subject " is struck through in the original.

an agreeable companion for life, wh: I am convinced you never would have done while Mary Anne remaind to you—indeed from possessing her society you have already become so fastidious that it will require no small time of Solitude to teach you to be contented with any thing less than her equal and where my dear Willy is she to be found ?—Your Sister and I sat in *dark* divan, I think the last evening but one, that I was with you, on this very subject—I little thought then that the period was so very near when you was to be doomd to find that it is evil for Man to be alone—Enough of this for the present—I shall expect to hear from you were it but two lines to inform me *when* I am to be at liberty to adopt my future toast in the round of married ladies " Mrs. Campbell Clathick "—You do me justice in believing my impatience on the subject will be truly energetick. I must have a bottle extraordinary somewhere upon the score, and I am just thinking how in this howling wilderness I shall find any person worthy of sharing it—Let me hear as soon as settled all your motions and arrangements—What a cursed pity it is that none of them can possibly lye in this direction— I could be excessively foolish just now, as I have been whistling, hallooing and I verily believe almost crying this whole morning to the utter astonishment of my Uncle and Cousin—Tell Mary Anne how inconceivably mortified I shall be if I do not retain the same interest in her freindship as formerly—that I expect she will deviate from the fashion so far as to give *petits soupers* as well as *routes*—that tho she must form many acquaintances in the valley, yet she is not to forget the mountain— Do you know that amidst all my other motives for exaltation I entertain a kind of malicious satisfaction at the mortification of a certain unhallowd Ourang-Outang who " presumed to lift his surly eye " towards our gentle freind—Besides all this it will be no small satisfaction to me in the midst of my own uncertainties and dilemmas to think upon the probable happiness of a freind who is dear to me—For " *Dot & carry one* " is certainly gone to F——n—But the pleasant tidings you have sent must be as a rope and six horses to drag me out of this slough of Despond—Let it be the same to you whenever you think on the deprivation you are about to suffer—Let me end with what according to the Compleat Letterwriter ought to have begun my letter—My best Compliments of Congratulation to our freind—to Mr. Campbell also whenever you tell him I am acquainted with his approaching happiness—When you send the news to Thompson you will certainly drive the breath out of him altogether with joy—Once more God bless all and each of you— Adieu   WALTER SCOTT

[*Campbell-Colquhoun*]

To WILLIAM ERSKINE [1]

William Erskine Esq Advocate Crieff
To be left at the Post Office till calld for.

THY much esteemd favour of 18th Inst. dear Willy, was this day followd up by a letter from Miller on the important subject of the Ballads—In point of Time the publishers are certainly entitled to dictate and I do not know whether I may not admit their authority even as

[1] This letter, in the possession of Sir Alfred Law, is written after the marriage of Mary Erskine on the 19th of September, and shows Scott still uncertain of his own fate with Miss Belsches. The first paragraph refers to the forthcoming volume containing his translation of *Lenore* and *Der wilde Jäger*, for which Erskine had been arranging with Manners and Miller. Scott already adopts the independent attitude he was always to maintain to publishers.

The Roger Aytoun mentioned was the father, Joan Keir the mother, of William Edmonstoun Aytoun. Joan Keir " was the youngest daughter of James Francis Edward Keir of Kinmonth and West Rhynd, in Perthshire, and of Margaret Orme of Balvaird, in Fifeshire. She was, in many respects, a remarkable person. When young, she was very handsome, and she retained all the traces of beauty in old age. To marked originality of character she added superior culture. Early left an orphan, her youth was spent with her grand-uncle, Mr. Alexander Keith of Ravelstone, who had adopted

to the title page but that I take to be the *ne plus ultra*
of a Bookseller's dominion. As to expressing in a preface
feelings which I do not feel apprehensions which I do not
apprehend and motives by which I am no whit moved,
I hold it (so to speak) to be all *Blarney* and therefore
shall certainly not indulge Mr. Mundell by the insertion
of any of these common place apologies for publication
which are in fact no apologies at all—Either the things
are worthy the attention of the public or they are not,
in the one case an apology would be superfluous in the
other impertinent—*Sat est*—

I suppose of course . . . ¹ the new married folks, now no
longer bride and bridegroom are not distant from you—
Where do you hang out? Are you to racket it hard in
giving and receiving visits &c. All this I long to know.
I did not fail to drink on Monday an additional Bumper
to the happiness of a pair in whom I am so warmly
interested, and ranged the whole country for an Edinr.
paper that I might have the pleasure of seeing their union
announced in due form—The news gave great pleasure
to two of your neighbours whom I unexpectedly saw in
the City of Kelso on their return from visiting the Lakes
of Westmoreland—I mean the gentle Shepherds Patie

her. . . . Mrs. Keith was the grand-aunt of Walter Scott, who was a
constant visitor at Ravelstone. His sister, Anne Scott, was Miss Keir's
earliest and most intimate friend, and she saw much of Scott himself at
Ravelstone when a boy. Some of the anecdotes of his youthful days, which
are recorded in Lockhart's life of the poet, were supplied by Mrs. Aytoun ;
but so sensitive was she about appearing in any public way, that she would
not allow her name to be attached to them. She was herself a staunch
Jacobite. . . .It was from her that her son took his love of the White Rose.
From her, too, he imbibed . . . his deep devotion to the ballad poetry of
Scotland."—SIR THEODORE MARTIN, *Memoir of William Edmonstoun Aytoun.*
She was present at the meeting between Burns and Scott.

It has been suggested to me that Joan Keir had mentioned, possibly to
Anne Scott, a rumour that Miss Belsches was engaged to William Forbes,
or that she suspected something was on foot, as his father and he were, or
had been, paying a visit to Fettercairn.

¹ Here a pen has been drawn through three words. The first seems to
begin with a character somewhat similar to the mystery hieroglyphic in
the next paragraph. The third word is " friend."

and Roger Ayto[u]n—The day being diabolical I had
it not in my power to shew them the beauties of this place
and I could not even prevail on them to visit Rosebank.

To return to a subject which is never long absent from
my mind I am not sure but what your judgement may be
more correct than mine in what regards M—and therefore your sailing orders are—If the subject is casually
introduced to treat it lightly. No body can be surprised
that such a Don Quixote as your friend should have a
Dulcinea—you understand—I am satisfied Joan Kier
regarded it in that light otherwise she would hardly have
mentioned it—*verbum sapienti*—Your Sisters situation
will in all probability give her opportunities of getting
acquainted with the Lady in question. I am sure she
will like her for her own sake and I need not say how
much I should be delighted to see a union take place
between such kindred minds in each of whom I take such
interest—that is if nothing has occurrd from the campaign
of the formal Chevalier and his son and heir Don
Guglielmo—I endeavour to treat the recollection of
this visit and its consequences with levity, and yet upon
my word Dear Erskine it requires an exertion to do
it—Down busy devil down—But I run about the
country and gallop over stock and stile after the " gude
graer[1] dogs " so that if Horaces *Atra Cura*[2] insist upon
riding the pillion *sedere post equitem* as honest Flaccus
has it, I must een do my best to drop her jadeship into

---

[1] So I read Scott's word. Lord Sands makes it " Graca." What is
meant is the " grew " or " gray " dog, the Scottish greyhound, used in
Scott's favourite pastime of coursing : " ' I have six terriers at hame, forbye
twa couple of slow-hunds, five grews, and a wheen other dogs ' " . . .
" almost every farmer had with him at least a brace of large and fierce
grey-hounds of the race of those deer-dogs which were formerly used in that
country, but greatly lessened in size from being crossed with the common
breed."—*Guy Mannering*, cc. 23, 25.

Sed timor et minae
scandunt eodem quo dominus, neque
decedit aerata triremi et
post equitem sedet atra cura.
HORACE, *Carm.* III. 1.

a Teviotdale bog. I must not allow you to forget so good a habit as that of regular correspondence so if a sugar plum will have any effect upon you I must inform you that your letters are one of the chief sources of amusement I have here and that the more frequently you write the better you enable me to banish the Blue Devils and white black Devils and grey which insist upon being the companions of my Solitude—A thousand Compliments of Congratulation to our friends if they are within reach of receiving them—We will all busy ourselves in Winter to look out for a fellow-mind for you and I have no doubt you will meet one— Ever dear Willy ever thine

WALTER SCOTT

ROSEBANK 26 *Sept* 1796

[*Sir Alfred J. Law*]

TO MR. MILLER, BOOKSELLER, PARLIAMENT SQUARE, EDINR.

ROSEBANK 2*d. Octr.*, 1796

DEAR SIR,—I am favour with your letter accompanying a Copy of Fiesco [1] which I shall look over—You may word the advertisement as you please, the name in the Original is " *Lenore*," & that of the Chace " *Der Wilde Jäger* "— The time you propose will suit me very well. I hope to receive all or at least some of the copies I mentiond in my last by Tuesdays Coach as I leave this place on Wednesday [2]

[1] Schiller's *Die Verschwörung des Fiesco zu Genoa*, 1783. To a translation of this by himself, later lost, Scott refers in a much later letter.

[2] This is apparently the journey of which Lockhart tells : " On turning to James Ballantyne's *Memorandum* . . . I find an account of Scott's journey from Rosebank to Edinburgh, in the November after the Ballads from Bürger were published," and he goes on to give the well-known account of Ballantyne's meeting Scott in the coach and of their talk on literary matters. Lockhart's account is not very clear. What happened is probably that Ballantyne, journeying to Glasgow, found at Kelso Scott in the coach going to Edinburgh. The journey to Edinburgh was a whole day

& shall not return for some days—I am Sir   Your obedt.
servant

WALTER SCOTT

(1)

[*Stevenson*]

To ROBERT SHORTREED

DEAR SHORTREED,—I am extremely sorry to find that it
will not be in my power to visit our Liddesdale friends
this season.   The marriage of my friend James Edmonstone, at which I have received a summons to assist, will,
I hope, be admitted as a substantial apology for this
breach of appointment.   I am doubly sorry as I fear I
may have occasioned some inconvenience by the delay
of your journey, but you see the thing was unavoidable.
Present the Ballads to Doctor Elliot, with best compliments to him and all our friends on the Liddle and at
Falnash.   With best compliments to Mrs. Shortreed, I will
be extremely obliged if she will send the *two* old shirts
down to Rosebank, as they will get spoiled from not being
used, not to mention that I lost about half my stock in
the north.   Ever yours

WALTER SCOTT

HALYARDS 16 *October* 1796

[*Abbotsford Copies*]

trip, the travellers dining on the way.   They would part on reaching
Edinburgh.   From this letter to Miller the printer we gather that Scott
left Rosebank on the 5th of October, and in the next he writes from Halyards, the residence of Professor Ferguson in Peeblesshire, on the 16th.
Edmonstone's marriage took place on the 19th.   Scott left Halyards on
the 17th or 18th.   After the marriage he returned to Rosebank, and came
to Edinburgh again at the beginning of November.

[1] Red seal, female figure with motto " Reparabit Cornua Phoebe."

To WILLIAM TAYLOR[1]

EDINBURGH, 25*th November,* 1796

SIR,—Though I have not the honour of your acquaintance, I find myself under the necessity of intruding upon you with a double request : it is to entreat that you will do me the favour of accepting a copy of two Ballads, translated from Bürger, with an elegant version of one of which the world has been favoured from your hand ; and that you will further have the goodness to pardon a plagiary which I have committed in borrowing two energetic and expressive lines from your translation.

You will find the theft fully acknowledged to the public

---

[1] The letters to Taylor (1765-1836) are here printed, the first from *Memoir of William Taylor of Norwich,* compiled by J. W. Robberds ; the second from the original in the collection of Mr. Owen Young, New York. Taylor was a pioneer of German studies but also (which appealed less to Scott) an enthusiast for " enlightenment " and the Revolution. This is probably why we hear no more of any intercourse. In his *magnum opus, Historic Survey of German Poetry interspersed with various Translations,* London, 1830, he says, speaking of *Goetz von Berlichingen* : " It was admirably translated into English in 1799 by William Scott, Advocate ; no doubt the same person who, under the poetical but assumed name of Walter, has since become the most extensively popular of British writers." Scott refers to this later, and Carlyle in reviewing the work, after indicating this and other errors, says : " Of errors in doctrine, false critical judgements, and all sorts of philosophical hallucination the number . . . is also unfortunately great. Considered indeed as in any measure a picture of what is remarkable in German poetry this Historic Survey is one great Error." Taylor was misled by the name " William " on some of the copies of *Goetz,* 1799. See letters of 1831 later.

Taylor's letter to Scott was as follows :

. . . I need not tell you with how much eagerness I opened your volume, —with how much glow I followed " The Chase," & with how much alarm I came to " William and Helen." Of the latter, I will say nothing ; praise might seem hypocrisy,—criticism, envy. . . . The ghost nowhere makes his entrance so well as with you, and nowhere his exit so well as with Mr. Spencer. I like very much the recurrence of

" The scourge is red, the spur drops blood,
The flashing pebbles flee."

But of " William and Hellen " I had determin'd to say nothing. Let us return to " The Chase," of which the metre stanza style pleases me entirely. Yet I think a few passages written in too elevated a diction for the general spirit of the poem. This age leans too much to the Darwin-style. Mr. Pye's " Lenore " owes its coldness to the adoption of this, and it seems

in the preface ; but I should but ill satisfy my own
feelings, without the present further personal apology
to yourself.

My friend Mr. Cranstoun, brother-in-law to Professor
Stuart, who heard your translation read by a lady in
manuscript, is the gentleman alluded to in the preface to
my Ballads, to whose recollection I am indebted for the
two lines which I took the liberty to borrow, as a happy

peculiarly incongruous with the ballad, where habit has taught us to expect
simplicity. Among the passages too stately and pompous, I should reckon,

> " The mountain echoes startling wake,"
> " And for Devotion's choral swell
> Exchange the rude discordant noise,"
> " Fell famine marks the madding throng,"
> " With wild Despair's reverted eye,"

and perhaps one or two more. . . . In the twenty-first stanza, I prefer Bürger's

> " Trampling the corn into chaff and dust,"

to your more metaphorical, and therefore, less picturesque,

> " Destructive sweep the field along."

In the thirtieth,

> " On whirlwind's pinions swiftly borne,"

to me seems less striking than the still dis-apparition of the tumult and
bustle. The earth has opened at the altar's foot, and he is sinking with his
evil genius to the nether world. As he approaches,

> " Dumpf rauscht es wie ein fernes Meer."

It should be rendered, therefore, not by

> " Save what a distant torrent gave,"

but by some sounds which shall necessarily excite the idea of being *hell-
sprung* :—the sound of simmering seas of fire, pinings of goblins damned,
or some analogous noise. The forty-seventh stanza is a great improvement of the original. The profane & blasphemous speeches need not have
been softened down ; as, in proportion to the impiety of the provocation,
increases the poetical probability of the final punishment. I should not
have ventured upon these criticisms, if I did not think it required a microscopic eye to make any, and if I did not on the whole consider *The Chase* as
a most spirited and beautiful translation. . . .

I remain (to borrow in another sense a concluding phrase from the
Spectator), Your constant admirer, WILLIAM TAYLOR, JUNR.

NORWICH, 14*th December*, 1796.

[*Memoir of Taylor, corrected in some details from the original in Walpole
Collection*].

assistance in my own attempt. As I had not at that time seen your translation, I hope the circumstance will prove some apology for my bold effort to bend the bow of Ulysses.

Long afterwards, when I had the pleasure of reading Leonora, I found it so rich in beauties, that I could not consider a robbery in a very heinous light, where the plunder could so easily be spared, and really could not find in my heart to relinquish what formed so brilliant an ornament to my own little essay. I am very sensible that you are entitled to consider me as a hardened criminal, since I venture at once to claim forgiveness and justify my theft. Still, however, I have the courage to throw myself upon your mercy, and to hope you will pardon the present intrusion, which, had I been in town, you would have been troubled with much earlier. I remain respectfully, Your most obedient Servant,

WALTER SCOTT

P.S.—The book I have directed to be sent, per the coach, from London, and hope it will come safe. My address is W. S., Advocate, George-square, Edinburgh.

[*Taylor's Memoir*]

To WILLIAM TAYLOR

DEAR SIR,—I delayed acknowledging your favour of which I have a very high sense, till I should have it in my power to acquaint you that *Ellenore* had come safely to hand—I have now to return you very many thanks for my old favourite in her new attire, and with all her improvements. I shall imitate with much more reason your silence as to my version, and I have much to regret that you had not favoured the public with an attendant to Ellenore,[1] upon which I might have bestowed its due tribute of praise without the appearance of affectation.

---

[1] So Taylor called the ballad when he published his version.

To some of your criticisms upon the Chase, I feel much inclined to plead guilty ; for some other passages I have defences to offer such as they are.

I do not for example think quite so severely of the Darwinian style,[1] as to deem it utterly inconsistent with the Ballad, which, at least to judge from the examples left us by antiquity admits in some cases of a considerable degree of decoration—Still however I do most sincerely agree with you that this may be very easily overdone, and I am far from asserting that this may not be in some degree my own case, but there is scarcely so nice a line to distinguish as that which divides true simplicity from flatness and *Sternholdianism*[2] (if I may be allowd to coin the word) and therefore it is not surprising that in endeavouring to avoid the latter so young and inexperienced a Rhymer as myself should sometimes have deviated also from the former.—As for the "*fernes Meer*" I still feel half inclind to believe it an earthly sound or at least a supernatural sound heard upon the surface of the *earth* ; as I rather think Bürger meant that we should believe the Graf does not descend to the infernal regions but remains in the wood after the evanishing of the Deer, Hermit and suite to abide his doom—Thus, after the appearance of the hell-hounds, the bard proceeds,—

"Er rafft sich auf durch *Wald* und *Feld*,"

which words obviously imply his having continued in the forest instead of sinking with the Altar &c., as you seem to explain the passage. I ought to apologize for differing with you upon a language in which you show so much critical skill, especially as I can by no means boast of my own altho it is considerably increased since I made out these translations—I was at that time but a Tyro indeed

[1] Probably the first use of an adjective which has since acquired another and more disturbing significance.

[2] The style of Sternhold's versification of the Psalms, 1547.

and shall upon some future occasion avail myself of your friendly and polite criticisms to correct some of the many errors into which my ignorance has led me.

I most sincerely hope that you mean to favour the world with some further specimens of your skill in transfusing into the ancient English Ballad the spirit of the German. If you are engaged in any literary researches in which a correspondence with our northern capital could assist I should deem myself happy in having an opportunity to show by any little services in my power how much I wish to have a claim upon your friendship. From my own stores, I can offer little, but I can boast of some acquaintances among our literary gentlemen here who are neither few in number nor contemptible in talents. Permit me to return the compliments with which you honourd me, and to assure you how much I am your sincere admirer, as well as respectfull humble servant,

WALTER SCOTT

EDINBURGH, 22nd January, 1797

[Owen D. Young]

To CAPT. PATRICK MURRAY OF SIMPRIM OF THE PERTHRE. CAVALRY, PENRITH

DEAR SIR,—How you & I should have past so many months without exchanging a line is one of those problems in Ethics which is too deep for my philosophy; well however do I know that forgetfulness had no share on either side in the intermission of our correspondence. It is now a long time since in the month of October last, I expected to have had the pleasure of shewing you our border lions of which I have told you so many tales. All of Rosebank from the Master to Oscar the House Dog were prepared to receive you. Abercairney had told me your day of march and the cold beef & porter were standing ready to refresh the Captain after his fatigues—

but behold—another came, & we learned the unwelcome news that your route had been changed. You are now in a country in which I am sure you must meet with much entertainment from your vicinity to the Lakes of famous name—I should like to hear how you like it, &c. and in the mean time shall endeavour to send you some Auld Reekie news—Be it known to you in the first place that I have the honour to be Secretary & Chargé d'affaires to the Royal Corps of Edinr. Volunteer light Dragoons, & am in consequence quite a military man. Our number is 80 at present, and we mean to compleat two troops of 50 Gentlemen each mounted on horses worth from 30 to 60 guineas a piece, armed equipped &c at our own expence. I find the exercise, for we are drilled two or three hours every day by the officers of the Cinque Porte Cavalry, does my health much good, and am flattered that, in spite of natural deficiencies, I shall be able for the duty. So frere Cavalier, Je vous baise les mains. We can perform most of the common manœuvres at the hard trot & Gallop—I mean such of us as have drilled from the beginning, that is about a fortnight ago. Oh how I wish we may be able to merit some portion of your applause when you return among us— In addition to the old Volunteers, who are now very strong, we have raised a body of tradesmen, arm'd cloathed & paid by government under the Volunteer act—a 3rd Corps intended to consist of Highlanders, is also on foot & filling fast. Linton goes as an officer into this last, for these new Corps are chiefly officer'd from the old Volunteers who in that respect have proved of admirable service. Clerk, mirabile dictu, volunteers as an artillery man. You will rejoice with me that his natural gallantry & amor patriae have led him compleatly to throw aside party at this momentous period— Thus you see we are all alive, & I flatter myself you will be not a little proud upon glancing over an estimate of our Volunteer force which I shall subjoin— There is now no division amongst us— In case of an invasion one & all will be the word, unless with some very *black hearted* or *lily livered* rascals indeed. Health & fraternity from Dear Murray your truly affectionate

WALTER SCOTT

EDINR 8*th March* 1797

[*Abbotsford Copies*]

TO MISS CARPENTER, PALMER'S LODGINGS, CARLISLE [1]

[About 21*st September*, 1797]

SINCE Miss Carpenter has forbid my seeing her for the present, I am willing to incurr even the hazard of her displeasure by intruding upon her in this manner. My anxiety which is greater than I can find words to express leads me to risque what I am sure if you could but know my present [condition] would not make you very—very angry —Gladly would I have come to Carlisle tomorrow and returnd here to dinner but dearly as I love my freind, I would ever sacrifice my own personal gratification to follow the line of conduct which is most agreeable to her. I likewise wish to enter more particularly into the circumstances of my situation which I should most heartily despise myself were I capable of concealing or misrepresenting to you—Being only the second brother of a large family you will easily conceive that tho my father is a man in easy circumstances, my success in life must depend upon my own exertions. This I have been always taught to expect and far from considering it as a hardship, my feelings on that subject have ever been those of confidence in myself—Hitherto from reasons which have long thrown a lassitude over my mind to which it is not naturally liable, my professional exertions have been even culpably neglected, and as I reside with my father I gave myself little trouble provided my private Income did but answer

---

[1] For Miss Carpenter and the letters see the Introduction.

I   E

my personal expence and the maintainnance of a Horse or
two. At the same time none of those who were calld
to the Bar with myself can boast of having very far
outstripd me in the Career of Life or of Business.
I have every reason to expect that the Sheriffdom of a
particular County presently occupied by a Gentleman in
a very precarious state of health [1] may soon fall to my lot.
The Salary is £250 pr. ann: and the duty does not
interfere with the exercise of my profession but greatly
advances it. The only Gentleman who can be entitled to
dispute this situation with me is at present Col: of a
Regt. of Dragoons an office which he will not readily
quit for that of a provincial Judge. Many other little
resources which I cannot easily explain so as to make you
comprehend me induce me to express myself with confidence upon the probability of my success—and O how
dear these prospects will become to me would my beloved
freind but permit me to think that she would share them—
If you could form any idea of the Society in Edinr.
I am sure the prospect of living there would not terrify
you. Your situation would entitle you to take as great a
share in the amusements of the place as you were disposed
to, and when you were tired of these it should be the
study of my life to prevent your feeling one moments
Ennui. When Care comes we will laugh it away, or if
the load is too heavy we will sit down and share it
between us till it becomes almost as light as pleasure
itself. You are apprehensive of losing your liberty but
could you but think with how many domestic pleasures
the sacrifice will be repaid you would no longer think it
very frightful. Indisposition may deprive you of that
liberty which you prize so highly and Age certainly will.
O think how much happier you will find yourself

---

[1] "Andrew Plummer of Middlestead, a scholar and antiquary, who
had entered with zeal into his ballad researches, and whose name occurs,
accordingly, more than once in the notes to the Border Minstrelsy."—
LOCKHART. Plummer died in the autumn of 1799.

surrounded by freinds who will love you than with those who will only regard even my beloved Charlotte while she possesses the power of interesting or entertaining them. You seem too to doubt the strength or at least the stability of my Affection. I can only protest to you most solemnly that a truer never warmd a mortals breast and that tho' it may appear sudden it is not rashly adopted. You yourself must allow that from the nature of our acquaintance we are entitled to judge more absolutely of each other than from a much longer one trammelld with the usual forms of Life—and tho' I have been repeatedly in similar situations with amiable and accomplishd women the feelings I entertain for you have ever been strangers to my bosom except during a period I have often alluded to. I have settled in my mind to see you on Monday next.[1] I stay thus long to give you time to make what inquiries you may think proper—and also because you seemd to wish it. All Westmoreland and Cumberland shall not detain me a minute longer. In the mean while I do not expect you to write—you shall do nothing to commit yourself. How this week will pass away I know not but a more restless anxious being never numberd the hours than I have been this whole day. Do not think of bidding me *forget you* when we again meet—O do not— the thing is really impossible—as impossible as it is to express how much I love you and how truly I believe our hearts were formd for each other. Mr. and Mrs. B[ird] [2] are Hospitality itself but all will not do. I would fain make you laugh before concluding but my heart is rather too full for trifling. However if it will amuse you to know that my Brother is arrived this day and has lost his horses by the road pray receive the intelligence

---

[1] Probably 25th September.

[2] Mr. Bird was the perpetual curate of St. Mary's, Carlisle. He has been frequently described as a Minor Canon of Carlisle Cathedral by a confusion with the Mr. Brown who married Scott. Who Hodge and Davies and Mr. Green were I do not know.

& laugh if you please at the doleful conjectures he makes
on the subject. Sometimes he thinks Hodge & Davies
have borrowd them for pursuing their fair fugitives—
sometimes that Mr. Green in one of his reveries has
carried them to the gates of Jericho. I think I must go
in search of them tomorrow—it is the fittest employment
for one who has lost himself. I hope Miss N[icolson] is
better. Adieu—adieu. Souvenez vous de moi—

W. SCOTT

[*Law*]

TO MRS. SCOTT

N.D. [*c.* 21 *Sept.*, 1797]

MY DEAR MOTHER,—I should very ill deserve the care
and affection with which you have ever regarded me
were I to neglect my duty so far as to omit consulting my
father and you in the most important step which I can
possibly take in Life and upon the success of which my
future happiness must depend. It is with pleasure I think
that I can avail myself of your advice and instructions in
an affair of so great importance as that which I have at
present on my hands. You will probably guess from this
preamble that I am engaged in a Matrimonial plan
which is really the case. Tho my acquaintance with
the young Lady has not been of long standing this circumstance is in some degree counterbalanced by the intimacy
in which we have lived, and by the opportunities which
that intimacy has afforded me of remarking her conduct
and sentiments on many different occasions, some of
which were rather of a delicate nature, so that in fact I
have seen more of her during the few weeks we have been
together than I could have done after a much longer
acquaintance shackled by the common forms of ordinary
Life. You will not expect from me a description of her
person for which I referr you to my brother, as also for a
fuller account of all the circumstances attending this
Business than can be comprised in the compass of a Letter.

Without flying into raptures, for I must assure you that my judgement as well as my affections are consulted upon this occasion—without flying into raptures, then, I may safely assure you, that her temper is sweet and cheerfull, her understanding good, and, what I know will give you pleasure, her principles of religion very serious. I have been very explicit with her upon the nature of my situation and expectations, and she thinks she can accomodate herself to the situation which I should wish her to hold in society as my wife, which, you will easily comprehend, I mean should neither be extravagant nor degrading. Her fortune, though partly dependent upon her Brother who is high in office at Madrass, is very considerable—at present £500 a year. This, however, we must, in some degree, regard as precarious, I mean to the full extent, and indeed when you know her, you will not be surprised that I regard this circumstance chiefly because it removes those prudential considerations which would otherwise render our union impossible for the present. Betwixt her income and my own professional exertions I have little doubt we will be enabled to hold the rank in Society which my family and situation entitle me to fill.

My dear Mother, I cannot express to you the anxiety I have that you will not think me flighty nor inconsiderate in this business. Believe me that Experience, in one instance, you cannot fail to know to what I allude, is too recent to permit my being so hasty in my conclusions as the warmth of my temper might have otherwise prompted. I am also most anxious that you should be prepared to shew her kindness, which I know the goodness of your own heart will prompt, more especially when I tell you that she is an Orphan without relations and almost without freinds. Her guardian is, I should say *was*, for she is of age,[1] Lord Downshire, to whom I must write for his consent, a piece of respect to which he is

---

[1] She was then in her 27th year. Lord Downshire's consent was insisted on by her notwithstanding that she was of age.

entitled for his care of her—and there the matter rests at present. I think I need not tell you that if I assume the new character which I threaten, I shall be happy to find that in that capacity I may make myself more usefull to my brothers, and especially to Anne, than I could in any other. On the other hand I shall certainly expect that my freinds will endeavour to shew every attention in their power to a Woman who forsakes for me prospects much more splendid than what I can offer, and who comes into Scotland without a single freind but myself. I find I could write a great deal more upon this subject, but as it is late and as I must write to my father I shall restrain myself. I think (but you are best judge) that in the circumstances in which I stand you should write to her Miss Carpenter, under cover to me at Carlisle.

Write to me very fully upon this important subject— send me your opinion, your advice, and above all, your *Blessing*. You will see the necessity of not delaying a Minute in doing so, and in keeping this business *strictly private*, till you hear further from me, since you are not ignorant that even at this advanced period, an objection on the part of Ld. Downshire, or many other accidents, may intervene in which case I should little wish my disappointment to be public. Believe me, My dear Mother, ever your dutiful and affectionate son,

WALTER SCOTT

[*Law and Lockhart*]

To MISS CARPENTER [1]

[*6th* or *7th October* 1797]
Rosebank near Kelso.

MY DEAREST FRIEND,—I wrote you a few days ago a long and wise letter anticipating situations which I hope will never arrive but which we certainly ought to consider as

---

[1] This letter to Miss Carpenter is printed for the first time from the Law Collection. It was written after Scott had heard from his parents but before he had heard from Lord Downshire.

possible. These considerations will I hope only serve to
make us enjoy the more pleasant scenes that are reserved
for us and if Misfortune or Disappointment does come
my dear Charlotte shall we not find in each other some
protection against its shafts ? I have every reason to hope
that among my friends you will meet for my sake a most
wellcome reception, and as they learn to know you, how
well will they be convinced that you deserve it for your
own. If that noble friend of yours would but write soon.
By the way there is a circumstance which to me seemd
of so little consequence that I really forgot to make any
enquiry upon the subject, nor ever thought about it till
I felt awkward at not being able to answer my Uncle's
questions on the point. It relates to your fathers country
and profession and to your Brothers situation at Madrass.
You must have the goodness to furnish me with some
answer to these questions. Do not think these enquiries
on the part of my friends and you never can think that
they do upon mine, originate in the pride of family which
you think us all so plentifully furnishd with. I only
suppose that interested as they are in every particular
relating to the young Lady with whose alliance they have
a prospect of being honoured they naturally wish to
know all about her that they can. They have not my
apology for Indifference upon the subject which is that
my regard for Miss Carpenter herself was so great as to
make me utterly careless upon all such matters. I went to
Mertoun [1] yesterday in order to talk over the most interesting subject which can ever engage me with Mr. and Mrs.
Scott, as by themselves or their connexions they may have
access to Lord Downshire. But I found there Mr. and
Mrs. Morton Pitt from London so that I had no opportunity to accomplish what I proposed and finding their
visit was to last some days I took my horse & came back
here this Morning. You will like Mrs. Scott much. She
is considerably addicted like some people of my acquaint-

[1] Mertoun House, the seat of the Scotts of Harden.

ance to the practice of *quizzing* and like these same good folks is always careful not to give pain to the subject quizz'd. My employments here have been various chiefly calculated if that were possible to beguile the heavy Anxiety which I must feel till I hear from Cumberland. I have been doing the sword exercise to the astonishment of the native yeomanry cavalry. I have been fagging at partridge shooting till I convinced myself that I had lost all taste for the amusement, if breaking fences and wading thro stubble deserve the name. In grouse shooting there is something grand, the solitude of the wild scenery about you gives a sportsman the feeling of savage independence—but partridge-shooting is a paltry business. And now let me ask you what have *you* been doing ? Are you reconciled to the *pomp* and *glory* of the City of Carlisle or do you still think of changing it for the Solitude of Allonby.[1] Only think how dull—to abandon all the spectacled cousins whose conversation must be so infinitely interesting—to a herald or genealogist. I shall not wonder if you find the sacrifice difficult. And besides I had forgot the hunt with all its attendants of Balls and Assemblies in which I really hope you will find some amusement for tired I am sure you must be of Carlisle in its natural state. All I entreat of my lovely friend is not to be so very *very* much amused, as to forget my claims upon *one hour* in the day. At 10 o clock you know, folks neither visit nor receive visits nor do they dance, nor do they (except at Gilsland) play at Cassino, and so you may spare an hour to an absent friend who dedicates all his with little interruption to thinking of you. I am engaged as Counsell in a trial[2] which comes forward on Monday and am in consequence obliged to

[1] In Cumberland, the home of Mr Bird.

[2] The trial took place at the High Court of Justiciary, Edinburgh, on Monday, 9th October, 1797. It concerned a riot in which Scott acted for the defendant, as he did in another such case on the 12th May. Riots had been provoked by the Militia Act of 1797. See note, p. 195.

go to Edinr. tomorrow—two days sooner than I proposed
when I last wrote to my beloved freind.   I cannot express
to you how anxious I am to hear from you.   I fancy a
thousand difficulties many of which have I hope no other
origin than in my own ingenuity in tormenting myself.
Little as I have been accustomd either to look up to the
great or indeed to have much intercourse with them I
recoil from the reflection that my happiness or misery
may depend upon the modes of thinking of one of their
number—but I cannot forget that the ultimate decision
must come from you and O I hope you will not easily
be biassd from a resolution you have been pleased to
adopt.   By going into town just now I avoid the Kelso
races and Balls.   Why should I carry into scenes of mirth
and happiness feelings of uneasy solicitude which I can
so ill disguise.   Let me think that the bustle of professional engagements will more easily divert my attention
from what gives me pain—And therefore

> Wellcome, business, wellcome, Strife,
> Wellcome, the cares the thorns of Life—

You would think this quotation very apropos, could I
explain to you what unpleasant Bickerings are likely to
take place among my brethren the faculty of Advocates.
As I am both personally and politically attachd to the
Lord Advocate I will be expected to take share in the
squabble however disagreeable to me.

I beg to be most respectfully and if she will permit me,
kindly rememberd to Miss Nicolson.   Say that I esteem
her so much that I should think myself very unhappy did
I not hope one day to possess her good opinion, especially
considering she has so long been your attachd and firm
friend.   I remain my beloved Charlotte ever *ever* your

WALTER SCOTT

I formerly mentiond my direction in Edinr.

W. S. Advocate—Georges Square—Edinr.

[*Law*]

To MISS C. RUTHERFORD

[Late October 1797]

HAS it never happend to you my dear Miss Critty in the course of your domestic oeconomy to meet with a drawer stuffd so very, so *extremely* full, that it was very difficult to pull it open however desirous you might be to exhibit its contents—In case this miraculous event has ever taken place you may somewhat conceive from thence the cause of my silence which has really proceeded from my having a very great deal to communicate, so much so that I really hardly know how to begin—As for my Affection & Freindship for you, beleive me sincerely they neither slumber nor sleep, & it is only your suspicions of their drowsiness which incline me to write at this period of a business highly interesting to me, rather than when I could have done so with something like certainty —Hem ! Hem !—It must come out at once—I am in a very fair way of being married to a very amiable young woman—with whom I formd an attachment in the course of my Tour—She was born in France her parents were of English extraction,[1] the name Carpenter—She was left an orphan early in life & educated in England & is at present under the care of a Miss Nicolson, a daughter of the late Dean of Exeter, who was on a visit to her relations in Cumberland—Miss Carpenter is of age, but as she lies under great obligations to the Marquis of Downshire who was her guardian she cannot take a step of such importance without his consent—and I daily expect his final answer upon the Subject—Her fortune is dependant in a great measure upon an only & very affectionate Brother—He is commercial Resident at Salem in India and has settled upon her an annuity of £500„—Of her personal accomplishments I shall only say that she possesses very good sense with un-

[1] On what ground this statement rests I do not know. In a much later letter to his son Charles at Oxford Scott tells him that his mother was of purely French origin.

common good temper which I have seen put to [the] most severe trials. I must bespeak your kindness & freindship for her—You may easily believe I shall rest very much both upon Miss R. & you for giving her the *carte de pays*, when she comes to Edinr.—I may give you a hint that there is no *Romance* in her composition & that tho born in France, she has the sentiments & manners of an Englishwoman and does not like to be thought otherwise—a very slight tinge in her pronunciation is all which marks the foreigner—She is at present at Carlisle, where I shall join her as soon as our arrangements are finally made—Some difficulties have occurrd in settling matters with my father owing to certain prepossessions which you can easily conceive his adopting —One main article was the uncertainty of her provision which has been in part removed by the safe arrival of her remittances for this year with assurances of their being regular & even larger in future, her brothers situation being extremely lucrative—Another objection was her birth " Can any good thing come out of Nazareth "— but as it was *birth merely* & *solely* this has been abandond— *You* will be more interested about other points regarding her, & I can only say that tho our acquaintance was shorter than ever I could have thought of forming such a connection upon—But it was exceedingly close & gave me full opportunities for observation—and if I had parted with her, it must have been for ever, which both parties began to think would be a disagreeable thing—She has conducted herself thro' the whole business with so much propriety as to make a strong impression in her favour upon the minds of my father & Mother prejudiced as they were against her from the circumstances I have mentiond—We shall be your neighbours in the new town, and intend to live very quietly Charlotte will need many lessons from Miss R— in Housewifery—Pray shew this letter to Miss R. with my very best Complimts. Nothing can now stand in the way except Ld. Downshire

who may not think the match a prudent one for Miss C—
but he will surely think her entitled to judge for herself
at her age in what she would wish to place her happiness—
She is not a beauty by any means, but her person and
face are very engaging—she is a brunette—her manners
are lively but when necessary she can be very serious—
She was baptized [1] & educated a protestant of the C. of
England—I think I have now said enough upon this
subject—Do not write till you hear from me again
which will be when all is settled—I wish this important
event may hasten your return to town—I send a goblin
story with best complimts. to the Misses & ever am yours
affectionately   WALTER SCOTT

THE ERL-KING

(The Erl-King is a goblin that haunts the Black forest in Thuringia ;
to be read by a candle particularly long in the snuff)

1.

O who rides by night thro the woodland so wild,
It is the fond father embracing his Child,
And close the Boy nestles within his loved arm
To hold himself fast & to keep himself warm

2.

" O father see yonder ! see yonder ! " he says
" My boy upon what doest thou fearfully gaze "—
" O 'tis the Erl King with his crown & his shroud "—
" No my son it is but a dark wreath of the cloud "—

3.
(THE ERL KING SPEAKS)

" O come & go with me thou loveliest Child
By many a gay sport shall thy time be beguiled
My Mother keeps for thee full many a fair toy
And many a fine flower shall she pluck for my boy "

4.

" O father, my father, & did you not hear
The Erl-King whisper so low in my ear ? "—
—" Be still my hearts Darling my Child be at ease
It was but the wild blast as it sung thro the trees "—

[1] At St. George's Church, Hanover Square, 13th May 1787.

5.

ERL KING

" O wilt thou go with me, my loveliest boy
My daughter shall tend thee with care & with joy.
She shall bear thee so lightly thro wet & thro wild
And press thee & kiss thee & sing to my child"

6.

" O father, my father & saw you not plain
The Erl-kings pale daughter glide past thro the rain "—
—" O yes my loved Treasure I knew it full soon
It was the grey willow that danced to the moon "—

7.

" O come & go with me, no longer delay
Or else silly Child I will drag thee away "—
" O father ! Oh father ! now now keep your hold
The Erl King has seized me—his grasp is so cold—"

8.

Sore trembled the father—he spurnd thro the wild
Clasping close to his bosom his shuddering child
He reaches his dwelling in doubt & in dread
But claspd to his bosom the Infant was Dead.

You see I have not altogether lost the faculty of rhiming
—I assure you there is no small impudence in attempting
a version of that Ballad as it has been translated by *Lewis*.
All good things be with you—   W. S.

[*Miss Mary Lockhart*]

To THE MARQUIS OF DOWNSHIRE

MY LORD MARQUIS,—It is impossible to express the
pleasure with which I received this morning your Lordships favour—& I must add that as far as was possible
the very handsome manner in which the Obligation was
conferred even enhanced its value—In return for your
Lordships good wishes it shall be ever my earnest hope
that you enjoy thro' life the happiness which you are so
willing to confer upon others—I shall be proud to think
that I am contributing to your Lordship's stock of

pleasant reflection, while I exert myself to promote the happiness of the valuable charge you have thought me not unworthy of receiving from your hands.

I am thus far on my road to Carlisle to see Miss Carpenter—I understand it is her wish to retain that name for some time, tho I hope for as short while as she can possibly think consistent with propriety—this will remain to be settled at our meeting—I shall be most anxious that any settlement made by her Brother in her favour shall be upon her & her children exclusively.

I cannot conclude without assuring your Lordship that it shall be my future study to retain the favourable place in your Lordship's opinion with which I think myself so highly honourd and that I am with the highest sentiments of gratitude & respect My Lord Marquis Your Lordship's Most Obedient & most Humble Servant

WALTER SCOTT

SELKIRK 4 *Oct.* [*probably* 5 *Nov.*] 1797

[*Glen*]

To ROBERT SHORTREED [1]

DEAR BOB,—This day a long train of anxieties was put an end to by a letter from Lord Downshire, couched in the most flattering terms, giving his consent to my marriage with his ward. I am thus far on my way to Carlisle, only for a visit—because, betwixt her reluctance to an immediate marriage and the imminent approach of the session, I am afraid I shall be thrown back to the Christmas holy days.

In the meanwhile, let me know how I shall replace the article—by paying in to the British Linen Coy. or how? I shall be home in about eight days. I hope Mrs. S and child are both well. Ever yours sincerely   W. SCOTT

SELKIRK 4 *October* [*probably* 5 *November*] 1797

[*Abbotsford Copies*]

[1] Lockhart dates this letter 8th October and omits some sentences.

To MISS CARPENTER

[Postmark : *Nov.* 17] [1797]

AND Did my Love really think that I had forgot her or
was going to turn a negligent Correspondent, at the very
time when I would give the world to be with her and tell
her every hour how much I love her.   And why do you
think I should regret leaving Carlisle if it were not
because I leave my Charlotte behind me—if *you* were
out of that ancient and illustrious city I am sure I should
think it one of the dullest holes that ever *Ennui* set up her
throne in and far from regretting my departure I should
certainly not care a farthing if I was told at the same
time I should never see it more.   That you should be
melancholy my sweet friend at contemplating your
approaching change of State is not surprizing, but I
am glad you promise not to give way to such feelings
and that your *gaieté de cœur* is returning—if it will help
to banish *Tristesse* let me again assure you that every
thought of my heart shall be directed to insure your
happiness.   I admire of all things your laughing
Philosophy and shall certainly be your pupil in learning
to take a gay view of human life.   *On s'ennuyent* [sic] *d'être
tristes* [1]—*n'est ce pas.*   I suppose by this time you have
the few lines which I wrote from Ashesteel,[2] and which
my Sister filld up.   The place is seven miles distant
from the Post Town, which prevents them from having
regular opportunities of sending off letters.   Is it not
very strange that I should never have an answer from
Mr. Bird.   I really begin to be surprized.   He may'
perhaps have directed to Hardesty's tho' even then they
would have had the sense to forward the letter to me.

[1] Scott's French is corrected by Lockhart, who gives the singular verb
and adjective.

[2] The residence of Scott's cousins.   Colonel Russell had married a half-
sister of Scott's mother.   On the death of the Colonel, the heir being in
India, Scott resided at Ashestiel from 1804 to 1812.

We are getting a household servant with a very
excellent Character. She has been a long time in two
very genteel families and understands Marketing &c and
can set down a decent dinner or supper—not however
when there is *nothing* in the house. I am likewise buying
such things as are immediatly necessary for us—my
mother is to give us some linnen and buy us some more—
and in short we are endeavouring to put matters in train.

The precious lock came safe—do you think I did not
kiss it a hundred times. I could hardly part with it out of
my own custody—it is setting according to my special
directions and I have the vanity to think you will
approve my taste—but no more of that till you see it.
I am highly honord by Miss Ns kind intentions in my
favour—but I will not allow my pretty Charlotte's tresses
to be *all* converted into Jewellery ware. I love them better
where they naturally grow than when they are set tho
in gold & silver. You may easily believe I did not permit
Mr. Russell to remain a minute in his error as far as you
were concernd, leaving the Lady in full possession of the
imaginary treasures he had so liberally endowd her
with, so that if the Swain should be seized with any
desperate inclination my report will not stand in the way.
You will have by this time a letter from my Mother two
pages of which were coverd by your freind. She is a
very good woman & none of her faults lye in her heart
which is a very essential circumstance. I am likewise
busy just now in making Calls that my inattention to my
Lady acquaintances which has been very great may not
be rememberd in judgement against me when you come
to Edinr. I have sold my Servants horse and am looking for
stabling for my own Mare near us. I do not like to leave
the Cavalry tho' attended with some expence because my
situation in the Corps gives me access to the Duke of
Buccleuch & several other persons who may be useful
to me—besides all my dress and accoutrements have
been long bought so that the chief Expence is already

incurrd—add to all this, the Service is a little *Stylish* which I dont think you will dislike it for. When you write, do let me know if you have heard any thing of the Birds. I am afraid that what makes me so happy a Man will break the heart of our old friend Green. I do believe he had taste enough to be a little cut with a fair friend of mine altho her affection did not counter balance his dislike to the inside of a post Chaise or rather to the expence attending that useful conveyance.

I wish I was in *our own* house, tho I know I shall tire as much as our great grandfather Adam, who first made the notable discovery that it was not good for Man to be alone.

I shall be most happy to cultivate the acquaintance of any of your friends—if your freinds in Town really love you it must recommend them strongly to me. We shall be most happy if Lord D can honor us with a visit. I have no doubt that personal acquaintance will serve to increase the esteem & affection with which his kindness to you & his extreme politeness to me induce me to regard him. Does he mention having heard from me?— You will of course inform him of our little plans. Be a good Girl & think often of your friend—Do not be downcast but laugh as you are wont & believe me my Dearest Charlotte ever your faithful

WALTER SCOTT

Pray remember my best Respects to Miss Nicolson

[*Law*]

To MISS CARPENTER

In consequence of your letter, my dearest freind, I shall by tomorrows post transmit to Lord Downshire a scroll of a Contract of Marriage for his inspection and approbation, settling upon my sweet Charlotte as well what is her own already as what her Brother may be pleased to endow her with—a very slender piece of Justice on my part. Alas! my Love it is all I can at present do for you ; but I hope better days will come, when I shall be able to repay you for your disinterested attachment to your poor freind, *poor* indeed in everything but his attachment to you and your love to him.

Lord Downshire, when the paper is revised, must return it for your signature and mine, after which there will be no obstacle to our immediate marriage, and I shall endeavour to banish every disagreeable idea as it rises in my gentle Charlotte's bosom. In less than a month, if this paper is returnd, you *must* be mine, for I know you [are] above desiring any causeless delay of what is so very necessary to my happiness, and give me leave to say, to your own comfort, for I am sure you must be tired of the *Noblesse* of Carlisle.

I heard today from Mr. Bird—a very polite letter, and arrived just in the time that my Highland Blood began to boil over. I am no longer surprised at his silence. He had written me when I was in Edinr. which I had answerd, and sent him a small pamphlet, the receipt of which, to be sure, he never acknowledged, for it happend the bearer had faild to deliver it till the other day ; so I suppose we were mutually accusing each other of very ill breeding.

He has given me a commission to get a *seal*[1] engraved for him in a particular way ; now, if I can get (being, as you are pleased to acknowledge, a Man of Taste) something very uncommon and handsome, don't you think it would be a more genteel compliment than offering him money for making me the happiest man in the world. Ask Miss Nicolson. I am most happy you are pleased with the ring and still more that she is so because she is a

[1] This letter is in *Familiar Letters*. In a note to that edition we read : " The seal . . . is now the property of Mr. Dobinson of Stanwix. It is a Scotch crystal nearly an inch in breadth, set in open goldwork. The figure of a falcon with wings expanded is engraved on the stone with some Persian characters which may be read as John Bird."

more impartial judge of my Taste. In one instance I am sure it will be acknowledged by the whole world, tho' I fear the same instance will throw some imputation upon that of my petite amie. I had a visit from Mr. Haliburton to day, and asked him all about your Brother [1] who was two years in his house. My father is Mr. Haliburton's relation and Chief as he represents a very old family of that name. When you go to the South of Scotland with me, you will see their burying place, now all that remains with my father of a very handsome property—it is one of the most beautiful and romantic scenes you ever saw, among the ruins of an old Abbey. When I die Charlotte, you must cause my bones to be laid there—but we shall have many happy days before that I hope. My headaches are rather better—not quite gone yet tho. I must work at preparing that Scroll—so farewell my dear *dear* Charlotte. Write as often as you can find a spare moment. I love you dearly—encore adieu.

W. S.

22d Novr. 1797.

[Familiar Letters, corrected from Law]

To THE MARQUIS OF DOWNSHIRE

MY LORD MARQUIS,—I have the honour to transmit to your Lordship for your inspection & approbation a Scroll of a Contract of Marriage settling upon Miss Carpenter & her heirs whatever fortune she is presently possessed of and whatever provision her Brother may be pleased to settle upon her—your Lordship & Mr Slade

---

[1] " On my Brother's going to India he was very intimately acquainted and indeed under the charge of a relation of Mr. Scott's a Mr. Haliburton, he speaks in the highest terms of him, and also does another gentleman, I am very fortunate to have so good a Brother who is so generally respected. It will set me off to some advantage. I am more pleased with this circumstance on account of the Father and mother of Mr. Scott as they are not *in love*, and Scotch, they hold a great deal to family."—Charlotte Carpenter to Lord Downshire, 26th November 1797.

(with whose Christian name & particular designation your Lordship will have the goodness to acquaint me) doing her the honour to act as her trustees—It is I believe in the most approved form known in Scotland but I should still be desirous that it was subjected to the inspection of any professional Gentleman acquainted with the law of *both* countries There is no case in which I should be less willing to rest implicit confidence in my own legal knowledge limited especially as it is to the law of Scotland—Upon the scrole being returned to me with any additions which may be thought necessary and there are none which can be devised for Miss Carpenter's farther security to which I will not with pleasure subscribe, I will have it formally drawn out on stampd paper for her subscription & mine & then forward it to your Lordship—As all this must be previous to our marriage I need not mention to your Lordship how impatient I shall be till the Business is concluded.—But no selfish consideration would make [me] wish it hastily or imperfectly settled—

I am very much ashamed of the repeated trouble I give your Lordship but I will not add to it by fatiguing you with Apologies—

I learn with very great pleasure indeed that there is a chance of your Lordship visiting Edinr on your return from Ireland—Your protegee has indeed very many favours to thank your Lordship for & on my part there is nothing would gratify me so much as a personal opportunity of most respectfully acknowledging your Lordship's goodness—

When your Lordship or any person upon whom you devolve the trouble returns the Scrole of the Deed you will have the goodness to address No 50 Georges Street a house to which I have removed & which I hope will shortly call Miss C[arpenter] Mistress—My father's state of health has of late been very precarious, having been slightly affected by some paralytic disorder—In this situation I cannot immediately press him to make me any specifick settlement—Whatever sum I receive from that quarter will I think most likely be nearly equal to purchasing a comfortable House which saves more than 5 p.c. in rent & it is my intention to take the Titles to my wife & myself & the longest liver in liferent & to our children in fee—If all this little detail appears trifling to your Lordship I must be ungrateful enough to say that you have *your own* goodness to thank for the encouragement you have given to My Lord Marquis Your Lordship's most obliged & most respectful humble servant

WALTER SCOTT

EDINR. 23 *Novr.* 1797

[*Glen*]

To CAPT. P. MURRAY OF THE PERTHRE. LIGHT DRAGOONS, HEXHAM.

Anticipated

GAZETTE EXTRAORDINARY

xxiid. DECR: 1797

YESTERDAY WAS MARRIED AT CARLISLE WALTER SCOTT ESQR. ADVOCATE TO MISS MARGARET CHARLOTTE CARPENTER, DAUGHTER TO JOHN CARPENTER, LATE OF THE CITY OF LYONS ESQR.

Annotations upon the Gazette Extraordinary.

20th Decr.

" We hear from Edinr. that the celebrated Counsellor Scott, of that City set out this day for Carlisle to shew cause to the Bishop of that City why a license should be granted to solemnize the holy Sacrament of Matrimony." . . .

21st Decr.

" We hear from Carlisle that the Miss Carpenter whose name *is* to appear in the Gazette Extry. shortly to be published, is no relation whatever to the Indian Chief

called the little Carpenter late Sachem of the Shawanese,
but that she was born in the south of France, & was a
ward of the present Lord Downshire

21*st Decr.* As the public curiosity has been so much
excited about Miss Carpenter, it may be proper to say
that this *fortunate* young Lady is in the opinion of the
whole world, the delight of the male sex, & the envy
of her own." . . .

In a word, for I am tired of my newspaper mode of
communication, I am—I am—my dear Murray how
shall I say it—I am to be married tomorrow or next day
at farthest— Of this, my intended deed of desperation
you should not have remain'd so long ignorant had I
known how to address [you]— You may perhaps
have remark'd Miss C. at a Carlisle Ball, but more likely
not, as her figure is not very frappant—a smart looking
little girl with dark brown hair would probably be her
portrait if drawn by an indifferent hand— But I, you
may believe, should make a piece of work of my sketch
as little like the original as Hercules to me— We shall
have enough to live upon without being independent of
my profession which you may believe I shall now cultivate
with double assiduity— As from being a sorner I am
becoming a sornee, it is proper to acquaint you that my
dwelling is No. 50 Georges Street, where I hope you will
upon your first coming to town, retaliate some of the
hundred visitations with which I have favoured you.—
You shall pay your club by a lesson at the Hungarian
and then "Ware Bystanders"— Our Corps comes
merrily on, and makes a good appearance. I have to
thank you I believe for your political communication.
I read it over with as much attention as the present state
of my poor head would permit and I find the Dogs
behaved just as ill as any one acquainted with their
insolence and ill faith might have expected— I would
march tomorrow—mark me even tomorrow—with all
earthly pleasure to cut *One* & *Two* at the army of

England.[1]—Success to the English Army & Damnation to the Army of England. Hurrah ! Ever yours

WALTER SCOTT

21 *Decr.* 1797

[*Abbotsford Copies*]

To THE MARQUIS OF DOWNSHIRE[2]

MY LORD MARQUIS,—I again trouble your Lordship with a few lines to express in the name of the *late* Miss Carpenter as well as in my own, our very deep sense of the obligations under which we lie to your Lordship— I know only one circumstance that could add to the favours you have already been pleased to confer, and that is your Lordship's affording us an opportunity of returning our thanks in person—your extreme goodness hitherto encourages us to hope that at least your Lordship will not deem us intrusive if we take the liberty of hoping that on your return from Ireland you will perhaps take Edinr in your way to see how your protegee is settled in her new situation—It is an honour which I desire as ardently as I am diffident in requesting it.

Your Lordship was acquainted by Miss Nicolson of the circumstances under which we were obliged to leave Carlisle before the arrival of the deeds from Mr Slade— I am happy to find by these deeds, that that which was executed at Carlisle is such in tenor & form as Miss Carpenters friends desire—Indeed as I felt no small hesitation upon the subject, I had taken care that the Attorney, who is eminent in his profession, should insert a Clause binding me to execute any farther securities which might be thought necessary—we shall therefore execute the new deed also, as explanatory of the first and your Lordship & Mr Slade will hold under *both* or under

---

[1] The army raised by the French Directorate for the invasion of England. The title was applied later to Napoleon's army of 1803.

[2] This letter was written on the second day after the marriage.

either which shall be most advantageous to Mrs Scott—
I think nothing but the risque of a threatend snow storm,
which must have blocked us up in the most unpleasant
situation at Carlisle, which the Revd. Mr. Bird, Miss
Nicolson's cousin, & our only confidant was under the
necessity of leaving, could have made me anticipate the
arrival of these papers—I observe in those drawn by Mr
Slade, a stipulation in my favour in case of my surviving
—this is the single difference betwixt the deeds—Had the
advantage proposed by that Clause which was unsought
by me been upon the other side, I should not easily have
forgiven myself for our hurry—All the Deeds shall be
forwarded to Mr Slade duly executed—Miss Nicolson &
Mrs Scott join in respectful Compliments to your Lordship
& in hopes that we may perhaps see you—They are very
well notwithstanding a very fatiguing Journey which only
concluded last night—I have the honour to be ever
My Lord your Lordship's most obliged & faithful humble
servant   WALTER SCOTT

EDINBURGH 26 *Decr* 1797

[*Glen*]

To THE MARQUIS OF DOWNSHIRE [1]

MY LORD MARQUIS,—I am honord with your Lordship's favour & the affectionate & consolatory inclosure
for Charlotte I read it to her & I need not, indeed
cannot express how much she felt its well timed kindness
—I am happy to say that she continues to recover wonderfully, we observe however all manner of caution. Yesterday being the ninth day I hope everything like danger is

---

[1] The Marquis had written to Scott on the 10th October to congratulate
him on the birth of a son. He will serve as godfather " when the little
infidel is made a Christian " . . . " the anxiety care and tenderness you
feel & have shewn for my late ward are highly gratifying to me & I can
assure you that I am your very sincere friend &c."   The child died on the
15th and Downshire wrote to Charlotte and to Scott to console on a
" Friday," when he received the news.—*Walpole Collection.*

now past—My Mother has been her constant attendant till now & she now resigns the post to my Sister

Charlotte has been much gratified this morning by a very kind letter from Miss Dumergue indeed the attention of all her friends, more especially of your Lordship calls for our warmest gratitude—I understand from the King's counsel here, that there is at least a chance of our having an opportunity of personally expressing our thanks to your Lordship in case of your being Evidence on the Trial of a person here—We are so selfish as hardly to be able to regret that the cause of your Lordship's journey (if it takes place) is not a pleasant one.

We have been kept for some days upon the *Alerte* here owing to the appearance of a foreign fleet which turns out to be Russians—to my great joy, as your Lordship may easily conceive with what feelings I should at present have left Charlotte for the Discharge of any military Duty—

Charlotte sends her kindest respects & I am ever My Lord Marquis Your Lordship's much obliged & most respectful humble servant   WALTER SCOTT

EDINR. 23 *Oct.* 1798

[*Glen*]

To MRS. SCOTT [1]

MY DEAR MOTHER,—I conclude you will be anxious to hear of our safe arrival which took place yesterday after much bad weather & heavy snow on the Road— Charlotte however stood the journey remarkably well & we have been most affectionately receivd by her freinds here—I saw Lord Downshire yesterday who was very kind and I dine in company with him today at the

---

[1] This letter records Scott's first visit to London after the marriage and after the death of a child in October 1798. It was indeed his first visit since the days of his infancy. Thomas Scott, his favourite brother, apparently travelled up with the Walter Scotts, and Daniel, who was in training or business in England, met them at Stilton. M. G. Lewis wrote to Scott in December 1798, but Scott's answer is not extant. His father died while Scott was in London.

Dumergues who are excellent people—The Gentlemen at Sir W. Forbes house promised to lay the State of Setons Business before him immediatly I hope he has by this time had a meeting with Mr Trotter—Daniel dined with us at Stilton—he looks well & happy—we bought two Cheeses there—one a present from Tom to you & one for Castle Street—Neither will be fit to eat till we return—they come down by the Waggon—We saw Miss Nicolson at Longtown who sends her best Compliments—in which & all love Charlotte & Tom join me— we hope soon to hear how my father is—how you & Anne &c all are—Our address is No 55 New Bond Street London where we have very good lodgings just opposite the Dumergues & the attendance of their servants when we want any thing—Believe me ever Your affectionate dutiful son   WALTER SCOTT

LONDON 8 *March* 1799

Compliments to Jack.

[*Abbotsford Original*]

To MRS. SCOTT

LONDON, 19 *April* 1799

MY DEAR MOTHER,—I cannot express the feelings with which I sit down to the discharge of my present melancholy duty, nor how much I regret the accident which has removed me from Edinr. at a time, of all others, when I should have wishd to administer to your distress all the consolation which sympathy and affection could have offerr'd. Your own principles of virtue and religion will, however, I well know, be your best support in this heaviest of human aflictions—the removal of my regretted parent from this earthly scene, is to him, doubtless, the happiest change, if the firmest integrity and the best spent life can entitle us to judge of the state of our departed friends. When we reflect upon this we

ought almost to suppress the selfish feelings of regret
that he was not spared to us a little longer, especially
when we consider that it was not the will of heaven that
he should enjoy the most inestimable of its earthly
blessings, such a portion of health as might have enabled
him to enjoy his family. To my dear father then, the
putting off this mortal mask was happiness, and to us
who remain a lesson so to live that we also may have
hope in our latter end. And with you my dearest Mother,
remain many Blessings and some duties, a grateful
recollection of which will, I am sure, contribute to calm
the current of your afliction. The affection and attention which you have a right to expect from your children,
and which I consider as the best tribute we can pay to the
Memory of the parent we have lost, will also, I am sure,
contribute its full share to the alleviation of your distress.
The situation of Charlotte's health in its present delicate
state prevented me from setting off directly for Scotland,
when I heard that immediate danger was apprehended.
I am now glad that I did not do so, as I could not with
the utmost expedition have reachd Edinr. before the
lamented event had taken place.

The situation of my affairs detain me here for a few
days, I am uncertain for what precise time—the instant
I can I will set off for Scotland. Charlotte is getting
better, altho the late shock has depressd her spirits very
much. I am very well excepting a continual nervous
headache, the consequence of anxiety. I hope my sister
is well and that Tom has sufferrd nothing by his journey.
I need not tell you that you will not do well even
to attempt to answer this letter, indeed such an exertion
would be both unnecessary and improper. John or
Tom will write and let me know how my sister and
you do. Charlotte's most affectionate sympathy and
condolance attend you and Anne in your present distress,
and I am ever Dear Mother, your dutiful and affectionate
Son   WALTER SCOTT

Permit me my dear Madam to add a line to Scott's letter to express to you how sincerely I feel your loss, and how much I regret that I am not near you to try by the most tender care to soften the pain that so great a misfortune must inflict on you and on all those who had the happiness of being connected with him. I hope soon to have the pleasure of returning to you and to convince you of the sincere affection of your Daughter.

M. Charlotte Scott

My kind love and best wishes wait on Miss Scott. Compts to Capt Scott.

[Law]

To CAPT. PATRICK MURRAY OF THE PERTHRE. LIGHT DRAGOONS, MANCHESTER.

EDINR. 30 June, 1799

My dear Murray,—I am already much a debtor to you for your attention to my commission, and should have long ago acknowledged the rect. of one of the most admirable cloaks which ever wrapt a light Dragoon— Unfortunately I deferred writing till my worthy friend Mr. Bink [1] received a very unmerited, & what he calls a very smart reproof from you— I have set his mind at ease—truth was, I waited till I should hear of your being fairly settled at Manchester—Meanwhile I will not undergo the double censure of leaving unanswered your letter which was this day delivered to me by Adam— I cannot tell you how happy I should be to make the little tour you propose, & in your company, but to tell you a Benedict kind of truth, I cannot just at present, part from the little Lady you saw at Newcastle. We were unfortunate in losing our first child, & you must be married yourself before you can conceive in the slightest degree the interest which one takes in an event which is

---

[1] Probably the military tailor. I can find no such name in old Edinburgh *Directories*, but Burck appears as a tailor at the end of the eighteenth century.

likely to perpetuate his memory, tel qu'il soit. We go in next month to our little Cottage near Laswade to rest there for the four months vacation, unless perhaps a little trip to Tweedside may vary our plans—

As to Suwarrow,[1] I agree with you that he will wait the advance of a fresh army before he hazards the fruit of his victory—at the same time it appears to me impossible but what the Austrians must attack Macdonald or sustain his attack, which last defensive mode of warfare they have hitherto (unless in the affairs against Kray in the beginning of the Campaign) found unfavourable— If Macdonald is able to unite with Moreau, having the Swiss Alps for an appui upon their left wing, & the sea upon their right, they will be able either to make an obstinate stand or to advance, as shall best suit their purpose. Divide et impera is a maxim in war as well as in politicks— All this I speak under correction, for knowing the country you must be the best judge of their operations—

The ghost story shall be forthcoming & accompanied by a Border Ballad which I think better than the other— let me know how I shall send them— They are of some length, & will require some time to copy,[2] so I think the Session will be over before I can send them—

[1] More correctly Suvòroff (the name is spelt Sir Warron in the copies), the celebrated general commanding the Russian armies in Italy. " Macdonald . . . defeated the Austrians at Modena thereby paralysing the allied advance westwards. Moreau who reached Genoa on June 27, thereupon ordered him to strike at the communications of the Allies between Piacenza and Mantua, and so draw Suvòroff away to the east, while he himself assailed his rear. This plan came near to success, but Suvòroff by a rapid concentration and forced march threw himself on Macdonald while Moreau was still in Genoa, dealt the Army of Naples terrible blows in three days' fighting on the banks of the Tidone and Trebbia (June 17-19) and compelled it to retreat towards the Appenines. . . . The Russian leader, after routing Macdonald, had faced about and forced him to retire through the Bocchetta Pass. For these brilliant achievements Suvòroff received the title of Prince with the cognomen Italiski (Italian)."—Cambridge Modern History, viii. p. 657.

[2] A copy of the Eve of St. John in Lady Scott's handwriting, prepared for Scott's uncle at Rosebank, is now in the Library of the Writers to the Signet.

We do not pretend to judge of the expedition—I think with you it is destined for Holland.[1] I remember a prophecy of yours at Stirling, that Holland must be twice conquered & reconquered before a general peace—that was at the time of its recovery from Dumourier—if we really beat out the Sans culottes & peace follow—why Eris mihi magnus Apollo— I take this opportunity of recalling your vaticination to your memory (that you may claim in due time the full merits of a Diviner)—

Let me know if you please, the damage of my Cloak & tell me how I can get you anything that may be more useful to you or agreeable than the cash—otherwise I shall be your Debtor till some one of *yours* come this way —or till you come here yourself in winter, when I hope you will not forget that I have a claim upon you for my guest. We have plenty of room, & you shall find yourself no stranger. Believe me ever yours most faithfully

                                   WALTER SCOTT

Address Castle Street, Edinr.

[*Abbotsford Copies*]

TO WILLIAM RIDDELL [2]

MY DEAR SIR,—Presuming upon the friendship you have always shewn me I take the liberty of requesting

[1] " The autumn likewise brought disaster to the Allies in the north. In pursuance of an Anglo-Russian treaty of June 11-22, 1799, a joint expedition was prepared against Holland."—*Cambridge History*, viii. p. 662. It ended in nothing, and the English force had to evacuate with permission of the French commander, Brune. Murray's prophecy was *not* fulfilled.

[2] William Riddell of Camieston (1746-1829), in Roxburghshire, the grandson of Sir Walter Riddell, fourth Baronet of Riddell. In 1776 he married Elizabeth Carre of Cavers Carre, and the present representatives of the family bear the name of Riddell-Carre of Cavers Carre, Lilliesleaf, Roxburghshire. Scott in later life was not *very* fond of Riddell. In a letter to the Duke of Buccleuch in 1819, the year of his cramps, he writes of the sympathy his illness has evoked, and adds : " The only unwellcome resurrection was that of old Camie whose feud with me (or rather dryness) I had well nigh hoped was immortal but he came jinking over Bowden

your assistance in a matter of considerable consequence to my future prospects—I have with the approbation of the Ld. Advocate started as a candidate for the Sheriffdom of Selkirkshire, and have good reason for believing I shall also have Mr. Pringle's interest with the Duke of Buccleuch & Lord Napier. The Advocate thinks it advisable that I should procure the approbation of as many gentlemen of the County as possible, & may I hope my dear Sir you will add to your many favours by assisting me on this occasion. The opinion of your relation & friend Sir John Riddell from his rank & influence in the County & its vicinity must be attended with great weight & I flatter myself you will not be averse to using your interest with him on my behalf. I w'd have waited on you myself but am confind to bed by a feverish complaint   Ever yours mo: faithfully   W SCOTT

Saturday morng. 22nd Novr. 1799

[*Capt. Ralph Riddell Carre*]

moor with daughters and ponies and god knows what to look after my precious health. I cannot tolerate that man—it seems to me as if I hated him for things not only past & present but for some future offence which is as yet in the womb of fate." In 1809 Riddell had succeeded to Lenthill, which accounts for his coming over Bowden Moor. Sir John Riddell of Riddell was, I presume, Sir John Buchanan Riddell, ninth Baronet, M.P. for the Burghs of Selkirk, Lanark, etc., who in 1805 married Frances, eldest daughter of Charles, Earl of Romney, and grand-daughter of Charles, Earl of Egremont. He died in April 1829.—Burke's *Peerage*.

1800

To JAMES BALLANTYNE [1]

CASTLE STREET, 22d *April*, 1800

DEAR SIR,—I have your favour, since the receipt of which some things have occurred which induce me to postpone my intention of publishing my ballads, particularly a letter from a friend, assuring me that "The Tales of Wonder" are actually in the printer's hand.[2] In this situation I endeavour to strengthen my small stock of patience, which has been nearly exhausted by the delay of this work, to which (though for that reason alone) I almost regret having promised assistance. I am still resolved to have recourse to your press for the Ballads of the Border, which are in some forwardness.

I have now to request your forgiveness for mentioning a plan which your friend Gillon and I have talked over together with a view as well to the public advantage as to your individual interest. It is nothing short of a migration from Kelso to this place, which I think might be effected upon a prospect of a very flattering nature.

Three branches of printing are quite open in Edinburgh, all of which I am well convinced you have both the ability and inclination to unite in your person. The first is that of an editor of a newspaper, which shall

[1] This is the first mooting of the connection with the Ballantynes in business. The Gillon referred to was "Joseph Gillon . . . a solicitor of some eminence ; a man of strong abilities and genuine wit and humour, for whom Scott, as well as Ballantyne, had a warm regard. The intemperate habits alluded to at the close of Scott's letter gradually undermined his business, his health, and his character ; and he was glad, on leaving Edinburgh . . . to obtain a humble situation about the House of Lords—in which he died."—LOCKHART.

[2] But in May Lewis writes that "only 17 Ballads are yet printed out of 60."

contain something of a uniform historical deduction of events, distinct from the farrago of detached and unconnected plagiarisms from the London paragraphs of "The Sun." Perhaps it might be possible (and Gillon has promised to make inquiry about it) to treat with the proprietors of some established paper—suppose the Caledonian Mercury—and we would all struggle to obtain for it some celebrity. To this might be added a "Monthly Magazine," and "Caledonian Annual Register," if you will ; for both of which, with the excellent literary assistance which Edinburgh at present affords, there is a fair opening. The next object would naturally be the execution of Session papers, the best paid work which a printer undertakes, and of which, I dare say, you would soon have a considerable share ; for as you make it your business to superintend the proofs yourself, your education and abilities would insure your employers against the gross and provoking blunders which the poor composers are often obliged to submit to. The publication of works, either ancient or modern opens a third fair field for ambition. The only gentleman who attempts anything in that way is in very bad health ; nor can I, at any rate, compliment either the accuracy or the execution of his press. I believe it is well understood, that with equal attention an Edinburgh press would have superior advantages even to those of the metropolis ; and though I would not advise launching into that line at once, yet it would be easy to feel your way by occupying your press in this manner on vacant days only.

It appears to me that such a plan, judiciously adopted and diligently pursued, opens a fair road to an ample fortune. In the meanwhile, the "Kelso Mail" might be so arranged as to be still a source of some advantage to you ; and I dare say, if wanted, pecuniary assistance might be procured to assist you at the outset, either upon terms of a share or otherwise ; but I refer you for particulars to Joseph, in whose room I am now assuming

I   G

the pen, for reasons too distressing to be declared, but
at which you will readily guess. I hope, at all events,
you will impute my interference to anything rather than
an impertinent intermeddling with your concerns on the
part of, dear Sir, your obedient servant,

WALTER SCOTT

[Lockhart]

To UNKNOWN CORRESPONDENT

DEAR SIR,—I have had before the Committee the very
extraordinary process commenced agst you & Pillons [?]
for riding upon Leith Links wh: was put into my hands
by Mr. Mowbray. As he consider[s] the sentence as
highly improper & considerably aggravated by the mode
in which the Action has been conducted on the part of
the prosecutors, we have to request you will upon no
account submit to payment of the fine As we consider
it further as a matter highly interesting to the honor of
the Corps, we think it our duty to request you will
permit us immediatly to bring the Case before the Court
of Session the Expence to be defrayd from the funds of
the Corps, which will be very trifling as we flatter ourselves we have have [*sic* : ? law] enough among ourselves
& will spare neither pains nor time to see our brother
Dragoons righted—We beg an answer in course & believe
me ever Yours mo: faithfully

WALTER SCOTT Secy R.E.L.D.

EDINR. 1*st June* 1800

[Abbotsford Original]

To CHARLES ERSKINE [1]

DEAR CHARLES,—The Mare came quite safe & bids
fair to answer the purpose perfectly well. Pray have the

[1] Charles Erskine, ninth Laird of Shielfield, writer in Melrose, was born
in 1771 and married Barbara, only daughter of George Pott of Todrig,

goodness to settle the price for me with the Laird—I would not willingly be *his* Debtor a minute longer than possible. I reckon on seeing you in town in the course of two or three weeks—if an earlier opportunity occurs of sending the ready I shall embrace it.

I have written to my uncle requesting him to use his interest with the Adml. on your behalf if the old Commodore is not already secured I am in hopes his application may be successful—I enclose a letter from Baird of the Excheq. which will speak for itself, pray obtain from Lang[1] the list theirin mentiond & forward the same to me wt. the form of the Rate & assessment which I shall lodge in Excheqr. agreeable to the Act. I suppose the list will be a very concise one. Many & best thanks for all your trouble about the Mare & believe me Dear Charles ever yours faithfully

WALTER SCOTT

EDINR. 19*th June* 1800

[*Curle*]

To THE DUKE OF BUCCLEUCH [1]

MY LORD DUKE,—I trust your Graces goodness which I have so often experienced in matters of greater consequence will excuse the request I am now about to make.

I have for several years availd myself of every opportunity to collect such Border Ballads as may tend to illustrate the ancient state of the Southern Counties of

---

in 1806. See later letters. He served as Scott's Sheriff-Substitute at Selkirk from 1800 till his death in 1825, when he was succeeded by William Scott, younger, of Raeburn. The Lang of this letter is John Lang, Sheriff-Clerk at Selkirk. In 1805 his place was taken by his son, Andrew Lang, born 22nd December 1783 and died 10th November 1842. This last was the grandfather of the poet, critic, historian and writer on comparative mythology and religion.

[1] Henry, third Duke of Buccleuch, who had been influential in securing for Scott the office of Sheriff-depute of Selkirkshire. The Earl of Dalkeith, afterwards Charles, fourth Duke, and his brother Lord Montague had been fellow soldiers with Scott.

Scotland & those to whom I have communicated my collection have thought that these remnants of antiquity may not be an unacceptable present to the public. I have therefore determined upon publishing a small work containing these old poems with the necessary historical illustrations—Your Grace I hope will pardon me if I say that such a work has in some degree a legitimate claim to your protection for besides your being the Chieftain of an ancient & illustrious Border Clan, there are several poems in which the exploits of your Ancestors are particularly commemorated in a strain of poetry which would do honor to a more polishd age

I can only add that my desire of dedicating this publication to your Grace (if you are pleased to honor me with your permission) is peculiarly dictated by the gratitude with which I have ever the honor of subscribing myself My Lord Duke Your Graces most respectful & much obliged humble Servt

WALTER SCOTT

EDINR. 24*th June* 1800

[*Buccleuch*]

To DR. R. ANDERSON,[1] CARE OF MR. CONSTABLE,
BOOKSELLER, CROSS, EDINBURGH.

DEAR SIR,—I this day received a letter from Mr. Jamieson [1] a friend of yours & the intended publisher of a collection of Scottish Ballads As he proposes being in Edinr. this week I hope the inclosed which I have taken the liberty of addressing to your care will find him there. I have taken the liberty of asking him to spend a day with

---

[1] Robert Anderson, M.D. (1750-1830), editor and biographer. This is Scott's first introduction to Robert Jamieson, for whom see a later note on p. 335. On 15th October Heber writes to Scott : " I understand Jamieson called on you some time ago . . . and found you beforehand with him in the greater part of the provincial poetry he had collected."—*Walpole Collection*.

me here to talk over the proposed publications & as far as possible prevent the possibility of interference.

Will you permit me to hope you will do me the favour of accompanying him   I am disengaged every day this week & the beginning of the next & a note by the penny post over night will be sufficient notice of your intended approach.   We dine at 4 but I would wish to see you early as I think Mr. Jamieson may be pleased to see some of our walks if he is not already acquainted with them. Excuse this unceremonious liberty in Dear Sir Your very faithful humble Servant   WALTER SCOTT

LASWADE COTTAGE 13 *Augt* 1800

[*Watson Collection*]

To CHARLES ERSKINE

DEAR CHARLES,—I have your two letters & am happy to see that you have some prospect of throwing light upon the mischief which has been done among the Citizens of Selkirk.   We want something of a workhouse very much

I return pro: Elliot v. Sangster You will see I have appointed the Petition to be seen & answerd.   I shall certainly be at Selkirk on the 3d. next, the Circuit is on the 6th or 7th

There begins to be once more some prospect of plenty in this country   Believe me ever Yours very faithfully

WALTER SCOTT

LASWADE COTTAGE 17 *Augt.* 1800

[*Curle*]

To CHARLES ERSKINE

DEAR CHARLES,—Some particular business has prevented me from being at Selkirk on the Head Court day as I had proposed when I last saw you.   I am the more sorry for this as I must give you the trouble of a piece of Business which I should have liked to overlook myself.

You will have the goodness with your first conveniency to cause a strict examination be made of the weights & measures in Galashiels & also in Selkirk unless the Magistrates chuse to take it on themselves to do so—Let the Pror fiscal [1] be instructed to inform agt. the Delinquents that they may be properly & handsomely fined according to their abilities : the Bakers & Butchers must be particularly attended to. The high price[s] of every necessary of life render this mode of peculation very common at present—I trust this matter to your usual care & diligence : secresy must above all be observed.

When you happen to be in Selkirk, pray remember my commission about Brydones old sword & believe me ever yours faithfully WALTER SCOTT

LASWADE COTTAGE 8*th October* 1800

[*Curle*]

[*To* CHARLES ERSKINE]

DEAR [CHARLES],[2]—I have your letter—if you find it impossible to get a Standard I will apply to the Lord Lieutenant for his concurrence to procure a set here upon the model of Those lately made for the town of Edinr. which have been adjusted by the best Mathematicians—Meanwhile *keep quiet*—Lang was I understand in the habit of making the monthly returns of grain for the County for which there is a perquisite from Excheqr. of £10, or £12, he paying all expences—

I have directed him to continue this practice as I would not have him think I mean to deprive him of any of these emoluments & I know you will not grudge it to him—

---

[1] The Procurator Fiscal is the public prosecutor of a shire or other local district in Scotland. Acting for the Crown he conducts the preliminary inquiry into any accident, uncertified death, or other circumstance which might lead to a criminal prosecution. See *Guy Mannering*, c. x, where, however, the Sheriff conducts the inquiry in person. I understand there has been some change of practice since Scott's day, with a view to keeping the Sheriff in a more purely judicial capacity.

[2] Name cut out in MS.

The first time you are at Selkirk, will you get a sight of the Old Charter from James 5th it lies in a little odd looking Box on the top of their Charter Chest & copy for me the Inductive Clause of the grant with the date. If you cannot do this easily perhaps on granting a full rect. it may be trusted on my hands as I wish to publish it for the credit of the ancient Burgh & the refutation of those slanderers who deny its military glory. The sooner you can favour me with your attention to this little commission so much the better & more acceptable as I am about to begin to print—Excuse this trouble in Dear [Erskine] Yours faithfully

W SCOTT

18 *Octr.* 1800 LASWADE COTTAGE

Write me if you hear of a canvass in the Country & how Bowls run—this shall be *betwixt us.*

My little girl is quite recoverd of the Small pox— Peace be with the Burgh & its contentions—should these gentlemen ever get to heaven they must I suppose be quarterd in opposite corners of the firmament—

[*The remainder of the MS. has been cut off.*]

[*Craig Brown*]

TO DR. CURRIE, LIVERPOOL [1]

SIR,—I can only hope for pardon for my present intrusion from the interest which I am convinced the

[1] I print this letter, with permission, from the *Proceedings of the Hawick Archaeological Society*. Dr. Currie was editor of *The Works of Robert Burns, with an account of his Life and a Criticism on his Writings*, 1800. He died in 1805. It was Heber who, in a letter of 9th October, told Scott that Currie, whom Heber had met in Liverpool, had possibly material " from Burns's papers " which might be of use to Scott. Hence Scott's letter.
     Currie replied on the 28th November. He had not had time to make a careful examination of the Burns MSS. " The unfortunate bard never arranged his papers." Among the poems sent to him there are, however, some ballads : " O wha will lace my stays " ; Young Hunting ; " There won'd three ladies in a Bower " ; Auld Ingram ; Lady Mazery ; " What aileth ye my doctor Dysmall " ; The Battle of Corrichie on the Hill of Fair, Oct. 28, 1662 ; The Laird of Lamington ; Clerk Sanders. " There is

Biographer of Burns cannot fail to take in the success of any attempt to promote the cause of Scottish literature. It is not, I believe, entirely unknown to you that I have been for some time engaged in forming a collection of ancient Scottish Ballads, chiefly such as relate to the Border Counties or are popular in that part of Scotland. In this pursuit I have been more successful than at first I durst have ventured to hope, and have recovered many valuable originals. I am induced, however, to believe (from some passages in the interesting correspondence of Burns) that our late lamented Bard may have had among his numerous collection of Scottish songs some of the description I am in search of. I do not mean entirely to limit my collection to the Riding Ballads, as they are called in our country, those namely which relate to Border feuds and forays; but, on the contrary, to admit Scottish Ballads of merit upon romantic and popular subjects, provided they have been hitherto unpublished; indeed, my second volume will consist chiefly of the latter class.

It would confer a particular favour upon a stranger who is ambitious of the acquaintance of Dr. Currie if he would have the politeness when more important avocations will permit to inform him whether any materials for such a work could be recovered from the papers of Mr. Burns, and whether, if that be the case, it would be consistent with the plans of the Trustees to grant copies for the enlarging and improvement of such a work as I have described. My enthusiasm in this hobby horsical pursuit having led me thus to overstep the usual bounds of form, I cannot conclude without expressing my

also Rob Roy's address to his mistress whom he had carried off by force; Lochmaben Harper; Fair Janet; 'There was a maid as I heard say'; The Lads of Wamphray, an old Border Ballad." "I have read," Currie continues, your 'green Ladies.' It is a very noble poem." By the Green Ladies Currie means *Glenfinlas, or Lord Ronald's Coronach*, which Scott contributed to Lewis' *Tales of Wonder*, which appeared in 1801, printed, not by Ballantyne at Kelso (as is often asserted), but by W. Bulmer & Co., Cleveland Road, London. Currie's letter is in the National Library.

reverence for the man who has hung the last garland upon the grave of the first of Scotland's poetical sons. I have the honour to be, Sir, Your most Obedient Servant

WALTER SCOTT, Advocate

18th Oct., 1800. EDINBURGH

[Hawick Arch. Soc.]

TO CHARLES ERSKINE

DEAR ERSKINE,—I am concernd to observe by your last the very violent effervescence of the political disputes at Selkirk With these we have however nothing to do, unless to prevent any breach of public peace & order.— The Bail which may be demanded by the late Act is £1200 for a Nobleman £600 for a landed gentleman £300 for any other Gentleman Burgess or Householder & £60 for any inferior person—You must [illegible] the Bail within 24 hours after a petition has been lodged to that effect— As no blows seem to have been given I think the Bail should be moderate this you will arrange according to the mans circumstances & situation in Life, & the atrocity of the assault—You will forward the precognition to me without delay—that I may consider what is to be done— I beg you will intimate to those whom it may concern that if any more of these violent proceedings take place, my hand will fall heavy upon the perpetrators be they of what party they may, & I recommend it particularly to your attention to look after the quiet of the place till these elections are over—Believe me Dear Erskine Ever yours faithfully

WALTER SCOTT

EDINR. 21 Octr. 1800

[Curle]

To CHARLES ERSKINE

DEAR ERSKINE,—Your letter with the old Charters came safe to hand they shall be taken particular care of & be ready for you at the time you mention being in Town. I [am] much obliged to the Magistrates for the trouble I have given them.

I shall be glad if the party squabble is made up without recurring to judicial decision & I shall be still better pleased if there is no county Contest—Surely Selkirkshire has suffered sufficiently from such feuds.

I am not much given to be rigorous in exacting dues, particularly in the case of Mr. Pringle I should not wish from personal motives to be thought exorbitant. At the same time I suppose Mr. Gibson would not think of lowering his own dues for taking an Infeftment, because a former Notary had been paid for making out an inept Sasine. Mr. Pringles proper claim would be upon the heirs of Mr. Plummer or Mr. Cockburn as he cannot expect that we should put the blunders of his Agents to rights gratuitously. I shall however have no objection to compound upon reasonable terms & leave it to you to settle matters with Mr. Gibson for yourself & me *secundum bonum et aequum.* Whatever you do I shall be well satisfied with.

The melancholy loss of poor Willie Scott of Woollie in the Queen [?] Indiaman has shocked us all very much. Believe me ever Yours faithfully

WALTER SCOTT

COTTAGE LASWADE 2*d. Novr.* 1800—

Remember the Weights & measures

[*Curle*]

To CHARLES ERSKINE

DEAR CHARLES—I received your packet which I am sorry to find contains fresh instances of folly and absurdity on the part of the Selkirk people—Who ever heard of a Sheriff Judging in a case of Scandal—if they wish to empty their stomachs of gall & their pockets of money in Gods name have they not the Commissary court?[1] No consent of parties can extend the Jurisdiction of a Judge to causes from which he is excluded by express Law.— The Pror. fiscal is certainly bound to lend his name to every private prosecutor who brings forward a cause competent to the court, for example if Riddle had laid his action as for an assault which would have rendered it cognisable in my Court. But he cannot be compelled to lend his authority to a complaint which is ex facie exclusively proper to the Decision of the Commissaries. You will understand he has nothing to do with the merits of the cause but solely with the regularity or incompetency of the Complaint.

You will see I have thrown out the action—I have deliverd your letter to Gillon this morning Ever yours

WALTER SCOTT

EDINR. 4th Decr. 1800

[Curle]

[1] Scott was wrong on the point of law. The Sheriff *could* try an action for scandal, but might not order a public palinode or recantation which Riddle had demanded, declaring that Henderson had described him as " Damned Liar, Damned Villian and Scounderal and Blackguard."— JOHN CHISHOLM, *Sir Walter Scott as Judge*, 1918.

1801

TO BISHOP PERCY [1]

My Lord,—I shall not trouble your Lordship with an attempt to express the pleasure I felt at the receipt of the letter with which you honoured me, because the task would be equally difficult to me, and disagreeable to your Lordship.

Were I to compare it to any thing, it would be to the sensation I felt when the Reliques of Ancient Poetry were first put into my hands, an era in my poetical taste which I shall never forget.

The very grass sod seat to which (when a boy of twelve years old) I retreated from my playfellows, to devour the works of the ancient minstrels, is still fresh and dear to my memory. That you are pleased to approve of my intended work, will prove to me an additional stimulus in the execution. An early partiality to the tales of my country, and an intimate acquaintance with its wildest recesses,

[1] My attention was called to this letter by Mr. Glen. In the third paragraph Scott describes the same experience as he recorded later in his fragment of Autobiography : " It was beneath a huge platanus tree, in the ruins of what had been intended for an old-fashioned arbour in the garden I have mentioned. The summer day sped onwards so fast, that notwithstanding the sharp appetite of thirteen, I forgot the hour of dinner, was sought for with anxiety, and was still found entranced in my intellectual banquet. To read and to remember was in this instance the same thing, &c." The garden was at Kelso, so that the playfellows were not the High School boys. Percy had replied to an earlier letter from Scott, not now extant, regretting that his attention to graver subjects had impaired his taste and judgment for these things, and " still more unfortunately I lost a great part of my black-letter collections in the fire that happened at Northumberland House in London in 1780." From what remains his nephew is meditating a selection for a fourth volume of the " Reliques." His Border ballads relate chiefly to the English side of the Border, which will make Scott's collection all the more interesting by contrast. " I shall be very glad to oblige you by procuring you the Ballad on the escape of the Earl of Westmoreland which you desire, but it is a very poor dull performance."

acquired partly in the course of country sports, and partly in pursuit of antiquarian knowledge, will, I hope, enable me at least to preserve some of the most valuable traditions of the south of Scotland, both historical and romantic.

My want of knowledge and experience in these pursuits will, I hope, be in some measure supplied by the enthusiasm with which I have pursued my object, and the obscure path through which I have traced it.

I am very much obliged to your Lordship for the urbanity with which you have offered me a copy of the Earl of Westmoreland's escape ; but, under the circumstances you mention, I can have no wish to give your Lordship's amanuensis the trouble of transcribing it upon my account. On the contrary (did I not think that Mr. Percy's own researches must be far more accurate than mine), I would with pride contribute to the 4th vol. of the Reliques such particulars regarding the " Rising in the North Countrye " as I had arranged, with a view to some notices in my own publication ; and if this would be acceptable, your Lordship has only to give a hint to that purpose.

I have published (that is, printed) in the Minstrelsy of the Scottish Border, the Scottish account of the Battle of Otterbourne ; a ballad evidently much more modern than that published in the Reliques on the same subject.

In the notes upon the poem, I have been led to express doubt with regard to the account given in the Reliques of one of the heroes of the tale—I mean John of Agurstone —whom your Lordship, certainly not without probability, has conjectured to be one of the family of Hagerstoune, in Northumberland. At the same time, considering that the English, at the period of the battle of Otterbourne, possessed Roxburgh and Berwick, together with the intermediate fortresses on the south of the Tweed—Wark, Norham, Ford, Cornhill, Twisel, &c.—I think it unlikely that the Hagerstons could at *that time* acknowledge the

Scottish sovereignty, and am rather induced to think (*salva auctoritate tanti viri*) that the warrior was one of the Rutherfords of Edgerstone, anciently spelled Adgurstone, an ancient family, followers of the house of Douglas, and long established on the Scottish Borders, five or six miles above Jedburgh.

I am sure your Lordship's goodness and liberality will easily excuse my requesting your farther opinion on this hypothesis, although in making this request I am conscious I intrude upon time dedicated to much more valuable and important avocations.

Your Lordship may probably know my excellent and kind friend, the Marquis of Downshire, whose name I take the liberty of using as some security for my personal character ; and I flatter myself he will bear testimony, that in honouring me with an occasional continuance of your correspondence, your Lordship will not entirely misplace your favour. If there is any thing to be done here which can further the 4th vol. of the Reliques, your Lordship will honour me by commanding my best services.—I am, my Lord, your Lordship's obliged and very humble servant,   WALTER SCOTT

EDINBURGH, 11*th January* 1801.

[*Chambers's Journal*, 29 *Dec.* 1832]

To GEORGE ELLIS [1]

[*March* 27, 1801]

SIR, as I feel myself highly flattered by your inquiries, I lose no time in answering them to the best of my ability. Your eminence in the literary world, and the

---

[1] This is Lockhart's extract from the first of Scott's Letters to George Ellis (1753-1815), the founder with Canning of the *Anti-Jacobin* and an enthusiast for mediaeval antiquities and literature, though his temper is quite that of the eighteenth century. Ellis, Ritson, Douce and Richard Heber are among the antiquarians who come into Scott's correspondence while preparing his edition of *Sir Tristram*. In connection with the ballads his

warm praises of our mutual friend Heber, had made me
long wish for an opportunity of being known to you.
I enclose the first sheet of Sir Tristrem, that you may not
so much rely upon my opinion as upon that which a
specimen of the style and versification may enable your
better judgment to form for itself. . . . These pages are
transcribed by Leyden,[1] an excellent young man, of
uncommon talents, patronised by Heber, and who is of
the utmost assistance to my literary undertakings.

[*Lockhart*]

correspondents are especially Robert Surtees and James Ellis of Otter-
bourne. Unfortunately I have not been able to trace the letters of Scott
to George Ellis except one in the collection of Mr. Owen D. Young, of New
York, and another in the collection of Sir Alfred J. Law. I can print only
Lockhart's extracts. In the National Library is preserved a volume of
Ellis's letters and a few in loose form. I cite them occasionally to illustrate
Scott's.

   [1] The early life of John Leyden illustrates well what use could be made
by a man of great ability or genius and greater determination of the
opportunities for education afforded in Scotland even to the humblest for
he was *not* entirely self-educated. Born of humble parents in 1775, taught
to read from the Bible by his grandmother, he was sent to the village school
at the age of nine. His striking abilities pointing to the Church, he
received some special training in Latin and Greek from a Cameronian
minister, and entered Edinburgh University in 1790. There he studied
till 1797, and after a year in St. Andrews was licensed in 1798. Availing
himself of the free admission to classes allowed to candidates for the ministry,
he extended his knowledge in all directions, including natural science and
some elements of medicine, while indulging his antiquarian and linguistic
tastes in his private studies. By 1794 he was contributing poems, mainly
translations from various languages, to the *Edinburgh Magazine*, and had
acquired the friendship of Robert Anderson, the editor of that paper as
well as of a collection of the British poets. As he formed the acquaintance
of Constable the publisher, Richard Heber the collector and others,
Leyden's literary activities increased, and he published in 1799 *A Historical
and Philosophical Sketch of the Discoveries and Settlements of the Europeans in
Northern and Western Africa at the close of the Eighteenth Century.* Introduced
to Scott by Heber, he threw himself passionately into the quest for old
ballads, of which he had always been a lover. Failing to get a parish he
contemplated exploring, under the African Association which had sent
Mungo Park on his travels. Scott and others came to the rescue, and
through William Dundas of the Board of Control an appointment was
found for him in India, one which required a medical qualification.
Reviving his earlier studies Leyden quickly qualified as a surgeon in
Edinburgh and secured an M.D. from the complaisant University of St.
Andrews. In December 1802 he journeyed to London, being ordered to sail

To GEORGE ELLIS

LASSWADE COTTAGE, 20th *April*, 1801

My DEAR SIR,—I should long ago have acknowledged your instructive letter,[1] but I have been wandering about in the wilds of Liddesdale and Ettrick Forest, in search of additional materials for the Border Minstrelsy. I cannot, however, boast much of my success. One of our best reciters has turned religious in his later days, and finds out that old songs are unlawful. If so, then, as Falstaff says, is many an acquaintance of mine damned. I now send you an accurate analysis of Sir Tristrem. Philo-Tomas, whoever he was, must surely have been an Englishman ; when his hero joins battle with Moraunt, he exclaims—

" God help Tristrem the Knight,
    He fought for Ingland."

This strain of national attachment would hardly have proceeded from a Scottish author, even though he had laid his scene in the sister country. In other respects the language appears to be Scottish, and certainly contains the essence of Tomas's work. . . . You shall have Sir Otuel in a week or two, and I shall be happy to compare your Romance of Merlin with our *Arthur and Merlin*, which is a very good poem, and may supply you with

for India on the *Hindostan*. Delayed by ill-health he escaped the wreck of that ship and enjoyed for three months the friendship of George Ellis, Richard Heber, Lord Castlereagh, the Marquis of Abercorn and others. He sailed for India on the *Hugh Inglis* in April 1803. His life there, his study of Indian and other languages, do not concern us here. Scott will be found writing to him, and deploring deeply his death at Puloo Penang, in Batavia, in 1811. His work before leaving Scotland includes, besides the work on Africa, contributions to the *Minstrelsy of the Scottish Border*, an edition of the *Complaynt of Scotland* (1801), *Scottish Descriptive Poems* (1802), a collection with notes, and various poems of which the most popular was *Scenes of Infancy* (1803), a long descriptive and reflective poem in the usual couplet form. He was too indifferent to form, too eager and hasty, to leave any work of great, purely literary merit.

[1] Probably a letter of 2nd April, in which Ellis gives his views concerning Tomas and other topics.

some valuable additions. . . . I would very fain lend
your elephant *a lift*,[1] but I fear I can be of little use to
you. I have been rather an observer of detached facts
respecting antiquities, than a regular student. At the
same time, I may mention one or two circumstances,
were it but to place your elephant upon a tortoise. From
Selkirkshire to Cumberland, we have a ditch and bulwark
of great strength, called the Catrail,[2] running north and
south, and obviously calculated to defend the western
side of the island against the inhabitants of the eastern
half. Within this bulwark, at Drummelzier, near Peebles,
we find the grave of Merlin, the account of whose madness
and death you will find in Fordun.[3] The same author
says he was seized with his madness during a dreadful
battle on the Liddle, which divides Cumberland from
Scotland. All this seems to favour your ingenious hypothesis, that the sway of the British Champion [Arthur]
extended over Cumberland and Strathcluyd, as well as

[1] Lockhart cites from a letter of 1830 to William Brockedon, author of
the *Passes of the Alps*. " My friend the late George Ellis, one of the most
accomplished scholars and delightful companions whom I have ever
known, . . . used to tell me an anecdote of the eminent antiquary General
Melville, who was crossing the Alps, with Livy and other historical accounts
in his post-chaise, determined to follow the route of Hannibal. He met
Ellis . . . and pushed onwards . . . after a day spent with his brother
antiquary. After journeying more slowly than his friend, Ellis was
astonished to meet General Melville coming back. ' What is the matter,
my dear friend ? How come you back on the journey you had so much at
heart ? '—' Alas ! ' said Melville very dejectedly, ' I would have got over
myself well enough, but I could not get my *elephants* over the pass.' He
had, in idea, Hannibal with his train of elephants in his party. It became
a sort of bye-word between Ellis and me ; and in assisting each other
during a close correspondence of some years, we talked of a lift to the
elephants." I suppose Scott means especially the giving of assistance to
the support of a favourite hypothesis, such as Scott's regarding the influence
of Tomas on the French romantic poets.

[2] " A thousand thanks for your hints about the Catrail. My Elephants
are now in high spirits. I am now determined to *convince* the world . . . that
the French minstrels borrowed very many (though certainly not all) of their
legends concerning Arthur's Knights from the minstrels of the ' north
country.' Ritson will break my head but I dont care."—ELLIS, May 1801.

[3] Scott is referring to the *Scotichronicon* of John of Fordun, author or
part author of that work in the fourteenth century.

Wales.   Ercildoune is hardly five miles from Catrail.

. . .

Leyden has taken up a most absurd resolution to go to
Africa on a journey of discovery. Will you have the
goodness to beg Heber to write to him seriously on so
ridiculous a plan, which can promise nothing either
pleasant or profitable. I am certain he would get a
church in Scotland with a little patience and prudence,
and it gives me great pain to see a valuable young man of
uncommon genius and acquirements fairly throw himself
away. Yours truly,

W. SCOTT

[*Lockhart*]

To GEORGE ELLIS

MUSSELBURGH, 11*th May*, 1801

. . . I CONGRATULATE you upon the health of your
elephants—as an additional mouthful of provender for
them, pray observe that the tale of Sir Gawain's Foul
Ladie, in Percy's Reliques, is originally Scaldic, as you will
see in the history of Hrolfe Kraka, edited by Torfæus
from the ancient Sagas regarding that prince. I think
I could give you some more crumbs of information were
I at home ; but I am at present discharging the duties
of quartermaster to a regiment of volunteer cavalry—an
office altogether inconsistent with romance ; for where
do you read that Sir Tristrem weighed out hay and corn ;
that Sir Lancelot du Lac distributed billets ; or that any
Knight of the Round Table condescended to higgle
about a truss of straw ? Such things were left for our
degenerate days, when no warder sounds his horn from
the barbican as the *preux chevalier* approaches to claim
hospitality.—Bugles indeed we have ; but it is only to
scream us out of bed at five in the morning—hospitality
such as the seneschals of Don Quixote's castles were
wont to offer him—and all to troopers, to whom, for

valour eke and courtesy, Major Sturgeon himself might yield the palm. In the midst of this scene of motley confusion, I long, like the hart for water-brooks, for the arrival of your *grande opus.* The nature of your researches animates me to proceed in mine (though of a much more limited and local nature), even as iron sharpeneth iron. I am in utter despair about some of the hunting terms in *Sir Tristrem.* There is no copy of Lady Juliana Berners' [1] work in Scotland, and I would move heaven and earth to get a sight of it. But as I fear this is utterly impossible, I must have recourse to your friendly assistance and communicate a set of doubts and queries, which, if any man in England can satisfy, I am well assured it must be you. You may therefore expect, in a few days, another epistle. Meantime I must invoke the spirit of Nimrod.

[*Lockhart*]

To GEORGE ELLIS

EDINBURGH, 10*th June*, 1801

MY DEAR SIR,—A heavy family misfortune, the loss of an only sister [2] in the prime of life, has prevented, for some

---

[1] " The last book from Caxton's press is well known under the title of the *Book of St. Albans.* It contains three treatises, the first on hawking, the second on hunting, and the last on coat-armour or heraldry. Much has been written on the authorship of this book, which is probably not all from one hand. The part on hunting, which is in verse, ends with the words ' Explicit Dam Julyana Barneys in her boke of huntyng,' and this is generally considered to refer to a somewhat mythical Juliana Berners, traditionally prioress of the nunnery of Sopwell near St Albans &c."— *Cambridge History of Literature,* ii. 318.

[2] " I had an only sister, Anne Scott, who seemed to be from her cradle the butt for mischance to shoot arrows at."—SCOTT's *Autobiography.* He goes on to tell of her hand being injured by the gate of the George Square garden ; her being nearly drowned in an old quarry-hole ; and her cap accidentally taking fire. " After a lingering and dangerous illness she recovered but never to enjoy perfect health. . . . At length in 1801 poor Anne was taken ill and died after a very short interval . . . she was at heart an affectionate and kind girl, neither void of talent nor of feeling, though living in an ideal world which she had framed to herself by the force of imagination." She was buried on the 25th May in Greyfriars' Churchyard.

time, my proposed communication regarding the hunting terms of *Sir Tristrem*. I now enclose the passage, accurately copied, with such explanations as occur to myself, subject always to your correction and better judgment. . . . I have as yet had only a glance of *The Specimens*. Thomson,[1] to whom Heber intrusted them, had left them to follow him from London in a certain trunk, which has never yet arrived. I should have quarrelled with him excessively for making so little allowance for my impatience, had it not been that a violent epidemic fever, to which I owe the loss already mentioned, has threatened also to deprive me, in his person, of one of my dearest friends, and the Scottish literary world of one of its most promising members.

Some prospect seems to open for getting Leyden out to India, under the patronage of Mackintosh, who goes as chief of the intended academical establishment at Calcutta. That he is highly qualified for acting a distinguished part in any literary undertaking, will be readily granted ; nor do I think Mr. Mackintosh will meet with many half so likely to be useful in the proposed institution. The extent and versatility of his talents would soon raise him to his level, even although he were at first to go out in a subordinate department. If it be in your power to second his application, I rely upon Heber's interest with you to induce you to do so.

[*Lockhart*]

To CHARLES ERSKINE

[*4th July*, 1801]

DEAR CHARLES,—I return you the processes betw. Sanderson & Walker. I rather suspect both parties are

---

[1] Ellis's *Specimens of Early English Metrical Romances* (1805). Thomas Thomson, Scott's early friend, "the first legal antiquary of our time" (Lockhart), an elder brother of the painter John Thomson of Duddingston. In 1806 (see Vol. I. p. 284) he was appointed Deputy Chief Register of Scotland. See, *inter alia*, Florence MacCunn's *Sir Walter Scott's Friends*, 1909.

rascals—A document has been sent me rather irregularly. I do not however rest the decision upon it as Walker has an undoubted right to manage for his nephew during his minority—

I shall be in Selkirkshire immediatly after the races to make some stay. I think of taking up my head-quarters at White Banklee [1] where I suppose they can give my servants myself & horses decent accommodation. As I intend to ride a great deal I hope I shall have fine weather   Yours faithfully

W. SCOTT

In the course of your rides I wish you would give a call at Whitebanklee. I should wish to give a piece of money, so much a week for my accomodation so that I may drink what I please &c.

[LASWADE]

[*Curle*]

TO GEORGE ELLIS

EDINBURGH, 13th July, 1801 [2]

... I AM infinitely obliged to you, indeed, for your interference in behalf of our Leyden, who, I am sure, will

---

[1] Mr. William Pringle of Hillside, Lingfield, Surrey, tells me that " Whyt-banklee, known as Whytebanklee Cottages, was the original Clovenfords Inn. After the stage coaches between Edinburgh and Carlisle ceased running it was found that with the loss of the principal trade a small house would suffice. The licence was accordingly transferred to a small house at the corner which had been previously occupied by the village joiner and is now the post-office. . . . The original inn was then turned into two dwelling houses . . . known as Whytebanklee Cottages and remained as such till 1901 when it . . . became the Clovenfords Hotel. Sir Walter Scott made his headquarters at the Inn in 1799 . . . ere he went to Ashestiel . . . and the room he slept in there has often been shown me."

[2] Between this and the next extract, 7th December, there must have been at least one other letter of Scott's and one illustrating his strange habit of misdating his letters, for on the 2nd October Ellis writes to him : " judge of the pleasure I must have felt at reading on the 29th of September a letter to be written by you on the 24th of October. Whether that letter was written by yourself in your natural shape or in the inspired character of

do credit to your patronage, and may be of essential
service to the proposed mission. What a difference from
broiling himself, or getting himself literally broiled, in
Africa. " Que diable vouloit-il faire dans cette galère ? "
. . . His brother is a fine lad, and is likely to enjoy some
advantages which he wanted—I mean by being more
early introduced into society. I have intermitted his
transcript of *Merlin*, and set him to work on *Otuel*, of
which I send a specimen.

[*Lockhart*]

To DR. CURRIE

MY DEAR SIR,—I have to acknowledge with my best
thanks your very interesting packet [1] which I received as

Moy, whether Ritson has actually been with you, or whether the events
you relate as past are in fact to come is a matter of indifference to me as a
mere chronological question, &c." On the 14th Ellis acknowledges a
letter of the 9th and says : " I shall look forward with no small anxiety
to the moment when the border minstrelsy shall arrive and am afraid that
their appearance may realize the farce of *three weeks after marriage* and
produce a family dispute for I certainly shall not be so uxorious as to suffer
their contents should be enjoyed without my participation." He will add
his name to the list of subscribers to Campbell's intended publication ; and
he congratulates Scott on the imminent birth of a child—*i.e.* Walter, born
28th October 1801.

[1] Scott had written to Currie (see pp. 103-5 above) about the same
time as he wrote to Percy. In his reply (now in the National Library)
Currie apologises for delay ; sends a copy of Rob Roy's address to his wife,
which as not being of importance he had laid aside to await a convenient
messenger. " I have observed the use Mr Lewis made of your beautiful
poems and am sorry for it. Two volumes of Wonderful Tales selected for
no rule but that of their being wonderful do not I think make a very
judicious publication—the wonders put each other out of countenance.
I am happy you are going to intersperse your poems in your projected
publication where they will appear to much greater advantage when
relieved by the real language of manners and poetry of the ' Olden times.'
The song of ' Evan Banks ' was not written by Burns. It was written by
Helen Maria Williams. Who really wrote the Flowers of the Forest ? . . .
I am glad you have a copy of the old ballad ' I wish I were where Helen
lies.' I have seen the tomb of the lover Fleming a thousand times."
Two ballads on Rob Roy's abduction of his wife are among the Abbotsford ballad papers now in this library, two versions of the same. The one
is given in full ; the other in part with a summary of the rest. The former

I was upon the point of leaving town ; a circumstance which I regretted as it prevented my having an opportunity of waiting upon the Gentleman who took the trouble of delivering it, & offerring him any little civility in my power. The song of Rob Roy (as you readily conjectured) is not at all to my purpose. I was very much interested indeed by your anecdote of the drowning traveller so affecting in itself & so strikingly told. I intend to mention the incident in a little note subjoind to [*MS. torn here*] Annan Water [1] which is unfortunately

is headed " Rob Roy, an antient ballad.   Tune, Gipsy Laddie " ; the latter simply " Tune, a rude set of Mill, Mill O."   The first verse runs :

> Rob Roy from the Highlands came
>   unto the lallan border
> To steal awa a gay ladie
>   To haud his house in order :
> He cam owre the lough o' Lin,
>   Twenty men his arms did carry ;
> Himself gaed in and fand her out
>   protesting he would marry.

Both versions contain two lines that struck Scott's imagination and were made use of in his letters :

> He was a hedge unto his friends ;
> A heckle to his foes, Lady.

With the second version goes, on the third page of the sheet, a copy of a letter from Burns, which had accompanied the ballad, addressed to Mr. Tytler, Senr., Young Street.   At the end of this is written :

> " from the original in my possession "
>   A. CONSTABLE
>   July 1817

[1] In the introduction to that ballad in the *Minstrelsy* we read accordingly : " The Editor trusts he will be pardoned for inserting the following awfully impressive account of such an event, contained in a letter from Dr. Currie of Liverpool, by whose correspondence . . . he has been alike honoured and instructed.   After stating that he had some recollection of the ballad which follows, the biographer of Burns proceeds thus : ' I once in my early days heard (for it was night, and I could not see) a traveller drowning ; not in the Annan itself, but in the Frith of Solway, close by the mouth of that river.   The influx of the tide had unhorsed him, in the night, as he was passing the sands from Cumberland.   The west wind blew a tempest, and, according to the common expression, brought in the water *three foot abreast*. The traveller got upon a standing net, a little way from the shore.   There he lashed himself to the post, shouting for half an hour for assistance— till the tide rose over his head. . . .   No one could go to his assistance—no one knew where he was—the sound seemed to proceed from the spirit of

[*MS. torn here*] very striking. I wish it had possessd more of that locality which I account among the highest graces of which the old Ballad is susceptible, but as this is not the case I have made it an invariable rule to attempt no improvements upon the genuine Ballads which I have been able to recover. It will be necessary for me to be more particular in this respect because I shall give to the public many songs which have never before been publishd & some of which perhaps it may be now difficult to produce the Reciters. Indeed as our old Sennachies are yearly dying out & as the present generation " care little for these things " the sources of traditionary knowledge are fast drying up. Since my recollection Songs which I have often heard recited have been entirely forgotten. It is however my intention to produce my authorities in as many cases as possible although doubtless as [in] the course of ten & more years I have been a ballad collector, some facts may have escaped my recollection. I mention all this because having been guilty of the sin of rhyming & being therefore a suspicious person I have no doubt that many people may be ready enough to suppose that I have interpolated my originals—an accusation which whenever it may be made, will I do [*MS. torn here*] be totally unmerited. Still no [*MS. torn here*] Heber, I suppose he has met with some sale catalogue in his journey which would possess as to him all the attractions of Sindbads mountain of Adamant. I shall be content to pray for his disenchantment & his speedy arrival in Caledonia.

the waters. But morning rose—the tide had ebbed—and the poor traveller was found lashed to the pole of the net, and bleaching in the wind.' "

This incident was doubtless in Scott's mind when he described the escape from drowning of Sir Arthur Wardour and his daughter, for he uses the same phrase : " The tide will be running on Halket-head by this time like the Fall of Fyers. . . . It was coming in three feet abreast." So again in *Redgauntlet* : " He that dreams on the bed of the Solway may wake in the next world. The sky threatens a blast that will bring in the waves three feet abreast." Moreover, from the Solway one might see the sun sink in the sea, not from the coast of Forfarshire.

You have excited my curiosity (a very inflammable part of my constitution) very strongly by your hint about the Welch & Scottish apparitions. It was truly tantalizing to say so much and then to stop short : let me hope at a leisure hour you will favour me (I am you know an initiated Ghost-Seer) with the mysterious communication. Ghosts like many other things have of late been put out of fashion by a promiscuous & ill-judged introduction of tales relating to them. I differ from many of my contemporary Ghost-raisers upon this subject. I think the Marvellous in poetry is ill-timed & disgusting when not managed with moderation & ingrafted upon some circumstance of popular tradition or belief which sometimes can give even to the improbable an air of something like probability. I have not attempted lately any thing of the kind—One ballad I did begin but was not able to conclude it to my mind so it is with [?] [*MS. torn here*] the story of the Bear & Fiddle   Should I ever [*MS. torn here*] your acceptance of a copy & that you will favour me with your criticisms—

From all the enquiries I have been able to make I now understand Miss Elliot to be the Authoress of the words of the Flowers of the Forest excepting the burden

"Our braw foresters are a' wede away"

Miss Elliot says she has heard some lines of the old Dirge, particularly one which I think singularly pathetic

"I ride single on my saddle
Since our braw foresters are a' wede away"

Such are the only particulars I have been able to procure concerning this celebrated song   Miss Elliot [1] transmitted them to me thro' Somerville the historian but requested that her name might be conceald which I think somewhat prudish—I congratulate you on the success of Burns works. What subject for regret that the Bard cannot

[1] Jane Elliot (1727-1805), daughter of Sir Gilbert Elliot, first Earl of Minto, wrote the song in 1756.

share in the benefit procured by the exertions of such a freind. But poor Burns was doomd to be unfortunate. Believe me ever Dear Sir Your obliged & faithful Servt.

WALTER SCOTT

LASWADE COTTAGE 30 *July* 1801

[*Glen*]

To J. HANDLEY, CLERKENWELL, LONDON

SIR,—I have received your favour of the 10 Nov advising me that the Marchioness of Dounshire had received a packet addressed to the late Marquis [1] covering certain Certificates for the use of his sister Mrs Scott. I presume the proper mode of conveying them will be by an Indorsation by the Marquis' Executors altho' I am little acquainted with the forms of the English law. Upon the opposite side you will find an order subscribed both by my wife & by me for delivering the papers to Mr Dumergue Piccadilly or to his order. If you have occasion to mention this transaction to the Marchioness I beg you will have the goodness to express to her Ladyship how sensible we are of her attention & how deeply we join the universal regret excited by the late most unexpected & melancholy event.[2] I hope this will not be deemd an intrusion on the part of one who tho' personally unknown to her Ladyship was honoured by the friendship & protection of the late Marquis. It may be proper to add that his Lordship was one of Mrs Scott's trustees appointed by her Marriage settlement in conjunction with Mr Slade of Doctors Commons—About £1512 stock was purchased in 1799 on my wife's account in the £3 per cent Consols I am not sure whether in the name of the Marqs or of the Messrs Drummonds his Bankers. If the former be the case some reconveyance may be necessary to vest the stock in the person of Mr Dumergue or of Mr Slade Mrs Scott has made choice

[1] From Charles Carpenter.   [2] Lord D. died 7th September 1801.

of the former to supply her late noble protector in the
Trust. I remain Sir with thanks to your attention Your
very obedient servant   WALTER SCOTT

EDINR. 15 *Nov* 1801

[*Glen*]

TO GEORGE ELLIS [1]

EDINBURGH, 7*th* [8*th*] *December*, 1801

. . . MY literary amusements have of late been much
retarded and interrupted, partly by professional avocations, and partly by removing to a house newly furnished,[2]
where it will be some time before I can get my few books
put into order, or clear the premises of painters and
workmen ; not to mention that these worthies do not
nowadays proceed upon the plan of Solomon's architects,
whose saws and hammers were not heard, but rather
upon the more ancient system of the builders of Babel.
To augment this confusion, my wife has fixed upon this
time as proper to present me with a fine chopping boy,
whose pipe, being of the shrillest, is heard amid the storm,
like a boatswain's whistle in a gale of wind. These
various causes of confusion have also interrupted the
labours of young Leyden on your behalf ; but he has
again resumed the task of transcribing *Arthour,* of which
I once again transmit a part. I have to acknowledge,
with the deepest sense of gratitude, the beautiful analysis
of Mr. Douce's Fragments, which throws great light upon
the romance of Sir Tristrem. In arranging that, I have
anticipated your judicious hint, by dividing it into three
parts, where the story seems naturally to pause, and

---

[1] Lockhart dates 7th.   Ellis writes " your very kind letter of the 8th."
He replies to various questions in that part of Scott's letter which Lockhart
has omitted and adds :   " All you say about Leyden is very vexatious !
Le premier pas is in his case the only one about which you can have any
uneasiness because his merit once known could not fail of making its way."
He will use all the influence he can.

[2] He was moving from South Castle Street to 39 North Castle Street.

prefixing an accurate argument, referring to the stanzas as numbered.

I am glad that Mrs. Ellis and you have derived any amusement from the House of Aspen.[1] It is a very hurried dramatic sketch ; and the fifth act, as you remark, would require a total revisal previous to representation or publication. At one time I certainly thought, with my friends, that it might have ranked well enough by the side of the Castle Spectre, Bluebeard, and the other drum and trumpet exhibitions of the day ; but the *Plays of the Passions* have put me entirely out of conceit with my Germanized brat ; and should I ever again attempt dramatic composition, I would endeavour after the genuine old English model. . . . The publication of *The Complaynt* is delayed. It is a work of multifarious lore. I am truly anxious about Leyden's Indian journey, which seems to hang fire. Mr. William Dundas was so good as to promise me his interest to get him appointed Secretary to the Institution ; but whether he has succeeded or not, I have not yet learned. The various kinds of distress under which literary men, I mean such as have no other profession than letters, must labour, in a commercial country, is a great disgrace to society. I own to you I always tremble for the fate of genius when left to its own exertions, which, however powerful, are usually, by some bizarre dispensation of nature, useful to every one but themselves. If Heber could learn by Mackintosh, whether anything could be done to fix Leyden's situation, and what sort of interest would be most likely to succeed, his friends here might unite every exertion in his favour. . . . Direct Castle Street, as usual ; my new house being in the same street with my old dwelling.

[*Lockhart*]

[1] The MS. of which Heber had handed on, at Scott's request, to Ellis. Kemble had rejected it in October 1800.

1802

EDINBURGH, *8th January*, 1802

. . . Your favour arrived just as I was sitting down to write to you, with a sheet or two of *King Arthur*. I fear, from a letter which I have received from Mr. William Dundas, that the Indian Establishment is tottering, and will probably fall. Leyden has therefore been induced to turn his mind to some other mode of making his way to the East ; and proposes taking his degree as a physician and surgeon, with the hope of getting an appointment in the Company's service as surgeon. If the Institution goes forward, his having secured this step will not prevent his being attached to it ; at the same time that it will afford him a provision independent of what seems to be a very precarious establishment. Mr. Dundas has promised to exert himself. . . . I have just returned from the hospitable halls of Hamilton,[1] where I have spent the Christmas. . . .

[Lockhart]

[1] " It was in the course of this autumn (1799) that he first visited Bothwell Castle, the seat of Archibald Lord Douglas, who had married the Lady Frances Scott, sister to Henry Duke of Buccleuch ; a woman whose many amiable virtues were combined with extraordinary strength of mind, and who had, from the first introduction of the young poet at Dalkeith, formed high anticipations of his future career. Lady Douglas was one of his dearest friends through life ; and now, under her roof, he improved an acquaintance (begun also at Dalkeith) with . . . the Lady Louisa Stuart, daughter of the celebrated John Earl of Bute. These ladies, who were sisters in mind, feeling, and affection, he visited among scenes the noblest and most interesting that all Scotland can show."—LOCKHART.

The members of the family mentioned in the letter which follows in 1802 are the Duke ; Lord Archibald Hamilton, later a rather bitter Whig and opponent of the Tories and their organ the *Beacon* ; Lady Anne Hamilton, lady-in-waiting to Queen Caroline, whose *Secret History of the Court*

To LADY ANNE HAMILTON

I REGRET extremely that it was not in my power to have the parcel of pebbles ready to send to your Ladyship by Lord Belhaven—I cannot say upon the whole that I have been very successful in my search—The Cairn Gorms run from £2 „ 2 „ to £5 „ 5 „ I have chosen one of the cheapest & sent it with a dark pebble of the same size & I think superior lustre which is only a Guinea. The little packet contains also some other pebbles with the prices markd upon them. Your Ladyship will have the goodness to chuse what you wish to keep & return the others (or the whole of them if you please) with your farther instructions to your faithful & devoted Servant— I inclose a Copy of the *Entail*[1] which I found in Lord Orfords works—I hope his Grace will do me the honor to accept it with my respectful Compliments & that it will recall to his recollection the beautiful french translation of which he repeated so many lines—I also inclose some verses which Campbell has just composed [2] & which he gave me in the blotted copy—they are I think ex-

(1832), published in her name but without her sanction, created rather a scandal ; and Lady Susan, who married in 1803 her cousin, the sixth Earl of Dunmore.

[1] An elegant but not very pointed fable in octosyllabics by Horace Walpole, Lord Orford : a note in pencil on the National Library copy of Lord Orford's Works (1798) suggests that the poem may be by Gray, which is not at all likely. Apparently the Duke of Hamilton had read to Scott a French translation of the verses.

[2] *Stanzas to Painting :*

O thou by whose expressive art
Her perfect image Nature sees
In union with the Graces start,
And sweeter by reflection please.

In whose creative hand the hues
Fresh from yon orient rainbow shine ;
I bless thee, Promethean Muse !
And call thee brightest of the Nine !

Possessing more than vocal power,
Persuasive more than poet's tongue, &c.

quisitely beautiful & the subject entitles them in a very
particular manner to your ladyships peculiar notice.
I dare not affirm so much for the fair Lady Susan who
I fear will be offended at the pre eminence which the
Bard has given to Painting over Music but I hope her
resentment will not extend to excluding the lines from the
honor of the *lockd Book*.   I returnd her Ladyships slippers
to Mr Murray who is to make her a pair like those she
had last.   If he is not more fortunate in his next essay
he deserves to share the fate of the unsuccessful shoemakers of the Princess of Jutland whose catastrophe is
narrated by Count Hamilton.

I have been making some notes concerning the Scotish
Law of Marriage as it presently stands which I hope may
in some degree facilitate the researches which Lord
Archibald seems disposed to make into a subject so very
interesting to the country.   There never was a period
during the history of this country apparently more
favourable to the improvement of its laws than that in
which we are now placed   The pressing & peremptory
duty of national Defences swallowd up till lately every
lesser consideration & our legislators thought as little of
amending our laws where they might be imperfect as a
sailor would do of painting his cabbin during a hurricane.
But as we are now I hope safely moord for some time &
there is surely no reason why a thorough repair should
not take place were it only to fit us to weather the next
gale.   There is at present no establishd Minister for
Scotland to throw cold water upon any measure which
might be brought forward independent of his participation.   Are we not therefore entitled to expect at this
crisis the exertions of our native Nobles whose forefathers
led us to battle for the independence of our country.   It
is an excuse often made by men of Rank for withdrawing
themselves from active political exertion, that they leave
it in the hands of those who are what is calld *bred to
business*.   By this means the natural rules of political

influence have been often inverted and the rudder of the state has been abandond to a professional Adventurer. I am so far from acquiescing in this principle that I really think, paradoxical as it may appear, important & valuable alterations in the Law of a Country are most likely to be accomplishd by those who have *not* received a professional education. The mind of the Student of Law is early bent to the existing system, the principles which he has been taught in youth become engrafted with his habits of thinking & he himself incapable of viewing with an enlightend & unprejudiced eye the beauties or defects of what he has been taught to regard as alike sacred. On the contrary an intelligent & well educated Man who brings with him to the task of surveying & amending the laws of his country a good head & a good heart will easily surmount any difficulty which may arise from his not having been bred to the legal profession. Divested of the professional *Charlatanerie* there is no particular point which such a Man as I have described might not make himself master of by a fortnights study. I may mention in illustration of what I have said that the famous system of Naval Tactics [1] which comprehended so many important discoveries was written by a Man who never was at sea in his life.— How ardently would I join the general acclamations of applause should a brother of your Ladyships be disposed to take that distinguishd share in managing the affairs of Scotland to which his birth & talents so well entitle him ; & so to gain a civic wreath as glorious in the eye of Reason & philosophy as those which were gatherd by his ancestors upon the field of battle.—Here have I been led into a long *tirade* but your Ladyship knows that there

[1] John Clerk of Eldin : *An Essay on Naval Tactics, systematical and historical.* 1790-97. Clerk was the father of Scott's friend, William Clerk. " This elderly man sailing his miniature boats on an artificial pond had the reputation of having revolutionised naval warfare. All Scotland, at any rate, was convinced that Rodney owed his victories to careful study of Clerk's *Naval Tactics* "—MacCunn : *Sir Walter Scott's Friends.* 1909.

are some subjects upon which I can neither *think speak* nor *write* with sang froid. But I must hasten to relieve your Ladyship My most respectful homage attends the Goddess of the Vale of Clyde I hope she sometimes recollects the poetical critique which I had the honor to offer at her shrine— To Lord Archd I beg to be respectfully rememberd I hope his indisposition is quite gone— I am just interrupted by a visit from the Hero of Copenhagen[1] He has promised to dine with me Tuesday to meet Campbell & Leyden. If I can keep my two poets from disputing I shall think myself cleverer than Gil Blas —I am ever Lady Anne Hamilton's very faithful & most respectful humble Servt   W Scott

EDINR 17 *Jany.* 1802

[*Nat. Lib. Scot.*]

To LADY ANNE HAMILTON

[*1st February,* 1802]

I AM honord with your Ladyships letter. How greatly do I regret that the chain which binds me to my professional oar must detain me from visiting the towers of Hamilton for at least six weeks before which time I presume they will have lost their fair Inhabitants. But if the military authority of Field Marshall the Duke of

---

[1] Probably Captain Murray, afterwards Vice-Admiral Sir George Murray, who led Nelson's squadron into the attack on the Danish fleet and forts. For the first half-hour his *Edgar* with the *Polyphemus, Isis, Monarch* and *Ardent* bore the brunt of the fighting. In an early version of the *Battle of the Baltic*, stanza x. runs :

'Twas the Edgar first that smote
Denmark's line ;
As her flag the foremost soared
Murray stamped his foot on board,
And a hundred cannon roared
At the sign !

Murray had, probably, at the dinner described his experiences. But Campbell wisely suppressed the verse. From such crudities may a great poem emerge by way of trial and failure. The first version of the poem is given at length in a letter to Scott of 27th March 1805.

I   I

York detain you till that period I will most certainly have the honor of paying my respects at Hamilton. Lord Archibald was so good as to let me know when he was in town so I had the pleasure of a few minutes conversation with him—he made me a half promise to spend the evening in Castle Street, and I regreted he had not found it convenient as Lady Charlotte Campbell [1] Lord John and Col: Campbell were so good as to scramble for bread and Cheese with us and between reading reciting and music the time glided very pleasantly away.

I am very happy to hear that what Mrs Tabitha Bramble [2] calls *the litel box with the jowls* was acceptable. But when your Ladyship passes through Edinr. you will have an opportunity of chusing among a greater variety than I could offer to your selection—

I am much mortified to learn that there is a great prospect of Col. Stuart losing his election. It is a woful picture of the feelings of the Country that such a man should fail in a contest of this nature with an opponent of whom I shall say nothing for it is enough to make one sit down with Jaques to rail against all the first born of Egypt. To change the subject I will transcribe a few verses which I picked up from hearing Campbell recite them.[3] They are part of a poem which he is composing

[1] " The two leaders of society in Edinburgh, in the winter of 1801-2, were the celebrated Duchess of Gordon and Lady Charlotte Campbell, the lovely daughter of the lovelier Gunning," later Lady Charlotte Bury.— MacCunn, *Sir Walter Scott's Friends*.

[2] From Smollett's *Humphrey Clinker*. Lady Anne replied on 28th January : " You can hardly be under any uneasiness as to the fate of your *Jewel Box* and still more valuable *Fiesco* considering by whose favour it was convey'd— and the contents were everything I could wish and much more than I expected. . . . Both her [*sic—i.e.* Lady Susan) and I envy our dear cousin the delightful feast he must have had with *Three Poets* in the present age that's born and such poets." Scott's translation of Schiller's *Fiesco* disappeared.

[3] The obvious variants from the poem as we know it may be due to Scott's memory or be early variants. It was printed, along with *Lochiel's Warning*, by James Ballantyne in 1801, and dedicated to the Rev. Archibald Alison. The subscription papers referred to were for the volume *Pleasures of Hope with other Poems*, Edinburgh, 1803.

upon the dreadful action at Hohen Linden where nearly 30000 Men were left upon the spot. I think I have mentioned to your Ladyship that the Poet was upon the field of Action at the time when the battle was raging. The verses are uncommonly sublime—

On Linden when the sun was low,
All bloodless lay the untrodden snow,
And dark as winter was the flow
    Of Iser rolling rapidly !

But Linden showed another sight
When the Drum beat at dead of night
Commanding fires of Death to light
    The darkness of her scenery !

Then shook the hills with Thunder riven
Then flew the steed to Battle driven
Then volleying like the bolt of heaven
    Far flash'd the red artillery !

And redder yet these flames shall glow
On Linden's hills of purpled snow
And bloodier yet the torrent flow
    Of Iser rolling rapidly.

'Tis Morn ! but scarce youn level sun
Can pierce the war-cloud rolling dun
Where furious Frank and fiery Hun
    Shout in their sulphurous canopy !

The Battle deepens—On ye Brave
That rush to Glory or the Grave—
Wave Munich all thy banners wave,
    And charge with all thy chivalry !

*   *   *   *   *

Pray shew these energetick lines to Lady Douglas.— I have set the Bard Lady Susan's task tho' I am tempted to wish he may *not* accomplish till I have an opportunity of seeing her Ladyship in her state of *fury* so very congenial to the usual gentleness of her feelings. I will endeavour to procure and send by Col. Campbell one of the sub-scription papers upon which your Ladyship may mark the names you have been kind enough to procure for the Bard. I am sorry I shall again miss Lady Charlotte [Campbell] at Hamilton but it would be too great good fortune to meet so many of my first-rate favourites together—by the way this is a very mean way of distinguishing those whose disposition and talents claim yet more respect than their Rank—I direct to his Grace but I suppose he is by this time gone to the Castle of John of Gaunt [1]—if not I have the honor to offer my most respectful Compliments. Need I add my wish to be remembered *to* and *by* Lord Archibald and Lady Susan—Believe me ever most faithfully Lady Anne Hamilton's respectful and devoted humble Servant

W. S.

I have pick'd up one or two old pamphlets of no great value but which have some reference to your illustrious family. One is a Latin Elegy upon the Duke of H. who was slain in Hydepark—I will send them to Hamilton one of those days—the Bookbinder is stitching them into a cover and moreover the elegy must be translated but whether by Campbell, Leyden or your Ladyship's humble Servant is not yet decided. I will hunt about for some good devices.

EDINR. 1*st Feby*. 1802.

[*Owen D. Young*]

To GEORGE ELLIS

[14*th February*, 1802]

I HAVE been silent, but not idle. The transcript of *King Arthur* is at length finished, being a fragment of about 7000 lines. Let me know how I shall transmit a

---

[1] Ashton Hall, near Lancaster, the seat of the Duke of Hamilton, which had formerly belonged to John of Gaunt, Duke of Lancaster.

parcel containing it, with the *Complaynt* [1] and the Border
Ballads, of which I expect every day to receive some
copies. I think you will be disappointed in the Ballads.
I have as yet touched very little on the more remote
antiquities of the Border, which, indeed, my songs, all
comparatively modern, did not lead me to discuss. Some
scattered herbage, however, the elephants may perhaps
find. By the way, you will not forget to notice the
mountain called *Arthur's Seat*, which overhangs this city.
When I was at school, the tradition ran that King Arthur
occupied as his throne a huge rock upon its summit, and
that he beheld from thence some naval engagement upon
the Frith of Forth. I am pleasantly interrupted by the
post ; he brings me a letter from William Dundas, fixing
Leyden's appointment as an assistant-surgeon to one of
the India settlements [2]—which, is not yet determined ; and
another from my printer, a very ingenious young man,
telling me, that he means to escort the " Minstrelsy " up
to London in person. I shall, therefore, direct him to
transmit my parcel to Mr Nicol. . . .

[Lockhart]

[1] *The Complaynt of Scotlande vyth an Exortatione to the Thre Estaits to be
vigilante in the Deffens of their Public veil* : the earliest important example of
Scottish vernacular prose. It was written by someone unknown about
1549 and was an appeal to the Scottish people to defend themselves against
the pressure of the English " rough wooing." It is based, in the main, on the
French work of Alain Chartier, *Le Quadrilogue Invectif*. For Chartier's Dame
France the writer substitutes Dame Scotia, and for her enfants Le Peuple,
Le Chevalier and Clergie, Scotia's three sons Labour, the Nobles and
Spiritualty. Leyden's edition with . . . dissertation and glossary was
issued in 1801, and it is this, presumably, which Scott is forwarding. It was
edited later for the Early English Texts' Society by Sir J. A. H. Murray.
The *Minstrelsy of the Scottish Border* was published in January 1802, the first
two volumes " from the respectable house of Cadell & Davies in the
Strand." It was printed at Kelso by James Ballantyne.

[2] See note on Leyden, p. 111.

To LADY ANNE HAMILTON

[*February* 23, 1802]

Modesty and Diffidence, my fair friend, are very heavy charges against a Man of my Profession—they are supposed to be as inconsistent with the Practice of a Lawyer as with that of a Statesman *et c'est beaucoup dire*. But to do your Ladyship justice if you point out the weakness of my character with freedom, you take a most effectual mode to fortify me on the vulnerable side, for whose vanity and self-conceit would not be excited by the praises of Lady Anne Hamilton. I have not failed to profit by your Ladyships hint and have endeavoured to secure the Dutchess of Gordons Interest on behalf of Campbell [1] in which I flatter myself I have succeeded. I am no stranger to her Grace's activity when she is pleased to set seriously about such matters. I now inclose one of the Subscription papers on which your Ladyship can mark with more accuracy than I might do the names which your generous patronage has procured for our unfortunate Bard.—Will your Ladyship have the goodness to express to the Duke the high sense I entertain of his attention in sending me a copy of the beautiful french translation of the *Entail* which is quite a model of what a translation should be. I am quite delighted with it and still more with his Grace's recollecting my wish to be possessed of it.

I am very happy that the pamphlets were acceptable—really in sending you these trifles I always remind myself of the *bequest* which once upon a time the Wren made to the ffamily of Hamilton. Now as your Ladyship may not be acquainted with the nature of this legacy and as the last will and testament of the said wren will in all probability hardly be found upon record in Doctors

---

[1] *i.e.* towards the publication by subscription of Campbell's poems, a project with which the poet was busy throughout the autumn and winter. In February he moved to Liverpool. See later in the letter.

Commons I have the honor to inform you, that this magnanimous and patriotic bird after disposing of his personal property to useful and public purposes such as one of his legs to prop the Bridge of Forth and the other to prop the Bridge of Tay at length instructs his Executors thus—

> " And then ye'll take my gallant *bill*
> My bill that pecks the corn
> And give it to the Duke of Hamilton
> To be a *hunting horn*—"

Now I cant help thinking that my communications will be about as useful to your great work as the Wren's bill to waken the echoes of the Chase of your forefathers. The valuable packet was safely sent to the Thane of Buchan. I inclose, or rather send under a separate cover a copy of sublime verses addressed by the Noble Lord to the Dutchess of Gordon which I do not doubt that your Ladyship will understand although they are not calculated for the meridian of such plebian understandings as mine. An eccentric Irish friend of mine[1] was so delighted with

---

[1] Who the Irish friend was I cannot discover. Mr. Forbes Gray has pointed out to me that the lines addressed by Lord Buchan to the Duchess were printed in the *Scots Magazine* for 1802. They are reproduced in *Archibald Constable*, etc. :

> Thou beauteous star whose silvery light
> Enchanting came upon my youthful sight !
> Ah ! what a blaze has hid thy virgin rays,
> While I, in woods retired, have past my days !
> Now, silvered o'er by Time's eventful hand,
> I greet the evening beam on Scotia's strand, etc.

To Leyden is attributed, in the same work, a satirical " Irregular Ode to the Duchess of Gordon by the Earl of Buchan " (second edition) :

> Thou beauteous star,
> Seen from afar
> Than Phoebe's silvery beam more bright—
> As yet a boy
> And somwhat coy,
> I first beheld thy dazzling light, etc.

lines which recall Pyramus' speech in *A Midsummer Night's Dream*.
Mr. Gray suggests that these *may* be the lines to which Scott refers in his letter, but this is unlikely, for what Scott's Irish friend has written is a reply *from* the Duchess.

the effusions of his Lordships muse that he could not forbear writing an answer in her Graces name which I have transcribed for your amusement.

The Saxon seal is said to be in forwardness—when it is finishd I will settle with the Engravers for the jewel and cutting which will be the only accot. betwixt your Ladyship and me unless I can pay any other bills for you or Lady Susan in this place in which case I know you will have the goodness to command me without ceremony. The sudden march of Lord Archd leads me to expect that we may soon have the pleasure of seeing you in Edinburgh which will indeed afford me much satisfaction.

Your Ladyship does me justice in believing that I am sincerely interested in behalf of my literary friends Campbell and Leyden and think of them even oftener than of myself. For tho' it would be absurd affectation for me to pretend to renounce the wish and hope of improving my own situation as my advance in life and the increase of my family may render necessary and as fortune may afford me opportunity, yet I cannot in the mean time but feel myself highly fortunate in possessing a competence however limited when I see men of so much greater talent condemnd to seek their bread in a foreign land or what is yet more painful, to mendicate their way through life and solicit the Merchants of Liverpool to subscribe to what they neither can read nor understand.

The Bothwell anecdote has somehow fallen aside but it shall be recoverd. I am very curious to know how Lady Douglas likes the Border poems. You will be pleased to learn that the sale here is rapid—how they will suit the London *market* (as the Booksellers say) I cannot even guess. Remember me kindly & respectfully to Lady Susan. I long to see your Brother *The Douglas*. Did I ever tell you that my Ancestors were armour bearers to the Douglases, so that my attachment to you and all your family is feudal and hereditary.

(4 *sheets photostats end here.*)   ? *Close of letter probably on address side.*

[*Owen D. Young*]

To GEORGE ELLIS [1]

[*2nd March, 1802*]

I *hope* that long ere this you have received the Ballads, and that they have afforded you some amusement. I hope, also, that the *threatened* third volume will be more interesting to Mrs. Ellis than the dry antiquarian detail of the two first could prove. I hope, moreover, that I shall have the pleasure of seeing you soon, as some circumstances seem not so much to call me to London, as to furnish me with a decent apology for coming up some time this spring ; and I long particularly to say, that I know my friend Mr. Ellis *by sight* as well as *intimately*. I am glad you have seen the Marquess of Lorn, whom I have met frequently at the house of his charming sister, Lady Charlotte Campbell, whom, I am sure, if you are acquainted with her, you must admire as much [as] I do. Her Grace of Gordon, a great admirer of yours, spent

---

[1] On the 5th March 1802 Ellis writes : " The volumes are arrived and I have been devouring them, not as a pig does a parcel of grains . . . but as a schoolboy does a piece of gingerbread ; nibbling a little bit here and a little bit there, smacking his lips, surveying the number of square inches which still remain for his gratification, endeavouring to look it into larger dimensions, making at every mouthful a tacit vow not to lose the pleasure of devouring it at his leisure but protracting his enjoyment by restraining his appetite." He sends thanks to Leyden for his part of the precious parcel and deplores his forthcoming departure, not for the " fines atticae " but for those of Asia, and " that the Genius of Scotland instead of a poor *complaint* and an address in the style of ' Navis, quae tibi creditum debes Virgilium—reddas incolumen precor ' should not interpose to prevent his loss." He then passes to praise of the printing and the volume generally, and especially Scott's own ballads, which show what the ruder poems could become " when the age of good taste should arrive." No more than Miss Seward, apparently, is he prepared to admire them as they are.

some days here lately, and, like Lord Lorn, was highly entertained with an account of our friendship *à la distance*. I do not, nor did I ever, intend to fob you off with twenty or thirty lines of the second part of Sir Guy. Young Leyden has been much engaged with his studies, otherwise you would have long since received what I now send, namely, the combat between Guy and Colbronde, which I take to be the cream of the romance. . . . If I do not come to London this spring, I will find a safe opportunity of returning Lady Juliana Berners,[1] with my very best thanks for the use of her reverence's work.

[*Lockhart*]

To JOHN PINKERTON [2]

Lasswade Cottage, *April 24th,* 1802

I ESTEEM myself highly honored by the polite reception which you have given to the *Border Minstrelsy*, and am

---

[1] On the 12th October Ellis acknowledges having received from Nicol the " good Lady Abbess accompanied by a short note from you, but without one word from him, or any indication of the means by which I may have a chance of getting a sight of your brother. Heber . . will perhaps be more communicative. He has promised to bring Leyden hither as soon as he can lay hands upon him and I shall be very anxious to see your *friend*, though much more to see your brother." Ellis was helping to find Daniel a post in Jamaica. Lockhart's suggestion that he did not know Daniel to be Scott's brother is not borne out by this letter, unless the brother here is Tom.

[2] The Scottish antiquarian and historian. He had in 1783 published *Select Scottish Ballads*, with the sub-title " Hardy Knute : an Heroic Ballad now first published complete with various dissertations." " *Hardyknute. A fragment of an old heroic ballad* had appeared in Allan Ramsay's *Tea-Table Miscellany,* 1729. The ballads Ritson declared and Pinkerton acknowledged to be wholly or in part modern or of Pinkerton's own composition. The portrait of the Flower of Yarrow was possibly desired for a further edition of his, *The Scottish Gallery ; or Portraits of Eminent Persons of Scotland,* 1799. Of this and other letters Lockhart says : " I might fill many pages by transcribing similar letters [to one he gives from Ellis] from persons of acknowledged discernment in this branch of literature. John, Duke of Roxburgh is among the number. . . Pinkerton issues his decree of approbation as *ex cathedra* ; Chalmers overflows with heartier praise ; and even Joseph Ritson extols his presentation copy as ' the most valuable literary treasure in his possession.' "

particularly flattered that so very good a judge of poetical antiquities finds any reason to be pleased with the work. There is no portrait of *the Flower of Yarrow* in existence ; nor do I think it very probable that any was ever taken. Much family anecdote concerning her has been preserved among her descendants, of whom I have the honor to be one. The epithet of the *Flower of Yarrow* was in later times bestowed upon one of her immediate posterity, Miss Mary Lillias Scott,[1] daughter of John Scott, Esq. of Harden, and celebrated for her beauty in the pastoral song of Tweedside ; I mean that set of modern words which begins, " What beauties does Flora disclose." This lady I myself remember very well ; and I mention her to you lest you should receive any inaccurate information, owing to her being called, like her predecessor, " *The Flower of Yarrow*." There was a portrait of this latter lady in the collection at Hamilton, which the present Duke transferred, through my hands, to Lady Diana Scott,[2] relict of the late Walter Scott, Esq. of Harden ; which picture was vulgarly, but inaccurately, supposed to have been a resemblance of the original Mary Scott, daughter of Philip Scott[3] of Dryhope, and married to *auld Wat* of Harden in the middle of the sixteenth century. I shall be particularly happy if, upon any future occasion, I can in the slightest degree contribute to advance your valuable and patriotic labors.

[*Pinkerton Correspondence*]

[1] John Scott of Harden married, 1719, Lady Jean Erskine, daughter of the Earl of Kellie, and had two daughters, Anne and Mary.

[2] Walter Scott of Harden had married, in 1754, Lady Diana Hume Campbell, third daughter of Hugh, third Earl of Marchmont.

[3] According to Douglas' *Baronage*, p. 214, " of John Scott of Dryhope."

To R. CLEATOR, CROPTON LODGE, NEAR PICKERING, YORKSHIRE.[1]

SIR,—I am honored with your very obliging favour, and beg leave to express my best thanks for the information which it so handsomely communicates. In the late Mr. Riddell of Glenriddle's MS.,[2] which I have frequently referred to in the late compilation, there is a copy of the Ballad called *Jock of Milk*, which I examined very attentively. I was only deterred from publishing it by the strong doubts I entertained of its authenticity, as it appeared to me to bear more the character of an imitation than of a real ancient ballad. It is very possible, however, that I may be mistaken, or that the copy I have seen may be interpolated, and I shall be very much gratified indeed by your furnishing me with the copies which you

[1] This letter is given in *Notes and Queries* as " exhibited at the Manchester Literary and Philosophical Society on Jan. 21, 1879." It is followed there by a letter of 9th April 1802 from a certain R. Liddesdale, East Wood, to Cleator indicating the source of the ballad supplied and the notes : " The old ballad Jock o' the Milk was given to me by Mr Bell Irving of Whitehill and the notes thereon were collected from old tradition. . . . Mr Bell Irving's grandfather . . . was many years factor to the family of Castle Milk, and having access to the Repository of all the deeds and papers he found this ballad among them, so the present Mr Bell Irving informs me. From many inquiries amongst the old people now no more I could perceive there had been such a ballad but of which they had a very imperfect idea, but sometimes it strikes me that two verses were added by the present Mr Bell Irving." The ballad sent to Scott has disappeared, but the "notes thereon " are still extant. The ballad, with identical notes, as in the Glenriddel MS. as Scott says, is a poor affair. One note on the line " When at the Galliard or the court " runs : "The Castle of Galliard upon the River Seine was the place of residence of King David when in France— it was there the League between Scotland and France was said to be renewed." Another on a line " And called him cousin Duke of Milk " runs : " David created many knights (and made Douglas an Earl) before his intended invasion of England . . . but of the creation of a Duke of Milk in the Feild the Historians are silent and perhaps of some other of the dignities conferred. . . . There was no Court Gazette in those days." To both these notes Scott refers in this and the next letter. It is interesting evidence of the care he took to secure genuine ballads.

[2] The Glenriddell MS., 1791. Preserved in vol. xi. of Robert Riddell's collection of Scottish Antiquities in the Library of the Society of Antiquaries of Scotland.

have so handsomely offered to send me, with as much of the traditionary history as you recollect. I should be also much interested to know whether the verses were taken down from recitation or from a MS., ancient or modern. I have been very desirous as far as possible to ascertain the authenticity of the old poems which I have given to the world, as literary forgeries have been but too often and too justly imputed to the Scottish antiquaries. The Galliard mentioned in your fragment was, I believe, a castle upon the *Seine* belonging to the French monarchs, which gave a name to the favourite dance there practised, just as a more modern dance was called the *Louvre*, and as we call our Highland dance a *Strathspey*. I beg you to believe that I am extremely sensible of your polite attention to the researches of a total stranger, and that I feel myself very much gratified by the interest you have taken in them. I have the honor to be, Sir, Your obliged and faithful servant,

WALTER SCOTT

LASWADE COTTAGE, NEAR EDINBURGH, 2 *April*, 1802.

[*Notes and Queries*, 5th Ser., xi. 284]

To WILLIAM LAIDLAW,[1] JUNIOR, BLACK-HOUSE UPON DOUGLAS WATER, CARE OF MR. CLARKSON, SURGEON, SELKIRK

Edinr. 12*th May*, 1802

SIR,—In order to testify as much as possible my sense of your politeness in relation to the objects of my pursuit, I have to request your acceptance of two volumes of the

---

[1] This is the first letter to Laidlaw I have come upon. It is addressed to his father's farm. Scott had made his acquaintance in 1801 when hunting for ballads, and through him of Hogg who was a shepherd in the older Laidlaw's family. Laidlaw's *Recollections of Sir Walter Scott* are among the Laing MSS. in Edinburgh University Library. They were used by Dr. Carruthers in his Abbotsford Notanda appended to Robert Chambers' *Life of Scott*, 1871. See Lockhart *passim*, Mrs. MacCunn's *Sir Walter Scott's Friends*, and Hogg's *Domestic Manners of Scott*.

Minstrelsy of the Scottish Border, which I hope may afford you some amusement.

I beg you will keep on the look out for any old stories [which] may fall in your way, whether in rhime or otherwise, and preserve a Memorandum of them against I come to the country. I hope you will not forget your promise to let me see you when you come to town & I remain Your obedient servant,

WALTER SCOTT

[*Abbotsford Copies*]

To R. CLEATOR

SIR,—You have doubtless by this time set me down as guilty of great ingratitude and unworthy of your farther correspondence for so long and unjustifiable a delay in answering your letter enclosing " Jock o' Milk." The truth is, I have been absent from Edinburgh for some weeks, and since my return my professional engagements have obliged me to leave the tales of the East, West, and Middle Marches as quiet in my desk as the bodies of their quondam heroes rest in their graves. At length I have an opportunity to acknowledge your obliging favour. My incredulity with regard to the ballad you have been so good as to send me is not yet entirely obviated. If it is not entirely and radically a modern fabrication, the ancient verses are what the French call *beaucoup brodées*. " Virtue is its own reward," trite as the sentiment is, can hardly be supposed quite so old as the reign of David II. The title of duke was first introduced into Scotland in the reign of Robert III, and was only conferred upon immediate relations of the royal family till at a very late period the Hamilton family got that title. There never was, as far as I can learn, a peer, whether duke, earl, or baron, of the name of Irving ; and although there were many landholders of the name in the south-west of

Scotland, the principal seat of their chieftain was Drum, in Aberdeenshire. So far with regard to historical fact ; but a ballad-maker is entitled to use great latitudes in that respect, and accordingly it is not upon the ana-chronisms that I chiefly found my disbelief in the anti-quity of the poem. It is rather upon the mixture of ancient and modern phraseology, and especially upon the different attempts at sentiment and pathos, inconsis-tent with the simplicity of the minstrel style, that I ground my opinion, which will always, however, be subject to alteration upon reasonable and convincing evidence. The copy you have been so good as to send me is nearly the same with one which I found in Glenriddell's MS. collection of ballads, and with another procured from Mr. David Herd,[1] of this place. The last copy has this memorandum : "This fragment was taken down from the recitation of some of the country people in Annandale, by William Bell, a writer there, who communicated it to D. H., but in a very bad case, about the year 1776, and he was afterwards informed that Dr. Clapperton, a surgeon in Lochmaben, was in possession of a complete copy of the ballad, which never could be got, the Dr. intending, as was said, its publication along with several other curious ancient songs." As this account in a great measure tallies with that with which you have favoured me, I hope it may be yet possible to recover some account of the original copy of this curious ballad, by which means we may perhaps be able to determine what parts are modern and what really ancient. I shall wait with impatience the result of your inquiries of your friend Mr. Liddesdale. The battle in question, if such there was, must have been fought in the course of the four years intervening betwixt 1342, the date of David's return from France, and 1346, when the battle of Durham was fought, in which Randolph E. of Murray was slain, and the King himself led into captivity.—Believe me, sir,

---

[1] The Herd MSS. are now in the British Museum.

with many thanks for your obliging communication, your
faithful humble servt.,   WALTER SCOTT
EDIN., 4 *June*, 1802.

[*Notes and Queries*, 4th Ser., i. 456]

To ANNA SEWARD

[Extract]

EDINBURGH, *June* 29, 1802

I HAVE some thoughts of attempting a Border ballad
in the comic manner ;[1] but I almost despair of bringing
it well out.   A certain Sir William Scott, from whom I
am descended, was ill-advised enough to plunder the
estate of Sir Gideon Murray of Elibank, ancestor to the
present Lord Elibank.   The marauder was defeated,
seized, and brought in fetters to the castle of Elibank,
upon the Tweed.   The Lady Murray (agreeably to the
custom of all ladies in ancient tales) was seated on the
battlements, and descried the return of her husband with
his prisoners.   She immediately inquired what he meant
to do with the young Knight of Harden, which was the
petit titre of Sir William Scott.   " Hang the robber,
assuredly," was the answer of Sir Gideon.   " What ! "
answered the lady, " hang the handsome young knight
of Harden, when I have three ill-favoured daughters
unmarried !   No, no, Sir Gideon, we'll force him to
marry our Meg."   Now, tradition says, that Meg Murray
was the ugliest woman in the four counties, and that she
was called, in the homely dialect of the time, *meikle-
mouthed Meg*[1] (I will not affront you by an explanation).
Sir Gideon, like a good husband and tender father,

---

[1] For Miss Anna Seward, the Swan of Lichfield and friend of Dr. Darwin,
see among other works Mrs. Oliphant's *Literary History of England* (1882).
The earliest letter of her's to Scott extant is dated 29th April 1802.   She
acknowledges the receipt of the *Border Minstrelsy* and expresses her own poor
opinion of ballad poetry :   " Yet are there critics who seem to mistake the
squalid dress of language for poetic excellence provided the verse and its

entered into his wife's sentiments, and proffered to Sir William the alternative of becoming his son-in-law, or decorating with his carcase the *kindly* gallows of Elibank. The lady was so very ugly, that Sir William, the handsomest man of his time, positively refused the honour of her hand. Three days were allowed him to make up his mind ; and it was not until he found one end of a rope made fast to his neck, and the other knitted to a sturdy oak bough, that his resolution gave way, and he preferred an ugly wife to the literal noose. It is said, they were afterwards a very happy couple. She had a curious hand at pickling the beef which he stole ; and, marauder as he was, he had little reason to dread being twitted by the pawky gowk. This, either by its being perpetually told to me when young, or by a perverted taste for such anecdotes, has always struck me as a good subject for

---

mean garb is ancient. Of that number is Mr. Pinkerton in some of his notes to those old Scottish ballads which he published in 1781 and the late Mr. Headly more than so seems in that collection of ancient English ballads which he soon after gave to the press. We find there an idiot preference of the rude and in itself valueless foundation on which Prior raised one of the loveliest poetic edifices in our language, the *Henry and Emma*." She reviews various ballads, praises Scott's notes, and closes with the announcement that "a bright luminary in this neighbourhood recently shot from its sphere with awful and deplored suddenness. Dr. Darwin &c." Scott's letter, of which I know only this extract, is a reply in which he defends his love of the old ballads. Miss S. replied on the 10th July acknowledging the force of Scott's apology "for estimating the poetry of the *Border Minstrelsy* higher than I think its merit." "If the local partialities have biassed the criticism of Scotland they have given exquisite interest and beauty to her metrical compositions since they ceased to be merely metrical." . . . "Your poetry is among ballads what *Clarissa* and *Grandison* are among novels. . . . On the subject of the *Eve of St. John* and *Glenfinlas* . . . preference is divided . . . the folk who are dead to almost all other sublime poetry were charmed with the former and gave *Glenfinlas* but cold acquiescent praise. . . . Those who taste the higher orders of verse are also charmed with the *Eve* but unanimously assert the superiority of the Highland poem." The omitted opening of Scott's letter was, Lockhart says, a polite acceptance of the ballad by Miss Seward, *Rich Auld Willie's Farewell*, which was afterwards included among the *Imitations*. The story of Meg on which Scott composed a fragment *The Reiver's Wedding*, printed in Lockhart, and on which Browning later in *Asolando* tried his hand in a very different manner, is, I am told, apocryphal. But the wife of Sir William Scott *was* Agnes, daughter of Gideon Murray.

a comic ballad, and how happy should I be were Miss Seward to agree in opinion with me.

This little tale may serve for an introduction to some observations I have to offer upon our popular poetry. It will at least so far disclose your correspondent's weak side, as to induce you to make allowance for my mode of arguing. Much of its peculiar charm is indeed, I believe, to be attributed solely to its *locality*. A very commonplace and obvious epithet, when applied to a scene which we have been accustomed to view with pleasure, recalls to us not merely the local scenery, but a thousand little nameless associations, which we are unable to separate or to define. In some verses of that eccentric but admirable poet, Coleridge, he talks of

> " An old rude tale that suited well
> The ruins wild and hoary."

I think there are few who have not been in some degree touched with this local sympathy. Tell a peasant an ordinary tale of robbery and murder, and perhaps you may fail to interest him ; but to excite his terrors, you assure him it happened on the very heath he usually crosses, or to a man whose family he has known, and you rarely meet such a mere image of Humanity as remains entirely unmoved. I suspect it is pretty much the same with myself, and many of my countrymen, who are charmed by the effect of local description, and sometimes impute that effect to the poet, which is produced by the recollections and associations which his verses excite. Why else did Sir Philip Sydney feel that the tale of Percy and Douglas moved him like the sound of a trumpet ? or why is it that a Swiss sickens at hearing the famous Ranz des Vaches, to which the native of any other country would have listened for a hundred days, without any other sensation than ennui ? I fear our poetical taste is in general much more linked with our prejudices of birth, of education, and of habitual thinking,

than our vanity will allow us to suppose ; and that, let
the point of the poet's dart be as sharp as that of Cupid,
it is the wings lent it by the fancy and prepossessions of
the gentle reader which carry it to the mark. It may
appear like great egotism to pretend to illustrate my
position from the reception which the productions of
so mere a ballad-monger as myself have met with from
the public ; but I cannot help observing that all Scotchmen prefer the Eve of St John to Glenfinlas, and most of
my English friends entertain precisely an opposite
opinion. . . . I have been writing this letter by a
paragraph at a time for about a month, this being the
season when we are most devoted to the

> " Drowsy bench and babbling hall."

I have the honour, &c. &c. . . .

[*Lockhart*]

To WILLIAM OWEN [1]

SIR,—As a stranger I ought to apologize for this
intrusion but I flatter myself an appeal to your own zeal
for the promotion of literature will be my best excuse.

I have been for some time past engaged in a work of
some Interest to those who have made Antiquities their
study in which I have had occasion to be very troublesome
to my literary friends—I mean an edition of an ancient

---

[1] Later Owen-Pughe (1759-1835), the Welsh antiquary and lexicographer. He replied to Scott's letter on the 15th of July from Penton
Street, Pentonville : " We have in Wales large collections of the ancient
tales alluded to, written on vellum of the date of the 12th and 13th centuries
under the title Mabinogion or Juvenilities. They are all in prose, it being
a maxim of the Bards not to employ verse in fiction (just the reverse of this
is supposed in them). . . . They are not so wild as the romances, their
incidents pass before us rapidly like a pantomime, and generally within
the scope of possibility, and develope a great deal of ancient manners in
the colloquial language of the times, and there is very little chivalry and
combat in them," which seems a strange account of the tales. He goes on
to tell Scott of his forthcoming *Cambrian Biography* and to describe Trystan
as he is classified with other heroes in the Welsh Triads.

metrical Romance calld *Sir Tristram* preserved in the Advocates Library here and which announces itself to be the composition of Thomas the Rymer of Ercildoune who flourished in the end of the 12th Century. This poem is essentially different in all its parts from the Voluminous ffrench Romance in prose bearing the same title, but it resembles very nearly in the conduct of the story a *ffrench metrical romance* of which I have a copy and which is obviously much more ancient than that in prose as you doubtless are well aware that all the celebrated ffrench romances were originally composed in Rhime. The Romance is obviously of *Celtic* extraction, but there occurs a curious query in solving which I venture to hope for Mr. Owen's Assistance. Did the Minstrel of the Scotish Borders borrow his subject from the Normans who might have picked it up in A[r]morica among other traditions of Wales? Or are we entitled to suppose that Thomas of Erceldoune residing very near to Silva Caledonia & other districts of Scotland long possessed by the Cumraig, collected his materials from the Celtic traditions which must have continued to float for a length of time through the countries which they had so long inhabited? In this uncertainty as to the derivation of the Romance I am tempted to think that the works of Welch Bards wt. which Mr. Owen is so intimately acquainted & which he has so well illustrated must contain much curious matter upon the subject of Sir Tristram, who was a favourite warrior of your famous Arthur & of whom I observe frequent mention in such books relating to British antiquities as have come to my hand. What I am particularly desirous of knowing is the history of Sir Tristram as told by the Bards, the names of the personages occurring in his history, also whether he has been the subject of any particular poem & if so whether such a poem is printed or in Ms.—

I cannot flatter myself it will at all facilitate my enquiries at you to add that I am the Editor of a late work

on poetical Antiquities called the Minstrels[y] of the Scotish
Border, but it will at least tend to shew that I am a
labourer in a different inclosure of the same Vinyard
which Mr. Owen cultivates with so much success. May
I further request that you will have the goodness to add
my name to the subscription for the Welch Dicty. which
the publishers may forward to Mr. Constable Bookseller
Edinr.

My address is W. S. advocate Castle Street Edinburgh.
I have the honour to be Sir Your very obedt. servant

WALTER SCOTT

EDIN. 15 *July* 1802

[*Mrs. Meilir Owen*]

To LADY ANNE HAMILTON

[*July* 29, 1802]

INCLOSED the long promised Ballad [1] kisses your Ladyship's hands. It is not so good as I could wish (indeed
how was that possible) but I prefer keeping my promise
as an honest man to my poetical reputation. The poem
is rather a piece of historical painting than a narrative
Ballad & will need many notes. To *you* it is only necessary to say that Woodhouselee whose ruins near the Eske
are still supposed to be haunted was the property of which
Bothwellhaugh (who killed regent Murray) was deprived
by tyranny. One or two old words are used *Pryse* " The
note blown when the Deer or other game falls "—*Quarry*
" The slaughtered game "—*Genzie bent* [2] " a cocked gun "
—how was it possible to say all this in modern language &
a very few others. The wild cattle of Cæsar were long
preserved at Hamilton and serve to vary the uniformity
of a Scotish hunting. Upon the whole Cadzow Castle

---

[1] Cadzow Castle, *Minstrelsy*, iii. p. 386.

[2] For " Genzie bent " Scott wrote and printed " hackbut bent."

will crave much indulgence from your Ladyships criticism being hastily written like everything that is long delayd & still capable of great improvement. I should like to have your opinion Lady Susans & Lady Douglas's if you think it worthy of going farther than the Halls of Hamilton where it is in some measure entitled to a partial audience.

I am going to a vile Election so must conclude in great haste with begging to be kindly remembered to Lady Susan who I hope has recovered in the woods of Hamilton the roses which Indisposition had stolen—also to my Lord Archd. Need I add how faithfully I am Lady Anne's most respectful humble Servt

WALTER SCOTT

LASWADE COTTAGE NEAR EDR.

[*Owen D. Young*]

To LADY ANNE HAMILTON

I CANNOT express how happy I am that Cadzow Castle has found favour in the sight of those whom it was principally designed to gratify and interest. Lady Douglas' request of a copy does me very much honor and I shall be most proud to comply with it. I have in the mean time been endeavouring to render the Ballad rather more worthy of its patroness—most of the alterations are minute and will be contain with the notes & illustrations in a copy which Mrs. Scott is engaged in making for your Ladyships acceptance. But if in the meanwhile Lady Douglas wishes to have a copy from that which I had the honor of sending to you I would wish the following improvements to be adopted. They chiefly regard the arrangement of a verse or two in Bothwellhaugh's Speech, but *for connexion's sake* (as a worthy Clergyman said in reading his text from the 119th Psalm) I must recite nearly the whole of the said speech

[*Eight stanzas of Cadzow Castle, from* " From the wild
Border's humbled side," *to* " The death-shot parts—"] [1]
as in your copy untill you come to the verse immediately
subsequent to Bothwellhaugh speech which I have
altered thus—

> Vaults every warrior to his steed,
>   Loud Bugles join the wild acclaim—
> " Murray is fallen and Scotland freed,
>   Couch, Arran, couch thy lance of flame," &c.

I think these alterations are improvements especially
that which introduces Lord Lindesay of the Byres. Your
Ladyship will recollect that this caitiff was the agent
employd by Murray's faction as the most unrelenting
of the party to force Mary when imprisond in Lochleven
Castle to sign a deed abdicating the throne : he executed
his office with the most savage brutality and even pinchd
with his iron glove the arm of his weeping sovereign when
she averted her eyes from the fatal parchment which she
was compelld to sign.

I shall be very much gratified indeed if the young
Douglas thinks these verses at all worthy of the subject,
but I cannot be more so than by the approbation of the
Weird Sisters.[2] As to the little *yellow* spot I am afraid
your observation for once has deceived you for you do
not know how beautiful a poem Mr. Lewis has written
upon Bothwell Castle at Lady Douglas request. In
return for Cadzow, pray ask for the *Three Sisters* which
Lewis shewed me in Edinr. I am meditating just now
quite a grand work being nothing less than a tragedy
the title of which is to be " *the perilous Castle of Douglas.*"
Should I carry on my plan which is a great chance, and
succeed at all to my liking which is a still greater I think
seriously of encountering the stage—this is a formidable
intimation to my few friends in the higher circle as I must
teaze them for interest to bring it out &c. &c., so beware

[1] The stanzas from *Cadzow Castle* are here just as they stand in the printed
text.
[2] So Lady Anne refers to herself and Lady Susan.

Lady Anne, how you prematurely tax an author with so unfashionable a quality as *mauvaise honte*. But do not be too soon afraid neither there is not a line of the tragedy written.

I beg always to be respectfully and kindly remembered to my fair friend Lady Susan no one rejoices more sincerely than I do at her convalescence—I hope to see the Ladies of Hamilton some time before our Courts resume their labours and I shall assume my minstrel privilege of *rebuke* if Lady Susan is not *dans tout son brillant*.

Once more remember me respectfully to Lady Douglas —her noble friends at Dalkeith are well and often grace our cottage with a call—I hope you will soon have your Brothers and the excellent Chief to enliven Hamilton.

Believe [me] ever most respectfully and with great regard Your Ladyships very humble Servant

WALTER SCOTT

10 *Augt.* 1802 LASWADE COTTAGE.

[*Owen D. Young*]

To CHARLES KIRKPATRICK SHARPE [1]

SIR,—I beg your acceptance of my very best thanks for your valuable and obliging communication, which I received yesterday, and which will form an interesting addition to the 3d volume of Ballads which I intend shortly to publish. I have been very anxious to open some literary communication with your part of Dum-

[1] This is the first of Scott's letters to Sharpe, several of which are printed in the volumes of *Kirkpatrick Sharpe's Letters*. Some are printed here from these volumes, others from originals in the Hornel collection at Dumfries. For a character and life of Sharpe see also MacCunn's *Sir Walter Scott's Friends*. For all the ballads mentioned in this and the next letter to Sharpe, *The Twa Corbies*, *The Douglas Tragedy*, *Mary Hamilton* (*The Queen's Mary*), Sharpe's own ballad *Lord Herries Complaint*, and the three on the battles, see *The Minstrelsy* and Scott's notes. Sharpe's versions were generally blended with verses from other sources. See also Henderson's notes in *Sir Walter Scott's Minstrelsy of the Scottish Border*, edited by T. F. Henderson. William Blackwood and Sons, 1902.

frieshire, and am truly happy in embracing the opportunity which your politeness has offerd me.

The wild and beautiful tale of the Corbies resembles in the outline an old English poem published by Ritson from an ancient MS. with this important and remarkable difference that in the English verses the hawk, hound and lady all remain faithful to the slain warrior and the moral of the tale runs thus:—

" God send every gentleman
    Such hawks, such hounds and such a lemman."

I had a very corrupted and inferior copy of the Douglas tragedy, which is doubly acceptable to me, as I had been long desirous of obtaining a good set. Popular tradition has pointed out the scene of this fatal story and assignd it to Blackhouse in Selkirkshire where there are ruins of a very ancient castle said to have belonged to a Lord William Douglas who sat in a parliament of Malcolm Canmore. The scenery around it is savage and desolate : a stream called the *Douglas-Burn* is said to have been that where the lovers stopd to drink, and seven huge stones are averrd to have been erected in memory of the seven brothers : the Douglas-craig is in the immediate vicinity, and takes its name from the same family. All these circumstances seem to argue that the uniform tradition of the country people has some foundation in fact. I am just going to that part of the country, and shall carry the Douglas Tragedy along with me.

The ditty of Mary Hamilton will be *most* acceptable to me. I have several fragments of it, but not a complete copy. I also am greatly indebted to you for your offer of Lady Dismal which I think I have either seen or heard of. To the ballad of " *Lady Anne sate in her bower* " I am a perfect stranger,—at least I do not remember any which begins with that line.

I am to make some excursions through the Borders in the course of this month, it is not impossible but I may have the pleasure of meeting you, but at any rate when business or pleasure calls you to Edinr. or its neighbourhood I shall *claim* the privilege of returning you my personal thanks for the obligation you have conferred on me. My usual summer residence is at this little retreat, where it would give the greatest pleasure to receive a call from you. Should you write to me in the course of a fortnight, direct to me Sheriff Clerk's office, Selkirk, as your letter will probably find me wandering in Ettrick fforest, after which I return here.—I remain, sir, your obliged and faithful   WALTER SCOTT

LASWADE COTTAGE,

Near EDR., 13 *Augt.* [1802]

Nota Bene.—Every scrap of legendary intelligence, prosaic or poetical, will be most thankfully received.

[*Curle*]

TO ANNA SEWARD

To Miss Seward, High-Lake near Neston, Chester

[P.M. *August* 16, 1802]

I AM very sorry to have left you under a mistake about my third volume. The truth is, that highly as I should feel myself flatterd by the encouragement of Miss Seward's name, I cannot, in the present instance, avail myself of it, as the Ballads are not publishd by subscription.[1] Providence having, I suppose, foreseen that my literary qualifications, like those of many more distinguished persons, might not, *par hazard*, support me exactly as I would like, allotted me a small patrimony, which, joined to my professional income, and my appointments in the characteristic office of Sheriff of Ettrick Forest, serves to render my literary pursuits more a matter of amusement than an object of emolument.

[1] Miss Seward in her letter of 20th July had apologised for not sooner asking to have her name placed among the subscribers to the third volume.

With this explanation, I hope you will honour me by accepting the third volume as soon as publishd, which will be in the beginning of next year, and I also hope, that under the circumstances, you will hold me acquitted of the silly vanity of wishing to be thought a *gentleman-author.*

The ballad of the Reiver's Wedding is not yet written, but I have finished one of a tragic cast, founded upon the death of Regent Murray, who was shot in Linlithgow, by James Hamilton of Bothwellhaugh. The following verses contain the catastrophe. Told by Hamilton himself to his chief and his kinsmen :—

"With hackbut bent," &c., &c.

[10 stanzas of Cadzow Castle]

Bothwellhaugh has occupied such an unwarrantable proportion of my letter, that I have hardly time to tell you how much I join in your admiration of Tam o' Shanter, which I verily believe to be inimitable, both in the serious and ludicrous parts, as well as the singularly happy combination of both. I request Miss Seward to believe that among the numerous admirers of her talents none is more sincere than her faithful and respectful friend and Servant   W. SCOTT

LASWADE COTTAGE

[Lockhart and Owen D. Young]

To CHARLES KIRKPATRICK SHARPE

LASSWADE COTTAGE, 8 *Septr.* [1802]

MY DEAR SIR,—I have to acknowledge with my very best thanks your second packet. Mary Hamilton was most welcome & will be a valuable addition to my 2d. Edition. I have got one or two verses from other hands but cannot hope to make any material improvement upon that which you have so obligingly sent me— I have seen a fragment like Lady Anne but in a different

measure. I have little doubt that the foundation is
ancient though it may possibly have received a little &
but a very little modern decoration. At any rate it is
highly worthy of publication. As to Lady Dysmal[1]
I cannot say quite so much—she is, as the reviewers say,
under consideration, but I fear it will be difficult to
expect that she should excite much interest considering
the extreme degradation of her *Liaison*.

But now " like musick sweetest at the close " I haste
to notice your concluding poem, which notwithstanding
your modest entreaties to the contrary I have examined
with the most microscopic criticism which has only
resulted in confirming the judgement I formd at first
reading when it struck me as being one of the most
happy imitations of ancient strains of minstrelsy which
I had ever the good fortune to peruse. I hope you will
add to your other favours permission to ornament my
3d. volume with *Lord Herries' complaint*, a request which I
would not venture to make were I not certain that the
author's modesty is the only bar to its being made public.
If you are pleased to grant me this favour by which I
shall hold myself particularly gratified I must farther
draw upon your time & indulgence for a prose account
of the Tradition & scenery. The beautiful Locality of
which you have so well availd yourself is in fact calculated
to give to fiction itself the charms of truth or at least of
vraisemblance. Lest you should distrust indiscriminate
praise I add two minute observations which alone occurd
to me in the way of criticism

" Ere *that* heart *light* can be "

Would not this line read better thus

" Ere *light* that heart can be "

[1] " I fear greatly that poor ' Lady Dysmal ' hath not beauty enough to
save *her* from oblivion. I am sensible that her age—a thing at present much
admired in ladies—is her only merit."—Sharpe to Scott, Aug. 27th, 1802.
The other ballads mentioned are in the *Minstrelsy*. The spelling " Scotch "
is retained.

My second remark regards the words "*cut* the throat" which perhaps fastidious criticism may regard as rather too plebeian & unbaronial a mode of committing murder "*pierced*" might be substituted without injury either to the sense or rhyme. The simple beauty of the next verse has made its chime in my ear ever since I have read it. *Scotch* must be spelld *Scots* to keep up the orthography of the antique age. You see to what minute investigation I have descended in order to find fault & avoid the imputation of sending a vague & unqualified panegyric.

I have been just two days returnd from Ettricke fforeste & found your letter here on my arrival. It would have gratified me exceedingly to have extended my ride to Dumfrieshire nor do I yet entirely dispair of doing so. Should there be a chance of my being within 36 miles I will not fail to visit Hoddam Castle, & the mysterious tower concerning which you have composed a tale of Repentance[1] never to be repented of. I am much obliged to you for consulting the old Lady of Ecclefechan[2] on my account, & shall be anxious to hear the result of your enquiries. To save you trouble in copying if you give me any idea of the names & scope of her stories I will let you know if I have them in my collection which is now very extensive. I have got three covenanting ballads which I think curious altho' God knows their share of poetical merit is but small. They celebrate the battles of Philiphaugh, Loudon hill & Bothwell Bridge. That of Loudoun hill is the same with the skirmish at Drumclog & I am informd that a better edition of the ballad than mine is still in circulation in Dumfrieshire— perhaps it may fall in your way.

[1] Of his own ballad Sharpe says, " It is founded on a tradition respecting the Tower of Repentance, and I fear will inspire you with no great opinion of the author's modesty or abilities. . . . Pray, when *you* read it, do not clap on a pair of critical spectacles, like those which the merciless Dr. G—— used at the dissection of poor Burns's 'Wounded Hare.' "

[2] " I heard yesterday of a woman in the village of Ecclefechan, who can repeat a number of auld sangs, as they call them, whom I will send for as soon as possible to sing or say her collection."

I met a college friend of yours at Mertoun—Alexr. Scott who tells me you add drawing to your other accomplishments. How I envy you such an advantage in the study of antiques. Yours faithfully

W Scott

[*Hornel*]

TO THE EDITOR OF THE " SCOTS MAGAZINE " [1]

SIR,—The inclosed letter is the first of a series received by me from a young man born in Etterick Forest, and literally bred there in the humble situation of a shepherd. Various causes have concurred, in Scotland, to excite and encourage acuteness of observation, and strength of character, even among those who have reaped few or no advantages from fortune and from education. From the remarks of such men, especially upon subjects which they have been accustomed to consider with accuracy, more information may be derived than perhaps the pride of lettered rank will readily allow. We often hear the trite remark, that a stranger usually sees more of a town which he visits upon his travels, than those who have all their life been its inhabitants. Something like this may occur in the fields of knowledge. Those whose education has commenced with the first opening of their ideas, who have never known what it was to be at large from the trammels of an instructor, who have been as it were, " rocked and craddled, and dandled " into men of literature, may be considered as the denizens of the realms of taste and science. But the uneducated and hardy intruder, whose natural strength of mind impels

---

[1] Hogg had contributed *The Mistakes of a Night* to *The Scots Magazine* in 1794, but his first direct introduction " was made in October 1802 by Scott, who sent some letters which Hogg had addressed to him, and explained in a covering letter that the author really was a shepherd of Ettrick. These letters were published from October 1802 to June 1803 under the title of A Journey through the Highlands of Scotland in the months of July and August 1802, in a Series of Letters to —— Esq."— EDITH C. BATHO, *The Ettrick Shepherd*.

him to study, and to whose researches novelty gives all its charms, may, while bewildering himself in unknown streets, and occasionally mistaking gewgaws and trinkets for real treasures, view nevertheless recesses untrod before, and discover beauties neglected by those who have been bred up among them.

I felt myself deeply impressed with the truth of those observations, on perusing part of the journal which my correspondent had kept during a distant highland tour, and at my request, he undertook to digest his travelling observations into a series of letters. Should you think them worthy of a place in your Publication I should hope many of your readers may be amused, and even instructed, in following the views and ideas of such a character as I have described, especially when I assure you, that it is not assumed to give a factitious interest to the letters, which are really and unaffectedly the production of a shepherd of Etterick Forest. I remain, Sir, Your humble servant,

S. W.[1]

EDINBURGH, 26*th Sept.* 1802.

[*Scots Magazine*, lxiv. p. 812]

To ARCHIBALD CONSTABLE

DEAR SIR,—I leave this place today for Selkirkshire from whence I shall not return till the 13th about which time I suppose Mr. Mawman[2] will be arrived in Edinr. & I shall be glad to have some conversation with him & you. I re-inclose his letter with my best thanks for your attention & am very sincerely Yours

WALTER SCOTT

LASSWADE COTTAGE [3*rd*] *Octr.* 1802.

I hope Mr. M. & you will spend a day here.

[*Stevenson*]

[1] " S. W." So in the *Scots Magazine*, for " W. S."

[2] Joseph Mawman, the first London publisher of the *Edinburgh Review*, but owing to dissatisfaction with his management, the London sale was transferred to Messrs. Longmans. See *Constable and his Literary Correspondents*, I. 55.

To CHARLES KIRKPATRICK SHARPE

I MUST not delay to express to you my dear Sir how much I am gratified by your permission to insert the *Complaynt* [1] in the 3d. Volume more particularly as it is accompanied by so beautiful a companion as the Murder of Caerlaverock.[1] I perfectly remember the subject of that tragical tale & taking your leave for granted shall prefix it as it is narrated by Fordun & the Prior of Lochlevin. I beg pardon for mentioning on the same page the wretched Duke of Milk of which I have no less than two if not three copies, but it is only to remark the difference betwixt a beautiful *imitation* & an impudent *forgery*. The latter class (ex. gratia the said D. of Milk & the Bedesman of Nidside) abound with an extravagant use of old words & are in fact usually composed chiefly from the glossary of some old author without the ingenious imitator being capable of discovering the proportion which the words requiring explanation in old compositions bear to those which are still in common use. Something of this may be observed in Chatterton & in fact such impositions are usually liable to detection from their out heroding herod. You will find a splendid example of this in some verses intitled the " Mort o' Lauch " if in your copy of the Bedesman[2] as in mine. They are subjoined to that Ballad. Bad as the Bedesman is I think it must have been rather beyond Glenriddell at least if I can judge from some of his prose compositions now in my hands which are truly the most extravagant compositions that ever ever a poor Man abandond by providence to the imaginations of his own heart had the misfortune to devise—To return to a more interesting subject I am greatly pleased with Caerlaverock which is in the very best Ballad taste & unacknowledged by you

[1] *The Lord Herries, his Complaint* and *The Murder of Caerlavrock* were included in the *Minstrelsy*, vol. iv.

[2] " The Bedesman of Nithside " which Sharpe, in his letter, ascribes to a Dr. Clapperton of Lochmaben, " a very poor production.".

might readily pass for a first-rate ministrel composition. It puts me out of conceit with some things I have been attempting in the same style for in endeavouring to preserve the track of true Ballad simplicity I feel it difficult to avoid slipping into the morass of bald & childish doggrel which you so happily avoid.

I have recoverd three Covenanting Ballads—The defeat of Montrose at Philiphaugh—the Battle of Bothwell Brigg & the preceeding Skirmish at Drumclog or Loudoun hill. They are all as you will readily suppose, indifferent enough the genius of the sect turning them rather towards psalmody but they will afford room for some curious notes. I have Lagg's elegy & am acquainted with the traditions of the period respecting most of the persecutors and persecuted saints. These traditions in many cases have extinguishd the more early history of the Border feuds tho' in themselves far less valuable. The effects & dregs of *whiggery* to use a word of those times has left some of the worst impressions on the character of the South Country peasantry. I must not omit to answer the Query of your postscript. The print in the Minstrelsy is intended to represent the Castle of Hermitage in Liddesdale famous in Border history & tradition. It is very poorly executed which is not altogether the Artist's fault for it was taken from a sketch of mine (copied by an Artist). Now I was famous when I drew at all for making representations of houses & churches which if they were not geese & turkies to the beholders as the originals were to the Dragon of Wantley had at least a much greater resemblance to *thrawn* hay-stacks than to any thing else.— I am very gratful for the account of Lord Herries & the tower of Repentance which you have added to your other favours. I have read somewhere a curious debate about the mode of garrisoning that fortalice.—The Queen's Maries are mentioned both by Buchanan & Keith. They were 4 young Ladies of high family sent to France along with their Mistress. Their names were

I   L

Seton, Beton, Fleming & Livingston. The two last are
in the Ballad exchanged for Hamilton & Carmichael.
But the Mary Hamilton of the ballad is a creation
of tradition, the real sufferer was a french waiting
woman.

Permit me while I return my best thanks for your most
acceptable correspondence earnestly to solicit its continuance & at the same time to regret that circumstances
have not permitted me to return those thanks in person.
I hope to hear of you from the Banks of Isis & ever am
Dear Sir Yours most faithfully

                                                        W. SCOTT

LASWADE COTTAGE, 17 *Octr.* 1802

Charles Kirkpatrick Sharpe, Esq.
Hoddam Castle By Ecclefechan

[*Hornel*]

To ANNA SEWARD

SHORT Letters are vile things—at least with my feelings
the beginning of an epistle is like the first start of a race
horse & I would always wish to continue it till I had run
over paper enough to have gaind as jockeys say my speed
or in plainer language till exertion had become pleasure.
I have therefore deferrd from time to time the pleasure
of continuing this valuable correspondence which has
commenced under such flattering auspices untill I should
be able to say something more than " yours received &
note the contents." Both Miss Sewards favours arrived
safe & I have been forming the resolution of answering
them tomorrow for certain for several weeks. But my
country amusements & journies were succeeded by the
necessity of attending to some family affairs & besides
I can plead with too much justice the feeling apology of
the sturdy Neopolitan Lazarone to a person who urged
him to work "My dear friend did you but know how
lazy I am." A disease for which no Pharmacopeia I

believe affords a remedy unless the sharp *stimulus* of
absolute necessity.—

Since I had the pleasure of hearing from you I have
disposed of the property of the Border Minstrelsy for
£500 ! I only mention this circumstance that you
may hold me acquitted of the vile vanity of wishing to
hold myself forth as despising to reap any profit from
his literary pursuits which I should hold to be ineffable
conceit & folly in a man much richer than myself.
The mode of publishing by subscription is one which in
itself can carry nothing degrading & which in many of
the more extensive & high priced publications is perhaps
essentially necessary.   Still however it is asking the public
to become bound to pay for what they have not seen, &
carries with it if not the reality at least the appearance
of personal solicitation & personal obligation. Yet
our most brilliant authors have had recourse to it &
alas ! too often from circumstances of necessity disgrace-
ful to the age in which they lived & which perhaps may
hereafter be distinguishd more by the honor of having
produced them than by any other attribute. As for
Mackenzie [1] he was only a subscriber to my 3^{d} vol: in the
same way in which Miss Seward is viz by contributing
to its contents not to its Sale.—I mean not *directly* to
the sale—for I know how valuable the contributions of
my friends have proved to me in securing the benevolence
of the public & have often likend myself to a general
who tho' neither the bravest nor most skillful soldier
in the army runs away with all the profit & half the
applause acquired by the prowess of those who have
fought under his banners.

I am highly flatterd by your approbation of Cadyow
Castle which is founded upon a fact in Scottish hist^{y}—
for which I referr you to the death of the Regent

---

[1] *i.e.* Colin Mackenzie, Esq., of Portmore, one of the Principal Clerks of
Session and through life an intimate friend of Scott. His contribution to
the *Border Minstrelsy* is *Ellandonan Castle : a Highland Tale.*

Murray as narrated in Robertsons history at the end
of the 1st vol: where you will find the story told in
a manner highly picturesque. Hamilton of Bothwellhaugh by whom he was slain had received the most
poignant injury at his hands : his dwelling of Wood-
housilee having been plunderd by the Regents minions
& his wife, a few days after child-birth having been
turnd naked into the fields when coverd with snow—
in consequence of which barbarous usage she went
raving mad & died shortly after. She is the Margaret
of the Ballad. I have meditated upon your criticism
of the *death-deafend ear* [1] & as I deeply distrust my own
judgement when opposed to that of those whom I
esteem I have consulted Dugald Stuart & some of our
literati here. What they submit in answer to your
ingenious remark is that *deafend* by no means implies total
deafness but rather the act of becoming deaf through the

---

[1] I cannot find the letter in which Miss Seward criticised this epithet, but
on 19th March 1803 she writes congratulating him on the financial
success of the *Minstrelsy* : " Since I received your last letter I have seen
the assassination of the Regent Murray in Robertson. Do you follow the
history strictly respecting the manner in which it was performed ? The
fragment you sent me commences here
                    With hackbut bent my bold scout stand
which implies a band of rebel conspirators in a balcony. I resign my
objection to *death-deafend*. The expression struck me as having somewhat
of an Hibernian complexion and I hold it very stuff of conscience to communicate to a friend every objection to his unpublished work, however
trivial, because it costs no trouble to do away questionable verbalisms. . . .
When and how is the *sublime* tragic ballad to appear ? Such from the
sample I have no scruple to pronounce it. Will it find a place in your
third volume of *Border Minstrelsy* ? "—*Unpublished letter in National Library*.
    She goes on to intimate the part she is to take in the Life of Darwin :
" I shall not attempt more than the outline of his Derby History." The
rest is to be the work of a Pupil and late years' friend Mr. Bilsbury. " From
his pen I suspect we shall see one of those faultless monsters with which
Biography abounds. *Fidelity* and not *emblazonry* is my plan. . . . Mr
Hayley's Life of Cowper has disappointed me. . . . He claims approachless
excellence for Cowper's letters which any person of sense and education
might have written. They have neither the critical interest and instruction
of Pope's ; the humorous strength of Johnson's ; the sprightly grace of
Madame Sevigné's nor the brilliant elegance of Gray's . . . in sublimity of
idea and strength of expression the Night-Thoughts extremely transcend
the Task." To all this Scott replies in his next letter.

approach of death.   Besides *death-deafning* rather seems to
convey an active idea as we talk of a *deafning sound* &
moreover all even of Murrays ear was actually finally
closed by death there was nothing to prevent the ghost
from hollowing into it since like many good people she
may be supposed more intent to express her own feelings
than either to convey reproach or admonition to the
person to whom she addressd herself. --While we talk of
verbal criticism I must not omit to mention that Miltons
metaphor

> Fame is the *spur* which the clear spirit doth *raise* [1]

retains its accuracy in Scotch tho as you justly observe
it is lost in the modern English.   We still say that a Man
or a horse is *raised* when by any violent impulse he is
thrown into a state of extraordinary exertion of mind
or body & to *raise* a horse with the spur would be an
expression perfectly legitimate in Scotland.   The word
you will of course understand relates not to the action
but to the effect of the spur.

I Rejoice that you have met the ladies of Llangollen [2]
of whom I have heard so much that I think you must
have found them kindred spirits.   My friends Mr. &
Mrs. Dugald Stuart are well acquainted with them and
great admirers of their accomplishments & manners—
a eulogium which conveys a great deal to all who know
Mr. & Mrs. S.—

As I hope you read the bible & are acquainted with the
propriety of heaping coals of fire upon the head of a lazy
correspondent I venture in virtue of that precept to solicit
the pleasure of hearing from you when you can spare
me an hour for so idle a purpose—I am at present busy

[1] " Milton should have said *doth goad* to have kept his metaphor accurate."
—ANNA SEWARD.

[2] Miss Sarah Ponsonby and Lady Eleanor Butler of the Bessborough and
Ormonde families.   See later letters and Lockhart.   Professor Dugald
Stewart is too well known to need a note.   Born in 1753 he survived till
1828.   A coldness between Scott and Stewart followed the Melville trial
and banquet.

with the second edition of the Minstrelsy & preparations for the third volume particularly a sort of Romance of Border Chivalry & inchantment which will extend to some length. When it has made any progress I will send you a few stanzas which unworthy as they are will I hope serve as a sort of peace-offering for the offences with which I reproach myself towards Miss Seward. I have ever the honor to be Miss Sewards obliged & very respectful Servant

WALTER SCOTT

EDINR. 30*th Novr.* 1802

[*British Museum*]

To WILLIAM OWEN

SIR,—I must have been suffering deeply in your esteem on account of permitting your very obliging favour to remain so long unnoticed.

I beg you will impute my doing so to anything rather than a want of sense of the value of your correspondence from which I derived much & curious information. The truth is that avocations partly of a literary partly of a professional nature have of late very much interfered with my labours upon the old Romance of Sir Tristrem concerning which I consulted you. I am now anxious to introduce to your knowledge my friend Dr. Leyden [1] who is about to leave this country for India. We lose in him an able Scottish Antiquary whose mind was greatly turned to the illustration of our early history & who is anxious in common with myself to learn the

---

[1] On the 10th of January 1803 Owen replies to this letter and says : " Your letter by favour of Dr. Leyden gave me great pleasure. . . . I am glad a man of such talent as Dr. Leyden should be going to India : for I consider that country as abounding with magnificent treasures of primitive monuments and only just opened to our curiosity.—There are surprising affinities between some of our Druidical Triads &c. and the Braminical mythology. Take as an instance that those Triads &c. preserve the memorial of Menw the son of the Three Waedds (Loud Utterances) with similar attributes as are preserved among the Bramins who represent him as the promulgator of the three Veds."

lights which can be thrown upon it from the ancient British Authors. You know that the Western part of Scotland formed long an independant British Kingdom under the name of Strath Clwyd which I believe can be proved to have extended over the greater part of Peebles & Selkirkshires—

Now although this kingdom had ceased to exist some time before the date of Tomas of Erceldoune the author of Sir Tristrem (who flourished about the middle & end of the 13th. Century) yet many traces of British manners language & poetry must have been floating among his neighbours of Ettricke forest.

Even at this remote period we can distinguish from the names of places & some obscure & faint traditions that these hills were long inhabited by a British tribe. In the time of Tomas all their history real or fabulous must have been fresh in memory & I think it highly probable that he took the subject immediately from the British traditions without its having past to Armorica & returned from thence in a french dress which was the case of many of those Romances which were termed *Lais* of Brittany. The names of all the personages in the Romance seem to me to be British for example—Morgan—Rowland Rus— Urgan—Ysoude or Yseult. Caer—Leon—Brengwain— Meriadok—The only place that stumbles me is *Ermonie* —Is it possible that this can mean—" The land opposite to Mona " as Armorica is said to have meant the Land upon the sea-coast. If so the names and geography will be purely British & we may perhaps see reason to think that the Romance did not come to us from the French but was of domestic & British origin. I lay no stress upon the *Morte Arthur* nor indeed upon any of the prose Romances of Chivalrey in the decision of this question because there is hardly one of them which was not originally written in verse to be sung by the Minstrels. It was at a much later period about the reign of Charles VIIth of France that the fas[h]ion was introduced (I presume to gratify the increasing number of readers) of *transprosing* the old songs of the Minstrels & Trouveurs into those massive volumes of prose Romances. I have in particular a copy of the metrical Romances of King Arthur as translated from Wace's poem of the Brut upon which Geoffrey of Monmouth grounded his history. I therefore do not look at the prose Romances where the metrical originals are to be come at.

Forgive me for this rhapsody which I write in great haste Leyden after long expectation being at length summoned away in a great hurry. If I have not forfeited so great a favour by ungracious silence may I request to be favoured with a translation of the dialogue betwixt Tristrem & Gwalchmai which you so obligingly offered me. I think I requested to be enrolled among the subscribers to your Dicty. & that my copy might be forwarded to Constable Bookseller here. You have contrived to make a Dicty. which offered both instruction & amusement even to those unacquainted with the language so curious are the illustrations & examples.

Wishing every success to your literary labours I remain Dear Sir Your obliged humble servant

EDIN. 22 *Dc.* 1802   WALTER SCOTT

[*Mrs. Meilir Owen*]

1803

21 January, 1803

All happiness of the season
to you your father & brothers

MY DEAR SIR,—So many acceptable things as accompanied your last letter demand a very speedy acknowledgement. Graeme & Bewick[1] will be at the press in a fortnight & will form an early article of the third volume with which I am now busy. I have used your copy literally with the exception of a verse which I heard Hogg repeat in which he made the conclusion rather different in word though not in sense : & also with one or two literal alterations to restore rhyme as " *came* " for " *same* " &c. I also read Liddisdale for Lauderdale as the more probable seat of war betwixt the Graemes and the Scottish. You have excited my curiosity strongly about Tushilaw lines if they can be recovered for God's [sake] spare no pains, & *speedily good Tyrrel* as Shakespeare I think somewhere says or as I say whether he does or not. I am sorry you should be disappointed about the Rannoch farm which after a conversation I had with Mr. Niel Fergusson a friend of Sir — Menzies I considered as in a very fair train. He was quite satisfied with the account I gave of my Black-house friends—but I suppose you have been out-bid. I hope you will secure the Craig—at any thing like a rent you should not hesitate—it

---

[1] See *The Minstrelsy of the Border*. Of the version there Henderson says : " Scott's is a mere corruption of the broadside, of which there are copies in the Douce and Roxburghe collections, the original date being *c.* 1698 and the date of the reprint c. 1778."

lies at your door you are young and active & depend
upon it while you & I live (unless some extraordinary
event take place) the value of land and of tacks will
continue to rise. Our fathers thought it at it's height
sixty years ago, so if you can get a reasonable length of
lease dont be afraid of rent. When I say the value of
land rises perhaps I ought to add that the rise is only
apparent consisting in a good measure though not
entirely in a depretiation of the value of money. If
my name can serve you with Mr. George Stuart refer
him to me freely but he knows your Father well.

   Mrs. Scott is very much obliged to George for the game
& so are my books for the Tod's tail which I have *bane'd*
and mounted on a stick to give them a weekly switching.[1]
I am afraid their are too many of them which have the
dust seldom removed in a more legitimate & honourable
way. I had however a struggle with my wife before I
could rescue it from her for being packed with the game
she claimed it as being part and pertinent thereof & I
think would have mounted it on some sort of Montero cap
like Corporal Trim's if I had not promised her to replace
it with a Selkirkshire brush whenever any of my correspondents could get one. So if such a thing should
again fall in your way have the goodness to secure it for
her. The [verse]s respecting the Devils wooing are curious
and pathetic. I never saw the whole song though I have
a distant recollection of hearing parts of it. When you
have leisure to write it out I will thank you for a copy
though I think I shall have no room for it in the volume.
I would much prefer Tushilaw. I would make a point
of squeezing them in. The locality and traditional
history of such a ballad gives it great interest above a
mere legend. Whenever this said third volume is
finished you shall have a copy & you will see how very
much it owes to our Selkirkshire collections. Auld
Maitland laced & embroidered with antique notes and

---

[1] Used later as a duster for his books. See *Lockhart*, c. xli.

illustrations makes a most superb figure. I will also send you a copy of the second edition of the 2 first vols. the others may gratify any of your friends who likes such things. I have got through the intervention of Lady Dalkeith a copy of Mr. Beattie [of] Muckledale's [1] Tamlane it contains some highly poetical stanzas descriptive of Faery land which after some hesitation I have adopted although they have a very refined and modern cast. I do not suspect Mr Beattie of writing ballads himself but pray will you enquire whether within the memory of Man there has been any poetical clergyman or schoolmaster whom one could suppose capable of giving a coat of modern varnish to this old ballad what say you to this for example.

> We sleep in rosebuds soft & sweet
> We revel in the stream
> We wanton lightly in the wind
> Or glide on a sunbeam.

This seems quite modern—yet I have retained it—I am curious to see his other traditionary treasures so pray hint to no one my doubts of their authenticity—Yours truly

W. Scott

[Abbotsford Copies]

To WILLIAM LAIDLAW

My dear Sir,—I am very much obliged to you for your letter & the Inclosure. The Laird of Logie [2] is

[1] But this memory of mine was a very fickle ally . . . and might have enabled me to adopt old Beattie of Meikledale's answer when complimented by a certain reverend divine on the strength of the same faculty. "No, sir," answered the old borderer, "I have no command of my memory. It only retains what hits my fancy, and probably, sir, if you were to preach to me for two hours I would not be able, when you finished, to remember a word you had said."—*Autobiography*. Scott's version of *Tamlane* in the *Minstrelsy* is obviously inferior to that supplied to Johnson's Musical Museum. See Henderson's note in his edition of the *Minstrelsy*.

[2] This appeared in the second edition of the *Minstrelsy*, and the introductory note says : " An edition of this ballad is current under the title of *The Laird of Ochiltree*, but the editor, since the first publication of this work, has been fortunate enough to recover the following more correct and ancient copy as recited by a gentleman residing near Biggar."

particularly acceptable as coming very near the real history. Carmichael mentioned in the Ballad was the ancestor of the Earl of Hyndford & Captain of James VIths guard so that the circumstance of the prisoner being in his custody is highly probable. I will adopt the whole of this Ballad instead of the common one called Ochiltree. *Geordie* I have seen before—the ballad is curious tho very rude & although it does not fall within my plan I am glad to have a copy of it. *Ormond* may be curious though modern— The story of Confessing the Queen of England is published by Bishop Percy so I will neither trouble you about that nor about *Dundee.* The latter is a very curious Ballad but I have a compleat copy of it with the tradition to which it relates. *Glendinning* is a wrong reading, the name of the Highland Chief who carries off the Lady is Glen Lyon one of the Menzies's.— Among Hogg's Ballads was a compleat & curious set of Laminton or Lochinvar which I incline to adopt as better than that in The Minstrelsy. Quaere? who was Katherine Jeffray the heroine? She could hardly be a damsel of great rank as the estate of Whitebank is an ancient patrimony of the Pringle's. I dont know what to make of Cokburns [1] name unless it be Perys the modern Pierce, which is not a very common name in Scotland.— I am

---

[1] Laidlaw, in the letter Scott is answering, writes :

"A copy of the inscription on Cockburn's tombstone at Henderland had been taken by one Armstrong who surveyed & published a map of Tweeddale some time ago. The stone would be there entire, & the letters not so much defaced. . . . Armstrong has recorded the Outlaw's Epitaph in his Companion to the map : it is here lyes perys of Cockburn & his wife Marjorie. I got it from one of our herds at Bowerhope. . . . Only this day a woman in the town here was singing *Tushielaw's* lines which I have some times heard but always judged it to relate to some of the Andersons & of newer date ; but she happened to call him Scott of Tushielaw—I said I thought he had been Anderson—she didna ken she said she aye heard him ca'd Scott—I wish this could be made out—it is a story of much lore & witchcraft—I had the surprise of a visit from my crackbraind acquaintance Mr. Bartran of Biggar the other day. He brought me a copy of the Laird of Laminton . . . likewise . . . the Laird of Logie (Ochiltree) which I will transcribe & enclose. . . . I wrote to Bartran as strongly & as artfully as I could & since I saw him he has fallen in with Leyden *at*

very much interested about Tushiclaw's lines which from what you mention must be worth recovering.

I shall be at Whitebanklee for two days Saturday, namely & Sunday—on Friday evening I shall sleep at Selkirk as we have a County meeting that day. If you can take a ride down any of these days I will be happy to see you as wherever I may be in the course of the day I will always be at home in the Evening.

I forgot to bring with me from Blackhouse your edition of the Gosshawk in which were some excellent various readings. I am so anxious to have a compleat Scottish Otterburne that I will omit the Ballad entirely in the first volume hoping to recover it in time for insertion in the third. I would myself be well pleased to delay the publication of all three for some time, but the Booksellers are mutinous & impatient as a Book is always injured by being long out of print. As to the Liddesdale traditions I think I am pretty correct although doubtless much more may be recovered. The truth is that in these matters as you must have observed old people are usually very positive about their own mode of telling a story and equally uncharitably critical in their observations on those who differ from them— Hoping you will find it convenient to let me see you I remain Yours faithfully

WALTER SCOTT

Wednesday WITEBANKLEE

Complt to your father & brothers & service to our ingenious Shepherd.

[*Abbotsford Copies.*]

a private Ball in Edinr. & between us I believe we have set the whole bent of his mind (it is strong though uncommonly eccentric) in search of antient Ballads & he makes no discrimination. . . . . I do not know your reasons for publishing a second edition of your first volume now, therefore I cannot suppress a wish that you would postpone it for a little—It seems the Liddesdale people say you got your information there from Dr. Elliot & they persist in saying his knowledge is very shallow. But if you have seen Mr. Beattie Muckledale it answers this objection."

To G. ELLIS

January 30, 1803 [1]

THE idea of a map pleases me much but there are two strong objections to its being prefixed to this edition. *First,* we shall be out in a month, within which time it would be difficult, I apprehend, for Mr. Arrowsmith labouring under the disadvantages which I am about to mention, to complete the map. *Secondly,* you are to know that I am an utter stranger to geometry, surveying, and all such *inflammatory* branches of study, as Mrs Malaprop calls them. My education was unfortunately interrupted by a long indisposition, which occasioned my residing for about two years in the country with a good maiden aunt who permitted and encouraged me to run about the fields as wild as any buck that ever fled from the face of man. Hence my geographical knowledge is merely practical, and though I think that in the *South Country* " I could be a guide worth ony twa that may in Liddesdale be found " yet I believe Hobby Noble or Kinmont Willie would beat me at laying down a map. I have, however, sense enough to see that our mode of executing maps in general is anything but perfect. The country is most accurately defined, and had your general marched through Scotland by the assistance of Ainslie's map, his flying artillery would soon have stuck fast among our

[1] On the 16th January 1803 Ellis had written acknowledging a letter brought by " John of Leyden," and in it had urged that a map of the Border district should be supplied, which Longman is perfectly willing to prefix to the third volume. " Leyden whom I carried to Arrowsmith was unable to point out to me on the best map of Scotland the situation of Erceldoun or even to trace the several dales and heights which are the scenes of your ancient ballads. He tells me that *you* have a *survey* of the *forest* which does exhibit, with tolerable precision, the scenery of that curious part of the country." He tells how he had once made a map of a country he had never seen : " I attempted to give a bird's-eye view of Mount Caucasus," which a Russian general had been able later to use with advantage. He praises Scott's continuation of Sir Tristrem, and describes Leyden's arrival without the ballad of Cadzow Castle (*Lockhart,* c. x.).

morasses and his horse broke their knees among our cairns. Your system of a bird's-eye view is certainly the true principle . . . the map then must be deferred until the third edition about which, I suppose, Longman thinks courageously. . . . I am almost glad Cadzow Castle miscarried, as I have rather lost conceit of it at present being engaged on what I think will be a more generally interesting legend. I have called it the Lay of the Last Minstrel and put it in the mouth of an old bard who is supposed to have survived all his brethren and to have lived down to 1690. The thing itself will be very long but I would willingly have sent you the Introduction had you been still in possession of your senatorial privilege ; but double postage would be a strange innovation on the established price of ballads which have always sold at the easy rate of one halfpenny.

[*Lockhart*]

To CHARLES CARPENTER [1]

EDINBURGH, 6 *March*, 1803

MY DEAREST BROTHER,—I have just received your letter of Septr. 1802 the first I have had from you since you had received the melancholy intelligence which I transcribed to you with so much pain. I am more concerned than surprised at the deep impression which such a loss must necessarily have made upon your mind but you must give me leave to hope that your reflections are now in some degree turn'd from so very painful a subject to your own fair & flourishing prospects. I know that good news from Scotland will have considerable effect in enlivening your spirits & therefore

[1] This letter from " I know that good news " is printed in *Familiar Letters* with some other omissions and some errors and corrections. The first sentences, omitted there, refer doubtless to the death of Lord Downshire in 1801. See also *Memoir and Correspondence of General J. S. Fraser*, 1885, and note later, p. 290.

I hasten to tell you that we are well happy & prosperous. Charlotte about four weeks ago presented me with a little damsel whom we have call'd Anne in compliment to my worthy mother : had it proved a boy it was to have been a little Charles. My little Sophia is a thriving little Scotch girl & the boy uncommonly stout healthy & robust : in short quite a model for a little Hercules. My worldly matters jog on very well. Government propose to increase the appointments of the Sheriffs which will put an additional £100 a year into my pocket. Moreover I have contrived to turn a very slender portion of literary talents to some account by a publication of the poetical antiquities of the Border Counties where the old people had preserved many ballads & ancient songs descriptive of the manners of the country during the wars with England. This trifling collection was so well received by a *discerning* public that after receiving £100 profit for the first edition, which my vanity cannot omit informing you sold off in 6 months, I sold the copy right for £500 more. I am seeking a mode of conveyance to transmit to you this precious compilation. You will hear a good deal of our motions from a Doctor Leyden who goes to Madras in this fleet should his fortune throw him in your way. Charlotte has given him a few lines to you merely as an introduction, but I must let you a little deeper into his history ; he was the son of a very petty farmer in Roxburghshire & had so little education that at 12 years old he did not know how to write. Nature had however been liberal in her gifts : he caught a taste for knowledge & under the most depressing circumstances made himself master of most of the learned languages, of those of modern Europe, & even dabbled in Eastern literature. When he found his way to Edinburgh College his merit by degrees became noticed & at length conspicuous. I had the good luck early to discover both his literary and personal worth & at different times he lived a good deal with us till it was in my power to procure him his

present appointment of Assistant Surgeon on the Madras
establishment, which I accomplished through Mr. W.
Dundas. Ld. W. Bentinck is to countenance him in his
labours which I suppose will be rather literary than
medical : he will certainly make an effort to see you if
it be possible : you must be prepared to encounter &
pardon some peculiarity of manner arising from his early
history & which even his intercourse with the first people
here & in London has not quite erased ; but you will find
this amply atoned for by a great fund of knowledge &
native kindness of disposition. He will be able to tell
you a thousand little anecdotes regarding our domestic
habits &c. for things of very little importance in themselves are pleasing & interesting when they relate to
separated friends. I am rejoiced to see that at length
you fix a period at which we may hope for your return
to Britain. Happiness depends so much less upon the
quantity of fortune than upon the power of enjoying what
we have that I am sure you my dear brother after
having spent your early years in acquiring a respectable
fortune will not delay enjoying it for the purpose of
making it still larger. Remember Scotland will have a
claim on you for one part of the year, if upon trial you
like its society & climate & I am so true a Scotchman
that I think it impossible you can dislike them. Besides
our women are generally reckon'd handsome & accomplished & I hope notwithstanding your attachment to
old England you will give our Nymphs a chance of
setting their caps at you. Your sister says you positively
must be married soon after your arrival so you must
prepare for fetters even in the land of liberty. I would
send you political news were there any worth sending !
Those from France are singularly gloomy. Subjected to
a very rigorous military government all attempt at
domestic happiness seems to be given up for the *fracas* of
public amusements & immense parties where none dare
tell his mind to his next neighbour should it involve

anything more important than an opinion on the merit of the newest *cantatrice* or *figurante*. Besides all this a pestilential disorder is now raging at Paris. At home the most remarkable event is the discovery of a plot to assassinate the best of Kings by a set of low ruffians the leaders of whom have been executed. Col. Despard the Ringleader of these Miscreants was once in the army & had a character for bravery & skill in his profession. Being intrusted with some presents intended to conciliate the Chiefs of the Mosquito Indians in the Bay of Honduras the worthy Colonel chose to appropriate the gifts to his own purposes for which peculation he was broken by a Court Martial in the W. Indies : having become totally desperate in consequence of this well merited disgrace he embraced eagerly the opportunity of avenging himself on government by embarking in all the seditious proceedings during the war which procured him a lodging in Cold Bath fields where his fate was deplored & howled over by Sir Frances Burdett & other reforming members of the house of commons : the first act of this worthy & oppressed patriot upon his liberation was to organize the murder of his Sovereign. It does not appear from his trial that any persons were associated with him excepting the Ruffians who were to be the immediate actors, but it is generally believed that he acted as the link betwixt these subordinate agents & a higher rank of conspirators as it is hardly to be conceived that a person of sense & education would embark in so desperate a project without being assured of more powerful allies than a set of low blackguards not exceeding 30 or 40 in number. Col. Despard died like a true Jacobin neither fearing God nor regarding man. The peace seems likely to hold notwithstanding it is confidently asserted that we are to retain Malta as the only security against the preponderance which the French have acquired in the Mediterranean by the cession of Elba & the chief Consul's having been placed at the head of the Cisalpine republic.

Those who talk of the retention of Malta (& I have heard some very high authority upon the subject) reason thus : If Bonaparte does not wish to quarrel with this country or again to possess himself of Egypt which would produce an immediate breach then our cession of Malta cannot be to him a matter of such importance as to precipitate him into war. But if he really wishes to have Egypt, the removal of our fleet & armies from Malta will be an indispensible preliminary & such a removal would be follow'd by his immediately invading Egypt & consequently by a war with this country under circumstances much more unfavourable than if we still held Malta so that the proposed cession might accelerate but could not possibly avert a breach with France. Such were the sentiments which I heard deliver'd by a very eminent statesman & I think there is good sense in them though I do not pretend to understand the subject. To return to domestic affairs—as soon as your sister is quite recovered I intend we shall go to London where I am call'd by some professional business so we shall have the pleasure of seeing all our good friends in Piccadilly which will be no small gratification to me as well as to Charlotte : she is recovering from her indisposition uncommonly well & desires a thousand expressions of the kindest affection to you. Joining cordially in all her good wishes I am ever most sincerely Your truly affectionate brother

WALTER SCOTT

[*Abbotsford Copies and Fraser Memoir*]

To ANNA SEWARD

[*March*, 1803]

I HAVE been for about a fortnight in this huge & bustling metropolis, when I am agreeably surprized by a packet from Edinburgh, containing Miss Sewards letter. I am truly happy at the information it communicates respecting the life of Dr. Darwin, who could not have wishd his fame & character intrusted to a pen more capable of doing them ample & above all discriminating Justice. Biography the most interesting perhaps of every species of composition, loses all its interest with me when the shades and lights of the principal character are not accurately & faithfully detaild nor have I much patience with such exaggerated daubing as Mr. Hayley has bestowd upon poor Cowper. I can no more sympathise with a mere eulogist than I can with a ranting hero upon the stage & it unfortunately happens that some of our disrespect is apt rather unjustly to be transferrd to the subject of the panegyrick in the one case & to poor Cato in the other.—Unapprehensive that even friendship can biass Miss Sewards duty to the public I shall wait most anxiously for the volume her kindness has promised me. From what I know of Mr. Billsbury and from what I have heard I should not suppose him likely to spare much time and pains upon a work which to be well executed would require a great deal of both.—As for my third volume it was very nearly printed when I left Edinr. and must I think be ready for publication in about a fortnight, when it will have the honor of travelling to Litchfield. I doubt you will find but little amusement in it as there are a good many old ballads particularly those of the covenanters which in point of composition are mere drivelling trash. They are however curious in a historical point of view & have enabled me to slide in a number of notes about that dark & bloody period of Scottish history. There is a vast convenience to an editor in a tale upon which without the formality of adapting the notes very precisely to the shape & form of the ballad, he may hang on a set like a heralds coat without sleeves saving himself the trouble of taking measure & sending forth the tale of ancient time ready equipd from the Monmouth street warehouse of a commonplace book. Cadyow Castle is to appear in v. 3$^\mathrm{d}$ I cannot conceive how I made the foolish blunder of writing *bold scout stand*, what I meant to write was *secret stand*, the error is not only inconsistent with history as you justly observe but seems moreover to be very like nonsense.

I proceeded thus far about three weeks ago & shame to tell have left my epistle unfinished ever since. Yet I have not been wholly idle about a fortnight of that period having been employd as much to my satisfaction as any similar space of time during my life. I was the first week of that fortnight, with my invaluable friend George Ellis & spent the second week at Oxford which I visited for the first time. I was peculiarly fortunate in having for my patron at Oxford, Mr. Heber a particular friend of mine who is intimately acquainted with all both animate & inanimate that is worth knowing at Oxford. The time though as much as I could possibly spare has I find been too short to convey to me separate and distinct ideas of all the variety of wonders which I saw. My memory only at present furnishes a grand but indistinct picture of towers & Chapels & oriels and vaulted halls and libraries and paintings. I hope in a little time my ideas will develope themselves a little more distinctly otherwise I shall have profited little by my tour. I was much flatterd by the kind reception & notice I met with from some of the most distinguishd inhabitants of the halls of Isis which was more than such a truant to the Classic page as myself was entitled to expect at the source of classic learning.— On my return I find an apologetic letter from my printer saying the 3ᵈ volume will be despatchd in a day or two. There has been it seems a meeting among the printers devils—also among the paper makers. I never heard of authors *striking work* as the mechanicks call it untill their Masters the Booksellers should increase their pay, but if such a combination could take place the revolt would now be general in all branches of literary labour. How much sincere satisfaction would it give me could I conclude this letter (as I once hoped) by saying I should visit Litchfield, & pay my personal respects to my invaluable correspondt. in my way northwards. But as circumstances render this impossible, I shall depute the poetry of the olden time in the Editors stead—My Romance is not yet finished. I prefer it much to any thing I have done of the kind   [*MS. ends here*]

ASHESTIEL BY SELKIRK

[*British Museum*]

To JAMES BALLANTYNE [1]

[*21st April*, 1803]

I HAVE to thank you for the accuracy with which the Minstrelsy is thrown off. Longman and Rees are delighted with the printing. Be so good as to disperse the following presentation copies with " From the Editor," on each :—

James Hogg, Ettrick-House, care of Mr. Oliver, Hawick
—by the carrier—a complete set.
Thomas Scott (my brother), ditto.
Colin Mackenzie, Esq., Prince's Street, third volume
only.
Mrs. Scott, George Street, ditto.
Dr. Rutherford, York Place, ditto.
Captain Scott, Rosebank, ditto.

[1] " Scott . . . hurried up to town as soon as the Court of Session rose for the spring vacation, in hopes of seeing his friend [Leyden] once more before he left England ; but he came too late. . . .   The letter is dated No. 15 Piccadilly West,—he and Mrs. Scott being there domesticated under the roof of the late M. Charles Dumergue . . . who had been intimately acquainted with the Charpentiers in his own early life in France, and had warmly befriended Mrs. Scott's mother on her first arrival in England."   But Leyden's letter from the Isle of Wight when on the point of sailing implies that he *had* met Scott in London : " When I got to Portsmouth neither ship nor purser had arrived and I then regretted most sincerely that I had left you with so much precipitation."

I mean all these to be ordinary paper. Send one set fine paper to Dalkeith house, addressed to the Duchess ; another, by the Inverary carrier, to Lady Charlotte Campbell ; the remaining *ten*, fine paper, with any of Vol. III. which may be on fine paper, to be sent to me by sea. I think they will give you some *éclat* here, where printing is so much valued. I have settled about printing an edition of the Lay, 8vo. with vignettes, provided I can get a draughtsman whom I think well of. We may throw off a few superb in quarto. To the Minstrelsy I mean this note to be added, by way of advertisement :—" In the press, and will speedily be published, The Lay of the Last Minstrel, by Walter Scott, Esq., Editor of the Minstrelsy of the Scottish Border. Also, Sir Tristrem, a Metrical Romance, by Thomas of Ercildoune, called the Rhymer, edited from an ancient MS., with an Introduction and Notes, by Walter Scott, Esq." Will you cause such a thing to be appended in your own way and fashion ?

NO. 15, PICCADILLY WEST

[*Lockhart*]

To M. BOULTON [1]

[13*th May*, 1803]

To M. Boulton, Esq.,
  Soho House, Birmingham

MY DEAR SIR,—He was a wise man who said " Trust not thy wife with a Man of a fair tongue." Now as I

---

[1] Matthew Boulton (1728-1809), engineer and partner of Watt, who made coins for the British and other Governments. Mr. A. H. Westwood of the Assay Office, Birmingham, to whom I am indebted for a copy of this letter, writes to me : " Boulton, as you may know, met Lady Scott, then Miss Charpentier, before her marriage, at the house in London of his firm friend Charles Dumergue, dentist to the Prince of Wales. There is a reference to her in a letter of Dumergue to Boulton which we have here, as well as several in those of Mrs. Nicholson, Dumergue's house-keeper. In view of the friendly relations of Boulton with the Scotts, it is hard to see how the anecdote in ' Lockhart ' originated, where Boulton is reported to

have very little wisdom of my own I am content to gather
all I can get at second hand and therefore upon the
faith of the sage whom I have quoted I should consider
myself as guilty of great imprudence were I to permit
Charlotte to wait upon you on her return or even to
answer your kind letter to Mr. Dumergue. That task
therefore I take upon myself and you must receive my
thanks along with hers for your very kind & flattering
invitation to Soho.—But independent of my just suspicion
of a Beau who writes such flattering Love letters to my
wife our time here (owing to the sitting down of our
Courts of Justice which I must necessarily attend) lays
us under an indispensible necessity of returning to
Scotland as speedily as possible & by the nearest road.
We can therefore only express our joint & most sincere
regret that we cannot upon this occasion have the honor
& satisfaction of visiting Soho & its hospitable inhabitants.
Mrs. Nicolson Mr. & Miss Dumergue join Charlotte &
me in the most sincere good wishes to Miss Boulton to you
and to all your friends & I suspect so foolish a letter will
make you believe you have escaped a very idle visitor
in Dear Sir Your very obedient Servt.

WALTER SCOTT

LONDON, 13 *May*, 1803

[*Westwood*]

have taken offence at being worsted during a verbal engagement with
Sir Walter. The fact that Boulton had been dead over ten years at the
time the encounter is alleged to have taken place is in itself sufficient proof
of its incorrectness, and a reference to ' Birmingham Buttons ' would have
certainly pleased, not offended, him, as he was proud of his factory.
Possibly Boulton has been confused with his son, who had none of the
pride of his father in the origin of his wealth." The anecdote referred to
(*Lockhart*, c. 1.) derives from Allan Cunningham's memoranda of Scott's
visit to London to witness the coronation of George IV in 1821.

To GEORGE ELLIS [1]

EDINBURGH, 25*th May*, 1803

MY DEAR ELLIS,—. . . I was equally delighted with that venerable seat of learning, and flattered by the polite attention of Heber's friends. I should have been enchanted to have spent a couple of months among the curious libraries. What stores must be reserved for some painful student to bring forward to the public ! Under the guidance and patronage of our good Heber, I saw many of the literary men of his Alma Mater, and found matters infinitely more active in every department than I had the least previous idea of. Since I returned home, my time has been chiefly occupied in professional labours ; my truant days spent in London having thrown me a little behind ; but now, I hope, I shall find spare moments to resume Sir Tristrem—and the Lay, which has acquired

---

[1] " Scott's principal object . . . (having missed Leyden) was to peruse and make extracts from some MSS. in the library of John Duke of Roxburghe, for the illustration of the *Tristrem* ; and he derived no small assistance in other researches of the like kind from the collection the indefatigable and obliging Douce placed at his disposal. Having completed these labours he went, with Heber and Mrs. Scott, to Sunninghill, where they spent a happy week, and Mr. and Mrs. Ellis heard the first two or three cantos of the *Lay of the Last Minstrel* read under an old oak in Windsor Forest."—LOCKHART. This accounts for the gap in the correspondence, but there had been letters. On the 29th May 1802 Ellis acknowledges a letter of the 10th of this month and tells of his reviewing Scott and Leyden in the *British Critic*. He adds, " I rejoice exceedingly that my young friend Lord Dalkeith has not quite forgotten me. He was quite the pearl of the young men whom I met in Italy and would have been a Tristrem, a Lancelot or a Gauvain had he lived in the days of Arthur, tant etoit-il courtois et bien appris." On the 1st of November of the same year he acknowledges a letter of the 17th October and says, " Heber was in daily expectation of Leyden's arrival," but " I conclude that your learned friend's journey is again postponed." Where is Tristrem ? Should it not form the fourth volume of the *Minstrelsy* ? Mrs. Ellis " is not less impatient to see the ballad upon the death of the regent Murray (Cadzow Castle) than I am for the pretended doggerel of Sir Tristrem." A letter of 11th December acknowledges Scott's reply to his views on *Richard Cœur de Lion* and reports the serious illness of Lady Parker. Ritson's book on animal food has appeared, but with the blasphemies cut out by the printer. Heber is in Paris.

additional value in my estimation, from its pleasing you. How often do Charlotte and I think of the little paradise at Sunninghill and its kind inhabitants ; and how do we regret, like Dives, the gulf which is placed betwixt us and friends, with whom it would give us such pleasure to spend much of our time. It is one of the vilest attributes of the best of all possible worlds, that it contrives to split and separate and subdivide everything like congenial pursuits and habits, for the paltry purpose, one would think, of diversifying every little spot with a share of its various productions. I don't know why the human and vegetable departments should differ so excessively. Oaks and beeches, and ashes and elms, not to mention cabbages and turnips, are usually arrayed *en masse* ; but where do we meet a town of antiquaries, a village of poets, or a hamlet of philosophers? But, instead of fruitless lamentations, we sincerely hope Mrs. Ellis and you will unrivet yourselves from your forest, and see how the hardy blasts of our mountains will suit you for a change of climate. . . . The new edition of " Minstrelsy " is published here, but not in London as yet, owing to the embargo on our shipping. An invasion is expected from Flushing,[1] and no measures of any kind taken to prevent or repel it. Yours ever faithfully,

W. SCOTT

[*Lockhart*]

To PATRICK MURRAY

MY DEAR MURRAY,—I have delay'd answering your letter not from indifference to its contents, but from a wish

---

[1] Ellis's letters abound in references to the possibilities of invasion and the country's unpreparedness. It is impossible to follow Scott's correspondence throughout the war and the years that follow without recalling the experiences and feelings of the dire years through which we passed a century later—enthusiasm, alarms, political resentments, reaction, fears of revolution as a consequence of unemployment, etc.

to make good my promise. But owing to my being in London when the little edition of Hohenlinden & Lochiel was thrown off I did not get the copies which the Printer promised me, and after several fair promises I fancy I must sit down contented with the disappointment. This is of little consequence to you as I learn to-day that Campbells new edition will be here in a day or two, & as you are an early subscriber I will see that your copy is directly forwarded to Meigle. It contains the poems you wish to be possessed of, & has saved my Clerk the trouble of copying them, on which he was employed when I was told that the subscription copies were sent off— I believe I told you I intended to throw off some copies of the Border Ballads upon royal paper for the acceptance of a friend or two— One of them, which I hope Mrs. Murray will honor me by accepting is sent by this weeks Coupar Carrier as I did not know any better mode of dispatching it— We are all here on the qui vive, except our rulers above stairs who seem to be of the phlegmatic race of beings who would roast potatoes at a Volcano, & go to sleep under the gentle agitation of an earthquake. About 3000 men are clamorous for arms, & there are 20,000 stored in the Arsenal in the Castle which cannot be deliver'd out, even by order of the Commander in chief until certain forms are gone through (i.e. *fees paid*) in the London Offices—Surely this is trifling cruelly with the spirit & safety of the country— The new rais'd Corps of Yeomanry are likely to be left to practise like so many Harlequins with lath sabres. Our Regiment goes into quarters on the 9th of next month to remain for a week or 10 days ; it has received numerous recruits, is very strong, & in good order. It will give me great pleasure when I can make a sally to Meigle which I shall certainly make out in the course of the Autumn & if possible, bring the Baronet or Adam along with me— But in this bustling time who can tell the obstacles which may occur to the plans they have most at heart. Char-

lotte joins in best Compliments to Mrs. Murray— I am
ever Yours affectionately

WALTER SCOTT

EDINR. 29 *June*, 1803.

[*Abbotsford Copies*]

To ANNA SEWARD

[Extract]

[MUSSELBURGH, Summer, 1803]

MISS SEWARD's acceptable favour reaches me in a
place, and at a time, of great bustle, as the corps of
voluntary cavalry to which I belong is quartered for a
short time in this village, for the sake of drilling and
discipline. Nevertheless, had your letter announced the
name of the gentleman who took the trouble of forwarding
it, I would have made it my business to find him out, and
to prevail on him, if possible, to spend a day or two with
us in quarters. We are here assuming a very military
appearance. Three regiments of militia, with a formidable park of artillery, are encamped just by us. The
Edinburgh troop, to which I have the honour to be
quartermaster, consists entirely of young gentlemen of
family, and is, of course, admirably well mounted and
armed. There are other four troops in the regiment,
consisting of yeomanry, whose iron faces and muscular
forms announce the hardness of the climate against which
they wrestle, and the powers which nature has given
them to contend with and subdue it. These corps have
been easily raised in Scotland, the farmers being in general
a high-spirited race of men, fond of active exercises, and
patient of hardship and fatigue. For myself, I must own
that to one who has like myself, *la tête un peu exaltée*, the
" pomp and circumstance of war " gives, for a time, a
very poignant and pleasing sensation. The imposing

appearance of cavalry, in particular, and the rush which marks their onset, appear to me to partake highly of the sublime. Perhaps I am the more attached to this sort of sport of swords, because my health requires much active exercise, and a lameness contracted in childhood renders it inconvenient for me to take it otherwise than on horseback. I have, too, a hereditary attachment to the animal—not, I flatter myself, of the common jockey cast, but because I regard him as the kindest and most generous of the subordinate tribes. I hardly even except the dogs ; at least they are usually so much better treated, that compassion for the steed should be thrown into the scale when we weigh their comparative merits. My wife (a foreigner) never sees a horse ill-used without asking what that poor horse has done in his state of pre-existence ? I would fain hope they have been carters or hackney-coachman, and are only experiencing a retort of the ill-usage they have formerly inflicted. What think you ?

I am infinitely amused with your sagacious critic. God wot, I have often admired the vulgar subtlety of such minds as can with a depraved ingenuity attach a mean or disgusting sense to an epithet capable of being otherwise understood, and more frequently, perhaps, used to express an elevated idea. In many parts of Scotland the word *virtue* is limited entirely to *industry* ; and a young divine who preached upon the moral beauties of virtue was considerably surprised at learning that the whole discourse was supposed to be a panegyric upon a particular damsel who could spin fourteen spindles of yarn in the course of a week. This was natural ; but your literary critic has the merit of going very far a-field to fetch home his degrading association.

[*Lockhart*]

To GEORGE ELLIS [1]

[*July*, 1803]

I CANNOT pretend immediately to enter upon the serious discussion which you propose respecting the age of " Sir Tristrem ; " but yet, as it seems likely to strip Thomas the Prophet of the honours due to the author of the English " Tristrem," I cannot help hesitating before I can agree to your theory ;—and here my doubt lies. Thomas of Ercildoune, called the Rhymer, is a character mentioned by almost every Scottish historian, and the date of whose existence is almost as well known as if we had the parish register. Now, his great reputation, and his designation of *Rymour*, could only be derived from his poetical performances ; and in what did these consist excepting in the Romance of " Sir Tristrem," mentioned by Robert de Brunne ? I hardly think, therefore, we shall be justified in assuming the existence of an earlier *Thomas*, who would be, in fact, merely the creature of our system. I own I am not prepared to take this step, if I can escape otherwise from you and M. de la Ravaillere [2]— and thus I will try it. M. de la R. barely informs us that the history of Sir Tristrem was known to Chretien de Troys in the end of the twelfth century, and to the King of Navarre in the beginning of the thirteenth. Thus far his evidence goes, and I think not one inch farther—for it does not establish the existence either of the metrical

---

[1] This letter is an answer to one by Ellis, now lost. To Scott's letter he replies on the 24th July, accepting, generally, Scott's dating. He will transmit to Douce the dilemma " shall Tomas be considered." Macpherson has told me that " Rymer " is a not uncommon surname and does not imply a calling more than Taylor to-day, so that the Thomas of Robert de Brunne's poem may not be Scott's Tomas. To this Scott replies on 27th August. Ellis, replying, has been visited by Douce and his wife (would that Scott had been there). Douce is a sort of Tristram, " for I am convinced that nothing short of a drink of might could have conducted him to the arms of Mrs Douce who though neither his aunt nor grandmother . . . has more powerful negative electricity surrounding her than either relationship or ugliness could bestow."

[2] Révolutions de la langue Française. Poésies du Roi de Navarre.

romance, as you suppose, or of the prose romance, as M. de la R. much more erroneously supposes, at that very early period. If the *story* of Sir Tristrem was founded in fact, and if, which I have all along thought, a person of this name really swallowed a dose of cantharides intended to stimulate the exertions of his uncle, a petty monarch of Cornwall, and involved himself of course in an intrigue with his aunt, these facts must have taken place during a very early period of English history, perhaps about the time of the Heptarchy. Now, if this be once admitted, it is clear that the raw material from which Thomas wove his web, must have been current long before his day, and I am inclined to think that Chretien and the King of Navarre refer, not to the special metrical romance contained in Mr. Douce's fragments, but to the general story of Sir Tristrem, whose love and misfortunes were handed down by tradition as a historical fact. There is no difficulty in supposing a tale of this kind to have passed from the Armoricans, or otherwise, into the mouths of the French ; as, on the other hand, it seems to have been preserved among the Celtic tribes of the Border, from whom, in all probability, it was taken by their neighbour, Thomas of Ercildoune. If we suppose, therefore, that Chretien and the King allude only to the general and well-known *story* of Tristrem, and not to the particular edition of which Mr. Douce has some fragments—(and I see no evidence that any such special allusion to these fragments is made)—it will follow that *they* may be as late as the end of the thirteenth century, and that the Thomas mentioned in them may be *the* Thomas of whose existence we have historical evidence. In short, the question is, shall Thomas be considered as a landmark by which to ascertain the antiquity of the fragments, or shall the *supposed* antiquity of the fragments be held a sufficient reason for *supposing* an earlier Thomas ? For aught yet seen, I incline to my former opinion, that those fragments are coeval with the *ipsissimus Thomas.*

I acknowledge the internal evidence, of which you are so
accurate a judge, weighs more with me than the reference
to the King of Navarre ; but, after all, the extreme
difficulty of judging of style, so as to bring us within
sixty or seventy years, must be fully considered. Take
notice, I have never pleaded the matter so high as to say,
that the Auchinleck MS. contains the very words devised
by Thomas the Rhymer. On the contrary, I have always
thought it one of the spurious copies in *queint Inglis*, of
which Robert de Brunne so heavily complains. But
this will take little from the curiosity, perhaps little from
the antiquity, of the romance. Enough of Sir T. for the
present.—How happy it will make us if you can fulfil the
expectation you hold out of a northern expedition.
Whether in the cottage or at Edinburgh, we will be
equally happy to receive you, and show you all the lions
of our vicinity. Charlotte is hunting out music for
Mrs. E., but I intend to add *Johnson's* collection, which,
though the tunes are simple, and often bad sets, contains
much more original Scotch music than any other.

[*Lockhart*]

To ANNA SEWARD [1]

[. . .] that you may not *scout* this poetical communication as you most justly did the former. The *Laird* of
Logan a humourist of this part of the world used to lay
the blame of his bad spelling upon his bad pens so I hope
you will admit the same apology on my behalf. The
scene is Branxholm Castle a Border fortress inhabited by
the Lady of Buccleuch and her daughter—the latter is
the Margaret of the following verses—she is crossed in

---

[1] This fragment of a holograph letter was sent me by Mr Shirley of the
Dumfries Public Library. The address is gone but the letter is clearly to
Miss Seward implementing the promise made to her in the letter of 30th
November, 1802, promising to send her a few stanzas of the Lay. Scott
cites from memory, and there are some variants due to forgetfulness or to
earlier work later amended.

love and sits upon the *Castle Wa'*, circumstances and
a situation peculiarly natural to the heroines of romance.

>So past the day—the evening fell
>The sound had ceased of Curfew bell
>The stream was smooth, the sky was calm
>The wind was down, the dew was balm
>E'en the rude watchman on the tower
>Enjoyed and blessed the lovely hour
>Far more fair Margaret loved and blessed
>The hour of silence and of rest
>On the tall turret sitting lone
>She waked at times the lutes soft tone
>Struck a wild note and all between
>Thought of the Bower of Hawthorns green
>Her golden hair flow'd free from band
>Her fair cheek rested on her hand
>Her blue eye sought the west afar
>For lovers love the western star
>Is yon the Star o'er Pencryst-pen
>That rises slowly to her ken ?
>And spreading broad its wavering light
>Shakes its loose tresses to the night
>Is yon red glare the western star ?
>O, 'tis the beacon blaze of war !
>Scarce could she draw her tighten'd breath
>For well she knew the fire of death.
>
>The warder viewed it blazing strong
>And blew his war-note loud and long
>Till at the high and haughty sound
>Rock, wood, and river rung around
>The blast alarm'd the festal hall
>And startled forth the warriors all
>Far downward in the castle yard
>Full many a torch and cresset glared,
>And helms and plumes confusedly toss'd
>Were in the glare half seen half lost
>And spears in wild disorder shook
>Like reeds beside a frozen brook.

(Another hurly-burly verse I have forgotten)

Fair Margaret from the turret's head
Heard far beneath the charger's tread
And loud the harness rung
As to their seats with clamour dread
The ready horsemen sprung
And stamping hoofs and iron coats
And leaders voices mingled notes
And out and out
In hasty route
The warriors gallop'd forth
Dispersing to the south to scout
And east and west and north
To view their coming enemies
And warn their vassalls and allies.

A ready page with hurried hand
Awaked *the need-fires* [1] slumbering brand
And ruddy blush'd the heaven
For a sheet of flame from the turret high
Waved like a blood-flag on the sky
All flaring and uneven
And soon a score of fires I ween
On hill and tower and cliff were seen
They glimmered on each dusky tarn [2]
Haunted by the lonely earn. [3]
And on each cairn's [4] grey pyramid
Where many a heroe's urn is hid
Each with warlike tidings fraught
Each from Each the signal caught
Each after Each they glanced to sight
As stars arise upon the night
Till proud *Dun-edin* [5] the blazes saw
From Soltra and Dumpender Law
And Lothian heard the regent's order
That all should bowne them for the Border.

[1] The beacon lights in border castles were so called.

[2] Mountain lake.   [3] Eagle.

[4] Those heaps of stones piled on the tops of our hills usually places of sepulture.

[5] Edinburgh.

(All these are Scott's notes.)

I can proceed no further being alarmed by the Bugle Call not indeed to summon to battle but to the less hazardous task of a Mess Dinner where our Society tho' somewhat noisy is very good humoured and where

> None are unwilling and few are unable
> To sing a wild song or to tell a wild tale.

In these interesting circumstances I have only time to add that Longman & Rees, London will forward for me Darwin's Life when published which I am certain to value for its own intrinsick merit and yet more highly as a mark of the Authoress' esteem and friendship. Believe me, Very faithfully, and sincerely, Your most respectful servant,

WALTER SCOTT

MUSSLEBOROUGH, 10th July, 1803.

When you favour me with a line address Laswade Cottage, near Edinburgh.

[Shirley]

To JAMES LAING, CLERK TO THE LIEUTENANCY OF
THE CITY OF EDINR.[1]

SIR,—As I observe by the inclosed summons that I am drawn a soldier of the army of reserve, I beg to

---

[1] " In June 1797 an Act was passed for embodying a militia force in Scotland. By its provisions 6000 men were to be called out in the following manner. The school master in each parish was to make a list of the able-bodied men between the ages of nineteen and twenty-three. The names were to be posted up at the Church door on the Sunday preceding the date fixed for the meeting of the deputy-lieutenants of the district where complaints were to be heard, the lists revised, and a date appointed for the ballot. Married men with more than two children, *and all Volunteers, privates as well as officers*, were to be exempt."—MEIKLE, *Scotland and the French Revolution*. The volunteers had been raised in 1793, and in 1796 their numbers had been largely increased under fear of rebellion. In fact they had been regarded more as a protection against internal disturbance than even as a protection against invasion. To join them had been a sign of loyalty to the constitution. The exemption of them from the militia was a source of irritation to the lower classes, "who felt that they were being made to pay for either their poverty or their former disloyalty."—MEIKLE, *op. cit.*, p. 182. Scott here is pleading that as a volunteer he is exempt.

inform you it is my intention to claim the exemption provided in favour of Volunteer Cavalry, having been for several years a member of the Edinburgh Troop of the R.M.Lothian V. Cavalry. I understand from Col. Dundas that the Adjutant Mr. Adams is to supply the Lieutenancy with a List of the Corps in which you will find my name regularly inserted, if further verification of the exemption is requisite have the goodness to acquaint Mr. Adams or me. I remain Sir Your obedient Servt

WALTER SCOTT

LASWADE COTTAGE 22 *July* 1803.

[*Edin. Corp. Mus.*]

To GEORGE ELLIS [1]

LASSWADE, *August* 27, 1803

DEAR ELLIS,—My conscience has been thumping me as hard as if it had studied under Mendoza,[2] for letting your kind favour remain so long unanswered. Nevertheless, in this it is, like Launcelot Gobbo's, but a hard kind of conscience, as it must know how much I have been occupied with Armies of Reserve, and Militia, and Pikemen, and Sharpshooters, who are to descend from Ettrick Forest to the confusion of all invaders. The truth is, that this country has for once experienced that the pressure of external danger may possibly produce internal

---

[1] Ellis replied to this on the 10th September, deploring the fright to which Mrs. Scott has been exposed and accepting Scott's views on Thomas and raising further points. " What you tell me about your Cornish fisherman is very curious ; and I think with you that very little reliance is to be placed on Welsh geography and that Caerleon on Usk is by no means the Caerleon mentioned to have been Tristram's country. The name Wales has covered *all* the country not conquered by the English—the whole western coast nearly from Cornwall to Dumbarton."

[2] Daniel Mendoza (1764-1836), a famous pugilist of Jewish stock. " His advent was a new feature in the practice of boxing, and his style caused much discussion . . . the ' school of Mendoza ' marks a period in the history of pugilism. . . . When he encountered Richard Humphries, ' the gentleman boxer ' . . . Sir Thomas Apreece, Bart., acted for Mendoza."

unanimity ; and so great is the present military zeal, that
I really wish our rulers would devise some way of calling
it into action, were it only on the economical principle
of saving so much good courage from idle evaporation.—
I am interrupted by an extraordinary accident, nothing
less than a volley of small shot fired through the window,
at which my wife was five minutes before arranging her
flowers. By Camp's assistance, who run the culprit's
foot like a Liddesdale bloodhound, we detected an unlucky
sportsman, whose awkwardness and rashness might have
occasioned very serious mischief—so much for interruption.—To return to Sir Tristrem. As for Mr. Thomas's
name, respecting which you state some doubts, I request
you to attend to the following particulars :—In the
first place, surnames were of very late introduction into
Scotland, and it would be difficult to show that they
became in general a hereditary distinction, until after
the time of Thomas the Rhymer ; previously they were
mere personal distinctions peculiar to the person by
whom they were borne, and dying along with him. Thus
the children of *Alan Durward* were not called *Durward*,
because they were not *Ostiarii*, the circumstance from
which he derived the name. When the surname was
derived from property, it became naturally hereditary at
a more early period, because the distinction applied
equally to the father and the son. The same happened
with *patronymics*, both because the name of the father is
usually given to the son ; so that Walter Fitzwalter would
have been my son's name in those times as well as my
own ; and also because a clan often takes a sort of general
patronymic from one common ancestor, as Macdonald,
&c. &c. But though these classes of surnames become
hereditary at an early period, yet, in the natural course of
things, epithets merely personal are much longer of
becoming a family distinction. But I do not trust, by
any means, to this general argument ; because the
charter quoted in the Minstrelsy contains written

evidence, that the epithet of *Rymour* was peculiar to our Thomas, and was dropped by his son, who designs himself simply, *Thomas of Erceldoune, son of Thomas the Rymour of Erceldoune* ; which I think is conclusive upon the subject. In all this discussion, I have scorned to avail myself of the tradition of the country, as well as the suspicious testimony of Boece, Dempster, &c., grounded probably upon that tradition, which uniformly affirms the name of Thomas to have been Learmont or Leirmont, and that of the Rhymer a personal epithet. This circumstance may induce us, however, to conclude that some of his descendants had taken that name—certain it is that his castle is called Leirmont's Tower, and that he is as well known to the country people by that name, as by the appellation of the Rhymer.

Having cleared up this matter, as I think, to every one's satisfaction, unless to those resembling not Thomas himself, but his namesake the Apostle, I have, secondly, to show that my Thomas is the *Tomas* of Douce's MS. Here I must again refer to the high and general reverence in which Thomas appears to have been held, as is proved by Robert de Brunne ; but above all, as you observe, to the extreme similarity betwixt the French and English poems, with this strong circumstance, that the *mode* of telling the story approved by the French minstrel, under the authority of his Tomas, is the very mode in which my Thomas has told it. Would you desire better sympathy ?

I lately met by accident a Cornish gentleman, who had taken up his abode in Selkirkshire for the sake of fishing— and what should his name be but *Caerlion* ?[1] You will not doubt that this interested me very much. He tells me that there is but one family of the name in Cornwall, or as far as ever he heard, anywhere else, and that they are of great antiquity. Does not this circumstance seem to prove that there existed in Cornwall a place called Caerlion, giving name to that family ? Caerlion would

[1] See note, p. 207.

probably be *Castrum Leonense*, the chief town of Liones, which in every romance is stated to have been Tristrem's country, and from which he derived his surname of Tristrem *de Liones*. This district, as you notice in the notes on the *Fabliaux*, was swallowed up by the sea. I need not mind you that all this tends to illustrate the *Caerlioun* mentioned by Tomas, which I always suspected to be a very different place from Caerlion on Uske— which is no seaport. How I regret the number of leagues which prevented my joining you and the sapient Douce, and how much ancient lore I have lost. Where I have been, the people talked more of the praises of Ryno and Fillan (not Ossian's heroes, but two Forest greyhounds which I got in a present) than, I verily believe, they would have done of the prowesses of Sir Tristrem, or of Esplandian, had either of them appeared to lead on the levy *en masse*. Yours ever,

W. SCOTT

[*Lockhart*]

To JOSEPH RITSON

MY DEAR SIR,—I embrace the opportunity of Mr. Rees being here to transmit you a parcel which you should have received long ago. But my duty both official & military has for some months past greatly interfered with my literary pursuits which I flatter myself you will readily excuse. I now inclose a translation of Chastellains [1] recollections with the Original. You will readily see I have studied fidelity & literal translation more than any attempt at elegance. The latter is also in some degree precluded by the nature of the poem in which the same ideas recur very often in the original & where I am also occasionally hamperd by my ignorance of the

---

[1] Presumably Georges Chastellain, author of *Chronique des ducs de Bourgogne* (1420-74), and *Histoire du bon chevalier messire Jacques de Lalain, frère et compagnon de l'ordre de la Toison d'Or*. The poem may be the *Poème sur la bataille de Liège en 1469*, which is printed with the *Chronique des ducs*, etc., in the edition in the *Collection des chroniques nationales*, Paris, 1824-1827.

subject. The places in which I have found this most
puzzling are 1mo The stanza commencing with line 116th
of the Original. To what historical transaction does this
allude. I should be ashamed to ask the question but I
am here without books or learned freinds from whose
recollection of the history of Burgundy I might be assisted.
2do. The line 281 & the following Stanza What monarchs
are here meant ? Is it supposed that they are complimented by the poet for agreeing to hold the states of
" Le grant Duc de Virtu " as expressing some real
potentate probably he to whom the poem is inscribed.
Or are we to understand that the expression is that of
personification & only means that they were to hold their
power of Virtue as their grand Superior & Liege Lord ?
The ambiguity of these two stanzas perplexes me : in
the others tho' the expression may be faulty the meaning
is in general clear. If you think of publishing this
translation I will [be] happy to have an opportunity of
more fully correcting it, & of profiting by your criticisms
both in the above & other respect.

Your criticism on the translation of Killicrankie verse
8th [1] is quite just pray let it run thus

> He left the boar on Speys bleak shore
> He left the wolf at bay
> The whiggish race like hares to chase
> And course the false Mackay.

I inclose in this packet Pennicuikes [2] poems from which I
have renderd Kennedys poem.

In my last parcel I returnd your MS book containing

---

[1] " With respect to the eighth (stanza) I know not what to say without
applying to yourself with great humility for another line if the present rime
cannot be rendered more analogous :

> To course like stags the Lowland Whigs

this my dear Sir, cannot remain for your own sake : all the rest being
conceived in your usual fluency which I have ever regarded with pleasure
and admiration."—Ritson to Scott, 2nd July 1803.

[2] Pennecuik's (Alex.) *Collection of Scots Poems*, 1769, is in the Abbotsford
Library.

Richards song not fully understanding that you wishd
me to give a poetical version. If you will favour me with
a copy of the original accompanied with your own
illustrations I will at least do my best to do it some
justice.

I am glad you have had a sight of the Dukes copy of
Leader Haughs. I think I told you that the tradition
of our country is that the Author was a dependant of the
famous Duke of Lauderdale and lost his favour on account
of the faint praise (as his Grace thought it) expressd of
his house of Lauder Castle compared to Newark. The
Song I think says

> It stands *as fair* on Leader side
> As *Newark* does on Yarrow.

I think it is said the Author was a clergyman but the
story will apply as well to Burns the violer who may have
depended in some shape on his graces favour. At any
rate Burns clearly seems to have been the Author, & not
Hume of whom I never heard but from Dr. Douglas, a
worthy & able man but who has not greatly attended to
the minutiæ of antiquarian lore.

I am sorry we are not immediately to expect your
king Arthur yet I hope we are not altogether to lose him.
In perusing your Romances one or two trifling remarks
have occurrd which I require you to consider as an
instance at least of the extreme attention with which
I regard every thing coming from your hand. They
are chiefly glossarial.

Crowlandi III. 36. Seems to be *crowing* or *chuckling*.

Dour II. p. 189. Seems an arbitrary spelling for *Daur*
or day assumed rythmi gratia no uncommon thing with
Romancers.

Fiytes III. p. 155. Fights : this does not quite suit the
association but the stile of the composition is so very
rambling that I cannot help thinking it is the true meaning.

Lyngell In Scotch signifies a string or strap particularly

such as is used by Shoemakers. For instance in the
petition of the Shoemakers apprentices

> When Lads of the trade in company mingle
> Can they Bind Leather shoe, or lick a cold *lingle*.

Applied to armour it would appear to mean the thongs
by which the various pieces were laced together.

Fyle. According to the Blackguard Idiom calld flang,
in which many curious & ancient phrases are retaind, *fyle*
signifies Thief, e.g. file-frow—a pickpocket girl or whore.

Hyllynges III. p. 180. Whatever be the precise
meaning seems to be derived from Helyng covering or
concealing.

But I find my time wasting & will not longer detain
you reserving my other notices for some future letter.
In the mean while I shall hope to be favourd by your
remarks on the new Edit. of the Border Ballads particularly v. 3d.—

I send you Robin Hood & the Pedlar with which I
fear you will be disappointed. It is but a poor song & I
incline to think that which I heard long ago was better &
considerably longer. But I was then very young.—As
it is I suppose you will be glad to have any thing hitherto
unknown which relates to the Woodland heroe of
Sherwood whose fame your collection has tended so
powerfully to preserve & to revive.

I am grieved at the interruption which has arisen to
the publication of the Scottish biography but I hope we
shall not be ultimately deprived of the information
collected by so accurate & zealous an investigator upon
so curious a point of Ancient Scottish or rather British
history.

The description of Geo. Wallace Author of the Peerage
& of a Prospect from the Hills of Fife (a very poor
performance) is his profession of Advocate & office as a
Commissary of Edinr. He is still alive though an
old Man.

I beg you to believe it will at all times give me
the most sincere pleasure to assist your interesting
pursuits & that I am with great respect & regard Your
very faithful humble Servant

WALTER SCOTT

LASWADE COTTAGE 11 *Septr.* 1803

[*Edin. Univ. Lib.*]

TO GEORGE ELLIS

[*14th September* 1803]

I AM very sorry that you flag over those wild and
interesting tales.[1] I hope, if you will not work yourself
(for which you have so little excuse, having both the
golden talents and the golden leisure necessary for
study), you will at least keep Owen to something that is
rational—I mean to *iron horses,* and *magic cauldrons,* and
Bran the Blessed, with the music of his whole army upon
his shoulders, and, in short, to something more pleasing
and profitable than old apophthegms, triads, and
" blessed burdens of the womb of the isle of Britain."
Talking of such burdens, Camp has been regularly wedded
to a fair dame in the neighbourhood ; but notwithstanding the Italian policy of locking the lady in a stable, she
is suspected of some inaccuracy ; but we suspend
judgment, as Othello ought in all reason to have done,
till we see the produce of the union. As for my own
employment, I have yet much before me ; and as the

---

[1] Of the *Mabinogion,* which Ellis had contemplated editing. Scott is probably answering Ellis's letter of 10th September, which was an answer to Scott's
of 27th August : " As your last volume announced your Lay of the Last
Minstrel I begin, in common with all your friends, to be uneasy about the
future disposal of your time. Having nothing but a very active profession,
and your present military pursuits, and your domestic occupations to think
of, and Leyden having monopolised Asiatic literature, you will presently
be quite an idle man ! You are, however, still in time to learn Erse and
it is, I am afraid, very necessary that you should do so to stimulate my laziness
which has hitherto made no progress in Welsh. Indeed even my introduction goes on so slowly that what I have hitherto done will not exceed, when
in print, two pages." Scott's industry was the amazement of his friends.

beginning of letting out ink is like the letting out of water, I daresay I shall go on scribbling one nonsense or another to the end of the chapter. People may say this and that of the pleasure of fame or of profit as a motive of writing. I think the only pleasure is in the actual exertion and research, and I would no more write upon any other terms than I would hunt merely to dine upon hare-soup. At the same time, if credit and profit came unlooked for, I would no more quarrel with them than with the soup. I hope this will find you and Mrs. Ellis safely and pleasantly settled.

—By the way, while you are in his neighbourhood, " In Yorkshire near fair Rotherham," I hope you will not fail to inquire into the history of the valiant Moor of Moorhall and the Dragon of Wantley.[1] As a noted burlesque upon the popular romance, the ballad has some curiosity and merit.—Ever yours,   W. S.

[*Lockhart*]

To GEORGE ELLIS

[Extract]

[*14th October* 1803]

THE necessity of the present occasion has kept almost every individual, however insignificant, to his post. God has left us entirely to our own means of defence, for we have not above one regiment of the line in all our ancient kingdom. In the meanwhile, we are doing the best we can to prepare ourselves for a contest, which, perhaps, is not far distant. A beacon light, communicating with that of Edinburgh Castle, is just erecting in front of our quiet cottage. My field equipage is ready, and I want nothing but a pipe and a *schnurbartchen* to convert me into a complete hussar. Charlotte, with the infantry (of the household troops, I mean), is to beat her retreat into Ettrick Forest, where, if the Tweed is in his

---

[1] For the *Dragon of Wantley*, see Percy's *Reliques*, vol. iii. book iii.

SIR WALTER SCOTT 205

usual wintry state of flood, she may weather out a descent from Ostend. Next year I hope all this will be over, and that not only I shall have the pleasure of receiving you in peace and quiet, but also of going with you through every part of Caledonia, in which you can possibly be interested. Friday se'ennight our corps takes the field for ten days— for the second time within three months—which may explain the military turn of my epistle.

Poor Ritson [1] is no more. All his vegetable soups and puddings have not been able to avert the evil day, which, I understand, was preceded by madness. It must be worth while to inquire who has got his MSS.,—I mean his own notes and writings. The " Life of Arthur," for example, must contain many curious facts and quotations, which the poor defunct had the power of assembling to an astonishing degree, without being able to combine anything like a narrative, or even to deduce one useful inference—witness his " Essay on Romance and Minstrelsy," which reminds one of a heap of rubbish, which had either turned out unfit for the architect's purpose, or beyond his skill to make use of. The ballads he had collected in Cumberland and Northumberland, too, would greatly interest me. If they have fallen into the hands of any liberal collector, I dare say I might be indulged with a sight of them. Pray inquire about this matter.

Yesterday Charlotte and I had a visit which we owe to Mrs. E. A rosy lass, the sister of a bold yeoman

---

[1] In his reply to this letter, 10th November 1803, R. Ellis, after apologising for his delay, writes : " Now as to your question about Ritson, our friend Heber is, I believe, at this moment no less actively employed than the rest of his Majesty's faithful subjects in preparing for invasion. . . . Yet I am persuaded he will not have lost a moment in going to town on all sorts of commissions, & for the purpose of securing as much as he can of the strange farrago compiled by his deceased friend. I am afraid, however, that the ballads collected for the Cumberland and Northumberland Garlands will not be forthcoming, as I have a sort of recollection of having heard Heber say that a very large collection of such things had been disposed of at a sale which the little man thought fit to make a little before his death." Ritson died on 23rd September 1803.

in our neighbourhood, entered our cottage, towing in a monstrous sort of bull-dog, called emphatically Cerberus, whom she came on the part of her brother to beg our acceptance of, understanding we were anxious to have a son of Camp. Cerberus was no sooner loose (a pleasure, which, I suspect, he had rarely enjoyed) than his father (*supposé*) and he engaged in a battle which might have been celebrated by the author of the "Unnatural Combat," and which, for aught I know, might have turned out a combat *à l'outrance*, if I had not interfered with a horse-whip, instead of a baton, as *juge de Camp*. The odds were indeed greatly against the stranger knight —two fierce Forest greyhounds having arrived, and, contrary to the law of arms, stoutly assailed him. I hope to send you a puppy instead of this redoubtable Cerberus. Love to Mrs. E.   W. S.

[*Lockhart*]

1804

To REV. R. POLWHELE [1]

CASTLE-STREET, EDINBURGH, 27 *Jan.* 1804

SIR,—I am honoured with your letter of the 16 January, and lose no time in communicating such information about Sir Tristrem as I think may interest you.

Tristrem (of whose real existence I cannot persuade myself to doubt) was nephew to Mark King of Cornwall. He is said to have slain in single combat Morough of Ireland, and by his success in that duel to have delivered Cornwall from a tribute which that kingdom paid to Angus King of Leinster. Tristrem was desperately wounded by the Irish warrior's poisoned sword, and was obliged to go to Dublin, to be cured in the country where the venom had been confected. Ysonde, or Ysende, daughter of Angus, accomplished his cure, but had nearly

---

[1] Richard Polwhele (1760-1838), a clergyman, " by turns poet, topographer, theologian and literary chronicler " (*D.N.B.*), enters Scott's correspondence by a side wind. Clement Carlyon (1777-1864), having graduated at Pembroke College, Cambridge, and gained a travelling fellowship, made the acquaintance of Coleridge at Göttingen, and later studied medicine at Edinburgh. In July 1803 he spent six weeks with a young friend at the romantic little village of Clovenfords on the Tweed, mainly fishing. The sudden arrival of the Sheriff, whose regular abode when on official duty was at this inn, threw the landlady into distress, which was overcome by the young men sleeping together and Scott taking the smaller bed, the parlour being shared. Scott, whose mind was full of *Sir Tristrem*, no sooner heard the name of Carlyon than he was on the quest for information : " You are a Cornishman, of course, and can tell me whether there is any seaport at present in Cornwall of your name, for such there certainly was in former days, as you will see by the history which I have here, and which if it suit your taste and you can find time you may read and tell me what you think of it, as I am preparing the manuscript for the press." Just so Mr. Oldbuck in *The Antiquary* took Lovell in hand. Carlyon referred him to his friend Mr. Polwhele, then engaged on the subject of the Morte d'Arthur for his History of Cornwall, and a letter was written which, though signed by Carlyon, was clearly

put him to death upon discovering that he was the person who had slain her uncle. Tristrem returned to Cornwall, and spoke so highly in praise of the beautiful Ysonde, that Mark sent him to demand her in marriage. This was a perilous adventure for Sir Tristrem, but by conquering a dragon, or, as other authorities bear, by assisting King Angus in battle, his embassy became successful, and Ysonde was delivered into his hands, to be conveyed to Cornwall. But the Queen of Ireland had given an attendant damsel a philtre, or aphrodisiac, to be presented to Mark and Ysonde on their bridal night. Unfortunately, the young couple, while at sea, drank this beverage without being aware of its effects. The consequence was the intrigue betwixt Tristrem and Ysonde, which was very famous in the middle ages. The romance is occupied in describing the artifices of the lovers to escape the observation of Mark, the counterplots of the courtiers, jealous of Tristrem's favour, and the uxorious credulity of the King of Cornwall, who is always imposed upon,

dictated by Scott : " Of course," the letter proceeds after indicating the drift of the story, " the story abounds in wondrous exploits, but from the frequent references that have been made to it, and the veneration which still attaches to the author, the fiction perhaps is more closely interwoven with truth than usually happens. The topography may, for the most part, be ascertained at the present day ; and the few exceptions, fairly referable to the stroke of time, may consequently be looked upon as no inaccurate guide towards the former existence of places now withdrawn from view. Mention is more than once made of a Cornish port of the name of Carlion." Compliments follow of the kind in which Scott abounded : " Has his *Minstrelsy of the Scottish Border* fallen into your hands ? If not, I shall not incur the risk of having to apologise to you for calling your attention to a very interesting and elegant specimen of the fruits of *Local Attachment*. Mr Scott is likewise desirous that Mr Whitaker, our worthy historian of Manchester, should be informed of the high esteem in which he is held on his side of the Tweed ; nor does anyone esteem him more highly than Mr Scott himself. As my sheet will admit of it I may as well send you the first stanza of the Romance." Polwhele wrote to Scott on the 16th January 1804 (in Walpole Collection), and the above letter is Scott's reply.—CAR-LYON, *Early Years and Late Reflections*, London, 1843, vol. ii.

Polwhele's *Traditions and Recollections* (1826) and *Reminiscences in Prose and Verse* are not without interest, but one gets the feeling later that he was one of the bores whom Scott suffered too patiently. *Local Attachment*, a poem of his, is frequently referred to by Scott, but is now forgotten.

and always fluctuating betwixt doubt and confidence.
At length he banishes Tristrem from his court, who
retires to Brittanye (Bretagne), where he marries another
Ysonde, daughter of the Duke of that British settlement.
From a vivid recollection of his first attachment he
neglects his bride, and, returning to Cornwall in various
disguises, renews his intrigue with the wife of his uncle.
At length, while in Brittanye, he is engaged in a perilous
adventure, in which he receives an arrow in his old
wound. No one can cure the gangrene but the Queen of
Cornwall, and Tristrem dispatches a messenger entreating
her to come to his relief. The confident of his passion is
directed if his embassy be successful to hoist a white sail
upon his return, and if otherwise a black one. Ysonde
of Brittanye, the wife of Tristrem, overhears these
instructions, and on the return of the vessel with her rival
on board, fired with jealousy, she tells her husband falsely
that the sails are *black*. Tristrem concluding himself
abandoned by Ysonde of Cornwall, throws himself back
and dies. Meantime the Queen lands and hastens to
the succour of her lover—finding him dead she throws
herself on the body, and dies also.

This is the outline of the story of Tristrem, so much
celebrated in ancient times. As early as the eleventh
century his famous sword is said to have been found in the
grave of a King of the Lombards. The loves of Tristrem
and Ysonde are alluded to in the songs of the King of
Navarre, who flourished about 1226, and also in Chretien
de Troyes, who died about 1200. During the 13th
century Thomas of Erceldoune, Earlstown in Berwickshire, called the Rhymer, composed a metrical history
of their amours. He certainly died in 1299. His work
is quoted by Robert de Brunne with very high encomium.
For some account of this extraordinary personage I
venture to refer you to a compilation of ballads, entitled,
the Minstrelsy of the Scottish Border, v. II. p. 262, where
I have endeavoured to trace his history. It is his metrical

I   O

romance which I am publishing, not from a Scottish manuscript of coeval date, but from an English manuscript apparently written during the minority of Edward III.   The transcriber quotes Tomas as his authority, and professes to tell the tale of Sir Tristrem as it was told to him by the author.   The stanza is very peculiar, and the language concise to obscurity ; in short what Robert de Brunne called, in speaking of Sir Tristrem, " queinte Inglis," not to be generally understood even at the time when it was written.   The names are all of British, or, if you please, Cornish derivation, as Morgan, Riis, Brengwain, Urgan, Meriadoc, &c.   Tomas of Erceldoune lived precisely upon the Borders of what had been the kingdom of Strath Cluyd ; and, though himself an English author, naturally adopted from his British neighbours a story of such fame.   Perhaps he might himself be *utriusque linguæ doctor*, and a translator of British Bards.

It happens by a most fortunate coincidence, that Mr. Douce, with whose literary fame and antiquarian researches you are probably acquainted, possesses two fragments of a metrical history of Sir Tristrem in the French, or I should rather say in the Romance language. One of them refers expressly to Tomas as the best authority upon the history of Tristrem, though he informs us that other minstrels told the story somewhat differently. All the incidents of these fragments occur in my manuscript, though much more concisely narrated in the latter. The language resembles that of Mademoiselle Marie. Tintagel Castle is mentioned as Mark's residence, a fairy castle which was not always visible. In Tomas's Romance, the capital of Cornwall is called *Caerlioun*, as I apprehend *Castrum Leonense*, the chief town of the inundated district of Lionesse, from which Sir Tristrem took his surname. The English and French poems throw great light upon each other.

When the art of reading became more common, the books of chivalry were reduced into prose, the art of the

minstrel being less frequently exercised. Tristrem shared
this fate, and his short story was swelled into a large folio
now before me, beautifully printed at Paris in 1514. In
this work the story of Tristrem is engrafted upon that of
King Arthur, the romance of the Round Table being
then at the height of popularity. Many circumstances
are added which do not occur in the metrical copies. It
is here that the heresy concerning the cowardice of the
Cornish nation first appears ; there is not the least
allusion to it in the ancient poems, and it is merely
introduced to give effect to some comic adventures in
which Mark (le roy coux) is very roughly handled, and
to others in which certain knights, presuming upon the
universal poltroonery of the Cornish, attack Tristrem,
and according to the vulgar phrase " catch a Tartar."
This volume is stated to be compiled by Luce, Lord of the
castle of Gast, near Salisbury, a name perhaps fictitious.
But Luce, if that *was* his real name, is not singular in
chusing the history of Tristrem for the groundwork of
his folio. There are two immense manuscripts on the
same subject in the Duke of Roxburghe's Library, and
one in the National Library at Paris, and probably many
others. The Morte Arthur which you mention, is a book
of still less authority than the Paris folio. It is not a
history of the Cornish hero in particular ; but a bundle
of extracts made by Sir T. Mallory, from the French
romances of the Table Round, as Sir Lancelot du Lac,
and the other folios printed on that subject at Paris in
the beginning of the 16th century. It is therefore of no
authority *whatever*, being merely the shadow of a shade,
an awkward abridgement of prose romances, themselves
founded on the more ancient metrical *lais* and *gests*. I
suppose, however, Gibbon had not Mallory's authority
for his observation ; which he probably derived from the
elegant abridgement of Sir Tristrem (I mean of the prose
folio) published by Tressan, in " Extraits des Romans de
la Chevalerie."

I would willingly add to this scrambling letter a specimen of the romance of Tomas of Erceldoune ; but I am deterred by the hope of soon having it in my power to send the book itself, which is in the press.

I fear that in wishing fully to gratify your curiosity I have been guilty of conferring much tediousness upon you ; but, as it is possible I may have omitted some of the very particulars you wished to know, I have only to add that it will give me the highest pleasure to satisfy, as far as I am able, any of Mr. Polwhele's enquiries, to whose literary and poetical fame our northern capital is no stranger. On my part I am curious to know if any recollection of Sir Tristrem (so memorable elsewhere) subsists in his native county, whether by tradition or in the names of places. Also whether tradition or history points at the existence of such a place as Carlioun, which Tomas thus describes :

> Tristrem's schip was yare,
>   He asked his benisoun,
> The haven he gan out fare,
>   It hight Carlioun ;
> Nyen woukes and mare,
>   He hobled up and doun,
> A winde to wil him bare,
>   To a stede ther him was boun
>   Neighe hand,
>   Deivelin hight the toun,
>   An haven in Ireland.

I may just add that Tristrem is described as a celebrated musician and chess-player, and as the first who laid down regular rules for hunting.

I beg to be kindly remembered to Mr. Carlyon, to whom I am much obliged for giving me an opportunity to subscribe myself, Sir, your most obedient humble servant,   WALTER SCOTT

P.S. Do you not conceive it possible that the name of our friend *Carlyon's* family, which I understand is of original Cornish extraction, may have been derived from the lost *Caerlioun* ?

[Letters of Sir Walter Scott, 1832]

MEMORANDUM OF AGREEMENT BETWIXT MR. SCOTT AND MR. LAIDLAW [1] RELATIVE TO ASHESTIEL FARM

I. Mr. Scott is to offer £325 for the whole farm. Of which for the sheep part presently occupied & markd as such Mr. Laidlaw is to pay £240. And if the rent is settled at more he is to pay a proportion as £240 is to £85.

II. Mr. Laidlaw is to have the houses on that part of the lands which he is to occupy, and they are to be repaired kept and left by him on the same terms as the other houses.

III. The fences between Mr. Laidlaws & Mr. Scotts possessions to be mutually upheld by them, the Landlord paying one half of the whole expence.

IV. Public burdens exclusive of House and window duty to be paid in proportion to the real [?] rents of each.

V. The privilege of fishing & of the boat to be mutual while Mr. Scott is in the country, but [if] he is in Edinr. with his family Mr. Laidlaw to enjoy the exclusive liberty of fishing. Two keys to be made for the boat & one given to each   WALTER SCOTT

[Curle]

To CHARLES ERSKINE

[*10th March*, 1804]

DEAR CHARLES,—I forgot to tell you this morning that I had sent you Laidlaws letter. Having seen you it will

---

[1] This is not the Laidlaw who was Scott's friend and helper in ballad collecting but Laidlaw, " Laird Nippy," who held the farm of Peel, a distant kinsman of the former. Scott was trying to get this Laidlaw to take the greater part of the farm which lies on the upper side of the main road passing Ashestiel. It was he who later wrote to Sir Walter telling him the Abbotsford land was in the market (Mr. James Curle). See *Lockhart*, c. 17.

be necessary for you to give yourself the trouble of calling tomorrow. I want no more ground that I can dung for I will have nothing to do with Lime. I wish I could have some understanding with Laidlaw about lamb & mutton. My family is large & markets distant everything else I think I mentiond—Believe me ever Yours truly

W SCOTT

Write me what Laidlaw says

[EDINBURGH]

[*Curle*]

To GEORGE ELLIS

[19 *March* 1804]

As I had a world of things to say to you, I have been culpably, but most naturally silent. When you turn a bottle with its head downmost, you must have remarked that the extreme impatience of the contents to get out all at once greatly impedes their getting out at all. I have, however, been forming the resolution of sending a grand packet with Sir Tristrem, who will kiss your hands in about a fortnight.[1] I intend uncastrated copies for you, Heber, and Mr. Douce, who, I am willing to hope, will accept this mark of my great respect and warm remembrance of his kindness while in London.—Pray send me without delay the passage referring to *Thomas* in the French " Hornchild." Far from being daunted with the

---

[1] Replying on the 10th of May Ellis declares that he had sent by return " an extract from the French Horn (*i.e.* the French version of the romance *King Horn*) and a translation of the *Lai du Chevrefoil*." " Did you receive that letter or did some other Mr. Scott purloin it by the way . . . take notice that I begin to grow very impatient for the arrival of the hero of Leonois without whose aid I cannot possibly bring my prefatory matter to a conclusion. I had as I think made out a good case for the southern Welsh and those in Armorica, but all I have been able to attain is what appears to me a strong probability that the Norman minstrels borrowed a great deal from them. Now it has been your business to show that they have also borrowed from the Northern Britains indirectly, that is, through the medium of your Saxon bard Tomas, and it will remain to be seen

position of the enemy, I am resolved to carry it at the point of the bayonet, and, like an able general, to attack where it would be difficult to defend. Without metaphor or parable, I am determined, not only that my Tomas *shall* be the author of Tristrem, but that he shall be the author of Hornchild also. I must, however, read over the romance, before I can make my arrangements. Holding, with Ritson, that the copy in *his* collection is translated from the French, I do not see why we should not suppose that the French had been originally a version from our Thomas. The date does not greatly frighten me, as I have extended Thomas of Ercildoune's life to the three-score and ten years of the Psalmist, and consequently removed back the date of " Sir Tristrem " to 1250. The French translation might be written for that matter within a few days after Thomas's work was completed— and I can allow a few years. He lived on the Border, already possessed by Norman families, and in the vicinity of Northumberland, where there were many more. Do you think the minstrels of the Percies, the Vescies, the Morells, the Grais, and the De Vaux, were not acquainted with honest Thomas, their next door neighbour, who was a poet, and wrote excellent tales—and, moreover, a *laird*, and gave, I dare be sworn, good dinners ?—and would they not anxiously translate, for the amusement of their masters, a story like Hornchild, so intimately connected with the lands in which they had settled ? And do you

whether I can add any fresh confirmation to your proof, or whether it will be wiser to quote you *purement et simplement* as having proved the fact beyond the possibility of confutation." On May 20th he writes, " I have to announce to you that I have received, not indeed my own uncastrated copy but at last Longman and Rees copy of Sir Tristram and that having perused both the introduction and notes (the former two or three times) I am in strict truth delighted with them." After much antiquarian discussion he goes on to say that his projected visit is likely to fall through owing to the illness of Admiral Parker (" Anne's only brother "). " He may indeed have died before the period fixed for the journey, but then poor Sir Peter [Parker] will be left principally on our hands." It is also clear that Ellis has provided Scott with an introduction for Daniel (Scott's brother) to a Mr. Blackburn in Jamaica.

not think, from the whole structure of Hornchild, however often translated and retranslated, that it must have been originally of northern extraction ? I have not time to tell you certain suspicions I entertain that Mr. Douce's fragments are the work of one Raoull de Beauvais, who flourished about the middle of the thirteenth century, and for whose accommodation principally I have made Thomas, to use a military phrase, *dress backwards* for ten years.

. . . I quite agree with you as to the general conduct of the Review, which savours more of a wish to display than to instruct ; but as essays, many of the articles are invaluable, and the principal conductor is a man of very acute and universal talent. I am not regularly connected with the work, nor have I either inclination or talents to use the critical scalping knife, unless as in the case of Godwin, where flesh and blood succumbed under the temptation. I don't know if you have looked into his tomes, of which a whole edition has vanished—I was at a loss to know how, till I conjectured that, as the heaviest materials to be come at, they have been sent on the secret expedition, planned by Mr. Phillips and adopted by our sapient Government, for blocking up the mouth of our enemy's harbours. They should have had my free consent to take Phillips and Godwin,[1] and all our other lumber, literary and political, for the same beneficial

[1] William Godwin's *Political Justice*, which had for Scott none of the appeal it had for Wordsworth or Shelley, appeared in 1793 ; his *Caleb Williams* in 1794, and *St. Leon* in 1799. In 1803 he brought out a *Life of Chaucer*, which Scott reviewed in lively style in the *Edinburgh Review*. "The authenticated passages of Chaucer's life may be comprised in half a dozen pages ; and behold two voluminous volumes." Scott goes on to illustrate the kind of padding which produced this result. Godwin has discovered only one new fact, that Chaucer gave evidence in a case of heraldry between Scrope and Grosvenor. The political prejudice is not quite forgotten. " When he complains that private collectors declined ' to part with their treasures for a short time out of their own hands ' did it never occur to Mr Godwin that the maxims concerning property, contained in his *Political Justice*, were not altogether calculated to inspire confidence in the author ? " At a later period Godwin writes quite friendly letters to Scott (now in the National Library), and Scott to him.

purpose. But in general, I think it ungentlemanly to wound any person's feelings through an anonymous publication, unless where conceit or false doctrine strongly calls for reprobation. Where praise can be conscientiously mingled in a larger proportion than blame, there is always some amusement in throwing together our ideas upon the works of our fellow-labourers, and no injustice in publishing them. On such occasions, *and in our way*, I may possibly, once or twice a-year, furnish my critical friends with an article.

[*Lockhart*]

To CHARLES ERSKINE

[19*th March* 1804]

DEAR ERSKINE,—I am truly indebted to you for the trouble you have taken about the inscription & the farm. I hope I may be able to agree with Mr. Laidlaw finally although I am decided not to accept his present proposals, which are greatly too unfavourable for me. The Sheep-farm is a very desireable one & has usually paid the Miss Russells £300. Considering the saving in expence of management and in the chance of peculation it must be worth at least one third more to an active farmer. On the other hand the arable ground with the exception of the haugh is of a very inferior quality much of it not worth 10s. an acre. Now if Mr. Laidlaw chuses to take the ground lying on the upper side of the road leading past Ashestiel, I am willing to give £65 for the house garden & the remainder of the arable ground. In that case I will offer in my own name £325 £325 [*sic* : in MS.] or to take the farm at such higher rent as may be offerd by a respectable tenant and in case I shall get any preference, such advance of rent shall be paid by Mr. Laidlaw & me in the proportions of £260 and £65.

You may let Mr. Laidlaw know that these are my ideas on the subject from which I am not likely to depart

especially as I am a very poor farmer & do not expect
my farm to do more than keep my horses and save itself.
Fairnalie [?] which is a larger farm & much better land
than the arable part of Ashestiel is let for £80 and it is a
rackd rent.—I will certainly be with you on Sunday 1st
to arrange this important matter and in the mean while
I remain ever Your most faithful humble Serv.

WALTER SCOTT

EDINR. *Monday*

[*Curle*]

To CHARLES ERSKINE

DEAR CHARLES,—Just when I received your letter I
got one from Mr. Pringle informing me that my offer
could not be accepted unless it was advanced. He has
fixd Wednesday next for a meeting of the offerers at
Selkirk when the amount of the highest offer is to be made
known and the party preferrd unless some one will bid
more. I intend to be there certainly but as I am engaged
on Tuesday I must come off by post in the morning ; so
that I wish you to be present as well as Mr. Laidlaw in
case any unforeseen accident should stop me on the road.
I hope it will not be too much trouble to you to take a
ride up that morning ; & in case of need to bid for me.
It will be hard if we cannot secure it.

On Thursday I intend to proceed with the proof in the
Burgh politics & have apprized both parties parties [*sic
in MS.*] of my intention to do so. I suspect I will need
to borrow David Brown as Clerk for I cannot think of an
impartial scribe in Selkirk. Yours truly

WALTER SCOTT

EDINR. 14 *Apl.* 1804.

[*Curle*]

N.D., Postmark : *April* 15 [? 1804] [1]

My dear Mother,—I am at all times most happy to give you the best advice and assistance in my power in any of your little matters.   I think clearly that before selling your Stock which may [be] a very adviseable measure you should settle some mode of employing the money as it is certainly unnecessary that it should lie long in the hands of a Banker.   Mr. Setons Commissioners are to give us good heritable security over a free estate for £4000 , with an obligation from Sir W. Forbes &c for the regular payment of the Interest.   I would advise you to speak to Mr. Fergusson about investing your money on that security which I understand to be indisputable and it will also I dare say be an accomodation to my fathers Trustees who may want the money to pay off other claims.   I do not know if I make myself very intelligible to you, but I would advise you to consult with Mr. W. Keith and Mr. Fergusson.   I am very busy here at present and not able to come into town my horse being lame—the first time I am in town I shall certainly see you.   Meanwhile believe me ever my dear Mother. Yours very affectionatcly

W Scott

[LASSWADE] COTTAGE *Tuesday*

The wife and bairns are well and join in Love and duty.

[*Law*]

---

[1] Scott left Lasswade Cottage in the summer of 1804 for Ashestiel.   See next letter.

To GEORGE ELLIS

[*4th May* 1804]

I HAVE been engaged in travelling backwards and
forwards to Selkirkshire upon little pieces of business,
just important enough to prevent my doing anything to
purpose. One great matter, however, I have achieved,
which is, procuring myself a place of residence, which will
save me these teasing migrations in future, so that though
I part with my sweet little cottage on the banks of the
Esk, you will find me this summer in the very centre of
the ancient Reged, in a decent farm-house [1] overhanging
the Tweed, and situated in a wild pastoral country.

[*Lockhart*]

[*From a copy of* " *Sir Tristrem ; A Metrical Romance of the
Thirteenth Century, by Thomas of Ercildoune, called the
Rhymer.*" *Edited from the Auchinleck MS. by Walter Scott,
Esq., Advocate. Edinburgh : Constable,* 1804.]

[*The following letter is affixed in front of the title page*]

To THE CURATORS OF THE ADVOCATES LIBY.

GENTLEMEN,—With my best thanks for the indulgence
you have shewn me I have the honor to return the
Auchinleck Ms to its place in the Library. To convince
you that your kindness has not been altogether misplaced
I have the honor to request that you will accept an
uncastrated copy of the Romance of Sir Tristrum from
which you will see that I have endeavoured to analyze &
announce to the public the contents of this very curious &

---

[1] Ellis received this letter while he was in the act of writing to Scott, and
adds, " God bless you ! Anne desires her very best love to you and your
Charlotte and begs to assure you that a ' decent farm-house ' in Ettrick
forest will be sufficient to inspire her with romantic ideas for the rest of
her life. Pray *mettez-moi aux pieds* of Mrs. Scott, etc."

valuable volume   I remain Gentlemen Your very obedt.
humble Servt   WALTER SCOTT
CASTLE STREET 7th May [1804]

*On a fly-leaf of this copy, which is in the National Library of
Scotland, Scott has written the following inscription :*
To the Library of the Honble Faculty of Advocates—
this copy of a Romance published from a valuable manuscript in that collection is respectfully offerd

[*Nat. Lib. Scot.*]   By the Editor

TO FRANCIS DOUCE [1]

EDINBURGH, CASTLE-STREET, *May* 7, 1804

SIR,—The warm recollection of your kindness, during
my short stay in London, would have induced me to find
out some means of acknowledgment, however trifling,
even if the volume which I have now the honour to
request you to accept had not derived a great share of any
interest it may be found to possess, from the curious
fragments upon the same subject which you so liberally
communicated to me. I hope that in both points of
view, the copy of Sir Tristrem now sent will be thought
deserving of a place among your literary treasures. It is
one of twelve thrown off, without a castration which I
adopted in the rest of the edition, against my own opinion,
and in compliance with that of some respectable friends :
for I can by no means think that the coarseness of an
ancient romance is so dangerous to the public as the mon-
grel and inflammatory sentimentality of a modern novelist·
By honouring with your acceptance a " Tristrem
entier," you will greatly oblige, Sir, your most obedient
humble servant,   WALTER SCOTT

[*Letters of Sir Walter Scott,* 1832]

[1] Francis Douce (1757-1834) was a good deal older than Scott. His best
known and most valuable work, *Illustrations of Shakespeare*, 2 vols., appeared
in 1807.

To GEORGE ELLIS

[*19th May*, 1804]

FOR more than a month my head was fairly tenanted by ideas, which, though strictly pastoral and rural, were neither literary nor poetical. *Long sheep* and *short sheep*, and *tups* and *gimmers*, and *hogs* and *dinmonts*, had made a perfect sheepfold of my understanding, which is hardly yet cleared of them.—I hope Mrs. Ellis will clap a bridle on her imagination. Ettrick Forest boasts finely shaped hills and clear romantic streams ; but, alas ! they are bare, to wildness, and denuded of the beautiful natural wood with which they were formerly shaded. It is mortifying to see that, though wherever the sheep are excluded, the copse has immediately sprung up in abundance, so that enclosures only are wanting to restore the wood wherever it might be useful or ornamental, yet hardly a proprietor has attempted to give it fair play for a resurrection . . .

. . . You see we reckon positively on you[1]—the more because our arch-critic Jeffrey tells me that he met you in London, and found you still inclined for a northern trip. All our wise men in the north are rejoiced at the prospect of seeing George Ellis. If you delay your journey till July, I shall then be free of the Courts of Law, and will meet you upon the Border, at whatever side you enter.

[*Lockhart*]

[1] Writing the next day, therefore, before he received this letter, Ellis, after saying much about Sir Tristram, goes on : " Our long projected and anxiously wished for journey is likely to be postponed by the illness of Admiral Parker," and later, on the 6th of June, he announces the death of the Admiral and the postponement indefinitely of his visit. He will review *Sir Tristram* for the *Edinburgh*.

To WILLIAM SMITH, SOLICITOR, KELSO

DEAR SIR,—I have adopted your advertisement with
an alteration or two of little consequence, and one which
is of great importance, namely, fixing upon a public sale.
My friends here tell me so many stories of higher sums
drawn in this way than could have [been] had otherwise
&c., &c., that I am resolved to let the place go to the
highest bidder, that I may have no reflections on myself
afterwards. I shall desire Joseph Gillon, who does any
little jobs for me, to send you a copy of the advertisement
to be inserted in the Kelso paper once a fortnight till the
time of sale, and in the Northumberland and Dumfries
papers as often as you think proper. I will also advertise
in the three Edinburgh papers, and give the matter as
much publicity as I can. Will you have the goodness to
send Gillon a copy of the Inventory of the Title Deeds.
I may say, with Romeo's apothecary, that in this business
my poverty and not my will consents. I hope to be at
Rosebank on Monday 23rd, when my uncle [1] will meet me
upon the affairs of the Trust, and of course we will see
you there. Believe me, Dear Sir, Your faithful Servant,

EDINR., 11*th July*, 1804.   WALTER SCOTT

[*Smith's Kelso Grammar School*]

To GEORGE ELLIS

[*18th June* 1804]

HE [2] was a man of universal benevolence and great
kindness towards his friends, and to me individually.
His manners were so much tinged with the habits of
celibacy as to render them peculiar, though by no means

[1] *i.e.* Thomas Scott.

[2] On the 10th of June 1804 died, at Rosebank, Captain Robert Scott,
his uncle. Ellis sends condolences on the 4th of July, and reports the
dispatch of a review of *Tristrem* to the *Edinburgh*. The letter to William
Smith concerns the sale of Rosebank, which had been left to Scott.

unpleasingly so, and his profession (that of a seaman) gave a high colouring to the whole. The loss is one which, though the course of nature led me to expect it, did not take place at last without considerable pain to my feelings. The arrangement of his affairs, and the distribution of his small fortune among his relations, will devolve in a great measure upon me. He has distinguished me by leaving me a beautiful little villa on the banks of the Tweed, with every possible convenience annexed to it, and about thirty acres of the finest land in Scotland. Notwithstanding, however, the temptation that this bequest offers, I continue to pursue my Reged plan, and expect to be settled at Ashestiel in the course of a month. Rosebank is situated so near the village of Kelso, as hardly to be sufficiently a country residence ; besides, it is hemmed in by hedges and ditches, not to mention Dukes and Lady Dowagers, which are bad things for little people. It is expected to sell to great advantage. I shall buy a mountain farm with the purchase money, and be quite the Laird of the Cairn and the Scaur.

[*Lockhart*]

To GEORGE ELLIS

[1 *August* 1804]

HAVING had only about a hundred and fifty things to do, I have scarcely done anything, and yet could not give myself leave to suppose that I had leisure to write letters. 1*st*, I had this farm-house to furnish from sales, from brokers' shops, and from all manner of hospitals for incurable furniture. 2*dly*, I had to let my cottage on the banks of the Esk. 3*dly*, I had to arrange matters for the sale of Rosebank. 4*thly*, I had to go into quarters with our cavalry, which made a very idle fortnight in the midst of all this business. Last of all, I had to superintend a removal, or what we call a *flitting*, which, of all bores under the cope of Heaven, is bore the most tremendous.

After all these storms, we are now most comfortably settled, and have only to regret deeply our disappointment at finding your northern march blown up. We had been projecting about twenty expeditions, and were pleasing ourselves at Mrs. Ellis's expected surprise on finding herself so totally built in by mountains as I am at the present writing hereof. We are seven miles from kirk and market. We rectify the last inconvenience by killing our own mutton and poultry; and as to the former, finding there was some chance of my family turning pagans, I have adopted the goodly practice of reading prayers every Sunday, to the great edification of my household. Think of this, you that have the happiness to be within two steps of the church, and commiserate those who dwell in the wilderness. I showed Charlotte yesterday *the Catrail*, and told her that to inspect that venerable monument was one main object of your intended journey to Scotland. She is of opinion that ditches must be more scarce in the neighbourhood of Windsor Forest than she had hitherto had the least idea of.

ASHESTIEL

[*Lockhart*]

To CHARLES ERSKINE [1]

DEAR CHARLES,—After much debate in my own mind I have finally determined to sell Rosebank as I find my prospects of inhabiting it are very remote and should like much better to have a place higher up the country. You will therefore see it in the papers shortly. Mrs. Scott is very much obliged to you for the very smart compl[i]ment of the calf and hopes you will soon give her an opportunity of thanking you in person as she will be at Ashestiel

---

[1] This letter seems to be wrongly dated. Scott has written " March " for, I think, " July." Compare the letter about the sale of Rosebank to William Smith. Captain Scott died on the 10th June. 10th July was a Tuesday.

about the end of this week. I expect to be there Sunday
se'enight the instant our quarters break up. . . .

I have presented an application to the Court in my own
name & that of the Magistrates for their warrant authoriz-
ing us to send prisoners to Jedburgh jail the town of
Selkirk paying all expences as if they were confined in
their own Burgh. This I observe from the Acts of
Sederunt is the form. The petition will be moved tomorrow.

I was present at Browns declaration today—he stoutly
& impudently denied stealing the cow. The Sheriff & I
thought it as well to cause him enact himself Banishd
from the Count[r ?]y & put him aboard a Man of war,
as to have him tried since in all probability the Court
would only have banishd him from Scotland. So this
business is at an end of which pray apprize Mr. Roger.
I will write to Baillie Clarkson whenever I learn the
success of the petition. I inclose a paper which had
fallen out of the process betwixt Sir I. P. & his tenant.
Yours ever truly

W. SCOTT

EDINR. *Tuesday* 10 *March* [*July*] [1804]

[*Curle*]

To GEORGE ELLIS

[*21st August* 1804]

I SHOULD have liked very much to have had appropriate
embellishments. Indeed, we made some attempts of the
kind, but they did not succeed. I should fear Flaxman's [1]
genius is too classic to stoop to body forth my Gothic
Borderers. Would there not be some risk of their
resembling the antique of Homer's heroes, rather than

---

[1] In closing his letter of 4th July Ellis writes : " Why dont you make
Flaxman draw some sketches for the Lay . . . and why dont you publish
it on the same sized paper as Sir Tristram ? "

the iron race of Salvator ? After all, perhaps, nothing is more difficult than for a painter to adopt the author's ideas of an imaginary character, especially when it is founded on traditions to which the artist is a stranger. I should like at least to be at his elbow when at work. I wish very much I could have sent you the Lay while in MS., to have had the advantage of your opinion and corrections. But Ballantyne galled my kibes so severely during an unusual fit of activity, that I gave him the whole story in a sort of pet both with him and with it. . . . I have lighted upon a very good amanuensis for copying such matters as the *Lay le Frain*, &c. He was sent down here by some of the London booksellers in a half-starved state, but begins to pick up a little. . . . I am just about to set out on a grand expedition of great importance to my comfort in this place. You must know that Mr. Plummer, my predecessor in this county, was a good antiquary, and left a valuable collection of books, which he entailed with the estate, the first successors being three of his sisters, at least as old and musty as any Caxton or Wynkyn de Worde in his library. Now I must contrive to coax those watchful dragons to give me admittance into this garden of the Hesperides. I suppose they trouble the volumes as little as *the* dragon did the golden pippins ; but they may not be the more easily soothed on that account. However, I set out on my *quest*, like a *preux chevalier*, taking care to leave Camp, for dirtying the carpet, and to carry the greyhounds with me, whose appearance will indicate that hare soup may be forthcoming in due season. By the way, did I tell you that Fitz-Camp is dead, and another on the stocks ? As our stupid postman might mistake *Reged*, address, as per date, Ashestiel, Selkirk, by Berwick.

[*Lockhart*]

To UNKNOWN CORRESPONDENT

ASHESTIEL, 3*rd Septr.*, 1804

SIR,—I am very sorry (as you came to Ashestiel on purpose to see me) that I happened to be from home for two days when you called there. At the same time it is in some degree of less consequence as I have laid it down for an unchangeable resolution upon no account to give an opinion upon other authors poems, as I am too distrustful of my own taste & too fond of the leisure my profession permits but rarely to enjoy, to think of undertaking a task so delicate & laborious.

I beg you will not impute my declining your request to any dislike of your MSS. which are herewith returned, on the contrary the suffrage of the friends you mention is sufficient to induce me to put my name down for two copies which please forward to Sir, Your servant,

[*John T. Scott*]   (Signed) WALTER SCOTT

To THOMAS THOMSON [1]

DEAR TOM,—I was favoured with your estimable letter by Nelson who has been with me ever since. He is a very well behaved pleasant inmate so I detain him untill you summon him back to the *grande opus* as he has nothing else to do in Town & would only waste his time & cash. My own time has been entirely spent in field sports of which I have not taken so good a swing this many a day. I only lament I have seen so little of the chosen but still hope Miss Thompson & you will make out your expedition here when I think I can promise you good amusement. Erskine I almost despair of & Cranstoun will I suppose roost in Ayrshire till the accursed 12 of November.

[1] See note, p. 116.

I have not been able to touch Irving [1] for the want of books & also because I disagree with the man of the leaden mace about the Celtic derivation of the Picts on which subject he is entêté. I will return the MSS by Mr. Nelson. Irvings book is *beggarly* beyond description & only my extreme politeness prevents my spelling the epithet with a ŭ. Tell Jeffrey when you see him that I have never been able to put pen to paper & certainly cannot till I come to town unless there comes a bitter bad day. On Wednesday we had a rousing *kirn* the evening concluded with the utmost conviviality in the morning the dead like those in Chevy Chace were carried off in *carts & wains* by their weeping spouses. I conclude this will find you returnd & I hope thinking of moving toward the forest were it only to seek Admiral Nelson Yours ever sincerely WALTER SCOTT

ASHESTIEL 6 *Oct:* 1804

[*Stevenson*]

To GEORGE ELLIS

[*November* 1804]

I FEAR you fall too much into the sedentary habits incident to a literary life, like my poor friend Plummer,[2] who used to say that a walk from the parlour to the garden once a day was sufficient exercise for any rational being, and that no one but a fool or a fox-hunter would take more. I wish you could have had a seat on Hassan's tapestry, to have brought Mrs Ellis and you soft and fair

[1] Irving (David), *The Lives of the Scotch Poets ; with preliminary dissertations on the literary history of Scotland and the early Scotch drama.* 2 vols. Edinr., 1804. Readers will recall the quarrel as to the Celtic or Gothic origin of the Picts between Oldbuck and Sir Arthur in *The Antiquary.* Irving was for the Goths. "That the Picts were Gothic colonies has, I apprehend, been sufficiently evinced by Mr. Pinkerton." Scott held the same opinion. See his review of Ellis's *Specimens of the Early English Poets* (*Periodical Criticism,* vol. i.).

[2] Scott's predecessor as Sheriff-Depute of Selkirkshire, himself an antiquary.

to Ashestiel, where, with farm mutton at 4 p.m., and goat's whey at 6 a.m., I think we could have re-established as much *embonpoint* as ought to satisfy a poetical antiquary. As for my country amusements, I have finished the Lay, with which and its accompanying notes the press now groans ; but I have started nothing except some scores of hares, many of which my gallant greyhounds brought to the ground.

EDINBURGH

[*Lockhart*]

To GEORGE ELLIS

[*November* 1804]

I AM sorry for the very pitiful catastrophe of Dr. Young's publication,[1] because, although I am altogether unacquainted with the merits of the controversy, one must always regret so very serious a consequence of a diatribe. The truth is, that these gentlemen reviewers ought often to read over the fable of the boys and frogs, and should also remember it is much more easy to destroy than to build, to criticise than to compose. While on this subject. I kiss the rod [2] of my critic in the Edinburgh,

[1] In a letter of 10th November Ellis, after accounting for his silence by illness, goes on to complain of the tone in which the *Edinburgh* has treated " a most amiable and uncommonly able man (Dr. Young) in whom I am sincerely interested. He was for some time lecturer in Natural Philosophy at the Royal Institution and having determined to publish his lectures had received from one of our booksellers the offer of £1000 for the copyright and was actually preparing for the press when the bookseller came to him and told him that the ridicule thrown in the *Edinburgh Review* on some papers of his published in the *Philosophical transactions* had so frightened the whole trade that he must request to be released from his bargain. The work therefore now lies upon his hands."

[2] On the 4th of July Ellis had written : " You will find when the article appears . . . that you had no occasion to stimulate me to severity for in truth I do feel very angry, not indeed with you, but with your bookseller. It is quite scandalous in him to make the book scarce at the moment of publication by printing off no more than 150 copies and selling them at a high price to save himself the trouble of distributing. . . . Your name must have sold 500 copies just as easily as 150, . . . it is your wish to popularise learning and you are known to possess the talent of doing this

on the subject of the price of Sir Tristrem ; it was not my fault, however, that the public had it not cheap enough, as I declined taking any copy-money, or share in the profits ; and *nothing*, surely, was as reasonable a charge as I could make.

[*Lockhart*]

To GEORGE ELLIS

[*30th December 1804*]

THE *Lay* is now ready, and will probably be in Longman and Rees's hands shortly after this comes to yours. I have charged them to send you a copy by the first conveyance, and shall be impatient to know whether you think the entire piece corresponds to that which you have already seen. I would also fain send a copy to Gifford, by way of introduction.[1]   My reason is, that I understand he is about to publish an edition of Beaumont and Fletcher, and I think I could offer him the use of some miscellaneous notes, which I made long since on the margin of their works. Besides, I have a good esteem of Mr. Gifford as a manly English poet, very different from most of our modern versifiers.—We are so fond of Reged, that we are just going to set out for our farm in the middle of a snow-storm ; all that we have to comfort ourselves with is, that our march has been ordered with

insomuch that those who do not care about the old English would be sure to buy your book (if they could) for the sake of the introduction, the notes and the epitome of the story." Later, 3rd December, he writes : " I did not mean to offend Constable *very much* . . . about the price . . . but as you had desired me to say something against it, I took what I thought the only vulnerable point. I am glad you agree with me in my calculation about Tomas's birth."

[1] In his letter of 9th January 1805 Ellis writes : " I rather believe it is Massinger, not Beaumont and Fletcher, that little Gifford is going to publish, but if he would attempt an edition of the latter I am sure that he would be extremely grateful for your communications and I am quite sure that few things would delight him so much as receiving from you a copy of the *Minstrel*. I forget where he sleeps—somewhere in Westminster I think, but he *lives* principally in Hatchard's bookshop."

great military talent—a detachment of minced pies and brandy having preceded us.   In case we are not buried in a snow-wreath, our stay will be but short.   Should that event happen, we must wait the thaw.

[*Lockhart*]

1805

TO GEORGE ELLIS

FRERE[1] is so perfect a master of the ancient style of composition, that I would rather have his suffrage than that of a whole synod of your vulgar antiquaries. The more I think on *our* system of the origin of Romance, the more simplicity and uniformity it seems to possess ;—and though I adopted it late and with hesitation, I believe I shall never see cause to abandon it. Yet I am aware of the danger of attempting to *prove*, where proofs are but scanty, and probable suppositions must be placed in lieu of them. I think the Welsh antiquaries have considerably injured their claims to confidence, by attempting to detail very remote events with all the accuracy belonging to the facts of yesterday. You will hear one of them describe you the cut of Llywarch Hen's beard, or the whittle of Urien Reged, as if he had trimmed the one, or cut his cheese with the other. These high pretensions weaken greatly our belief in the Welsh poems, which probably contain real treasures. 'Tis a pity some sober-minded man will not take the trouble to sift the wheat from the chaff, and give us a good account of their MSS. and traditions. Pray, what is become of the *Mabinogion*? It is a proverb, that children and fools talk truth, and I am mistaken if even the same valuable quality may not

---

[1] See Lockhart (chap. xiii.) for Frere's opinion and Ellis's comment, in which Lockhart has introduced some errors. Ellis continues where Lockhart stops (9th January 1805) : " I think I can trust you for having concluded the *Last Minstrel* with as much spirit as it was begun, but if I should not think so you may depend upon my telling you the truth. Indeed it shall be my duty, I shall say it with all possible rage and fury, for if you have been capable of writing anything unworthy of the highest mountains of Reged there is an end of everything like inspiration."

sometimes be extracted out of the tales made to entertain both. I presume, while we talk of childish and foolish tales, that the Lay is already with you, although, in these points, *Long-manum est errare*. Pray inquire for your copy.

[*Lockhart*]

The following is written on the first page of the manuscript copy of " The Lay of the Last Minstrel " :

THE LADY DALKEITH

from her Ladyships much attached and very respectful humble servant   WALTER SCOTT

CASTLE STREET 10 *January* 1805

Copy of letter on opposite page :

Will your Ladyship with your usual goodness honor with your acceptance the enclosed Manuscript.

The little ornaments would have been better executed had it not been for the shortness of the days which obliged the Transcriber to work by candle light. Mrs. Scott joins in offering most respectful compliments to all at Dalkeith House & I am with all the zeal of a faithful vassal Your Ladyships very faithful humble Servant

CASTLE STREET *Saturday*   W. SCOTT

[*Buccleuch*]

To LADY MOIRA [1]

[*10th February* 1805]

YOUR ladyship's genealogical deductions gave me much amusement and information ; they are the keys of history and often its touchstone, and it is scandalous that the

---

[1] This is a fragment of a longer letter in the possession of the Earl of Granard, who has been good enough to search for the original, but in vain. The Earl of Moira (also Earl of Rawdon and Marquess of Hastings) married, on 12th July 1804, Flora, daughter of James Mure Campbell, fifth Earl of

history of our most noble families should be, as they are, abandoned to the interested tribe of heralds and pedigree makers. Till of late years, I believe, these matters were better managed in Scotland, but we have long grown nearly as careless as the neighbours whom we are daily aping. I think your Ladyship's conjecture with respect to the origin of the song " Queen Eleanor was a sick woman " is quite a ray of light ; hardly anything was so likely to be of advantage to the Lancastrians as to slur the descent of the house of York.

[*Hist. MSS. Commission*]

To DR. CURRIE, CLIFTON MALL NO 5, BRISTOL [1]

My DEAR SIR,—I am favoured with your letter covering that of Mrs. Riddell & the very curious extract which she has taken the trouble to make in my behalf from Mr. Grays papers. I do not know whether I have been more entertaind with the last or flattered by the obliging manner in which Mrs. Riddell has been pleased to communicate it. I hope you will add to your goodness on this occasion the trouble of making my most respectful [thanks] to that Lady for the [*MS. torn here*] she has been pleased to confer on me & to assure her that I am highly sensible of it.

Loudon, and at the time of the marriage she was Countess of Loudon in her own right. As commander of the forces the Earl had been very popular in Edinburgh at the beginning of the century. A letter from Lady Charlotte, a sister of the Earl, to Scott of 21st June 1804 speaks of her interest in antiquities but adds : " Alas ! all researches after antiquity, taste, literature, all ! all ! are destroyed in this unfortunate country and I cannot forbear remarking that I see since the Rebellion a ferocity of character gaining ground among the common people that certainly did not exist formerly and suspicion seems cherished as a virtue."

[1] This letter is dated 25th September but is endorsed 25th February. Currie died at Sidmouth on 31st August of this year. Mrs. Riddell is probably Mrs. Walter Riddell (for whom see Lives of Burns) and Gray is presumably James Gray, the friend of Burns to whom in 1816 Wordsworth addressed his letter on Currie's *Life of Burns*. He was master of the Dumfries High School, a teacher at the High School, Edinburgh, and at Belfast. He went later to India as a chaplain.

Edinburgh news we have little or none—except that Sir John Sinclair of pastoral fame proposes an excursion into the regions of metaphysicks wherein all the powers & faculties of the Human Mind according to the most approved division are to be illustrated by the various events of a cockeneys expedition from London to Windsor. I was favoured with a sketch of this curious performance which is to constitute an introduction to a work upon Longevity which I suppose may claim the title of the ancient " & verie pithie comedie, entitled The longer thou livest the more fole thou art." If the introduction does not put down Dugald Stuart & the work occasion physick being thrown to the Dogs as altogether superseded by the worthy Bart's rules for prolonging life the author will be contented to chuse for his mottoe the exclamation of a brother Shepherd

Ah silly I more silly than my Sheep

I am truly happy that your letter gives a favourable account of your progressive amendment & I hope you will not return to Bristol [1] untill you carry mild weather [?] [*MS. torn here*] along with you & even then will be cautious of over exertion. Believe me with great regard Dear Sir Your very faithful humble Servant

WALTER SCOTT

EDINR. 25 *Septr.* [*February*] 1805.

There has been a very pretty poem published here lately under the title of the Sabbath—it has been so successful that the Author Mr. James Graham [2] Advocate after remaining long incognito has steppd forward to claim his renown. I think you will have great pleasure in perusing it—

[*Glen*]

[1] This letter is addressed to Bristol, but the writing of the address does not look like Scott's hand. It is possible it may have been enclosed in a letter to someone to address.

[2] More correctly Grahame. Published his *The Sabbath* in 1804 and *Sabbath Walks* in 1805. The poem is chiefly remembered by Byron's scoffing lines in *English Bards and Scotch Reviewers*.

To MRS. GREENWOOD [1]

MADAM,—I am honord with your letter covering a copy of the Ballad of Mary Hamilton for which as well as for the very flattering manner in which you mention my collection of the time worn songs I can only offer my most respectful thanks. It is now some time since I published a 2d Edition of the Minstrelsy containing a full copy of Mary Hamilton arranged as I best could from several editions which were sent to me from different persons favourers like Mrs. Greenwood of the ancient Scottish poetry. Should the work come to a 3d. Edition I will not fail to avail myself of several improvements which may be adopted from the copy with which you have favoured me. Upon the whole it is very similar to that which I have printed & I do not doubt that it has been handed down by tradition from a remote period though perhaps modernised and altered by the reciters. I have lately amused myself with throwing together into the shape of a metrical romance a number of the Border traditions which I picked up in the course of my researches after old songs and which I had not found an opportunity of inserting in the Minstrelsy. As I have no pretensions to the power of writing regular or polished poetry I have put the narrative into the mouth of an old Minstrel the last of the race and therefore entitled it the Lay of the Last Minstrel. Should this poem fall in your way I should be much flattered by learning that you approve of it which I am encouraged to hope from your attachment to Legendary Lore and more especially to that respecting Teviotdale. You will

---

[1] Mrs. Greenwood of Brookwood Park, Alresford, Hants. She came from the Borders and knew a number of ballads which had been handed down by tradition. Two letters from her to Scott are in the Walpole volumes. This letter I owe to her grandson, Mr. C. J. P. Cave, Stoner Hill, Petersfield. The letter from Mrs. Greenwood enclosing the ballad of Mary Hamilton is dated 21st February (no year), but is inserted among the 1806 letters in the Walpole collection.

probably meet among the actors with some of the old heroes of Kirston Scott.[1] The book is published in Londn otherwise I would beg your acceptance of a copy. Although I do not think that I will ever again renew my researches into these subjects I am not the less anxious to collect materials for improving and amending what I have already published when the good or bad taste of the public gives me the opportunity by demanding another edition of the Minstrelsy. With this view I will deem myself highly favoured if when quite at leisure you would favour me with copies of the Ballads you mention. I have a Johnie Scott beginning

> Johnie Scotts to fair England
> This quarter of a year
> And Johnie Scotts to fair England
> The Kings braid banner to bear

The tale of the Fenwick is I think in a little collection published by the late Mr. Ritson called the Northumbrian garland but probably much corrupted. It is a story of a Lady who died in child-birth. Thomas the Rhymer I should very much like to see. I hope the same good nature which led you to countenance my pursuits will readily excuse the trouble I am giving you by so readily snatching at your obliging offer. I have no prospect of being very soon in town when I am I will take an early opportunity of expressing in person how much I am Mrs. Greenwoods much obliged very humble servant

    EDIN. 1 *March* [1805 ?]   WALTER SCOTT

    Mrs. Greenwood

[*Cave*]

---

[1] " It (the ballad) is so far *genuine*, that it is about fifty years since they (her mother and aunt) learned it & then from an old woman who lived where they were born at Longnewton near Jedburgh. . . The old woman *Kirstan Scott* was quite a chronicle of old songs and stories." *Mrs. Greenwood.*

To WILLIAM WORDSWORTH, GRASMERE BY
KENDALE CUMBERLAND

MY DEAR WORDSWORTH,—I duly received both your
letters and before the last arrived had deeply sympathised
in your late melancholy loss.[1] The same dreadful
catastrophe deprived me of a near relation a delightful
& promising youth the hope and pride of his parents.
He had just obtained a cadetship & parted from us in all
the ardour of youthful hope & expectation leaving his
father (a brother of my mother) almost heartbroken at
his departure. But I will not dwell on the grief &
despair which his fate occasioned except to assure you
that in the scenes of distress which I was obliged to
witness & in which indeed I shared sincerely I often
thought of the similar effects which the same disastrous
event must necessarily have produced in your little
family of Love. I hope you will struggle against the too

[1] The death by shipwreck of John Wordsworth. The similar loss to
which Scott refers is the death of his young cousin, son of Professor Daniel
Rutherford, who was lost in the *Lady Jane Dundas* on 5th February of this
year.

On 16th January Wordsworth had written : " Your letter announcing
your Border Romance as being on its way to my sister I received yesterday.
The Romance has not arrived yet. . . . My sister is very anxious as I am
to see a work the fragments of which gave us so much pleasure. . . . On
the other side you will find a few stanzas which I hope for the subject at
least will give you some pleasure. I wrote them not without a wish of
pleasing you soon after our return from Scotland though I have been too
lazy to send them to you till now. They are in the same sort of metre as
the Leader Haughs and I have borrowed the name *Burn-mill* meadow from
that poem for which I wish you would substitute some other that may
really be found in the Vale of Yarrow—I only mean the verses for your own
personal perusal." On the opposite page is then transcribed " From
Stirling castle we had seen " without the later title " Yarrow Unvisited."
On the 7th March he wrote again announcing the arrival of the poem,
but excusing his sister's silence " from the late deplorable loss which we
have sustained in the person of our Brother. . . . This affliction weighs so
heavily on the hearts of all in this house that we have neither strength nor
spirits for anything. Our Brother was the pride and delight of our hearts,
as gentle, as meek, as brave, as resolute, as noble a spirit as ever breathed."
—*Walpole Collection.*

great indulgence which grief is apt to exact and that Miss Wordsworth will call her admirable good sense to assist her in calming her feelings under this unexpected and dreadful blow. It is a vile selfish maxim to say " Sorrow not for what cannot be recalled " & those who can give the advice are I hope the only persons who could accept of the consolation it affords. But that which *is* has stronger claims on us than that which is gone & I hope in the discharge of your mutual duties & in the taste of mutual consolation your sorrow will in time be robbed of its bitterness.

I am truly happy that you have found anything to interest or amuse you in my romance. It has the merit of being written with heart & goodwill and for no other reason than to discharge my mind of the ideas which from infancy have rushed upon it. I believe such verses will be generally found interesting because enthusiastic. Having thus expelled from my brain the Fiend of Chivalry & sent him to wander at will through the world I must sweep & garnish the empty tenement & decorate or rather fill it with something useful, least the former tenant should return with seven devils worse than himself & take possession for good & aye. And now let me tell you that I am very much flattered by your choosing Yarrow for a subject of the verses sent me in your first letter which shall not pass out of my own hand nor be read except to those worthy of being listeners. At the same time I by no means admit your apology however ingeniously & artfully stated for not visiting the bonny holms of Yarrow & certainly will not rest till I have prevailed upon you to compare the ideal with the real stream. We are usually now (during the vacation of the court) within three miles of the dale of Yarrow by a wild & mountainous pass. Our own farm is on Tweedside, a sweet & simple spot which I hope you will one day visit. I intended a poetical request of this nature in your own measure & versification but postpone it for the present. We have Broad-meadow [1] upon Yarrow which with the addition of green or fair or any other epithet of one syllable will give truth to the locality & supply the place of Burnmill meadow which we have not. There are some good lines in the old Ballad—the hunted hare for instance which mourns that she must leave fair Leaderhaugh and cannot win to Yarrow and this which from early youth has given my bosom a thrill when sung or repeated

> For many a place stands in hard case
> *Where blythe folks ken'd nae sorrow*
> Mongst Homes that dwelt on Leader side
> And Scotts that lived on Yarrow

I like your swan upon St Mary's Lake—how came you to know that it is actually frequented by that superb bird ?

My mind is much set upon accepting your flattering invitation to the Lakes this approaching [summer?] Our Courts do not rise till the 12th of July when we have some liberty & I would fain hope that I may be then able to see you on the banks of Derwent among the scenes you have immortalized. But I have many duties to discharge & cannot always be the absolute Master of my own time. May I hope to hear from you at your leisure moments. I beg kindest compliments to your sister & Mrs. Wordsworth in which Charlotte cordially joins. Yours truly

W. SCOTT

EDIN. 16 *March* 1805

I am to be in the country for the next six weeks : my address Ashestiel by Selkirk.

[Abbotsford Copies]

---

[1] Scott is correcting Wordsworth's *Yarrow Unvisited* :

> Let beeves and home-bred kine partake
> The sweets of Burn-mill meadow ;
> The swan on still St. Mary's lake
> Floats double, swan and shadow.

I   Q

To MISS SEWARD [1]

EDINBURGH, 21*st March* 1805

MY DEAR MISS SEWARD,—I am truly happy that you found any amusement in the Lay of the Last Minstrel. It has great faults, of which no one can be more sensible than I am myself. Above all, it is deficient in that sort of continuity which a story ought to have, and which, were it to write again, I would endeavour to give it. But I began and wandered forward, like one in a pleasant country, getting to the top of one hill to see a prospect, and to the bottom of another to enjoy a shade ; and what wonder if my course has been devious and desultory, and many of my excursions altogether unprofitable to the advance of my journey? The Dwarf Page is also an excrescence, and I plead guilty to all the censures concerning him. The truth is, he has a history, and it is this : The story of Gilpin Horner was told by an old gentleman to Lady Dalkeith, and she, much diverted with his actually believing so grotesque a tale, insisted that I should make it into a Border ballad. I don't know if ever you saw my lovely chieftainess—if you have, you must be aware that it is *impossible* for any one to refuse her request, as she has more of the angel in face and temper than any one alive ; so that if she had asked me to write a ballad on a broomstick, I must have attempted it. I began a few verses to be called the Goblin Page ; and they lay long by me, till the applause of some friends whose judgment I valued induced me to resume the poem ; so on I wrote, knowing no more than the man in the moon how I was to end. At length the story appeared so uncouth, that I was fain to put it into the mouth of my old Minstrel—lest the nature of it should be misunder-

---

[1] In a letter of 7th March Miss Seward had declared of the *Lay of the Last Minstrel* : " If I proceed to remark every excellence of which I am susceptible in this fine work, my comment will be scarcely less extensive than the work itself. Yours and Burns' poetic journeys transcend those of every other Poet."—*Walpole Collection.*

stood, and I should be suspected of setting up a new school of poetry, instead of a feeble attempt to imitate the old. In the process of the romance, the page, intended to be a principal person in the work, contrived (from the baseness of his natural propensities I suppose) to slink down stairs into the kitchen, and now he must e'en abide there.

I mention these circumstances to you, and to any one whose applause I value, because I am unwilling you should suspect me of trifling with the public in *malice prepense*. As to the herd of critics, it is impossible for me to pay much attention to them ; for, as they do not understand what I call poetry, we talk in a foreign language to each other. Indeed, many of these gentlemen appear to me to be a sort of tinkers, who, unable to *make* pots and pans, set up for *menders* of them, and, God knows, often make two holes in patching one. The sixth canto is altogether redundant ; for the poem should certainly have closed with the union of the lovers, when the interest, if any, was at an end. But what could I do ? I had my book and my page still on my hands, and must get rid of them at all events. Manage them as I would, their catastrophe must have been insufficient to occupy an entire canto ; so I was fain to eke it out with the songs of the minstrels. I will now descend from the confessional, which I think I have occupied long enough for the patience of my fair confessor. I am happy you are disposed to give me absolution, notwithstanding all my sins.

We have a new poet come forth amongst us—James Graham, author of a poem called the Sabbath, which I admire very much. If I can find an opportunity, I will send you a copy. Your affectionate humble servant,

WALTER SCOTT

[*Lockhart*]

To THE REV. EDWARD FORSTER [1]

DEAR SIR,—I will not delay to acknowledge the receipt of your favour. I hope by this time Mr. Skenes Sketches are in your hands & will be happy when you can favour me with your opinion of them. My idea of the publication has been formed on some conversation with the Booksellers who wish to be concerned. As Mr. Skene furnishes the original drawings & copy for the letter press he will of course expect what every author is entitled to—half profits upon the trade price when an edition shall be disposed of—But he also wishes to retain a share in the work perhaps to the extent of a fourth, he contributing in that proportion to the expences of the work i.e. to the printing & engraving advertising &c. When the edition is disposed of Mr. Skene's claims will stand thus $\frac{1}{2}$ of the free profits on the work at the trade price, & a fourth of the residue, this last sum being subject to a per centage of 10 per cent. in favour of the actual publishers which I think is reasonable as they run the risque of bad debts &c. So much for money matters.

---

[1] When Scott made the acquaintance of Forster (1769-1828), clergyman and miscellaneous writer, I do not know. It was probably through Lord Somerville, Scott's sporting neighbour on the Tweed (in summer) at Alwyn, or The Pavilion, some eight or nine miles below Ashestiel, and a patron of Forster. In his *Memories of Sir Walter Scott* Skene says : " The two following notes have reference to a project which my friends had probably induced him to entertain, but to which I never felt cordially disposed to concur, that of having a series of my foreign drawings engraved and published. For this purpose a few of them had been sent to London for the inspection of the Rev. Edward Forster, a friend of Sir Walter, engaged in literary pursuits, and particularly conversant with works in the line of the Fine Arts. He was pleased with the drawings, and some of them were engraved upon trial, but it afterwards appeared that they could not be executed within such an amount of expense and risk as it would not have been prudent to encounter, and accordingly the intention was for the time abandoned. And although in after years, when the taste for publications of that class had become a little more prevalent, Sir Walter frequently recurred to the idea, and with a view to its success was willing to add the now effective aid of his pen, it was never put into practice." The letter here printed is not one of those given by Skene. I owe it to the kindness of Mr. C. F. Bell, Ashmolean Museum, Oxford.

The plan of the work is—that it shall be published in detached Numbers (four etchings in each) with perhaps a sheet or more of letter press to each view—this last will be my concern & I will endeavour to make them as interesting as possible, by translations from the Sicilian poetry, historical anecdotes, account of manners &c. Mr. Skene has kept an admirable journal but declines publishing it for many reasons. In particular the great expence necessary to finish so many etchings is of itself an absolute bar to publishing the whole at once ; of course I will transfer every thing from it that is interesting.

As to finishing the etchings Mr. Skene wishes them to be executed in the best possible stile & I believe most artists think it necessary to finish some parts with the graver in order to produce the full effect : but so that the Artist *does justice* to the drawings he may take his own way of doing it & calculate his price accordingly. We will be very happy to have one etched as a specimen.

Now for the Magnum Opus.[1]—I would have no objection in the world to one half of the work being printed in London if it was not for the stipulation that my name was to be in it & as you think a good name is better than great riches I must be very chary of mine when it stands in such very good company. I am aware that you have every right to make the same objection

---

[1] The Magnum Opus referred to is the edition of Dryden's works in which Forster and Scott were to have co-operated : " In commencing this task, the Editor had hopes of friendly assistance, which might have rendered his toil more easy, and the result more accurate. Deprived of this by a concurrence of unlucky circumstances, etc."—*Advertisement* to Scott's edition (1808). Forster had contemplated an edition before Scott.

From letters of James Ballantyne in September and December it is clear that Millar objected to including Forster's name with Scott's in the work. " If, as you have reason to think, his name would injure the work it would be absurd to pay for it ; if it would ruin the work it would be madness to retain it. You only can feel the pulse of the London trade." Scott, he goes on, has written to Forster " immediately on your leaving us at Ashestiel, letting him down in the gentlest manner possible. Forster expresses less acrimony than I had anticipated." Scott will stand firm : " Mr. Scott, though the most honourable and delicate, is one of the most resolute men in the world."

to my part of the work being executed without your
superintendence—but an edition of Dryden has been a
hobby of mine for a long time & I think I could throw in
some touches even upon those parts which had undergone
your inspection ; besides you are aware that this will be
absolutely necessary to prevent our repeating explanations
which may have been already given. I do not mean (I
hope you will not suppose that I *can mean*) by this objection
either to engross the merit or the profit of that part of
the work which you may execute I only wish to have
an opportunity of securing the accuracy & above all
the uniformity of the edition, I mean in matter as well as
manner & unless you could prevail upon yourself to take
the whole in your own name it must land in being
printed here.—I am aware that you have stated a difficulty very hard to be got over yet there remains the
alternative of not publishing till 1808 which I would
greatly prefer to a hurried and ill-concocted edition in
1807. If you fear the market being pre-occupied or the
advance becoming heavy we will bring out the life with
the Dramatic Works and so stop the way. Another
convenience would be that it might go on here as silently
as death. But whether it goes on in your name solely
or in yours and mine jointly I can see no reason why we
should not go to press *instantly* when time is so precious.

Ballantyne tells me he has good paper & I think in a
post you may settle your terms with him as to printing.
You are best judge of the price & I suppose he will be
disposed to do it as low as another only in making your
bargain you will recollect it is impossible for me to go on
unless with an Edinr printer and we have no other that
I would trust wt printing a penny ballad. The [This ?]
extreme accuracy too must save us both much trouble.

In your calculation I think you make the selling price
too low 10s. a volume will add one 9th to your proposed
profit of £133 „ 6 „ 8 & will not be higher than the
Shakespeare. I shd think about £150 being 50 per cent

a reasonable profit considering we have the editorship ; however certainly the more the better. But suppose we pay dearer for the first volumes (I mean those which we print first) than for the others I think that if the contract is to be months in making we had better begin to print in the mean time especially as I can send a volume or two of plays to Ballantyne upon a weeks notice.

I should be truly grieved if we were not able to carry on this work in conjunction after we have gone so far and wish you to consider seriously both points of view in which I have placed it you sole editor—half the edition printed in Londn & brought out in 1807 or we joint editors & the edit printed here & brought out or at least compleated a year later.—

A very important part of this matter will devolve almost entirely upon you vizt the collecting materials both from the Museum and private hands. Malone in his Life of Dryden has pointed out some valuable sources & we must move heaven & earth to get at them. You will find this trouble at least equal to that of superintending the press here of which according to my second plan I propose in some measure relieving you. Of course always consulting you before any material alteration in your MS notes—I wish any means could be fallen upon to know what Malone proposes to—if he can be brought to look with a propitious eye on our undertaking it would be very agreeable. Believe me Yours truly

WALTER SCOTT

EDINR. *Friday 29th March* [1805]

[*C. F. Bell*]

To JAMES BALLANTYNE

ASHESTIEL, *April 12th,* 1805

DEAR BALLANTYNE,—I have duly received your two favours—also Fo[r]ster's. He still howls about the expense

of printing, but I think we shall finally settle. His
argument is that you print too fine, *alias* too dear. I
intend to stick to my answer, that I know nothing of the
matter ; but that settle it how you and he will, it must
be printed by you, or can be no concern of mine. This
gives you an advantage in driving the bargain. As to
everything else, I think we shall do, and I will endeavour
to set a few volumes agoing on the plan you propose.

I have imagined a very superb work. What think you
of a complete edition of British Poets, ancient and
modern ? Johnson's is imperfect and out of print ; so
is Bell's, which is a Lilliputian thing ; and Anderson's,
the most complete in point of number, is most contemptible in execution both of the editor and printer. There
is a scheme for you ! At least a hundred volumes, to be
published at the rate of ten a-year. I cannot, however,
be ready till midsummer. If the booksellers will give
me a decent allowance per volume, say thirty guineas, I
shall hold myself well paid on the *writing* hand. This is a
dead secret.

I think it quite right to let Doig [1] have a share of
Thomson ; but he is hard and slippery, so settle your
bargain fast and firm—no loop-holes ! I am glad you
have got some elbow-room at last. [2] Cowan will come
to, or we will find some fit place in time. If not, we *must*
build—necessity has no law. I see nothing to hinder
you from doing Tacitus with your correctness of eye, and
I congratulate you on the fair prospect before us. When
you have time, you will make out a list of the debts to be
discharged at Whitsunday, that we may see what cash we
shall have in bank. Our book-keeping may be very
simple ;—an accurate cash-book and ledger is all that
is necessary ; and I think I know enough of the matter
to assist at making the balance sheet.

[1] An Edinburgh bookseller. Scott's project of a Life of Thomson was
only given up in 1807 or 1808.

[2] Some place to establish James's press.

In short, with the assistance of a little cash I have no doubt things will go on à *merveille*. If you could take a little pleasuring, I wish you could come here and see us in all the glories of a Scottish spring. Yours truly,

W. SCOTT

[*Lockhart*]

TO JAMES SKENE

April 1805

DEAR SKENE,—The enclosed arrived yesterday. I think you had better, to save time, etc., answer it yourself. Mr. F.'s address is Rev. Edward Forster, South Audley Street, Berkeley Square. Adam Ferguson came yesterday opportunely to supply in part the blank your departure made in our fireside circle. He is just setting off, so no more, except that we hope to hear of your speedy return to Ashestiel. Yours truly,   W. S.

[*Skene's Memories*]

TO REVED. EDWARD FORSTER

MY DEAR SIR,—I am favoured with your two letters and am very much pleased with your plan for Dryden. It quite obviates my objections & gives me the advantage of your assistance by which I shall be glad to profit. The original part of the work bears so small proportion to the re-print that there can be neither delay nor trouble in sending you the proofs of the former the latter will be unnecessary as accuracy alone will be required. As to Ballantynes prices I am truly no judge, there is no other printer here whom I can trust to, so I must e'en leave you to make the best bargain you can. The great rise of wages has I believe enhanced his charges.

Holding our plan as settled, I will, as soon as you have settled with Ballantyne put into his hands the second volume which I think ought to consist of The wild

See page 271 for letter of 19th April 1805.

gallant, The rival ladies, The Indian queen. The Essay
on Dramatic poetry should I think be thrown to the end
of the first volume the rest of which will be occupied by
the life general critique & other prolegomena. I presume
in the plays you will use Congreve's edition correcting it
(which I assure you is absolutely necessary) by the
original quartos which are easily to be had and the two
folios. I am clear his alterations of Shakespeare should
be reprinted and also the Indian Queen omitted in your
list, for although Sir R. Howard shared in the composition
the greater part is Drydens and it is not only connected
with the Indian Emperor but alluded to in his controversy
with Settle. Malone's dates are very accurate & should
be followed in arranging the plays—they differ considerably from those of Dr. Johnson & Congreve. The
other plays which I should like to superintend are the
vols containing the conquest of Grenada, Spanish friar
Duke of Guise Don Sebastian King Arthur—on each of
which I have a good deal to say. I suppose you will
think three plays enough in each volume— If Malone
be tractable it will be a pleasant circumstance : he is a
very laborious editor though I think confused and
tasteless. You must look out anxiously for original
materials in which article the labouring oar will be yours.
Surely many of Dryden's letters may yet be recoverd.
Mr. Bindley of Somerset house[1] has most of the rare
controversial tracts relating to that period. I can get at
him through my friend Heber to whom when the work is
fairly set afloat I will intimate our intentions.

Skene is now with me in this wilderness. I have made
him jot down on a slip of paper his own ideas of the mode

[1] In the advertisement of Dryden's works Scott tells how the collection
of fugitive pieces of the reigns of Charles II. to Queen Anne collected by
Narcissus Luttrell, but dispersed after his death, passed in large number into
the possession of James Bindley of Somerset Place, " who, with the utmost
urbanity, permitted the Editor the unlimited use of these, and other literary
curiosities in his valuable library." This was in London in 1806. Bindley was
Commissioner of Stamps for fifty-three years. " At the sale of his library,"
says Lockhart,' ' a collection of penny ballads . . . produced £837."

of executing his etchings which I enclose though it will
put you to the expence of double postage. I am happy
to hear you still look northward. When you see Lord
Somerville tell him I was three hours on the water last
night & killed some salmon, the boat sunk with us however & concluded our sport with a sound ducking. I
hope his Lordshp will not forget to get grates for the
lights made in Londn on the construction we spoke of.
Believe me Yours faithfully

W. SCOTT

ASHESTIEL BY SELKIRK *Sunday* 21 [*April* 1805]
P.M. *April* 26 1805

Reverend Edward Forster,
South Audley Street Berkeley Square London

[*C. F. Bell*]

To GEORGE ELLIS

EDINBURGH, *May* 26, 1805

MY DEAR ELLIS,—Your silence has been so long[1] and
opinionative, that I am quite authorized, as a Border
ballad-monger, to address you with a " Sleep you, or
wake you ? " What has become of the " Romances,"
which I have expected as anxiously as my neighbours
around me have watched for the rain, which was to
bring the grass, which was to feed the new-calved cows,

---

[1] Ellis, replying on the 28th August, apologises on the ground that he
had heard of a possible visit of Scott to London, and had hoped for a longer
visit than on the last occasion. He has heard of the projected edition of
the Poets (see letter to Ballantyne) from Longman. He would prefer
" another minstrel lay by the last and best minstrel," but if Scott will not
take a " second ride on Pegasus " why not undertake what Gibbon once
undertook, an edition of our historians. . . . " I have never been able to
look at a volume of the Benedictine edition of the early French histories
without envy. . . . John Murray who was here lately seems to think that
the *Edinburgh Review* is on the point of being discontinued . . . Heber the
most locomotive of mankind seems to have a project of becoming quite a
Terminus. He has expended this year, as he tells me, £1000 on wine.
Life, I should think, is scarcely long enough to exhaust such a quantity."

—and to as little purpose, for both Heaven and you have obstinately delayed your favours. After idling away the spring months at Ashestiel, I am just returned to idle away the summer here, and I have lately lighted upon rather an interesting article in your way. If you will turn to Barbour's Bruce (Pinkerton's edition, p. 66), you will find that the Lord of Lorn, seeing Bruce covering the retreat of his followers, compares him to Gow MacMorn (Macpherson's Gaul the son of Morni). This similitude appears to Barbour a disparagement, and he says, the Lord of Lorn might more mannerly have compared the king to Gadefeir de Lawryss, who was with the mighty Duke Betys when he assailed the forayers in Gadderis, and who in the retreat did much execution among the pursuers, overthrowing Alexander and Thelomier and Danklin, although he was at length slain ; and here, says Barbour, the resemblance fails. Now, by one of those chances which favour the antiquary once in an age, a single copy of the romance alluded to has been discovered, containing the whole history of this Gadefeir, who had hitherto been a stumbling-block to the critics. The book was printed by Arbuthnot, who flourished at Edinburgh in the seventeenth century. It is a metrical romance, called " The Buik of the Most Noble and Vauliant Conquerour, Alexander the Grit." [1] The first part is called the Foray of Gadderis, an incident supposed to

---

[1] See *The Buik of Alexander or The buik of the Most Noble And Valiant Conqueror By John Barbour Archdeacon of Aberdeen* Edited . . . from the unique printed copy in the possession of the Earl of Dalhousie. . . . By R. L. Graeme Ritchie, D.Litt., Professor of French Language and Literature in the University of Birmingham. Edinburgh, 1925. The first volume contains Part I. of the *Buik of Alexander* and *Li Fuerres de Gadres*, edited from MS. 264 of Bodley's Library. The second and third volumes contain the French *Les Vœux du Paon* with the Scottish translation : " The significance of the Scottish translation, its literary value, the personality of the translator and the much disputed relation in which he stands to John Barbour cannot be determined without the French originals. One step towards the solution . . . is to provide a better text of *Li Fuerre de Gadres* than that edited many years ago by M. Michelant, and to produce the *Les Vœux du Paon* hitherto unpublished."—Introd. to vol. ii.

have taken place while Alexander was besieging Tyre ; Gadefeir is one of the principal champions, and after exerting himself in the manner mentioned by Barbour, unhorsing the persons whom he named, he is at length slain by Emynedus, the Earl-Marshal of the Macedonian conqueror. The second part is called the Avowis of Alexander, because it introduces the oaths which he and others made to the peacock in the " chalmer of Venus," and gives an account of the mode in which they accomplished them. The third is the Great Battell of Effesoun, in which Porus makes a distinguished figure. This you are to understand is not *the* Porus of India but one of his sons. The work is in decided Scotch, and adds something to our ancient poetry, being by no means despicable in point of composition. The author says he translated it from the *Franch*, or *Romance*, and that he accomplished his work in 1438-9. Barbour must therefore have quoted from the French Alexander, and perhaps his praises of the work excited the Scottish translator. Will you tell me what you think of all this, and whether any transcripts will be of use to you ? I am pleased with the accident of its casting up, and hope it may prove the forerunner of more discoveries in the dusty and ill-arranged libraries of our country gentlemen.

I hope you continue to like the Lay.[1] I have had a flattering assurance of Mr. Fox's approbation, mixed

---

[1] In his letter of 4th June Ellis, after some talk about his own romances, writes : " And now for your Minstrel—Though I had previously made up my mind upon the subject, or rather perhaps because I had done so, I was very anxious to compare my sentiments with that of your Edinburgh critic, and I found that in general we were perfectly agreed but that there were parts of the subject which we consider from very different points of view. Frere, with whom I had not any previous communication about it, agrees with me, and trusting very much to the justice of his poetical feelings, I feel some degree of confidence in my judgement though in opposition to Mr. Jeffery whose criticism I admire upon the whole most extremely as being equally acute and impartial and as exhibiting the fairest judgement that could be formed by the mere assistance of good sense and general taste without the particular sort of taste which arises from the study of romantic compositions." He goes on to state his and Frere's answers to Jeffrey's points, but says they both feel doubtful about the songs at the end.

with a censure of my eulogy on the Viscount of Dundee. Although my Tory principles prevent my coinciding with his political opinions, I am very proud of his approbation in a literary sense.

Charlotte joins me, &c. &c.   W. S.

[*Lockhart*]

To CHARLES ERSKINE

[12*th June*, 1805]

Dear Charles,—I send you the processes with judgements on all but Hutson v. Dobson. The reason I have not decided upon the last is, that one of Mr. Laidlaws herds stop'd Dobson on the Dukes property who behaved very insolently on the occasion & I wish this to appear on the face of the proof lest Lord Traquair should think himself obliged to pay the fine. You can hint this to Park & let him consider the propriety of giving in a note craving leave to adduce farther evidence. Laidlaw will tell the man's name—it was not Fletcher but another.

The cheese is admirable many thanks for it the cloth came safe & is now converted into frocks for the Infantry. I suppose the trout spear should have four prongs with withers about an inch & a half separate I have often seen them. I hope to be soon at Ashestiel & to see you there trusting you will not have so good an excuse as last time for staying at home. Believe me ever Yours very truly   Walter Scott

[*Curle*]

To REV. EDWARD FORSTER

[20*th June* 1805]

Dear Sir,—I have the pleasure to enclose a proof of Dryden from which you will perceive the plan I have adopted with respect to his plays. I suppose it will be quite unnecessary to send you those proofs which contain a mere re-print, because doing so will materially delay the work—accuracy being all that is required for which I will be answerable. I beg you will return the enclosed *quam primum* that it may be thrown off and the work fairly set going. I am anxious to save post, believe me, yours truly, W. S.

[*C. F. Bell*]

To JAMES SKENE [1]

ASHESTIEL, 23*rd July* 1805

DEAR SKENE,—I enclose you what Forster calls and I think a poor impression of the drawing. The background seems almost effaced, and the cows in the front look like rabbits. I think, however, the manner, independent of the execution, conveys some notion of your style.

I presume this will find you wandering among the Highlands, and will be happy to hear from you both how you were entertained, and what is to be said about the etching. Forster says he is to write me further particulars. I hope he will send me a better sample of his friend's labours. We are all here as idle as usual, only I have prepared a second edition of the *Lay*,[2] 1500 strong, moved thereunto by the faith, hope and charity of the London booksellers. Comps. to Mr. Greenough. Charlotte sends you kind respects.—Believe me, ever, dear Baron, yours sincerely, WALTER SCOTT

[*Skene's Memories*]

[1] Skene replied to this letter from Oban on 25th August, describing the voyage and a gale which had driven them off the north coast of Ireland : " We passed the body of a man floating in the water but could not have picked him up if it had been the King, the sea ran so high . . . Scott, our friend Foster has really no taste and no knowledge of drawing . . . the trees are like old wigs hung upon hop poles, the cows as you say like rabbits and standing *upon* the river withall instead of the neighbouring meddow, &c."

[2] Lockhart took the portion of this letter which refers to the " Lay " and used it as the beginning of another letter which he misdated " 18th August 1805."

To JAMES SKENE

CASTLE STREET, 3*rd August* 1805

MY DEAR SKENE,—Mr. Alexander Campbell,[1] drawing-master, is upon an expedition through your glens, and has begged from me a card to you as a brother of the brush. He is a very good-natured man whom fortune has pleased to deal rather hardly with. He is, moreover, a little flighty, which you must brave for a day for the sake of his good-nature and misfortunes. Or if he is more *bore* than is permissible, pray set down the overplus to value in accompt with your truly faithful,
WALTER SCOTT

[*Skene's Memories*]

To JAMES SKENE

ASHESTIEL, 25*th August* [1805]

DEAR SKENE,—I lately forwarded you an etching which I hope came safe to hand, though I have heard nothing of it since. But I presume your motions in the Hebrides have been too uncertain to admit of much correspondence. In this persuasion, as you know the great value of my time in this place and season, I will employ no more of it than is necessary to forward the enclosed. All our little household are in usual health, and beg to be kindly remembered to you, and I am always, dear Skene, truly yours,
W. SCOTT

We hope to see you soon after your return.

[*Skene's Memories*]

To WILLIAM SCOTT [2]

MY DEAR WILLIE,—I return the bond duly executed and am very happy to have at all contributed to smooth

---

[1] Scott's old music master, who was touring in quest of Scottish songs and airs. There are repeated references to him and his activities.

[2] Probably William Scott of Raeburn (1773-1855), eldest son of Walter Scott of Raeburn. He married Susan, eldest daughter of Alexander Horsburgh of Horsburgh, Peebleshire.

the way for your entrance into life. Your proposal with respect to your sister's provision is very liberal and affectionate. I trust your success in life will be such as soon to enable you to carry your kind intentions concerning her into effect. In the mean time I will willingly continue to be her trustee and to do any thing in my power to be of service to her, as the daughter of a man to whom I owed much kindness, the memory of which ought not to be buried with him.

As you are now setting out in a *quasi* military career, the advice of a worthy old clergyman to his son will not perhaps be misplaced, especially as it breathes rather more liberality and knowledge of the world than might have been expected from the person by whom it was originally given. " There is a thing called Religion, think of it in the morning, there is something called honour, do not forget that in the transactions of the day, and for the rest, drink and whore—as little as you can."

From the tenor of your letter I suppose you soon leave Scotland, but I hope I shall have a chance of seeing you either here or at Edinburgh before you go. Believe me always Yours very truly   WALTER SCOTT

ASHESTIEL 26*th August* [1805]

I only received your letter yesterday as it had been sent to Keswick in pursuit of mine. The Witnesses are David Ross my servant and Mr. Ebenezer Clarkson Surgeon Selkirk.

[*Blackwood Copy*]

To CHARLES ERSKINE

[*3rd September* 1805]

DEAR CHARLES,—I send the processes & also inclose a petition for Law Burrows at Nicol Milnes instance agt. John Hutson. I have made some enquiry into this business & understand Hutsons bail is ready (Mr. Curver

I   R

of Howford) You will therefore renew the order for bail allowing such time for giving it in as shall seem proper to you on speaking to the prors. I had suspended process till the petition was laid before me & I beg you will explain to Mr. Borrowman [1] that he is *upon no account* to take it upon himself to grant Lawburrows as a matter of course without consulting either you or me. I know no such summary proceeding in our law against personal liberty & therefore it is not to be used without some discretion.

Have the goodness to give Curver a proper lecture for his insolence to Lord Dalkeith & warn him to be on his guard, I do not mean in his behavior to gentlemen but to persons of all descriptions as such another frolic may cost him very dear I understand he scrambled over the Dukes fences also upon this memorable occasion & so made himself liable in a trespass I enclose Lord Ds letter that you may be quite at home in your text. We will be most happy when you can come up & spend a day with us Believe me very truly yours   WALTER SCOTT

ASHESTIEL *Tuesday*

[*Curle*]

The *pot* being bespoken, the *porter* will be forth-coming at Broughams I will make him send a line to Peter to say where your cart shall call.

[*Curle*]

To GEORGE ELLIS

[*About 5th Sept.* 1805]

I HAVE had booksellers here in the plural number. You have set little Rees's head agog about the Chronicles, which would be an admirable work, but should, I think, be edited by an Englishman who can have access to the MSS. of Oxford and Cambridge, as one cannot trust

[1] William Borrowman, surgeon, Selkirk, Hon. Sheriff-Substitute entitled to act in the absence of Charles Erskine and of Scott.

much to the correctness of printed copies. I will, however, consider the matter, so far as a decent edition of
Holinshed is concerned, in case my time is not otherwise
taken up. As for the British Poets, my plan was greatly
too liberal to stand the least chance of being adopted
by the trade at large, as I wished them to begin with
Chaucer. The fact is, I never expected they would
agree to it. The Benedictines had an infinite advantage
over us in that *esprit du corps* which led them to set labour
and expense at defiance, when the honour of the order
was at stake. Would to God your English Universities,
with their huge endowments and the number of learned
men to whom they give competence and leisure, would
but imitate the monks in their literary plans ! My
present employment is an edition of John Dryden's
Works, which is already gone to press. As for riding on
Pegasus, depend upon it, I will never again cross him in
a serious way, unless I should by some strange accident
reside so long in the Highlands, and make myself master
of their ancient manners, so as to paint them with some
degree of accuracy in a kind of *companion* to the Minstrel
Lay. . . . I am interrupted by the arrival of two *gentil
bachelors*, whom, like the Count of Artois, I must despatch
upon some adventure till dinner time. Thank Heaven,
that will not be difficult, for although there are neither
dragons nor boars in the vicinity, and men above six feet
are not only scarce, but pacific in their habits, yet we have
a curious breed of wild cats who have eaten all Charlotte's
chickens, and against whom I have declared a war at
outrance, in which the assistance of these *gentes demoiseaux*
will be fully as valuable as that of Don Quixote to
Pentalopin with the naked arm. So, if Mrs. Ellis takes a
fancy for cat-skin fur, now is the time.

[*Lockhart*]

To JAMES BALLANTYNE [1]

DEAR BALLANTYNE,—As I have full confidence in your applying the accommodation received from Sir W. Forbes in the most economical and prudent manner, I have no hesitation to return the bond subscribed as you desire. This will put you in cash for great matters. I have had a visit from Rees yesterday. He is anxious about a Corpus Historiarum or full edition of the Chronicles of England—an immense work.

I proposed to him beginning with Holinshed, and I think the work will be secured to your press. I congratulate you on Clarendon, which under Thomson's direction will be a glorious publication.

I am glad you like Helvellyn. Without affectation. I was dubious about it, but am reassured by your approbation and that of Mr. Graham.

I hope Mr. White [2] understands that he is not to give the words to any publication unless a musical one, and that he is satisfied with them.

I am impatient to see Graham's new poem, and have racked my imagination for a name which is a matter of consequence.

After all, the most simple is perhaps the best, if sufficiently descriptive of the contents and if it glides trippingly off the tongue.

What think you of " The Birds of Britain," a poem. This title, though simple, sounds well and is quite new. The British Choristers might do, but then the owl,

---

[1] This letter is given in part by Lockhart. The references in it are to the suggested collected edition of the historians, of whom Clarendon was to be entrusted to Scott's friend Thomas Thomson ; to Scott's poem *Helvellyn*, composed on his visit to Cumberland in summer—the occasion of Wordsworth's *Fidelity* ; to a new poem by Grahame of the Sabbath, which appeared in 1806 as *The Birds of Scotland* ; the printing of Dryden ; and a new issue of the *Lay*. What error Dugi was I have not discovered.

[2] William White, an Edinburgh music publisher, to whose *Collection of Scottish Airs*, 2 vols. (1806-7), Scott contributed five songs, one of which was *Helvellyn*.

eagle, raven, &c, could hardly be included under that description.

I will send much of Dryden very soon : the circuit and review have been in the way.

The Lay looks beautiful. I hope Dugi is cancelled. It remains in the copy Rees brought me.

To save drawing when you have next occasion to write, be so good as to enclose a £20 note and £10, which is all I shall want till Mart', when my cash comes in. If you direct under cover to Lord Somerville by Melrose I will receive it safely and free of postage.

I had your parcel of Dryden, and have detected no errors. Yours truly

WALTER SCOTT

ASHESTIEL, *Wednesday, 2nd Sept.* [*Oct.*] [1805] [1]

The bond was signed to-day. Witnesses both my servants.

[*Hawick Arch. Soc.*]

To GEORGE ELLIS

ASHESTIEL, 17*th October* 1805

DEAR ELLIS,—More than a month has glided away in this busy solitude, and yet I have never sat down to answer your kind letter. I have only to plead a horror of pen and ink with which this country, in fine weather (and ours has been most beautiful) regularly affects me. In recompense, I ride, walk, fish, course, eat and drink, with might and main, from morning to night. I could have wished sincerely you had come to Reged this year to partake her rural amusements ;—the only comfort I have

---

[1] This letter is wrongly dated. The 2nd September 1805 was a Monday ; the 2nd October a Wednesday. The bond referred to was a cash credit bond for £800 granted by James Ballantyne & Co. and the dates of the bond are 24th September and 2nd and 5th October.

is, that your visit would have been over, and now I look forward to it as to a pleasure to come. I shall be infinitely obliged to you for your advice and assistance in the course of Dryden. I fear little can be procured for a Life beyond what Malone has compiled, but certainly his facts may be rather better told and arranged. I am at present busy with the dramatic department. This undertaking will make my being in London in spring a matter of absolute necessity.

And now let me tell you of a discovery which I have made, or rather which Robert Jamieson has made, in copying the MS. of " True Thomas and the Queen of Elfland," in the Lincoln cathedral. The queen, at parting, bestows the gifts of harping and carping upon the prophet, and mark his reply—

" To harp and carp, Tomas, where so ever ye gen—
    Thomas, take thou these with thee."—
" Harping," he said, " ken I nane,
    For Tong is chefe of mynstrelsie."

If poor Ritson could contradict his own system of materialism by rising from the grave to peep into this MS., he would slink back again in dudgeon and dismay.[1] There certainly cannot be more respectable testimony than that of True Thomas, and you see he describes the tongue, or recitation, as the principal, or at least the most dignified, part of a minstrel's profession.

Another curiosity was brought here a few days ago by Mr. Southey the poet, who favoured me with a visit on his way to Edinburgh. It was a MS. containing sundry

[1] Ritson had contended against Percy that the minstrels were not in the habit of composing the verses which they sang to the harp and that the word *minstrel* " in its ordinary acceptation meant no more than musician." In reply " Dr. Percy showed that at no period of history was the word . . . applied to instrumental music exclusively ; and . . . produced sufficient evidence that the talents of the profession were as frequently employed in chanting or reciting poetry as in playing the mere tunes."—*Introductory Remarks on Popular Poetry.* Scott now has a fresh proof of his and Percy's view. Jamieson writes on 30th May : " I have copied the fragments of *True Thomas* and *Little Musgrave*."

metrical romances,[1] and other poetical compositions, in the northern dialect, apparently written about the middle of the 15th century. I had not time to make an analysis of its contents, but some of them seem highly valuable. There is a tale of Sir Gowther, said to be a Breton Lay, which partly resembles the history of Robert the Devil, the hero being begot in the same way ; and partly that of Robert of Sicily, the penance imposed on Sir Gowther being the same, as he kept table with the hounds, and was discovered by a dumb lady to be the stranger knight who had assisted her father the emperor in his wars. There is also a MS. of Sir Isanbras ; *item* a poem called Sir Amadis—not Amadis of Gaul, but a courteous knight, who, being reduced to poverty, travels to conceal his distress, and gives the wreck of his fortune to purchase the rites of burial for a deceased knight, who had been refused them by the obduracy of his creditors. The rest of the story is the same with that of Jean de Calais, in the Bibliothèque Bleue, and with a vulgar ballad called the Factor's Garland. Moreover there is a merry tale of hunting a hare, as performed by a set of country clowns, with their mastiffs, and curs with " short legs and never a tail." The disgraces and blunders of these ignorant sportsmen must have afforded infinite mirth at the table of a feudal baron, prizing himself on his knowledge of the mysteries of the chase performed by

---

[1] Southey refers to the MS. in a letter to Wynne of 3rd October 1805 : " Froude a clergyman of Devonshire happened, some time ago, to tell me that a lady in Nottinghamshire had an old MS. volume of poetry which nobody could make out. I expressed a wish to see it—and in short, here it now lies on my desk. It contains all sorts of things and among others three romances, Sir Isambras, Sir Ghother, and Sir Amadas &c. &c." On the 20th he adds : " We were three days at Scott's, a much superior man, whom it is impossible not to like. He was delighted with the MS., and has commissioned me to offer fifteen guineas for it, for the Advocates Library." Scott later sends the price, twelve guineas. The MS. is now in the National Library (19.3.1.), with the table of contents entered in Scott's own hand. The Froude in question was father of the historian. The name of the lady who sold the MS. was Mrs. Sherbrook. This with other MSS. had been saved from " the wreck of a parochial library at the Reformation."

these unauthorized intruders. There is also a burlesque sermon, which informs us of Peter and Adam journeying together to Babylon, and how Peter asked Adam *a full great doubtful question*, saying " Adam, Adam, why didst thou eat the apple unpared ? " This book belongs to a lady. I would have given something valuable to have had a week of it. Southey commissioned me to say that he intended to take extracts from it, and should be happy to copy, or cause to be copied, any part that you might wish to be possessed of ; an offer which I heartily recommend to your early consideration.[1]—Where dwelleth Heber the magnificent, whose library and cellar are so superior to all others in the world ? I wish to write to him about Dryden. Any word lately from Jamaica[2]?— Yours truly,   W. S.

[*Lockhart*]

TO GEORGE ELLIS

[*About the end of Oct. or beginning of Nov.* 1805]

I WILL not castrate John Dryden.[3] I would as soon

[1] To this Ellis replies : " I can only say that *mon livre est fait*, and that nothing will induce me to read another romance until you, by a sufficiently long converse with Highlanders, shall have composed a paulo post ultimum lay of the last minstrel. It will however probably be right that I should desire Longman to thank Mr. Southey (with whom I have at present no personal acquaintance) for his very kind offer."

[2] Ellis writes on 11th December : " Your Daniel (who I am afraid is no prophet) did not perhaps foresee the advantages in point of intoxicating power which a vertical sun gives to rum over whisky imbibed in Scotland. Such at least was the inference I drew from the information of Blackburn." It is not clear that Ellis knew that Daniel was a brother.

[3] In his letter of 26th October Ellis had suggested that Scott might do what Warton had projected and edit Dryden on the " same principle as the castrated edition of Cowley." In reply to this protest by Scott, Ellis waived all moral considerations but argued that " whatever is in point of expression vulgar, whatever might have been written by any fool, whatever might be suppressed without exciting a moment's regret in the mind of any of his admirers *ought* to be suppressed by any Editor who should be disposed to make an appeal to the public taste upon the subject." It will be found later that Scott *does* confess to some difficulties and that Ellis keeps him to his word.

castrate my own father, as I believe Jupiter did of yore.
What would you say to any man who would castrate
Shakspeare, or Massinger, or Beaumont and Fletcher?
I don't say but that it may be very proper to select correct
passages for the use of boarding schools and colleges, being
sensible no improper ideas can be suggested in these
seminaries, unless they are intruded or smuggled under
the beards and ruffs of our old dramatists. But in making
an edition of a man of genius's works for libraries and
collections, and such I conceive a complete edition of
Dryden to be, I must give my author as I find him, and
will not tear out the page, even to get rid of the blot, little
as I like it. Are not the pages of Swift, and even of Pope,
larded with indecency, and often of the most disgusting
kind? and do we not see them upon all shelves and
dressing-tables, and in all boudoirs? Is not Prior the
most indecent of tale-tellers, not even excepting La
Fontaine? and how often do we see his works in female
hands? In fact, it is not passages of ludicrous indelicacy
that corrupt the manners of a people—it is the sonnets
which a prurient genius like Master Little sings *virginibus*
puerisque—it is the sentimental slang, half lewd, half
methodistic, that debauches the understanding, inflames
the sleeping passions, and prepares the reader to give way
as soon as a tempter appears. At the same time, I am
not at all happy when I peruse some of Dryden's comedies:
they are very stupid, as well as indelicate; —sometimes,
however, there is a considerable vein of liveliness and
humour, and all of them present extraordinary pictures
of the age in which he lived. My critical notes will not
be very numerous, but I hope to illustrate the political
poems, as Absalom and Achitophel, the Hind and
Panther, &c., with some curious annotations. I have
already made a complete search among some hundred
pamphlets of that pamphlet-writing age, and with
considerable success, as I have found several which throw
light on my author. I am told that I am to be formidably

opposed by Mr. Crowe,[1] the Professor of Poetry at Oxford, who is also threatening an edition of Dryden. I don't know whether to be most vexed that some one had not undertaken the task sooner, or that Mr. Crowe is disposed to attempt it at the same time with me ;—however, I now stand committed, and will not be *crowed* over, if I can help it. The third edition of the Lay is now in the press, of which I hope you will accept a copy, as it contains some trifling improvements or additions. They are, however, very trifling.

I have written a long letter to Rees, recommending an edition of our historians, both Latin and English ; but I have great hesitation whether to undertake much of it myself. What I can, I certainly will do ; but I should feel particularly delighted if you would join forces with me, when I think we might do the business to purpose. Do, Lord love you, think of this *grande opus*.

I have not been so fortunate as to hear of Mr. Blackburn. I am afraid poor Daniel has been very idly employed— *Cœlum non animum*. I am glad you still retain the purpose of visiting Reged. If you live on mutton and game, we can feast you ; for, as one wittily said, I am not the hare with many friends, but the friend with many hares.

W. S.

[*Lockhart*]

To REVEREND EDWARD FORSTER

MY DEAR SIR,—I am extremely sorry to learn by your letter of the 21st that you are finally resolved to abandon

---

[1] William Crowe (1745-1829), poet and divine, public-orator at Oxford 1784-1829. In the letter already cited Ellis after some remarks about the library of Mr. Bindley writes : " With regard to your competitors I feel perfectly at my ease because I am convinced that though you should generously furnish them with all your materials they would not know how to use them as you will do. ' Non cuivis homini contingit ' to write critical notes which the world will read and though the ramage of *Maître Corbeau* has its admirers he will never rank either as poet or critic with you & Gifford."

Dryden—it will be a serious disappointment to me as I reckoned much on your assistance and will I believe cost me a journey to London in the spring besides double the labour I had expected but there is now I am afraid no help for it.

I heard from Ballantyne accidentally that you intend to go on with some additional volumes of the Drama besides the Shakespeare. I hope you will give us a handsome & complete Ben Jonson which I have long thought a great desideratum—he is one of our neglected classics— Believe me it would give me great pleasure could I hope to be of use to you in this or any future undertaking which would be compensation to my feelings for the very untoward disappointment to which I have been subjected. I look on our old plays as the best possible record of manners which can be traced no where else & I trust as you you [sic] have set your hand to the plough you will suffer nothing to prevent your proceeding with them in some shape or other.

Skene was much disappointed about the engraving which he will not on any account publish. The gentleman in his note to me mentioned 20 Guineas as an average without reference to the engraving sent which he admitted was not worth that sum & which I should think dear at the half. Skene left me some days ago and promised to write to you himself upon this subject. I fear his disappointment will occasion suspension of the design perhaps till Spring.

I am just leaving this place for Edinburgh & am therefore rather in a hurry at present. My address in Edr. is Castle Street—I will write you at large soon my ideas about ornamented books. Dear Sir, Yours truly

WALTER SCOTT

ASHESTIEL, 27 October [1805]

Lord Somerville left us about a fortnight ago—

[C. F. Bell]

To GEORGE THOMSON, YORK PLACE [1]

[November 1805]

DEAR SIR,—I will be happy to see you in the course of the forenoon, altho I have great diffidence in undertaking the task you propose. Should I be successful I will exchange the Musical property of the song against a copy of Ducange's Glossary now in Laing's shop, I retaining the literary property, that is the exclusive right of printing the words when unconnected with Music. The Book may be worth about ten or twelve guineas. I am Dear Sir your mo. obedt. servt.   W. SCOTT

Sunday

[British Museum]

To CHARLES ERSKINE

DEAR CHARLES,—I am just returned from quarters where we have been living jollily & have an opportunity of a frank to acknowledge your kind present of pigeons & cheese. I have this day proved the goodness of both & find them admirable.

I had a letter from Park with a petition from Gownlock complaining of the cold &c of the jail—this I referred to the Magistrates at the same time I wish you would give a look at his condition when you are at Selkirk—it is not meant to be comfortable but should not be unhealthy—the windows for example ought directly to be glazed in this bitter weather.

We got all well to town. Mrs. Scott joins in kind Compliments and thanks to your attention to her Larder. She is still holding out but I believe must take to the bed in a day or two.

[1] So many Thomsons come into the letters that it is well to distinguish. This is the collector of Scottish music, officially principal clerk on the Board of Trustees for the Encouragement of Manufactures in Scotland. See J. Cuthbert Hadden's *George Thomson, the Friend of Burns : his life and correspondence,* 1898. On the MS. of this letter Thomson notes that the proposal was for a song on Lord Nelson's death.

Mrs. P A was at Mussellburgh when I was there.
I called on her and saw her frequently at Shorthope's
Yours truly   WALTER SCOTT

EDINBURGH 6 *Nov.* 1805

[*Curle*]

To LONGMAN AND CO.

DEAR SIR,—I have a letter[1] from your house of the 11th
covering the bills for £500 in moieties of £167 at 6 12 &
18 months as agreed.   I would have instantly proceeded
to copy the Assignation upon a stamp but for the following
reflections that occurred in looking over the Minstrelsy
to make the selection you propose.   I observe that my
own verses ballads &c will run to about 150 pages of
extract from the Minstrelsy & I have lying by me a
tragedy and a few minor pieces which would run to about
200 pages more and which I intend one day to publish
Now if you prefer purchasing these just now & so making
up a complete volume of my own compositions exclusively
[?] the greater part of which will be new to the public
I am willing to treat about them.   Or if you would like
to have the minor pieces I mentioned without the tragedy
in order to give some novelty to your proposed volume of
selections you shall have the copyright at a reasonable
rate I reserving to myself & assignees the right of using
them in any musical publication along with the tunes to
which they are set and no otherwise. This must be understood as a stipulation in either case.

The tragedy is in prose and has been thought interesting.   Of the other things I can only say that they are
written with due regard to my poetical reputation.

---

[1] Messrs. Longman's letter is in the Walpole collection ; " We accept of
your proposal of £500 for the copyright of the Lay &c. . . .   We must claim
your promise of making a selection of your own pieces from the Minstrelsy
to be published in a similar volume to the Lay. . . .   We annex a copy of
an Assignment for the Lay &c."

I do not by any means press either of these plans upon you : if you prefer adhering to our first idea of a selection it shall be instantly put into Ballantynes hands.

I will be greatly obliged to you for a sight of the . . . you may depend upon it it shall never be exhibited. The 4th volume of Turners history is come safe & gave me great pleasure I wish it were possible to bring it into the circulation which its merit so well deserves. Many thanks for that & the last No. of the Censure I remain Yours very truly   WALTER SCOTT

EDINB. 15 *Novr* 1805

[Abbotsford Copies]

To MISS NICOLSON, LYME REGIS, DORSET [1]

MY DEAR MISS NICOLSON,—I have the pleasure to acquaint you that Charlotte last night added a little boy to our family and that they are both as well as you could wish that is as well as possible—In every other respect your Castle Street friends have every reason to be contented & happy. Our family are healthy & strong your little favourite Sophia turns out a very clever girl of her age & gives great content to her instructors. I am at pains with her education because you know " learning is better than house or land "—At the same time my own prospects are so fair that I have every reason to think I shall soon be able to make a very decent provision for my little people. This little fellow is to be called Charles after brother Charles whose sudden marriage gave us both pleasure & surprize. I incline to think this con-nection will induce him to remain some time longer in India. As my Countrywomen like my Countrymen go all over the world I have taken it into my head he may have lighted upon one of them.

[1] Jane Nicolson, sister of Sarah Nicolson, the housekeeper to Mr. Du-mergue. It was with Jane Nicolson that Miss Carpenter visited Gilsland and met her future husband. We shall hear of her again in some of Scott's later letters. See Introduction.

Adieu my dear Madam I hope you will let me know you are well & happy—Believe me your very faithful humble Sert　　WALTER SCOTT

EDINR. 24 *Dec.* 1805.

[*Abbotsford Copies*]

To THE RIGHT HONBLE. LADY CHARLOTTE RAWDON [1]

DEAR LADY CHARLOTTE,—Accept my best thanks for the translations which Lord Moira was so good as to forward from which I expect to derive both pleasure & information. I have also to make my respectful acknowledgements for the beautiful poems of the Welch bard with which I am so much delighted that in my present state of indolence & solitude I think of imitating some of them or at least particular passages. If I am at all successful I will have the honour of presenting my imitations to your ladyship when we meet.

All Edinburgh is delighted with Lord M's return rendered double [*sic*] agreeable by the reports that we were to be deprived of the advantage of his talents & pleasure of his society. Of the last I have had no share not being in Edin. for this month past. I am quite happy you like the lay—it is a wild story wildly told, & though I have no reason to complain of its reception yet I would rather have the sanction of the few who profess taste like Lady Charlotte Rawdon than the indiscriminating applause of the public. Indeed whatever recalls the author to your recollection will always acquire a double value with Your Ladyships much obliged & very respectful humble Servant　　WALTER SCOTT

ASHESTIEL SELKIRK 19 *April* 1805

Mrs Scott has the honour to offer her respectful compliments.

[*Maggs Bros.*]

[1] This letter was discovered too late to be inserted at its proper date on p. 249.

1806

[*11th January* 1806]

DEAR CHARLES,—I send the process with a judgement
which I think I will not be easily induced to alter.   I also
recommend to your charge a letter for the Magrs. of
Selkirk

Mr. Park Carterhaugh complaind to me yesterday that
he had been stop'd on the road insulted & even threatend
by Gownlock for having been a witness on his trial.
When you return will you cause the fellow to be informd
that if I hear of the slightest repetition of such intolerable
insolence either to Mr. Park or any other person I will
make him rue it severely.   Should there be any farther
complaint he must go back to Bridewell or on board a
Man of war.   Send an officer to let him know as much

I suppose I shall hardly see you before the running
noose is slipped over your head   All happiness & good
things attend you   Believe me ever Yours truly

EDINR. *Saturday*   WALTER SCOTT
[*Curle*]

To GEORGE ELLIS [1]

EDINBURGH, *January* 25*th*, 1806

MY DEAR ELLIS,—I have been too long in letting you

---

[1] On the 2nd February Ellis writes from Bath still awaiting news of the
expected " further increase to your family " and of Dryden.   He wishes to
have family news, to hear what Scott thinks of Frere's verses [translations
from the *Cid*] sent in his last letter, and to know if he (Ellis) could get an
article into *The Edinburgh* on Macpherson's *Annals of Commerce*.   By the 6th
he had just received Scott's letter, for in a letter of that date, also from Bath,
he speaks of the long interruption of their correspondence.   The rest of the
letter deals with Scott and the Ministry and is given by Lockhart.

hear of me, and my present letter is going to be a very selfish one, since it will be chiefly occupied by an affair of my own, in which, probably, you may find very little entertainment. I rely, however, upon your cordial good wishes and good advice, though, perhaps, you may be unable to afford me any direct assistance without more trouble than I would wish you to take on my account. You must know, then, that with a view of withdrawing entirely from the Bar, I had entered into a transaction with an elderly and infirm gentleman, Mr. George Home, to be associated with him in the office which he holds as one of the Principal Clerks to our Supreme Court of Session ; I being to discharge the duty gratuitously during his life, and to succeed him at his decease. This could only be carried into effect by a new commission from the crown to him and me jointly, which has been issued in similar cases very lately, and is in point of form quite correct. By the interest of my kind and noble friend and chief, the Duke of Buccleuch, the countenance of government was obtained to this arrangement, and the affair, as I have every reason to believe, is now in the Treasury. I have written to my solicitor, Alexander Mundell, Fludyer Street, to use every despatch in hurrying through the commission ; but the news of to-day giving us every reason to apprehend Pitt's death, if that lamentable event has not already happened, makes me get nervous on a subject so interesting to my little fortune. My political sentiments have been always constitutional and open, and although they were never rancorous, yet I cannot expect that the Scottish Opposition party, should circumstances bring them into power, would consider me as an object of favour : nor would I ask it at their hands. Their leaders cannot regard me with malevolence, for I am intimate with many of them ;— but they must provide for the Whiggish children before they throw their bread to the Tory dogs ; and I shall not fawn on them because they have in their turn the superin-

tendence of the larder.   At the same time, if Fox's friends
come into power, it must be with Windham's party, to
whom my politics can be no exception,—if the politics of
a private individual ought at any time to be made the
excuse for intercepting the bounty of his Sovereign, when
it is in the very course of being bestowed.

The situation is most desirable, being £800 a-year,
besides being consistent with holding my sheriffdom ; and
I could afford very well to wait till it opened to me by
the death of my colleague, without wishing a most
worthy and respectable man to die a moment sooner than
ripe nature demanded.   The duty consists in a few hours'
labour in the forenoons when the Court sits, leaving the
evenings and whole vacation open for literary pursuits.
I will not relinquish the hope of such an establishment
without an effort, if it is possible without dereliction of
my principles to attain the accomplishment of it.   As I
have suffered in my professional line by addicting myself
to the profane and unprofitable art of poem-making, I am
very desirous to indemnify myself by availing myself of
any prepossession which my literary reputation may,
however unmeritedly, have created in my favour.   I have
found it useful when I applied for others, and I see no
reason why I should not try if it can do anything for
myself.

Perhaps, after all, my commission may be got out before
a change of Ministry, if such an event shall take place, as
it seems not far distant.   If it is otherwise, will you be
so good as to think and devise some mode in which my
case may be stated to Windham or Lord Grenville,
supposing them to come in ?   If it is not deemed worthy
of attention, I am sure I shall be contented ; but it is one
thing to have a right to ask a favour, and another to
hope that a transaction, already fully completed by the
private parties, and approved of by an existing Administration, shall be permitted to take effect in favour of
an unoffending individual.   I believe I shall see you very

shortly, unless I hear from Mundell that the business can
be done for certain without my coming up. I will not,
if I can help it, be flayed like a sheep for the benefit of
some pettifogging lawyer or attorney. I have stated the
matter to you very bluntly ; indeed, I am not asking a
favour, but, unless my self-partiality blinds me, merely
fair play. Yours ever,

WALTER SCOTT

[*Lockhart*]

To CHARLES ERSKINE

[*27th January*, 1806]

DEAR CHARLES,—I suppose you are fairly turned off &
beg Mrs. Erskines & your acceptance of kindest & best
congratulations in Mrs. Scotts name as well as my own.
A piece of express & important business hurries me to
London on a moments warning. I hope my stay will be
short but as it cannot be less than a month I recommend
the County to you in my absence. A letter will always
find me if addressd Care of Charles Dumerguc Esq White
Horse Street Piccadilly Londn   Yours in haste

Monday   W SCOTT

[*Curle*]

To LORD DALKEITH

LONDON, 11*th Feb.* 1806

MY DEAR LORD,—I cannot help flattering myself, for
perhaps it is flattering myself, that the noble architect
of the Border Minstrel's little fortune has been sometimes
anxious for the security of that lowly edifice during the
tempest which has overturned so many palaces and
towers. If I am right in my supposition it will give you
pleasure to learn that notwithstanding some little rubs, I
have been able to carry through the transaction which
your Lordship sanctioned by your influence and approbation & that in a way very pleasing to my own feelings.

Lord Spencer upon the nature of the transaction being explained in an audience with which he favoured me was pleased to direct the commission to be issued as an act of justice regretting he said it had not been from the beginning his own deed. This was doing the thing handsomely & like an English Nobleman. I have been very much fêted and caressed here almost indeed to suffocation but have been made amends by meeting some old friends. One of the kindest was Lord Somerville who volunteered introducing me to Lord Spencer as much I am convinced from respect to your Lordship's protection and wishes as from a desire to serve me personally. He seemed very anxious to do anything in his power which might evince a wish to be of use to your protégé. Lord Minto was also infinitely kind and active & his influence with Lord Spencer would I am convinced have been stretched to the utmost in my favour had not Lord Spencer's own view of the subject been perfectly sufficient.

After all a little literary reputation is of some use here. I suppose Solomon when he compared a good name to a pot of ointment meant that it oiled the hinges of the hall doors into which the possessors of that inestimable treasure wished to penetrate. What a *good* name was in Jerusalem a *known* name seems to be in London. If you are celebrated for writing verses or for slicing cucumbers for being two feet taller or two feet less than any other biped, for acting plays when you should be whipped at school or for attending schools & institutions when you should be preparing for your grave, your notoriety becomes a talisman, an " Open Sesamum " before which everything gives way till you are voted a bore & discarded for a new plaything. As this is a consummation of notoriety which I am by no means ambitious of experiencing I hope I will be very soon able to shape my course northward to enjoy my good fortune at my leisure & snap my fingers at the bar and all its works.

There is, it is believed, a rude scufle betwixt our late commander in chief & Lord Lauderdale for the patronage of Scotland. If there is to be an exclusive administration I hope it will not be in the hands of the latter. Indeed when one considers that by means of Ld. Sidmouth & Ellenborough the King possesses the actual power of casting the balance betwixt the five Grenvillites & four Foxites who compose the cabinet I cannot think they will find it an easy matter to force upon his Majesty any one to whom he has a personal dislike. I should therefore suppose that the disposal of St. Andrews Cross will be delayed till the new Ministry is a little consolidated, *if that time shall ever come.* There is much loose gunpowder amongst them & one spark would make a fine explosion. Pardon these political effusions. I am infected by the atmosphere which I breathe and cannot refrain my pen from discussing state affairs. I hope the young ladies and my dear little Chief are now recovering from the hooping cough if it has so turned out to be. If I can do anything for any of the family here you know your right to command & the pleasure it will afford me to obey. Will your Lordship be so kind as to acquaint the Duke with every grateful and respectful acknowledgment on my part that I have this day got my commission from the Secretarys office. I dine to-day at Holland house ; I refused to go before lest it should be thought I was soliciting interest in that quarter as I abhor even the shadow of changing or turning with the tide.

I beg to be respectfully reme[m]bered to my Lady Dutchess, Lady Dalkeith, Lord & Lady Montagu & Lady Douglas if at Dalkeith.

I am ever, with grateful acknowledgment your Lordships much indebted faithful humble Servant,

79 JERMYN STREET 11*th febry.*   WALTER SCOTT

[*Buccleuch and Lockhart*]

To this Lord Dalkeith replied in a letter now at Abbotsford :

DALKEITH HOUSE *Feb 20th* 1806

MY DEAR SIR,—I do most cordially and sincerely felicitate you on having obtained your commission at last from the Secretary's Office—I should have said my " Gratulor " sooner, had I not been occupied lately more than usual with a variety of avocations ; none very pleasant . . . Lord Spencer (as a professed patron of literature) has done what he ought to have done in regard to you ; independent of the fairness of the request—You are now to snap your fingers at the Bar—*But* you are not to be idle—We shall expect much from your leisure—Why have we no good compendious *Border History ?* . . . You are too modest in comparing yourself to anything extraordinary in the deficiency or superabundance of nature (vide your own letters)—For the credit of London, let it be said that The Last Minstrel is not unnoticed ; but that he is " High Placed in Hall, a welcome Guest." This shows the intrinsic merit of your work.—*We* have many Local reasons for admiring the Poem—The Londoners have no reason for admiring it, but that it possesses real general merit and might be read by an erudite and judicious Englishman as well as by a partial Borderman or Scott—

Talk not, think not of Politics. Go to the Hills and converse with the Spirit of the Fell ; or any spirit but the spirit of Party ; which is the foulest fiend that ever disturbed Harmony and social pleasure : one cannot keep quite clear of its clutches but thank God it has only slightly scratched me as yet— My star of attraction is set—I shall only say he [Pitt] was the mightiest man (take him for all in all) that ever lived—His last effort to recover the lost Liberties and independence of Europe ; the means he imagined and those he realised were truly gigantic—He could not controll fate ; nor less could he make Mack a General or Francis a rational Being—Peace to his Manes and honor to his memory and in my mind unutterable grief and eternal regret— Lady D. desires to be kindly remembered yours sincerely

DALKEITH

To GEORGE ELLIS

LONDON, *Feb.* 20, 1806

My DEAR ELLIS,—I have your kind letter,[1] and am infinitely obliged to you for your solicitude in my behalf. I have indeed been rather fortunate, for the gale which has shattered so many goodly argosies, has blown my little bark into the creek for which she was bound, and left me only to lament the misfortunes of my friends. To vary the simile, while the huge frigates, the Moira and Lauderdale, were fiercely combating for the dominion of the Caledonian main, I was fortunate enough to get on board the good ship Spencer, and leave them to settle their disputes at leisure. It is said to be a violent ground of controversy in the new Ministry, which of those two noble lords is to be St Andrew for Scotland. I own I tremble for the consequences of so violent a temper as Lauderdale's, irritated by long disappointed ambition and ancient feud with all his brother nobles. It is a certain truth that Lord Moira insists upon his claim, backed by all the friends of the late administration in Scotland, to have a certain weight in that country ; and it is equally certain that the Hamiltons and Lauderdales have struck out. So here are people who have stood in the rain without doors for so many years, quarrelling for the nearest place to the fire, as soon as they have set their feet on the floor. Lord Moira, as he always has been, was highly kind and courteous to me on this occasion.

Heber is just come in, with your letter waving in his hand. I am ashamed of all the trouble I have given you, and at the same time flattered to find your friendship even equal to that greatest and most disagreeable of all trials, the task of solicitation. Mrs. Scott is *not* with me, and I am truly concerned to think we should be so near, without the prospect of meeting. Truth is, I had half a mind to make a run up to Bath, merely to break the spell

[1] That of the 6th February from Bath, referred to above.

which has prevented our meeting for these two years. But Bindley, the collector, has lent me a parcel of books, which he insists on my consulting within the liberties of Westminster, and which I cannot find elsewhere, so that the fortnight I propose to stay will be fully occupied by examination and extracting. How long I may be detained here is very uncertain, but I wish to leave London on Saturday se'ennight. Should I be so delayed as to bring my time of departure anything near that of your arrival, I will stretch my furlough to the utmost, that I may have a chance of seeing you. Nothing is minded here but domestic politics, and if we are not clean swept, there is no want of new brooms to perform that operation. I have heard very bad news of Leyden's health since my arrival here—such, indeed, as to give room to apprehend the very worst. I fear he has neglected the precautions which the climate renders necessary, and which no man departs from with impunity. Remember me kindly and respectfully to Mrs. Ellis ; and believe me ever yours faithfully,   WALTER SCOTT

P.S.—Poor Lord Melville ! how does he look ? We have had miserable accounts of his health in London. He was the architect of my little fortune, from circumstances of personal regard merely ; for any of my trifling literary acquisitions were out of his way. My heart bleeds when I think on his situation—

> " Even when the rage of battle ceased,
>   The victor's soul was not appeased."

[*Lockhart*]

To CHARLES KIRKPATRICK SHARPE

[3 *March* 1806]

MY DEAR SIR,—I inclose the Tale of the Bard of Caithness which I like very much. Some parts are quite

delighful. Should you not say something of the effect
produced on the Earl by the wasting of the waxen figure
& its removal. I might mention one or two criticisms
to give value to my general applause but have not time
at this moment.

I left my name at Cleveland House when I came to
town & shall do the same today when I am about to
leave it. I would have been very glad to have had an
opportunity of expressing to the Marchioness of Stafford
my continued sense of her civility the last time I was in
town but I must now trust to you to do it for me, as I set
out tomorrow. Believe me Yours ever truly

W. SCOTT

BURY STREET *Monday*

Do you go to the Tower with Lady Douglas etc
tomorrow ? I wish you would—

Charles Kirkpatrick Sharpe Esq
St James Hotel Jermyn Street.

[*Hornel*]

TO GEORGE ELLIS

LONDON, Saturday, March 3, 1806

MY DEAR ELLIS,—I have waited in vain for the happy
dissolution of the spell which has kept us asunder at a
distance less by one quarter than in general divides us ;
and since I am finally obliged to depart for the north
to-morrow, I have only to comfort myself with the hope
that Bladud will infuse a double influence into his tepid
springs, and that you will feel emboldened, by the
quantity of reinforcement which the radical heat shall
have received, to undertake your expedition to the
tramontane region of Reged this season. My time has been
spent very gaily here, and I should have liked very well
to have remained till you came up to town, had it not
been for the wife and bairns at home, whom I confess I

am now anxious to see. Accordingly I set off early to-morrow morning—indeed I expected to have done so to-day, but my companion, Ballantyne, our Scottish Bodoni, was afflicted with a violent diarrhœa, which, though his physician assured him it would serve his health in general, would certainly have contributed little to his accomplishments as an agreeable companion in a post-chaise, which are otherwise very respectable. I own Lord Melville's misfortunes affect me deeply. He, at least his nephew, was my early patron, and gave me countenance and assistance when I had but few friends. I have seen when the streets of Edinburgh were thought by the inhabitants almost too vulgar for Lord Melville to walk upon ; and now I fear that, with his power and influence gone, his presence would be accounted by many, from whom he has deserved other thoughts, an embarrass-ment, if not something worse. All this is very vile—it is one of the occasions when Providence, as it were, in-dustriously turns the tapestry, to let us see the ragged ends of the worsted which compose its most beautiful figures. God grant your prophecies may be true, which I fear are rather dictated by your kind heart than your experience of political enmities and the fate of fallen statesmen. Kindest compliments to Mrs. Ellis.—Your next will find me in Edinburgh.

WALTER SCOTT

[Lockhart]

To GEORGE THOMSON, YORK PLACE

[March 1806]

MY DEAR SIR,—I am greatly to blame for not having before informed you of what I have myself been long sensible, my total incapacity to compose anything on the subject of Lord Nelson's glorious victory and death that could be in the least serviceable to your elegant collection. I assure you I have not relinquished a task so pleasing to

myself without repeated attempts to execute it, but what
would not even please the author was still less likely to
stand any competition with its companions in your
selected specimens of poetry and music. I have given
Mr. Laing directions to transfer the " Ducange " to
another account, but in relinquishing the prize of my
intended labours I am much more mortified by my own
failure in not producing anything that could be creditable
to myself or agreeable to you. I remain Dear Sir your
obedt. serv.

WALTER SCOTT

EDINR. *Saturday.*

[British Museum]

To GEORGE ELLIS

ASHESTIEL, *April* 7, 1806

MY DEAR ELLIS,—Were I to begin by telling you all
the regret I had at not finding you in London, and at
being obliged to leave it before your return, this very
handsome sheet of paper, which I intend to cover with
more important and interesting matters, would be
entirely occupied by such a Jeremiade as could only be
equalled by Jeremiah himself. I will therefore waive that
subject, only assuring you that I hope to be in London
next spring, but have much warmer hopes of seeing you
here in summer. I hope Bath has been of service ; if not
so much as you expected, try easy exercise in a northward
direction, and make proof of the virtues of the Tweed and
Yarrow. We have been here these two days, and I have
been quite rejoiced to find all my dogs, and horses, and
sheep, and cows, and two cottages full of peasants
and their children, and all my other stock, human and
animal, in great good health—we want nothing but Mrs.
Ellis and you to be the strangers within our gates, and
our establishment would be complete on the patriarchal
plan. I took possession of my new office on my return.

The duty is very simple, consisting chiefly in signing my name ; and as I have five colleagues, I am not obliged to do duty except in turn, so my task is a very easy one, as my name is very short.

My principal companion in this solitude is John Dryden. After all, there are some passages in his translations from Ovid and Juvenal that will hardly bear reprinting, unless I would have the Bishop of London and the whole corps of Methodists about my ears.[1] I wish you would look at the passages I mean. One is from the fourth book of Lucretius ; the other from Ovid's Instructions to his Mistress. They are not only double-entendres, but good plain single-entendres—not only broad, but long, and as coarse as the mainsail of a first-rate. What to make of them I know not ; but I fear that, without absolutely gelding the bard, it will be indispensable to circumcise him a little by leaving out some of the most obnoxious lines. Do, pray, look at the poems and decide for me. Have you seen my friend Tom Thomson, who is just now in London ? He has, I believe, the advantage of knowing you, and I hope you will meet, as he understands more of old books, old laws, and old history, than any man in Scotland. He has lately received an appointment under the Lord Register of Scotland, which puts all our records under his immediate inspection and control, and I expect many valuable discoveries to be the consequence of his investigation, if

---

[1] Replying on 13th May, Ellis writes : " First then, with regard to Dryden, whatever the Bishop of London and all the corps of Methodists may say, I am clearly of opinion that, having undertaken a complete edition of Dryden, you are not at liberty to leave out the obnoxious passages to which you have directed me, though I admit it might have been better for Dryden's reputation that such lines had never been written ; or perhaps ... it would have been much better if the general state of the manners of the times in which he lived had not been so gross as to induce him to select among the classical poets such passages as were calculated to please the frequenters of a brothel and to bestow on his translation all the ornaments of his diction." Scott might have been better to act as censor morum, but he chose that of editor and had made a compact with his readers.

he escapes being smothered in the cloud of dust which his researches will certainly raise about his ears. I sent your card instantly to Jeffrey, from whom you had doubtless a suitable answer. I saw the venerable economist and antiquary, Macpherson,[1] when in London, and was quite delighted with the simplicity and kindness of his manners. He is exactly like one of the old Scotchmen whom I remember twenty years ago, before so close a union had taken place between Edinburgh and London. The mail-coach and the Berwick smacks have done more than the Union in altering our national character, sometimes for the better and sometimes for the worse.

I met with your friend, Mr Canning, in town, and claimed his acquaintance as a friend of yours, and had my claim allowed ; also Mr. Frere,—both delightful companions, far too good for politics, and for winning and losing places. When I say I was more pleased with their society than I thought had been possible on so short an acquaintance, I pay them a very trifling compliment and myself a very great one. I had also the honour of dining with a fair friend of yours at Blackheath—an honour which I shall very long remember. She is an enchanting princess,[2] who dwells in an enchanted palace, and I cannot help thinking that her prince must labour under some malignant spell when he denies himself her society. The very Prince of the Black Isles, whose bottom was marble, would have made an effort to transport himself to Montague House. From all this you will understand I was at Montague House.

I am quite delighted at the interest you take in poor Lord Melville. I suppose they are determined to hunt him down. Indeed, the result of his trial must be ruin from the expense, even supposing him to be honourably acquitted. Will you, when you have time to write, let

---

[1] Presumably David Macpherson (1746-1816), deputy-keeper in London of Public Records and editor of Wyntoun's *Orygynal Cronykil of Scotland*, 1795.

[2] The Princess of Wales, then living at Montague House.

me know how that matter is likely to turn ?   I am deeply
interested in it ; and the reports here are so various, that
one knows not what to trust to. Even the common
rumour of London is generally more authentic than the
" from good authority " of Edinburgh. Besides, I am
now in the wilds (alas ! I cannot say *woods* and wilds),
and hear little of what passes. Charlotte joins me in a
thousand kind remembrances to Mrs. Ellis ; and I am
ever yours most truly,

WALTER SCOTT

[*Lockhart*]

To MISS SEWARD [1]

ASHESTIEL, 10th *April* 1806

I HAVE at once to acknowledge the copy of your last
favor and that which contains it, to regret that I should
have been so long of receiving what does me so much
honor & to express my thanks for the high gratification
Miss Sewards approbation must always confer on the
feelings of a commoner of Parnassus. I believe I can
account for the miscarriage of the Letter of 1805 as I had
been at that time so great a wanderer that several Letters
were for a length of time missing. One of them was only
returnd to the nobleman by whom it was addressd this
spring from Keswick in Cumberland. Yours I may yet
recover if it has not fallen into the hands of some curious
Namesake who may consider it as too great a literary
treasure to be resignd to the right owner— The Lay of
the Last Minstrel has been for a long time so much out of
my thoughts that your approbation recalls very pleasingly

---

[1] Miss Seward had written to Scott on 7th March 1805 acknowledging
the receipt of the *Lay*, on which (after some account of her health) she
dilates in great detail.   Scott answered this on the 21st March (see above,
p. 242), and on the 17th April 1805 Miss S. had written defending the poem
against Scott's own strictures.   This had not reached him at the time.
This letter, with the verses to Father Tweed, is in the Walpole collection, as
also a letter of 26th March 1806, in which she recopies the address.

the feelings with which I composed it & is something like
the eulogium upon a departed friend— Could I have
thought it would have attracted so much of your attention
I would have endeavourd to have written it better & in
consequence might very likely not have done it so well.
Still the flimsiness of the story might have been corrected
by a little thought and attention which I now regret not
having bestow'd upon it— This is the second [1] day of
my retreat to this farm and I have read your beautiful
verses to Father Tweed who is of opinion that in the
course of his poetical experience which you know has been
rather extensive he never heard better poetry employd
upon so idle a subject. He joins however with the
honoured Bard in expressing his grateful sense of the high
privilege of being celebrated by your Pen and would you
only add to the favor by visiting this wild retreat the
river & the Bard would be proud to exhibit all their
treasures from legendary tales & fine scenery down to
the humbler tribute of trouts & salmon— The other
verses inclosed are so beautiful that I exceedingly regret
not having received them when I was in Cumberland as
my poetical friends Wordsworth & Southey must have
been as much delighted with them as I am— I spent
some time in their society very pleasantly and Southey
repaid me by visiting my farm. They are certainly men
of very extraordinary powers, Wordsworth in particular
is such a character as only exists in romance virtuous,
simple, and unaffectedly restricting every want & wish
to the bounds of a very narrow income in order to enjoy
the literary and poetical leisure which his happiness
consists in— Were it not for the unfortunate idea of
forming a New School of Poetry these men are calculated
to give it a new impulse, but I think they sometimes lose
their energy in trying to find not a better but a different
path from what has been travelld by their predecessors—
I saw nothing in Southeys manner like literary jealousy &

[1] He says, in letter above to Ellis, he has been here " two days " on the 7th.

should think him above it ; Certainly they are not always
& altogether so easy & pleasing as those of Wordsworth
but I think it is mere manner—individually as I was not at
all a subject for his jealousy I am certain that neither did I
excite any though much kind and free discussion took place
amongst us. I agree with you in admiring Madoc very
much : the descriptions of natural objects are most admirable and may certainly rank with any that our Poetry
affords. Mr. Southey seems to excell in seizing either
those circumstances which give character to a Landscape
or such as are so closely connected with them that the one
being suggested to our imagination naturally & almost
necessarily recalls the rest. I am not quite sure that the
subject of such & so long a poem is altogether so well
chosen. The exploits of Madoc necessarily recall the
history of Cortez & the voyage of Columbus & this
mixture of truth & fancy is not pleasant : Whether it is
owing to this or that the heroes & heroines considered
as men & women have little of that discriminating
character which is absolutely necessary to interest a
reader I am unable to decide but so it is that Madoc
sometimes requires an effort on the part of the reader to
accompany him on his journey. It is however an effort
amply repaid by the fine passages which perpetually
occur throughout the poem— To the admirers of Southey
I fear Thalaba will prove most interesting in spite of the
heretical structure of the measure if indeed it deserves
that name— I think were you to know my little friend
Jeffery the Aristarchus of the Edinr Review you would
perhaps have some mercy on his criticisms—not but he
often makes his best friends lose patience by that love of a
severity which drives justice into tyranny but in fact I
have often wonderd that a man who loves & admires
Poetry as much as he does can permit himself the severe
or sometimes unjust strictures which he fulminates even
against the authors whom he most approves of & whose
works actually afford him most delight. But what shall

we say ? Many good natured country Tonies [1] (myself
for example) take great pleasure in coursing & fishing
without any impeachment to their amiabilities &
probably Jeffery [*sic*] feels the same instinctive passion for
hunting down the bards of the day. In common life the
lion lies down with the Kid for not to mention his
friendship for me now of some standing he had the
magnanimity (absolutely approaching to chivalrous
reliance upon the faith of a foe) to trust himself to
Southeys guidance in a boat on Windermere when it
would have cost the poet nothing but a wet jacket to
have overset the Critic & swam triumphantly to shore &
this the very day the review of Madoc was published.[2]
I am afraid however you will hardly allow my apology
any more than for an arcadian slaughtering & cutting
up his favorite lamb. Owing to my removal to this place
I have not had it in my power to wait on Mrs. Jackson [3]
but when I return to Edinbr perhaps in a month I will
lose no time in endeavouring to secure the personal
knowledge of a friend whom you esteem.

I hope this Letter will find your complaints abated or
removed : gentle exercise & light study would be I think
the best remedies. Believe me dear Miss Seward Very
faithfully Your obt Servt

WALTER SCOTT

[*Shirley*]

[1] That is Tony Lumpkin I presume.

[2] Southey met Jeffrey in Edinburgh in October 1805 : " Jeffrey is
amusing from his wit ; in taste he is a mere child ; and he affects to despise
learning because he has none. . . . I cant feel angry with anything so
diminutive ; he is a mere *homunculus*." The review of *Madoc* in the *Edinburgh* appeared in the same autumn. Of his visit Southey says : " Jeffrey
came back in the stage with us to visit the Lakes, and supped here ; so you
see we are good friends. What I condemn in him is a habit of speaking of
books worse than he thinks of them. . . . But his praise and censure are
alike hap-hazard and worthless."—7th November 1805.

[3] Mrs. Jackson figures as a very intelligent and much-loved friend of
Anna's throughout her correspondence.

I   T

To MRS. CARPENTER [1]

EDINBURGH, *April* 10, 1806

My DEAR MADAM,—With my best congratulations on the happy event which permits me to have the honour of addressing you will you allow me to request your acceptance of a few idle books which the encouragement of an idle public has induced me to give to the world. As they have been favourably received I will not so far drown the vanity of an author as not to hope that you will receive some pleasure from them. At any rate they are the best acknowledgment I can make of the sincere pleasure with which we received the news of your union with my brother Carpenter & I would have sent them a month ago but for a new edition being in the Press which I thought would be more worthy your acceptance & would be ready by this time. I have written a long letter to Mr. Carpenter giving a full account of our little family & our prospects : the first are well & the other flattering. It gives me pleasure to think that your connection with Scotland may perhaps occasion your having some commissions to discharge or acknowledgments to make in the country : in which case may I venture to solicit the honor of your commands ; I dare not recommend myself as a faithful at least a punctual correspondent but I am allow'd to maintain a very respectable character for accuracy in executing any commissions that may devolve on me & it would give me sincere pleasure if you would make the experiment. Mrs. Scott joins me in the most

[1] Charles Carpenter, Mrs. Scott's brother, was married on 23rd May 1805 at Mount Capper, Cuddalore, to Isabella, third daughter of Colonel Charles Fraser, son of Thomas Fraser of Ardachie (the Frasers of Ardachie were cadets of Lovat) and Charlotte, daughter of the Hon. Charles Campbell, third son of Archibald, ninth Earl of Argyle, beheaded in Edinburgh in 1685. Two of Mrs. Carpenter's brothers, General Hastings Fraser and General James Stuart Fraser, were distinguished soldiers in the East India Company's service. See *Memoir and Correspondence of General James Stuart Fraser* by his son, Colonel Hastings Fraser, 1885, in which some of Scott's letters to his brother-in-law are printed.

sincere congratulations on your marriage with her brother & in the most affectionate wishes for your mutual happiness. Believe me with great regard Dear Madam Your affectionate brother   WALTER SCOTT

[*Abbotsford Copies*]

To ROBERT SOUTHEY,[1] GRETA HALL, KESWICK

[*April,* 1806]

MY DEAR SIR,—The least thought you can have had of me during my long and most unreasonable silence must have been that I intended to play you a slippery Border trick and carry off the old M.S. without value. You will probably however have since learned from your brother that I have been in London " pursuing fortunes slippery ball ", and have been fortunate enough notwithstanding the change of men and measures to secure the reversion of a considerable patent office which was destined for me by W. Pitt and Lord Melville. I venture to hope my success has given some pleasure to my friends at Greta Hall and Grasmere : it is particularly acceptable to me as it enables me without imprudence or indeed injustice to my family to retire from the bar which I have always thought and felt to be an irksome and even hateful profession— I am truly sorry to think there should be any uncertainty about Coleridge : surely the return by land was a slow and circuitous route during the course of which he could have but little communication with home. I am surprised he chose it yet with his knowledge of the

---

[1] Southey had written Scott on the 4th February intimating the dispatch of the MS. and mentioning his uneasiness about Coleridge in Italy. Coleridge left Malta on the 21st September 1805 and had not been ten days there when " the French torrent rolled down on Naples." He went on to Rome in January 1806 and, according to his own rather inconsistent accounts, was warned to escape and made his way to Leghorn and sailed thence. On the 18th August Wordsworth writes to Scott regretting his inability to come to "Ashysteel," and " to this bad news, for such I assure you I consider it, I have the pleasure of adding some good viz. that Coleridge is arrived and is now performing quarantine off Portsmouth."

continental languages I think there is nothing to be apprehended but bad health and of that I would fain hope there is no risk.

I will not fail to put Mr. Duppas [1] work under Judge Jefferie's view in the light you would have it. He is not you know the most tractable of critics and I never venture to answer for him as indeed we differ in many most material points of taste but he will not willingly do an illnatured thing to a person of your friends description. In fact he is the old character the best good man with the worst natured Muse (if there be a Muse of criticism) that ever wielded the quill of an Aristarchus.

I grieve we are to lose you in Summer and were it not that I expect so much from your history I would willingly hope that your visit to the Douro and the Tagus should be converted into another trip to Tweedside and your embarkation on the bay of Biscay into such a voyage as we made together on Derwentwater or at worst into another perilous pilgrimage in my frail bark where the ponderous Grecian proved more than a counterpoise for the two bards. [2] Seriously if you do not go to Portugal

---

[1] Richard Duppa (1770-1831) was both artist and author. He matriculated at Trinity College, Oxford, in 1807 ; became a student of the Middle Temple in 1810 ; graduated LL.B. at Trinity Hall, Cambridge, in 1814, and wrote on botanical, artistic and political themes. His *Life and Literary Works of Michel Angelo Buonarotti, 4to, London,* the work Scott refers to, appeared in 1806. Among Duppa's other works are : *Dr. Johnson's Diary of a Journey into North Wales in* 1774, first printed and elaborately edited by Duppa in 1816 with Mrs. Piozzi's help (incorporated in Croker's *Boswell*), pamphlets on literary copyright (1813), on Junius (1814), on the price of corn (1815), and classical school-books. In his letter, already quoted, Southey had ventured a request of Scott. " My friend Duppa is about to publish a Life of Michel Angelo. The book will be a good book, for no man understands his art better. I wish when it comes in course of trial you would save it from Judge Jeffray, or intercede with him for as favourable a report as it may be found to deserve. Duppa deserves well of the public because he has at a very considerable loss published those magnificent heads from Raffaello & Michel Angelo, & is publishing the present work without any view whatever to profit,—indeed he does not print copies enough to pay his expences."—*Walpole Collection.*

[2] In the same letter Southey had written : " I know not whether I shall ever see the Tweed and the Yarrow : yet I should be sorry to think I should not. Your scenery has left upon me a strong impression, more so

what think you of varying the scene by a winter in Edinr. you will find plenty of books and I will venture to assure you plenty of friends. I am extracting from the Border Minstrelsy those Ballads which I wrote myself with a few other fugitive pieces of a similar nature. I will send you a copy as soon as they are printed.

Mrs. Scott begs kind compts to Mrs. Southey Mr. Coleridge and Mrs. Lozd in which I have the honour to join, Believe me ever dear Southey Yours sincerely

WALTER SCOTT

Your brother was so kind as take charge of the price of the M.S. (twelve guineas) as I did not know exactly where you would wish a draught made payable—

[*Abbotsford Copies*]

To MALCOLM LAING, ADVOCATE, EDINBURGH

ASHESTIEL BY SELKIRK 14 *April* 1806

DEAR SIR,—Since I came here I have rummaged at the original copies of the ballad of Sir Patrick Spens as taken down from the mouth of the Reciter. One was picked up by Leyden with some other little things from a woman in Kelso. The other was furnished in the state in which you see it by Mr. William Laidlaw of Blackhouse. Laidlaw and Leyden never met except once when I was present. Blackhouse is forty miles from Kelso & in the most wild & sequestered nook perhaps you ever saw : so there is not even a probable chance that the same fabrication should be imposed on me from two different quarters.

from the delightful associations which you and your country poets have inseparably connected with it. I am going in the autumn, if Bonaparte will allow me, to streams as classical and lovely—of the Mondego of Camoens, the Douro and Tagus ; but I shall not find such society on the banks. Remember me to my two fellow-travellers. Heaven keep me also from being the subject of any further experiments upon the infinite com-pressibility of matter." He, Jeffrey, and Peter Elmsley, editor of Sophocles and Euripides, " the ponderous Grecian," had been too heavy for their boat on Derwent Water.

I received Leyden's first which I scrupled to use on account of one verse containing these lines which I still think are an interpolation

> When the lift grew dark and the wind blew loud
> And gurly grew the sea.

But when I received the copy from Blackhouse I thought myself entitled to use both with Hamiltons fragment assisted by the printed copies.

I cannot find the copy of Cowden knowes but I will make a further search & at any rate if the original copy sent to me has been lost I will procure an exact history of the song from the person who sent it me. I trouble you with these little explanations because I would not willingly leave the impression on your mind that I have interpolated these ancient Ballads. Had I meant to put a trick on the Public I would have taken care it should have been attended with more interest from its poetical merit than these dull songs. But I utterly disclaim the idea of writing anything that I am not ready to own to the whole world & though the ancients have " stole my good things " as the frenchman complaind I will not indemnify myself by imputing to them the discredit of my nonsense.

I suppose the Diary of Bannatyne is by this time out and the 2nd Part of James the Sext in forwardness. When do you appear in the monthly Magazine against the North British Critic ? If you could come here I would be very happy to shew you the wonders of the forest particularly a monument dug up where the scene of the ballad of the Dowie Dens of Yarrow is said to be. It has an inscription but unfortunately illegible. Believe me Dear Sir yours truly

WALTER SCOTT

Malcolm Laing Esq Advocate Edinburgh

[*Abbotsford Copies*]

To CHARLES ERSKINE

DEAR CHARLES,—You are very wellcome back from London I hope we will be more fortunate in seeing Mrs. Erskine at Ashestiel on our return there which this delightful weather makes me very anxious for.

I enclose Mr. Innes' petition : it would have been more regularly made to the Justices but it is competent to the Sheriff to restrict the execution of a Servitude & therefore I have pronounced the enclosed Interloqr. It will not be proper to pronounce a final decreet till the enclosures are put up for fear of encroachments.

My Mother is anxious to have Daniel's business finishd and is willing to agree to the terms last proposed by them which though high are I think little enough for getting rid of such a scrape.[1] The money is ready in Sir William Forbes's. In short you must just close on the best terms you can & write (if you please to my mother on the subject) as I do not care to be seen in it myself Believe me ever Dear Charles Yours truly   W SCOTT

25 *May* EDINR. [1806]

[*Curle*]

To GEORGE THOMSON, FAVOURED BY MR. ERSKINE

[1806]

DEAR SIR,—My freind Mr. William Erskine who is just leaving me takes charge of a few verses for the Monks March [2] if you have not been able before now to procure other assistance. I have been really engaged very much since I came here besides some family misfortunes which rather put me *out of tune*. I am so ignorant of music that I do not know whether the lines will answer but if they are otherwise agreeable to you, I can easily alter them to suit the measure. There is a Catch note which I have

---

[1] Probably a reference to the aliment of Daniel's natural child.

[2] See note 1, p. 296.

not always applied a syllable to, but I can easily supply one. Believe me Yours very truly   WALTER SCOTT

If these answer I will forthwith finish " the Sheriffs fancy " [1]

[Watson Collection]

To JAMES BALLANTYNE [2]

[1808]

DEAR BALLANTYNE,—What *can* I say to you except that I feel for what I know by never to be forgotten experience is a situation scarcely susceptible of comfort but from generous disdain of the wanton cruelty by which you suffer. The young Lady's conduct has been most singularly & abominably profligate, or there may be something in vanity which really renders the heart as hard as a nether millstone

At all events you have had a most happy escape—the same vanity in a wife what might it not have produced ? I give today to yourself—tomorrow I must see you that the ice may be broken ; we will speak of the matter once & then forget it forever   I will call in St. John Street as I come from the Court   W. S.

Remember my breaking the wine-glass upon a similar recollection

On second thoughts I will call as I come from the Register House but dont receive me unless it will give you rather comfort than additional distress.

[Glen]

[1] " When the heathen trumpets clang." That to *The Sheriffs Fancy* was probably " On Ettrick Forest's mountains dun." Both were written for Thomson in 1806, though erroneously dated 1817 and 1822 in collected editions of Scott's poems.

[2] The date of this letter is uncertain. I think it should have been included in the 1808 letters, after the letter to Ballantyne, vol. ii. p. 82, and the reference to marriage, vol. ii. p. 135. We shall hear of his more prosperous suit later. It is clear that Scott still thinks of himself as having been hardly used by Miss Belsches.

To ROBERT SURTEES.[1]

[*Probably* 1806]

SIR,—I have to beg your acceptance of my best thanks for the obliging communications with which I am this day favoured ; and am much flattered to find that my collectns have proved at all interesting to a gentleman whose letter proves him so well acquainted with Northumbrian antiquities. I have only to regret that a new edition of the Minstrelsy of the Scottish Border has just issued from the press, so that I must treasure up your remarks for a future opportunity.

I had begun to suspect that Whitfield of Whitfield might be the person of whom Hobbie Noble expresses some apprehensions ; and as I see in Wallis's history of Northumberland that about the close of the sixteenth century, *Ralph* Whitfield was at the head of the family, I have expressed my opinion that *Ralph* Whitfield had in recitation been corrupted into Earl of Whitfield, as the words are very similar in sound, though not in sense or spelling. But your very curious observations lead me to hesitate, and think the original reading of Earl may be the right one.

I am here so far from books and authorities that I cannot say anything with certainty on the subject of Ralph Eure. Certain it is that the Scottish historians call him Lord Eure ; but that, according to the loose practice of giving the father's title to the son, common in these days, is no argument against your proofs, which indeed seem irrefragable.

The Knights of St. Michael were, according to the best of my recollection, called Knights of the Cockle ; but having no authority to consult, I may be mistaken. The

---

[1] This is the first of many letters to Surtees (1779-1834), the antiquarian, historian of Durham, and ballad-monger. They are printed from the *Memoir of Surtees* and compared with the copies in the Abbotsford volumes. The points raised all concern the *Minstrelsy* and the notes to the ballads there.

ornament or badge seems more appropriate to the knights of St. James of Compostella.

Your story of the Goth who melted Lord Eure's chain, reminds me of the fate of a beautiful set of rosary-beads, which James V of Scotland gave to one of his godsons, and which fell into the hands of an old lady, who had the cruelty to dispose of the best part of it, *à la façon* of the proprietor of Witton Castle.

Poor Ritson's MSS. were sadly dispersed. Indeed, in the alienation of mind which preceded his death, he destroyed many which contained the memoranda of the labours of years. There is a copy of Musgrave,[1] in the Roxburghe or Pearson Collection of Ballads, which I hope to get copied when I go to London. It seems to be that very favourite song of " Plumpton Park," which is often referred to as a popular air. There was another ballad in the collection of poor Ritson, of which he would not give me a copy, and which I fear is lost. It was called the " Raid of Rookhope," and, as I think, was picked up from recitation somewhere in the Bishoprick of Northumberland. It contained some account of a skirmish between the Tynedale men and those of Rookhope, in which the former were beaten ; with a curious enumeration of the clans on both sides. Perhaps these hints may

---

[1] In a letter of Joseph Frank (nephew of Ritson) to Surtees, 9th February 1807, which Surtees has forwarded, he says : " I am glad of this early opportunity of sending you *Rookhope Ride* and *Musgrave's Lamentation.*" He begs for the loan of any letters of Ritson Scott may have and will omit any objectionable passage. He hopes " by these letters to convince the public that my poor uncle was neither so fierce and ferocious, nor so incapable of kindness and friendship as some of his enemies have endeavoured to represent him." On the back of the letter Surtees cites from another letter a note by Ritson on the Lykewake dirge. In a postscript Surtees adds : " I forgot to mention one ballad which I have recovered (tho not relative to the rebellions). It begins :

Lord Ewrie was as brave a man
As ever stood in his degree ;
The King has sent him a braid letter
For his courage and loyaltie."

Rookhope Ride and *Lord Ewrie* are given in the *Border Minstrelsy*, with acknowledgments to Surtees and Ritson and Frank.

enable you, or some friend curious in these matters, still to recover it.

The fragment with which you favoured me seems to refer to a ballad current in Scotland, the burden of which runs,

"With a hey and a lily gay
And the rose it smells sae sweetly."

But one or two verses of your fragment are much more poetical than those of our old song. The bride's brother kills the bride. It is printed by Jamieson,[1] in his Select Ballads, lately published by Constable of Edinburgh, in which you will, I think, find some other curious matter. I am, Sir, with my best thanks for your polite attention, Your obliged and very humble Servant

WALTER SCOTT

ASHESTIEL, BY SELKIRK

[*Abbotsford Copies*]

To LADY DALKEITH

Monday [Spring 1806][2]

MY DEAR LADY DALKEITH Our Ettrick Shepherd has laid by his pastoral reed for the more profitable employment of valuing Sheep Land in which he has given great satisfaction to those who engaged him being a remarkably

---

[1] See note later, p. 335.

[2] These two letters about Hogg's affairs are undated, but belong to the spring of 1806. On 17th March 1806 Hogg wrote to Scott : " For my sake, my dear Scott, if you think there is any chance for a farm of the Duke, push your request. . . . What would you think of my writing a line to one of the family myself. I have no time to lose, else I would wait for your advise in this ; and now I think I will write to Lady Dalkeith. If it do no good, it can do no ill."—(*Private Letter-Books of Sir Walter Scott*, p. 87). In April he writes, " I wrote to Lady Dalkeith on the same day I wrote you last, simply thanking her for her kind attentions. . . . I have met with no disappointment from his Grace's refusal. . . . I had a present of a very elegant copy of the *Lay*, lately, from a gentleman in Edinburgh, to whom I was ashamed to confess that I had it not. This is just to give you a hint that the present should have come from some other hand." See *Familiar Letters*, i. p. 44.

intelligent clever fellow in the line of his business. His present object is to have the Dukes patronage in case his Grace wishes the service of such a person as is reported. If there is the least chance of such an application being successful I will take care to procure & send to the Duke or Mr Riddell the necessary attestations of his skill & character. His charge seems moderate and I will answer for his honesty : and he might be tried on a small scale at first.

Lord D. being absent on his Roxburgh campaign, I entreat your Ladyship (though I know you do not meddle with business) to take an opportunity of putting the inclosed into the Dukes hands. If I did not think he might really be of use I would not on any consideration recommend him. Indeed I fear the Duke will think his business is getting a little too much out of sober prose when one poet is dabbling in his elections & another proffering his services to value his sheep farms. But I really do not feel entitled to suppress this application which carries something in it more feasible than anything hitherto proposed for this poor man & also promises some advantages for the property from his local knowledge & skill in the business

I trust to your Ladyships usual goodness to pardon this intrusion & am with great respect Dear Lady Dalkeith your much honoured & obliged humble Servant

WALTER SCOTT

[*Buccleuch*]

To LADY DALKEITH [1]

[*Spring* 1806]

DEAR LADY DALKEITH,—I was rather surprized to learn by a letter received yesterday from my friend the Shepherd that he had taken the liberty of applying personally to your Ladyship about his affairs which I

[1] See footnote on p. 299.

certainly should not have recommended to him to do. I have no reason to think that his disappointment can be violent as I had expressd to him my strong conviction that his Grace must from the mode in which he manages his estates have many claims entitled to precedence both upon his justice & liberality. I have communicated to him your Ladyships letter & I am sure that your sympathy with his situation & extreme delicacy of expression must tend greatly to alleviate his feelings of disappointment if he indeed harbours any. It is one of the inconveniences attached to exalted rank that the expectations of suitors are apt to be unreasonable because founded on ignorance but a kind answer to a petitioner even when unfavourable is often [more than] equivalent to an ungracious grant of his request.

I certainly hope to pay my respects at Langholm— perhaps to bring with me my friend Mr. Skene of Rubislaw an amiable & accomplished young man & for a gentleman the best draughtsman I ever saw. I wish him to take a peep at Hermitage etc. Lord Dalkeith was so good as to say I might use the freedom to bring him to Langholm. Mrs. Scott desires her most respectful compliments to your Ladyship & I am with great respect Ever your Ladyships Devoted humble Serv.

W. Scott

CASTLE ST. *Monday.*

[*Buccleuch*]

To LADY ABERCORN [1]

9th June 1806

MY DEAR LADY MARCHIONESS,—Did you ever hear the ffrench parrot's apology for its silence—" Je pense plus "

---

[1] This is the first of the series of letters to Lady Abercorn, the third wife of John James Hamilton, Earl (after 1790 Marquess) of Abercorn, Viscount Strabane, Viscount Hamilton. The Marchioness was Anne Jane, the

because if you have not I intend to adopt [it] for my own ungracious taciturnity because during the period of busy idleness which has elapsed since I saw the cottage at the Priory I have very often thought of it and its kind and condescending mistress. When I had rejoined my little family which I found at our own mountain farm closed in by many a dark blue hill I had a great number of trifles to adjust which the head of a family among us little people generally finds it best to look after himself. There were sheep to be bought and bullocks to be sold—there was a sick horse and a lame greyhound to be cured—there were Salmon to be caught and poachers to be punished. Now though I know very little about some of these matters yet I find it very convenient to let it be supposed I am very knowing and anxious upon the subject although it costs me a good deal of trouble to keep up my credit. When I came to town I had to take possession of [my] new office which your Ladyship will hardly suppose a very difficult one when you are informed that I am actually scribbling at my bureau amidst the clamour of the lawyers—" the drowsy bench the babbling hall," being my immediate neighbours. I have however acquired such a happy command over my imagination that even in these untoward circumstances I can represent

daughter of the second Earl of Arran and the widow of Henry Hatton of Great Clonard, co. Wexford. Douglas was the first to print from the series, for Lockhart merely refers to them. But only some half of the letters are reproduced in *Familiar Letters*, and that with large omissions. I have printed them in full from the originals in the Library of the late Mr. Pierpont Morgan. Scott's connection with the family was due to the fact that his father, and after him his brother, had been their man of business in Scotland where they owned the estate of Duddingstone. The letters will show that Tom mismanaged the estate and Scott had in 1809 to lay aside other tasks and straighten out the affair at some cost to himself. He gained the close friendship and support of the lady. The Marquess was a man of enormous vanity who hunted and travelled with all his orders displayed, and insisted that the maid in making his bed should wear white kid gloves. Scott generally refers to him as the Marquess of Carabas, but Lockhart discreetly drops the addition. The Marchioness died at Naples in 1827. His seat in England was Bentley Priory near Stanmore in Middlesex.

to Myself how beautiful [the] groves of the Priory must now appear in all the glory of Midsummer foliage. I have not forgot a promise so flattering to my vanity as that you would permit me to have a share in ornamenting the interior of the cottage. I am not coxcomb enough to use the common phrase that the Muses have been unpropitious but the truth is that I have not been able to do anything lately that has pleased me and consequently nothing that would be worthy of so honourable a station as the walls of the Cottage. I did two little things for Welch tunes some time ago and when I can furnish them with companions I will do myself the honor of sending them to the Priory. I am much flattered by your Lady-ship's enquiries about my literary engagements. My grand edition of Dryden's Works is advancing I hope prosperously. The booksellers are publishing a fourth edition of the Lay and also some of the ballads which call me father extracted from the Border collection that I formerly published. I intend to add to these last a few little things so as to make them into a little volume, which I will take an early opportunity of laying at your Lady-ship's feet. Besides all this I have a grand work in contemplation but so distant, so distant that the distance between Edinburgh and Stanmore is nothing to it. This is a Highland romance of Love Magic and War founded upon the manners of our mountaineers with my stories about whom your Ladyship was so much interested. My great defficiency is that being born and bred not only a lowlander but a borderer I do not in the least understand the Gaelic language and therefore am much at a loss to find authentic materials for my undertaking. Mrs. Scott is deeply obliged by the message with which your Lady-ship has honoured her She has a grateful remembrance of her late Protector & friend Lord Downshire which extends to all his friends but Lady Abercorn in particular has a thousand other claims to her respectful regard.— Adieu, my dear Lady Marchioness. Believe me with

the greatest respect and regard, ever your Ladyship's
much obliged & most obed. humble servant,

WALTER SCOTT

EDINBURGH 9*th* *June* 1806

This letter has waited two days to accompany me to
the Marquis

[*Pierpont Morgan*]

To LADY ABERCORN

[EDIN., *June* 1806]

DEAR LADY MARCHIONESS,—I enclose a trifling song
which was sung with immense approbation at a meeting of
five hundred select friends of Lord Melville [1] from which
your Ladyship will probably be of opinion that they
approved too much of the sentiment to be very critical
about the poetry.   I also scratched down another ballad
[the] morning of the day of meeting, of which a few copies
have been printed and if I can get one in time to save
the post I will also enclose it.   I am sure your Ladyship,
with your usual goodness will not suppose that by sending
you these little foolish things I think them at all worthy
of your acceptance, but will just receive them as graciously
as the Duchess in Don Quixote accepts of the half dozen
of acorns from the wife of Sancho Panza.   There is in
the printed ditty a little attempt at a tribute to the
memory of the never to be forgotten Pitt which drew
tears from many of the jovial party to whom it was
addressed.   I have only room and time to add how much
I always am the Marchioness of Abercorn's most faithful
and respectful humble sert.,   WALTER SCOTT

[*Pierpont Morgan*]

[1] Lord Melville's impeachment was commenced in Westminster Hall on
29th April 1806 and he was acquitted on the 12th June.   The public
dinner for which Scott wrote this and another political song took place on
27th June.

To COLONEL ROBERT DUNDAS

My dear Colonel,—I have deferrd saying my *Gratulor* on the late glorious decision of the House of Peers till I should be able to tell you at the same time how splendidly our great gaudeamus went off yesterday which indeed I soon found bafled all description. It was impossible for the warmest friends of Lord Mellville to have anticipated that so huge a meeting should have been entirely made up of respectable materials & animated with the same general soul. I had the happiness to add something to the mirth, & I will say the enthusiasm of the Meeting, by the inclosed ditties, which I got Ballantyne the printer to hollow forth with the voice of a Stentor. I should be happy Lord Mellville saw them, as no man ought to feel or can feel more happy than I have done on this occasion, which I beg you to express to his Lordship in the strongest and most respectful language. I wish you would look at the Selkirk address which I sent off to the Burgh by express & am happy to see they were among the foremost. Remember me kindly to Mrs. D. & excuse brevity, for my head akes somewhat & my throat as Falstaff says is hoarse with hollowing & singing of anthems. Yours most truly

EDINBURGH 28*th June* (1806)   WALTER SCOTT

The Honble Robert Dundas M.P. London

[*Nat. Lib. Scot.*]

To DR. LEYDEN

EDINBURGH 5 *July* 1806

My dear Leyden,—You cannot doubt that the receipt of your letter from Pulo Penang [1] dated 20th November

---

[1] Pulo Penang, officially Prince of Wales Island, at the northern extremity of the Straits of Malacca. Leyden had gone thither from the Malabar coast to recruit in " the delightful climate of P. P.," arriving on 22nd October 1805.

I   U

gave Charlotte and me the greatest pleasure more especially as it contains the very first lines which we have received from you since you went to India or indeed which have ever reached Europe excepting a letter of some length to your father. But it was doubly acceptable in the present moment because the reports of your illness reached Europe in such an exaggerated form that we had every reason to apprehend we had lost you entirely which you may imagine gave us sincere distress. Letters have also arrived safe to Heber to Ballantyne to Constable and I believe to some of your other friends. I am happy to see your health is mending pray take care of it for the sake of your friends and of literature. You may sow the seed & raise the crop of Oriental acquisitions in India. But we in Europe are by all the rules of the East India Company entitled to the exclusive profit of the harvest and should you disable yourself from transmitting us our lawful dues it will be but a sorry account of your stewardship. I wish from my soul the Brass cauldron in which you traversed the Indian torrent had possessd the qualities of Medea's kettle and renewd your blood liver lights & limb to the full vigour of a true Moss trooper. In the circumstances however I should have been rather alarmed that the previous process of hewing to pieces might have preceded the embarkation without producing the same marvellous effects experienced by Osen, or whatever his name was. Now as I know you must be gasping for European intelligence I will endeavour to gratify you with such particulars as I think will be interesting to you. In the first place as to my own affairs your little freind and hostess continues the same kind & affectionate companion. She begs to be very kindly remembered to you & we very often talk of you and mourned long over what then seemed to me your unaccountable silence. We beg you will take the greatest care of your letters in future and you may depend upon hearing from me very often. Indeed I should

have written long ere now but had no means of directing
to you. The Cottage is no longer in our possession we
abandoned it with regret ; but it was growing too small
for my increasing family & the neighbourhood began to
be inconveniently populous. I therefore have taken a
lease of the house and estate of Ashestiel. You remember
this little mansion upon the Tweed where we dined with
the Miss Rutherfords and the Miss Russells. I have
sublet the whole of the Sheep farm which is valuable and
extensive & retaind in my own hands a small arable
farm for cows horses sheep for the table etc. Here we
live all the summer like little kings and only wish that you
could take a scamper with me over the hills in the morning
and return to a clean tablecloth a leg of forest mutton &
a blazing hearth in the afternoon. Walter has acquired
the surname of Gilnockie being large of limb and bone
and dauntless in disposition like that noted chieftain.
Your little friend Sophia is grown a tall girl and I think
promises to be very clever as she discovers uncommon
acuteness of apprehension. We have moreover a little
roundabout girl with large dark eyes as brown as good
humourd and as lively as the Mother that bore her and
of whom she is the most striking picture. Over and
above all this there is in rerum natura a certain little
Charles so called after the Knight of the Crocodile, but
of this gentleman I can say but little as he is only five
months old and consequently not at the time of life when
I can often enjoy the honour of his company.—I have ex-
changd my practice at the bar in order to become one of
the principal Clerks of Session which with my Sheriffdom
forms a very good official appointment. The worst of it
is that I draw little immediate profit from my new office
till the death of an old gentleman who resigned in my
favour but it is to be supposed he will soon make a final
resignation of his soul to him who gave [it] when I succeed
to near £1000„ a year which as you [know] my habits are
more for comfort than show will amply supply my turn.

About literary labours I must inform you that the fourth
edition of the Lay is just come out, and is to be followed
by an Edition of the Minstrelsy and of Sir Tristrem.
I will take the safest measures I can to forward to you
sets of these books and of any others which I think likely
to interest you. The reception of the Lay has been very
flattering and the sale both rapid and extensive. I am
somewhat tempted to undertake a highland poem upon
the same plan. Meanwhile my present grande opus
consists in an uniform edition of Drydens works which
as you know have never been collected ; with notes
critical and illustratory by the Editor. This fills up most
of my leisure hours and as the duties of my office are very
slight which was indeed my principal motive for asking
it these leisure hours are numerous. I only wish I
could have your assistance as formerly in arranging
digesting and contributing to my labour or rather to my
amusement. I have one or two trifling undertakings
besides Dryden but they are hardly worth mentioning
though I may probably detail them in another letter
before these ships sail. Camp is as much in favour as
stout and hearty as ever. He had a very violent illness
about a year ago which had like to have carried him off.
He was unable to stir for about two days & eat nothing
but some milk which I forced into his mouth with a tea
spoon ; but by dint of using that noble remedy un petit
lavement frequently repeated we brought on a crisis and
his health was restored to the general joy of the family—
enough of myself let me now tell you of some other
friends. I was in London in last spring when I saw
Heber frequently. His father being now dead and he in
possession of a large property, his diligence indefatigable
and his taste undoubted he will be soon in possession of
the noblest library in England. Ellis poor fellow is a
martyr to the liver but carries on his studies with vigour.
He has finished his Romances in three volumes—a most
lively & entertaining performance. Most of those in the

Auchinleck MS our old friend were well ransacked upon this occasion. Yet though I cannot tell why this work has not been quite so popular as the Specimens. To come nearer home—Ballantyne continues to flourish like a green bay tree but instead of being planted by a river he has established at the bottom of St. Mary's Wynd a hall equal to that which the Genie of the lamp built for Aladdin in point of size but rather less superbly furnished being occupied by about a dozen of presses. Constable goes on to improve in circumstances trade and size. He has associated with him young Hunter of Blackness who bringing £3000 or £4000 to the stock has enabled him to outdo his former outdoings. Tom Brown [1] is well but having published a collection of poems which were rather too metaphysical for the public taste he has become shyer than ever.

We are now assured that after a vigourous contest with the India Directors on the subject of Lord Lauderdale, Lord Minto is finally to go out as Governor General. You know he is one of my most intimate freinds in that rank of life. I intend to press your pursuits and person very strongly on his notice before he leaves Europe. He is a man of taste & literature ; so pray arrange matters so as to keep in his way—Charlotte sends you *mille choses* but I will write soon and tell you all about her messages. Ever Yours truly

WALTER SCOTT

Dr Leyden
    Care of Messrs Binnie & Dennison
      Armenian Street Madras East Indies

[*Edin. Univ. Lib.*]

---

[1] Dr. Thomas Brown, afterwards Professor of Moral Philosophy, Edinburgh University. The collection referred to is, *Poems*. In two vols. 12mo. Edinb. 1804. He published several volumes later.

To GEORGE THOMSON

[*July* 23, 1806]

DEAR SIR,—I have not been inattentive to your request, though much pressed with business, both literary and official. I enclose you the beginning of a war song imitated from the Morlachian—it is a fragment but could easily be completed if you think it will suit the character of the tune called " The Sheriff's fancy." The verses are uncommonly dashing.

The Massacre of the Monks of Bangor contains a subject, which is always a great advantage. I therefore prefer it to " Black Sir Harry," [1] and will endeavour to send you some verses suited to it before I leave town. In case you have not seen the enclosed squib I beg your acceptance of a copy. It has made much noise in London. Yours truly

W. SCOTT

[*British Museum*]

To LADY ABERCORN

ASHESTIEL, BY SELKIRK, 6*th August* 1806

MY DEAR LADY MARCHIONESS,—Almost ever since I had the pleasure of receiving the delightful bundle of persiflage with which your Ladyship honoured me I have had neither leisure nor inclination to do one single thing that was at all entertaining. This was owing to the arrival of my youngest brother from the West Indies with ruined

---

[1] On the 12th June Thomson had written expressing regret that no poem on Nelson's death had been forthcoming, but he will still pay for the Ducange if the poet will write " two charming songs on *any* subject." He sends as airs " The Monks of Bangor " and " The Sheriff's Fancy," and states that there is another very favourite Welsh air called " Black Sir Harry," for a song to which he would give " two beautiful drawings, the one of the Abbey of Dunfermline, the other of Doune Castle."—J. CUTHBERT HADDEN, *George Thomson, the Friend of Burns: his life and correspondence,* p. 155.

health & blasted prospects : [1] after a tedious struggle he died last week. It was not for many reasons an event to sit down & mourn over deeply but still it gave us all sufficient distress. I am sure your Ladyship will be sorry I can plead so unfortunate an excuse for not more early acknowledging what gave me so much pleasure as well as honor—I am now thank God got to my little farm, and I really wish I had the lamp of Aladdin or the tapestry of some other eastern Magician, whose name I have forgot but you will find the story among the records of the immortal Scheherazade. Could I possibly command so easy a conveyance I would certainly transport your Ladyship to this retreat with which I have the vanity to think you would be pleased for a day were it only for the extraordinary contrast between the scenery here and at the Priory. Our whole habitation could dance very easily in your great Salon without displaceing [sic] a single moveable or endangering a mirror. We have no green pastures nor stately trees but to make amends we have one of the most beautiful streams in the world winding through steep mountains which are now purple with the heath blossom. We are eight miles from the nearest markettown and four from the nearest neighbour. The last circumstance I by no means regret, but the first is productive of very curious shifts and ludicrous distresses well worthy of being recorded in the *Miseries of Human Life* [2]—a very diverting little volume which if your Ladyship has not seen I beg you will add to your bookshelves on my recommendation. For example my scrutoire having travelled by some slow

[1] I have inserted a colon here to make the sequence a little clearer. The reference is to Daniel.—See *Lockhart*, c. xix.

[2] In the course of the former year (1806) Scott found time and (notwithstanding their political bickerings) inclination to draw up three papers for the *Edinburgh Review*," including " that exquisite piece of humour, his article on the *Miseries of Human Life*, to which Mr. Jeffrey added some, if not all, of the Reviewer's groans with which it concludes."—*Lockhart*, c. xvi. This is probably the squib referred to in previous letter.

conveyance I was obliged, not to mention searching half an hour for this blasted [?] solitary sheet of letter paper, to sally forth and shoot a crow to procure a quill which performs its duty extremely ill, as your Ladyship is witness. I am afraid that this candid declaration of our wants, and the difficulty of supplying them will make the Marchioness bless her stars that the lamp and tapestry is out of fashion. But don't be afraid too soon : for the main business of the day we have the best mutton in the world and find by experience that the air of our hills makes an excellent sauce. Then we have pigs and poultry, and a whole apparatus of guns fishing-rods salmon spears and nets for the employment of male visitors, who do not find their sport less agreeable because part of their dinner depends upon it. Then grouse-shooting begins bye and bye and I have some very good coveys on the moors, besides the privilege of going far and wide over those of my neighbour the Duke of Buccleuch a favour not the less readily granted because like many other persons in this world I make more noise than I do mischief. Then if all this is insufficient you shall have hare soup for am I not the Sheriff of the County and may I not break the laws when I please and course out of season Besides all this you shall have one of the kindest welcomes which our hospitable mountaineers can afford. So pray don't quarrel with my lamp or tapestry any more. I only wish it was possible for you to make good this little dream.

I saw Lord and Lady Melville before I left town and dined at Melville Castle. I never saw the veteran statesman looking better or in more high spirits. He was very full of the pleasant visit he had made at the Priory just before he set out. His journey too had been very flattering to his feelings—nothing but huzzaing and cheering in almost [all] the towns they had occasion to pass through. I was much tempted to accept of a kind invitation they gave me to their seat in the Highlands where I could have collected some materials for my projected romance. But my mind was on this little crib, and I could not find [it] in my heart to leave it.

I am a good deal interested in the discussions which have been proceeding concerning the Princess of Wales. Having had the honour to eat of her salt I should be extremely sorry to think there was the least chance of her being trammelled either by her own imprudence or otherwise in the toils of her accusers. Of this however I hope there is no danger. I must now break off as I must ride about ten miles to a County meeting about roads being the dullest of all dull amusements though country gentlemen have such a peculiar pleasure in it that one of my neighbours used to travel with the Turnpike Act of Parliament in his pocket till I told him it was against the law which prohibits [bis] carrying concealed arms. I shall however see my friend and fishing crony Lord Somerville and get a cover for this letter as the Marquis is I suspect long since in green Erin. Mrs. Scott has the honour to offer her respect and I am with sincere respect and regard, Ever your Ladyship's most faithful humble servant,   WALTER SCOTT

[*Pierpont Morgan*]

(P.S.) On the other side I have copied a few verses which I intend to begin one of the Tales in my Highland Romance. They are supposed to be sung by an old *Seannachie* or Man of Talk, or in short Tale-teller, who by what accident I know as little as your Ladyship has strolled into the Lowlands. While I am on this subject I may mention that I or rather my Bookseller has collected into one small volume all the little tales & songs I have written & which have hiterto been dispersed in the Border Minstrelsy Tales of Wonder etc [1] & that I hope your Ladyship will do me the honour to accept of copy [*sic*] the instant it is finished.

---

[1] *Ballads and Lyrical Pieces.* By Walter Scott, Esq. Edinburgh : printed by James Ballantyne and Co. 1806.

To JAMES SKENE

ASHESTIEL, *Monday,* 11*th August* 1806

MY DEAR SKENE,—I am favoured with your letter giving me an account of the transactions of the Meeting of Officers relating to our corps, which is such as I expected and indeed wished. I should have been sorry that the *pet* had had the least share in our breaking up, having seen so little of it in the Troop while embodied. I wish I could promise to add to your convenience by accommodating the boarder, but our grass has been so scanty that, upon consulting with James and Mr. Laidlaw, they both agree we could not do him justice. I have indeed cut grass for the horses in the house, but that you know requires exercise, and I have no one to whom I could trust your horse when Peter is out of the way, which must sometimes happen. I have plenty of forage for the winter, and should it then continue to be an accommodation to you, I will gladly take care of Billie as usual.

I am truly sorry for Sir William's [1] bad health, both as a friend and as one of the most estimable characters in Scotland. I also feel for your situation, which is an unpleasant one in its way, but I hope the worthy Bart.'s health will soon admit of execution being done on Cawdor. If in the interim you could find a moment to spend here, you know the way, and the ford is where it was ; which by the way is more than I expected, after Saturday last, which was the most dreadful storm of thunder and lightning I ever witnessed. The lightning broke repeatedly in our immediate vicinity, *i.e.* betwixt us and the Peel Wood. Charlotte resolved to die in bed like a good Christian, the servants thought it was the preface

---

[1] The letter, Skene says, "was written on the occasion of my approaching marriage, which had for some time been retarded by the illness of my future father-in-law, the late Sir William Forbes of Pitsligo, to whose estimable character Sir Walter alludes in this letter, and also in the Introduction to the Fourth Canto of *Marmion*." Lockhart prints an extract from this letter misdating it 18th August 1805.

to the end of the world, and I was the only person that maintained my character for stoicism, which I assure you was some merit, as I had no doubt that we were in real danger. It was accompanied with a flood so tremendous that I would have given five pounds you had been here to make a sketch of it. The little Glenkinnen brook was unpassable for all the next day, and indeed I have been obliged to send all hands to repair the ford, which was converted into a deep pool.

Will you slip into my book-room, and on the ground shelves next the window you will see some volumes of the *Biographia Britannica*. Will you give that containing the article " Burnet, Gilbert, D.D." to our old house-keeper, and tell her to send it out to Ashestiel with the basket which she will receive by the carrier, and which is to return this week. Also to clap in parcels, letters, etc. Excuse, my dear Skene, this trouble from, yours truly,

[*Skene's Memories*]   WALTER SCOTT

To LADY ABERCORN

ASHESTIEL, 20*th September* 1806

NOTHING except the fairy Goodwill or the Marchioness of Abercorn could possibly supply the minute wants of their friends' domestic economy, at the distance of so many hundred miles as are between the Priory and the Forest of Ettrick. The little parcel of quills is quite a treasure and as to their everlasting duration I shall be happy to find that they possess a quality which we some-times miss in Love Friendship and Fidelity however fondly ascribed to them. The worst of the little packet is that it removes all apologies for a very indifferent hand and transfers the blame so often laid on the innocent goose quil to the fingers of the clumsy writer himself.

I am quite delighted with the little heroine of your thunder-storm : I hope she will not lose the benefit of your Ladyship's protection as she is certainly reserved for some great things. The state of our own weather has been most calamitous. Land floods river floods water spouts and torrents and tempests of all kinds and denominations, have almost laid waste our country. One day the thunder was so tremendous as actually to affect my hearing for some time. The lightning broke within a hundred yards of our farm house but fortunately did no damage except that the concussion threw down the bricks etc. from the top of the chimneys : we thought it quite near enough. There were however no tragic incidents in our immediate neighbourhood except the death of a poor pony. Our rivers and brooks always sufficiently rapid became the most furious torrents which it was possible to behold. Ricks of hay whole acres of young and old trees even cattle and horses came swimming past us without the possibility of our giving any assistance. One gentleman of this country Ogilvie of Chesters has sustained more than a thousand pounds worth of damage much of which is absolutely irreparable as the very soil is carried away. Another gentleman has totally lost a large and valuable garden which a small rivulet, that in general winded very peaceably through it, chose to carry off entirely. Minto House was in great danger, the inhabitants driven to the upper rooms as the lower part of the mansion was quite filled with water. A heroic cook-maid secured a sirloin of beef in her retreat, otherwise the plague of famine would have been added to the distresses of the sufferers.

I have been several days out upon the moors in hopes of making up a box of game for the Priory but the wet weather has made the grouse so wild that neither by my own exertions nor those of my friends have I been ever able to get above a brace or two in the day and as they have not like your Ladyship's kind present the faculty of everlasting duration, to be fit to send they should all be killed on the same day. I still hope to be more fortunate.

I observe from the papers that the Marquis is still in Ireland and has received the thanks of the Country for his unceasing exertions in bringing Judge Fox [1] to account. I suppose however his stay will not be very long in that country ; as I presume there will be much bustle in the political world in consequence of Mr. Fox's death. He was certainly a great man, yet it so happened that there was never a human being whose talents were of less service to his country. How different from Pitt ! I am not apt to be very much exalted with any success which my literary essays have obtained because I know very well how much is owing to chance how much to novelty and how little to any actual merit they may possess. But in telling me I have been so fortunate as to please Mr. Pitt your Ladyship gives me something to be justifiably proud of till my dying day ; and I can say without affectation that I would rather have the satisfaction of having been approved by him, though now dead, than by all the living statesmen and nobility in Europe. From the pilot-less state in which the political vessel has remained since his death his worst enemies may be taught to appreciate the extent of his unequalled talents.

We have been *threatened* with a visit of the Heir Apparent—a very serious business to the poor Scottish nobility who might have deemed it necessary to receive him and some-how [*sic*] not very acceptable to the people at large. It certainly requires ingenuity in a personage whose very smile is a favour and therefore who has popularity so much at his own commands to contrive so totally to get rid of what naturally attaches to one from whom much might have been hoped and little feared ; if he had chosen it should be so.

Your Ladyship is very good to enquire after Dryden. I have I assure you been labouring very hard through the old libels and pamphlets of the time to complete the

---

[1] A Justice against whom a petition had been presented for misconduct during the assizes at Donegal about two years before.

historical notices upon his political poems ; and I am at least willing to hope that I have been in some degree successful. I am very anxious to procure copies if possible of three original letters that are among the Duke of Dorset's papers written by Dryden to his Grace's ancestor the witty Earl of Dorset. I am quite at a loss for a channel to approach this great man : perhaps your Ladyship may be able either to give me some assistance or at least your kind advice. If he is accessible to any of our Scottish nobles I could contrive, directly or indirectly to procure their mediation. It is of the greatest consequence to me to procure them if possible.

I hope with my next to send one or two little songs for the decoration of the Cottage. I have kept this letter two days expecting Robert Dundas who had promised to spend them with me but he has not appeared either prevented by the vile weather or it is still again a hurricane or by something else. So it must go without a frank for which & all it's other imperfections I hope your Ladyship's usual goodness will excuse your very respectful & faithful,   W. SCOTT

[*Pierpont Morgan*]

To HIS GRACE THE DUKE OF BUCCLEUCH &C &C &C
DALKEITH HOUSE

MY LORD DUKE,—I have the honor to inclose to your Graces address a Copy of Minutes of Committee of some Gentlemen in Roxburghshire who are desirous to have your Grace's countenance in erecting a Monument in memory of the poet Thompson near Ednam the place of his nativity.[1]

Although I think the design is highly laudable I could have wished the Gentlemen had chosen some other channel for communicating it to your Grace as it has

---

[1] Why Scott should spell the poet's name in this very English way I do not know.

been so often my lot to be troublesome to you with solicitation : it was perhaps the less proper as I have now
very little connection with Roxburghshire & yet am
requested to address your Grace as Lord Lieutenant of
that County. At the same time I rather chuse to trust
your Grace's often-tried goodness for pardoning any
impropriety which may be in the mode of communication, than contribute by declining it to a second failure
or rather I believe a *third*, of a purpose honourable to the
County which gave birth to so great a Poet. I was not
at the meeting where the plan was concerted otherwise
I should have suggested the propriety of the application
to your grace being made by the president rather than by
an individual. I am with the greatest respect Your
Graces much obliged very faithful humble Servant

WALTER SCOTT

ASHESTIEL 30*th Septr.* [1806]

[*Buccleuch*]

To ANNA SEWARD [1]

ASHESTIEL [probably *September* 1806]

MY DEAR MISS SEWARD,—I am quite ashamed of the
date of your valuable favour yet when you have made
allowance for real business, for family calamity by the
illness & death of a near relative [2]—and after all for a

---

[1] Lockhart prints this letter in part and dates it 1805, but it is a reply
to a letter from Anna of 20th June 1806 : " Apropos of Ossian ; you and
I have never interchanged our sentiments on the reality or pretence of that
bold poetic source. . . . Dr. Johnson's scornful assertions on the subject
have no weight with me, etc." She replied to this letter on the 23rd
September 1806, commending his intention of writing a Highland poem
and thanking him for his " ingenious and ingenuous dissertation . . . concerning the long disputed claim of originality for Ossian." Scott's remarks
on Madoc are in reply to high-flown encomiums of his own and Southey's
poems, which are in the originals at Abbotsford but were, doubtless at Scott's
instance, left out in the printed edition of the letters, 1811. Of the Ossian
question, see a full and interesting history in the late J. S Smart's *James
Macpherson : An Episode in Literature* (1905).

[2] Daniel Scott died 20th July 1806.

gentle degree of procrastination I hope the last ingredient which I admit to be a sin that easily besets me
in my correspondence will not be found to bear so undue
a proportion as usual in my delay. I have first to thank
you for making me acquainted with Mrs. Jackson, a very
good-humoured and agreeable Lady who did us the
pleasure to spend the day with us once before we left
Edin.ʳ and whom we hope to see a good deal of when
we return.

You recall to me some very pleasant feelings of my
boyhood, when you ask my opinion of Ossian. His works
were first first [sic] put into my hands by old Dr. Blacklock
a blind poet of whom you may have heard ; he was the
worthiest and kindest of human beings, and particularly
delighted in encouraging the pursuits & opening the
minds of the young people by whom he was surrounded.
I though at the period of our intimacy a very young boy
was fortunate enough to attract his notice and kindness ;
and if I have been at all successful in the paths of literary
pursuit I am sure I owe much of that success to the books
with which he supplied me and his own instructions.
Ossian and Spencer were two books which the good old
bard put into my hands and which I devoured rather
than perused. Their tales were for a long time so much
my delight that I could repeat without remorse whole
cantos of the one & Duans of the other & woe to the
unlucky wight who undertook to be my auditor for in the
height of my enthusiasm I was apt to disregard all hints
that my recitations became tedious. It was a natural
consequence of progress in taste that my fondness for
these authors should experience some abatement. Ossian
in particular has more charms for youth than for a
more advanced stage. The eternal repetitions of the
same ideas & imagery however beautiful in itself, is
apt to pall upon a reader whose taste has become
somewhat fastidious and although I agree entirely with
you that the question of their authenticity ought [not]

to be confounded with that of their literary merit yet
scepticism on that head takes away their claim for
indulgence as the productions of a barbarous & remote
age, & what is perhaps more natural, it destroys that
feeling of reality which we should otherwise combine
with our sentiments of admiration. As for the great
dispute I should be no Scottish man if I had not very
attentively considered it at some period of my studies
& indeed I have gone some length in my researches
for I have beside me translations of some twenty
or thirty of the unquestioned originals of Ossians
poems. After making every allowance for the disadvantages of a literal translation & the possible debasement
which those *now* collected may have suffered in the great
& violent change which the Highlands have undergone
since the researches of Macpherson I am compelled to
admit that incalculably the greater part of the English
Ossian must be ascribed to Macpherson himself and that
his whole introductions notes &c &c is an absolute tissue
of forgeries. In all the ballads I ever saw or could hear
of Fin and Ossian are described as natives of Ireland ;
although it is not unusual for the reciters sturdily to
maintain that this is a corruption of the text. In point of
merit I do not think these Gaelic poems much better
than those of the Scandinavian Scalds ; they are very
unequal often very vigorous and pointed often drivelling
and crawling in the very extremity of tenuity. The
manners of the heroes are those of Celtic savages and I
could point out twenty instances in which Macpherson
has very cunningly adopted the beginning, the names
of the leading incidents of an old tale and dressd it up
with all those ornaments of sentiment & sentimental
manners which first excite our surprize and afterwards
our doubt of its authenticity. The Highlanders themselves recognising the leading features of tales they had
heard in infancy with here and there a tirade really taken
from an old poem were readily seduced into becoming

I   x

champions for the authenticity of the poems. How many
people not particularly addicted to poetry who may have
heard Chevy Chace in the nursery or at school & never
since met with the ballad might be imposed on by a new
Chevy Chase bearing no resemblance to the old one save
in here & there a stanza or an incident : Besides, there
is something in the severe judgment passd on my countrymen " that if they do not prefer Scotland to truth they
will always prefer it to enquiry." When once the
Highlanders had adopted the poems of Ossian as an
article of national faith you would far sooner have got
them to disavow the Scripture than to abandon a line of
the contested tales. *Only* they all allow that Macphersons
translation is very unfaithful & some pretend to say
inferior to the original, by which they can only mean if
they mean any thing that they miss the charms of the
rhythm & vernacular idiom which pleases the Gaelic
natives, for in the real attributes of poetry Macphersons
version is far superior to any I ever saw of the fragments
which he seems to have used. The Highland Society
have lately set about investigating, or rather, I should
say collecting materials to defend the authenticity of
Ossian. Those researches have only proved that there
were no real originals using that word as is commonly
understood to be found for them. The oldest tale they
have found seems to be that of Darthula but it is perfectly
different both in diction & story from that of Macpherson
—it is, however, a beautiful specimen of Celtic poetry &
shews that it contains much which is worthy of preservation—indeed how should it be otherwise when we know
that till about fifty years ago the Highlands contained a
race of hereditary poets. Is it possible to think that
perhaps among many hundreds who for such a course of
centuries have founded their reputation & rank on
practising the art of poetry in a country where the scenery
& manners gave such effect & interest & imagery to their
productions, there should not have been some who have

attained excellence? In searching out those genuine
records of the Celtic Muse & preserving them from
oblivion with all the curious information which they must
doubtless contain I humbly think our Highland antiquaries would merit better of their country than confining
their researches to the fantastic pursuit of a chimera.
I am not to deny that Macphersons inferiority in other
compositions is a presumption that he did not actually
compose these poems.   But we are to consider his advantage when on his own ground.   Macpherson was a
highlander and had his imagination fired with the
charms of Celtic poetry from his very infancy.   We know
from constant experience, that most highlanders after
they have become compleat masters of English, continue
to *think* in their own language and it is to me demon-
strable that Macpherson *thought* almost every word of
Ossian in Gaelic although he wrote it down in English.
The specimens of his early poetry which remain are also
deeply tinged with the peculiarities of the Celtic diction
& character so that in fact he might be considered
as a highland poet even if he had not left us some Earse
translations or originals of Ossian unquestionably written
by himself.   These circumstances gave a great advantage
to him in forming the style of Ossian which though
exalted and modified according to Macphersons own
ideas of modern taste is in great part cut upon the
model of the tales of the Sennachies & Bards.   In the
translation of Homer he not only lost these advantages,
but the circumstances on which they were founded were
a great detriment to his undertaking for although such a
dress was appropriate & becoming for Ossian few people
cared to see their old Grecian friend disguised in a tartan
plaid & philabeg.   In a word the style which Macpherson
had formed however admirable in a Highland tale was
not calculated for translating Homer, and it was a great
mistake in him, excited however by the general applause
his first word received, to suppose that there was anything

homogeneous betwixt his own ideas & that of Homer. Macpherson in his own way was certainly a man of high talents & his poetic powers as honourable to his country, as the use which he made of them and I fear his personal character in other respects was a discredit to it. Thus I have given you with the utmost sincerity my creed on the great national question of Ossian : it has been formed after much deliberation & enquiry. I have had for some time thoughts of writing a Highland poem, somewhat in the style of the Lay ; giving as far as I can a real picture of what that enthusiastic race actually were before the destruction of their patriarchal government. It is true I have not quite the same facilities as in describing border manners where I am as they say more at home. But to balance my comparative deficiency in knowledge of Celtic manners you are to consider that I have from my youth delighted in all the Highland traditions which I could pick up from the old Jacobites who used to frequent my father's house and have . . . which I learned from . . . [*MS. defective*] . . . decaying tradition, actually excited in the Highlands within the memory of many now alive : so that the publicity of the circumstances annexed to it will I hope make some amends for my having less immediate opportunities of research than in the Border tales. What does Miss Seward think of this plan ? Assuredly I will be impatient to learn her opinion.

Agreeably to your advice I have actually read over Madoc [1] a second time, & I confess have seen much beauty which escaped me in the first perusal—*Yet* (which *yet* by the way is almost as vile a monosyllable as *but*) I cannot feel quite the interest I would wish to do. The difference of character which you notice reminds me of

[1] Miss Seward had defended the blend in Madoc of history and fiction as traditional in the epic and maintained that in " discrimination and variety of character Madoc appears to me far to exceed Virgil and Tasso's epic."

what by Ben Jonson & other old Comedians were called *humours* which consisted rather in the personification of some individual passion or propensity than of an actual individual man. Also I cannot give up my objection that what was strictly true of Columbus becomes an unpleasant falsehood when told of some one else. Suppose I was to write a fictitious Book of travels I would certainly do ill to copy exactly the incidents which befel Mungo Park or Bruce of Kinnaird. What was true of them would incontestably prove at once the falsehood & plagiary of my supposed journal. It is not but what the incidents are natural but it is their having already happened, which strikes us when they are transferrd to imaginary persons. Could any one bear the story of a second city being taken by a wooden horse (*MS. ends here—conclusion from Lockhart*).

Believe me, I shall not be within many miles of Lichfield without paying my personal respects to you ; and yet I should not do it in prudence, because I am afraid you have formed a higher opinion of me than I deserve : you would expect to see a person who had dedicated himself much to literary pursuits, and you would find me a rattle-sculled half-lawyer, half-sportsman, through whose head a regiment of horse has been exercising since he was five years old ; half-educated—half-crazy, as his friends sometimes tell him ; half everything, but *entirely* Miss Seward's much obliged, affectionate, and faithful servant,

WALTER SCOTT

[*British Museum*]

To CONSTABLE & CO. [1]

GENTLEMEN,—I am much obliged to you for forwarding Sir W. Slingsby which makes a very handsome volume.

[1] With this letter is a letter from Sir Thomas Slingsby apologising for having demurred to the publication of the Journal and adding : " In the

I have written to Sir Thomas concerning the circumstances of the publication in a manner which cannot fail to be satisfactory to him & may induce him to communicate something for the improvement of the next edition. All that you have done in the business is marked with your usual prudence & consideration & I take it particularly kind that you left me to mention my name myself to Sir Thomas though I had no wish to conceal it. I hope the book will answer.

Mrs. Scott makes her best acknowlegement for the splendid copy of Jamieson which will be a great ornament to her shelves. I really hope for the poor authors sake that this book will answer & when I come to town I will write to him to go with your parcel—this will be on the 13th. Current.

My principal cause of writing just now is to beg Sir Tristrem may be stoppd till I come to town. There are some papers relative to Thomas of Ercildoune particularly a genealogy of which I am promised the inspection when I come to Edinburgh. They have been discovered in the Register House & of course I am anxious to examine them before the new edition goes out as I think you will not grudge some expence if necessary to make it more complete. I am ever with regard Your very faithful Servant

WALTER SCOTT

ASHESTIEL 7 *Octr.* 1806

Messrs. Constable & Co. Booksellers Edinr.

[*Stevenson*]

form in which these Memoirs appear in your Work I can have no possible objection to their publication, on the contrary, from whatever source the information concerning them (& which as far as I have yet had time to compare with the MS. in my possession seems perfectly correct) has been obtained, I rather congratulate myself that it has fallen into the hands of Persons so judicious & respectable— I remain Gentlemen Your very obdt Sert THOMAS SLINGSBY."

To GEORGE THOMSON

[October 1806]

DEAR SIR,—Be so good as to receive fair copies of the two songs. You will see I have attended to your criticism in most instances, and I have added another stanza to the " Monks of Bangor." I have also altered and I think improved " The Sheriff's fancy," and beg you will be so kind as to destroy the foul copy which you have. I think I have made as much of both as I can do at present, but I would like to see them in the proof copy in case any minute alterations may yet occur to me, and also to ensure their being correctly printed. I hope they will answer your wishes, and I am Dear Sir Yours very truly

W. SCOTT

My critical friends think the Monks improve by wanting the double rhymes. I will take care to give no copies.

[<i>British Museum and Hadden's George Thomson</i>]

To LADY CHARLOTTE CAMPBELL [1]

December [October] 12th [1806]

WILL you, my dear ——, allow an old, and, I hope,

---

[1] Lady Charlotte Bury (1775-1861), novelist, youngest child of John Campbell, fifth Duke of Argyll. Married Col. John Campbell in 1796 and the Rev. Edward John Bury in 1809. It was at one of her parties that Sir Walter Scott became acquainted with Monk Lewis. She became Lady-in-Waiting to the Princess of Wales, afterwards Queen Caroline. Her *Diary* was published anonymously in 1838 in two volumes, followed in 1839 by other two edited by John Galt. Probably it was her Court connection which misled the editor of *Familiar Letters* into doing her an injustice. In one of Scott's letters to Lady Abercorn (1st June 1820) there is a reference to " Lady C." This is indexed in *Familiar Letters* as an allusion to Lady Charlotte Campbell. The " Lady C." in question was Lady Conyngham, mistress of the Prince Regent.

The letter is dated December, but I think Scott has, as often, given the wrong month, for Lady Charlotte Campbell's reply (in the Walpole collection) is dated 9th of November 1806 (P.M. Nov. 10 1806). She writes from " Hartwell House near Aylesbury Bucks an excellent place for Ghosts and Horrors " and says, " I . . . have been busily engaged trying to procure subscribers for our friend," which suggests some interval of time since Scott wrote.

not an unremembered friend, the privilege of intruding
upon you, by letter, in a cause which, I know, will somewhat interest you, who unite so remarkably the power of
procuring much with the wish to assist distress. I allude
to my old friend, and your acquaintance, the Ettrick
Shepherd (for I will not mention him by the unpoetical
name of Mr. James Hogg) who is now, as you will perceive
by the enclosure, venturing upon the public with a
collection of ballads. Some of them, if I (myself a ballad-
monger) may be permitted to judge, have a very uncommon share of poetical merit ; and the author of
these beautiful pieces, some of which I used to repeat to
you at the delightful attic evenings of —— street, is now
actually an hired servant. I have been exerting all the
little influence I possess to fill up such a subscription as
may enable him to stock a small farm from the profits ;
and I have been very successful here. I believe I may
claim something of a promise from —— and you to assist
me in this matter ; and as I know your influence in every
society which has the honour to possess your countenance,
I hope you will get me a few names for this miserable
son of the Muses.

I will not attempt to tell you the blank your absence
has made among your friends here. Pray remember me
most kindly to ——, and tell him I have not smoked a
single cigar since I saw him. I am sure it will give you
all pleasure to learn that Mrs. Scott and my little people
are well, and that the world is smiling on us through the
clouds. I have got an excellent situation ; it is however,
for the present, but a kind of Irish sinecure ; being all
work and no pay. But I have the word of my predecessor,
a very worthy gentleman, that he will not live unreason-
ably long, and on his death I succeed to a thousand a
year ; and meanwhile have the world, as they say, for the
winning.

I find Lord —— is in town, so I will endeavour to
procure a frank from him for this epistle ; for it would

be too bad to receive begging letters and pay postage
too.

I am, with great respect and regard, your most devoted
and faithful humble servant,   WALTER SCOTT

[*Diary illustrative of the times of George IV.*]

To LORD DALKEITH [1]

EDINR., CASTLE STREET,

23 *Nov.* [1806]

MY DEAR LORD DALKEITH Since I had the pleasure
of seeing you I have not had a moment till today to
think of the question you put to me ; for the printers
Devils & the fiends of the Law (the worst harpies of the
two) have had their fangs upon me for some time past.
And I now wish I may not fall far short of the satisfaction
I would always [want] to give any enquiry of yours
within the compass of my limited studies. But I will
do the best I can. I *understood* you *wishd* to know for
the information of my old friend and fellow collegian
Lord Selkirk [2] the circumstances which attended the
dismission of the superfluous population who occupied
the estates of the Border Chieftains when they were
converted into sheep-walks. There are particular difficulties which attend this investigation & make it in a

[1] This very interesting letter is printed in part by Lockhart with a good
many inaccuracies.

[2] Thomas Douglas, fifth Earl of Selkirk (1771-1820), a college friend of
Scott, had early interested himself in the economic condition of the Highlands and in 1792, after a tour through the districts, had resolved on a
large policy of emigration. Between 1802 and 1804 he settled large
numbers in Prince Edward Island. In 1806 (he succeeded to the title
in 1799) he was chosen one of the representative peers of Scotland, and
spoke and wrote on the question of defence. In 1805 he published *Observations on the Present State of the Highlands of Scotland with a View of the Causes
and Probable Consequences of Emigration* (second edition, 1806). It is doubtless
in this connection that he has asked about the earlier history of the Borders.
In 1811 he began his efforts to colonise the Red River, which led to such
long and bitter conflict with the North-West Company.

great measure obscure compared to the history of the same change which has taken place in our own day in the Highlands.

The State of the Borders before the accession of James VI. & of the Highlands strictly resembled each other with respect to internal circumstances. The patriarchal right or dominion of a Chieftain of a Clan over those of the same name & who were presumed to be of the same family with himself a right of dominion the most ancient in the world was acknowledged in both countries while the authority exercised by the lowland Scottish nobles & barons depended upon the feudal principle of Superior & vassal or upon that of Landlord and tenant. This is proved by the Act of James VIths parliament 1587 where a roll is made up of the clans in the Borders & Highlands who lived under the patriarchal dominion of the Captains & Chieftains " oftimes " says the Statute " against the will of their landlords on whose grounds they live." The change which took place at the union of the Crowns upon the border clans chiefly respected the crushing of this patriarchal or *clannish* authority if I may call it so. There were also measures taken & apparently very prudently to remove from the country many of those fiery and unruly spirits who had hitherto been maintaind by the Border chiefs to serve in their quarrels & who had subsisted chiefly by spoil & depredation. Your Lordships Ancestor Walter the first Earl of Buccleuch formed a Legion of these free-booters who served under him in the Dutch wars against the Spaniard from which probably few of them returnd.

A whole Clan (the Graemes[1]) were transported to Ireland by an order of James's privy Council. Repeated and severe executions under the authority of the Earl of Dunbar thind or dispersed the rest of the Border Riders who had subsisted by depredation. But it would be a

[1] See Scott's Introduction to the *Minstrelsy*. Scott's reference to this brought him into correspondence later (1817) with one of the Irish Grahams.

mistake to suppose that these changes (although un-questionably they draind off the more enterprizing and warlike of the Borderers) had any immediate effect upon the population at large.

Sir William Scott of Harden who wrote in the end of the 17th century an account of Roxburghshire and who is the best possible authority as the representative of a Border Leader of great note says that before the accession of James to the English Crown no rent was paid on the border excepting man service in war & some little ack-nowledgements known by the name of hereyeld & other feudal prestations. Some change must very shortly have taken place in this respect so soon as the safety of the country was so ascertaind that the Laird had more need for money than for men. But the change seems to have been very slow & gradual. The Borders were not like the Highlands surrounded by a country in a civilized state whose stock & farmers were ready to rush in upon this change of manners to fill the purses of the Landlords & to empty the land of its ancient military tenants. On the contrary the rest of Scotland was so poor & its inhabitants so uninstructed in the art of farming to advantage, in short the difference between the Borders & the interior was comparatively so small that I suspect no change of inhabitants took place at all but that the descendants of the old *reivers* or such of them as were reclaimd beat their own swords & their fathers into ploughshares & sat down to do their best in cultivating their own country instead of plundering their neighbours. Besides as I have already mentiond although the patriar-chal power of the Chieftains was broken, those who were landed proprietors retaind their feudal authority over their vassals & tenants. Neither was the 17th Century so secure as to induce any one to increase his rent-roll at the risk of greatly diminishing his retainers. The frequent civil wars, and the unsettled state of the country must have greatly retarded the progress of those causes of depopulation which have operated with such rapidity in the Highlands where there was nothing to balance the Landlords natural desire to make the most he could of his property except the pride of some individuals & the compassion of others. It must also be considered that during the 17th Century there was comparatively little of our Border country occupied by sheepwalks. Black cattle were in high estimation & the number of hands necessary to attend this kind of stock is much more numerous than that requisite for sheep. I do not therefore think that the union of the Crowns although it broke the warlike & turbulent spirit of the borders had any immediate effect on the extent of the population. But within 80 years after that event the bond between chieftain & kinsman seems to have been much broken. To take the individual case of our own Clan these patriarchal notions seem to have been much diminishd by the Duchess of Monmouth [1] marrying & residing in England. Scott of Satchells [2] whose doggerel poetry contains sometimes a peep at manners complains heavily of the alteration this had produced to the poor kinsfolk of the family.

In England now the Duchess dwells
Which to her friends is a curs'd fate
For if they famish starve or die
They cannot have a groat from that estate.
The times of old are quite forgot
How inferior friends had still relief
And how the worthiest of the name
Engaged themselves to hold up their chief etc.

[1] Ann, Countess of Buccleuch, second daughter of the second earl, was married in her twelfth year (1663) to the Duke of Monmouth, when they were created Duke and Duchess of Buccleuch. The Duke's honours were forfeited on his execution in July 1673 but that of the Duchess was unaffected. She married secondly Charles, Lord Cornwallis.

[2] See *Lockhart*, c. ii. for Walter Scott of Satchells and his *True History of several honourable Families of the Right Honourable Name of Scott in the Shires of Roxburgh & Selkirk and others adjacent gathered out of Ancient Chronicles, Histories and Traditions of our Fathers*. The author describes himself as " an old Souldier and no Scholler And one that can write nane But just the letters of his Name."

About this time as appears from the writing of the same elegant poet the sheep were universally introduced. Satchells served in the Regiment which Buccleuch carried to Holland & enlisted about 1627—he wrote his book in 1688 so he is tolerable traditional authority

A cause which hastend the conversion of the Border into sheep walks was the downfall of the small proprictors. Satchells names an hundred landed proprietors of the name of Scott living on the Borders in 1688 in which he could hardly be mistaken. I think in the same track of country we cannot now find ten. Each of these persons maintaind his little stile & had a few cottages round his old tower whose inhabitants made a desperate effort to raise some corn by scratching up the banks of the stream which winded through their glen. These are all gone & their followers have disappeard along with them. I suppose it became more & more difficult for them after the union of the Crowns to keep the " name & port of gentlemen " ; they fell into distress, sold their lands, & the farmers who succeeded them & had rent to pay to those who bought the estates got rid of the superfluous cottagers with all despatch. I have often heard my Grandmother & other old people talk of the *waefu'* year when seven Lairds of the Forest (all Scotts) became bankrupt at once but how or why I know not. The farmers when they had got rid of the inactive retainers of the small proprietors seem to have gone on for a long time reducing the number of the people on their farms. The ruins of cottages about every farm-house in the country show that this last cause of depopulation continued to operate till a very late period & indeed within the memory of Man. I could name many farms where the old people remember twenty *smoking chimneys* & where there are now not two. From all these considerations I am induced to think that the causes of depopulation on the Border although quite the same with those in the highlands occurd gradually & were insensible in their operation ; while the singular circumstance of the Highlands retaining their ancient manners till the Lowlands had attaind the highest pitch of civilization has occasiond their passing from a race of warriors into a handful of Shepherds in the course of fifty years a change not completely operated on the Border within three times the period. In evidence of this last circumstance I forgot to mention that in the time of the late Duke of Douglas [1] the Jedwood forest estate (now entirely a sheep-walk) was divided among sixty or seventy tenants who were bound to furnish three armd men on horseback each for their landlords military service. This was within the memory of man & Lord Douglas's tacks will show it.

I cannot but mention though it has no immediate reference to your Lordships inquiry that there seems to be an alteration of management fast creeping into the sheep-farms. It is now found impossible to put a full stock of sheep upon the farm during the summer unless provision is made to assist them with food in winter. This can only be done by the turnip husbandry & as that requires a great number of hands the farmers who do not lie near a town or village are as anxious to have cottagers upon their estates as they were formerly desirous of banishing them ; & this the more as they find by experience that they are more regular sober and manageable than hired servants, or labourers. In this way we may hope that our vallies will be gradually repeopled with a hardy and virtuous peasantry. As to our military propensities and attachment to such of the ancient Chiefs and Landholders as have retaind the ancient ideas towards their tenants I think I know one estate on which the proprietor might for a brush raise at least three

[1] Archibald, Marquess of Douglas, etc. (1694-1761) was in 1703 created Duke of Douglas, but died s.p. when the dukedom became extinct and the honours he inherited devolved on his cousin. He aided the Government in the rising of 1715, serving as a volunteer at Sheriffmuir, and in 1745.— The Complete Peerage. (See also D.N.B.) He was the brother of the heroine of the famous Douglas case, Lady Jane Douglas.

thousand men by the summons of his Baron officers. But in the general case the vulgar saying of " no longer pipe no longer dance " applies to Landlord & tenant Chieftain & clan Superior & vassal & in short to all the relations of mankind. Excuse this hurried and confused statement. I have been long in endeavouring to satisfy your Lordship's request & at length have done so in too great a hurry— My respectful Compliments to her Grace and all the family at Dalkeith but particularly to Lady D. I am anxious to hear that her Confinement has taken place & I am ever my dear Lord your Lordships most obedt & much obliged　　WALTER SCOTT

EDINR. CASTLE STREET 23 *November* [1806]

[*Buccleuch*]

To ARCHIBALD CONSTABLE [1]

ASHESTIEL *friday* [1806]

DEAR SIR,—I have given Mr. John Ballantyne the Dedication for Jamiesons Ballads [2] to the Dutchess of Gordon. You will I suppose think it right to bind up a copy smartly & send it to her Grace who may do much for the work. I will write to her on the subject when I hear your packet is about to go. Copies as from the Author should be sent, to the Reverend Mr. Smythe

---

[1] This letter is undated but the letter of 16th December to Jamieson implies that the book was out some time before, and so this letter must be at latest November.

[2] " Popular Ballads And Songs From Tradition, Manuscripts, And Scarce Editions with Translations Of Similar Pieces from the Ancient Danish Language And A Few Originals By The Editor By Robert Jamieson, A.M. and F.A.S. Edinburgh : Printed for Archibald Constable and Co., Edinburgh ; Cadell and Davies, and John Murray, London, 1806." Jamieson, a classical teacher at Macclesfield and later at Riga, had been at work collecting independently when he became aware of Scott's intention and work. Thereafter he found in Scott an active friend, and through his aid became assistant to the depute-clerk-register in the Register House, Edinburgh. We shall find him also co-operating with Scott and Weber in *Illustrations of Northern Antiquities*, Edinburgh, 1814.

St Peters College Cambridge—to Heber—to Dr. Jamieson —& to Dr. Robert Anderson perhaps you may know farther of his wishes than I do in this particular. Do not omit to send the Bard himself a copy. I will write to him on the subject & I hope the Book will do. I was much obliged by your kind attention in sending the Highland books of which I hope to give you news. I inclose an order on the Advocates Liby. for one or two books & I will be greatly obliged to you to send me "Foxes Martyrology" even your imperfect copy if you have not a better. Perhaps you can find me the books in case Mr. Gib has them not. Mr. Millar who takes me in his way to London will probably take charge of these books for me if you will have the goodness to cause them be tied up. When you or Mr. Hunter are in motion I should be happy to see you at this farm & am very truly always yours

WALTER SCOTT

Is there any news of Mr. Cliffords grande opus.[1]

Archibald Constable Esq

[*Stevenson*]

To ROBERT SYM, W.S., GEORGES SQUARE [2]

MY DEAR SIR,—I beg you to believe that it would have been the last thing in my thoughts to have taken offence at your observations on the lay when anonymous much more when avowd for *yours*. I would rather have a much more moderate portion of applause than you have thought meet to honour the Lay with, when accompanied with the flattering assurance which the critique infers of

---

[1] Clifford's *grande opus* was the *Sadler Papers* : see later.

[2] The Timothy Tickler of Wilson's (his nephew's) *Noctes Ambrosianae*. In April 1805 he wrote a detailed critique of the *Lay* which was transmitted to Scott through Constable. Scott appended defensive or explanatory notes and returned the MS., which is now in the National Library. Sym acknowledged on the 21st of November, and begged permission to keep the notes.

your having considerd it with critical accuracy than the
indiscriminate & unapropriate applause of most general
readers.   The little remarks I made on the criticism are
most heartily at your service.   I only designd them for a
freindly Critic but am much gratified at their falling into
the hands of a *critical freind*.   Believe me Sir with great
regard Your very humble Servt

 CASTLE STREET *Decr. 2d.* [1806] WALTER SCOTT

[*Mrs. Wilson*]

To ADAM FERGUSSON [1]

HAVING a few moments time at our black table & the
Bart in the abundance of his parliamentary connections
& freindships having promised to get me a *kiver* I think I
cannot employ time or a frank better than be [*sic*] enquiring
whether you have got rid of the unlucky Typhus which
I hear from the valiant knight aforesaid has laid its claws
upon you.   I hate to hear any of my freinds talk of a
disorder by its scientific name ; it is a sign it has taken a

[1] Adam Fergusson was at this time secretary to the Governor of the
Channel Islands and stationed at St. Helier. Braxie is Macqueen of
Braxfield (the "Weir of Hermiston") ; Cardrona is Mr. Williamson of
Cardrona, whose humours Scott celebrated later in Malachi Malagrowther ;
Hermand, Polkemmet and Bannatyne are three judges of the Court of
Session. The murdered man was Begbie, whose murderer was never
discovered.   In a note on the case Scott says : " Circumstances have gone
far to fix this cruel and mysterious crime on one, a surgeon in Leith,
respectably connected and married to the daughter of a worthy and
substantial burgher of Edinburgh. . . . This lad was a profligate and
spendthrift, who had exhausted his patrimony, and was in great necessity
at the time of the murder. Soon afterwards he became possessed of money,
paid his debts, and seemed to live well without any sensible addition of
means.   His discourse frequently turned on the murder of Begbie, and the
story seemed to haunt him.   I have been told that suspicion had
approached him very nearly, when he committed suicide. The thing
was then smothered, through respect to the feelings of his connections."
Scott had seen the knife with which the crime was committed, " a
remarkable one, such as bread is sliced with, having a wooden handle ;
the blade was short, broad, and keenly tempered ; it had the shop-mark
of the person who sold it, and the shop grease was still upon it, so that it
had never been used but for the fatal purpose. It had been prepared for
the deed by grinding the extremity to a sharp point and double edge."
Compare Cockburn's *Memorials*, etc.

I   Y

little hold of his mind & that he has made further investigation about it than is consistent with the idea of its
being a transient guest. I beg therefore that the Typhus
may as speedily as possible assume the more humble
denomination of a feverish cold unless you mean to be set
down amond [*sic*] the learnd Lord Admirals catalogue
of scientific infirmities. You know our old freind Braxie
cut short one of Maconochies learned queries about the
vena cava " Hout awa' wi' your Macavas Mr. Macono-
chie " even so say I hout awa' wi' your Typhus Mr.
Secretary— When you shall have got quite stout which
I hope and trust will be by the time this reaches you I
will absolutely envy your situation in Jersey where there
must be so many things both curious and entertaining.
Claret in plenty for noonday and right nantz for discussion of a midnight chat. Blithe French lasses with
their black eyes and national vivacity scratching each
other for the honour of dancing & flirting with Mr.
Secretary. With what contempt you must recollect
a nipperkin of whiskey punch and the lang traind frost
bitten Dearies of your ci-devant freind Cardrona. But
instead of writing nonsense you will expect no doubt
that I should give you a little news from Auld Reekie.
I presume you will be little edified or entertaind by an
extract from my new work which is to be entitled Clerk
Scotts decisions & is to come out on cream coloured wire
wove paper printed by Ballantyne with a vignette to each
number :   the first to represent Hermand *rampant*,
Polkemmet *couchant* and Bannatyne *dormant*. I will
therefore tell you concisely that the country gentlemen
are cutting each others throats about politics while the
blackguards of the town have more sensibly *done* an
unfortunate porter who was loaded with £6000 belonging
to the British Linen Company & was murdered in
day light at the head of the Bank office close & within
20 yards of their secretary. He was most dexterously
dispatchd with a single stab through the very heart

so that he died without a single groan & the assassin escaped with his booty. I declare this story makes me growze whenever I think of it. The man is probably in the better ranks of life from the precautions & desperation of the action very likely somebody on the verge of bankruptcy that awful interval when the best men are apt to become knaves & those who are naturally bad are quite desperate. If this be the Case he will probably never be discoverd unless by some mere chance as he will not like a low ruffian be either suspected from the quantity of the booty or obliged to fly from his habitation.

I had but a lonely time at Ashestiel this year and often wished we could see you and Bob *looming* upon the Peebles road ; almost my only companion if that is not two [*sic*] free a word for a great Lord of the Bed Chamber was our neighbour Lord Somerville. It is a pity to think how we who were so inseparable in former days are now squanderd abroad & sequesterd at home. Poor Edmonstounes [1] health is I fear irrecoverable & what makes it more melancholy if possible his health I mean his bodily health seems I understand to gain ground as his mental faculties give way. I understand that there is a plan certainly the most advantageous in his situation that a pension equivalent to the salary of the Shruffdom [*sic*] shall be settled on him & Mrs. E. for their joint lives & then the Bart will I hope succeed to Bute.

Pray write to me soon and let me know that you are well and happy We very often think and talk of you and it [would] make you too vain were I to tell you how much you are regretted here.

Charlotte sends your [*sic*] her kindest remembrances— the Laird of Gilnockie has got short clothes & promises to be a strapper. Believe me ever yours affectionately

EDINR. 16 *Decr.* 1806   WALTER SCOTT

Given from our black table

[*Bayley*]

---

[1] See note, p. 26.

To ROBERT JAMIESON, RIGA

EDINBURGH, 16 *Decr.* 1806

My DEAR SIR,—I was yesterday surprised to find by a letter of yours, dated on the 15th November, that you have not got two of mine, written since the publication of your book. In the last I mentioned what I now have the pleasure to repeat, that the ballads have been very well received by the public, and Constable is pleased with the sale. Since that time there has been a pretty rough attack from the " Critical Review," arising, I suppose, from the connexion which Mr. Pinkerton has with that Journal. He is returned from Paris, and probably was not particularly gratified with the notice taken of him in your preface. This, however, is but a conjecture of mine. Constable long ago shipped for you the books you wanted from Leith. The vessel was driven back and the books re-landed and shipped in another vessel. There were also several sets, four or five [I] think, he says of your own work, and I am truly surprised and sorry to find that the package has not reached you. I cannot but hope you have ere now received one at least of my letters. I wish with all my heart you were safe in Scotland. Mr. Thomson, who has been lately named deputy of the Lord Register, has great occasion for assistance from some person as well acquainted as you are with old hands and Scottish antiquities. He is a noble-minded fellow, and would strain a point to make your situation comfortable, if you would think of assisting him in his department, which is the Ancient Records and Diplomata of Scotland. I suppose that as this sort of labour is very well paid, you might be sure of from £150 to £200 a year to begin with, and every effort would be made to place you on a more permanent footing. When I say £150 or £200, I mean that as this is a kind of piece-work—Mr. Thomson would put it in your power to execute work to that amount. You could easily combine this labour with that of teaching a scholar or two, if you were so disposed. We would, of course, keep the Library in our eye, as it must open one day. In short, you would be on the spot ; and although my friends are not at present in power, so that, like Noodle in Tom Thumb, I am on the side of the malcontents, yet things may turn round again when I will have some chance of being listened to. I am sensible this is a very small thing, but it gives you a footing in your native country, and connects you with a most excellent man whom I am sure you would have every reason to be pleased with.

I must not omit to mention that your Norse translations came safe and are printed in your collection. The principal blunder in the work was the mutilating the battle of Belrinnes, which has not been discovered by the " Critical " critic. As I am very uncertain as to this letter's fate, I will rather repeat what I have said in another than prolong it at present. All your friends are well, and the country is *one and all*. Believe me, yours most truly,　　　　　　　　　　　WALTER SCOTT

[*Rosebery*]

To ROBERT SURTEES

DEAR SIR,—I was much obliged and interested by your long and curious letter.[1] The fray between the Ridleys

---

[1] This is the letter in which Surtees palmed off on Scott as genuine a ballad on the " Feud between the Ridleys and the Featherstones, from the recital of an old woman of Alston Moor," with glossarial explanations and historical notes, and along with this a professed extract from a MS. note in a copy of Burthogge on the Nature of Spirits. Scott introduced the ballad as a valuable gem of antiquity into a note on the first Canto of *Marmion*. The extract is also given in a note and from it Scott derived the episode of Marmion's encounter with an Elfin Knight. Both ballad and Latin extract were concoctions of Surtees. In the same letter Surtees goes on to urge Scott to take up " the interesting periods of 15 and 45. Whilst Scotland can boast a minstrel, why is posterity to trace those interesting periods only in the cold pages of a professed historian ? . . . Your poems, original and collected, and the wonderful fund of information and entertainment in the Notes, already incontestably present the best existing history of the times you undertake to illustrate ; and the periods I allude to must, I think, afford materials little less interesting." This is probably the impulse which led to the tale of *Waverley*.

and the Featherstonehaughs is extremely curious, and seems to have been such a composition as that in the Border Minstrelsy called the " Fray of Suport," [1] which I have heard sung. I will certainly insert it, with your permission, in the next edition of that work ; and I am only sorry that it will be some time before I can avail myself of it, as the third edition is just out of press. Your notes upon the parties concerned give it all the interest of authenticity, and it must rank, I suppose, among those half-serious, half-ludicrous songs in which the poets of the Border delighted to describe what they considered as the *sport* of *swords*. It is, perhaps, remarkable, though it may be difficult to guess a reason, that these Cumbrian ditties are of a different stanza, character, and obviously sung to a different kind of music, from those on the Northern Border. The gentleman who collected the words may, perhaps, be able to describe the tune. That of the Fray of Suport is a wild rude kind of recitative, with a very outrageous chorus. The Raid of Rookhope, such parts of it at least as I have seen, resemble extremely the Fray of Suport, and the verses you have so kindly sent me ; and none of them are like any Scottish ballad I ever saw.

You flatter me very much by pointing out to my attention the feuds of 1715 and 45 :—the truth is, that the subject has often & deeply interested me from my earliest youth. My great-grandfather was *out*, as the phrase goes, in Dundee's wars, and in 1715 had nearly the honour to be hanged for his pains, had it not been for the interest of Duchess Anne of Buccleuch and Monmouth, to whom I have attempted, *post longo intervallo*, to pay a debt of gratitude. But, besides this, my father, although a Borderer, transacted business for many Highland lairds, and particularly for one old man, called Stuart of Invernahyle, who had been out both in 1715 and 1745, and whose tales were the absolute delight of

[1] An ancient Border gathering song in very irregular verse.

my childhood. I believe there never was a man who united the ardour of a soldier and tale-teller, or man of talk, as they call it in Gaelic, in such an excellent degree ; and as he was as fond of telling as I was of hearing, I became a valiant Jacobite at the age of ten years old ; and, even since reason & reading came to my assistance, I have never quite got rid of the impression which the gallantry of Prince Charles made on my imagination. Certainly I will not renounce the idea of doing something to preserve these stories, and the memory of times and manners, which, though existing as it were yesterday, have so strangely vanished from our eyes. Whether this will be best done by collecting the old tales, or by modernizing them, as subjects of legendary poetry, I have never very seriously considered ; but your kind encouragement confirms me in the resolution that something I must do, and speedily. I would be greatly obliged to you for the " Good Night of Lord Derwentwater." I have a stale copy of a ballad so entitled, very similar to that published by Ritson, in a small thin 12mo. entitled the Northumberland Garland, or some such thing. Ritson's copy and mine agree in the main, and begin

> " Mackintosh was a soldier brave,
> And of his friends he took his leave,
> Toward Northumberland he drew, . . .
> Marching along with a valiant crew."

This is a miserable ditty in all respects ; and, as it does not contain either of the verses in your letter, I hope yours is either entirely another song, or a very superior edition of the same.

The extract of the ghostly combat, between Bulmer and his aerial adversary, is like the chapter of a romance, and very curious. I am much obliged to you for the trouble you have taken of transcribing it. The story of the nocturnal proclamation at the cross of Edinburgh, summoning all the leaders of the Scottish army to appear before the tribunal of Plotcock (Pluto, I suppose,) occurs in Pitscottie's History of Scotland.[1] I think he gives it on the authority of the person who heard the proclamation ; and, hearing his own name in the citation of the infernal herald, appealed from Plotcock's tribunal to that of God, and threw a florin over the balcony in which he was walking, in evidence of his protest. He was the only man of the number cited who escaped death at the fatal field of Flodden. I have some part of a poem or tale upon this subject, which I will be happy to shew you one day.

Once more, my dear sir, pray persevere in your kind intentions towards me, and do not let me lose the benefit your correspondence holds out to, Dear Sir, Your most obliged humble servant, WALTER SCOTT

EDINBURGH, 17 *December*, 1806.

[*Abbotsford Copies and Surtees Memoir*]

To GEORGE HOME [2]

[1806]

MY DEAR SIR,—Will you pardon the vanity of an author in hoping a copy of a new edition of his work may not be unacceptable to you as a man of letters & an ancient borderer. It contains some lines on p. 138 relative to the Homes of Wedderburn & the Swintons (my own maternal ancestors) with a few others which were added since the Quarto edition I am ever with great regard Dear Sir Your obliged & faithful Servant

CASTLE STREET *Friday* W. SCOTT

[*1871 Exhibition Catalogue*]

---

[1] See Notes to *Marmion*.

[2] The Clerk of Session whose work Scott took over, leaving the salary to Home till a later period, when, as the letters will show, difficulties arose under the new Judicature Act.

1807

EDINBURGH, 13 *January* 1807

ACCORDING to all the usual forms of correspondence my dear Miss Seward I ought to apologise for not having long ere now done myself the honour of replying to your very flattering and interesting letter. But what shall I say unless I were to lay the blame on that vile to-morrow in favour of which we make so many unfullfilled vows and promises. Moreover the Dœmin of politics being unchained has for some time passd involved even the most peaceable and retired in the whirlwind which he guides. Thank heaven the storm is over for a few years & leaves us only the mournful prospect of the torn friendships and wrecked honour which [we] have sufferd in its transit. As for my own affairs [1] about which you enquire a little in the end of your letter I believe they are rather different from yours and therefore I shall say very little about them. I was not only very early disposed to what have been called Tory principles by the opinions of those whom I respected & was bound to respect but the favours I received the intimacy in which I lived with many of Lord Mellville's family his nephew & son in particular, was founded as much upon attachment to their measures in 1792-3 as to gratitude for favours received at a time when they were truly valuable. And so we will let that matter rest only that I sympathize deeply

---

[1] Miss Seward in the letter of Sept. 23 had written : "Politics having never been a theme of our letters, I know not whether you deplore with me the extinction of that bright luminary whose fifteen years earlier ascent in the zenith would have preserved, by its benign and pacific influence, the freedom of the continent, and averted from Britain all her present difficulties and dangers." The reference is to Fox.

in the loss of Mr. Foxes high talents at a time when the country never needed them more & that I am candid enough to esteem the principles & cherish the [friendship] of many whose political opinions are different from my own, because I know they are adopted by those who hold them from an internal conviction of their rectitude.

I am quite delighted with your enthusiasm about Madoc and begin to be a convert to your arguments on the discrimination of his character Still I stop short with Agrippa & it is only " almost thou persuadest me." To the extreme beauty of his landscape painting and to much of his energetic description of battles and more peaceful [scenes] I have always renderd full justice. I am aware of the connection which his tale has with the ancient history of Wales but Sir Richard Hoares translation of Giraldus will make that connection more generally known. It is a very splendid work although I think the price is renderd injudiciously extravagant by the number of engravings. Indeed the price of new Books in general is an increasing evil and will be producing bad consequences by placing new publications beyond the reach of those to whom the[y] would be most acceptable and probably most useful. But books are no longer solely respected for their insides since they have been honourd with admission into the drawing room which although a very pleasing & sensible transition from the stiffness of ancient manners when every guest was obliged to sit with hands across & listen to the prosing of such as could prose, has nevertheless contributed greatly to render Books expensive as elegant pieces of furniture. The great genius who invented the gilded inlaid or Japan bookstands for boudoirs & drawing rooms did a great service to the print engraver & bookseller, but I question if literature in general has not sufferd from the invention.

We had the pleasure of Mrs. Jacksons company a few

days ago upon our return from the Country where we had passed the Christmas holidays, & will endeavour to shew her every attention in our power, as well for the sake of her own lively & good-humourd conversation as for your highly valued recommendation. I wish I could promise myself that I had any prospect of paying my personal respects to you at Litchfield which your name & that of the great Lexicographer have made so classical. But although I have some thoughts of being in London in spring I doubt much whether I can achieve my long intended purpose of returning by the western side of the island & visiting in my journey many [friends][1] of which I have only heard and some [others with whom][1] I have only corresponded. [You[1] will I feel sure] be interested in learning that I have [now][1] laid aside my Highland poem. The truth is it would require a journey of some length into the country not only to refresh my faded or inaccurate recollection of the scenery ; But also to pick up some of the traditions still floating in the memory of the inhabitants. I am at a great loss also from not understanding the language of that enthusiastic . . . [bottom of page (probably 7 lines) missing] . . . the fatal battle of Flodden & I think I will call it Flodden Field. Each canto is to be introduced by a little digressive poem which for want of a better name may be calld an epistle. I have disbanded on this occasion all my border riders although I may come to want their assistance as much as the King is said to have done that of Johnie Armstrong after he was hanged. In . . . [end of MS. missing—probably six lines and signature].

 Miss Seward Litchfield

[British Museum]

     [1] Damaged by seal.

To JAMES LONGMAN

[Draft]

DEAR SIR,—I have your favour and I am truly sorry to see that you are disposed to consider continuance of the connection of Constable & Co [1] as an absolute bar to your accepting my new work—I cannot suppose any performance of mine of sufficient consequence to induce you to surmount the feelings which you express & upon my own part I can add little to what I have said in my former letter. I did not think it necessary upon former occasions nor indeed upon the present to state an explicit condition on this subject in the outset of the transaction because I was sensible & the event has proved it that your own delicacy would prevent your changing the Edinburgh Editor of any of my publications without previously consulting me. Indeed knowing the unfortunate disagreement between the houses has not prevented your names standing together on the Lay and Edinburgh Review I certainly hoped that so far as I a mutual friend was concernd matters might have tacitly gone on in the same channel without even the appearance of my interfering. I beg to assure you that I am neither actuated in this matter by caprice or obstinacy but feel

[1] " It was during his first visit to London, in March 1795, that my father was introduced to Mr. Longman. Their acquaintance soon ripened into friendship, and it is much to be regretted that misunderstandings, from apparently conflicting interests which afterwards arose, should even occasionally have interrupted a commerce so advantageous to both parties. It had been well for Archibald Constable and Co. had it been otherwise. The unfortunate experiment of the establishment of a London House in 1809 would thereby have been averted, and the catastrophe of 1826 might never have occurred."—*Archibald Constable and his Literary Correspondents*, i. 43-44. The trouble seems to have begun in 1804 and been at its height in 1806, when John Murray took Longman's place in Constable's intimacy. It was probably Hunter who here, as with Scott, was the cause of trouble. " Mr. Hunter was a high-minded and I must say honourable man, but of warm temper, and out of that perhaps these quarrels originated, more than anything else."—Note by Constable, *op. cit.*, i. 339. In the letter of 13th January which Scott is here answering, Longmans speak of " the yet unexplained insults we have received from them."

that by giving up this point I would sanction a severe treatment of a house which has been very useful to Scottish literature : [1] whatever their demerits may be towards you [they] have certainly deserved no slight at my hand.

I regret perhaps with more reason than you that any thing should happen to interrupt the connection which has so long subsisted between us with mutual satisfaction. I beg Mr. Rees & you will accept my assurances of uninterrupted regard & that all the gentlemen of your house will believe that nothing will give me more pleasure than a renewal of our correspondence on some more fortunate occasion.   I am etc.

[Unsigned]

EDINBURGH 27th January [1807]

[Stevenson]

To ARCHIBALD CONSTABLE & CO.

GENTLEMEN,—I am favoured with your letter in which referring to our previous communing you agree to pay one thousand guineas for the poem [2] which I am now engaged in ; the copy money to be paid at my conveniency & the property to be divided between you Mr. Miller & Mr. Murray [3] in the proportions you mention in all which I acquiesce with pleasure and am wishing you all success. Gentlemen Your most obedient Servt

WALTER SCOTT

EDINR. 31 January 1807

Messrs. Archd. Constable & Co

Booksellers Edinr.

[Stevenson]

[1] I have inserted a colon and the word [they] to clear up this sentence. Scott was to find Hunter as disagreeable a person to deal with as Longmans had.

[2] i.e. Marmion.

[3] Murray took the place of Longmans, writing to Scott on 25th January.— Walpole Collection.

To LADY ABERCORN

Mrs. Scott is quite ashamed and sorry that she has not been able to furnish the transcript which she intends for your Ladyship's acceptance. The trifles it contains have been so long dispersed that she has found it a very difficult matter to get copies of them from those into whose possession they had gone. She has now recovered all she thinks worth preserving and is busy with her copy.

Meanwhile in acknowledgement of your Ladyship's kind & flattering enquiries after my engagements I have put under two covers the first sheet of a poem with which I have been for some time closely engaged when my official attendance upon the Court here & my engagements with Dryden would permit. I beg that the verses may not go out of your Ladyships own hand as I may probably make some alterations in them before the final publication. The sheet now sent forms the Introduction to the 1st Canto of a legendary poem called " Marmion or a Tale of Flodden Field." Each canto is to have an introductory epistle of the same kind & I hope to have the pleasure of shewing your Ladyship this new poem at least a considerable part of it very soon as I hope I may get to town about the beginning or rather towards the middle of March. I am quite pleased that your Ladyship has forgot the ancient ditties with which I had the honour of entertaining you at the Priory last spring because I may in that case hope you will not be displeased to hear some of them again. One of my principal reasons for visiting London this spring is that I may avail myself of your ladyships goodness in procuring me a passport to the Dorset papers. I am much bent on rendering the edition of Dryden as perfect as I can & I find my northern situation is too remote for procuring all the necessary information.

Lord Melville is here for the present with his lady. I have seen them several times & dine there today. We

are all in a bustle here with a new Bill introduced by
Lord Grenville to alter the organisation of our Courts of
Justice in which I am deeply concerned as they intend
totally to change the nature of our offices & what is more
formidable the mode of paying us—I suppose however
we shall not be losers for of course no administration is
anxious to reduce the value of situations which fall
within their own gift—I hope to bring up Mrs. Scott's
Manuscript along with me & to have the honour of
presenting it myself.

There has been a new Edition of the Minstrel : [1] the few
additional verses are printed apart & I shall bring a
sheet or two of them with me to complete the copies of
my friends & particularly that at Stanmore priory.

I have not troubled your Ladyship with these leaves [?]
sooner partly because they were not finished to my mind
(as indeed they are not yet) & partly because I know that
the holidays are always a busy as well as a merry time
at the Priory. Believe me with every sentiment of
respect & regard in which Mrs. Scott sincerely joins [2]
Lady Abercorn's most faithful humble servant

W. Scott

11th Feb. 1807.

[Pierpont Morgan]

To MISS SEWARD

My dear Miss Seward,—I take an early opportunity
to send you the promised specimen of my new poem
and at the same time to request your acceptance of a
small volume of poetry[3] written by one of our Country

---

[1] I have inserted a colon.

[2] " Tell Mrs. Scott not to be jealous of my admiration of her Husband
and tell her how very kind I think it of Her to take so much trouble to
collect all those TRIFLES of yours."—Lady Abercorn to Scott, 10th February.

[3] *The Mountain Bard*, by James Hogg, the Ettrick Shepherd. Edinburgh
1807. Dedicated to Walter Scott, Esq., Sheriff of Ettrick Forest.

Shepherds[1] which, if you can wade through the Scotch will repay you for the labour. If upon perusal you should like the poems you would do me a great kindness to give the little volume that celebrity among your literary friends which you can so easily confer by your recommendation. The Author gives a most literal & very curious account of his life and studies in the preface & is upon the whole a very interesting person. The success of his Book is of some consequence to him as it may assist him in stocking a small farm which he has taken & where he will probably succeed very well as he is not only a good Ballad writer but a most excellent shepherd. I know nobody that understands the diseases of the sheep so well or faces the tempests more hardily. In short he is a very deserving character and I am deeply interested in his fate now that he is about to emerge from his state of Servitude. A friend who goes up to London has promised to find some mode of sending this safe to Litchfield. I have not yet seen Capt. Hastings [2]—I returnd his call after a days interval but I find he is gone to the country for fourteen days. I will undoubtedly wait upon him at his return & solicit his acquaintance ; from which I need not say I promise myself much pleasure when I consider the terms in which you mention him.

I have at length fixed on the title of my new poem which is to be christend from the principal character

[1] Miss Seward replies to this letter on the 16th April, and of Hogg she writes : " Now to your mountain bard, James Hogg,—luckless name ! . . . He is another poetic miracle, rising up from the lowest of your peasantry. Though I do not believe that he will ever reach the heights which Burns ascended, or ever produce a poem of such length, consequence, and interest as Bloomfield . . . yet . . . I perceive vivid and not infrequent flashes of real genius."

[2] In her letter of 29th January Anna writes : " Captain Hastings, the deprived, the intelligent, the excellent, sets out in a day or two for your city." He had lost an arm in the 1807 attack on Copenhagen. The story of his sensibility and heroism, worthy of Captain Toby, is related in the sixty-ninth of her printed letters. He thought the subject of *Marmion* " tender ground for your patriotism ; to question if it might not wound the known nationality of the Scotch to see celebrity and poetic immortality given, and that by a native, to the most disastrous event in their military annals."

Marmion or a Tale of Flodden Field. There are to be
six Cantos & an introductory Epistle to each in the stile
of that which I send to you as a specimen. In the
legendary part of the work " Knights Squires and Steeds
shall enter on the Stage." I am not at all afraid of my
patriotism being a sufferer in the course of the tale. It
is very true that my friend Leyden has said

> Alas that Scottish Maid should sing
> The Combat where her lover fell
> That Scottish Bard should wake the string
> The triumph of our foes to tell.

But we may [say] with Francis I that at Flodden ' all
was lost *but our honour* ' an exception which includes
everything that is desirable for a poet.

As to my editorial labours they are not in the state of
forwardness which Mr. White supposes.[1] It is very true
that for two years past I have been occasionally labouring
on a complete edition of Drydens Works which have
never been collected. I hope it will be out by Xmas
next the illustration of the poetical & historical passages
have cost me much labour

> From my research the boldest spiders fled
> And moths retreating trembled as I read

As for poetry it is very little labour to me indeed 't were
pity of my life should I spend much time on the light &
loose sort of poetry which alone I can pretend to write.
Were all the time I wasted upon the Lay put together
for it was laid aside for long intervals I am sure it would
not exceed six weeks—the last Canto was written in
three forenoons when I was lying in quarters with our
Yeomanry. I leave it with yourself to guess how little
I can have it in my most distant imagination to place

[1] " Mr. White has recently told me that you had published a voluminous
edition of Dryden. . . . I almost grieve that you . . . should employ your
golden hours in removing the leaden incrustations of former editors."
" Dryden, Spencer and Chaucer have, in my opinion, been overpraised . . .
not one of them equals yourself or Southey."

I   Z

myself upon a level with the great bards you have mentiond the very latchets of whose shoes neither Southey nor I are worthy to unloose. My admiration of Chaucer Spenser and Dryden does not blind me to their faults for I see the coarsness of the first the tediousness occasiond by the continued allegory of the second and the inequalities of the last but my dear Miss Seward " in these days were giants in the land " and we are but dwarfs beside them.

I am infinitely obliged by your sending me your tribute to the memory of the immortal Garrick. How much I envy those who have seen that abridgement of all that was pleasant in man. But we have Siddons though less extended in her range yet not surely less excellent and for what we have received let us be thankful in Gods name. I think I must be in London about the middle of next month. My stay will be but short and I dare not flatter myself that my time will permit me to execute the plan I have so often projected of returning by the western road. Should I be so fortunate as to find it otherwise I will not fail to take an early opportunity of endeavouring to accomodate my motions so as might best suit your time for it would be mortifying to run any risque of disappointing myself of the pleasure of being personally known to you. I am with great regard Dear Madam Your most faithful humble Servant

EDINR. 20th feby [1807]   WALTER SCOTT

May I beg particularly that you will on no account trust the verses out of your own custody or suffer them to be copied—

[British Museum]

To ROBERT SURTEES.

MY DEAR SIR,—I cannot express how much I am obliged to you for your kind communications, which

I value as I ought to do. The Raid of Rookhope,[1] so
unexpectedly recovered, is a very curious piece ; and
rendered much more so by your illustrations. I willingly
acknowledge Mr. Frank's kindness, by sending such of
his uncle's letters as I have been able to recover. I think
I have one or two more, but I fear they are at my farm
in Ettricke Forest. Mr. Frank is perfectly at liberty to
print any part of them he pleases, excepting those
passages round which I have put a circumflex with a
black-lead pencil, which he will see reasons for my wishing
omitted. I had a great kindness for poor Mr. Ritson ;
and always experienced from him the readiest, kindest,
& most liberal assistance in the objects of our joint pursuit,
in which he was so well qualified to direct the researches of
an inferior antiquary. One thing I observed in his
temper, an attention to which rendered communication
with him much more easy than if it was neglected : it
was, that Mr. Ritson was very literal and precise in his
own statements, and, expecting you to be equally so, was
much disgusted with any loose or inaccurate averment.
I remember rather a ludicrous instance of this. He made
me a visit of two days at my cottage near Laswade, where
I then spent the summer. In the course of conversing on
such subjects, we talked of the Roman Wall ; and I was
surprized to find that he had adopted, on the authority of
some person at Hexham, a strong persuasion that its
remains were nowhere apparent, at least not above a foot
or two in height. I hastily assured him that this was so
far from being true, that I had myself seen a portion of
it standing almost entire, high enough to break a man's
neck. Of this Ritson took a formal memorandum, and
having visited the place (Glenwhelt, near Gilsland), he
wrote back to me, or rather I think to John Leyden, " that
he had seen the wall ; that he really thought that a fall
from it *would* break one's neck ; at least it was so high as

---

[1] Surtees had got for Scott from Mr. Frank, Ritson's nephew and executor,
a copy of *The Raid* from among Ritson's papers. Frank had asked for
letters of Ritson for a projected biography. See note, p. 298.

to render the experiment dangerous." I immediately
saw what a risk I had been in, for you may believe I had
no idea of being taken quite so literally. I was very
indignant at the insult offered to his memory, in one of
the periodical publications, after his decease, imputing
the unfortunate malady with which he was afflicted to
providential vengeance and retribution, for which the
editor, in exact retributive justice, deserved to be damned
for a brutal scoundrel.

As a friend going towards London has promised to drop
the parcel containing Ritson's letters at Rushyford, I add
a small volume of ancient modern ballads and traditions,
composed by one of our shepherds,[1] (I do not speak in
Arcadian phrase, but in literal Ritsonian strictness) of
which I beg your acceptance. You will, I think, be
pleased both with the prose and verse of this little publication ; and if you can give it any celebrity among your
friends who may admire ancient lore, you will do service
to a worthy and ingenious lad, who is beating up against
the tide of adversity.

I must now tell you (for I think your correspondence
has been chiefly the cause of it) that, by calling my attention back to these times and topics which we have been
canvassing, you are likely to occasion the world to be
troubled with more border minstrelsy. I have made
some progress in a legendary poem, which is to be
entitled, " Marmion, or a Tale of Flodden-Field." It is
in six Cantos, each having a *l'envoy*, or introductory
epistle, in more modern verse. In the first Canto I have
introduced a verse of the Thirlwalls, &c. Marmion, on
an embassy to Scotland, is entertained at Norham Castle,
by Heron, the Captn of that fortress.

> " He led Lord Marmion to the dais,
>   Placed o'er the pavement high,
> And placed him in the upper place ;
>   They feasted full and high.

[1] That is, of course, Hogg.

Meanwhile a Northern harper rude,
Chaunted a rhyme of deadly feud :—
' How the fierce Ridleys and Thirlwalls all,
    Stout Willemoteswick,
    And Hard-Riding Dick,
And Hughie of Hawdon, and Will of the Wall,
Have set on Sir Albany Featherstonehaugh,
And taken his life at the Deadman's Shaw.'
Scantly Lord Marmion's ear could brook
    The harper's barbarous lay ;
Yet much he praised the pains he took,
    And well those pains did pay ;
For lady's suit and minstrel's strain
By Knight should ne'er be heard in vain."

In the notes I will give your copy of the ballad and your learned illustrations. Holy Island is one of my scenes : also Whitby. I have occasion for an Abbess of Whitby, and also for a Nunnery at Lindisfarne. There were nuns in both places, as well as monks ; both of the order of St. Benedict : but I suspect I am bringing them down too late by several centuries ; this, however, I shall not greatly mind. I fear I shall be obliged to go to London this spring, which may throw me behind in my poetical labours, which, however, are already pretty well advanced.

I wonder what other ballads Mr. Ritson intended to insert in the little collection, of which the Raid of Rookhope is one ; and should like very much to have a complete set of the leaves, if Mr. Frank could favour me so far. If he has any intention of publishing them, I will with pleasure postpone my curiosity. The Latin song, which you mention as a favourite of the old heroe of 1745, was probably Kennedy's *Praelium Gillicrankiense*, in leonine Latin, which I translated into doggrel verse, at Ritson's instance, and for his collection. If Mr. Frank wishes to have those verses which are alluded to in Mr. R.'s letters to me, I will send them. They are absolute doggrel, but very literal. I also translated for him *Les*

Souvenirs de Chastelain. " Down Plumpton Park " seems to have been a favourite tune. There are many references to it. As the Duke of Roxburghe's library is in a state of abeyance, I may not easily find access to the copy which is there. Will you, therefore, excuse my requesting you— not to write out the song yourself (which if you hate copying as much as I do will be but a tedious task), but to find some one to make me a copy. The Dialogue between Jenny Cameron and her Maid I have seen. I like some of the simple strains in Lord Derwentwater's Complaint very much indeed, and am impatient to see it ; though I should be ashamed to say so, after the trouble I have already given, and am to give you. Ritson had a ballad with a simple northern burden—

" The oak, the ash, and the ivy tree,
    O, they flourish best at hame, in the North country."

Do you know any thing of it ?

I dare not again read over this scrawl, which has been written at our Court table, while the Counsel were pleading the great cause of the Duke of Roxburghe's succession. So pray excuse mistakes, and believe me, Dear Sir,

[*The remainder has been cut out*]

21 *Febry* EDINR. 1807

Of course Mr. Frank will take [care] of and return the originals of Mr. Ritson's letters to me.

[*Abbotsford Copies and Surtees Memoir*]

To CHARLES ERSKINE

MY DEAR CHARLES,—The very interesting discussions concerning our Court here which have deeply engaged my attention both as a Scotchman & an individual nearly concernd have interfered greatly wt. my Sheriff matters & I now find myself obliged to set off for London instead of coming out to Ashestiel. The alarming illness of Colin Mackenzie [1] to whom we Clerks had entrusted our pleas for compensation occasions this rapid change in my motions. I am therefore obliged to turn over upon you the process of the Magistrates which I wish you to decide upon this principle that the pursuers are entitled to have their time compensated when they were *bona fide* off work. But they are not entitled to take a catch & either charge those days when they were actually employd by others or those on which they might have been so employd had they chosen. This is the equitable view of the case. I send you also a petition for White of which you are a more competent Judge than I am. Also two letters from litigants which pray attend to. . . .

I have no hopes of being at the Circuit so you must put on the Belt & sword. I hope to have pleasant news of Mrs. Erskine by & bye—If you have occasion to favour me with a letter direct to the care of Mr. Miller Bookseller Albemarle Street

Tell Baillie Clarkson I received his letter. I understand I have a chance of meeting him in town. I am with great regard Dear Charles yours truly

WALTER SCOTT

EDINBURGH 14 *March* [1807]
I set off tomorrow

[*Curle*]

To ROBERT SURTEES.

DEAR SIR,—I am constrained to answer your very kind and acceptable letter [2] by a few hurried lines. The

---

[1] Scott's colleagues as Clerk of Session included David Hume (the nephew of the philosopher) ; Hector Macdonald Buchanan of Drumalkiln, " at whose beautiful seat of Ross Priory on the shores of Loch Lomond " Scott was a frequent visitor ; Sir Robert Dundas of Beechwood ; and the friend of his boyhood, Colin Mackenzie of Portmore. For his letter on *Marmion* see *Lockhart*, c. xvi.

[2] A letter of Surtees of the 28th February, sending ballads from Ritson's papers ; promising to inquire about the song, " The Oak, the Ash and the Ivy Tree " ; rejoicing in the prospect of *Marmion* and sending £5 for Hogg.

truth is, I hoped in my way to town to have had an opportunity to avail myself of your kind invitation, and to have personally offered my thanks for your repeated favours. But I find I must deny myself that pleasure till my return ; for the illness of a particular friend, charged with a commission of some delicacy, in which we are both deeply interested, obliges me to make the best of my way to town : his physicians have advised him to go down to Devonshire, and I am aware he will not obey them until I relieve him upon his post. I inclose a letter of poor Ritson's, which had fallen aside when I last wrote. Lord Derwentwater's Lament, as you have improved it, is beautiful. There are also some uncommonly happy touches in the original ; and I am particularly pleased with the expression of devoted loyalty in his address to Collingwood, where the sense of his own misfortunes is completely lost in his feelings for his dethroned sovereign. But I will resist the temptation of entering upon this subject, and recollect that I have papers to arrange, and a portmanteau to pack up. In about a month I hope my business in town will be finished, and in my way down I reckon upon the pleasure of waiting upon you at Mainsforth. I will duly apprize you of my motions.

I must not omit to thank you for your very liberal inclosure for the Ettrick Shepherd, who was doubly happy at learning from whom it came. I hope the books were regularly despatched, and have duly reached you. I am happy to say that the bard's success has been such as to induce him to look forward to the power of stocking his little farm very comfortably at Whitsunday. Believe me, dear Sir, Yours most truly,

WALTER SCOTT

EDINBURGH, 15 *March*, 1807.

[Abbotsford Copies and Surtees Memoir]

To LADY ABERCORN

[1807]

I HAVE the pleasure my dear Lady Marchioness to send you the little Ballad of Queen Auragua.[1] It does not look quite well in writing as I was uncertain about some of the lines & besides to produce the proper dramatic effect it should always be read aloud or recited. I am also dubious about the spelling of some of the Spanish names which I picked up from the recitation only. But such as it is, it will shew the pleasure I have in executing any of your Ladyships commands altho neither that nor any thing I can do or say can express my sense of the value of your friendship. I had a most stormy passage to Scotland for the tempest of disputed election was raging in every town almost through which I past. Post horses were generally speaking out of the question and the public coaches on the outside and in the inside of which I performed the greater part of my journey were crowded with drunken voters whom the candidates were transporting in that manner through the country and who drank brandy at every furlong for the good of their country. I arrived here on Wednesday without having been in bed for three nights but without experiencing either fatigue or inconvenience from my vigils. The cry of King and Constitution was the favourite through every part of the country I passed. My route extended a good way to the westward by Liverpool Lichfield Sheffield, etc. till I joined the great North road at York finding it difficult to return, as I had intended by Carlisle. Here Lord Melville is at work with Election business from morning till night & I think will give a very good account of the returns. I hardly think that Opposition

---

[1] Southey's fine ballad of *Queen Orraca*, first printed in the *Morning Post* on 1st September 1803, but which Scott seems to have picked up from Southey's recitation and sent copies of to friends. It was afterwards printed in the *Edinburgh Annual Register* for 1808 (issued 1810) and in the *English Minstrelsy*, 1810.

will be able to make ten out of the forty-five although they supposed they would have double that number. The interests of the Duke of Argyle & Marchioness Stafford are their only support here for the Foxites themselves are weaker than water.

Charlotte is quite delighted with the cap which your Ladyship selected for her. It looks very smart & will I dare say be the envy of the Edinburgh Belles. She desires me to make her respectful thanks acceptable to your Ladyship I found all my little people in great health and spirits and beginning to talk a little French under their mother's instructions. I am very anxious that my sons in particular shall be masters of the modern European languages an accomplishment which although much neglected in our common mode of education may be of the utmost use to them in future life. Your Ladyship will I hope commend my early and fore-casting prudence in this matter when you consider that the eldest boy is only five years old and the youngest cannot speak his mother tongue yet.

I find myself treated with an unusual degree of respect in this country from the idea which the good people are pleased to entertain of my favour with the ministers and their strongest supporters. As the only course in my power I look wise say nothing and gain the credit of being in the secret and knowing how to keep it. I need not tell your Ladyship that I laugh in my sleeve, and yet I daresay I have often looked up with profound respect to some person or other who had no better claim to it than being personally known to his betters like myself.

You will expect to hear something of *Marmion*. He begs his respectful compliments to the Marchioness, and will have the honor of kissing her hand at Christmas having adjourned his introduction to public life till that period. The whirlpool of politics run such risque of absorbing all the public interest, and my own labours have been so effectually interrupted by the gaieties of your Metropolis that this arrangement will be most convenient for both parties.

I send Queen Auragua under the Marquis's cover and will be happy to hear how your Ladyship likes it in Manuscript ; and still more so to know that you are tolerably well and taking care of your health, to which London air and London hours are I fear not very favourable. I beg my respects to all the family in James Square who may do me the honour to enquire after me & I ever am Dear Lady Marchioness your obliged & faithful

WALTER SCOTT

EDINBURGH 15 *May* [1807]

I have not seen Tom nor learned the nature of his request to Lord Melville in which he was so fortunate as to have your Ladyship's powerful mediation. I hope he has well considered what he asked as I am certain your interest will (as it ought) secure it for him if it be practicable.

[*Pierpont Morgan*]

To JAMES BALLANTYNE [1]

[*c. May*, 1807]

DEAR JAMES,—I am much obliged for the rhimes. I presume it can make no difference as to the air if the first three lines rhime—& I wish to know with your leisure if it is absolutely necessary that the fourth should be out of Poetic rythme as " the deserting fair one " certainly is— for example would this

> Should my heart from thee falter
> To another love alter
> (For the rhime we'll say Walter)
> Deserting my lover.

There is here the same number of syllables, but arranged in cadence.

[1] This letter is a note about the song in Canto III of *Marmion* beginning " Where shall the lover rest."

I return the proof & send the copy which please return when you have made the calculation—there will be six cantos.   W. S.

If we could make the tune suit anything like verse we might have it engraved on a scroll as a Vignette.

[*Abbotsford Copies*]

TO ROBERT SURTEES

MY DEAR SIR,—The dissolution of Parliament hurried me down to Scotland, where I had some duty to discharge in consequence ; so that I was compelled to pass Mainsforth without soliciting an opportunity of personally acknowledging the favours you have so frequently conferred on me. Since my return, my leisure has been partly occupied in preparing for the press a mass of curious state papers[1] belonging to the representatives of the famous Sir Ralph Sadler, who you must remember makes such a figure in history in the reigns of Henry VIII. Edward VI. & Queen Elizabeth. There are many particulars in these letters which I am persuaded will be very interesting to you ; and I would be particularly happy to profit by your assistance in the task I have undertaken, of adding a few notes of occasional illustration. As an introduction, we intend (for Mr. Clifford the proprietor is properly the publisher) to reprint the curious negotiation concerning the proposed marriage of Queen Mary with Edward VI. These you are doubtless no stranger to, as they are contained in a small 8vo. volume published about the beginning or middle of the last century. These letters are to be followed by the whole correspondence between

[1] This finally appeared as *The state papers and letters of Sir Ralph Sadler Knight Banneret. Edited by Arthur Clifford Esq. In three volumes. To which is added a memoir of the life of Sir Ralph Sadler with historical notes by Walter Scott Esq.* 2 vols. Edinburgh. Printed for Archibald Constable & Co. Edinburgh ; and for T. Cadell and Davies, William Millar and John Murray, London, 1809.

Sir R. Sadler & Sir James Crofts on the one side, and the Scottish Reformers, the English Privy Council, and Randolph, Queen Elizabeth's agent to the Lords of the Congregation, on the other. The intrigues of the English Court in that bustling period are very clearly developed ; and though I cannot say that any new facts occur of great importance, yet the minuter springs by which so great a machine was agitated may be thence more distinctly and accurately traced than they have heretofore been. The letters referring to this period of 1549 or 1550 are very numerous, and all either autographs or copies in Sir Ralph Sadler's handwriting. There follow some very curious letters during the rebellion of the Northern Earls, in the 12th of Queen Elizabeth, particularly a very long and curious letter from Robert, afterwards Sir Robert Constable, who took upon him the dishonourable office of a spy for Sadler, and in that capacity visited the Earl of Westmerland, while sheltered in Fairnihirst Castle, near Jedburgh, whom as well as Richard Forster, a noted insurgent, he attempted, under the masque of friendship, to prevail upon to return, and take shelter in his house in England. He prays Sadler, that if this plan should succeed, his (Constable's) house may be their sanctuary, but adds, that the parties must take their own risk in coming and going. If I had an opportunity I would gladly send you this letter, which is altogether a very curious piece ; and would probably convey to you some information in the way of your particular researches. You would also probably know much more than I can easily find out concerning the Northumbrian gentlemen mentioned in the letter. The last part of this collection refers to the part which Sadler had in the confinement of Queen Mary in Tutbury Castle. Some of these last letters appear in the Shrewsbury Collection, published under the inspection of Mr. Lodge, in 3 vols. 4to. Will you be so good as to consider whether you would like to look over these letters, at least such as are connected with North-

umberland, and in what way they will reach you safely.   I
mean to send the copies, as the originals remain with Mr.
Clifford.

This by-job has a little interfered with the progress of
my new Poem MARMION, in which I think I told you I
had upon the stocks, and in which I have availed myself
of your curious old ballad of the Featherstonhaugh feud.
But this I intend to resume at a later period of the year,
for I have been too much fretted by election bustle to
have my pipes in very good tune for poetry.

I am very much interrupted in my letter by the pleading
of a vociferous counsel at the bar, (for I write from the
Court), who is discussing a battle or battery fought out in
the ancient style, between a Highland Chieftain and a
gentleman of another family ; the scene of contest being
a churchyard after an interment, and the accompaniment
a pair of great war bagpipes blowing " The Cameron's
Gathering." It is a shame that what was so chivalrously
commenced, should be finished with lawyers' tongues
instead of the dirk & glaymore. At any rate I must give
way to it, and subscribe myself in haste, And very truly,
yours,   WALTER SCOTT

EDINBURGH, 12 *June*, 1807.

[*Abbotsford Copies and Surtees Memoir*]

To LADY ABERCORN

20 *July* 1807

I DID myself the honour about two months ago to send
my dear Lady Marchioness the Manuscript of the Ballad
of Queen Auragua : I must flatter myself that your
Ladyship not liking it so much in writing as when
repeated was owing entirely to the want of the graces
of my recitation or rather that your Ladyships time has
been so fully [and so pleasantly] occupied that you have

not had a moment for your northern correspondent.[1] In the mean while a most woeful mischance has befallen me which is likely to silence the Muse for a good while. My brother as your Ladyship too truly augured has proved but too faithfully a *living witness* that his faults were of a kind never to have been capable of correction. Finding himself pressed to make up the money belonging to another client with which according to his usual custom he had most improperly interfered he did not hesitate to apply the term's rents of the Duddingstone estate to make up his deficiency and has [now] absconded leaving me to settle his account with the Marquis as I best can. I am not afraid of being able to make up this loss to the Marquis [ultimately] for I have never exceeded my income and am worth about six thousand pounds independant [*sic*] of my House furniture Books and farm stocking which are worth at least £4000 more. So that I can easily meet my loss by making some œconomical restrictions in my expences indeed I would rather become a hack author for my own and my familes [*sic*] daily bread than the Marquis should lose a penny by having on my account and at my intercession reposed Confidence in my brother after in his Lordship's most justly formed opinion he had ceased to deserve it. But as I know how much interest your Ladyship & the Marquis have with Lord Melville I trust I do not greatly intrude upon your goodness if in this very disagreeable situation of doubt and expected loss I should pray for some exertion of it on my behalf. Lord Melville who has always been my noble friend & every Member of his family have always expressed themselves not only willing but desirous that

[1] Lady Abercorn replies on the 23rd apologising for her silence. She is removing to Ireland : " Lord Abercorn has told me all that has happened respecting your Brother. I really cannot tell you how much I grieve upon the occasion for every one concerned in the business, how could a Brother of yours act ill, there certainly never was a greater contrast in two minds so nearly connected and living so much together. I am truly sorry for Him. . . . I am more angry with Him for His deceiving you than for anything else."

I should be in some way enabled to receive the appointments of my office as Clerke of session which are at present entirely drawn by my predecessor MR. George Home. I spoke to Lord M. himself on this subject when last in Scotland and he expressed himself in the kindest and most favourable manner. I had no idea of intruding upon his goodness by harrassing him with repetitions of my application well knowing how many demands he has to gratify & that it is impossible for him to *make* opportunities of complying with them. In a word I intended to have [waited] quietly my income being sufficient for my expenses till the revenue of my office should open & give me a prospect of saving something for my children. But I own I am not quite philosophic enough to see my capital so far diminished by the necessity of paying for the folly of another without placing my case before your Ladyship & begging your interference with Lord Melville in hastening the progress of any good office he may intend me. For the trouble I am about to give you Lady Abercorn I will make no apology because in stating my situation you will do a good & kind action such as I am sure is more congenial to your own disposition and not inconsistent with the marks of friendship which I have always considered as the highest & most gratifying honour. As to Lord Melville it is true I have but little title to teaze him for favours & yet I have some little. More than one distinguished individual of the party who were last in power paid me much attention till they saw I would not be coaxed to leave Lord M's standard in Scotland by any prospect which could be held out to me. Neither was my assistance totally insignificant for although I have neither family nor pecuniary influence yet in the circle in which I live I have always had something of that consideration which is usually given to any person of a decided character by those who cannot form general opinions for themselves. I am sure I prevailed on at least thirty people to declare themselves for Lord M.

by attending the jubilee at his acquittal & most of them were persons of more consideration than myself. As I did not fear to expose myself to the storm I may be considered as not unreasonable in wishing to share the Sunshine ; more especially as I only desire to reap the emolument of my own daily labour at a time when innocently & even not illaudably I am likely to be involved in the misfortunes of another. I am sure your Ladyship must remember the story of the Old Man of the Sea who established himself on the shoulders of Sinbad the Sailor. My old gentleman is as well fixed in his position & as determined to maintain it. It would be a shame to the present Ministry to suffer a literary Adherent of some notoriety to be ridden to death in the manner I am likely to be. Had it not been this last misfortune I could have trotted on very well for a good many stages. But as it is I have at least the same claim to attention which Dugald Stuart & Tom Campbell had from the Grenvillites. I am far from comparing myself either [to] the Bard or the philosopher but then I am not asking either a pension or a sinecure but merely admission to the regular profits of a laborious office, & that at a time of (I will say) undeserved misfortune.

I could indulge on this occasion the usual loquacity of people in distress & tell your Ladyship that the charge of my brother's wife & children must devolve in a great measure on my shoulders—& that Pitt not long before his death made enquiry after & recommended me to be provided for—with sundry other pleas of various kinds. But I am sure I have said enough to interest & I do not mean to distress you. If Lord M. is sincerely disposed to serve me of which I cannot harbour a doubt more especially if my solicitation is backed by your powerful intercession it may be either done by a pension to Mr. Home as a superannuated officer (being in fact as deaf as a post & as capable of discharging his duty as I am of dancing a hornpipe) or under the various provisions of

I 2 A

the new Judicature Bill some of which will doubtless require the creation of new offices.

I have resolved not to trouble Lord A. with a word on this subject. He is my noble & kind friend & has behaved with all the consideration to my feelings & situation which I could possibly have expected & I hope to live to repay him by putting his affairs in a better situation than they have ever been before they pass into the hands of a mere mercenary Agent. But I must not forget that I have been the innocent cause of his present uneasiness. My own mortification has been so great that I was very feverish for three days & if I had [had] leisure would have been most heartily sick with vexation anxiety & grief.

Who could have thought this miserable young man would have behaved so cruelly ill after your Ladyship & the Marquis remonstrating so kindly with him. Indeed this very improbability threw me off my guard so that I was not much startled when I found he had sent off his accounts to Lord Abercorn without sending them to be inspected by me. His wife who is just recovering from confinement & is nursing an Infant has stood this shock surprisingly. Excuse all this egotism & nonsense & believe [me] ever Dear Lady Marchioness Your Ladyships most respectful Much obliged humble Servant

[*Pierpont Morgan*]   WALTER SCOTT

To ROBERT SURTEES.

MY DEAR SIR,—Accept of my best congratulations on your change of condition,[1] and may you long experience, as I have done, that mutual affection is the surest, as it is the most natural support in a pilgrimage through this nether vale. Your line, as the Scripture somewhere says, has fallen in pleasant places ; for, with a taste for litera-

---

[1] Surtees was married on the 23rd June 1807. He reports the event to Scott in his letter of 9th July : " Your letter reached Mainsforth after I had left home, and has since been pursuing me through the several stages of a short tour we have been making."

ture, and the means of supporting with independance an elegant retirement, I know nothing but an affectionate partner which would add to your means of happiness.

It will give me sincere pleasure, should I have an opportunity of waiting upon you and Mrs. Surtees at Mainsforth ; but I dare not flatter myself it will occur till next Spring, when probably I may look towards London. Do you never think of taking a peep at our northern wonders, now so much the object of curiosity and attention ? Should Mrs. Surtees and you think of a Scottish trip this season, you will find Mrs. Scott and me at our little farm on Tweedside, to which we go on Friday fortnight. I have just finished some unpleasant business which has robbed me of some part of my vacation. I cannot express the pleasure it will give us to see you ; and for shewing our lions—

> " I'll be a guide worth any two
> That may in Teviotdale be found."

I willingly embrace your obliging offer of looking through Sir Ralph Sadler's letters during the Great Northern Rebellion, which I am apt to think will interest you considerably. Be so good as mark any illustrations which occur to you upon the blank side ; and never mind my scribbling, which was hastily [jotted] down from the readiest authorities. I have not had time to look over these notes, or rather memoranda, since I marked them down. You will see but too much reason for this apology.

I should be glad to see Ritson's Songs,[1] although they are all old acquaintances. It is not likely that the Minstrelsy will be re-published in a hurry ; being a book of rather a confined sale. But, should such an event happen in my day, I would seek to have the means of making the poems as perfect as possible by collating them accurately.

[1] Surtees had reported that " Mr. Frank has sent the following songs," and he gives a list of thirteen.—*Surtees Memoir*, pp. 58-9.

I am scarce able to write, with a violent nervous headache, which I take the more unkindly with, as I am little
accustomed to indisposition of any kind. There is no
hurry whatever in returning the papers, which will not
be wanted for some time for the press. Will you make
my respectful compliments acceptable to Mrs. Surtees, as
those of an unknown, but sincere well-wisher, and believe
me, Ever yours faithfully,   WALTER SCOTT

EDINR. 28th July [1807].

My address henceforward is Ashestiel by Selkirk.

[Abbotsford Copies and Surtees Memoir]

To MISS SMITH [1]

MY DEAR MISS SMITH,—I send you the promised lines ;
which indifferent as they are have proved better than I
durst venture to hope considering that I have been
obliged to postpone the task of writing them till this
morning. The idea is better than the execution, but I
comfort myself that many better lines have wanted the
advantages which your recitation will give mine. Adieu
we hope to see Mrs. S and you on Sunday, at this farm—
Middleton & Bankhouse will be your first stages and
Ashestiel the third—In great haste I am ever with best
wishes for Saturday and deep regrets that I cannot partake
your triumph—Yours very faithfully & respectfully

WALTER SCOTT

ASHESTIEL BY SELKIRK Tuesday Morning [August 1807]

I have opened my letter again to beg you will not
mention the author of these lines for which I will give
you a reason when we meet.

[Abbotsford Copies]

---

[1] Sarah Smith, an accomplished actress engaged at Covent Garden.
She was in Edinburgh and Scott had apparently written some pro-
logue or other lines for her. She and her mother visited Ashestiel and
on 21st August she wrote from Margate to " thank you for the happiest

To MISS SEWARD [1]

MY DEAR MISS SEWARD,—I very little anticipated upon quitting your hospitable Mansion that my first letter should have begun with an apology for delaying to express the pleasure I had received from a personal acquaintance which I value so highly. But it has pleased God since that period to visit me with distress of a kind which least of all others I am able to bear— My younger Brothers affairs fell very suddenly into total and irretrievable disorder, at a time too when his wife was confined after the birth of a Son and under a variety of other circumstances tending to agravate a calamity in itself sufficiently severe. He had been for many years Manager of the Estates of the Marquis of Abercorn & I was security to his Employer for the regular payment of his rents. The consequence of my Brother's failure was that the whole affairs of these extensive Estates were thrown upon my hands in a state of unutterable confusion, so that to save myself from ruin I was obliged to bend my constant and unremitting attention to their re-establishment. In the course of this unfortunate business I was so absolutely worried to death that I had neither head nor heart to think of any thing else. Fortunately between Lord Abercorn's friendship & liberality of sentiment on the one hand, & unceasing attention on

hours I have known since my soul could of men distinguish, in your hospitable dwelling my mind was intirely free from the vexations ever attendant on my profession." In 1814 she married George Bartley and died in 1850.

[1] Scott had visited Miss Seward in the first week of May. See Lockhart and her letter to Cary the Dante scholar of 10th May. She replied to this letter on 26th August and tells him of a young prodigy, an actor Betty, and her plans for his education. She has had two letters from Southey, who tells her that the profits from Madoc amount to £3 12s. 2d., and she complains bitterly of the injustice of "your Judge Jefferies." " Surely Wordsworth must be mad as was ever the poet Lee " is her judgment on the 1807 volumes. This will explain several of the points in Scott's next letter, undated, but written in September. For William Henry Betty (1791-1874) the "Young Roscius." See D.N.B.

the other, I have put things into such a train as to avoid a personal loss which would not only have deprived me of the power of assisting my Brothers family but very much cramped me in maintaining my own or deprived me at least of that independance which in my opinion is essential to happiness. Thank God every thing has turned out better than I ventured to hope and I have found myself at liberty to escape to the banks of my dear Tweed without any apprehension of being obliged to quit them. I have also hopes by some kind & powerful friends to establish my brother in a line which will suit him better than that in which he has met with this misfortune. If this can be accomplished his youth and talents which are very considerable may easily repair to himself & his family the disasters which his illtimed speculations have occasioned. Meantime I have found the truth of an old Scottish proverb that " if a thing is kept for seven years some use will be found for it." After so many years spent at the Bar and in literary pursuits I never thought to have been so much obliged to an early part of my education in which I was trained to what you would call Attorney's business which my father thought I ought to understand although my practice was to be in the higher and theoretical branch of the Law. This has done me yeoman's service in the hour of necessity but most devoutly do I pray I may have no farther occasion to plague myself with rent rolls annuity tables purchase & redemption of Leases and all the endless train of complicated chicanery by understanding which one part of mankind enable themselves to live at the expense of the sons of fortune.

In the midst of all this bustle it is scarcely necessary to say that my harp has been hung on the willows ; my grand poem called Marmion has been entirely stopped even when half finished and Dryden has crept on very slowly. All this delay must now be compensated when leisure and renovated spirits enable me to resume my literary labours. I was much pleased with some verses by a certain Lady of Lichfield addressed to the young Roscius—what a pity some care is not taken of that boy's education—the father I fear is a sordid miscreant. Since I came here I have had a visit from Miss Smith of Covent Garden Theatre[1]—an actress of the Tragic Muse for whom I have an especial regard as a very good and pleasing Girl with high talents for her profession in which she is now second to Mrs. Siddons alone— I carried her to see Melrose with which she was delighted to a degree of enthusiasm. As she goes by the western road I would have ventured to give her a few lines of introduction to you had her time been such as to permit her to wait upon you. She is quite received every where & was introduced to us by the Buccleuch Ladies—

I have no literary intelligence of any consequence not having written a letter save on business for these two months & upward. It is said Tom Campbell is writing an Epic or narrative poem of some kind in which the Scene is laid in America— Believe me with every sentiment of regard My dear Miss Seward Your very faithful & indebted

WALTER SCOTT

ASHESTIEL BY SELKIRK
11 *August* 1807

[*Abbotsford Copies*]

TO MISS SMITH

DEAR MISS SMITH,—Everything that conveys good news of your health and prosperity must be wellcome to those who know [you] and especially whom you honour with your friendship. I need not then dwell upon the satisfaction with which we learned in our solitary retreat that you had made out your fatiguing

[1] See note, p. 372.

journey so well as to be able to resume the labours of your profession immediately on its conclusion. Remember however you are accountable to your friends in particular as well as to the public in general (as the advertisements have it) for the preservation of your power of charming us and we will not admit any excuse for over-exertion. In order to delight us long you must not labour too hard and if I had the power of my name sake Michael Scott I would certainly whisk you on a dragon's wing back to Ashestiel where you would be condemned to solitude and goat's whey for a few months to teach you [not] to endanger the public property in your health and voice by presuming under any pretext to travel all night. I assure you we felt a little pang of remorse when we considered that the day you so kindly spent at our farm had been the means of reducing you to the necessity of such violent exertions to be in due time at Margate. Seriously you must allow no consideration to do so in future ; the voice (especially so flexible a voice as yours) has a delicacy equal to its other powers and a bad cold might deprive it for a long time if not for ever of that command of tone which it now possesses. So pray as you value my regard take care of damp dressing rooms and of Night journeys— I am not ignorant that your profession and the eminence you have deservedly gaind in it expose you to sensations still more painful than those of colds and rheumatisms and that the heartache which is produced by lacerated feelings is more acute than the severest bodily pain. But you must look my dear young friend upon the livelier side of the picture and consider the pleasures of your profession when its highest rank is attained by one who is in every respect deserving of the elevation it gives her. Popular applause for which heroes you know bleed and grave folks write books is attaind by the performer in the highest degree and conferd upon him glowing from the feelings of the moment. The actor gives life to the poet

and embodies those passions which the author can but
sketches [sic] and the ardour with which a favourite part
is studies [sic] and masterd seldom fails in the keenest
degree to reward a performer who has given himself the
pains to understand it.   Every line of life has its advantages and usually is balanced with drawbacks of a nature
corresponding to them.   The performer whose enjoyment lies in exquisitely feeling and expressing the beauties
of poetry is by the acuteness of feeling which he must
cultivate renderd doubly sensible to mental distress and
as he lives by the applause of the public he is liable to be
wounded by all the tales of calumny and malice to which
the public is always too willing to lend an ear.   But your
powers with the good temper and propriety to which
they are united may safely defy all these inconveniences
and if you cannot avoid feeling them for a time you have
the pleasing consciousness that they arise only from a
sense of your excellence.

Mrs. Scott and I arrived here on Monday from Bothwell
Castle where we had made a visit to Lady Douglas.   I
never witnessed such a storm of rain and wind as took
place on Sunday.   We were unluckily travelling through a
highland country when the rivers were all swelld and the
bridges sometimes broke down—sometimes left standing
encircled with water all around.   All the inhabitants
of cottages in these wild glens had deserted their houses
and our situation was often not only disagreeable
but extremely dangerous.   Fortunately we reached home
in safety after walking and wading many miles.   It was
comparatively a trifling misfortune to find great part
of the crop on that level field up which we walkd on the
morning you were with us had been entirely swept off
by the flood.

To leave these moving accidents by flood and field I
have the pleasure to say I left Lady D[ouglas] in good
health.

All my little people about whom you enquire so kindly

are well. Mrs. Scott joins in kind remembrances to
Mrs. Smith. Believe me ever yours affectionately

ASHESTIEL 9th Sept. [1807].   WALTER SCOTT

Miss Smith
16 Great Roper Street, Covent Garden, London.
[Sir Alfred J. Law]

To MISS SEWARD

[September 1807]

SINCE I was favoured with your letter[1] my dear Miss
Seward I have brought the unpleasant transactions to
which my last letter alluded, pretty near to a conclusion
much more fortunate than I had ventured to hope. Of
my Brothers creditors those connected with him by
blood or friendship shewd all the kindness which these
ties are in Scotland peculiarly calculated to produce :
and what is here much more uncommon those who had
no personal connection with him or his family shewd a
liberality which would not have misbecome the generosity
of the English. Upon the whole his affairs are put in a
course of management which I hope will enable him to
begin life anew with renovated hopes & not entirely
destitute of the means of recommencing business. All
this is much more than I had ventured to hope of so
unfortunate & complicated transactions.

I am very happy (although a little jealous withal)
that you are to have the satisfaction of Southey's personal
acquaintance. I am certain you will like the Epic Bard
exceedingly, although he does not deign to enter into
the mere trifling intercourse of society yet when a
sympathetic spirit calls him forth no man talks with
more animation on literary topics & perhaps no man
in England has read and studied so much with the same
powers of making use of the information which he is so

[1] Of 26th August (see p. 373, n.)

indefatigable in acquiring. I despair of reconciling you to my little friend Jeffcrics although I think I could trust to his making some impression on your prepossession were you to converse with him. I think Southey does himself injustice in supposing the Edinburgh Review or any other could have sunk Madoc even for a time. But the size & price of the work, joind to the frivolity of an age which must be treated as nurses humour children are separate reasons why a poem on so chaste a Model should not have taken immediately. We know the similar fate of Miltons immortal work in the witty age of Charles II. at a time when poetry was much more fashionable than at present. As to the division of the profit I only think that Southey does not understand the gentlemen of the *trade*, emphatically so calld, so well as I do. Without any greater degree of *fourberie* than they conceive the long practice of their brethren has renderd matter of prescriptive right they contrive to clip the authors proportion of profits down to a mere trifle. It is the tale of the fox that went a hunting with the lion upon condition of equal division of the spoil. And yet I do not quite blame the booksellers, when I consider the very singular nature of their *mystery*. A Butcher generally understands something of black cattle, & woe betide the jockey who should presume to exercise his profession without a competent knowledge of horse flesh. But who ever heard of a Bookseller pretending to understand the commodity in which he dealt. They are the only tradesmen in the world who professedly & by choice deal in what is calld a pig in a poke. When you consider the abominable trash which by their sheer ignorance is publishd every year you will readily excuse them for the indemnification which they must necessarily obtain at the expense of authors of some value. In fact though the account between an individual bookseller & such a man as Southey be iniquitous enough yet I apprehend that upon the whole the

account between the trade & authors of Britain at
large is pretty fairly balanced & what these gentlemen
gain at the expense of one class of writers is lavishd in
many cases in bringing forward other works of little
value. I do not know but this upon the whole is
favourable to the cause of literature. A Bookseller
publishes 20 Books in hopes of hitting upon one good
speculation as a person buys a parcel of shares in a
lottery in hopes of gaining a prize. Thus the road is open
to all & if the successful candidate is a little fleeced
in order to form petty prizes to console the losing adventurers, still the cause of literature is benefited since none
is excluded from the privilege of competition. This does
not apologize for Southeys carelessness about his interest.
For

> —— his name is up & may go
> From Toledo to Madrid.

Pray dont trust Southey too long with Mr. White.
He is even more determined in his admiration of old
ruins than I am. You see I am glad to pick a hole in his
jacket being more jealous of his personal favour in Miss
Sewards eyes than of his poetical reputation.

I quite agree with you about the plan of young Beatties
education & am no great idolater of the learnd
languages excepting for what they contain. We spend
in youth that time in admiring the wards of the key
which we should employ in opening the cabinet &
examining its treasures. A prudent & accomplishd
friend who would make instruction acceptable to him
for the sake of the amusement it conveys, would be worth
an hundred schools. How can so wonderfully premature
a genius, accustomd to excite interest in thousands be
made a member of a class with other boys.

Your song is quite delightful but rather too melancholy.
I have not trusted myself with reading often in a temper
when I have had much . . . (continuation of MS. missing).

[British Museum]

To LADY ABERCORN

ASHIESTIEL, 10 *Sept.* 1807

I HAVE defered writing from day to day my dear Lady
Abercorn untill I should be able to make good my promise
of sending you the two first cantos of *Marmion*. The
printers have hitherto disappointed me under one pretext
or another but as I have now their solemn assurance that
it will be sent to Mr. Wright in a day or two who will get
a post office frank for this parcel I may venture to hope
that the doughty knight will cross St. Georges channel
about the same time with this letter.

I am sure it will give your kindness pleasure to hear
that the very unpleasant affair which distressed me so
much when I met your Ladyship at Longtown is taking a
turn much more favourable than I had ventured to augur
at that time. Lord Abercorn will I think sustain no loss
whatever, my own will be trifling and something will
even be saved out of the wreck of my brother's fortune,
to save his family from actual distress or dependence upon
the charity of their friends. Thus it is my dear Lady
in human life : the bad is not always so *very* bad and the
good is not always so *very* good as we at first fear or
expect ; and in this twilight sort of state in which good
and bad fortune are so strangely chequered, we find
something to make misfortune tolerable and something
to embitter prosperity itself.

Apropos of prosperity, our glens have been honoured
with a visit from the Duke and Duchess of Bedford [1] ; they
made some stay at a shooting hut of Lord Somerville's
(how he contrived to pack them I cannot imagine) and
looked around them at the antiquities and agriculture of
Teviotdale. I renewed my former acquaintance with
her Grace which commenced when she was the Duchess's

---

[1] John Russell, Duke of Bedford (1766-1839), had married, for his second
wife, Georgiana, fifth and youngest daughter of Alexander, fourth Duke of
Gordon, and his first wife, Jane, daughter of Sir William Maxwell of
Monreith. The latter was " *the* Duchess."

Georgie and they breakfasted at our farm on their road
to Hamilton. She enquired a great deal about your
Ladyship and was surprized to find that I had seen you
so lately ; I have seldom seen any person so happy at
revisiting their native country. She was quite ready
with the damsel in the old song,

" To throw off her gallant shoes
　　Made of the Spanish leather,
And to put on the Highland brogues
　　To skip among the heather."

Marmion has been sadly interrupted but is now making
some progress. I was under the necessity of going to
Edinburgh for a few days and as Mrs. Scott was with me
we returned by Bothwell Castle both to visit Lady Douglas
and that my wife might see the Falls of Clyde. But the
pleasure of this excursion had like to have cost us dear.
For on Sunday as we were travelling through a very wild
country between the towns of Lanark and Peebles, the
weather which had been rainy for several days became a
perfect hurricane. Many bridges were broke down.
Others were left standing with the water flowing round
both ends of them so that they seemed in the middle of a
lake. At other places the road was entirely under water ;
going forward and stopping seemed to be almost alike
impossible. However by walking, wading and riding
before the carriage when we came to those perilous spots
where my coachman could not see the road we did at
length to the Astonishment of all beholders reach the
town of Peebles which was half under water. Next day
all the roads being impassable for a carriage we had to
walk home being about eight miles intersected by brooks
and had on our arrival the displeasure to find a good part
of my crop had been carried off by the river which very
nearly made free with the persons of some people who had
made themselves busy in saving it. But as I remember
formerly terrifying your Ladyship with the description
of a Scottish *tornadoe* I will not inlarge upon this tempest

lest I should make you afraid of a country which I have so many reasons to wish you to love.

I learned by a letter from Lord A. that you [had] reached in safety " the green isle of the ocean " whose verdure and riches have I daresay long since obliterated the recollection of the dusky heaths and mountains which you traversed on your way to Portpatrick. When your Ladyship has an hour to dispose of so idly will you let me know how you have been since you reached Eirin & whether you did not suffer from your journey, but particularly whether I can do anything for you in this country though I suppose the communication with Dublin is so direct that your Ladyship will have no commissions for Edinburgh.

With respectful compliments to Lady Maria & all the family at Baronscourt I am ever Your Ladyships most respectful & very faithful   WALTER SCOTT

[*Pierpont Morgan*]

To HENRY MACKENZIE

[*10th September,* 1807]

I READ the poem about three years ago with very great pleasure and should be extremely sorry indeed were it to be suppressed when you are collecting your literary labours. I remember thinking that it held a rank nearer Pope's Satires than any that I had ever perused ; certainly it is much superier [*sic*] to Young's, and they are read with great pleasure. As to the applications real or imaginary which the world upon such occasions puzzle themselves to discover, I think the circumstance is quite below attention, especially below yours.[1]

[*Thompson's A Scottish Man of Feeling*]

---

[1] This note refers to Mackenzie's poem, *The Pursuits of Happiness*, " which, upon its original publication in 1771, had given offence to those who made personal application of the satire to such individuals as Henry Erskine."—THOMPSON, *A Scottish Man of Feeling*, p. 309. Mackenzie was gathering together his *Collected Works*, which appeared in eight volumes in 1808.

To LADY ABERCORN

ASHESTIEL, *Sept.* 19, 1807

I AM this morning honoured My dear Lady Abercorn
with your very kind & most friendly letter of the 10th.
Believe me that I am incapable of forgetting the interest
you have so generously taken in my fortune ; I am sure
that no success could give me more real pleasure than I
have received from the kind and liberal protection your
Ladyship has afforded me. I am sure my Lord Melville
is thoroughly disposed to serve me when circumstances
will permit him to do so with propriety. I have always
found his Lordship & everyone of his family my kind &
noble friends. It will give your Ladyship pleasure to
learn that from the state of my brother's affair I am not
likely to be a sufferer beyond the extent of the small sum
which I lent him & which I always regarded rather as a
gift than a loan. In these circumstances so much better
than what I had ventured to hope when I first ventured
to intrude my affairs on your Ladyship's consideration,
I am under no immediate necessity of hurrying the
progress of Lord Melvilles good intentions towards me,
but after having experienced so much & such kind
support I will wait till I see either the Chief Baron or
someone of the family when they will probably explain
his Lordships intentions. One thing I am determined
& that is that they shall not out of personal regard to me
do anything which may be matter of reproach to them
elsewhere. " I'll rather dwell in my necessity " than
anything done to serve me should be the handle of
accusation against Lord M. who has incurred so much
obloquy. I rather fear that a pension (which his Lordship
seems to allude to) might give rise to some reflections of
this kind. But of this I am no very competent judge.

I flatter myself your Ladyship has received a long
letter from me written about a week ago & that Marmion
is also despatched. I have worried the printer about it

almost every other day & Wright has promised to get an official frank from Edinr. which will save its going round by London.

Whenever I hear from the C[hief] Baron or Robert Dundas I will write to your Ladyship upon a subject in which you honour me by taking such an unmerited interest. I am going on with *horse* and *foot* that is *prose* and *verse* alternately. *Marmion* is now well advanced. Pray observe that in the character of Fox two lines are omitted ; they should follow that which says,

"Lest it should drop o'er Fox's tomb."

They run thus

"For talents mourn untimely lost
When best employed and wanted most
Mourn genius gone," etc.

Pray Lady Abercorn add these lines with a pen, They are an admirable improvement suggested by the M[arquis] when I was at the Priory.[1] The sheet was thrown off before the correction reached the printer, but the leaf is to be cancelled and printed anew before publication.

I see my neighbour Lord Somerville's carriage on the opposite side of the Tweed. I suppose he is coming to spend the day with us so conclude in haste. "Dear dear Lady Abercorn."—Your truly grateful and deeply obliged

[*Pierpont Morgan*]   WALTER SCOTT

To ROBERT SOUTHEY [2]

ASHESTIEL, 1*st October* 1807

MY DEAR SOUTHEY,—It will give me the most sincere pleasure to receive any token of your friendly remem-

---

[1] In April of this year. Some copies wanting these lines were thrown off, and Scott was accused of omitting them in copies sent to his Tory friends. See *Lockhart*, c. xvi.

[2] The letter to which this is an answer is in the Walpole collection. That which came between this and the next is printed in *The Private*

brance, more especially in the shape of a romance of knight-errantry. You know so well how to furbish the arms of a preux chevalier, without converting him *à la Tressan* into a modern light dragoon, that my expectations from Palmerin are very high, and I have given directions to have him sent to this retreat so soon as he reaches Edinburgh. The half-guinea for Hogg's poems was duly received. The uncertainty of your residence prevented the book being sent at the time proposed—it shall be forwarded from Edinburgh to the bookseller at Carlisle, who will probably know how to send it safe. I hope very soon to send you my Life of Dryden, and eke my *last* Lay —(by the way, the former ditty was only proposed as the lay of the *last* Minstrel, not his *last* fitt.) I grieve that you have renounced the harp ; but still I confide, that, having often touched it so much to the delight of the hearers, you will return to it again after a short interval. As I don't much admire compliments, you may believe me sincere when I tell you that I have read Madoc three times since my first cursory perusal, and each time with increased admiration of the poetry. But a poem whose merits are of that higher tone does not immediately take with the public at large. It is even possible that during your own life—and may it be as long as every real lover of literature can wish—you must be contented with the applause of the few whom nature has gifted with the rare

Letter-Books of Sir Walter Scott, ed. Wilfred Partington, 1930. He is sending Queen Orraca and congratulates Scott on his memory, for from this Scott had supplied Lady Abercorn and the Princess of Wales with copies. He discusses the profits of poetry. Would Constable take the *Curse of Kehama* ? He has the *Poema del Cid*, edited by Sanchez. Of Wordsworth's volumes, the " defects . . . seem to be more felt than their beauties. . . . He is probably compleating his *Recluse*." On 8th December Southey replies to the second of the two letters here, and referring to the suggestion that he might review for the *Edinburgh*, writes : " I have scarcely one opinion in common with it [the *Review*]," if he writes, " my moral feelings must not be compromised." Of Wordsworth he goes on, " That song to Lord Clifford, which you particularise, is truly a noble poem. . . . The sonnets are in a grand style. I only wish Dundee had not been mentioned. James Grahame and I always call that man Claverhouse, the name by which the devils know him below." This will explain most of Scott's remarks.

taste for discriminating in poetry. But the mere *readers of verse* must one day come in, and then Madoc will assume his real place at the feet of Milton. Now this opinion of mine was not that (to speak frankly) which I formed on reading the poem at first, though I then felt much of its merit. I hope you have not, and don't mean to part with the copyright. I do not think Wordsworth and you understand the bookselling animal well enough, and wish you would one day try my friend Constable, who would give any terms for a connexion with you. I am most anxious to see the Cid.[1] Do you know I committed a theft upon you (neither of gait, kine, nor horse, nor outside nor inside plenishing, such as my forefathers sought in Cumberland), but of many verses of the Queen Auragua, or howsoever you spell her name ? I repeated them to a very great lady (the Princess of Wales), who was so much delighted with them, that I think she got them by heart also. She asked a copy, but that I declined to give, under pretence I could not give an accurate one ; but I promised to prefer her request to you. If you wish to oblige her R. H., I will get the verses transmitted to her ; if not, the thing may be passed over.

Many thanks for your invitation to Keswick, which I hope to accept, time and season permitting. Is your brother with you ? if so, remember me kindly. Where is Wordsworth, and what doth he do ? I wrote him a few lines some weeks ago, which I suspect never came to hand. I suppose you are possessed of all relating to the Cid, otherwise I would mention an old romance, chiefly relating to his banishment, which is in John Frere's possession, and from which he made some lively translations in a tripping Alexandrine stanza. I dare say he would communicate the original, if it could be of the least use. I am an humble petitioner that your interesting

---

[1] " The Chronicle of the Cid is just gone to press,—the most ancient and most curious piece of chivalrous history in existence—a book after your own heart."—SOUTHEY.

Spanish ballads be in some shape appended to the Cid.
Be assured they will give him wings. There is a long
letter written with a pen like a stick. I beg my respects
to Mrs. Southey, in which Mrs. Scott joins ; and I am,
very truly and affectionately, yours,   WALTER SCOTT
[*Lockhart*]

To ROBERT SOUTHEY

EDINBURGH, *November* 1807

MY DEAR SOUTHEY,—I received your letter [1] some time
ago, but had then no opportunity to see Constable, as I
was residing at some distance from Edinburgh. Since I
came to town I spoke to Constable, whom I find anxious
to be connected with you. It occurs to me that the only
difference between him and our fathers in the Row is on
the principle contained in the old proverb :—*He that
would thrive—must rise by five* ;—*He that has thriven—may lye
till seven.* Constable *would* thrive, and therefore bestows
more pains than our fathers who *have* thriven. I do not
speak this without book, because I know he has pushed
off several books which had got aground in the Row.
But, to say the truth, I have always found advantage in
keeping on good terms with several of the trade, but never
suffering any one of them to consider me as a monopoly.
They are very like farmers, who thrive best at a high rent ;
and, in general, take most pains to sell a book that has
cost them money to purchase. The bad sale of Thalaba

[1] See previous note, p. 386. *Amadis de Gaula* (1508), the origin and
authorship of which is much disputed, between Spaniard and Portuguese,
is " the only chivalresque novel that man need read. . . . Later
stories are mostly burlesques of *Amadis ;* the giants grow taller, the
monsters fiercer, the lakes deeper, the torments sharper . . . the best of
its successors is *Palmerino de Inglaterra* which Cervantes' Priest would have
kept in such a casket as that which Alexander found among Darius's
spoils, intended to guard the works of Homer."—FITZMAURICE KELLY,
Spanish Literature. Southey issued a condensed translation of *Amadis.*
   The poem of Hindoo mythology is *The Curse of Kehama.* To the *Edinburgh
Annual Register* Southey contributed till 1813 the history of the year.

is truly astonishing ; it should have sold off in a twelve-month at farthest.

As you occasionally review, will you forgive my suggesting a circumstance for your consideration, to which you will give exactly the degree of weight you please. I am perfectly certain that Jeffrey would think himself both happy and honoured in receiving any communications which you might send him, choosing your books and expressing your own opinions. The terms of the Edinburgh Review are ten guineas a-sheet, and will shortly be advanced considerably. I question if the same unpleasant sort of work is anywhere else so well compensated. The only reason which occurs to me as likely to prevent your affording the Edinburgh some critical assistance, is the severity of the criticisms upon Madoc and Thalaba. I do not know if this will be at all removed by assuring you, as I can do upon my honour, that Jeffrey has, notwithstanding the flippancy of these articles, the most sincere respect both for your person and talents. The other day I designedly led the conversation on that subject, and had the same reason I always have had to consider his attack as arising from a radical difference in point of taste, or rather feeling of poetry, but by no means from any thing approaching either to enmity or a false conception of your talents. I do not think that a difference of this sort should prevent you, if you are otherwise disposed to do so, from carrying a proportion at least of your critical labours to a much better market than the Annual. Pray think of this, and if you are disposed to give your assistance, I am positively certain that I can transact the matter with the utmost delicacy towards both my friends. I am certain you may add £100 a-year, or double the sum, to your income in this way with almost no trouble ; and, as times go, that is no trifle.

I have to thank you for Palmerin, which has been my afternoon reading for some days. I like it very much, although it is, I think, considerably inferior to the Amadis. But I wait with double anxiety for the Cid, in which I expect to find very much information as well as amusement. One discovery I have made is, that we understand little or nothing of Don Quixote except by the Spanish romances. The English and French romances throw very little light on the subject of the doughty cavalier of La Mancha. I am thinking of publishing a small edition of the Morte Arthur, merely to preserve that ancient record of English chivalry ; but my copy is so late as 1637, so I must look out for earlier editions to collate. That of Caxton is, I believe, *introuvable*. Will you give me your opinion on this project ? [1] I have written to Mr. Frere about the Spanish books, but I do not very well know if my letter has reached him. I expect to bring Constable to a point respecting the poem of Hindoo Mythology. I should esteem myself very fortunate in being assisting in bringing forth a twin brother of Thalaba. Wordsworth is harshly treated in the Edinburgh Review, but Jeffrey gives the sonnets as much praise as he usually does to anybody. I made him admire the song of Lord Clifford's minstrel, which I like exceedingly myself. But many of Wordsworth's lesser poems are *caviare*, not only to the multitude, but to all who judge of poetry by the established rules of criticism. Some of them, I can safely say, I like the better for these aberrations ; in others they get beyond me—at any rate they ought to have been more cautiously hazarded. I hope soon to send you a Life of Dryden and a Lay of former times. The latter I would willingly have bestowed more time upon ; but what can I do ?—my supposed poetical turn ruined me in my profession, and the least it can do is to give me some occasional assistance instead of it. Mrs. Scott begs kind compliments to Mrs. Southey, and I am always kindly yours. WALTER SCOTT

[*Lockhart*]

[1] See letter to Southey of 10th September 1809.

To LADY LOUISA STUART[1]

[*November-December* 1807]

I SHOULD not have laboured so long under the charge
of ingratitude much worse than that of witchcraft (which
a ghost ballad writer is naturally subjected to) if I had not
hoped to have a personal opportunity of paying my
acknowledgments for Lady Louisas kindness. I take
great care of your correspondents curious letter as I shall
be within twelve miles of Bothwell on the 30th ; if Lady
Douglas spends the Christmas there I will have the
honour to deliver it upon that day. My errand at
Glasgow is to see the Lord Advocate[2] installed as Lord
Rector in the university : but if the family are to be at
Bothwell I will leave him when invested with his dignity.

I am more & more delighted with the tale of King
Henry, his cup & his blessing[3] but I will not willingly
allow that our good Scotch King meant to betray him.
You remember the lines of Chapelain on the succour he
received in Scotland, " Ever kind to banished princes
though so rude a country." I forget the French words
but that I think is the meaning which recurred strongly

---

[1] Lady Louisa Stuart, youngest daughter of John, fourth Earl of Bute, and
grand-daughter of Lady Mary Wortley Montagu. Scott first met her at
Dalkeith and then at Bothwell, the seat of Archibald, Lord Douglas, whose
wife, Lady Frances Scott, was one of Scott's friends.

[2] *i.e.* Campbell Colquhoun, husband of Mary Erskine ; see letters of
1796. He was installed on 20th December 1807. For Lady Louisa's
letter and the story of Henry VI.'s glass see *Familiar Letters,* i. pp. 85-86.
The original is in the *Walpole Collection.*

[3] Lady Louisa is speaking of Muncaster Castle and says : " Here
Henry VI. found an asylum when flying from the Yorkists and remained
some months inhabiting a part of the castle still known by the name of
the King's Apartment. When going away he lamented that his poverty
allowed of no suitable gift to his kind host . . . but said he would leave the
glass out of which he commonly drank ; then formally blessed it, and
prayed that while that glass remained unbroken the House of Muncaster
might never want a male heir. It has ever since been called the Luck of
Muncaster. It is a goblet of thick Venice glass." She goes on to describe
the veneration with which it was regarded by the peasantry. Henry was a
saint as well as a king.

to my mind when I saw Monsieur come to our old Abbey. I am going to discontinue all my dangerous intentions of giving poetic celebrity to Ld. Muncasters habitation (since you were pleased to think I can do so) for I think the story is far too good to be comprized in a stanza & a note which is all I could afford in Marmion. Besides the making it public would be giving the signal to build some vile milk & waterish legendary tale upon so beautiful a subject which would grieve me as deeply as it would Lord M. to see a trim, neat, white wash'd gothic castle almost as large as one of his ancestors goose pyes, arise upon the most romantic knoll in the environs of Pennington with its usual graces of slits & pigeon holes for loop holes & embrasures, petticoat flounces for parapets battled & embattled pepper boxes for turrets & old perspective glasses for watch towers. I therefore intend to lay bye the tradition in lavender till some occasion when I can give it its full interest or at least do my best to give it as much as I can. I am just now very busy dressing your cousin James 4th in his court suit : his cloaths are all cut, sew'd & ready to put on so I must bid your Ladyship farewell in order to attend his royal levee. I am ever with great respect Yr Ladyships most respectful & obliged humble servant W. S.

I go on Christmas to Mertoun but return immediately to make out my Glasgow party the most interesting part of which will be my visit to Bothwell should the time arrive.

[Abbotsford Copies]

To MISS HAYMAN [1]

MY DEAR MISS HAYMAN,—Whatever *you* admire will I am sure add greatly to the value of the work in which you

[1] To this letter Mrs. Hughes in the Abbotsford copies appends a note : " This letter was addressed to Mrs. Hayman the friend who introduced me to Sir Walter in the Spring of 1807. She was privy-purse to the late

arc pleased to request a place for it. I am just now finishing my romantic poem of Marmion a tale of war & wonder with notes like Noah's ark an ample receptacle for every thing that savours of romantic lore. I will take care to distinguish the poem in all honourable fashion of type & introduction ; but I must beg the favour that you will forward it as soon as possible as I am printing rapidly & must drive a peg somewhere into my own poem to hang your friend's ballad upon.

You do me but justice in believing that I was quite delighted with Mrs. Hughes. I have achieved a doleful song to an ancient Gaelic air & intend as soon as I can get it arranged to the music to send it as a little tribute of gratitude for the pleasure I received from her melody. I have destined a copy of Marmion for you and the promised ballad will give it double interest. Shall it be sent to Berkeley Street or how ? I have also one with some ornaments which I wish should reach Blackheath some time before the work is public which may I think be in February. Will you be so good as to inform me who will be in waiting on the Princess about that time. I should be happy if it happens to be your turn of duty. I visited Bothwell Castle this summer and returned in the most dreadful storm that ever was raised by Charlotte Smith or Mrs. Radcliffe. We narrowly escaped drowning more than once. I sincerely hope that I may have leisure (which according to the best definitions includes time & money) to visit Wales this summer : it is a scheme I have long had at heart & the pleasure of your acquaintance.

I have just abandoned my own hills & glens for this

Queen Caroline." The song set to the ancient Gaelic air was the ballad of the " Spirits blasted thee " given in the notes to *Marmion*, Canto 6. Montague House, Blackheath, was the residence of the Princess of Wales (later Queen Caroline). Mrs. Hayman lived at Berkeley Square when not in attendance. " Miss Hughes " at the end was a slip of the pen. See also Partington, *Private Letter Books* etc., pp. 8-9. It will be remembered that " Mrs." does not imply marriage necessarily.

city to which Mr. Wynne (to whom present my compliments) will be so good [as] to address the communication
which I expect with impatience. Believe me Dear Miss
Hughes with sincere respect & regard

[Yours WALTER SCOTT]

CASTLE STREET EDINBURGH. 10th Novr. [1807]

[Abbotsford Copies]

To LADY ABERCORN

MY DEAR LADY ABERCORN,—I did not answer your
Ladyship's kind letter untill I should hear something
about the subject which you make the object of your
friendly enquiries. Believe me I feel as I ought to do the
unmerited interest which you take in my success in life
& though I do not love to make professions even where
these are all I can offer in return for your active friendship
I must needs say in one word that the impression is
indelible. Hitherto I can say nothing about what Lord
Melville's kindness which I am sure is sincere intends to
do in my behalf. I have seen Mr. R. Dundas often but
only in his capacity of Colonel of our regiment of Yeomanry which was called out & quartered near Edinburgh
for about ten days for the sake of discipline. This was a
time of too much hurry & military bustle to have any
conversation with him The chief Baron has also been in
quarters for in our country almost every one has a military
as well as a civil capacity. I fancy there will be new
arrangements in our court very soon & then perhaps I
may be remembered among those whom the King
delighteth to honour. I hope your Ladyship has long
since had the sheets of Marmion—they were forwarded
by Mr. Wright in my absence to Lord Castlereagh the
inner cover addressed to your Ladyship. This is the
way that all the Marquis's heavy parcels reach him with

safety so I cannot doubt that your Ladyship's also will come safe although I think you should have had it before the date of your last card. If it has not yet come to hand I will try to send one by another channell [*sic*] Your stay in Ireland has already exceeded the time proposed & Ld Abercorn seems to think it will be still farther protracted perhaps beyond Christmas. At any rate I propose to meet the Marquis at Dumfries on his return so that I shall have the pleasure personally to assure you how much I feel your goodness—I hope you will visit Lord & Lady Aberdeen [1] the next season instead of the plains of green Erin. In that case you must pass through Edinburgh & I shall have the great satisfaction of showing you all the northern lions besides my own little fireside.

We have information here that Sir Walter Farquar's time is so absolutely & exclusively occupied at Carlton house that he cannot attend his other patients—this came to me from a very sure hand, that of a lady who went to London on purpose to consult him in the case of a son.— If ever the Princess has good cards in her hand I hope she will remember her friends in the North : I assure you I should beg hard to be made a Baron of Exchequer— These are pretty waking dreams—

Marmion after long repose has been resumed with spirit & the third canto is at length finished. Dryden's life is more than half printed. I think the latter will appear in about six weeks ; the poem perhaps a month later.

Yesterday I dined with Lord Advocate & a sort of Scottish privy council—all in high spirits—Mr. Dundas is just returning to superintend his Indian concerns.

Pray remember me kindly to Ladies Maria & Harriet not forgetting Miss Humphries & believe me ever your Ladyship's truly grateful

WALTER SCOTT

EDINBURGH 12 *November* 1807

---

[1] Lady Aberdeen was the Marquis of Abercorn's daughter.

I observe by the frank that Lord Chancellor [1] is at Baron Court—I hope Lady Manners has not forgotten me. If so will your Ladyship make my respects acceptable.

[*Pierpont Morgan*]

To MISS SEWARD [2]

[*23rd November*, 1807]

MY DEAR MISS SEWARD—I was honourd with your Letters some little time ago and moreover I last night received another kind mark of your remembrance by a card from Miss White who has just reached Edinburgh. To day when I leave the court where I am now writing I will do myself the honour to call upon that Lady. I am only sorry Mrs. Scott cannot as yet accompany me as she has been confined these few days with a rheumatic cold. But as Miss White makes some stay here Charlotte will take an early opportunity to pay her respects to a friend of Miss Seward & shew her any civility in our power.—I grieve for the misfortune of Captain Hastings & am now almost glad at my ill luck in not meeting him when formerly here. But what can we say—five hundred blockheads whose arms legs and headpieces are of no earthly service to themselves or any other person might have gone into a fire as hot as that at Vesuvius and

---

[1] Thomas, Lord Erskine (1750-1820), brother of Lord Buchan and Henry Erskine. For Scott's opinion of the brothers see note on p. 15.

[2] This letter was an answer to those of 26th August and 4th November. After congratulating him on the end of Tom's affair and thanking him for his account of the bookselling business, she tells him that she expects a visit from Southey and expresses her regret that her friend Captain Hastings had missed him in Edinburgh. She writes : " Alas ! he had his left arm torn off by a cannon ball in that infamous invasion of Denmark, which no apprehended peril to the State could justify or even extenuate, etc." She has reviewed the " Mountain Bard," *i.e.* Hogg, an unprecedented favour. Macneil's poems, sent her by Constable, are a " vapid collection."

In *Familiar Letters* this letter of Scott's is printed from a transcript. For " old Lady Lucas " is substituted " old Lady Tarras " ; and the letter is without indication amalgamated with one of date May 1808.

brought all their limbs safe off while the single man of worth & accomplishment was the sufferer. Your account of Captain Hastings interests me so much that I sincerely wish for the accomplishment of a hope which Mr White gives me that we shall see them both in Scotland in Summer 1808. Would your health would permit [you] to come about the same time but that we must not hope for— As for the affair of Copenhagen I know you will ascribe to my ancient freebooting border prejudices a latitude of morality which I think State necessity must justify because in the code of nations as in that of social order the Law of self-preservation must supersede all others. Indeed my patriotism is so much stronger than my general philanthropy that I should hear with much more composure of a general conflagration at Constantinople than of a hut being on fire at Lichfield. And as for the morality of an action in which the wellfare of the country is deeply concernd I suspect I feel much like the Laird of Kiers Butler. Keir had been engaged in the affair of 1715 & was tried for high treason ; the butler whose evidence was essential to conviction chose to forget all that was unfavorable to his master who was acquitted of course. As they returnd home Kier could not help making some observations upon the violent fit of oblivion with which John had been visited but that trusty domestic answerd with infinite composure that he chose rather to trust his own Soul in the Lord's hand than his Honour's life in the hands of the Whigs. But if I write any longer in this way you will lock up your plate as old Lady Lucas threatend to secure her cows when I should visit her suspecting that my distinctions between meum & tuum were hardly more accurate than those of Johnie Armstrong of Gilnockie.

I am very glad indeed that you have condescended to take upon you the task of reviewing my poor Shepherd. This dismal day of wind and snow is probably finding him a very different occupation from writing verses. A sailor when he hears the wind whistle always thinks of a sea tempest & such a night as last always sends my thoughts to the desert hills where my poor countrymen must be all night driving the sheep with their faces to the wind to prevent their lying down & being smotherd. In this service they very often lose their lives.

I do not at all like the task of reviewing & have seldom myself undertaken it—in poetry never—because I am sensible there is a greater difference of tastes in that department than in any other and that there is much excellent poetry which I am not now-a-days able to read without falling asleep & which would nevertheless have given me great pleasure at an earlier period of my life— Now I think there is something hard in blaming the poor cook for the fault of ones own palate or deficiency of appetite— There is a clever little Pamphlet come out against Jeffrey by Mr. Copplestone of Oxford. I gave it to the critic this morning & he is so much delighted with it that he says he means to request the favour of the authors contributions to his Review. To be sure he is the most complete *poco-curante* that I ever knew.

As for Macniels Poems [1] I perfectly agree with you & to complete the matter the man himself is as splenetic . . . [*MS. defective*] and conceited as his trumpery is insipid. I sometimes meet him in a booksellers shop & he has more than once threatend me with that most direful of evils the perusal of a Ms. poem written he does me the honor to say in my own Minstrel stile. What say the Laws of morality to this matter & am I at liberty to break his head for dishonouring my *manner*? The only case in point which I can recollect is that of Ariosto breaking the potters dishes who was singing his stanzas out of tune & I

---

[1] *The Poetical Works of Hector Macneill, Esq.* A New Edition Corrected and Enlarged. Veritatis simplex oratio est. Edinburgh. Printed by James Ballantyne for Mundell & Co. &c. 1806. The first edition is London, 1801. The poems, some of which date as far back as 1779, are ballads, elegies, etc. in the sentimental and elegant style of Gray and Collins or their imitators, and Scotch poems of the kind Burns had set the example of.

question professionally speaking if it can apply as a precedent my tales of Chivalry being as far below those of the Tuscan as the potters shards are superior to the ditties of Master Macniel. So peace be with him.

As to my own labours they are pretty well advanced. Since my brothers affairs have been put in a fair train I have resumed my pen in order to accomplish my engagement with the Booksellers which had been terribly retarded by the real avocations & other disabilities which these most unpleasant matters had occasiond. I am a pretty hard worker when once I set about [it] & in fact my literary life resembles the natural life of a savage absolute indolence interchanged with hard work. This is the interval of labour to which the gloomy weather & whistling wind are very favourable. Three cantos of Marmion are already printed—two will compleat the adventures of this doughty warrior. By the way I fetchd him from Tamworth in your neighbourhood—Colin Mackenzie when we heard of him was in great spirits & I hope as much amended as he thinks himself. Yet I wish he would seek a warmer winter climate. His absence is a dreadful blank to me in this place (our court house). I am now writing beside his empty chair & deprived of all the little intercourse & amusement with [which] we used to amuse our hours of official attendance. Will you excuse me requesting your servant may leave the inclosed for Mr. White— Believe me dear Miss

A general address to me at Edinburgh will always find me out.

Miss Seward, Litchfield.   [Franked "Dalhousie."]

[British Museum]

To ROBERT SOUTHEY

EDINBURGH, 15*th December* 1807

DEAR SOUTHEY,—I yesterday received your letter,[1] and can perfectly enter into your ideas on the subject of the Review :—indeed, I dislike most extremely the late strain of politics which they have adopted, as it seems, even on their own showing, to be cruelly imprudent. Who ever thought he did a service to a person engaged in an arduous conflict, by proving to him, or attempting to prove to him, that he must necessarily be beaten ? and what effect can such language have but to accelerate the accomplishment of the prophecy which it contains ? And as for Catholic Emancipation—I am not, God knows, a bigot in religious matters, nor a friend to persecution ; but if a particular sect of religionists are *ipso facto* connected with foreign politics—and placed under the spiritual direction of a class of priests, whose unrivalled dexterity and activity are increased by the rules which detach them from the rest of the world—I humbly think that we may be excused from intrusting to them those places in the State where the influence of such a clergy, who act under the direction of a passive tool of our worst foe, is likely to be attended with the most fatal consequences. If a gentleman chooses to walk about with a couple of pounds of gunpowder in his pocket, if I give him the shelter of my roof, I may at least be permitted to exclude him from the seat next to the fire. So thinking, I have felt your scruples in doing anything for the Review of late.

As for my good friend Dundee, I cannot admit his culpability in the extent you allege ; and it is scandalous of the Sunday bard to join in your condemnation, " and yet come of a noble Græme ! " I admit he was *tant soit peu sauvage*, but he was a noble savage ; and the beastly covenanters against whom he acted, hardly had any claim to be called men, unless what was founded on their

[1] See previous note on p. 386.

walking upon their hind feet. You can hardly conceive the perfidy, cruelty, and stupidity of these people, according to the accounts they have themselves preserved. But I admit I had many cavalier prejudices instilled into me, as my ancestor was a Killiecrankie man.

I am very glad the Morte Arthur is in your hands ; it has been long a favourite of mine, and I intended to have made it a handsome book, in the shape of a small antique-looking quarto, with wooden vignettes of costume. I wish you would not degrade him into a squat 12mo ; but admit the temptation you will probably feel to put it into the same shape with Palmerin and Amadis. If on this, or any occasion, you can cast a job in the way of my friend Ballantyne, I should consider it as a particular personal favour, and the convenience would be pretty near the same to you, as all your proofs must come by post at any rate. If I can assist you about this matter, command my services. The late Duke of Roxburghe once showed me some curious remarks of his own upon the genealogy of the Knights of the Round Table. He was a curious and unwearied reader of romance, and made many observations in writing ; whether they are now accessible or no, I am doubtful. Do you follow the metrical or the printed books in your account of the Round Table ? and would your task be at all facilitated by the use of a copy of Sir Lancelot, from the press of Jehan Dennis, which I have by me ?

As to literary envy, I agree with you, dear Southey, in believing it was never felt by men who had any powers of their own to employ to better purpose than in crossing or jostling their companions ; and I can say with a safe conscience, that I am most delighted with praise from those who convince me of their good taste by admiring the genius of my contemporaries. Believe me ever, Dear Southey, with best compliments to Mrs. S., yours affectionately,   WALTER SCOTT

[*Lockhart*]

To MRS. HUGHES [1]

[15*th December*, 1807]

MY DEAR MRS. HUGHES,—I was very much diverted with the quizzing article which you were so kind as to send me and particularly delighted as it was a mark of my retaining a place in your memory. I had the pleasure of shewing the critique to our great Judge Jeffries who considering the strength & sharpness of his teeth and claws is the tamest lion you ever saw in your life. He was extremely delighted with the imitations of his stile and proposes to write to the author without of course being supposed to know his name inviting him to contribute to the Edinburgh Review as he seems so well to understand the rules of criticism.

I heard from Miss Hayman some time ago with an

---

[1] Mary Ann Watts, born about 1770 at Uffington, a little village two miles north of King Alfred's White Horse Hill in Berkshire, married the Rev. Thomas Hughes, a canon of St. Paul's Cathedral considerably older than herself who, by an exchange of parishes, became Vicar of Uffington. She formed Scott's acquaintance in 1806 through Miss Hayman, a lady-in-waiting to Queen Caroline then living at Blackheath. Mrs. Hughes became much later a pretty steady correspondent, visited Scott at Abbotsford in 1824 and in 1828, and saw him from time to time in London. See *Letters and Recollections of Sir Walter Scott* by Mrs. Hughes (of Uffington), edited by Horace G. Hutchinson, 1904. Mr. Hutchinson says that of these letters " Lockhart does not seem to have suspected the existence." But in fact Mrs. Hughes supplied Lockhart with complete, or nearly complete, copies of the letters in her own handwriting, as well as copying for him the letters of Joanna Baillie and others. With Sophia Lockhart she was his chief copyist. There is another reason which may have influenced Lockhart in not making greater use of them—a distrust of the good lady's strict accuracy, and now that we are able to compare her copies with the original, to which I have had access through the kindness first of Mr. Heffer, Cambridge, and then of Mr. Gabriel Wells, New York, we can see that she touched them up throughout in a manner flattering to herself. But of this more later.

This letter is in reply to Mrs. Hughes' of 22nd December from Amen Corner " to keep alive an acquaintance which short as it was, afforded me so much pleasure." She encloses Coppleston of Oriel's *Advice to a Young Reviewer*, ' a parody of the method of criticism adopted in the earlier numbers of the *Edinburgh Review*, a marvellous piece of imitation, full of the finest irony."—*D.N.B.*

elegant Welch tale a contribution to Marmion for so is called the new ditty about which you express such flattering curiosity. The said doughty [knight] (for a knight he is and of merry England) is to sally forth in January—the printing is going on rapidly but my time is so much occupied with the discharge of my official duties that I have hardly time to keep up with its exertions.

My motions in spring are uncertain. I am always easily draggd up to London but the expense of the journey is an object to a poor bard with four small children ; but as this is merely a prudential [1] I am greatly afraid it will as usual give way to inclination. I need not add that the charms of Amen Corner will be a great additional temptation. There is in the 3d Canto of Marmion a certain doleful ditty adapted to a curious Gaelic air literally picked up from the Highlanders who have the same attachment to reaping in Scotland that the Irish have to making hay with you & always descend to the Low country (low comparatively speaking) in great bands to get down the harvest.[2] I will endeavour to get a noted copy of this same air which I think has some interest in itself and to which I am certain you could give a great deal. It has much the character of the beautiful Welch airs to which you give so much interest but is quite irregular in comparison.

[1] Perhaps " scruple " or " motive " accidentally not written.

[2] See *Marmion*, Canto III, ix. :
" A mellow voice Fitz-Eustace had,
The air he chose was wild and sad ;
Such have I heard, in Scottish land,
Rise from the busy harvest band,
When falls before the mountaineer,
On Lowland plains, the ripen'd ear.
Now one shrill voice the notes prolong,
Now a wild chorus swells the song :
Oft have I listen'd, and stood still,
As it came soften'd up the hill,
And deem'd it the lament of men
Who languish'd for their native glen."

I beg my best compliments to Mr. Hughes & am
with great regard My dear Madam your obliged humble
servant   WALTER SCOTT

EDIN. 15 *Dec.* [1807]

[*Abbotsford Copies*]

To ARCHIBALD CONSTABLE

Endorsed : 21*st December* 1807

DEAR SIR,—I inclose Mr. Murrays letter. I hope &
indeed believe that Mr. Millar has not quite been so
communicative as he has been informd but I have written
to him in a manner effectually to check any future risk.[1]
I promised him that if you askd a copy of the poem he
should have it also & it cannot have been a week in his
possession—I am very busy or would call on you. Yours
truly   W. S.

(private)

[*Stevenson*]

To LADY ABERCORN

DEAR LADY MARCHIONESS,—The effect of your kind &
undeserved attention is not lost on me for without your
friendly zeal I could hardly find in my heart to recur to
a subject which in its present situation is likely to
connect my chance of temporal advantage with the loss
of one of the kindest & most affectionate friends I have
in the world. Upon my return to Edinburgh I found
that the health of my colleague Mr. Mackenzie has
become much worse. He has been now in Devonshire
for nine months in hopes of overcoming a tendency to a
decline which is hereditary in his family. But lately the
symptoms have recurred & his mother & brother are
now gone to attend him. In these circumstances I can

---

[1] Millar had been showing parts of *Marmion* in advance to friends in
London.

have no doubt that there will be much solicitation to Lord Melville concerning an expected vacancy in his office. All I wish is that my interest should be so far kept in view that in case of the melancholy event taking place which is to be apprehended the person appointed to the vacant situation should relieve me of my bargain with Mr. Home. There is no one to whom Lord Melville would think of giving the situation that would not most willingly agree to this & think the favour almost as great as if granted unconditionally. And when in London I mentioned the possibility of such an event to Robert Dundas who seemed to think it most reasonable that any new Clerk should come into my place & that I who have served two years for nothing which may be considered as equal to paying between £2000 & £2400 should be put in full possession of the emoluments of my office.

As to my sheriffdom I shall think it hard if I am required to resign it. The offices have been held by the same person in a very late instance & I cannot think if together they produce me £1000 or thereabouts annually that it is more than (retiring from all professional pursuits or farther views of ambition) I may be thought to merit. But there is another reason of great delicacy why I think Lord Melville will be inclined to leave me in possession of this office. As the Duke of Buccleuch's estate composes two thirds of the County he is the natural patron of the situation & I think nay I am sure from my intimate connection & regard for that family they would much rather that no change should take place. But if a change were to take place I have reason to think that the Duke's Interest would be engaged in favour of a young country gentleman of his own class. Thus no point would be gained politically speaking except taking an office from a sincere zealous & sometimes an efficient friend to give it to a mere cypher—But in truth nobody seems to wish or think of a change in that sheriffdom & I leave the subject entirely at your Ladyship's discretion whether there be prudence in stirring that question unless it is proposed by Lord Melville.

I have thus my dear Lady Abercorn laid my full views before you ; they are not I think very ambitious as they if fullfilled [sic] to the uttermost will with my private fortune make me worth about £1500 a year out of which I must save something for my family but success to this extent would be fully adequate to my highest wishes & in fact I have lived hitherto honourably & indepently [sic] & not without a decent hospitality for a great deal less money—To be sure the public has been very favourable but this is a precarious resource, & the very circumstance of some literary celebrity carries with it temptations to expense. I commit the matter fully to your Ladyship in your own time & your own way to make such use as your friendship may dictate of this unreserved communication. I feel a natural shyness at opening my wants & wishes even to those who I know would have pleasure in assisting me & of this number I sincerely believe Lord Melville & his family. Should the renunciation of my sheriffdom be insisted upon as a preliminary to putting me on full pay sooner than the course of nature may dispose [?] of Mr. Home it would be more for my advantage not to give up £300 a year to come a year or two earlier to possession of £700.

If as I yet trust & hope may take place Mr. Mackenzie should recover his health I will enjoy from that event a pleasure far superior to the increase of my income [by] ten times the sum proposed.

I have filled this sheet so amply with those hateful personal details that I have but little room left to ask how you got up to London & whether you have experienced no inconvenience from the journey. I am also anxious to know how you like Marmion & whether the Marquis has seen it—I have some dread of his criticism as he understands the niceties of the English language better than anyone I ever met with. I am pushing on this poem to its conclusion & hope it will be out in the ensuing month greatly to my relief. Adieu my dear Lady & may God bless you for all your undeserved kindness to W. S.

MERTOUN 25*th Dec.* [1807]

I am spending my Xmas as usual with Mr. Scott of Harden my friend and relative but I go back to Edin^r to-morrow . . .

[Pierpont Morgan]

The vitally important letters which follow, and are now for the first time printed complete, were not discovered in time for them to be distributed chronologically through the first few volumes of the Centenary Edition.

As stated in my preface, there came to light at the very last moment in the offices of Messrs. Mackenzie & Kermack, W.S., Edinburgh, a volume of letters inscribed by John Ballantyne : OPEN NOT, READ NOT.

These letters (now in the National Library of Scotland), and six which Mr. Glen has provided, supplement in the most important way others we have printed in Vols. I-III ; but as these volumes were already in page and only Vol. I had room for additions, we have thought it well to print them together as an Appendix to this volume rather than to hold them over for a much later volume.   We have added cross references to other letters with which they connect.

We believe that the first volumes will thus provide much fresh material towards an unbiased verdict on Scott's relations with the Ballantynes.

H. J. C. G.

APPENDIX

LETTERS TO BALLANTYNE
1807-1818

To JOHN BALLANTYNE, JUNIOR [1]

DEAR JOHN,—I return the papers for revision. After mature deliberation I am still of opinion that we should average the clear divisible profits of Ballantyne & Co/ from this term to Marts. 1808 at £1200,, of which James to draw £800 and I £400,, by half yearly payments or as shall be most easy for the business. This will leave a sinking fund of £700,, or £800,, in the course of the year which will be applied to the payment of Interest or trade-interest and the balance to the gradual extinction of Company debts. Some sort of minute should be made of this engagement which must be held sacred. If James finds his £800 too much we can readily take any part of it back as payment of stock. But considering he has considerable sums of Interest to pay I fear he will not save much out of it. It is however a very handsome allowance & should be amply sufficient for the present. If all continues well I have no doubt the next years dividend may prudently be raised to £1000,, to James & £500,, to me. This simple plan will save you the trouble of all these half yearly calculations excepting

---

[1] This letter is printed in full in the *Reply* to Lockhart's *Ballantyne-Humbug.* John replies on the 1st December. The proposed division of profits seems " without objection, and it should immediately be acted upon," but owing to various causes " it cannot be *easily* acted upon." The partners have drawn from the business since Whitsuntide 1806 at the average rate of " £1130 a year." " These drafts the business has paid but encountering along with these the payment of wages in advance and the outlay to stock from encreasing trade, it has been disabled from clearing the encumbrances with which it set out and indeed has more than required

409

as a check upon our sale of profits : & will prevent were that likely to occur the least chance of disagreement. In striking James's stock I fear the balance of the cash accots. due by him at the commencement of the co-partnery must be deduced. In fact they should never have stood there as they were truly a burden on the valued stock which he transferrd to the Company. I have already explaind that I think the Company should pay the interest of these sums as hitherto incurd. When we see how the difference between his stock & mine stands all the advances of both parties to meet and pay the encreased demand, one cause of this will be easily understood from the following statement :

James Ballantynes Stock valued & carried to his credit at commencement March 14 1805 - - - - -	£2090
James Ballantyne & Co as under 25 Nov. 1807 - -	£6002
Printing Office including Marshall & Coy floor, new rooms, lead water stoves and furniture - - - - -	£2568
Founts of Types - - - - - - - - -	1630
Chases and all other printing furniture - - - -	340
12 Presses (1 French) - - - - - - - -	520
Ink & press room furniture - - - - - -	128
2 Hot presses - - - - - - - - -	110
Furniture in rooms, hot plates &c. - - - - -	78
House in Foulis close - - - - - - - -	450
Otranto - - - - - - - - - -	65
Paper Stock pd. for - - - - - - - -	113
	£6002

every farthing of which immense accession of dead stock . . . is paid for the calculation is made from James B's personal stock and the payments since made by Coy under his charge.

" It is therefore my decided idea that the Coy should take from the partner willing to advance it £1100 more at the Trade allowance of 15 p.c. and that the sinking fund should be appropriated (if not occupied in a still further extension of trade) towards *his* repayment. The trade would thus be clear and the dividends could easily be paid regularly." He goes on to argue that James's £500 due by him to the Royal Bank, being a personal loan for which the partners are not liable, cannot, he thinks, fairly be " a charge against his capital until it is *paid* by the Coy any more than the other sums procured by him on loan." He is personally liable for the interest and " should not be permitted to operate upon the account with the Coy's cash," but his doing so gives certain facilities with the Bank and saves him a small amount on the £25 interest. " . . . My payment of £200 to James (which I hoped to have employed differently, but this duty is paramount) will bring his present balance a little ahead of yours. Constable has the money & I can get it on demand, so that you will be so good as consider the usual equality maintained on the present balance."—
Nat. Lib. Scot.

a considerable part if not the whole of the Balance should bear 15 pr. cent in my favour.

With respect to accomodations in my opinion we ought to get rid of all that floating balance which with circumstances attachd to James's situation has hitherto kept us in a state of poverty. And in general when a partner is applied to for his individual security it should I think be optional to him to be the Banker himself if it suits his convenience better than to give a security. Bankers Interest seldom comes lower with one charge & another including renewals than £6,, or £7 & though to a partner the Company pay £15,, yet a proportion of the Balance is out of his own pocket in as far [as] it diminishes his interest in the free profit. On the other hand while Bills belonging to the Company are discountable without such security or if the Company on its own credit can procure a stationary loan at £5,, per Cent it would be unjust that a partner should force a loss upon them. I mention this because I shall have a large sum of money to dispose of at Whitsunday and the state of my family requires I make the most of it I can. What Ballantyne & Co/ have no occasion for I will probably employ in some literary speculation. Betwixt [now] and Candlemass this matter may be considerd more narrowly meantime I will lodge what money I can to assist against immediate demands. Believe me ever My dear John Yours truly   WALTER SCOTT

EDINR. 31 *Novemr* 1807

On looking back at the provision necessary for Whity. 1807 I see it was £1970. Since that we have received towards Stock

Shakespeare	- - -	£250,,
Cash by W. S. on trade profit		900,,
		1150

And although James overdrew considerably yet it was coverd by Mrs. Bruces loan. Yet the floating balance is still about £1500,, for although you reduce it to £900,, it is by reckoning the cash in hand & bills amounting to about £800 great part of which however cannot properly be placed against the floating Balance being the funds of paying the profits & carrying on the trade.   I observe however there is about £400,, laid out in stock which goes a great way to account for the debt remaining so large.

[*Glen*]

To JAMES BALLANTYNE

ASHESTIEL 23 *Oct.* 1810

DEAR JAMES,—I send you a wild sort of an introduction to a set of imitations in which I have made some progress for the Register.   But I want your opinion on the plan and preliminary vision.   Not having a Don Quixote here I cannot prefix the motto, but you will find the passage towards the end of the 4th vol : where Altesidore gives an account of her pretended death and of what she saw in the Infernal Regions.   I will make considerable improvements if you like the general idea.   You may take Counsellor Erskine into your deliberations.   I think the imitations will consist of Crabbe, Southey, W. Scott, Wordsworth, Moore and perhaps a ghost story for Lewis. I should be ambitious of trying Campbell, but his peculiarity consists so much in the matter and so little in the manner that (to his huge praise be it said) I rather think I cannot touch him, understand I have no idea of parody but of serious anticipation if I can accomplish it—The subject of Crabbe is " The Poacher " a character in his line but which he has never touched.

I wish John to take an exact account of his Quire Stock and compare it with his Catalogue.   This should be done every quarter at least and I suppose you can spare him the help of Hughes for a day or two to accomplish so useful a purpose.   His last Accounts state the Stock roughly from £7000 to £10,000.   Of this very

little excepting the Register can arise from our own
publications and I hope he will not increase it by purchases which have two bad effects *first* crippling our
publishing adventures by want of ready money—
secondly, giving ready money for that which we might
obtain by barter to much greater advantage. He
ordered £500 worth of Books from Rees which was
perhaps more than we shall be able to dispose of to
advantage at least without interrupting other speculations and his own experience of the profit of selling other
peoples things seems to argue our confining ourselves
as much as possible to our own—John has a little of the
spirit of purchase from old commercial habits but we
must now bend every nerve not to fill our warehouse
with other folks books but to sustain our presses by means
of our own publications which have hitherto answered
so well.

I make these observations chiefly to pave the way for
an adventure for which should Cash be wanted I will
willingly advance a few hundreds. I mean an Edition
of Shakespeare with a text as accurate as Weber and you
can make it, which would be to you both a labour of
love, and a selection of notes from former editions with
some original commentaries, exclusive of all trash and
retaining only what is necessary to the better understanding the Author or to justify disputed readings of
importance. I do conceive that such a Book printed
well, leisurely and accurately in an elegant but not an
expensive form would cut out all the ordinary editions
and afford a most respectable profit to the adventurers
as well as credit to the press. I should be willing to
take a few plays under my particular inspection and I
think Erskine would do the same, but Weber whose
romances and Ford will be soon out would be worth us
both. Pray take this into your anxious consideration. You
will perhaps startle at our doing more in the publishing
line, but as far as I can observe our overtrading if there

be any has arisen from our being obliged from various
reasons to take other peoples balderdash which from
our *bound* stock (which will cost us a loss of the interest
at least) to our Birmingham acquisitions of spelling
Books and Classics never has and never will answer. John
has neither patience nor capital for that sort of game, for
if he cannot get rid of a book in six months he will grasp
at ready money at any discount and thus make his
trade a losing one upon that bargain. His activity the
most valuable of all qualities in a tradesman is I think
in this sole respect apt to step over the line. He is
willing to give a great order rather than not be thought
to do as much business as other folks without reflecting
at the moment that the ready money which must be kept
to answer his Bill would bring into his shop at one half
the expense publications which would fetch double the
profit. All I have said on this subject is no doubt subject
to qualification and particularly does not apply to taking
other folks publications for our own when our own sell
slowly, nor yet to such purchases as may be absolutely
necessary to extend & confirm our Correspondences
which I am apt to think will be but few. You looked
I think at John's Acco^t of our own publications which
excepting the Register and the Immortal Georgics were
reduced to a very low ebb in almost every case. De Foe
was also then an exception but has since moved off. The
Register I will pawn my life upon and though the
Georgics be an affaire manque it is the only one [on]
which we have had to encounter loss and is but a trifle
after all.

Upon your part my dear James and as a corollary to
what I have been saying I must request your uttermost
exertions to make your presses up to 12 at least and to
keep your composition in as close a proportion to them
as possible. This may be no doubt difficult, but it is
the very difficulty which entitles you to 2/3ds profit—if
the business could be managed without your activity

good sense and unremitting exertion such an allowance would be unnecessary. You must be aware that Swift is gone,[1] that you are about to lose Somers, which I really cannot gainsay not a sheet having reached me this three weeks and that while your establishment declines, you will gradually lose the means of employing even the presses you have left. At least if we must retrench our business let us also retrench our Drafts upon it, for supposing 11 presses which have of late been our highest number to produce £2200 clear of all expense of superintendence &c. and we have never been able to bring out more, £400 is greatly too little for a sinking fund the object of which ought to be not merely to support the constant and necessary expenses of types &c &c with the discounts on Bills and a thousand other drawbacks but also to pay off debts and increase Capital. If therefore you are not able to put the establishment on a more productive footing the necessary though unpleasant consequence must be an abatement of the dividends to the partners from next Martinmas. For I think you will agree with me it would be a pity to make our Milk Cow yield blood and our last dividend was calculated expressly upon the understanding that the establishment could be maintained from 12 to 14 presses.

John whose communications are not always so full as I could wish upon such points has neither told me the state of your Law Suit nor whether you have done anything to recruit the presses. Surely it would not be difficult to get two journeymen for the little office on the plan I mentioned and I am sure it would break the confederacy of your apprentices as soon as any thing you could devise.

The various subjects of this letter so important in

---

[1] The first volume of Scott's edition of Swift was printed by G. Ramsay & Co., Edinburgh. The second, third, fourth and fifth by James Ballantyne & Co., but the sixth bears no printer's name, and the seventh to the nineteenth and last revert to G. Ramsay & Co. Ballantyne could not apparently keep his full twelve presses at work and so keep up with Constable's demands.

themselves and their consequences will make me anxious for a full reply. I mentioned the subject of the presses particularly to John as a subject of my deepest anxiety, but he might omit in the hurry of his business to communicate with you on the subject. You will readily believe I give both him and you credit for every exertion where your own interest and mine are so deeply concerned, nor do I think were the former out of the question, that the last would be indifferent to you. But unreserved intercourse where the stake is so ample, is highly necessary & needs no apology.

[*Copy among John Ballantyne Letters, Nat. Lib. of Scot.*] [1]

To JOHN BALLANTYNE

DEAR JOHN,—The note granted by you to me for £315,, dated this day is without present value further than what may be due to me by account for the Edition of Secret Memoirs [2] and the Register & of course I am to make up the difference before retiring the Bill. Yours truly   WALTER SCOTT

EDINR. 27 *May* 1811

[*Nat. Lib. Scot.*]

DEAR JOHN,—I reinclose the note endorsed—I think you should take measures to compell Murray & Longman to be *on* or *off* in their present state they hang on the book without aiding it and if they refuse their paltry money assistance I think you might express your peremptory wish that they would come to a point. Constables foot is in that business. He persuades them that he will make a better thing & give them a larger share &c. & they are

---

[1] A fragment of the original of this letter is in Mr. Glen's collection. For Lockhart's use of the letter see note, vol. ii. p. 526.

[2] *Secret History of the Court of King James*, 2 vols., 8vo. Edinburgh : Printed by James Ballantyne & Co. for John Ballantyne & Co., Edinburgh, and Longman, Hurst, Rees, Orme, & Brown. London, 1811.

asses enough to believe him—the old registers are also against us in the eyes of these honest gentlemen.

I sympathize in Sandie's distress which is too deep to be alleviated by considerations which must press on James's good sense & yours—for what could protracted life have [been] under such a disorder but protracted distress to the poor child & misery to its parents.

I wish to have my books very much especially the poets : as I intend to be in town about the 27th to see Jo: Kemble. I trust they will then be ready.

I inclose a most affecting letter from Polwhele.[1] James or you have his MS. I wish you would read the account of a dispute between an author & bookseller in Miss Edgeworths tale of Tomorrow. It is a good lesson for the danger of mislaying MSS. Pray write to him as you promised to do long since & say whether you will publish his work or no which is all he or I can require of you. I shall say you asked a little time to consider the matter.

Rokeby is advancing but slowly. James & Erskine have alternately thrown cold water about my ears so that I have lost much of my confidence. But I will do my best & make a bolt or a shaft of it.

When you write let me know when Mr Kemble is expected and what characters he first performs. I can spare but two or three days & am most anxious to see Cato. Yours truly   W SCOTT

ABBOTSFORD 19 *July* 1812

[*Nat. Lib. Scot.*]

DEAR JOHN,—I send you the note indorsed. I am aware your Necessity in the present instance has no law— the necessity of getting the poem forward becomes so pressing that I believe it will occasion my giving up my

---

[1] Polwhele's letters, full of anxiety regarding his MS., are in the Walpole Collection. For Scott's reply see Vol. III. p. 158.

English jaunt.¹ I have a letter from James very anxious about your health and state of spirits. If you suffer the present inconveniences to depress you too much you are wrong—and if you conceal any part of them are very unjust to us all. I am always ready to make any sacrifices to do justice to engagements & would rather sell every thing or any thing than be less than true men to the world.

If there is any thing worse than your last statement I intreat you will let me know it—if not I think that the poem will extricate all, & I am now in full sail. If James or you can come out any day next week I trust to shew you Canto I. I can not ask you both because I have but a bed for one. Yours truly   WALTER SCOTT

ABBOTSFORD *Monday* [PM. *August* 11 1812]
[*Nat. Lib. Scot.*]

DEAR JOHN,—I have your letter and can have no personal objection to your disposing of ¼ of your own three eigths [*sic*] of the poem. But I own that I think it a desperate expedient for yourselves since if my luck hold it is borrowing money at 100 per Cent besides proclaiming very legibly your wants to the whole book-selling world. If I could have foreseen this failure I could easily have been in high strength considering my late increase of income. But my buildings & plantings will cost me odds of £1000,, this season. Still however if it were possible by another discount to stave off matters till your bills came round I would do so rather than you made the proposed sacrifice which I trust you will pause

¹ " Scott, I believe, accepted Mr. Morritt's friendly offer so far as to ask his assistance in having some of Ballantyne's bills discounted ; and he proceeded the week after to Rokeby, by way of Flodden and Hexham, travelling on horseback, his eldest boy and girl on their poneys, while Mrs. Scott followed them in the carriage." Lockhart goes on to tell the story of the innkeeper of *Scott's Head* and the horse-doctor turned physician at Flodden. The visit took place in the last week of September and first of October. See Vol. III. pp. 157 *et seq.*, where these letters fall into their place.

on. I write by this post to Hay Donaldson to pay you
£200,,—£150 for the Lay &. the other £50 may remain
with you to answer in part a Note of mine to Messrs.
Yeoman & Co/ of Langholm for £70 value in slates
payable in three months after the date 24th Augt. I will
put you in cash for the balance between [now] & that
time & make the interim deposit for your convenience.
The note is payable at your shop.

Can you not get off some of your old stagers of bound
Stock—better lose on them than on the poem.

Consider what you want is only a temporary supply
which it shall be my business to render necessary as short
while as possible. Therefore do not be rash—it is a last
expedient to be resorted to when others fail : indeed it
is a kind of selling off if to carry on trade you part with
the *raw material* instead of the *manufacture*. I should like
to know precisely the sum you will thus raise before you
do more in the matter. Yours truly   W. S.

ABBOTSFORD 14 *August* [1812]

My books have never arrived unless they are come to
Melrose bridge tonight. You had better call on Donaldson for the money.

[*Nat. Lib. Scot.*]

DEAR JOHN,—I return the inclosed & shall be glad
when all that matter is finishd. Pray look over our
voluminous commissions & report progress. We country
folks are impatient. By the way James carried off my
black coat I suppose to persuade Mrs. Ballantyne that
he had fallen away through the abstinence of Abbotsford.
As the said garment is necessary upon official occasions
pray let it be returnd. I will send the proofs by next fly.

On thursday I have people here on business on friday
we are engaged at Yair—on Saturday Sunday or Monday
I will be happy to see Mr. Rees although we can give

him but beggarly accomodation. It will be very convenient to know the day and time of his arrival by post.
There is nothing else in yours requiring an immediate
answer.   Yours truly   W. S.

1st Septr 1812 [1] ABBOTSFORD
[*Nat. Lib. Scot.*]

DEAR JOHN,—I return the sheet. I begin to dread its
running out to the necessary length.

I wrote by the parcel advising you of a bill to Sterling
which proves to be £158,, 12,, 10 instead of £150 as
formerly advised.

I have been tortured to death by idle people & I hope
Rees will not come : indeed I cannot see any one here
with the least comfort except very intimate freinds.
Pray say Mrs Scott is unwell which is the case & make
my apology to him.   The poem requires my utmost labour
and I think is the signal for every one to interrupt me.

In the matter of the case [?] we will be guided by the
opinion of the artist.   My temper is really worn to a
hairs breadth—the intruder of yesterday hung on me
till twelve today.   When I had just taken my pen he was
relieved like a centry leaving guard by two other lounging
visitors & their post has been supplied by some people on
real business.   I shall write to Rees I think by this post
which may save you the trouble.   Yours truly   W. S.

2d Septr. 1812 [2]
[*Nat. Lib. Scot.*]

[1] The 1st was Tuesday, so that Thursday was the 3rd and Saturday the 5th,
accordingly the letter written from Edgerston at Vol. III. p. 157 must be
wrongly dated.   Lockhart leaves the date of the visit to Rokeby obscure, as
he does not date the letters he cites of Erskine and Morritt.   Morritt's is dated
the 10th September (*Walpole Collection*) and Erskine's the 18th.   Lockhart's
" week after " the receipt of Morritt's is therefore wrong.   The visit took
place at the end of September and beginning of October.   He is still at
Abbotsford on the 20th, and writes from Rokeby on 1st or 2nd October.

[2] Date added later.   An extract from this letter will be found at Vol. III.
p. 337, printed from Lockhart, who had dated it 2nd September 1813, a
year later.   Lockhart gives it as to James.

To JAMES BALLANTYNE

DEAR JAMES,—The packets came safe. I am greatly obliged by your criticisms though I dont subscribe to all of them. *Exempli gratia* the plume *hid* Bertrams face when he enterd but surely *not* when he smiled at the pains Oswald took to throw light upon it. Again you must remark that though Oswald knows him he is a stranger to the reader & his appearance must be minutely described. *Host* & *lost* are a perfect rhyme to the eye that satisfies the critics I believe. Most of your other criticisms you will find complied with by corresponding alterations.

John writes me he has got bills from Longman & Co/ for £2000 of quartos upon my guarantee. Surely this with £500 from hence should be much more than enough to meet all difficulties without farther incroachment on Sir W. Forbes. John reckond that £700,, would carry him through before Scholeys failure—Scholeys is £1200 so we have £2500 to meet £1900—besides what John has got in London from Scholey. I presume you were not apprized of Johns success when you applied to Sir W. I trust whatever facilities are now afforded will be strictly redeemd. We must not on any account consider them as a part of Capital. Of all this you are as sensible as I am but we must positively often recall it on all sides. I shall send the £500 so soon as I receive it but I believe the bill must go to London so it may be a week or more. But it is *certain*.

Lady Louisa Stuart & Morritt give me much heart on the opening of Rokeby. My being here will prove of the utmost consequence to the poem. Indeed I now think I should have slurd the business without it. I have got quite a new stock of ideas & subjects.

On Sheet A if it is yet time I incline to have the following alteration.

From Brackenbury's tower [1]   Instead of Old Baliols.

[1] But "old Baliols" remains. *Rokeby*, I. i.

There is I think nothing else of consequence. Your next letter must be addressd to Jedburgh where I shall be on tuesday [1] for two days. You will be surprized at the localities I have gotten. Pray get out of the Shop & send me Hutchinsons history of Durham & Northumberland. Hay Donaldson comes to Melrose on Saturday and may leave it at Erskines for me. Fail not to do this as it is necessary for my *localities* names &c. Yours truly

W. SCOTT

ROKEBY *Wednesday* [PM. *Oct* 2 1812]

Charlotte begs you will remember Mrs. Gills remittance & your promise to enquire after her lottery ticket.

[*Nat. Lib. Scot.*]

TO JOHN BALLANTYNE

MY DEAR JOHN,—After many *offs* and *ons* and as many *projets* & *contre-projets* as the treaty of Amiens I have at length concluded a treaty with Constable in which I am sensible he has gaind a great advantage but what could I do amidst the disorder & pressure of so many demands & scarce a farthing to pay either James household or my own. In short I have e'en sold him ¼ Rokeby at £800 & as many articles of one kind & [an]other as at a round discount makes up £1200—300 Registers for one article & 50 B. & Fletcher for another—this engages him on the Register & he promises his utmost for that work when you come down which I think now must be as soon as possible—your work at London is of course

---

[1] That is on the 6th October, and a letter to James from Chesters, near Jedburgh, written on the 6th, is printed in Vol. III. pp. 166-7 from the collection in the Signet Library, Edinburgh, and a second from Jedburgh on the same day, pp. 167-9. Other letters to the Ballantynes, filling the gap between this of 2nd October 1812 and the next of 19th May 1813, are in Vol. III. pp. 177, 178, 179, 187-91 (about text of *Rokeby*), 203-4 (ditto), 209 ; 4th May, p. 264 (which resumes the money question and the steps to be taken to meet the crisis). At pp. 271-2 follows a " manipulated " version of this letter.

ended when this news reaches them. The arrival of your
long-dated bills decided my giving in for what could
James or I do with them. I have askd the favour of Sir
W. Forbes to let me discount for £1500 which they have
agreed to but we must strain them no farther for I see
as I suspected it will not do. Constables bills are long,
but they are sure and will relieve this £1500,, Constable
has not said positively if he will take a future share in the
Regr. or no the expence of the management startled
him at once for at first he would have taken the whole
1000 copies rated as my stock at 40 pr. cent discot. but
went off on calculation of the profit. You will of course
keep in eye the beginning of June and the middle of July
& do what you can to meet them. I trust this last sacrifice
has cleard our way but many rubs remain nor am I after
these hard skirmishes so able to meet them by my proper
credit. Constable however will be a zealous ally & for
the first time this many weeks I shall lay my head on a
quiet pillow for I do think that by our joint exertions
we shall get well through the storm & save Beaumt.
from depreciation, get a partner in our heavy things reef
our topsails & move on securely under an easy sail &
if on the one hand I have sold my gold too cheap I have
on the other turnd my lead to gold. Brewster & Singers
are the only heavy things to which I have not given a
blue eye. Had your news of Caddells Sale reachd us
here I could not have harpoond my grampus so deeply
as I have done, as it was nothing but Rokeby wd. have
barbd the hook : his interest commences with the
present Editn., i.e. that which is at press—but I will
desire him to write to you himself. Adieu my dear John
I have the most sincere regard for you & you may depend
on my considering your interest with as much attention
as my own. If I have expressd myself with irritation in
speaking of this business you must impute it to the
sudden extensive & unexpected embarassments in which
I found myself involved all at once. If to your real

goodness of heart and integrity and above all to the quickness & acuteness of your talents you added habits of more universal circumspection and above all the courage necessary to tell disagreeable truths to those whom you hold in regard I pronounce that the world never held such a man of business. These it must be your study to add to your other good qualities meantime as some one says to Swift I love you with all your failings pray make an effort & love me with all mine. Yours truly

W. S.

PRINTING OFFICE 19 *May* [PM. 1813] [1]

We have just £1500 to go on with & £1770 to pay & more before 31st. but there be debts recoverd & James is to do your bidding about the discount—damn the very name—I shall hate it while I live.

[*Nat. Lib. Scot.*]

DEAR JOHN,[2]—On the other side I send a list of the stock sold Constable for which wt. the ¼ Rokeby I got £2000 at 6. 12. & 18 mos. It *is* a sacrifice but being pennyless and without credit what could we do? A few months earlier information would have made the whole affair easy and to the want of this alone the excess of our extremity is to be attributed. Let it never escape your recollection that shutting your own eyes or blinding those of your freinds upon the actual state of business is the high road to ruin. Meanwhile we have recoverd our legs for a week or two and James has got £150 out of the proceeds to pay some distressing claims of his own. His

---

[1] This letter, or at least a " manipulated " extract, is printed by Lockhart in his *Life*, and in that form will be found, for comparison, in Vol. III. pp. 271-2. See also there the letter to Constable of 18th May, p. 272.

[2] For Lockhart's version of this letter see Vol. III. p. 273. On the 20th of June Scott wrote to Constable with proposals for the new poem. See Vol. III. pp. 285-8, with the note on relative correspondence between Constable and Cadell. Scott writes again to Constable on the 21st and 25th June (Vol. III. pp. 289-91). John's address on both the letters printed here is " Care of Messrs. Barclay & Sons 95 Fleet Market London."

living and yours must be regulated and regularly provided in future with the wages or quarterly or partly both. I have also got money to pay my interests & servants with some tradesmens bills. Constable will I think come into the Register—Russell is to write the history and I think will bring it out in time : he seems most eager on the job—Constable is equally anxious to maintain the printing office—he sees most truly that the more we print the less we publish—for the same reason I think he will help us off with our heavy quire stock. I should like to guard the Beaumt. which *must* come round one day.

I was aware of the distinction between the State & Calendar as to the latter including the Printing office bills & I sumd & deduced them (they are marked with red ink) but there is still a difference of £2000 & upwards on the Calendar agt. the business. Dont forget Lord Somerville. Constable will take as much of that work as we chuse to part with—of course we will keep very little. When I can get James to send the fac-simile of old poems I will send 20 under one or two office franks. You can dispose of them well in London. I sometimes fear that between the long date of your bills and the tardy settlements of Edinburgh trade some difficulties will occur even in June—& July I always regard with deep anxiety. As for loss if I get out without public exposure I shall not greatly regard the rest. Ratcliff the physician said when he lost £2000 in the South Sea scheme it was only going up 2000 pair of stairs. I say it is only writing 2000 couplets & the account is balanced. More of this hereafter. Yours truly   W. SCOTT

EDINR. 21 *May* [PM. 1813]

Of course you lose the sale of ¼ of the 5th. Editn. Rokeby.

100 Tales of East £2,,	12,, 6	-	-	£262,,	10
220 Popular tales 17/4		-	-	-	190,, 13,, 4
146 Charles I 8/-		-	-	-	58,, 8,,
20 Royal Do 14/-		-	-	-	14,,
18 James Ist 16/		-	-	-	14,, 8

```
   25 Do. royal      28/      -    -    -   £35,,
  107 Do. Roderick 4to 10/-   -    -    -    53,,  10
  124 Do. Royal       8/-     -    -    -    49,,  12
  489 Demy Do.        6/      -    -    -   146,,  14
   50 Beaumont & Fletcher £5,, 12,,   -    280,,
   50 De Foe £2. 6         -    -    -    -  115,,
  119 Last nine vols 34/6    -    -    -   205,,  5,,  6
                                          ─────────────
                                         1425,,  0,,  10
   28 Annual Regr. 30/     -    -    -      42
  267    Do        30/  6 vols.   -    -   400,,
                                          ─────────────
                                         1867,,     ,,  10
          Discot. off  -    -    -    -    -   567
                                          ─────────
                                         1300
       Rokeby       -    -    -    -    -   700 with my
    book accot. about £120 more   -   £2000
                                          120
                                         ─────────
                                         £2120
```

James has behaved very well during this whole transaction & has been most steadily attentive to business.
I am convinced that the more he works the better his
health will be.   One or other of you will need to be
constantly in the Printing office, hence forward—it is
the sheet anchor.

In the anxiety wt. which I look forward to July &
August it has occurd to me that a sale might be advan-
tageously made to the public of our miscellaneous stock
& of such books especially of the showy kind as you can
collect by *exchange* (not *purchase*) in London.   This wd.
be Cent per cent more advantageous than a sale to the
trade who at present neither can nor will buy either
here or in London, & it is too obvious that we *must* sell
for I see discounts cannot be had.   I would half bind the
books as formerly & arrange them as miscellaneously as
possible.   We would sell none of our own publications
but let the others go as the public would take them.   The
booksellers would *rage* but we have all the ill effects of
their enmity already & never had the least advantage

from their favour & Constable & probably Blackwood
the only publishers may be secured to the printing house.
If you can propose a better measure I shall be glad—
if not this adopted about the 1st July or in the race
week will clear possibly £1200 or £1500. Of course if
you think of this you will endeavour to make your
exchanges miscellaneous. I would avoid Longmans
books for an obvious reason with Scholeys I would use no
ceremony.

I pray you to observe that supposing your June settlements clear June & they are all you have to trust to you
enter on July altogether unprovided with about £1800
to pay before the 14 July I having £3000 payable in the
same month. It is impossible we can proceed without
a sale to the public or the trade.

[*Nat. Lib. Scot.*]

DEAR JOHN,—I sent you the order & have only to
hope it arrived safe & in good time. I wakend the boy
at three o'clock myself having slept little less on account
of the money as on that of the time. Surely you should
have written three or four days before the probable
amount of the deficit & as on former occasions I would
have furnishd you with means of meeting it. These
expresses besides every other inconvenience excite surprize
in my family and the neighbourhood. I know no justifiable occasion for them but the unexpected return of a
bill. I do not consider you as answerable for the success
of plans but I do & must hold you responsible for giving
me in distinct & plain terms your opinion as to any
difficulty which may occur and that in such time that
I may make arrangements to obviate them if possible.

The inclosed letter will explain itself. You will inclose
the £666,, Bill in it & forward it to Constable immediatly
with a card from yourself if the note be indorsed by you
otherwise send it by a chairman or the penny-post as

there is no occasion he should know it has been in your hands. I shall discot. these two bills of £333,, at Selkirk & Galashiels place the produce of the one in my cash accot. as part payment of the money advanced to you by drat. & send you the produce of the other in the course of next week. Supposing therefore that you are clear till 1st Augt. or nearly so, this sum will help you over the first days of that month. You then have the sale £350 & you said you could renew the acceptance due upon the 8th for £179 & may probably do the same by a part of that due on the 13th. (Hartstongue has most kindly promised to get the Bill for £700 returnd from Miss Dumergue cashd in Dublin. You may speak with him on this subject to learn the mode of drawing which will be discountable here—it meets my Jedburgh drat. of the 15th—& is not payable untill April. I will write to him to make the remittance to you as the money is payable in Edinburgh & I shall be out of the way.)

It would be proper to try Sir W. F. with an acceptance say for £250 from you to me if that could be discounted about the beginning of Augt. & suffered to remain in my cash accot. till the end of the month it would help us a little. The date might be 6 months. Pray send me such a bill. I have no doubt of getting £500,, or £600 or more about the same period among the Levites here or otherwise & thus Augt. is pretty well disposed of. For Septr. I have less fear. Longman must renew his £500 so must Murray his £300. Your rejected bills then fall in with several others & I can get some cash at Jedburgh. Besides I hope you will get some aid from Rees. I have much more to say but am forced to conclude. Let me know your views & opinions plainly and candidly upon this statement. Yours truly   W. S.

Saturday [1] ABBOTSFORD. [PM. July 25, 1813.]

<hr>

[1] Lockhart dates this letter " 24th July 1813," which was a Saturday. The letter enclosed, to Constable, is dated " Saturday 25 " with Scott's usual carelessness. See Vol. III. p. 309. John is back in Edinburgh.

Seal Constables letter with a wafer.

Of course if any thing has gone wrong you will come out here tomorrow. But if as I hope & trust the cash arrived in due time you will write to me under cover to H. Grace the D. of Buccleuch Drumlanrig Castle Dumfrieshire. I shall set out for that place on Monday morning early.

[*Nat. Lib. Scot.*]

MY GOOD FRIEND JOHN,[1]—The post brings me no letter from you which I am much surprized at as you must suppose me anxious to learn that your express arrived. I think he must have reachd you before post hours & James or you *might* have found a moment to say so in a single line. I once more request that you will be a business-like correspondent & state your provisions for every week prospectively. I do not expect you to *warrant them* which you rather perversely seem to insist is my wish but I want to be aware of their nature & extent that I may provide against the possibility of their miscarriage. The Calendar to which you refer me tells me what is due but cannot tell your shifts to pay them which are naturally altering with circumstances, & of which alterations I request to have due notice. You say you *could not suppose* Sir W. F. wd. have refused the long dated bills : but that you *had* such an apprehension is clear both because in the Calendar these bills were rated two months lower & because, three days before, you wrote me an enigmatical expression of your apprehensions instead of saying plainly there was a chance of your wanting £350 when I would have sent you an order to be used conditionally.

---

[1] Scott has addressed this letter to " Mr James Ballantyne, printer, St. John Street, Edinr." For Lockhart's version of this letter see Vol. III. pp. 306-8 ; and for a letter to Constable of this day, Vol. III. p. 309.

Having more regard for your anxiety than you have for mine I must inform you I shall send you in two or three days £333 which with the sale £300,, which I do not see credited in July & your proposed renewals will carry you on I presume till about the 20th Augt. when I will rummage about for £500,, which if I succeed in will leave only £300 minus. In Septr. I have rated myself at £750,, Longman & Wardrope making together a sum of £850,, may all be renewd & Longman pitchd over to January feby. & even April. Thus the minus on that month is only £330,, In October Longman & Murray must again lend a lift of £800,, should it be necessy. & then the minus will not exceed £250,, In Novr. (if I succeed in getting £500,, from Lord Somerville at a long date in Augt.) I cannot make the debts exceed £2700 which are fully met by the funds supposing the poem sold. You see that according to this scheme little of the pressure will lie upon you but if you can do more than provide for a deficit of about £300,, in each month so much the lighter will my task be. All I desire is unlimited confidence & frequent correspondence · & that you will give me weekly at least the fullest anticipation of your resources & the probability of their being effectual. I may be disappointed in my own of which you shall have equally timeous notice. Omit no exertions to procure the use of money even for a month or six weeks for time is most precious. The large balance due in January from the trade & individuals which I cannot reckon at less than £4000,, will put us finally to rights & it will be a shame to founder within sight of harbour. The greatest risque we run is from such ill-considerd dispatches as those of friday. Suppose that I had been gone to Drumlanrig—suppose the poney had set up— suppose a thousand things & we were ruind for want of telling your apprehensions in due time. Do not plague yourself to vindicate this sort of management but if you have escaped the consequences (as to which

you have left me uncertain) thank God and act more
cautiously another time.   It was quite the same to me
on what day I sent the Drat. indeed it must have
been so if I had the money in my cash accot. & if I
had it not the more time given me to provide it the
better.

You will of course consider what I have stated and
looking over your own notes let me know if I have
mistated any thing.   I have reckond nothing on getting
in debts or on the sale—the latter Indeed cannot come
in till Decr.   I wish you wd. consider what I have said
about Constables proposal.

Now do not affect to suppose that my displeasure
arises from your not having done your utmost to realize
funds & that utmost having faild.   It is one mode to
be sure of exculpation to suppose one's self accused of
something they are not charged with & then to make a
querulous or indignant defence & to complain of the
injustice of the accuser.   The head & front of your
offending is precisely your not writing explicitly upon the
the deficit to be apprehended in such a time that it might
have been provided for & I request this may not happen
again.   It is your fault and I believe arises either from an
ill-judged idea of smoothing matters to me—as if I were
not behind the curtain—or a general reluctance to allow
that any danger is near untill it is almost irretrieveable.
I shall be very sorry if any thing I have said gives you
pain but the matter is too serious to all of us to be passd
over without giving you possession of my explicit sentiments.

Tomorrow I set out for Drumlanrig—& shall not hear
from you till Tuesday or Wednesday.   Make yourself
master of the post-town—Thornhill probably or Sanquhar
—& of the post hours.   As Sir W. F. have cash to meet
my order nothing I think can have gone wrong unless
your boy perishd from the way.   Therefore in Hope &
Faith and that I may lack none of the Christian Virtues

in Charity with your dilatory worship I remain very truly yours

W. S.

ABBOTSFORD 25 *July* 1813

How did you address Mr. Morritt. I fear the note has miscarried. Have you heard in answer.

[*Nat. Lib. Scot.*]

DEAR JOHN,—I inclose the order—unfortunately the Drumlanrigg post only goes thrice a week but the Marquis of Queensberry who carries this to Dumfries has promised that the guard of the Mail Coach shall deliver it by five tomorrow. I was less anxious as the £350 is markd in the Calendar as due 27th and your note said you could clear this month. It is a cruel thing upon me that no state you furnish excludes the arising of such unexpected claims as those for the taxes on the printing office. What unhappy management to suffer them to run a head in such a manner but it is in vain to complain. The Calendar bears only £231 & wages as due on the 15. I suppose the taxes make up the difference. I inclose both bills— that to Sir W. F. you will not present till I write at more leisure. Were it not for your strange concealments of debts & difficulties I should anticipate no difficulty in winding up these matters. But who can reckon upon a state where claims are kept out of view till they are in the hands of a *writer*. If you have no time to say that this comes safe to hand I suppose James may favour me so far. I write also by post but your answer cannot reach me untill *tuesday*. Yours truly

W. S.

DRUMLANRIG *friday* [29 *July* 1813]

Let the guard be rewarded.

You will take heed to procure a stamp on Saturday

cveng. & draw a bill on me at 3 mos. for £350 leaving
the date blank & send it here for acceptance. It will
reach me on Tuesday & I hope with a full letter on
affairs in general.

[*Nat. Lib. Scot.*]

As the Marquis does not set off immediatly I may
as well add all I have to say as write by the post. (I
intend to write Mr. Gilbert Innes to ask him to discot.
the £350 which I am aware he will do at my request.
If the £250 is also discounted at Sir W. F's I shall then
be in readiness to face £710 due on the 15th & also to
afford you some assistance if absolutely necessary). But
I wish to know supposing I send you money then what
you propose to do for the end of the month when according
to my view of the matter supplies will be at least equally
necessary. Let me know in short what you *can* do & *hope*
to do both for this & next month & what you think of
my proposals in my last letter—for it signifies nothing
raising money for you unless I see it is to be of real
service. Observe I make you responsible for nothing
but a fair statement of your probable funds & of the
times & periods when assistance will be necessary ; that
I may be at once provided at the proper times & not
subject to these irregular sort of demands which have
so often deranged the plans I have laid for retrieving the
business. This £200,, for instance—why was it not kept
in view ?—You must write often & fully stating what
effect every advance made is likely to have upon the
business. Did you speak to Hartstongue about the Bill.
If it arrives & I get £500 besides I shall be very easy.
But every thing must be renewd that is possible. Longman & Murray I will manage myself & I wish your
opinion distinctly in answer to my full letter of Sunday
last. I shall leave this on tuesday or Wednesday &
expect to hear from you on tuesday morning at length.
To tell you the truth I fear nothing in the business but

your odd ways of keeping all difficulties out of view till the very instant moment of ruin.

I have only with me the leaf of the Kalendar which relates to Augt. the book being too large for my writing box.

Do not forget to inclose in your letter £20 in B. of England notes as I think when I have made the necessary arrangements of going a little way into England I will send you a cheque when I can get a stamp.   Yours &c

W. S.

DRUMLANRIG CASTLE 30 *July* [1813]

The Guard is known to the Marquis who has promised good naturedly to give him the letter with his own hands so it must reach you in time though probably past five on Saturday.[1]

[*Nat. Lib. Scot.*]

DEAR JOHN,—I trust you got my letter yesterday by five o'clock with the Drat inclosed.   The strange circumstance of the Dukes post being so ill arranged occasiond the delay.   I return your Drat. accepted.   I expect to hear from you on tuesday by which post I shall apprize you of my motions.   On Wednesday I think of leaving this place where but for these damnd affairs I should have been very happy.   I shall be very anxious to know your opinion of my plans & whether you can do any thing to aid them.   (I keep my purpose of discounting £350 with the royal Bank in aid of my £700,, on the 15th). I will want a note of funds to enter in Kalendar ever since you were at Abbotsford also when the renewals &c fall in. I conclude from your last though not very distinct that

---

[1] For Lockhart's version see Vol. III. p. 313.   To the postscript he has added that portion of the first letter which begins : " Let me know in short what you *can* do and *hope* to do," but with some modifications.

with this £350 you can go on untill the middle of this
month which will do very well.　　W. S.

Sunday DRUMLANRIG [31 *July* 1813] [1]

[*Nat. Lib. Scot.*]

DEAR JOHN,—I inclose you an order for £350 on Sir
W. F. It is within my credit even if the £250,, be
declined which however I trust is not the case. I have
written to Mr Innes & have no doubt the R.B. will
discount £350 more as I formerly wrote you. I mentiond
to Mr. I. it was the remnant of the transaction in which
he formerly interested himself. These bills will retire
mine of the £710 from Jedburgh due 15 as I think. If
Hartstongues letter comes you may open it as it contains
no secrets. Be pleased to inclose a £10 english note in a
letter to me at Rokeby where I shall remain untill
Saturday or Sunday & I shall be at Abbotsford on
Wednesday at latest.

I hope the printing office is going on well. I fear from
the state of accompts between the companies restrictions
on the management & expence will be unavoidable
which may trench upon James's comforts. I cannot
observe hitherto that the P.O. is paying off but rather
adding to its embarassments & it cannot be thought
that I have either means or inclination to support a
losing concern at the rate of £200 per month. If James
could find a monied partner an active man who understood the commercial part of the business & would

---

[1] Scott leaves Drumlanrig on the 4th August, returning, I suppose,
to Abbotsford, whence he sets out for Rokeby, but at Brough on the 10th
receives Morritt's letter of the 8th putting off the Scotts' visit on account
of his wife's ill-health, not, as Lockhart states, because of John's worrying
letters. He writes to John from Penrith before he has heard the news, and
to Morritt on the same day from " Brough," presumably Brough-under-
Stainmore in Westmorland. He will go on to Keswick to visit Southey.
See Vol. III. pp. 315-16. He expects to be home by Saturday, 14th August ;
but he seems to have been in Carlisle on that day. He writes from Abbotsford on the 16th.

superintend the conduct of the cash it might be the best
for all parties for I really am not adequate to the fatigue
of mind which these affairs occasion me though I must
do the best to struggle through them.   I should like to
know the present state of expenditure at the Office
falling under the article of wages bookkeepers salary & so
forth.   I fear it is more than James & you are aware of
I mean that it bears a heavier proportion to the actual
receipts otherwise the business should clear itself faster.
Believe me yours &c.   W. S.

    PENRITH 10 *Augt.* [PM. 1813]

    Dont forget the £10,, as it is troublesome drawing in a
strange country.

[*Nat. Lib. Scot.*]

                              CARLISLE *friday night*

    DEAR JOHN,—I have your letter & regret to see that by
some fatality you have totally misunderstood my meaning.
I wrote to M[r] Innes to request the R.B. as before to
accept a drat of yours on me for £350—& I directed you
to send me such a drat for acceptance.   You did so but
with the view of discounting it yourself in which case
as I also wrote to you it would be necessary to send me
another.   As no other appeard I concluded you intended
to defer discounting for the Compys use that which [I]
had signd.   I therefore did not (as I once thought of
doing & now do) send you a blank acceptance to be filld
up for £350.   I concluded of course you would speak
with Mr Innes as *you* were to discot the bill though on my
credit.

    To crown all I did not get your letter till four hours
after post : so you will only have this on Sunday.   You
must see M[r] Innes as soon as you can & remedy any
evil that may have happend on the 15th.   When the Bill
is taken up you must write an apologetic letter to Fair/

.Jedburgh/ in case it has been dishonord, stating the real
fact that I was in England & my order came too late.
You say nothing of Sir W. F. & the £250,, acceptance.
Write to me at Abbotsford by return of post—remember
it is *two o clock*.   I will write at large on hearing from you.

W. S.

[PM. 15 *August* 1813]

[*Nat. Lib. Scot.*]

DEAR JOHN,—I received all your letters & hope the
business with M[r] Innes is settled if not I shall send a
Drat to M[r] Fair.   This will greatly hurt my means of
getting supplies in the country but the resolution I have
now taken renders that of less consequence.   I am quite
satisfied it is impossible for Jo: B. & Co/ to continue
business longer than is absolutely necessary for the sale
of stock & extrication of their affairs.   The fatal injury
which their credit has sustaind as well as your adopting
a profession in which I sincerely trust you will be more
fortunate renders the closing of the bookselling business
inevitable.   With regard to the printing it is my intention
to retire so soon as I can possibly do so with safety to
myself and with the regard I shall always entertain for
James's interest.   Whatever loss I may sustain will be
preferable to the life I have lately led when I seem
surrounded by a sort of magic circle which neither permits
me to remain at home in peace nor to stir abroad with
pleasure.   I have therefore resolved that all the copy-
rights be sold and I have to request you will take the
necessary measures for doing so immediatly & to the best
advantage : perhaps Longman should have the refusal
you may consider this.   As Gale is now down & Rees
will soon be so you will certainly have it in your power
to make a bargain as well as if you were in London, or
you may speak to Blackwood & Constable also : though
I fear the latter is too deeply dipd to make it possible at
this time for him to be a purchaser.   Get rid of them

however at such dates as will bring in cash for the exigencies of the business without giving me any farther trouble. I should imagine if you proceed cautiously they will fetch long prices. As I hereby give up our bargain of sale the Compy will fall to retire the drats. I granted so far as still outstandy. & to repay me the sums I have advanced for paymt. of the £3700,, If the money thus procured is inadequate to the relief of these affairs your first exertions as an auctioneer will probably be made on " that distinguishd select and inimitable collection of books made by an amateur of this city retiring from business." I do not feel either health or confidence in my own powers sufficient to authorize me to take a long price for a new poem untill these affairs shall have been in some measure digested. This idea has been long running in my head but the late fatalities which have attended this business have quite decided my resolution. Probably the copy rights may carry some stock with them if well managed. I will write to James tomorrow being at present annoyd with a severe headache. Yours truly

W. SCOTT

ABBOTSFORD 16 *Augt.* 1813

I trust I shall be able to get cash for the exigencies after the 24th. I wish to know if the £612,, of bills stated in the calendar as at maturity in Septr. are to be brought forwd. in the beginning of the month or how ?— [1]

[*Nat. Lib. Scot.*]

[1] For Lockhart's version of this letter see Vol. III. pp. 316-17. In the *Life* he says : " By his [Scott's] desire, the Ballantynes had, it would seem, before the middle of August, laid a statement of their affairs before Constable. Though the statement was not so clear and full as Scott had wished it to be, Constable, on considering it, at once assured them, that to go on raising money in driblets would never effectually relieve them ; that, in short, one or both of the companies must stop unless Mr. Scott could find means to lay his hand, without farther delay, on at least £4000 ; and I gather that, by way of inducing Constable himself to come forward with part at least of this supply, John Ballantyne again announced his intention of forthwith abandoning the bookselling business altogether, and making an effort to establish himself—on a plan which Constable had shortly before suggested —as an auctioneer in Edinburgh."

DEAR JOHN,—I received your two letters. No doubt I might raise money here to carry on business some little time longer but in the circumstances I cannot think it fair or honorable to do so not being assured that I could regularly repay the sums I might thus obtain. If the copy rights can be sold so as to make the price apply early in Septr. I will endeavour to provide for the gap. But if not I think the most fair & honble. way will be to state to the parties principally concernd our inability to go on and exhibit a state of our funds. As to myself my sufferings will be rather from the eclat of such an affair than any other circumstance—for no one shall lose a penny by me. If Rees was down he might be consulted with for I cannot help thinking it would be worth their while to buy these copy-rights which would give much relief to the business or rather insure a clearance with what I might be able to do.

I certainly can write a poem & I can sell my books either or both of which expedients I will have recourse to discharge these claims. I must reserve a quarter for Jo: Murray. Longman & Constable might have the rest Longman perhaps a half with the management. Two thousand pounds advance at Marts. is no more than I have always gotten & if that joind with debts & the price of the copy-rights will not clear out the concern there is no faith in figures. I cannot think that any of the trade with whom I have had concern will be very rigorous on this occasion but on the contrary I should look for such support & assistance as the view of the affairs may render suitable for them to give & us to expect. As Rees is not in Edinburgh Constable might be consulted with as to the time & mode of laying open these affairs to the persons principally concernd. But unless upon assurances that the copy-rights can be speedily converted into money it would be injustice to attempt going on & for me to raise money at the country banks here would be in the highest degree improper. The evil of this business is having carried on the concern so very long untill its credit was totally ruind before having recourse to my assistance for what I have done ought to have cleard it if the business had been in a situation to do any thing for itself.

But I will not do in my own case what I have condemnd in others that is attempt to support a falling business beyond the moment that it appears rational to hope for its being retrieved. I have no debts of my own of any consequence excepting such as have been incurrd in the unlucky business. I shall therefor[e] wait patiently till tomorrow when I hope to hear from you & if you give them no hope that the copy-rights can be sold why the affairs must go into the hands of trustees. Perhaps James or you if you are able to travel had better come out here yet I scarce see that your doing so or my going to town can be now of service.

I can only add that in the event of giving up the affairs you should speak to Mr. Scotland on your part as I shall to Hay Donaldson on mine & M[r] W. Erskine will I am certain give his advice to both.

It is a comfortable reflection that every thing (at least according to the states I have had) is fair & above board & threatens no ultimate loss to the creditors. In the event of your presenting me such a view of things as will authorise going on I will endeavour to make the necessary remittances & am Yours &c.   WALTER SCOTT

[PM. *August* 20 1813] [1]

[*Nat. Lib. Scot.*]

DEAR JOHN,—I am far from wishing to shrink from any responsibility which I may have incurd in this business & still farther from wishing to precipitate the bankruptcy of your firm. But you will attend that a very great change

[1] For Lockhart's extract from this letter see Vol. III. p. 317.

has taken place for the worse since I wrote the letter to
which you allude. Bills to the extent of at least £600,,
are there reckond upon as funds applicable to Septr.
but these are now anticipated & the proceeds gone.
Add to this £200 of taxes & the missing renewal of
Mundells bill & you will see matters are just £1000,,
worse than when I wrote from Drumlanrig. I will
manage however to send the funds for Monday as I
should not wish to injure Mundells house. I can perfectly well do all *I* proposed and even more for I kept
within the mark but then I do not see what will be the
use of my exertions unless you can take up your share
of the load. I shall however provide myself to pay the
£750 about the middle of the month ; sooner it cannot
be—this I must do by accepting M[r] H's offer [1] of £500
& therefore I must wait its being remitted from Ireland &
for the remaining £250 I must wait till the 21st. So that
after the present inclosure & another £100 which I shall
send against the 28th you will be left to your own funds
& devices but I should think Hartstongues money would
reach [you] before the 12th. I see no prospect of getting any
else where. If the copy rights can be sold to the extent
even of £1000 payable in Septr. it will make matters
endurable but if they can be entirely disposed of at
6, 8 & 10 mos. things will be quite easy. But I own I do
not at present see what you are to do in the interim
unless Sir W. F. once more extends his liberality to you.
I have been anxiously expecting Rees's arrival. It still
seems to me he is likely to purchase but of this you will
judge.

I have not had a proof of Somers since my return. It
is surely no time to neglect that work.

As the surest mode of remitting I send you an order on
Sir W. F. It is beyond my credit but the deficit will be

---

[1] *i.e.* Mr. Hartstonge's. See Scott's letter to him of 21st August (Vol. III.
pp. 317-19) and Scott's letter to Constable of 23rd August (Vol. III.
pp. 319-20).

made by remittances on Monday. I should like to know more particularly what passd between Gale & you also your views of providing for deficiencies in the end of the month & the beginning of September. You need not however write untill Monday. If there is any question made about the drat (which I do not expect) you will explain that Sir W. F. will receive cash from me on tuesday. We must keep up credit there.

I have only to repeat that I have every wish to support the credit of the house if it can be supported but I wish on the other hand to have some reasonable prospect that my exertions will be ultimately successful for hitherto while I have done everything that I had engaged for & calculated upon there has been always some back-stroke which has put us all to sea again. I can only look to a speedy sale of the copyrights as a certain means of extrication & it is certainly worth struggling to gain time for such a transaction. But if we are to fall behind a £1000 every month over & above what had been calculated & provided for who can stand it. Yours &c

W. SCOTT

ABBOTSFORD *Saturday* [PM. 22 *August* 1813]

[*Nat. Lib. Scot.*]

DEAR JOHN,—After some meditation last night it occurd to me I had some title to ask the Duke of Buccleuchs guarantee to a cash-accot. for £4000,, as Constable proposes. I have written accordingly stating that the purpose is to prevent the hasty sale of my copyrights & I have very little doubt that he will be my surety. The fact is between ourselves I once assisted him in a similar matter.

I shall hear by tuesday I hope. I will send the £350 produce of the bill discounted at Galashiels which will clear this week. By the 1st. we shall know if the cash

accot. can be had but I wish it were possible to renew
Blackwoods bill on that day though I shall look for cash
here for that & the remainder of the next week.   If the
Cash Accot. be in view M[r] Constable will certainly
assist us untill the necessary writings are made out or
Hartstongues bill arrives.

I calld your attention to the alteration of circumstances
since I wrote the letter you quoted against me somewhat
too keenly not as making you answerable for the short-
coming but as an answer to your allegation that *nothing
in the circumstances of the company had changed* since I had
engaged to advance certain sums.   Am I right in supposing that by paying £450 on the 2d. we recover £600 of
discountable bills because that will be a fund for several
days further.   I beg your pardon I dare [say] I am very
stupid but very often you dont consider that I cannot
follow details which would be quite obvious to men of
business of which this is an instance ; & was indeed my
purpose of asking *what* supplies you had for the beginning
of month.   If these bills be discountable when recoverd
they are good for so much.   If not when will they be
discountable ?   Is your drat. an acceptance which must
be paid on the 2d. or can it lie over if inconvenient.   All
this I dare say it is very ignorant to ask but yet it is what
I have been labouring to know from you & have never
learnd.   You always refer me to what is before me in the
book but that cannot teach me such details as have taken
place since you last adjusted it.   Your own answers
sometimes vex me : for instance you tell me drily that
if the sums I count upon [are] forthcoming the result
must be as I suppose—but in a week the scene is changed
& all I can do & more is inadequate to bring about these
results.   I protest I dont know at this moment if even
£4000 will clear us out.

After all you are vexd & so am I and it is needless to
wrangle who has a right to be angry—but pray try to be
as luminous as you can especially when present operations

are calculated to make alteration on what was formerly counted upon. Commend me to James. Yours truly

W. S.

ABBOTSFORD 24 *Augt.* [PM. 1813] [1]

I have written to Constable of the proposal I have made to the Duke & that I expect a favourable answer.

[*Nat. Lib. Scot.*]

DEAR JOHN,—I drew on you for £350 to replace with Sir W. F. the £400 drat. in part & discounted the Bill at Galashiels—please to accept it.

We have no occasion earthly for £6000,, the third part of the sum supplied in the course of the next two months will amply supply our wants providing I can sell a new poem & get £2000 to accot. in Novr.—Now I should think if Mr. Constable really has that deep & serious interest in our support which he seems to have he will have no objection on proper security being given to grant acceptances for such a sum. Or he might intimate to his Londn. Banker what is strictly true that he is in treaty for a work of mine & that I wish to be accomodated with £2000,, or £2500,, immediatly which on our joint security I should think might easily be had for a few months. By the term of Whitsunday I could put all matters straight whether the copy-rights be sold or no it is only the immediate pressure which gives me any embarassment or anxiety. I should be glad to come to town but I shall lose three days hard work at Swift, & I believe it would really be Mr Constables interest to favour me with a visit here. James & you could bring him out and I think I could easily show him that he would run no sort of risque by assisting us to the extent of £2000 or £3000 with his credit but would on the contrary reap advantages

[1] On the same day Scott wrote to the Duke of Buccleuch. See Vol. III. pp. 322-25.

both direct & indirect of a very important kind. It is a great mistake to suppose that I am insolvent for by disposing of my property of various kinds I could pay every farthing the company owes without the aid of their funds & have clear £2000 a year remaining. If our good friend thinks that by holding a synod here on Sunday first suppose or any day but Saturday we can chalk out any feasible plan of raising this sum it will fully answer our turn & as I wish not to enter into any farther engagements than are absolutely necessary I would rather decline assistance to a larger extent than £2000 or £2500. I do not mention among my resources that I am brother-in -law to one of the richest men in India who has been long married without any family & to whom my children are the natural heirs. But the circumstance should not diminish my credit & I have no doubt I could borrow a couple of thousands from him in the course of an Indian letter ; but I should not like to ask a relative whom I never saw for pecuniary assistance. I have written to M[r] Constable but James & you can also see him—it is quite in his power to serve us at this pinch for it is credit we want & not money. I really wish he could come out here & talk this matter over. I can give you all beds by sending the girls to Charles Erskines for one night. I should make many apologies for giving him the trouble of coming here in my affairs but by going to [*the remainder of the MS. is cut away*]

[PM. 26 *August* 1813]

[*Nat. Lib. Scot.*]

DEAR JOHN,—I inclose an order for £350,, for this week. I expect to hear from the D. by tuesday & I trust favorably. Yet even then there will be a great dilemma between the 1st. Sept and the adjustment of the credit. Constable cannot have an answer to his proposal till the 3d. at soonest then deeds &c must be exchanged & in the

mean while there is £700,, or £800,, to pay. You have
draind me as dry as hay & I believe any assistance I can
have here will be very trifling not above £200 or £300.
I could to be sure send a receipt for my salary due on the
20th & with that in his hands and the assurances of the
Dukes support without which nothing can be done I
should think Constable would help us forward in some
way or other. As for me I really can no more & I blush
to think of the straits I am reduced to—I—who could
have a thousand or two on my own credit in any previous
period of my life. As for sending me states they only
confuse me. If the Calendar be really perfect it is the
best state for me. I am afraid that all the acceptances
you counted for October & November are thrown back
as well as those for Sept. I must know how this is before
I engage further. It would be a fine thing if after getting
this credit if it can be got you should (that is the business
should) a third time leave me in the hole to struggle for
myself. For you must be sensible that by degrees I have
been left totally alone & to tell you a secret I would rather
the business stood on your acceptances than mine—so I
must look sharp to the provision for November. I need
not reply to James's letter. Yours truly   W. SCOTT

ABBOTSFORD 27 *Augt.* [PM. 1813] [1]

[*Nat. Lib. Scot.*]

DEAR JOHN,—I inclose the bill for £500,, which with
£450,, formerly sent makes £950 towards this month.
I can positively do no more for Sir W. F. have intimated
their dissatisfaction with my late heavy draughts though
very civilly—I am obliged in every case to prefer your

[1] For Lockhart's version see Vol. III. p. 328, where also follow Scott's
letter to Constable of the 28th, letters to John of the 29th, and to James of
the 30th and 31st (originals in the Signet Library). The hoped-for relief from
the Duke is announced in the last just as the end seems certain : " Scotland
and I must part as old friends have done before, for I will not live where
I must be necessarily lookd down upon by those who once lookd up to me."

wants to my own otherwise this bill would exactly have coverd Longmans & greatly facilitated Constables negotiation in the row.

For Gods sake look forward how your own funds & those provided in London will come in to extinguish debts & remember *mine* must be paid as well as yours. You know I cannot calculate how or when your bills will be discounted though you can by taking the worst view. It is comparatively easy to provide for a difficulty seen at the distance of months but who can trust to doing so at the warning of days & hours. Do take a well digested view of this matter upon a broad & extensive plan.

I think that those books of which you have small re-mainders should all go to [the] *public* not the *trade*—this is my decided opinion—you will realize (considering your own new profession) much more money more speedily & more safely than in any sale you can make to the Edr. booksellers. Do not quit sight of this : 10 or 12 copies of any book may easily be passd off in an extensive sale nay 20 or 30 in the course of a season. I find the Dukes books are to be sold at Kelso. Yours truly   W. S.

ABBOTSFORD *Sunday* 5*th* [PM. *September* 1813] [1]

Our carrier is the *Galashiels* not Melrose carrier he leaves Edinr. on Wednesday morning. I mention this for the green paint.

[*Nat. Lib. Scot.*]

DEAR JOHN,—I wrote fully to James before receiving his & yours today & just added a prospect. I have no means whatever of making you any remittance but as of course I must raise the money by way of annuity if it cannot be got otherwise I should suppose Constable could easily

---

[1] For Lockhart's extract from this letter see Vol. III. p. 355, and Vol. III. p. 358 for a letter to Constable (28th September) on the subject of raising money by " a redeemable annuity," to which Scott refers in the next letter.

help you through in the interim which can be but a few days. No letter of yours can reach me till thursday as no post comes into Melrose on Wednesday. You should always remember this.

The annuity plan must certainly be kept in view though I shall be a heavy loser for I dont see how I can have much expectation of relief from a concern which cannot relieve itself. I shall certainly not need above £4000,, at the outside—if Caddell & Davies will buy any part of the copy-rights at reasonable prices I shall not need so much. Some part of the sum will however be necessary in any point of view at least I fear so, for [I] doubt Caddell will not buy all the copy-rights out & out which would enable us to have recourse to the Bankers in London with his bills. As however they have made the offer let us see what they will do—Longman & Co/ have had their option & cannot complain & Constable may be taken care of. If matters press the securities must be drawn up for the money on annuity I fear that to wait Longmans answer will throw us too late for the £800,, bill. But of this you are to judge remembering that there will be a week at least required for sending the papers to the Duke & for signature then back to me & so to town. James having sent me £30,, I shant want more than £70,, of the £100,, you promise. Perhaps C. & D. will take some stock—would to heaven they would. In the circumstances I do not suppose that Rees's application will be successful it is a mere fetch to put off the unpleasantness of declining the arrangement from himself & I think the result need not be waited for. I think therefore James should canvass Davies after speaking with Constable. If he comes forward frankly good & well—but if not ; or if which is most likely he only chuses to buy *part* of the copy-rights then let the annuity transaction go forward—calculating the extent by the proposal of Davies. I expect £1000,, in the course of November so I think £4000 will be enough at the outside.

Besides it is the sum mentiond to the Duke. If Constable thinks the transaction should be gone into directly you had better transmit me the papers by express not by post as you know their importance. I shall send them to Drumlanrig by a servant of my own. In writing remember post-hours—James's of Saturday only reachd this morning which is very strange.   W. S.

Tuesday 28 *Septr.* [1813]

[*Nat. Lib. Scot.*]

Monday

DEAR JOHN,—I have been in daily expectation of hearing from you and am disappointed. Something must have been arranged by this time either with Rees or the Annuity loan. I am most anxious about the £800 due at the B. of Scotland where I am promised credit in the winter which I shall certainly forfeit if this Bill is not retired punctually. But I presume that if the annuity loan is settled the lender will have no absolute objection to advance a part of the sum say £1000 even though the securities are not executed. Will you mention this to Constable.

Wednesday

I have yours. I believe Constables intentions to be most friendly but it is hard he should be so often mistaken in his calculations concerning others. I inclose the bills but I wish that it could be managed otherwise for preserving credit with the B. of Scotland.

The £70 came safe and will keep me till I have cash of my own.

I own I wonder you have not sooner communicated with Davies—take my word you will make the best bargain before Rees is decidedly off : & I cannot consider his hesitation very favourably. The one seems to wish an arrangement and the other to be desirous of evading it. I wrote James fully as to the footing on which he might treat with D. always having an eye to Constables interest.

I should greatly prefer any reasonable arrangement for sale of the property to borrowing money on annuity. There is besides your copyrights the share of the Lay which they themselves rated so very highly. You must on the whole be governd by circumstances. If Rees after all comes forward frankly good & well but I doubt his doing so. If not why we must take the other house. The length of bills will be of little consequence as the Bankers profit can go forward.

You tell me the paint is gone to Ashestiel but you do not tell by what *carrier*. So I am just as wise as I was—& how the people should have sent it to Ashestiel where I never lived when corresponding with them I cannot conceive unless it was one of your lucky hits in the way of addressing parcels.

If the £800 could be taken up by any arrangement with Davies or Rees I would greatly prefer to attempting renewal.[1] Yours truly   W. S.

[PM. *Oct.* 7th 1813]

[*Nat. Lib. Scot.*]

To JAMES BALLANTYNE

DEAR JAMES,—I have thought so much upon the subject of a new poem that I have no hesitation in fixing the price at £4200—(four thousand guineas) but I have no objection that £1050 shall be made dependent on the success of the work, as I have no wish to have any undue advantage. Should this be agreeable I would propose that *the poem be publishd in January* 1815 & in case Rees persists in declining the arrangement proposed I should be very well pleased that Messrs. C. & D. had one half of the Copy right with the management & that Messrs. Constable & Co/ and you retain each a 4th. But as my coming under an engagement of this sort at present is owing to

[1] See letter to Constable of 16th October, Vol. III. pp. 363-64.

my wish to realize a sum of money for a particular purpose [1] it would be necessary that Messrs. C. & D. should accept for the whole sum in four bills at 12, 15, 18 & 24 months for £1050 each. The last bill I shall relieve them from if the work proves unsuccessful. Of course Messrs. C. & D. will settle with the other partners by taking bills in the usual way. I cannot think this proposal unreasonable because hitherto the first edition of every poem has cleard the copy money & because £5000 has not been thought an extravagant request by well informd booksellers with whom I have talkd over this subject, & also considering the price at which the copyrights have sold long after numerous editions. Neither should I be at all disposed to take a less sum than £5000 but for my wish to enter into the transaction alluded to which I cannot do without these bills. If the advance of the first £1050 should be objected to the bills could easily be renewd for a few months not however at my expence. But it would be highly imprudent to publish before 1815 besides it will be necessary that I go to the Long Island [2] next summer to complete some of my scenery. This statement you may communicate to Mr. Davies & I think you should shew him the state of former sales that he may be satisfied that my demand though large is not exorbitant. I am Dear James Yours   WALTER SCOTT

ABBOTSFORD 7th October [PM. 1813]

It may be necessary to add that I should call the poem successful if it clear the copy money advanced with a reasonable profit before the last bill becomes due—Or some other equitable principle may be adopted. You may shew Messrs. C. & D. that I have been always paid in advance & am making no new rule for them.

[Nat. Lib. Scot.]

[1] Scott is contemplating the purchase of the lands of Darnick called Kaeside, which in May 1816 he acquired from John Moss. The poem is The Lord of the Isles.

[2] i.e. the Outer Hebrides.

To JOHN BALLANTYNE

DEAR JOHN,—I am very glad to find by your letters this morning received (by the way you need never write to me on a *tuesday*) that Davies has been at last spoken to. James will shew you my letter which is so written that it may be communicated to Mr. D. if you judge it necessary. You may also shew it to Constable who I think will not stumble at the price being beneath what we talkd of by £1000,, But I wish this cursed business to be terminated some how or other. Should C. & D. object to want of security, the other copy rights might be pledged to them by *you* in security of my fullfilling my part of the transaction. I do not know what to say about Mr Rees—the time is long past since he promised a decisive answer : but I should not like to cut my old friends short so that the offer cannot be made in a peremptory manner to C. & D. Yet I have no hope of Rees doing any thing & it seems hard to keep us in suspense. Mr Constable will best know the sort of law which he expects & perhaps will take the trouble to write him if the treaty with Davies assumes a form of probable success. I hope he will think I have done what is right with respect to his house. I am sure I would willingly transact with them for the whole & we should make it an easy matter but for the emergency of the case. The share of property which I return in your name may be afterwards parted with if necessary but having a share in all the other publications except Marmion I wish at present to retain some right in this also.

The interest of the printing house must be kept in view —they will lose a good friend in Longman if any breach takes place but to be sure the sacrifice of the quarter might propitiate them bye & bye. You will understand my plan is if I can get these bills to proceed on the Cash accot in Londn. Yours   W. S.

7th October [PM. 1813]
[*Nat. Lib. Scot.*]

DEAR JOHN,—As Wednesday is a blank day for Melrose post I only got yours this morning. You receive my Exchequer money this week which is a large step toward your £310,, upon the second & I am confident that on my guarantee which is indeed implied Messrs. Constable will accomodate you in some shape with the balance untill I come to town about the ninth or tenth when I mentiond that I would be able to give you some assistance either towards this sum or that payable at Whitsunday. I have made up my mind and arranged all my affairs upon our last examination of the Calendar & I promise you I shall like very ill to be driven out to sea again. Why does not James hurry through the Lady of the Lake but he is a true Spaniard who will not mend his pace though the House were on fire. Jamiesons copy money should have been enterd in the Calendar nothing has tended so much to cause and prolong the confusion of these affairs as leaving out of view claims which ought to be paid & are certain to be made. I think he owed us an accompt. Webers will also be payable.

As to your Paris plan Mr Constable will be best judge but I see many difficulties. In the first place it is one thing to speak a language for ordinary purposes & another to understand it commercially. But besides there is little of our stock fit for the Paris market except the Register & Memoirs of Charles I which well introduced would do at this moment. And respecting the Register you are to consider that not only Bonaparte but the French Nation and many of those Generals who still are in power are treated with wonderfully slight ceremony which will not be very flattering to their feelings. We do not yet understand what facilities will be permitted for commerce in a country still in great confusion & you will I fear be a good [deal] vexd & harassd by various impositions & exactions. If however Mr. Constable from what he can hear in London thinks the adventure hopeful I am sure I shall not object to any probable experiment.

As to your going to London I think it is unavoidable and indispensible. I see no prospect of closing these affairs but by selling the stock & no prospect of doing so under any tolerable circumstances except by exertions in London. The very loss of interest will more than make up the profit you might make upon the sale. But the main argument is that in neither of your three letters do you point at any means of supplying the deficit which will take place if there is not a sale in the end of June & beginning of July and I am sure I know of none. The business will be when in London to make the journey as efficient as possible & this I readily trust to your dexterity & alertness. I believe such of your books as are fit for the Paris market will be bought in London or exchanged without your going there & I would recommend you to enquire among those who use that trade. But as I said before I only stated my objections hypothetically to the Paris journey. At all events you will not think of going to London without seeing me. If you go to Paris it will be proper that James applies to the Lord Presidt. stating your intention asking if you can do anything for his Lordship & requesting some credentials to Lord Cathcart or Lord Aberdeen &c to distinguish you from a mere adventurer. This will be very well taken and properly & modestly used will put you on a creditable footing at Paris. Yours truly

WALTER SCOTT

ABBOTSFORD 28 *April* [PM. 1814] [1]

I see Burns Bowl is for sale at Mr Mortons Jeweller. I wonder what they ask for it.

You do not say what you are doing about the £310 but I presume you are not idle above all not trusting to me after my explicit declaration. I sent James a large portion of W.[2] yesterday by Selkirk Mail coach. I hope he has it. Pray ask. The weather upon the whole has

---

[1] John's address is now " Sale rooms Princes Street."   [2] *Waverley.*

been charming & if your sale did not keep you in town you could not do better than drive out here with James.[1]

[*Nat. Lib. Scot*]

DEAR JOHN,—I have your two letters this morning—how that of *Monday* was not here on *tuesday* it is impossible for me to conceive : but your letters never come right. I never supposed that having sent you £655,, being £200,, more than I proposed that I was also expected to furnish the additional £110,, & if you read my last letter you will observe that I suppose you provided to the end of the month.

I never supposed that you did not do your best in these affairs but I have often regretted that you did not speak upon them more frequently. If you had opend your mouth during the last days of the Session you would have saved yourself and me great vexation. I do not see how I am favour by leaving me to the last moment & then dictating the way in which I am to employ the credit I have remaining in your behalf—whereas when I have a weeks notice I have at least the power of chusing my own expedients.

You say all the demands are before me—but I see no entry of the money due to Ross—I observe there are under acceptance for these sale room advances £661,, this sum of £300,, will make up the balance.

I shall inclose a cheque on Galashiels for £110,, for which purpose I shall draw a bill on you for £220,, as I shall need the balance myself and I do not want to abuse the patience of Sir William Forbes.

Upon affairs in general I can only say that my aid has been unceasing and constant and that all I want is to be treated like a man in return & not like a milk-cow. There may be inconvenience but there can be no disgrace

[1] For an extract from this letter see Vol. III. p. 434.

or ruin in the business if this is attended to. The whole debts are about £6000,, for which I shall probably be able to advance £3000 between [now] & Christmas. With your debts stock & credit you may surely help well on to the remaining Moiety of the debt. I will explain to you when I come to town how I think matters may be made tolerably easy. You will do me the justice to remember that in your views of anticipated resources I have always urged you to keep within the mark of just & moderate probability. I see no use in any other views except to mis-lead & perplex.

Let Mr Constable be so kind as to get you money for the Cheque as it would be awkward for you to indorse it. Yours etc.   WALTER SCOTT

ABBOTSFORD 21 *July* [PM. 1814]

I shall be in town on Monday. I intended to have sent the £110,, but concluded it included in the £300,,

[*Nat. Lib. Scot.*]

DEAR JOHN,—You were very right to write me that your drat. had come safe & for once your letter came by return of post. I do not begrudge you a bit of the vexation & doubt which you have had because all might have been arranged to your convenience eight days before I left town had you sought as you should have done a full communication on the subject. Accepting your trouble of mind as a penance for recurring to your system of expresses I have to inform you that I have on your calculation written to Constable that I will close with him for half the copy-right @ 1500 Gns. with which offer he must close if he wishes the work at all & which I dont anticipate his refusing. The term of acceptances for this sum cannot be fixd untill after a full conversation with you for which reason I shall wish to see you *all other engagements whatsoever laid aside* at six oclock on Monday evening bringing the means of making up the Calendar.

If you look in on Constable without saying anything of what I have told you, you will discover by a little address upon what trim he is & how he is like to be pleased with his bargain which it would be desireable to know. I want to know what the 3000 Waverleys should net of half profit you said I think between £500 & £600—Yours truly   W. S.

    ABBOTSFORD 23 *July* [1] 1814.

[*Nat. Lib. Scot.*]

DEAR JOHN,—I have your letter and send you inclosed a bill upon Constable for £300 ball: of Waverley. I have not the least doubt of your zeal in these matters nor do I the least doubt your integrity which if I doubted of course I would long since have endeavourd to put things in another course of management. I sometimes think you do not early enough speak out your thoughts upon business & are willing to avoid ungrateful communications untill the last moment—this I have said a hundred times and with some good effect for I have not had to make the complaint of late. As for Weber's bill I thought I had fully understood it when I left town but when James wrote me he could not discover how it stood. I supposed it might have happend that some other pressing demand not visible in the Calendar has as has sometimes chanced carried off the fund of provision. I never thought of your dilapidating the funds for yourself. Weber has no right to complain—he made his bargain & has been a gainer where the publishers have been sufferers.

I shall send £350 bill beginning of month which will be done at the R.B. But I see difficulty about discounting another bill of £300 unless it can be done in Edinburgh. Perhaps renewing Cowans £150 due on 1st. would lighten this matter somewhat but you are best judge of the

---

[1] See letter to Constable of this date, Vol. III. pp. 469-70.

propriety of asking it. This I know that I can & will do my best to serve them in their business as the only way to show my sense of their kindness. But they must give us good paper not greasy trash like this I am writing upon. —We shall certainly need their indulgence in December for £600 at least so we must not overwork it if we can do without. There is I presume no other temporary discounts which could be made in this month—On the business of the sale one ought to reckon nothing yet giving long credits to good people something may be done. It would be desireable to have it early in November & to sell off without reserve all that will not mend by keeping. Without however reckoning upon this I find that by the end of Jany. if the Register sells the debt will be reduced to between £2000 & £3000 & if money can be got on the P.O. proportionally lower. As to the Register James is in despair but his heart has been in his breeches about every thing since I came home. Whereas matters though bad enough are certainly mending with us & I would have given £1000 this time last year to have seen them so far on. Debts reversions from Bankrupt estates, the resources of the P.O. & my own with such small sums as can be had from stock will gradually melt down the remainder.

I hope you are taking books or bills from the Edinr. debtors—if books you must keep them by you for 40 days —I am sensible you are doing much to extricate these matters but as I am labouring very hard also we must reserve our mutual praises & congratulations till we are out of danger when I promise you shall have a civic crown were it made of nothing else but the best grey paper.—So let us have no more grumbling—I hope Waverley continues to go on. Yours truly   W. S.

Monday morning [PM. *Sep.* 27, 1814]

Should Constable decline to accept [1] the inclosed he

---

[1] For the enclosed letter to Constable of the 26th see Vol. III. p. 500, taken from Mr. Kilpatrick's volume.

must deliver up the remainder of Waverley & I will
through James or you treat with Blackwood. On consideration I have drawn only for £300. I wd. be loth
to give him a pretence to refuse me. I have said nothing
of your memorandum.

The Somerville conclusion goes by the Selkirk mail
to James—there is a letter in it that I trust will come safe.
You are like the crane in the fable when you boast of not
having got any thing from the business—you may thank
God it did not bite your head of[f] far from helping you
or anyone. Would to God I were at Let a be Let a be.
But you have done your best & so must I.[1]

[*Nat. Lib. Scot.*]

DEAR JOHN,—I have your letter of the 3d. Your
statement is so far incorrect that you omit to give me credit
in the first period for a bill of £300 accepted by Constable
which *I did & do* mean to come in place of the first £350
—I observe this will leave you about £100 short but you
must get acceptances for Somerville as I wrote you before
& I trust James will get in his £120,, minus. Supposing
he does so the first period is completed. Second period
will then stand thus reckoning your deficit of £351

Bill - - - - -	£350,,	£1210,,
Somervill instead of Waverley	250,,	
Jo. B - - - - -	200,,	
Constables Bill as @ - -	300,,	
	1100,,	
	3d. Divn.	£712
Kelso - - - £150,,		
New Edit. W. - 400,,		
	550	
Mr. S. repays - 50		
	£600	

[1] Lockhart has taken the last two sentences from " You are like, etc.,"
and added them to a letter of 17th October. See Vol. III. p. 507.

If you attend it is virtually the same thing whether I send you the £300,, on Constable or an acceptance for £350,, excepting to the extent of £50. So that I did not & do not intend to do both indeed my credit would be greatly prejudiced by attempting it. But I will take care to bring Somerville forwd. by the middle of the month should you experience difficulty about it. The only difference is that Waverly 2d. edn. has been sent for the 1st. period instead of the 2d—That Somerville must be brought to 2d period instead of the 3d—and Waverley 3d editn. (not counted upon at all in the schedule) comes as £400,, to the 3d & last period thus supplying £50,, under calculated being the difference between Constables bill *for* £300 & the proposed acceptance £350 not sent. It is merely a difference in name but not in substance & the change greatly in my favour & in that of the business. The title page of Somerville I think should be " The Memorie of the Somervills being historical Memoirs of the Baronial House of Somerville from the original Manuscript of James Lord Somerville A.D. 1679." I will be very glad to see James & you will let me know by him if I have made any mistake concerning the above. I think it is impossible. You will furnish Constable with the expence of Somerville & also send me a note of it by James—I think we should advertize the register without delay. I do not exactly know what I shall furnish but will let you know by James probably some poetry & some extracts from my journal— I write by return of post & flatter myself this explanation will make you easy. November will next require attention but your £500 or £600 on Decr. will come in prime though they would be still more acceptable about 12 Novr.—As for Constable he *must* & shall accept for the books before he gets them. I wish James could bring me Walkers Dicty. of rhymes from my liby. it is on a shelf on my right hand as I sit at desk.   Yours truly

W. SCOTT

Mr Erskine will be obliged to James to call in Albany & enquire if all are well & bring any letters. I beg the same favour.

[PM. *Oct.* 6, 1814]

[*Nat. Lib. Scot.*]

DEAR JOHN,—I am very sorry to find yesterday by a letter from James yesterday that he is stationary at Kelso from illness—he seems to know nothing of my last letter to you fully explanatory of our resources & does not send me the state of Somerville to enable me to draw for it. I have sent him a promy. note for £350,, which he will indorse & transmit to you by this days post. I have written to Mr. Innes on the subject & have little doubt of success. The funds will stand thus

Note	-	-	- £350,,	11th. to 15 Octr.	£820,,
Somerville abt.		-	280,,		
J. B.s loan	-	-	200,,		
			830	15 to 25	754
W. 3d. Editn.		-	£400,,		
Kelso	-	-	150,,		
W. S. repays		-	50,,		
			£600,,		
Minus	-	-	100,,		
			700		

The £100 you can probably provide by renewing a part of Hollingworths £254,, Thus October seems pretty well provided for if all strings hold. I am not afraid of mine. If you can do witht. my £50 it will be as well. I trust there will be no difficulty in discounting Constables £400,, I am more alarmd about the extent of his debt to us than any thing else chiefly from the fear of its

limiting our credit. Novr. will I think stand nearly
thus

Betwn. 15th. & 19—£1000,,
I trust to find @ £400 or £500 indi   -   - £500,,
Your sale   -   -   -   -   -   -   -   100,,

600,,
Ball   -   -   -   -   -   -   -   -   400

1000

This balance I imagine may be made up partly by
p.o. bills partly by renewals but you will let me know
how this stands & whether debts etc. will do any thing
at that term. I have written repeatedly about James
getting a few hundreds on the printing office but I cannot
learn if he has attempted it—it would make November
very easy for I conceive the last £350,, due 30th. may
be taken up by your proposed advance from sale rooms.

I trust to find   -   -   -   £500,,   December
Cowans will probably renew   600,,   £2700,, this
Sale room say   -   -   300,,   includes
May be renewd   -   -   -   500,,   J. B's £200
   & B of S. £500.
1900
800

2700

Towards this large minus of £800 the business I am
afraid can do little but I have taken my own resources
rather low considering the poem will be just coming out
& will endeavour to make further shift.

January
renewals for October excepting £500,,
& £200 payable in December —
£770
This month may surely
   be balanced by the Regtr. M. & M.   -   180

950
   if it be got out—£950,, 0,, 0

After this period the debts of the business must be considerably within £3000,, which I do not fear to sloken out mean while you will think of all within your power to lighten November & December—which must necessarily fall heavy—Let me know how W. gets on. James's absence is unlucky both for that work & the regr.—Pray write me your opinion of the above statement and mention particularly whether my proposed arrangement for this month is satisfactory. I will send the drats on C. & Longman the instant I get the state from James or you which I have been expecting impatiently. Above all get on W. I would not leave Constable a pretence for declining to accept about the 20th which he will not fail to avail himself of if the book be not near delivery. You will of course ship Longmans Somerville & advise them. Let me know if you think C's bills will discount freely because part of the £400 might be done here. But it would be at short date & will be much better let alone. Yours truly   W. S.

You must write fully as I have little chance I fear of seeing James soon. I shall get stamps for the bills here. I inclose James's letter—if he be out of town Barnet may open it & shew it to any of the other directors. Take care to ascertain its delivery or deliver it yourself.

[ABBOTSFORD, PM. *Oct* 9, 1814]
[*Nat. Lib. Scot.*]

DEAR JOHN,—Having no letter from you this morning and hearing nothing of James I have taken fright about the bills due next week. I therefore inclose a letter to Constable [1] with a drat. on him for £400,, I leave the letter open but you may wafer it. The contents will speak for themselves—if he does not accept the bill James has already paved the way for dealing with Murray & you may correspond with him in name of the Author of

[1] For letter to Constable of same date see Vol. III. pp. 504-5.

W. to accept to *you* for copies of present edition to extent of £440,, with promise of ½ future editions. Or you may make the same proposal to Longmans house—only Murrays could be done more readily through Blackwood. But I dont suppose Constable will quarrel with a work on which he has netted £612,, in four months with a certainty of making it £1000,, before the year is out. You will make him sensible the thing is serious for I cannot & will not want the money. I give you full powers to treat with the others in case he shufles. But thus far if I draw just now for Somerville on him & Longman I can postpone my drat. till nearer the end of month : you know better than me when it will be indispensible. Always I am supposing Constables bills are going readily. You will receive this day (Sunday) a long letter from me with a letter inclosed for Mr Innes referring to the £350,, which I accepted for to James on friday & which he has doubtless indorsed to you.

Observe I would not like to have Blackwoods own bills —I shall be anxious to hear the result of your conversation with C. Yours truly   W. SCOTT

ABBOTSFORD *Sunday* 9 *Octr.* [PM. 1814]

I trust you have got your own £200,, loan in which case you will with the inclosed & the £350 have assets for £1050,,

If Constable is restive he may lose the book entirely.

[*Nat. Lib. Scot.*]

DEAR JOHN,—I received your letter with the astonishing news of James's utter disregard to his own credit—he promised to let me have accurate accompts of his prospects & consult me upon the management of his cash affairs but has kept his word but lamely—he is even worse than you for you generally give a day or two's notice at least of the chance of dishonor & this pound^g is little better. His Kelso expectation has proved a fine one.—I have sent over a bill to Galasheils for £370 which I shall probably get & inclose the cheque—if not Sir W. F. must be tried—Both shifts are wretched and ruinous to our future operations but the last will be the worst. I shall receive my Excheqr. money on the 25 or 26th but shall need all but £50 for my own indispensible occasions.— Your expedients are all wretched so far as they regard me. I never will give Constable or any one room to say I have broke[n] my word with him in the slightest degree —if I lose everything else I will at least keep my honor unblemishd & I do hold myself bound in honor to offer him W. while he shall continue to comply with the conditions annexed. I am thirled to C. & L. & Co/ for half [the] poem & this I thought you knew. I reserve this to retire the bills @ B. of S. & R.B.[1] & will not break upon it—Indeed to let Murray in upon them would wreck all their prospects regarding the poem & give them just grounds of complaint. I mentiond to Jas. a speculation of which I think very well and which I shd. be willing to let Murray have if he fancies it but I have no idea he would advance money or credit for it.[2] Had it not been for the almost total failure of your provisions for this month I should have wanted neither but now I do not know what to say to it.—I intend the new novel to operate as something more permanent than a mere accomodation & if I can but be permitted to do so I will print it before it is sold to any one & then propose 1st. to C. & Longman 2d. to Murray & Blackwd. to take the whole at such a rate as will give them one half of the free profits—granting acceptances which upon an editn. of 3000 which we will be quite authorized to print will amount to an immediate command of £1500,, to this W. may also couple the condition that they would take £500 or £600,, of old stock. I own I am not solicitous to deal with Constable

[1] Bank of Scotland and Royal Bank.

[2] Probably the *History of Scotland for Young People.* See Vol. IV. p. 277 and elsewhere.

alone—nor am I at all bound to offer him the new novel on any terms—but he knowing of the intention may expect to be treated with at least—although it is possible we may not deal. However if Murray & Blackwood were to come forwd. with any handsome proposal as to the stock or regr. I should certainly have no objection to James giving the proposed pledge on the part of the Author of W. for his next work.

I inclose the drat. for £364,, 18,, 10d. which will be made up £400 from my Excheqr. money being the sum you want supposing James's bills discounted wh: I do not doubt if he goes rightly about it.—I wish you to make for him such a calendar as the Booksellers [use? or make?] & shew him how to make it up & the devil must be in him if I cannot keep him right—In discounting the inclosed see your own name does not appear. There is otherwise no small risque of stopping this most convenient channel should it seem this bill is discounted to meet the other of £220,, due this week. You will remember there is no Melrose post tomorrow but that it sets off on Wednesday so that you can write fully by that post. I think it would be right to let Caddell know you are fully provided. I hope yet to keep an equal tune [?] with the Cock of the Cross. Yrs in haste.   W. S.

17 *October* [PM. 1814] [1]

You told me you had the use of a small sum which will parry the time between the 24th and paymt of my Excheqr quarter.

[*Nat. Lib. Scot.*]

DEAR JOHN,—I have your two letters with the £50,,— Millers declining to renew will be a deficiency & I wish it may be filld up witht. me. This will probably depend

[1] For Lockhart's extract from this letter see Vol. III. p. 507 and note there. A distraint for debt ("pounding" or "pinding" Scott calls it) had been put in force against James while he was at Kelso on a visit.

on your settlements. I hope James hurries on with 4th W.—it will come in most opportunely at the end of the month. I shall make Constable " touch pot touch penny "—this settlement is very fair £213 upon every 1000 copies. You must bring him forward with the Somerville of which I now return the last proofs.[1] If half is to [be] accepted by Rees so much the better. The date will I fear be long—I wish you to be cautious of renewals with Constable for as he pleads being under heavy acceptances to us he should lighten them by paying his bills. This will require some delicacy on your part but you may plead my general desire to be informd before any bills are renewd. I do not mean we should *not* oblige him but he must not expect us to bolster him any more than he does us unless as a matter of favour. Indeed there is a great disadvantage in so many of his bills being afloat & I wish them reduced being fearful of checking discounts in Decr. on the poem-bills—If £1000,, can be got on heritable security at Martinmas it will be a gracious godsend. I hope James is looking for it—at Whitsunday I am pretty sure it can. This month will be a great relief £2000 nearly paid out of £3400 should lighten matters greatly. Yet we will need all we can scrape together to face Martinmas & December. Your £300 will be a great help. I wish it were twice the sum with all my heart—I shall write to Mr. Innes but this bill falls in on the 2d. period of this month & I should not like to antici-pate the fund for paying my own bills from Galasheils etc. I have little doubt that by Candlemas we shall be clear within £2000. As for the stock

> Twill be wearing awa, John,
> Like snow wreaths in thaw, John,

And were I once out of danger of thes[e] bills I could make a good shift to wait better times. Indeed if Constable is to get a new novel in spring he must take a

---

[1] *The Memorie of the Somervilles*, 2 vols., 8vo, was issued in 1814.

lug of stock with it, I promise him. Complimts. to James
—He has made some queer errata in Somerville—planted
Hawick upon the *Trent* for one thing instead of the
Teviot which I [would] scarce have expected. Yours etc.

W. S.

Saturday evening

You must send me the bill with first proofs not a double
letter if possible as postage comes to be a monstrous item—
When Somerville is finishd forward a copy without loss
of post to Lord Somerville Hill Street Berkeley Square.

[1814]

[*Nat. Lib. Scot.*]

DEAR JOHN,—I have your letter by which I regret to
see you are again short about £750 including James's
£450,,—I can promise you no assistance in this matter
having already provided £2000 for this month and having
no means of doing more. But I have no doubt that
James will get £500 as a temporary accomodn. on his
long dated bills. I will repay your £50,, on the 25th.
and you must shift for the rest. For me to attempt at
the present moment to draw on Sir W. F. would be utter
ruin. I assure you I calculate my exertions to the utmost
and do not save myself in the least. But I cannot throw
the means of two months into one. If you can fullfill
your engagements you may rely on mine. Consider what
I have to pay in Novembr. without the least prospect of
assistance unless James gets an heritable security. In
short he & you for this month must *pickle in your ain poke-
nook.* I cannot help—but next month if spared my
credit will revive or rather be strong enough to pay heavy
interests some debt of my own etc. etc.—I expect to pay
between Midsummer & Candlemass £5000,, and have
provided accordingly. But all this cash can only be

brought forward as wrought for—I think or rather am confident James will make an arrangement at Sir W. F.'s to the extent of £500. At any rate this experiment must be tried on the first instance. In all cases I wish you to consider accurately your own resources as I shall calculate mine—I have your apprehensions about *Goodman Puff of Bursen*.[1] But all his bills are @ six months of late & surely the poem etc. will make him stand that time. I shall have London Bills for half my copies that is determined—and you as you will be answerable to me & the copartnery will renew no bills without specially consulting me. What is sauce for the goose must be sauce for the Gander & our answer is ready " we have done enough "— this must be done in the quiet way of business and without the least appearance of irritation, merely as the natural and distressing consequence of evil times. Yours truly   W. S.

Wednesday evening [1814]
[*Nat. Lib. Scot.*]

MY DEAR JOHN,—I send inclosed Exchequer rects. for four sums—be so good as to receive the amot. which will [be] payable about 25th. or 26th. retain £50,, Send £20,, to my mother in George Street No. 37. and pay the rest in to my Accot. with the Leith Bank as I can draw it at Galashiels & it has a good appearance with our country Bankers. Call upon *Mr. Gardner Deputy Remembrancer* in Excheqr. & get his answer to the query in the postcript ; this will do when you get the cash.

I also inclose Caddells note of Bills which take care of. They have an unquestionable title to have the 3 Swift Bills renewd in the mode most convenient for them & for the term noticed. You will judge whether these matters may not be as well cleard by throwing part of the term of credit on other bills. I am much surprized at their

---

[1] Constable—so called from Puff the publisher in Foote's play, *The Patron*—but why " of Bursen " or " Burson " ?

deep engagements to the P.O. in the way of accomodn. and it certainly takes much off the feeling of displeasure which I entertaind at some parts of their late conduct & particularly refusing the printing bill for W.—James has really plied them pretty well—There is also £253 Jany. 2d. to you which does not appear in the Kalendar. All my bills are for value but Swift was put forward for a year. So they have actually given us a good lift & we cannot be surprized if they tire in these foul ways. But all you have to do is to *assume perfect good humour* leave me alone to manage with them—they shall have all they are entitled to get from me and I will take care to get what I have a right to from them. It is no doubt a great hardship to choke up our cash accot. But we must perform our obligations—& our engagements in the Parlt. Close have been and are decreasing. If you can pick up any cash by [?] Novr. good & well—if James gets his loan still better—but let the worst come to the worst " Coragio Bully monster." [1]   October is over & I will make the best fight I can till you like the God Thor bring your hammer to my aid.[2]   And in December the poem will be afloat—in January the regr.— in feby. the new Novel [3] which if presented in a state ready for publication will sell a lot of stock.   You may drop Caddell a hint that we are as sound as a roach [4] & will not need their aid.   I have mentiond Murrays visit to him as I want no jealousies or quarrels—I should like to know if they are speaking for themselves or us.   Make what remarks you can on Caddells manner.   My letter to him was quite civil & friendly but firm enough as you may believe.   Once more I think I can manage them very well if they will only keep their legs.   When C. comes down we shall know more.

[1] *The Tempest*, Act V. sc. i. 258.   [2] The auctioneer's hammer.

[3] *The Lord of the Isles* was actually published in January 1815, *Guy Mannering* in February.

[4] " Rock " is meant.

I desired James to give you a Ladys commission about cast-iron Elbow chairs for Lady Douglas at Bothwell Castle. I am anxious about the fate of a box containing some important papers & documents respecting Swift sent I think to your sale room in Augt. or to Constables pray enquire about it. Yours truly

W. SCOTT

ABBOTSFORD 21 *October* [PM. 1814]

Postcript

Mr. Walter Scott with best Compliments to Mr. Gardner would be glad to know the amount of the allowance made in Exchqer. for his accompts as he has mislaid the abstract of his charge & discharge for this last year.

If Caddell adverts to your dispute all you have to say is that I had desired you to renew no bills till I was furnishd with the accompt I wanted.[1]

[*Nat. Lib. Scot.*]

---

[1] On the 17th October Cadell wrote to Constable : " John and Richard & Co. are not doing any good. I sent you a copy of the Cos letter intimating a draft p £400 which to keep peace I accepted—I have since reason to understand it was refused at the Baronets at which I am not at all surprised —notwithstanding this I had a regular application from John on Saturday . . . for Bill or Cash p £310, he says he was set on by W. S. but I will not budge an inch and no consideration will make me give them our name for 1/- except for value. I am quite determined whatever may happen, they threaten the worst—they have all of them here a Black Sight. You will notice from the list with you that at the end of this month and beginning and Course of Novr. we have not under £2500 to pay to these people and their principle " [*sic.—i.e.* principal, to wit, Scott] " and we *must make a point of paying all of them off*—nothing else will do."

Cadell's letters indicate that Constable & Co. are labouring in as great difficulties as the Ballantynes. John's application on Saturday, 15th October, is probably explained by Scott's letter of 14th October. See Vol. III. pp. 505-6. On the 21st Cadell reports to Constable a letter from John Doe (so he calls John Ballantyne) stating " that without £310 on the following Tuesday he could not go on and an explosion would be the consequence of my refusal . . . a decided refusal of course was my reply and till the Tuesday when he called I did not know whether it was a sink or swim." " Richard " is Cadell's usual name for James in letters to Constable.

DEAR JOHN,—Caddell has sent me the inclosed two bills which he wishes to be negociated here.[1] The dates & sums alone would render this inconvenient which is what I have written him. But besides you are aware I applied to Galashiels at the last push & as to Selkirk I *must* reserve that for November. It will be much better if you can get him the Cash on acceptances to your firm— much better in every point of view than using these bills. He wishes the Bills not to go into Sir W. F's you will know how far he can be obliged. We must keep the terms of our treaty however & get him the money. Three smaller bills would make future renewals more easy—Thank God his bills fall on first after this. Yours in haste.   W. S.

ABBOTSFORD *Monday* [PM. *Oct.* 27, 1814]

This turn over I think you will have little or nothing to discount at all till the poem comes in excepting what we can do together in November.

[*Nat. Lib. Scot.*]

DEAR JOHN,—I have negociated the note at the Selkirk Branch & the cash is lying there ready for call. If you have my order for £300 I fancy it will do. I dont want to ask their cheque on the Parlt. Close for obvious reasons, & you can negociate my order through some other house as it requires no indorsation. If I am wrong in all this let me know & I will bring a cheque to town on Monday the £300 being due Tuesday.

Charles Erskine has written to me wishing to have his money as he has made a purchase of land—this is a new

---

[1] The bills are not to hand, but Cadell was having his own troubles. On the 25th he wrote to Constable : " It strikes me just now that no part of Scott's Copyrights could well be forced into the field at this moment but the moment after the Lord of the Isles has had its run and redeemed the name of the Author we might slip a share of the whole into some ones hands."

chapter of perplexity for paid he *must* be as his advance
was freindly & confidential. I do not at this moment
see *how* it can be raised but believe I shall find means.
In the mean while it will be necessary to propitiate the
Leviathans of Pater Noster row. My idea is that you
or James write to them to the following purport—that
a novel is offerd you by the author of Waverley with the
desire that you will print 2000 and publish yourself or
arrange with publishers—the name is Guy Mannering—
that you have proceeded accordingly & that the authors
further desire is that the work may be out either before
Mr. Scotts poem or as soon thereafter as may be—that
having resolved as they are aware entirely to relinquish
publishing you only wish to avail yourself of this offer to
the extent of helping off some of your stock & therefore
wish to know if it would be agreeable to them to take
such a work at prime cost vizt. Print paper & authors
half of profits & grant acceptance at six mos. along with
a handsome order on your other stock at usual credit.
I leave it to you to consider whether you should con-
descend on any particular work to offer them as bread to
their butter or on any particular amount—as an order to
amot. of £500,,—or whether you should leave matters
open untill their answer—One thing must be provided
& that is that Constable shares to the extent of the Scottish
sale—they however managing, for we must have *their* bills
for the whole. This should I think lay foundation for
£2000 at least early in february when it will be much
wanted—Keep a scroll of your letter & read mine over
carefully with James. My reason for letting them have
a scent of roast meat is in case it be necessary to apply to
them in Novr. or Decr. but not a hint of this must appear
in the letter as I trust we may do without them.

There must not & shall not be any delay as to the
Register—it MUST be out at such time as indisputably
to get into Xmas Accots. I will give my contribution
so soon as I come to town. It is a sheet anchor & it

must not slip. £1000 depends upon it which we have no means of doing without & fag'd as I am myself I will have no commiseration on printers & printers devils. In short the thing must be done sans faute.

Did you pay £4,, for me to Sir Wm. F. to accompt of Messrs. Will. Hunter Ayr—I desired James to tell you to do so but have no answer.

Wednesday. Eveng

I have not had an opportunity to send this. On the whole as the letter to L & Co/ is a matter of some delicacy you had better scroll it but not write it out till we go over it together—I think it should clear £2000—& if £500 of that be Stock it will come in at Xmas which will be very convenient.   W. S.[1]

[*Nat. Lib. Scot.*]

To JAMES BALLANTYNE

DEAR JAMES,—I have your letter & return the proof. By this you have the end of the canto and to further matters as much as I can I inclose one page beginning of the next. The financial operations you mention require attention & shall have it but *Nullum numen deest si sit prudentia.* I beg Johns attention to my last letter written yesterday—I always thought that Constables late conduct was the consequence of pressure not of humour. Longman must have the novel [2] through you & they must be allowd to smell the cheese while toasting for them but of this when I come to town—not sooner— I am glad you like the verses on the whole be as rough & plain in your criticism as you will. Yours in haste

W. SCOTT

ABBOTSFORD *Monday* [? 30 *Oct.* 1814]

[*Nat. Lib. Scot.*]

---

[1] Lockhart dates this letter 14th October 1814. In John Ballantyne's volume it comes among much later letters.
[2] i.e. *Guy Mannering*, published by Longman in February 1815.

To JOHN BALLANTYNE

DEAR JOHN,—I have your two letters & am rather disappointed to find from that recd. today that Constables bills have been after all renewd in *my name*. I trust you will get the other £500 in that of the compy. alone. It is of much more consequence to save my credit than theirs. Besides J. B. & Co/ will be no more when these bills come to be renewd & it will greatly increase any difficulty should the security sink from three names to two. You can split the £500 into two bills at different dates if possible. About Novr. I shd. be anxious to spare Sir W. F. as much as possible—observe I am *sure* of getting the money from them but prudence & futurity would make me anxiously wish to strain their kindness as little as possible. The first sum is about £1000,, of which I can I trust get £350,, here—say £350 more from Sir W. F. which will be granted without hesitation and there remains £300,, more. This I intended to do at Galashiels but it was anticipated at the last pinch. Do you think Caddell can be asked to renew his bill as it is the last time ? or that we could pick up £300 in Edinr. In short bustle about & let me know in good time. It will be I trust our *last* struggle and it is not one of vital importance though of *great convenience*—My own affairs will want a little assistance besides that I shall only get a bill from James for the cash due the annuitants at next term—so that upon the whole matter I would be most anxious to pay the bill of £300 at Sir W. F's on the 15th without renewal—You have not stated Mr. Gardners answer to my Memorand.—I am grieved and shocked at poor Constables misfortune [1]—to struggle with domestic afliction at such a moment must be hard indeed—No proposals have been made to me for renewal of any of his bills nor do I expect any at present. You may trust to my

[1] The first Mrs. Constable died on the 28th October 1814.

wish to get out as fast as possible—I trust the Regr. gets
on—it is a *sheet anchor* & you remember people scrupled to
accept for it last year on accot. of the late delivery : take
heed of this—The copy is much at your service. I wish
however you would state to enquiries that it was *returnd
to me by my order* which will prevent gurn [1] or dispute :
accordingly you may return it when I come to town & I
can give it to you formally.   Yours etc

W. S.

Sunday [PM. *Oct.* 31, 1814]

I sent a quantity of copy yesterday.

[*Nat. Lib. Scot.*]

DEAR JOHN,—I think it worth while to trouble you
with a line to cover an order for £300 on the Selkirk
Branch to meet £300 due at Sir William Forbes's. I
wish the note taken up on *Monday* in order to save the
calling of the Clerk in Castle Street which has to me a
most unpleasing effect. You can manage to send it in by a
strange hand with my Complimts. & *not* to send the Drat.
through their house—I received your note & extra post &
did inpeticos the gratility.[2] Since I came here my
postage has just cost £5,, over & above franks without
end.   Yours truly

W. S.

ABBOTSFORD *Saturday* [PM. *Nov.* 14, 1814]

[*Nat. Lib. Scot.*]

---

[1] Usually " girn " in Scotch—" growl."

[2] *Sir Andrew.* I sent thee sixpence for thy leman : had'st it ?

Clown. I did impeticos thy gratillity ; for Malvolio's nose is no whip-
stock ; my lady has a white hand, and the Myrmidons are no bottle-ale
houses.

SHAKESPEARE, *Twelfth Night*, II. iii. 24-7.

DEAR JOHN,—You had better call tomorrow as you proposed. I shall be at home all morning & as I have done with the Lord [1] (His name be praised). You wont interrupt me. Yours truly   W. S.

> Merit if thou art blessed with riches
> I pray thee buy a pair of Breeches
> And give them to thy naked brother
> For one good turn deserves another.[2]

[*Nat. Lib. Scot.*]

DEAR JOHN,—Inclosed is a cheque for £150,, part of £250,, due by a drat. on you @ 3 months Galashiels. Please as soon as possible to cash it and pay my brother Major Scott taking a receipt to accompt of Interest due to him at Whity. & Marts. last. The high state of the river prevented me sending to Galashiels till today & now I shall be anxious that this money which hangs about the neck of my conscience be paid as soon as possible. I conclude the calculation for your affairs holds good—indeed I cannot see how it should start.— We have had terrible winds here which has not prevented my transplanting some good half grown trees but how they will answer heaven knows.

We hold our purpose of starting about the 1st or 2d. I wish you would look at the smacks likely to sail about that time. My wife & daughter have two female friends so I would prefer taking the *after cabbin* (which generally contains I believe 4 *berths*) exclusively for them. Some male friends we shall have & I trust you will be of the number who will shift for themselves. The accomodation

---

[1] *Lord of the Isles*, published in January 1815. This letter must date from end of 1814 or beginning of 1815. It depends whether Scott has done with the composition of the poem or with the correcting of the proofs. On 21st October Cadell has told Constable that the poem is " at press ; " and on the 22nd that James B. says it " is *exquisite*—and I have ordered 1750,, total Print—how many Royal should there be 50 ? the third Edition of Waverley is ready."

[2] These lines are written on the address side of the letter.

for the ladies is all I am anxious about.   I think we shall be in town tomorrow se'nnight or Sunday at farthest.

I expect to hear from James whether he has got away the books as proposed to Longman of this date to make the necessary Drats. & generally about business.

Montfaucon [1] would be very useful to me in the Antiqy. indeed almost indispensible.   Will you advise with Constable what length I should go.   Do not forget the Chevalier & if the two Calots [2] the Infernal Regions & the Fair should go within compass I should not be sorry to have them.

I have had a few pleasant days here notwithstanding rough weather.   My complaint is giving place to moderate exercise & drinking whey instead of wine.

Take care in cashing the drat. but this you will do of course.   Yours truly   W. SCOTT

ABBOTSFORD 17th March 1815

If you have occasion to write remember there is no Melrose post leaves Edinr. on Tuesday—If you write mention any public news about Boney or otherwise as I am in a sort of desert here.

[Nat. Lib. Scot.]

DEAR JOHN,—I had your letter this morning.   I presume you will receive my quarters salary as today & I suppose it may be necessary for you to use it for a few days till the return of the drats. from London only I must have it on my return to arrange my affairs before going to

---

[1] Presumably Bernard de Montfaucon : L'Antiquité Expliquée et représentée en figures. 5 tom. divisées en 10. Supplément 5 tom. Paris, 1719-1724. The copy in the Abbotsford Library is said to be " the gift of his Majesty King George IV.," so that Scott cannot have bought it at this time.

[2] Jacques Callot, engraver (1592-1635), executed several Fairs. "The Infernal Regions" must be Purgatory and Hell, popularly known as Le Puits (the Pit), a vast composition in 4 plates apparently inspired by Dante. See Édouard Meaume, Recherches sur la vie et les ouvrages de Jacques Callot, 2 vols., Paris, 1860.

London. You say nothing particular of your provision —as calculated it carries you into the second week of April. I like *figures* & in my opinion they have been the means of extricating the business. I should therefore wish you had said something of means realized & in expectance amount of draughts etc. as to which you are silent.

I shall wish my bill of £350 paid the day before due— the calling of a banks clerk at my house in my absence will alarm my family & be most extremely unpleasant. I beg you will mind this.

We will make our voyage on the 4th. and it may be necessary that you secure our berths without loss of time. I said in my last letter we wish the after cabbin for the ladies exclusive use. I have been told it costs 14 guineas or thereabouts. Our females are four in number & as the two Mr. Bruces go with me we will require four male berths. You had better secure them & a place for my servant. I am chiefly anxious about Mrs. S. & her party as I can shift well enough for myself being easily satisfied in point of accomodation.

I am getting better daily by dint of walking much drinking whey and neither writing nor reading. I have been however obliged to use mercurial ointments & on the whole my winters labours have nearly cost me very dear.

Notwithstanding what you say I think you may mention to Constable my wish to have Montfaucon at a moderate price. You need not at any rate exceed the 30/ a volume but do not say what you have orders to bid.

We will esteem ourselves happy in securing you for a compagnon de Voyage, so pray arrange to be with us. You can send to the Bruces (at their father's Geo: Bruce Dep: Clerk of Session N. Fredk. Street) to ask if you shall take Berths for them. They are my neighbours & very good lads.

I expect to [be] at home on Sunday & should be anx[ious] to hear James's account of Kean. I wish you & he [would] dine with me on Monday or tuesday.

The news are clearing a little I understand today so I will keep my heart out of my breeches as well as I can. Yours truly   W. SCOTT

ABBOTSFORD 21 *March* [PM. 1815] [1]

[*Nat. Lib. Scot.*]

To JAMES BALLANTYNE

DEAR JAMES,—I have had little leisure to write though I cannot say my time has been very usefully occupied—it has passd agreeably however among many old acquaintances & some new. John will tell you what we have been doing here which is on the whole satisfactory. I shall begin the Anty.[2] on my return which will be about the 1st. week of June when I have arranged Miss Clephanes marriage settlements which alone delay me.

You will get on with Rokeby[3] with all dispatch it should be out by the end of June if possible. The management as it is calld will of course remain with your brother. I offerd to transfer that & all the other works upon certain terms which you recollect were not accepted. Of course he keeps his own in this & similar instances only I shall always wish him to offer the share to the co-publishers at good terms as has always been done.

John will have long ere this have acquainted you with any thing that is worth your knowing. I dined yesterday with the P.R.[4] who is an exceeding joyous companion & the party was very pleasant.

I inclose the proofs long delayd by the absence of Lord Somerville and I shall be glad that they are now got out while the season lasts. Yours truly   W. S.

LONDON *Sunday* [*April* 1815]

[*Nat. Lib. Scot.*]

---

[1] Scott went to London this year with Mrs. Scott and Sophia.
[2] *The Antiquary.*   [3] *i.e.* the sixth edition.
[4] *i.e.* the Prince Regent.

To JOHN BALLANTYNE

DEAR JOHN,—I will be glad to see you here tomorrow
as soon after ten as you can make it convenient—not very
late because I must dress to go to the drawg. room an it
please you.   Triermain must be thought of, if it is out.
Yours ever
                                                W. SCOTT
PICCADILLY Wednesday [PM. 3 May 1815]
[Nat. Lib. Scot.]

DEAR JOHN,—I have your letter and reinclose the
note accepted as it seems the only way at this distance to
get the balance of June made up, nor is it likely I could
help you otherwise were I even upon the spot.
   I wish you would attend to trifles.   White has sent
me a bill for £5,, a Book of St. Albans which you long
since told me you had settled.   Be so good as advise if
I am to pay it or no—and I do not find you have left the
money for Terry—the bill I mean—am I to settle with
him or how ?   I have arranged with Triphook he deducing your account.
   You reckon Somers among your means of the month.
But much of the volume is still in my hand.   I could not
get it forward while I was in Edinburgh.   I doubt its
being out in June.   I do not quite understand your
statement of funds but you will look at the subjoind & see
if I have calculated them rightly—

Due to the 10th June   -   -   -   - £1027,, 0,, 0
        to end of month   -   -   -   -   971
                                              _____
                                             £1998,, 0,, 0
Two weeks wages to P.O. not reckond in
    your account between 10 & 30 June -   160
                                              _____
        Funds   -   -   -   -   -   -   2158,, 0,, 0

I   2 H

P.O. bills in hand expected to be
discounted by Cowans -   -   £440,,
Other P.O. bills expected by the
end of the month supposed   -   400,,
I presume this includes the
Somers & farces.
Business & note Sir W. F.   -   -   200,,
Bill which I inclose   -   -   -   350,,   1390,, 0,, 0

768,, 0,, 0
Of this you mention being able to advance   250

But in my view there still remains a balance
to be provided of   -   -   -   -   £518,, 0,, 0

I shall be glad to find myself mistaken on this and
observe with pleasure that £1000 will be permanently
cleard off. Your memorandm. on the outside [of] the
letter was very attentive & saved me probably a turn of
the bile if I had read Sir W. F.s letter first.

You do not mention what arrangement you have made
with Mr Donaldson about his friends £700 or when the
Dividend will enable you to pay him.

Please to answer this letter in course as I shall sail
upon Monday or Tuesday 12th. & 13th.

I conclude you are pulling hard to get out Rokeby
which will cover the defalcation.

The Lord of the Isles has been strangely kept in hand.
Should you not get on with Triermain?—

I have been in the City since beginning this letter &
find that the vessels sail only on Sundays & Thursdays.
I think it likely therefore that I will come off next Sunday [1]
but as I shall send tomorrow by Mail-coach more copy
for James I will then state exactly on which day we sail.
I expect an answer in course with answers as to Terry &
White. I hate to be made to seem shabby in trifles.
Not to pay great sums may be want of means but to be
dilatory about small always shews either great irregularity
or covetousness or poverty. I wish I could beat this into
your head.

[1] 11th June.

I will write two lines to James by the parcel which please enquire for the day after you receive this. Yours truly

W. S.

[PM. *June* 5, 1815]

[*Nat. Lib. Scot.*]

DEAR JOHN,—As the Bill is too large for our small Banks here I have written to Mr Forester & have little or no doubt it will be discounted. I will get his answer on tuesday or Wednesday & should it be unfavourable of which I have no idea I will nevertheless get Mr Constable the money by Thursday. But it is really wrong not to have these things fully arranged when we have so many meetings on purpose & to trust them to all the chances of correspondence & of missing posts etc. I suppose though you say nothing of the matter that every thing else holds according to our last settlement & that the 24th. will produce my £400 & enable me to leave Edinr. on the next day. I shall have a packet for James in two days my progress is somewhat checkd by a visit from Adam Fergusson who keeps the whole house in uproar.

I will send the drat. so soon as I am assured the Bill is discounted. But at this rate what becomes of our £2000,, on the Antiqy. Yours truly   WALTER SCOTT

16 *July* ABBOT[SFORD] [PM. 1815]

It is possible I may have occasion to draw on you for £50 or £100 through Selkirk an additional reason for not sending this note there.

[*Nat. Lib. Scot.*]

DEAR JOHN,—I have not a line from you today at which I am surprized. The Note at B.S. [1] is gone quite right & very readily as I expected so that matter is quite

[1] Bank of Scotland.

easy. It will be better however to pay Messrs. C. the
£280,, out of my own funds and impress the Bank cash
with Coutts for travelling expences so they will know it
goes to my own use which has the best effect for all
parties.

I intend to be in town upon Sunday—pray let the old
woman in Castle Street know this & tell the Post office
people to send my letters there on Sunday—dont neglect
this—I expect to get away on thursday by which time my
Verses on recent events will be in proof. They are much
injured by the qualms which your financial operations
have given me. I take it for granted though you have
never so said that you have no spoke to put into my wheel
—I bring the verses with me to give them a little polishing.

W. SCOTT

ABBOTSFORD 21 *July* 1815

I hope to see you on Sunday eveng. or Monday
morning *early*.

[*Nat. Lib. Scot.*]

DEAR JOHN,—I arrived here last night [1] & found your
letter with the Bill which had followd me returnd from
London. I presume you have made some other shift or
I should have heard of it & I have a letter from James
dated 20th. saying all is well. I fear we shall be hampered
with the acceptances of C. but we must do the best we
can. I wish you could come here in the end of this week
& you could give Mr. W. Erskine a seat in your gig. We
could then arrange matters for the ensuing campaign.
Tell James I am obliged to him for his criticisms & will
endeavour to profit by them but we *must* have Waterloo
out in a day or two—this will bring forwd. Rodk. which
I think may be raised to 12/ which would afford a pretty
draught. I intend to add one or two things besides St.

---

[1] On his return from Waterloo, Paris, London, etc.

Cloud.[1] On thursday I am engaged so that on friday
I would wish to see you. Yours very truly

WALTER SCOTT

ABBOTSFORD 25 *Septr.* [PM. 1815]

[*Nat. Lib. Scot.*]

DEAR JOHN,—I write in some surprize at not having
seen or heard from you. My proof was regularly forwarded but no answer received from James & unless
you are on your way hither today I dont know what
to make of it. If the proof has been sent & has miscarried let another be sent under Mr. Kerrs cover which
is after all the safest. I have a load of Paul ready but
I do not like to send it till I know what has occasiond
this stop. Tomorrow I go to Bowhill for two days I
therefore inclose the drat on Coutts for £300 in case it be
needed. Yours truly   W. S.

ABBOTSFORD 5 *October* [PM. 1815] [2]

Take care in passing the within not to shew it has come
your own way.

[*Nat. Lib. Scot.*]

DEAR JOHN,—I am alway[s] sorry whenever I have
occasion to be dissatisfied. Your only faults arise from
a vivacity of temper which does not always allow you to
think *twice*. When you do so you think more correctly
than most folks. I am [not] angry or surprized at the
£80 occurring only at its being overlookd.

I grieve much to say that Cs note for £333,, has this
morning been returnd to me by the Selkirk Agent with
many apologies etc etc. But he is restricted for the
present to small sums which indeed I know to be true.

---

[1] See Vol. IV. p. 90.

[2] See Vol. IV. p. 102 for a letter to Constable on the same day.

This is very hard but I have no other means here to help the matter so I must needs return it to you. If you apply to Sir W. F. it will be best to do it on a bill to James on which my name should not appear because I may very probably have a similar application to make bye & bye. I am sure they will not refuse it if you show how compleatly your funds exceed your necessities.

Mr. Constable proposes 6000 of Waterloo to which I have no objection the price he proposes to be 5/. If so settled I presume I should have something handsome to draw for which will help out matters well. I pray you to push on Paul. Taking the edition at 6000—12/ & deducing £300 already received there will be £800 & upwards to draw which will do much to clear next month. I trust it will be out by 21st at farthest.

I do not write to Mr. Constable wishing to lose as little time as possible.

I reinclose the notes accepted & wish you well through with them. More I cannot write at present. I shall not hear from you I fear till Thursday which will be a period of some anxiety as you will only get this on Monday & there is no tuesday's post. Yours truly   W: S.

Sunday ABBOTSFORD [PM. *Oct.* 9, 1815]

In the presentation copies of Waterloo you will follow the list for those of Lord of Isles—only see that the Princes be finishd & sent off under Mr. Kerrs cover to Dr. Clarke as soon as possible & a day or two before one gets abroad. I shall wish to have half a dozen or so sent here.

[*Nat. Lib. Scot.*]

more land ! ! ! [1]

DEAR JOHN,—I reinclose the note indorsed—& am glad to find you have swum through. The funds are now rising & times will presently mend.

[1] This ejaculation is written at the head of the letter in another hand, whether that of John Ballantyne at the time or of Lockhart later I cannot say ; the latter, I think.

I inclose you another letter from those troublesome people White & Cochrane which I beg you to answer as we shall otherwise have a lawsuit. Write to the Attorney forthwith.

For heavens sake press on Paul to avoid hobbles in November. The proofs have been *very* long of arriving. I shall soon finish the work.

Our matters seem now so nearly ended that I have thoughts of entering into a transaction for a farm lying contiguous to Abbotsford.[1] It is very extensive & may be had cheap & as the owner wishes the money to remain in my hands will occasion no demand but for interest & will not therefore interfere with the redemption of the £4000. It may cost from £3000 to £4000 & I think in five or six years by judicious outlay I could double its value. It marches with Abbotsford & would add greatly to the value of this place which I think I may now hope to enjoy in peace. Let me know what you think I should do in this matter.

I want some good writing-paper—not greasy like this present. Pray send it me by Richardson Melrose carrier. He lodges at Bristow port & leaves town on Wednesday. I am foully out as Sir Andw.[2] says.

Does the inclosed imply a renewal of the £100 first paid or is it exclusive?—Also I want to have your opinion about my calculation respecting Paul. I trust the Publishers are at one about the size of impression & at any rate we are not as in another instance to have any thrown on our hands. Yours

W. S.

friday [*Oct.* 17, 1815]

I shall want my copies of Waterloo as soon as may be. [*Nat. Lib. Scot.*]

---

[1] *i.e.* Kaeside.   [2] Sir Andrew Aguecheek.

DEAR JOHN,—Your very acceptable letter reachd me this evening. I inclose a letter for Mr. Cranstouns inspection which you may shew him should you want to accelerate the delivery of the books before my coming to town. The getting the £500 is also agreeable as I am uncertain of getting even the £185,, discounted here. We shall now however make a complete rally & come up out of Egypt in triumph.

I send James 2d Canto Harold [1] & beg you as well as him to get it on. Give Rees as promised his full time to think of it : he will decide the reaction [?] that he sees it in hand—I dont quite understand the transaction of the Ly. of Lake but suppose it does not include the £250 mentiond in your letter of Saturday.

Paul is standing for want of my books from France which cost me £100,, if they are lost there will be a pretty job—they were to be addressd to Murray. I will write to him to night.

If you go to Abbotrule next week you had better take the other Abbot in your way. I shall budge on the 12th.

I had the inclosed flourishing epistle from a woman who modestly proposes I should lend her a hundred pounds. Will you enquire about her—if she is a decent person which is not likely send her the inclosed decent refusal & I may perhaps find the means of giving her something or other.

I think Harold will come within the month & with Paul will add £800 to your finances which will make them flourish as December has almost nothing.

I inclose a letter to my wife. Yours ever   W. S.

ABBOTSFORD *Wednesday* [*October* 1815] [2]

[*Nat. Lib. Scot.*]

---

[1] i.e. *Harold the Dauntless*, published January 1817 but, according to Lockhart, " begun several years back ; nay, part of it had been actually printed before the appearance of Childe Harold."

[2] See Vol. IV. p. 104 for letter to James Ballantyne on 21st October.

DEAR JOHN,—I have yours this morning by which I perceive Paul will be greatly less than I thought having understood from you that 6000 were going to press. James *must* press on with it however & without humming & hawing. I am surprized he has not more hands at work. Surely there has been time enough since you were here. The Antiqy. goes on instantly after or rather before Paul is done at press. I would give 100 guineas to have Paul out before next Quarterly when Southeys accot. of the battle will be given & surely with only 3000 this may be done. For GODS SAKE push it on what signifies my slaving myself to death if we do not get forward.

Inclosed is a proposal from a gentleman to whom I am obliged for some attention at Brussells. I wish you would throw it off in a modest way & stick it into all the copies of Waterloo. You may I think make bold with the names of Longman Murray & Constable to receive subscriptions & add your own (as an agent not as publisher) I mean *John* B. by himself.

I would do Mr Sasse some good if I could.[1] The note was returnd with copy under Mr Kerrs cover & I doubt not came safe.

When you write to Longman etc. say I desired you to use their name & tell C. of the matter immediatly.

W. S.

Sunday—

I intend for the Annual Register a short piece calld the Dance of Death. I am afraid I cannot let you have it before Wednesday having had the cramp in my stomach *very bad* as Paddy says by eating barley bannocks. I am now well again by dint of drinking gin.

[1815]

[*Nat. Lib. Scot.*]

---

[1] The actual word Scott has here written is " good."

DEAR JOHN,—I have your letter with Messrs. Cranstouns & Veitchs proposal on which two points ocur.

1st. Is the bargain a reasonable one that is will it pay you with your per. centage as auctioneer—but you can judge better of this than any one having I suppose sold most of the books. This I will assure you that very fine books of modern times like Boydells Shakespeare fetch half nothing at sales in London. If you make profit on the business of course it is your own but the prospect of a deficiency must be heedfully lookd at. We had too much of rash adventures.—One thing seems certain that half a year must be allowd to get in the money before any interest is expected. In other words if Books are sold between Xmas & spring no interest should be paid till Martinmas.

2dly. What security do they require. I will give none over my property though I have no objection to your proposing James & me for a personal bond. This will require great management & you must begin by learning the sort of security they demand before you name anyone & then you may propose me if you find it like to be agreeable as a person to whom you could give good counter security of a literary nature but not as having yet communicated with me on the subject. In this manner you can fish out what they expect before committing ourselves. If the books be really worth the money no doubt the cash would be convenient for us especially as I have two or three shabby borrowings from friends which I hunger & thirst to pay up. It would also make discounts etc easy or rather render them unnecessary for some time. But the great point is to know with what terms they will be satisfied—I mean with what security— I do not consider it as a matter of so much magnitude as to involve any friend in it and I would hurt my credit greatly by giving heritable security over Abbotsford more especially as things are clearing so fast.

You do not mention receiving my letter with a parcel of poetry for the Regr. nor what you think of it, nor whether you have got my parcel for Triermain or spoken to Rees about it.

James seems long about his wooing. I hope he will get it settled favourably this time. Yours truly W. SCOTT

ABBOTSFORD *friday* [PM. *Oct.* 28, 1815]

[*Nat. Lib. Scot.*]

DEAR JOHN,—I inclose a bill of £100 received from my brother this morning towards his drat. this you may use in the meanwhile keeping it in view it is only a fortnights loan.

I quite approve of what you have done about the Lady. I would deal with C. as little as possible untill his notes become more marketable.

I think it will help you with Rees to have a sheet to shew of Triermain Vol 2d. & I will endeavour to get you one. Mrs. Maclean Clephane has been a heavy draught on my time Mrs. S. being rather unwell.[1] I trust James will act well & prudently. He seems quite pleased with the arrangements I have made for him & I am very glad he is not suffering the iron to cool.

Yesterday I sent the poetry for the Register. Pray send a copy of the Waterloo to Mrs. Murray Keith & another to Miss Rutherford both to Miss Rutherfords house—Also one to Richard Heber Westminster. Yours truly   W. S.

I hope you sent Mr. Kerr Post office an early copy.

In computing November you must remember the ½ annuity from P.O.

private

[*October* 1815]

[*Nat Lib. Scot.*]

---

[1] See letter to James, Vol. IV. p. 105.

To [JAMES] BALLANTYNE

[Fragment]

[*no date*]

DEAR BALLANTYNE,—The Box has at length arrived
with the interesting inclosure. As we have fully discussed
that subject I need not attempt to express the interest I
so deeply feel in a point of such near interest to you. The
road is clear & fair before you and though Love &
Modesty should make the way faring man a fool yet I
think he can hardly err therein. A little ardour however
looks well throw off ten of your years for a month or two
and be as vehement earnest and solicitous as if you were
in your calf love. [*MS. torn away here*] . . . But you are
in an absolutely fair train, your play is on velvet &
nothing but your seeming too secure & being guilty of the
shadow of neglect can disconcert it. Though if after so
much frankness on her part she should suspect any thing
like want of assiduity on yours it will strike her that she
has made herself cheap—and then goodnight. Think
of this Mr. Brooke.[1]

I inclose a letter to Weber which pray forward & let
your Devils assist him in getting a parcel sent me by the
Coach when he has made it up which will be in a day or
two. [*The remainder of the MS. has been torn off.*]

[1815-16][2]

[*Glen*]

To JOHN BALLANTYNE

DEAR JOHN,—Your plan of a 4to/ is a good one. But
I doubt you must either agree with the publishers of the
8vo. Roderick abt. it or we shall be censured with justice
as acting unhandsomely by them. You can see what
Rees & Constable say to it, unquestionably they will not
wish their sale to be interfered with & if we do not agree

---

[1] *Fal.* Think of that,—hissing hot,—think of that, Master Brook.
                                —*Merry Wives of Windsor*, Act. iii, sc. v.
[2] But this fragment probably dates from 1808 and refers to James's *first*
affair. See Vol. I. p. 296 and Vol. II. pp. 82-5.

with them & Murray we must postpone your plan till their edition is out. I wish it had been thought of sooner. Constable you will see by the inclosed proposes the Lady of [the] Lake to go to press. I also inclose my answer leaving it to your arrangement. You will of course take care that no preference is given in the matter which can give offence in Pater Noster Row. I should be glad to see Rees at Abbotsford if he returns this way.

I shall proceed upon your recommendn. in the matter of Mosses land.

Probably by lumping the Lady with a 4to/ Rodk. we might make it all go down. But then Murray is to be settled with.

I have written to James fully upon our affairs : he will of course shew you the letter & I think you will be of opinion that although I cannot give up debts which are in a fair way of being paid by a thriving concern and which owes its subsistence & prosperity in a particular manner to my advances influence & exertions yet I have placed him in the situation of a free and unencumberd man with a decent present subsistence & very fair prospects. I shall be anxious to hear the result of his wooing.[1]

[1] The reference is to James's forthcoming marriage. He had written at length to Scott about his wish to be set free from debt and from further partnership in the business. Of Scott's reply I have only the following extract as given in the *Reply* to Lockhart's *Ballantyne-Humbug Handled*, 1839, p. 60. :

"Scott, in a letter dated 5th November 1815 (one of the few articles of James Ballantyne's correspondence with Scott that we happen still to have in our possession), says—

'Your future brother's wish of a complete discharge among the partners respectively of John Ballantyne & Co., not only fully meets my concurrence, but is *what I designed to request for my own sake, to put me in the exclusive possession of stock*, &c. But it will be impossible to disclose the business *to the public* till all current demands are out-and-out paid, and all the cash account is paid up, for which full provision has been made ; but I think it must be Whitsunday at soonest before it can be closed. *I am unconscious of having made any extraordinary exertion in your behalf.* I think it no more than you would have made for me in the like circumstances ; and your new friends may be assured that, however I may have opportunity of serving you, it is neither in my own nature, nor, in all human probability, in the nature of things, ·that my connexion should prove other than very advantageous to you.'"

You will wafer Constables letter & forward it & let the Lady go to press forthwith.   Yours truly

WALTER SCOTT

ABBOTSFORD *Tuesday* [*Nov.-Dec.* 1815]

I fear we shall have too much of Constables paper with Antiqy. so you must manage to get Longmans acceptances for as much as you can of Lady of [the] Lake—that is—I will have no management of C's to give us long bills. I think you may allow them good credits.

[*Nat. Lib. Scot.*]

DEAR JOHN,—I send you the poems for Register which I shall be glad to see in proof as I have hardly had time to look over the Dance.   There could be no objection to having a few quartos of that by the way & I should like at any rate to have a few separate 8vo copies for my freinds—What list of presentation copies did you send off? let one of your lads copy it for me in case of omission.

My brother [1] has drawn on me for £200,, at fifteen days sight.   I can manage £100,, but shall be pinchd for the rest unless you can help me about that time.   He tells me he is writing a novel [2]—if so I think it will prove a capital one—

I return two proofs one of Rodk. which I thought had been out & one of Paul.   I suppose James is set out. The paper came safe & was very acceptable also the copies.   Let me know your vidimus for Novr. so soon as you can—also what you settle in the matter of the Lady & the probable income.   These things tell well.   Yours truly

W. S.

ABBOTSFORD *friday* [*October* [?] 27, 1815]

I have been at Mertoun & now Mrs. Macleane Clephane has come here which has interrupted me somewhat. I have begun at odd times the 12 [two words illegible].

[*Nat. Lib. Scot.*]

---

[1] Tom.   [2] The actual words are " a writing novel."

DEAR JOHN,—I have a letter from Constable expressing a wish that 1500 Waverley should go to press directly which I request you will look after. I have referrd him to you for particulars. I mentiond to him formerly that I thought he should take some stock but as he has taken Thoms. of Reading & orderd the Register liberally of late I feel no wish to cram him and am better pleased with orders in the usual way of business. Of course you will be explicit in saying I will hear of *no* advertizing unless the over copies are carried to accompt. Better make a jotting of your whole agreement for you remember we had 4000 G.M. flung on our hands last year by Longms. people.

Murray has sold Paul (all his copies) to Longman so that work will soon be out. I think James has a copy with my corrections but as I have a great many to add I would wish to have it sent by our basket. It will reach me also by the Blucher. Some time I would like to have a copy of Waverley.

Mess[rs]. Constable & Longman wish to make the price of the Antiqy. 24/ instead of a guinea. I have no great objection but I will not connive for nothing at their picking the pockets of the public,—I must share like Falstaff I must have my eighteenpence I will not endanger my soul gratis. So if they charge 3/ one may go to the retailer one to the publishers & one to the author otherwise I will not boat. That sum & the Waverley 4th Edition will nearly make up what I want at this next term. I should think the last thousand G.M. & the Paul are also likely soon to be in. On the other side is the preliminary matter to the Antiqy.

I expected proofs today but have none.

W. S.

Thursday [*early in* 1816]

[*Nat. Lib. Scot.*]

DEAR JOHN,—Your explanation about the P.O. bills is equally pleasing & satisfactory. I wonder at C. & Co/ having chosen this time to be crusty since I really think all the danger is on our side and all chance of advantage on theirs—I am unwilling to butter Constables bills with my name (till I come to town at least) because I shall have to ask credit from Sir W. F. for November which assuredly will be the more readily given that my name is little in their books. I must be guided however by you. Whatever you do keep perfect good humour—do what they are entitled to and do no more. *They* will find themselves losers in the end but you are sensible a quarrel would put it in their power greatly to injure us by blabbing to which they are at all times sufficiently addicted. I will have a complete explanation with Goodman Puff upon his return.

And he may crack o' his winning
When he clears scores wi' me.

Do you push on the register Russell & James—you know I cannot—I thought there was no danger of its being out at Xmas & out it *must be* whatever it cost. Do not throw this on me who have to work for £3000 between [now?] & Candlemas & will win it too with fair play.

I think you may send the chairs at Thomsons price— they will not exceed £2,, 10,, if you show him the money for the packing charge is nonsense—if not he need not write or give himself any trouble as I have not a moment for useless correspondence. Yours truly

W. S.

[1816]

[*Nat. Lib. Scot.*]

DEAR JOHN,—I have seen the great Swab who is supple as a glove & will

Do ALL which some interpret NOTHING.

However we may rely on £600 there—press on the bills to get a deposit the 19th or 20th and we shall do well enough. W. S.

[*Nat. Lib. Scot.*]

DEAR JOHN,—James has made one or two important mistakes in the bargain with Murray. Briefly as follows.

Having only authority from me to promise 6000 copies he proposes they shall have the copy-right *for ever*. I will see their noses cheese first.

2dly. He proposes I shall have 12 mos. bills—I have always got 6 however I would not stand on that.

3dly He talks of volumes being put into the publishers hands to consider & decide on. No such thing—a bare perusal at St. John Street only.

Then for omissions.

It is NOT stipulated that we supply the print & paper of successive editions. This must be naild & not left to understanding.

Secondly. I will have London Bills as well as Blackwoods.

If they agree to these conditions—good & well—if they demur Constable must be instantly tried—giving half to Longman—& *we* drawing on *them* for that money or Constable lodging their bill in our hands. You will understand it is a 4 volume work a Romance totally different in stile and structure from the others—a new cast in short of the net which has hitherto made miraculous draughts. I do not limit you in terms because I think you will make them better than I can do. But he must do more than others since he will not or cannot

print with us. For every point but this one I would
much rather deal with Constable than any one for he
has always shewn himself both spirited judicious & liberal
& gets off his books faster than anybody our fathers in the
Row not ex[c]epted. Whenever Blackwood demurs &
he must be put to the point *instantly* Constable must be
treated with for there is no use in suffering the thing to
be blown on. At the same time you need not conceal
from him that there was some proposals elsewhere but
you may add with truth I would rather close with him.

Communicate with James on the matter who will
shew you my letter. It would be the height of folly to
reduce the price of the Antiqies. & your argument on
that is unanswerable. We shall have plenty of bills but
Disct. may be troublesome this is however a less evil.
I expect an accompt of my precepts having some matters
to pay but they will do in the end of the week should that
be matter of accomodation. Yours truly   W. S.

ABBOTSFORD *Monday* [PM. *Apr.* 30, 1816] [1]

I think Constable should jump at this affair for I
believe the work will be very popular. I need not say
I will be anxious to hear. I expect considerable accomodations to pay money about Whitsunday.[2]

[*Nat. Lib. Scot.*]

DEAR JOHN,—Shortly after you left me I discoverd
the mistake which originates as you conceived in your not
crediting the P.O. with £158,, as a part of the sum of
£280,, advanced by me on 15. It is very properly
enterd in the Calendar.

James's loan (Mr. Scott lent) 158—£280,,

[1] April 29 (Lockhart).

[2] Lockhart prints this letter in the *Life.* See also Vol. IV. pp. 222-3. The
bills for John's stock to value of £600 were granted by Murray and Blackwood early in May.

You had therefore understood the repayment at the time though afterwards I observe the jotting you had inaccurately made. The fact is that I just replaced that advance with the money from Couts as I see by looking at my rects. & of course considerd the printing debt as paid & took credit with James accordingly. I was sure I was not mistaken in that point. I will trouble you to call tomorrow that the balance may be settled & that the error may be corrected.

I wish you would bring James's cash with you minus his own balance & Cowans & a stamp for Constables money. You are quick in these matters & I slow and require great attention to prevent gross mistakes like the above. I hope you will let me see you sometimes not *upon the press* but to prevent it by deliberation. You see here has a mutual & unpleasant error gone on for a fortnight which two words of a morning or evening would have cleard up—It would insure any recurrence of mistake & I almost think of difficulty if you would appoint any time at least once a week to talk over these very important matters—Let me press it upon you that your own credit as well as mine depends upon this. Suppose you should join our Sundays breakfast as James docs.

[Unsigned]

[1816 ?]

[*Nat. Lib. Scot.*]

To JAMES BALLANTYNE

DEAR JAMES,—I observe by your letter the disappointment as to Hollingsworth [1] which cannot be helped.

---

[1] On 19th September of this year James writes to Scott explaining his accounts and that " I was correct in saying that only £500 was minus. That has been supplied & if I can discount Hollingworth's security bills the 21 will be weathered safely." He mentions other items and proceeds : " The pro[missory] note of £300 by John to Sir W. Forbes & Co. in November I explained or endeavoured to explain in a note accompanying the entry

But as there was a large lot of paper taken off their hands on express condition of their giving us this accomodation I would let them understand that the disappointment must be otherwise compensated as by long credit on that paper or otherwise.

As to the plan of finance to be substituted it occurs to me that you should get Cowans Security Bill of £414 & with the £350 & carry both to Sir W. F.'s Deducing between £250 & £300 owing to the House you will receive about £460,, or £500,, which will provide for the 1st. I will get Duncans £275 managed against the 10th & there is but little more to the end of the month, & I

... when I received from Blackwood & Murray their bills for £600 on account of Stock taken with Tales of my Landlord I gave them to John who at that period did all the pecuniary part of our business. They were deposited by him with Forbes & Co. in security of his own p. note to them for £300 which sum he advanced to me as wanted for the business. This note fell due on the 14th of August and he had left a fresh one with his clerk to be offered in payment on that day. This was accordingly done and the new note falls due as mentioned on 16 Nov. Why he did not enter this among the claims against us I really cannot explain. It is not possible I can be responsible for what he did or did not do when by general approbation he managed the pecuniary concerns of the business but this I will take on me to say that so long as that management is entrusted to me everything shall be laid and kept clearly before you . . . our concerns and Johns shall *never* be mingled by me, or with my good will . . . he is now (saving good will) no more to us than Johnie Anderson or Ro Miller. . . . I do not see why I should not transact all money business just as well as John. This leads me to notice an impression which you have many times stated as existing in your mind of me, that I am anxious & drooping & desponding. . . . Not a bit of it. I was once & who could avoid it ? for no man but yourself could have disentangled us ; and who could have thought that even you could have done what has been done. But for many months I have had no such feelings nor ever consciously expressed them." He goes on to a state of bills at Allans ; refers to John's doings in Paris and Rotterdam, where he has been seeking purchasers for the old stock and has arranged an agency in seeds and French wines. James then concludes "John is just arrived . . . no man can love or for many reasons respect another more than I do John. But with the Black man in the play

Cassio, I love thee but never
More be *Cash-keeper of mine.*"

Such were Scott's partners, but by this time John was out except as a literary agent and James, too, was no partner but a salaried manager.

hope you will claw in something more or less from the business. The only thing troublesome in these matters is the having so much in one name & the necessity of renewing his bills for him according to bargain. I had some conversation with young Smith at Glasgow about Constables business. The young man seemd to consider him as rather *too* enterprizing—these are hints which are seldom drop'd without reason. But he added he was very clever & had many resources.

I think you should have some conversation with Cadell —for if they are to give us business agreeably to their agreement we can do it cheaper & better now than at any other time. I really think the printers should lower their rates and recommend to you to speak to your brethren about it—better half a loaf than no bread. In your conversation with Cadell you will of course be amicable & confidential (indeed we have nothing to conceal) & endeavour to see what his feelings are as to the posture of affairs : he will scarce be able to conceal them if unfavourable.

To Longman it is only necessary to say that I have been making extensive copies from the records for their preface & am now in the highlands. It cannot be written in the country for want of books &c. I think they will get it about November.

I will trouble you to call in Excheqr with the inclosed receipts about the 25th. You will receive in the Auditors office 4 precepts which you will carry to the Receiver Generals office also in Exchequer & receive the contents amounting to £170 or thereabout which pay into the Leith Bank & take a receipt to account of Mr George Craig their Agent at Galashiels & inclose the receipt to me. It must be in my name " Received from W. S. &c to account of G. Craig " & so forth. The sooner you manage this the better as I have some heavey [1] sums to pay here.

[1] Spelt thus in MS.

You will also send me a bill for £300 drawn by you on me for my acceptance @ 3 months which can be discounted in Edinr. as [I have] a payment to that amount to make [*MS. torn here*] which the business has swallowd my funds.

I wish to know how far the Register is fward. I will send more copy in a few days to finish the volume which will produce some bills & then have at the tales. Yours truly

WALTER SCOTT

ABBOTSFORD 23 *July* [1816]

You had better be looking out & inquiring after some money-shop as we shall have enough of bills.

[*Glen*]

To JOHN BALLANTYNE

DEAR JOHN,—I have the pleasure to inclose Murrays acceptances. You will take up my £710,, bill at the Royal Bank & pray call to be certain of the day on which it is due it is the 14th or 15th. I think the last. You will have £200 over on Murrays bills or something less— £200,, on my Excheqr. precepts & I will send you £400,, agt. your long bills on the 24th. & it may happen some hundreds more. It will be uncertain whether I will not want this last money back against the 15 Augt. to retire my Jedburgh acceptance but I hope I shall not. I earnestly recommend to you to push *realising* as much as you can

> Consider weel gude man
> We hae but borrowd gear
> The horse that I ride on
> It is John Murrays mear.

You will of course write with the utmost regularity & tell me how to make my entries—let nothing escape you

that can be calculated upon as falling due under whatever
denomination. The states & balances will I trust be
ready about the middle of the month when James &
you will give us a Sunday at Abbotsford which I trust
will be a more pleasant one than we have been lately in
the habit of passing upon business. I go to Drumlanrig
about the end of the month so should like all these matters
settled.

Do not forget Winstanley who seems jealous of your
neglecting to write him & look over my books still at the
binding lest they find the way into your sale.

I have little else to say excepting to pray your earnest
and unremitted attention to calling in debts & making
sales where the latter is possible.   Yours truly

W. SCOTT

CASTLE STREET *Sunday* [1] [*August* 1816]

[*Nat. Lib. Scot.*]

DEAR JOHN,—I find Dr. Douglas has made *all his
arrangements* for disposing of his cash tomorrow. I must
therefore have £750,, before twelve o'clock get it how so
you can for I will be in very bad bread without it—I trust
you will have little difficulty in working it out with your
ammunition pouch filld as it is. But you must make a
point of it with some of your friends as the only pinch on
my side arises from my large advances to you.   Yours etc

W. S.

Monday [2] [*Aug.* 1816]

[*Nat. Lib. Scot.*]

[1] Lockhart prints a short extract from this letter in the *Life*, dating it
August 1816 (see Vol. IV. p. 264) on the strength of the reference to a
Jedburgh bill to be retired on the 15th.

[2] This follows the letter of August in the volume and is possibly, therefore,
of the same month and year.

DEAR JOHN,—I heartily congratulate you on your return [1] & hope your journey promises some effective advantages. You should immediately rigg out your rooms & advertize your things with the advantage of your return from abroad.

I perfectly remember the state of Allans accot. But it seems to me that as they state themselves to hold £750 undiscounted Edinburgh bills in expectation they will be calld on to advance £400 during this month (being the balance of your £1300 acceptances unextinguishd by London bills falling due during the month) it seems to me I say that if £400 is paid them to save them such advance they cannot refuse to render up these security bills. They will still have about £400 excresce [2] of the English bills to cover the chance of any dishonor with the interest on the accompt. I do not see how they can decently refuse this. But would it not be possible by collecting the funds destined for next month & borrowing on all hands to proffer them their full £1300. At any rate it seems ridiculous to permit them to hold fully £1200 for £400,, & something must be made of them if possible to save renewals which will be otherwise both disagreeable & difficult. About £1000 has emerged in different bills of James's & yours which did not appear in any of your books when I left town which alone occasions trouble.

James has gone on steadily with his money matters but must not be allowd to fall again into inactivity for besides that it would be unjust (the bookselling concern being at an end) to use your services as cash keeper without a remuneration which times will not afford you will I hope have enough to do with your own sales during the winter and have ample use for all your own credit. You will understand of course that I by no means relinquish our claim upon your advice confidence and

[1] John had been in Paris in August 1816.

[2] In excess, outstanding. See *New English Dictionary*.

assistance in these matters & in others which may arise
and I sincerely hope I will have it in my power to make
this advantageous to you. What follows therefore applies
to James under your advice & assistance.

DEAR JAMES,—I trust you have got matters arranged
with Constable & Millar. I fear there will be no means
of taking up the £280 save by renewal for which you
must send me a drat. for acceptance. Agt. the 9th. there
is £600 of mine at Sir W. F. this will open £300 of discot.
& if better means cannot be contrived they will take
my note for £300 at two months or three. To pay the
ballance you must with Johns assistance rub up Gale etc
and I think it possible that Orme might accept for the
balance of Guy Mannering at least in part. What other
funds & sources of credit there may be I know not but
I believe there is cash due in Glasgow & elsewhere—
also you have that fellows bill for a source of credit at
least—Morrison is I think the name but you will scrape
together what you can and report to me. Yours in haste

W. S.

BOWHILL *Wednesday* [*Septr.-Oct.* 1816]

If John can spare me a day I will be delighted to hear
his foreign news.

[*Nat. Lib. Scot.*]

DEAR JOHN,—I am glad to hear any reasonable
explanation of the unhappy protest but it seems to have
been a blunderd business for the money ought surely to
have been in the place where the bill was to be presented.
I must observe besides as I shall do to James that he
ought on no account to grant Compy. bills in his own
private affairs especially as they do not appear in the
books. It is extremely irregular. I also think he should
come to town & drive on the presses. If this work is not
out by the 15 & bills ready for it it will produce great

inconvenience—therefore no time should be lost in working off titles etc. and yet he will tell me the whole affairs of the company are before me. I sent copy yesterday & send more [on] Monday. As I pass through Galashiels I will get and inclose receipts for my precepts in Excheqr. which I beg you will receive and send me the proceeds which I need very much. I wrote to James a week ago about an Accot. due by Mrs. Scott to Mitchel & Harriot Milliners Princes Street £58 which I wishd to pay but he *never answerd me on the point.* If it is NOT paid will you take the trouble to pay it and send me the receipt with the balance of the precept money by next frank—if it IS paid you will retain the money and send the receipt. It should have been settled long ago but for James's distresses who seems to forget mine. Do not fail to send me the money having shearers etc to settle with. I have some hope of a goodish job for you—Will you get me a pruning knife at Marshals of the large kind the handle about nine inches long with a pruning blade & double edged saw— I have lost mine—make them chuse a real good blade. Send it by the Blucher to be left at the Post office. Yours truly   W. S.

26 *October* [1816] [1]

The 3d part of Vol iv is finishd so that with little exertion I can let you have the whole by Saturday or Sunday if I have no more worrying about other matters to put me off work.

The £400,, History Bill is to be renewd for Constable. This must be lookd to in time.

Sunday Morning.

I have just received yours & James's. I congratulate you on the order from Carleton House [2] & should be sorry

---

[1] John's address is now "Bookseller & Auctioneer, Hanover Street."

[2] On the 25th John had written : " I have had to-day the distinguished honour to receive the Prince Regent's command to send him your works

you missd it. Rather than you should not execute it creditably I will let you have my own quartos with all the prints thereunto belonging which are a matchless set you allowing me credit for the value at your sales. But I could not give you them till I come to town. I think you should write that you have a view of such a set also concerning the bound sets in case they should be more acceptable—The order does not give you any title to name yourself Bookseller to the Prince which is a title which I believe is only obtaind by paying for the same.

[*Nat. Lib. Scot.*]

DEAR JOHN,—I inclose the bill & wish you joy of your appointment which is honorable for certain & may be profitable. Do not let the gale of good fortune blow the pilot Prudence from the helm and you will make a good voyage. I think as H.R.H. has said so much about the books it may be worth while to make them more worth his acceptance. I am sure Kerr [?] will make drawings of some of the notable plans.

If Pauls bills are not discountable you had better give them to James to go with a lot he is sending to the banker. I write to wish him joy of this new production of the Ballantyne press. I am yours truly

W. SCOTT

ABBOTSFORD *Wednesday*.

I return on friday & bring No. 1. 2. & 3. Look early out for a light No. 4.

in royal 4to and James has to send him any thing he thinks good which is published here." James's letter of the same day—the 25th—expresses his regret " at the discreditable incident which has taken place. I shall limit myself to a naked statement (and a short one) of the circumstances that led to it." " The £200 bill lately dishonoured was given by me to John for an equal sum advanced by him and paid by me to Alexander," who was in difficulties. Scott's next two letters deal with this. The failure to take up the bill had been an accident. " Mr Cadell's conduct, in writing to you, seems to have been unnecessarily severe and precipitate." For similar incidents see Vol. IV. p. 387 and Vol. V. p. 270.

To JAMES BALLANTYNE

DEAR JAMES,—I have your letter and am unwilling to add to the pain you must have felt by reproaches. It is necessary however to say that secrets of all kinds in business are very hazardous and that it is extremely irregular to use the companys firm in raising money without advice to the partner principally concernd. It is indeed a thing most severely censurable and on sudden death or any other misfortune would expose the [*MS. faded here*] however innocent his purposes to the most [*MS. faded*] I have known it declared firm the [*MS. faded*] partner & not appearing [*MS. faded*] felt as a friend under cognisance of the criminal law. And you see to how many risques transactions out of the regular course of business are necessarily exposed. I cannot blame Constable & Co/—far from it I think they only did their bounden duty by me and I should be very sorry to think that a matter affecting my credit so deeply was considerd as a fit secret to be smotherd up, especially as it is possible it may influence deeply our schemes of provision. I expect the tales will be out of my hand by this day sennight and it is necessary the press should be forced on to meet the engagements in the middle of the month. What inconvenience may arise from this awkward & discreditable scrape I cannot pretend to anticipate. But I am glad you are in town to shew face as your absence gave a very critical air to the transaction.

I wishd much to see you here to consult you about the tales as well as to settle our accompts. I can end my story either tragically or otherwise—the last is the most commonplace but the most pleasing—on this I had wishd your advice particularly. You have never sent the running copy which makes me drop my notion of a glossary by Jedediah which will be now too late. I intreat title pages and all the dragwork may be got forward. I shall be glad to have your state of cash since forwarded to know if Cowan be paid & about my £200 note &c. Dont let these things fall again into arrear after all that has been said about them—*figures* is what I like. Also please to say at what dates the p. office bills will be coming in. Dont be caught napping again. Allans matter should also be very [*MS. faded*]. Do not let me waste time [*MS. faded*] all this over again but turn your [*MS. faded*] as time presses. Yours truly

W. S.

Sunday 27 *October* [1816]

I wrote you about an accompt due to Mitchell & Harriot. No answer aye or no. I inclose John the receipt for the precepts out of which I wish these people to be paid £58,, and the ballance sent in notes in the next parcel of proofs. Pray have an eye to this unless you would have me think Je suis ennuyé de lui et ses petites affaires. I leave Johns letter open that you may relieve him of the trouble of my commissions if you think fit.

[*Glen*]

To JAMES BALLANTYNE

DEAR SIR,—I got your letter [1] this morning and lose no time in answering it.

[1] That of 8th November. On the 28th October James had written in response to Scott's last letter : " I was not aware of the terrible consequences arising from an acting partner using the copartnery signature for his personal purposes. I assure you, Sir, I should very nearly as soon forge your own signature as use one which implicated your credit and property for what belonged to me personally." He recalls an unpleasant correspondence in 1814 on " the debt due to my brother." " I may now shortly restate that the money advanced by him went into the funds *of the business* and at periods when it was imperiously wanted. No doubt it went in my name, to keep up my share of stock equal to yours but I honestly confess to you that this consideration never went into my calculation . . . when my brother called up the money he had the company's obligation therefor and I thought myself warranted to pay him by means which did not increase the Coys responsibility nor pledge their credit one guinea further. . . . Sooner than pledge the Coys security again I would go to jail." James seems then to have gone to Abbotsford, and on 8th November he

When I enterd into my copartnery with you, your stock taken at your own valuation as worth rather what it would have been of value to the business than what it would have brought at a sale was £1500—to which I added in actual cash £1500.

For several terms the accompts were so made up that you carried two thirds of the *gross* profits instead of two third[s] of the *nett* profits to your own accompt of stock, which accot. I agreed to pass over and ratify although on the face of it grossly unequal.

For several terms also (owing to engagements as you stated in your fathers behalf) large portions of your stock were withdrawn & replaced as in an accompt current, against which I found it necessary to remonstrate very peremptorily as you & John must both remember.

You then informd me that you could make an addition to your stock through the means of a loan obtaind from Mrs. Bruce on condition the Co/ was to be pledged for the bills. To this I made no objection & I think there was another loan obtaind in the same manner.

wrote : " In consequence of what passed between us at Abbotsford I applied to my Brother Alexander to give up the Company's Bills for the £500 still due him, and to take mine in their stead, and this he has kindly done. The other £500 paid to him by funds raised by pledging the Coys security in other quarters I cannot get quit of in the same way. That sum *must* be carried on because I have no funds of my own to retire it." Adverting to what Scott has said of " a partner of the firm having used the security of the firm for a sum borrowed by him for my own personal purposes," he claims that Scott did exactly the same : " One of the sums paid in by you to the business and for which you drew 15 per cent for several years was borrowed by you from your brother Major Scott. For this sum you took the company bound to make over the security of the printing office when required. . . . Further when you indicated your displeasure upon this occasion about 3 years since I informed you that my Brother had agreed to give up the Company's security upon my making over to him in sale my house in St. John Street "—this Scott had not approved of. " Shortly afterwards this house, my personal property, was assigned over in security to Sir William Forbes & Co. for a Company debit to the extent of £1200. . . . I should humbly presume that this assignation . . . fully acquits me for having pledged the Coys firm for a personal one. At the present moment the Company are bound by my personal behoof for £500 ; but my personal property is bound for the Company's behoof for £1210." For a fragment from the 1814 correspondence see p. 530.

Of course I thought myself entitled to the same advantage & required security over the printing office for £1200,, advanced by my brother. This was agreed to and promised. But so far was my brother from getting the security as Mrs. Bruce did that I was afterwards told that there was a balance of an heritable bond due over the Office which was not paid up out of the £1200,, advanced. So that my brother *never got* the security and in point of fact requested and obtaind from me other caution.

All these were transactions in which I certainly had no advantage unless it were that I had the promise of security which could not be granted.

You & your brother keeping the accompts we both drew according to our rated stocks with such indiscretion as it proved that the concern was run £4000 in debt which £4000,, containing *your* draughts as well as *my own* I *alone* was under the necessity of replacing.

It was in these circumstances when the business was in every point of view deeply my debtor that you granted these bills to your brother without consulting me or intimating to me that I was to be so bound. Every other transaction had been the subject of some discussion between us—this was done without any & you are aware I challenged it so soon as it came to my knowlege. I do not say the purpose but certainly the effect of it was to save your brother at my expence & to involve me in a responsibility where I was not originally or properly liable. If your house in Johns Street stood pledged to Sir W. Forbes's house you must allow it was only for bills in themselves perfectly sufficient & through means of which you could sustain no loss. Whereas my advances were in actual cash & to a very large amount replacing your advances as well as my own.

My answers to your position therefore briefly are—

If my brother had got the proposed security he would only have got what was settled & agreed on between us in the same manner as I agreed Mrs. Bruce's debt should be guaranteed by the Company. And I cannot admit that you were entitled in consequence of a proposal *agreed to by us both* & in fact *never carried into effect* to grant the companys security *without my knowlege* for money advanced previously as a debt of your own. Again you say I received 15 pr. cent on the £1200. I believe this did not happen for above a term or two. But if I did I not only replaced every farthing of it but your draughts into the bargain so that it seems hard that this should be stated against me as [*MS. torn here*] an advantage. I think I have a title [not] to be made [*MS. torn here*] [1] than I chuse to make myself especially as I have been so heavy a loser in the other business and have to accomodate your views in life taken that loss exclusively on myself.

I hope we shall be able to put these things to rights when I come to Edinburgh which will be tomorrow. I will be glad to see you as soon as you can find it convenient. Believe me yours truly   W Scott

ABBOTSFORD *Sunday* [*postmarked* 12 *November* 1816]
[*Glen*]

To JOHN BALLANTYNE

DEAR JOHN,—With your fraternal aid of £400 James will be *bang up* till I return. As you are a collector of my fugitives I send you a trumpery thing to the tune of God preserve the Emperor Francis sung at the Provosts Gala with good approbation. Give no copies. Item I send you a companion to the View of Ashestiel for your 4to both should be marked Del: Harriet Scott of Harden Nee Comptesse de Bruhl von Martinskirken.—You promised to get me Giffords Johnson large paper—If you are successful send me the first volume or two by our carrier on Wednesday—& if there is any news in town I will be glad to hear it. Yours etc.   W. S.

[1816]
[*Nat. Lib. Scot.*]

[1] Probably "liable for more."

Dear John,—I have herewith returnd to James No: I & will be answerable for No II & III.[1] I think I can engage in your interest a classical scholar of uncommon genius.[2] I am very lazy or rather very fatigued just now as I walk out every glim[ps]e of daylight in spite of wind and weather. My bog which you remember I drained with so much difficulty proves to be a fund of very fine & almost inexhaustible marle—a circumstance almost invaluable to this property.

I think you had better keep the three £40,, for Paul to help out the acceptances on your account with me about the 5th. namely Johnstone Lang etc.

I have nothing to send you from this place but accounts of storms. Today I had near lost my life by a very singular accident. I was walking on the brink of the hill above the lake the wind blowing very high with some rain & as I tried to cast my plaid round to shelter me the wind got fairly possession and it was all I could do to prevent my being forced over the bank. I however saved myself and plaid by dint of main strength.

I will willingly wait till you get a copy of Johnson a bon marché. But it must be large paper to range with my other Dramatick authors.

The companion to Ashestiel is a view in the neighbourhood.

I will be obliged to you for any kindness you shew Mr Blore who has been very obliging in my matters here. Yours truly

W. S.

Thursday 26 *Decr.* [1816]

[*Nat. Lib. Scot.*]

---

[1] Of the *Sale-Room* (spelt and italicized thus). For details about this short-lived periodical see note, Vol. IV. p. 357.

[2] James Bailey. See Vol. IV. p. 139.

2 K

DEAR JOHN,—I inclose the Saleroom promised. I have a good subject for a work of fiction in petto. What do you think Constable would give for a smell of it ? [1] You ran away without taking leave the other morning or I wishd to have spoken to you about it. I do not mean a continuation of Jedediah because there might be some delicacy in putting that bye the original publishers. You may write if any thing occurs to you on this subject. It will not interrupt the history. By the way I have a great lot of the Register ready for delivery & no man asks after it. I shall want to pay up some cash etc at Whitsunday which will make me draw on my brains. Yours truly   W. SCOTT

ABBOTSFORD *Monday* [*April* 1817] [2]

[*Nat. Lib. Scot.*]

DEAR JOHN,[3]—I will be much obliged to you to come with Constable here on Monday as he proposes a visit & it will save some time as to the necessary arrangements. By the way you must attend that the usual quantity of stock is included in this arrangement that is £600 for 6000 copies. How will you manage with yours for of course we would not like that they should come to hammer ?—You must consider how this is to be managed, or whether any thing can be done instead of the stock to

[1] The work alluded to is *Rob Roy*.

[2] For Lockhart's version of this letter see Vol. IV. p. 429.

[3] For Lockhart's version of this letter see Vol. IV. pp. 439-40, and in the *Life* a shortened version of the following note from John :

½ *past* 3 *oClock Tuesday*

DEAR JAMES,—I am this moment returned from Abbotsford with entire & full success. I am obliged to go unshaven with a shirt of the third day to John Andersons sale instantly, & can only add wish me joy : I shall gain about £600* Constable taking my share of stock also. The title is Rob Roy by the Author of Waverley.

Keep this letter for me. Yrs truly   JN. B.

* I did gain above £1200.

give me a corresponding advantage. My sum is £1700 payable in May : a round advance by'r lady but I think I am entitled to it considering what I have turnd off hitherto on such occasions. Of course you will lay your account with staying all night. I can give you good accomodation as I have access to the spare rooms so you need not fear the cold hospitality of the stable.

James will give you his acceptance for £175 on showing him this letter. I am glad you like the Saleroom. I will give you another on the refitting of Old plays for the modern stage when I come to town.

I make a point of your coming with Constable health allowing. Pray bring any thing with you that is left for me in Castle Street & inform yourself of the health of the family there. Yours truly

W. S.

ABBOTSFORD *Saturday* [PM. *May* 4, 1817]

[*Nat. Lib. Scot.*]

DEAR JOHN,—I am sure nothing will be more agreeable to me than to do what you can show me is for your real advantage though from recollection of the past we must be cautious of more speculation seeing that I cannot afford to lose more money and should regret sincerely that you were to do so by my means. We will talk the matter quietly over when I come to town which will be ample time for my affairs. I am very truly Yours

WALTER SCOTT

ABBOTSFORD *Thursday* [PM. *May* 1817]

Will you be so good as to call in Castle Street & tell Sophia to send the Saleroom by the basket. You shall have another soon. If I want the £500 it will be on the 15th. or term day—the rest will do by the 25th—

[*Nat. Lib. Scot.*]

2 K 2

My DEAR JOHN,—Anent the £600 which completes my transaction I pray you this day to pay in to the *Bank of Scotland* two sums of £300 each, one to the accompt of the revd. Dr. Douglas & one to that of Charles Erskine Writer Melrose taking the proper receipts. I shall [1] advised them that these payments are so made of this date unless I hear from you to the contrary in which case you may send me a note to the Parliament House.

Pray have you not got a Swift of mine as well as the Dodsley ? I am pretty sure you have. Yours truly

W. S.

Tuesday [1817 ?]

I am sorry to see James so down in the mouth about his own affairs and ours. He seems more overwhelmd than ever & surely has no reason since he has a good income & with exertion might easily work off his debt. Had everyone abandond themselves to that senseless sort of despair *where* should we have been just now ?—

[*Nat. Lib. Scot.*]

DEAR JOHN,—I learn with pleasure your arrival in London & heard with concern your plagues losses and crosses. I hope you will have no loss by Ainslie [2]—I never could bear that man & am glad (were it not for your loss) to have a better reason for disliking him than his mere forward vulgarity. It was infamous in him to involve you knowing your situation.

James has just left me. He tells me nothing can be done in London respecting the money I want to pay off the Bond owing to Rees's absence. I must therefore enter into treaty with Constable (so soon as R. R. is out)

---

[1] Scott had written " have " and changed it into " shall."

[2] See letters to James, Vol. IV. pp. 498 and 505.

for the continuation Tales of my L[andlor]d 4 vols. which will make the £4000 forth coming especially if I change the publishers of the first four volumes. I wish while in London you would make particular inquiry into the state of all my works poems etc. and bring me a note of the result as specially as possible. I am ill satisfied with Longmans conduct in the Guy Mannering concern—that work one of the best of the kind has been managed to much less advantage than any other & I think seriously of putting it into Constables hands especially as they seem to have given up printing in Edinburgh.

To pay up Hogarths £1050,, and other incumbrancies of this month I must raise the wind on the owners of R. R. to the tune of £550,, each in addition to the £600 formerly levied.   Of this James will apprize you.   Your own moiety will be necessary on the 19th. & 20th.   You can probably arrange with Constable & Longman to make it easy for you.

I wish you would take the following commissions on my behalf.

To get from Longman & Co/ some drawings lent them for the Border Antiquities but never returnd though often promised.

To pay a small Accot. due by me to Mr. Tournerelle for the busts of Pitt Lord Mellville etc.   They were long of casting up owing to their being addressd to my fathers residence Georges Square & are now at your shop.   The amount is about £12,,   Also a small charge due by me to Rundell & Bridges Silversmiths of £2,, 14,,   Both of which sums I will replace the instant you come to Scotland.

If you can manage to get us some cash in London about the middle of October it will be convenient as from the 9th. to 17 includes some heavy claims & R. R. can scarce be out.

All this family are well—my new house coming on fast —affairs all prosperous and pleasing in prospect.

Pray read this letter attentively and do not neglect my commissions especially the small payments—if money be wanting I will send it up. I hope to hear of your wellfare and am always Very much yours

WALTER SCOTT

ABBOTSFORD 6 *Septr.* [PM. 1817]

I have heard nothing of the set of books.

[*Nat. Lib. Scot.*]

DEAR JOHN,—I was just going to beg to see you on the subject of the inclosed. The stipulated copies being exhausted this work will fall to be arranged something like the G. M. and the W[averle]y on the last occasion. I should like to look at both settlements the other two houses being the real publishers you will hold your third as my Agent. But as you had an original share in this work I propose that instead of a limited agency you and I should divide the profits of your third which I hope you will think handsome.[1] I have no objection to give reasonable time as the exertions of the publishers deserve every effort I can make. To prevent mistakes I think you had better call here after sale. I dare not come out today. I drank some claret yesterday & do not feel quite heart whole. I hope to be able to see our good friend Matthews very soon. At present I am confined except going to the court in a coach. Since you are so good as to admit Walter he will appear at four precisely. Yours Ever

W. S.

[1817]

[*Nat. Lib. Scot.*]

---

[1] Of *Rob Roy*. Ballantyne made over £1200.

DEAR JOHN,—I wrote you a few days since and have yesterday heard from you concerning Longmans proposal. I cannot think of agreeing to the proposed clause of valuation knowing how Murray sold some part of the stock which would have a sinister effect on the minds of the arbiters. I therefore beg to decline that part of the proposal and expect the stock to be taken off my hands at the former rate. Constable pushes books so much better than our London friends that I shall wish him to take the management if he comes into my terms of which I have little doubt. You observe that 10,000 of the Tales @ £1,, 8,, or more probably £1,, 11,, 6 must produce to the publishers between £4000 & £5000,, clear profit besides the command of triple that sum. Murray has made advantageous offers so Longman & Co/ must be sharp. If they are willing to take the bargain with the whole stock it will be unnecessary for you to delay your return. Do you propose to take any part of the bargain yourself at *argent comptant* as formerly—if so let me know that all interests may be keepd in view. Constables management is so much more advantageous than any other that I believe he must have it. But Longmans bills for their moiety must be granted to you or James directly & authors profits etc drawn for at the former credits. It is understood the parties will have the management of the old tales when the present edition is out. If they do wisely they will buy it up at some sacrifice before the publication of the continuation takes wind which should be kept an absolute secret.

I am very sorry for the distress of your family & need not say that I will be happy to see you here where you will find great changes for the better. The Waterloo stick will be most acceptable.

It is needless to point out to Longmans that their clearing decks just now will have the effect of putting the whole affair into their own management & prevent the stock being in future depreciated while on the other hand all being swept away future bargains will be burthend with no such clause.

I should like the bargain to be with Constable & Longn. the former managing and you if you can arrange it taking some slice for yourself.

I intreat your attention to commissions in my last particularly for cash in October to meet acceptances which ought not to be renewd.   Yours truly

W. SCOTT

ABBOTSFORD 10 *Septr.* [PM. 1817]

I shall wish to hear from you before you leave town.

[*Nat. Lib. Scot.*]

To JAMES BALLANTYNE

[*October ?* 1817] [1]

DEAR JAMES,—John will inform you all our matters have been finishd in great stile.   I inclose some copy. The exigencies of the month are thus provided for.   They amount I think to £1700,,

John gives me 2 Bills to London 350 each -	£700,,
I inclose one for which he says you will get cash at the Royal Bank where he has credit -	350
	1000
The other balance of £700 must be renewd by acceptances which must be sent to me forthwith - - - - - - - -	700
	1700

I have not had a note of receipts & payments this long time pray do not require jogging on this important point. It is but little trouble and may prevent much mischief. With November R. R. comes in if I should immure myself to get through with him.   I wrote for a running stitchd

[1] *Rob Roy* was published on 31st December 1817.

copy of Vol I also to Sheet A. vol 11d. but have received
neither.

I should like to know when Guy Mannering & Waverly
will be out.   Yours truly   W. S.

Monday morning

My English bills will be back on Saturday so make your
calculations to have the cash on Monday.

[*Glen*]

To JOHN BALLANTYNE

DEAR JOHN,—I send the Catalogue—look at page 173—
I did not wish to give you the trouble of calling today.
But said I would breakfast with you tomorrow.   If this
is not quite convenient you can come to me.   But at all
events let us have the Stock-book from James with the list
of what has been taken off since it was drawn up.   I
should like your plan very well.   But you will observe
it is necessary to be provided with a substitute if it fail.
For I must send the Creditor in the Bond intimation that
it is to be redeemd.   Now I think that supposing your
plan to fail—still an edition of 6000 Tales might be got
into such preparation by Marts. as almost to insure the
raising of £4000,, in some shape or other.   We must take
care as sailors say not to *miss Stays*.

I beg pardon for neglecting the Announce.   Remember
that you copy it over.   The first two chapters go to James
today.

Rob Roy in 3 Volumes
By the Author of Waverley etc etc
For why ?—Because the good old rule
Sufficeth them the simple Plan
That they should take who have the power
And they should keep who can.

[1817]   *Rob Roy's Grave.*   WORDSWORTH.

[*Nat. Lib. Scot.*]

DEAR JOHN,—I have all your favours. You will learn that your London Bankers have given you the slip so that it is most lucky you can yourself supply the £700,, I inclose a letter which came here for you. I rely on your attending to these matters & providing for all these engagements. James made an infernal blunder last week.

I return the two proofs & also a few sheets of copy. I have been liable to constant interruptions.

I also inclose a work (a novel) by a very clever person. I mentiond it to Constable. It is to be publishd on half profits accepted at publication at a reasonable date. If you approve of it you can secure a share for yourself but I w[ould] not have you dip farther in publications than you are s[ure] of being a gainer. Probably 700 will be a sufficient impression at first. It is in the stile of Richardson. Perhaps it had best go to press immediatly.

I expect your accot. of Waverley & will consider accurately what you say on that subject. As to G. M. I am quite determined to take a third. L. & R.[1] behaved very sorrily in that business. We will meet probably before the 22d. for I go to St Catherines on the 16th. to meet Lord Mellville & will probably spend the 17th there also in which case I will be in Edinburgh on the forenoon of that day.

At any rate we meet on 22d. Magraths letter has arrived. It was addressd by Galashiels which made small delay.

I am very glad of your good prospects. Still I cry *prudence prudence!* You see from Curries behaviour how little you can trust to bankers.

I have closed with Usher for his beautiful patrimony which makes me a great laird. I am afraid the people will take me up for coining. Indeed these novels while their attractions last are something like it.

[1] *i.e.* Longman and Rees.

I think it is shabby in Trotter to charge interest—however he will not make his plack a bawbee by it for I have a new house to furnish etc *avis au lecteur*.   Yours truly

W. S.

11th October [1817] [1]

Please let Jock throw the inclosed letters into the penny post.

[*Nat. Lib. Scot.*]

MY DEAR JOHN, I have your letter and leave it in your judgement to settle with Messrs. Constable for their over drat. as most convenient for keeping things in shape. I presume (for I have not my book here) that the £600 of Stock was drawn & accounted for in a separate transaction. I have not seen or heard any thing of Hogg but Walter poor fellow has got a bilious fit and is unable to shoot. He is not the less grateful for the bag which we will receive in due time. I am always very truly yours

W. SCOTT

ABBOTSFORD 31 *Decr.* 1817

All the good wishes of the year to you.

[*Nat. Lib. Scot.*]

[1] According to Lockhart it was in the autumn of 1817 that Scott completed the purchase of Toftfield for the price of £10,000. He secured it for Capt. Adam Fergusson (now at home on half-pay) and his sisters, who took up residence there in the following spring. At the ladies' request Scott altered the name to Huntly Burn. For Lockhart's extract from this letter see *Life*, chap. xxxix. He reverses the sequence of the sixth and seventh paragraphs, which are the two passages he quotes. His version runs : " I have closed with Usher for beautiful patrimony, which makes me a great laird. I am afraid the people will take me up for coining. Indeed, these novels, while their attractions last, are something like it. I am very glad of *your* good prospects. Still I cry, *Prudence ! Prudence !* " There is significance in the fact that Lockhart has italicised " your " ; Scott has not underlined the word in the original. See also letter to Constable of same date, Vol. IV. p. 540.

DEAR JOHN,—I have all your favours & am much obliged by the offer of the bear which however I beg leave to decline. Tony Lumkin says a Gentleman who is obligated to dance a bear must be in a concatenation accordingly & I do not find myself so at this moment. But I must request your attention to a little Stallion of the Dartmoor forest breed which comes in a present to me from Sir Thomas Acland. It comes by sea and I have desired it to be sent to your care : please give orders for its hospitable reception at Patriot Hall should it arrive in your absence also for paying expences of passage etc.

What you propose concerning the retention of a share in G. M. & Wy. to be kept in your name for the authors benefit seems quite reasonable. If a third amounts to £179 you may strike off £29,, which will be about £20 pr. cent discount as allowance to the publishers & some agent-fee to yourself. They should be allowd I think from £12,, to £15,, pr. cent. You will take your own time & manner to intimate this to the parties. I think the managing House should have the offer of this third in the first place that is Constable in the case of Waverley & Longman in that of Guy. I will not receive it as an objection to this plan that they have hitherto had these works on easier terms which rather forms a reason for my now making a little more by them. But I do not intend in any case to enhance the terms now proposed which I think are fully adequate & as there is every reason to believe that the works will remain with the same publishers (although of course I will come under no engagement to that effect direct or implied) it will I think be very proper to equalize the shares in both works ⅓d to each to Longman namely Constable & yourself as Agent for the author.

I am here to meet Lord Mellville & return today to Abbotsford. On Monday I go to Bowhill but will have some manuscript [sent] to you by that days post. I must

stay over the 22d. so you will not find me at Abbotsford
on the morning of that great day. But you will find
Peter with the carriage prepared to bring you all forward
not forgetting the Cremona.

Consider the List on the opposite side of means & tell
me at meeting if it is right calculated. Yours truly

W. S.

Stock of J. B. & Co/ say - - - -	£4000,,
Authors profit 10,000 new tales - - -	4000,,
Print & paper - - - - - -	2000,,
Authors profit 4000 old tales - - - -	1500,,
Print & paper - - - - - -	500,,
W[averle]y on plan proposed - - - -	650,,
Printing (Constable findg. paper) - - -	125,,
G. M. on plan proposed - - - -	650,,
Print & paper - - - - - -	375,,
	£13800

I look at this extraordinary result with astonishment
& yet I can discover no deception & if I go abroad as I
design I firmly believe the Travels will bring it up to
£20,000. Pray try your own hand on these calculations.
I put no value on R. R. Paul or other things which may
be wanted for the Printing acceptances.

[1818]

[*Nat. Lib. Scot.*]

DEAR JOHN,—I have yours with states of R. R. 4th.
Edition which seems quite right. You may hold the
authors copies to account till we balance my purchases
which have been considerable. I presume it will be very
convenient for James to be accomodated with discounts
so far as you can do it without inconvenience. I need not
add that I do not wish you to pinch yourself.

The cabinet is dear but I am glad to have it. I suppose
the best way is to have it packd carefully up at your shop

so as to admit of its being safely brought out here. My carts will be in town one of these days & can bring it out as well as a great package of busts still lying somewhere about your hand.

I intend to be in town on or before the twenty fourth for a few days. Yours truly   W. S.

ABBOTSFORD 15 *March* [1818/19]

[*Nat. Lib. Scot.*]

DEAR JOHN,—You were quite right to bid against Laing as far as he liked to go. I have not seen the books yet but shall have them tonight. The cabinet came quite safe. I have *found* the Douglas ring after it was lost in a plantation for three years. Sir Will: Forbes apprize[s] me of a bill of my brors. for £65,, 5,, 10 on me at 20/ days sight. Will you take it up out of the cash on precepts it is needless letting it lie till due. Yours truly

W. SCOTT

[30 *Ap.* 1818] [1]

[*Nat. Lib. Scot.*]

DEAR JOHN,—I fancy Constables people find our counter-bills convenient which makes them preserve the present five of the renewals.

I shall want the £200 in your hands or as much of it as can be spared for my own use for I have to pay a bill for building of £150 which leaves me almost pennyless.

I was positive the £6000 was totally independent of print & paper.

I find my banker is not disposed to take Constables bills as he only does business for two months date and for London bills direct. But at any rate he could only have been expected to take £600 or £700. I should think it

---

[1] Docketed this date.

possible to exchange or otherwise manœuvre some of these documents as the credit of the house is so good. You must lay your brain to this. A month later one or two could be easily renewd in the country but not at term time.

The work get[s] on but I am worried with all the interruptions of a damnd Election.[1]   Yours truly

W. S.

ABBOTSFORD *tuesday* [1818]

[*Nat. Lib. Scot.*]

DEAR JOHN,—I inclose an ostensible letter for Dr. Clarke & reinclose his own.   If you think it worth while I can easily get a sketch of Abbotsford as it will be, by means of the drawing by Wilson—Schetkey's illustrations are poor things but might be interesting.   W. S.

[1818/19]

I will send the Saleroom as soon as possible but I must complete my review of Lord Byron.

[1818]

[*Nat. Lib. Scot.*]

DEAR JOHN,—I received both your letters and inclose 3 drats. on Constable at 3, 4, & 6 mos. for £500 each which will put you smooth.

I doubt the measure of sending in your bills though it will answer by & bye.   I think you had better draw on me for a thousand or £1200 part in James name part in yours.   I would wish you could bustle about a little for the ballance which will be about £700—as we shall have some thing to renew in September.   Pray write on this subject to Drumlanrigg & send the bills.   I shall be there

---

[1] Parliament was dissolved in June 1818.   Opposition gained seats.

on the 11th. and the sooner you write the better after Sunday as the post goes only thrice a week. I wish to know if the Antiquary is at press yet. Also what is to be done about the 2d. Edition of Series 2d. & what Murray & Co/ are doing about the 1st. series. These things will come handsomely in to chalk off acceptances as I shall want no part of them.

Mr Milne is now here—he says his father in law M[r] Bell will call to receive the money on Monday so pray be in the way & prepared. You do not mention having paid the ball: into the Leith Banks.

Your workman is come & seems adroit & sensible. My address will be Drumlanrig Castle by Thornhill & you may inclose under cover to the Duke.

You will take Mr Bells receipt on Mr Milnes letter ordering him to receive the money. I am dear John Very truly yours

WALTER SCOTT

ABBOTSFORD 8 *July* [PM. *Aug* 8, 1818]

[*Nat. Lib. Scot.*]

DEAR JOHN,—I have your last letter & you ere this have mine with the bills. I leave this castle today & shall be at Rokeby on the 21st. not sooner as we shall travel slowly.

Much obliged for your attention in the matter of the Leith Bank & Mr Bell. I shall be glad to know what the price of the armour is like to be—of the full suit particularly.

I think the Antiqy. should go to press without waiting Constables return as we find paper etc there can be no difficulty & why should it not be got forward to fill the presses I cannot well perceive. It is *our* book & the progress will necessarily be interfered with by the other.

I wish this was attended to. Sir Tristram is in the same condition Edition 500—

This is heavenly weather & I am making the most of it as I shall have a laborious autumn before me. I may say of my head & fingers as the farmer of his mare when he indulged her with an extra feed

> Ye ken that Maggie winna sleep
> For this or simmer.

I have little prospect of being home till 1st. September so I hope you will organize your visit accordingly. I must stay a week with Morritt and the journey occupies three days as we have our own horses. I have my pony & ride when I find it convenient. Yours truly

W. Scott

DRUMLANRICK CASTLE 17 *Augt.* 1818

[*Nat. Lib. Scot.*]

DEAR JOHN,—I have your letter of the 13th. current & the subsequent one and now only write to say that I leave this tomorrow and will be home at Abbotsford on Sunday which may serve to arrange your visit or correspondence. It will cost me three days to return to my home as we have our own horses.

The armour will not be very dear of £30 if it is an entire suit & in good condition.

I wish to know why Sir Tristrem is not going on. I can make out no copy with convenience till I get home though I have several sheets ready. Probably you will convey back the first sample.

We will need also to look over our affairs for last & next month. Yours truly

WALTER SCOTT

ROKEBY 26 *Augt.* [PM. 1818] *Wednesday*

[*Nat. Lib. Scot.*]

[The following fragment, printed in an Appendix to the reply to Lockhart's *Ballantyne-Humbug Handled*, is all that remains of the 1814 correspondence referred to in the note on p. 509. When the whole business had hardly emerged from the shadow of bankruptcy Alexander seems to have demanded back his loan. All James Ballantyne's capital consisted of old machinery and loans. Scott alone supplied 'actual cash.'

This extract is not included in John Ballantyne's volume, OPEN NOT, READ NOT, but I have added it here as throwing additional light on the relations of Scott and the Ballantynes.]

To JAMES BALLANTYNE

[Extract]

[*24th September*, 1814]

You seem to think that, in making arrangements for clearing off your brother's debt, you give him no preference. I ask you, for what other creditor of the concern you are making similar provision? All those who advanced money to me would be equally glad, I promise you, to be paid, and I can hardly keep some of them quiet. Yet their money, to five times the amount, was equally advanced to the concern as this L.1000 of Mr A. Ballantyne; and I presume the circumstance of its having passed through *your* hands instead of *mine*, can give you no special right of preference. I presume your brother's pinch not to be extreme, since he was willing to take the house instead of cash; so I conceive he wants security rather than money. But if he choose to stop the house, of course he may. It is wholly in his power; for I *cannot* be responsible for paying these bills when they become due. Every farthing of my salary you have long received from the Exchequer as it fell due; and I assure you my family live bare enough. But I repeat it, if your brother choose to stop the house, it is quite in his power. He will hardly increase his chance of speedy payment, which seems morally certain if he choose to give time. The blow, too, will come from an unexpected quarter, but many uncommon things happen in this world; and he certainly may have the credit of ruining a man who has done, or at least tried to do, something for his family, with his two brothers into the bargain. I do not suspect you of any wish in this matter to pay off your own near relation at the expense of me and mine, and leave us all to the chance of the distress and disgrace which may happen, if all the spare funds go off to make good this obligation. You appear to have been a kind brother to him, and are surely entitled to some forbearance from him, and I cannot doubt that you will ask it. More unpalatable applications are wrung from me every day of my life. I put the case, that you have been misled in this matter by a very natural wish to comply with your brother, who as naturally wishes to have his money ; and truly sorry am I that it is impossible he can have it in the time and manner proposed, with any justice to others or safety to the concern. . . . I wish to God you could send me L.25 or L.30 just now, as I am almost penniless. You know where my last quarter from Exchequer went.

[*Reply to the Ballantyne-Humbug, Appendix.*]

PRINTED IN GREAT BRITAIN
BY ROBERT MACLEHOSE AND CO. LTD.
THE UNIVERSITY PRESS, GLASGOW